WITHDRAWN

The British Monarchy and Ireland

1800 to the Present

James Loughlin

University of Ulster

CAMBRIDGE
UNIVERSITY PRESS

CAMBRIDGE UNIVERSITY PRESS
Cambridge, New York, Melbourne, Madrid, Cape Town, Singapore, São Paulo,
Delhi

Cambridge University Press
The Edinburgh Building, Cambridge CB2 8RU, UK

Published in the United States of America by Cambridge University Press,
New York

www.cambridge.org
Information on this title: www.cambridge.org/9780521843720

First published 2007

Printed in the United Kingdom at the University Press, Cambridge

A catalogue record for this publication is available from the British Library

ISBN 978-0-521-84372-0 hardback

For Isabel and Ann

Contents

Illustrations

Preface

This book attempts to explain the role of the British monarchy in Anglo-Irish relations since the passing of the Irish Act of Union. It is one of the few remaining aspects of that relationship yet to receive sustained treatment from historians. Standard biographies of British royal personages treat Ireland only as a very minor topic, or merely in passing, while Irish, like British, historiography until very recently has been little attracted by an institution that in the modern period had lost its role as a central political actor. The work that has appeared has been less concerned with the nature of the monarchy's relationship with Ireland than with how opposition to the royal presence in Ireland has enhanced the organisational effectiveness of the groups engaging in it,[1] or to illuminate very narrow topics.[2] The exception to this neglect has been James Murphy's recent work on the Victorian monarchy and Irish nationalism.[3] The first substantial study of the subject, Murphy's book makes a significant contribution to knowledge. Victoria's engagement with Ireland is closely surveyed especially with reference to the major developments of the period.

This study differs from Murphy's in a number of respects. The timespan is much longer and the remit wider, taking account not only of nationalist Ireland but also of Ulster loyalism, a factor which complicated the role Westminster hoped the monarchy could play in Ireland as a whole. It also addresses more fully and directly the monarchy's relationship to the localist sphere of everyday life while situating the issue of allegiance to the throne within both the context of Government policies for Ireland

[1] Chantel Deutsch-Brady, 'The King's Visit and the People's Protection Committee, 1903', *Eire-Ireland*, 10 (1975), 3–10; Senia Paseta, 'Nationalist Responses to Two Royal Visits to Ireland, 1900 and 1903', *Irish Historical Studies*, 31 (1999), 488–505.

[2] Joseph Hone, 'Queen Victoria in Ireland, 1853', *History Today*, 3 (1953), 501–12; J. D. Fair, 'The King, the Constitution and Ulster: The Interparty Negotiations of 1913 and 1914', *Eire-Ireland*, 6 (1971), 35–52; Francis Costello, 'King George V's Speech at Stormont (1921): Prelude to the Anglo-Irish Truce', *Eire-Ireland*, 22 (1987), 43–57.

[3] James Murphy, *Abject Loyalty: Nationalism and Monarchy during the Reign of Queen Victoria* (Cork, 2001); also, 'Fashioning the Famine Queen' in Peter Gray (ed.), *Victoria's Ireland? Irishness and Britishness 1837–1901* (Dublin, 2004), pp. 15–26.

and the role of the Irish Viceroyalty, the monarchy's *surrogate* – as distinct from *representative* institution – in Ireland. It was an office that had its own court and all the forms and ceremonial appertaining to a court. In pursuing these issues, account is taken of the insights of relevant work on the British monarchy in general since the appearance of David Cannadine's seminal essay on the subject in the early 1980s.[4] Of particular relevance in the Irish context is Frank Prochaska's account of 'welfare monarchism',[5] the process by which royalty compensated for its loss of political power with a vast increase in social influence gained through the promotion of charitable works. Although Prochaska only incidently deals with Ireland, welfare monarchism, as we shall see, was no less an essential element of the royal – and viceregal – role in Ireland than it was in Britain.

A varied approach to the monarchy's relationship with Ireland in this period, going beyond the relatively narrow parameters of political history, is needed, not least to make sense of the contrast between recurrent constitutional and militant mobilisations against the state and equally recurrent and impressive popular receptions for royal personages; the one testifying to an enduring popular commitment to national independence, the other apparently evidencing that the Union could be secured if only the right strategy was found to cultivate on a permanent basis the loyalty royal personages called forth. Some respected historians have seen such occasions as providing opportunities the state foolishly failed to capitalise on.[6] It will be argued here, however, that popular receptions for royal personages and popular mobilisation for nationalist movements are very different kinds of phenomena, requiring different kinds of analytical approach. The former, especially, necessitates an understanding of the dynamics of ceremony and spectacle drawn no less from the discipline of anthropology than from historical inquiry.

---

[4] David Cannadine, 'The Context, Performance and Meaning of Ritual: The British Monarchy and the "Invention of Tradition", c. 1820–1977' in Eric Hobsbawm and Terence Ranger (eds.), *The Invention of Tradition* (Cambridge, 1983), pp. 101–64; also, Linda Colley, 'The Apotheosis of George III: Loyalty, Royalty and the British Nation 1760–1820', *Past and Present*, 102 (1984), 94–129; W. M. Kuhn, *Democratic Royalism: The Transformation of the British Monarchy 1861–1914* (Basingstoke, 1996); Richard Williams, *The Contentious Crown: Public Discussion of the British Monarchy in the Reign of Queen Victoria* (Aldershot, 1997); Antony Taylor, '*Down with the Crown*': *British Anti-monarchism and Debates about Royalty since 1790* (London, 1999); Vernon Bogdanor, *The Monarchy and the Constitution* (Oxford, 1999).

[5] Frank Prochaska, *Royal Bounty: The Making of a Welfare Monarchy* (New Haven and London, 1995).

[6] Frank Hardie, *The Political Influence of Queen Victoria 1861–1901* (2nd edn, London, 1938), pp. 177–8; Algernon Cecil, *Queen Victoria and Her Prime Ministers* (London, 1953), p. 83; Elizabeth Longford, *Victoria R.I.* (London, 1964), p. 191; Stanley Weintraub, *Victoria: Biography of a Queen* (London, 1987), p. 207.

The core positions of the historian and the anthropologist for understanding ceremony have been stated as follows: the historian is 'interested
in the working of ceremonial *in* society ... [He] wants to know how the
ceremonial image and the stability of the state relate to each other,
whereas the anthropologist wants to know how a society constructs a
transcendent symbolic idiom.'[7] In practice, however, there is much cross-
fertilisation between their approaches.[8] This is true of the present inquiry.
Discussions of the great Irish royal occasions are informed both by
historical assessments of the developments that underlay them and by a
number of studies that illuminate the workings of public ritual, spectacle
and the liminal conditions that surround them.[9] Moreover, the assessment of public ritual requires due attention to the public sphere, or arena,
in which it is performed.

The Anglo-Irish arena – the imaginative arena – in which British royal
ceremonial was exercised was the United Kingdom the monarchy
emblematised. It was, however, geographically riven by the Irish Sea,
often politically complex and dysfunctional, and informed by sectarian
and national divisions. Moreover, as the process of educational, communicative and political modernisation accelerated in the post-famine
period[10] its internal contradictions and lack of homogeneity became
ever more problematic, stimulated not least by British ethnocentric discourses that posited the Catholic Irish as culturally underdeveloped and
especially susceptible to royal charm. In this context, the significance of
Scotland as a model of the successful integration of a 'Celtic' nation into
the British state for Ireland to follow should be noted; persuasive not least
owing to the idyllic scenario of a socially 'organic' and hierarchical society
presented each year by Queen Victoria's sojourn at Balmoral. But for
profound historical, religio-cultural and political reasons Scotland was a
misleading paradigm for Ireland. Moreover, an overview of the Anglo-
Irish arena reveals the existence of a number of sub-spheres of meaning,

[7] David Cannadine, 'Introduction: The Divine Rites of Kings' in Cannadine and Simon
Price (eds.), *Rituals of Royalty: Power and Ceremonial in Traditional Societies* (Cambridge,
1992), p. 14.

[8] Ibid. pp. 14–15.

[9] A. M. Hocart, *Kings and Councillors: An Essay in the Comparative Anatomy of Human
Society* (1936; Chicago, 1970); Lucy Mair, *Primitive Government* (Harmondsworth,
1962); Victor Turner, *Dramas, Fields and Metaphors: Symbolic Action in Human Society*
(Ithaca, NY and London, 1974); Guy Debord, *Society of the Spectacle* (Detroit, 1983);
Clifford Geertz, 'Centres, Kings and Charisma: Reflections on the Symbolics of Power'
in Joseph Ben-David and T. N. Clark (eds.), *Culture and Its Creators: Essays in Honour of
Edward Shils* (Chicago, 1975), pp. 150–71; Steven Lukes, *Essays in Social Theory*
(London, 1977).

[10] For the role of the media in facilitating the social influence of monarchy in Britain, see
John Plunkett, *Victoria: First Media Monarch* (Oxford, 2003).

not just in Scotland and England, but in Ireland itself, in Ulster and the south.

In the latter the most important site for the exercise of royal ritual was Dublin, and in Britain a royal success in the capital was easily read as synecdochal of Ireland as a whole. Accordingly the cityscape was often the site of struggle between the authorities and opposition forces. This could take a number of forms, of which a situational conflict of competing symbols expressed in monuments and statuary was one of the most significant. It characterised the Irish landscape in general from the mid-nineteenth century, but especially the Dublin cityscape,[11] and close attention will be paid to it in this work. Furthermore, the constitutional fracturing of the Irish public sphere into two separate arenas following the Anglo-Irish Treaty of 1921 had a profound effect on the monarchy's relationship with Ireland.

In Northern Ireland a Government established on the basis of a Protestant majority would allow for a more direct engagement with monarchy that was denied Ulster loyalists in the nineteenth century, and almost inevitably in a way that served to compromise significantly the Bagehotian ideal the institution was believed to embody. In southern Ireland, the contested constitutional formation, the Irish Free State, ensured that the monarchy became a focus of conflict in a way that it had not been hitherto. And yet, if the status of the monarchy in Ireland has historically been a function of political and ethno-national conflict, as will become clear, the harmonisation of Anglo-Irish relations resulting from Northern Ireland's emergence from a long period of violent conflict has allowed a context to develop for the exercise of royal influence, one that allows royal personages to address concerns about the institution in Britain through contributing to the development of a shared Anglo-Irish culture.

This work has been in gestation over several years and the debts incurred several. I wish to thank Lady Sheila de Bellaigue, Pamela Clark and the staff of the Royal Archives at Windsor Castle for their unfailing helpfulness in accessing royal collections; Her Majesty Queen Elizabeth II for permission to quote from materials in the Royal Archives; Lady Mairi Bury and the Deputy Keeper of Records, Public Record Office of Northern Ireland, for permission to quote from letters of Sir

---

[11] Paula Murphy, 'The Politics of the Irish Street Monument', *Irish Arts Review*, 10 (1994), 202–8; Judith Hill, *Irish Public Sculpture* (Dublin, 1998); Elizabeth Darby and Nicola Smith, *The Cult of the Prince Consort* (New Haven and London, 1983); Yvonne Whelan, *Reinventing Modern Dublin: Streetscape, Iconography and the Politics of Identity* (Dublin, 2003).

Edward Carson to Lady Londonderry; the staff of the Bodleian Library at Oxford; the British Library; the British Library newspaper division at Colindale; the House of Lords Records Office; the National Archives at Kew; the Irish National Archives; Department of Folklore, University College Dublin; Public Records Office, Northern Ireland; the Libraries of Trinity College Dublin, Queen's University Belfast, the University of Ulster (especially at the Magee campus), the Irish section of Belfast Public Library, and the Central Library, Londonderry. Thanks are also due to David Cannadine and the anonymous readers of the articles related to this project, together with those who critically assessed the initial proposal for the present project; Michael Watson and the production staff of Cambridge University Press; Professor Mairead ni Craith of Ulster University for facilitating funds to pursue the final stages of archival research; Professor Bernice Hannigan for finance from the University of Ulster publication fund to acquire images and permissions for reproduction; and Terry Curran of IT User Services Division at the Magee campus for image preparation.

Introduction: the monarchy, Ireland and the Union

The Act of Union of 1801 completed the constitutional development of the United Kingdom through the incorporation of Ireland into a polity governed from Westminster. Henceforth the monarchy, as the hegemonic identifier of the state, was faced with a problem of representation, or embodiment, that had not existed before: could it give authentic expression to the identity and interests of the eight million Irish Catholics the Act had brought within its borders?

Ireland's connection with the monarchy had mythic, genealogical and constitutional strands. The history of the Stone of Scone – the coronation stone that until 1997 resided in Westminster Abbey – had been traced back to ancient Ireland, where for centuries it had been the coronation stone of the Irish High Kings at Tara; and from where it was believed to have gone, on loan, to Scotland early in the sixth century for the crowning of Fergus the Great, brother of Murtagh mac Erc, King of Ireland. The stone, it was believed, never came back to Ireland, and was removed to England by Edward I in 1297. Associated with it was a prophecy stating that wherever it resided a King of the Scotic (Irish-Milesian) race would reign – a prophecy that remained true, as the British royal family could trace its descent back through the Stuart line to the historic Kings of Ireland.[1] This account of Ireland's connection with the British monarchy is based on rather slim foundations; nevertheless the Irish–Scottish origins of the royal family are still, as we shall see, of importance to Ulster Unionists. Yet however strong the monarchy's genealogical link with Ireland – the title 'King of Ireland' was first assumed by Henry VIII in 1542, 370 years after the first invasion of Ireland[2] – there is little real evidence of a monarchical desire to acknowledge that genealogical strand; while the problems facing

---

[1] T. W. Rolleston, *The Myths and Legends of the Celtic Race* (London, 1905), p. 105; Michael McDonagh, *The English King: A Study of the Monarchy and the Royal Family, Historical, Constitutional and Social* (London, 1929), p. 69.

[2] Ibid. p. 83.

the monarchy in Ireland from 1800 were several, involving economic inequality, the coherence of the public realm, sectarian animosities, and antagonistic national traditions and objectives.

The example for the Irish Act of Union was clearly that of the Anglo-Scottish Union of 1707. The claim was made that a Union would open up Ireland for prosperity through the investment of British capital secured by the Westminster Parliament.[3] Henry Dundas, Pitt's Secretary of War, it is safe to assume, saw the path to progress being pursued by his own homeland in the late eighteenth century – a point made much of in Unionist arguments[4] – as a suitable model for Ireland; though the immediate factor pressing a Union was the Anglo-French war and associated problems of military strategy, resources and internal security.[5] In the event, the Union did not create a mutually beneficial economic and political arena. Ireland was, and would remain throughout the Union period, economically underdeveloped compared to Britain;[6] its sectarian divisions would remain entrenched, becoming exacerbated in Ulster as popular nationalism developed; while the overwhelming influence of British political opinion in shaping Irish policies determined that Anglo-Irish relations would remain deeply problematic. Geoff Eley's description of the public sphere in the nineteenth century as an 'arena of contested meanings, in which different and opposing publics manoeuvred for space' around questions of 'domination and subordination'[7] is an apt description of the Anglo-Irish context in which the Irish question was fought out. It was one that the monarchy was supposed to embody and give meaning to.

From the beginning that was difficult. Owing to a combination of political incompetence on the part of Pitt and Henry Dundas in failing to prepare the King adequately for the concession, and, more significantly, the King's entrenched belief that Catholic emancipation was fundamentally inconsistent with his coronation oath,[8] the Union was

---

[3] R. B. McDowell, *Ireland in the Age of Imperialism and Revolution 1760–1801* (Oxford, 1979), p. 687.

[4] E. A. D'Alton, *History of Ireland from Earliest Times to the Present Day* (London, n.d.), half-volume V, p. 103.

[5] Peter Jupp, 'Britain and the Union 1797–1801', *Transactions of the Royal Historical Society* (sixth series), 10 (2000), 202.

[6] Frank Geary and Tom Stark, 'Comparative Output and Growth in the Four Countries of the United Kingdom 1861–1911' in S. J. Connolly (ed.), *Kingdoms United? Great Britain and Ireland since 1500; Integration and Diversity* (Dublin, 1999), p. 168.

[7] Geoff Eley, 'Nations, Publics and Political Cultures: Placing Habermas in the Nineteenth Century' in Craig Calhoun (ed.), *Habermas and the Public Sphere* (Cambridge, Mass., 1992), pp. 235–6.

[8] For the difficulties of conscience the issue caused the King, see George Pellew, *The Life and Correspondence of Henry Addington, Viscount Sidmouth* (London, 1847), I, pp. 280–3.

enacted without this crucial accompaniment.[9] It was an entirely personal matter of principle, impervious to arguments for 'tranquillising Ireland, and attaching it to this country' through safeguards for the Anglican Church establishment; the demise of 'dangerous principles' among Irish Catholics; and state control through the part-payment of the Catholic clergy, together with superintendence and 'political tests'.[10] Against the logic of such arguments had to be set the place of the coronation ceremony and, more widely, the place of monarchy within a popular discourse of constitutionalism: 'If there was unanimity about anything in the world of nineteenth century politics it was that the English constitution was, or, at the very least had been, the best in the world ... the most sacred symbol of Englishness.'[11]

At the centre of English constitutional exceptionalism was the 'Glorious Revolution', a foundation myth focused on monarchy, a Protestant monarchy framed in opposition to the alien 'reference societies' of Catholic Europe.[12] Divine dispensation objectified in functional efficacy had invested the constitution with almost fetishistic dimensions. The centrality of monarchic constitutionalism to English history and politics was registered by Edmund Burke. His ideologically formative *Reflections on the Revolution in France* (1790) consecrated the existing constitutional order through an 'organic' theory of society: belief in the aristocracy as a governing class, and in the state as a great spiritual entity uniting the living and the dead. Burke claimed: 'we have given to our frame of polity the image of a relation in blood; binding up the constitution of our country with our dearest domestic ties; adopting our fundamental laws into the bosom of our family affections; keeping inseparable, and cherishing with the warmth of all their combined and mutually reflected charities, our state, our hearths, our sepulchres, and our altars'.[13]

In so doing Burke created a contemporary legitimising framework for an essentially archaic notion of the monarch as the overarching 'parent' of the people. Moreover, the monarchy was not only the master symbol giving identity to the system, but a proof of its efficacy and legitimacy based on ancient tradition. Radical as the events of 1689 appeared, 'the

---

[9] *Annual Register 1801* (new edn, London, 1813), pp. 118–20.

[10] William Pitt to George III, 31 Jan. 1801, in Pellew, *Sidmouth*, I, pp. 290–1.

[11] James Vernon, *Politics and the People: A Study of English Political Culture c. 1815–1867* (Cambridge, 1993), p. 298.

[12] Rheinhard Bendix, *Kings or People: Power and the Mandate to Rule* (Berkeley, Calif., 1980), p. 283.

[13] Edmund Burke, *Reflections on the Revolution in France*, ed. C.C. O'Brien (1790; Harmondsworth, 1968), p. 120; also 181–3, 194–204.

new [monarchical] line was ... still a line of hereditary descent ... in the same blood, though a hereditary descent qualified with Protestantism'.[14]

For his contribution to the state Burke was rewarded with a civil list pension of £1,200 a year,[15] and aided by the war patriotism of the Napoleonic era his version of nationality developed a hegemonic authority progressively throughout the nineteenth century, displacing earlier radical conceptions based on the 'Norman Yoke'.[16] By 1920, its influence was such that the historian A. F. Pollard could claim that the historical evolution of the constitution had a determining influence on the making of both the English-British state and nation: 'It is really coeval with them both.'[17] Moreover, in the nineteenth century the monarchic shift of 1688 could be read anthropologically as denoting the emergence of an era of not only political but cultural enlightenment. In his great work of armchair anthropology, Sir James Frazer saw it as indicative of a new progressive order that William III, unlike 'the dull bigot James the Second', refused to practise the royal touch as a cure for illness.[18] It was in this sense also that Sir Walter Scott, the pageantmeister of the great display of national tartanry that greeted George IV on his visit to Scotland in 1822, described Catholics as 'still with a touch of the savage about them' and their 'Popery' on a par with 'animal magnetism, [and] phrenology'.[19] The eminent constitutional lawyer A. V. Dicey thought that the people of England being 'ripe for Protestantism at a time when the people of Ireland had hardly *risen* [my italics] to the level of Roman Catholicism was to each country a grievous misfortune'.[20] Such opinions were the common currency of British popular Protestantism, which persisted until the twentieth century; indeed they were validated in the crude language of the Royal Declaration which each new monarch had to recite when first opening Parliament. Deriding the Catholic religion as 'superstitious and

---

[14] Ibid. p. 106. For a discussion of the English coronation ceremony as a ritual embodiment of fundamental aspects of English historical development, see Percy Schramm, *A History of the English Coronation* (Oxford, 1937), ch. 5.

[15] O'Brien, Introduction to Burke, *Reflections*, pp. 18–19.

[16] For a discussion of the radical dimension to British nationalism and its loss of influence, see Gerald Newman, *The Rise of English Nationalism: A Cultural History 1740–1837* (London, 1987); Hugh Cunningham, 'The Language of Patriotism' in Raphael Samuel (ed.), *Patriotism: The Making and Unmaking of British National Identity* I: *History and Politics* (London, 1989), pp. 57–89.

[17] A. F. Pollard, *The Evolution of Parliament* (London, 1920), pp. 4–5.

[18] Sir James Frazer, *The Golden Bough: A Study in Magic and Religion* (abridged edn, London, 1950), p. 50.

[19] Scott quoted in J. G. Lockhart, *Memoirs of Sir Walter Scott* (London, 1838), VI, p. 84; VII, p. 180.

[20] A. V. Dicey, *England's Case against Home Rule* (London, 1886), pp. 89–90.

idolatrous',[21] it continued in existence until George V insisted on its amendment in 1910.[22] A blend of theological contempt and cultural superiority, the attitudes it legitimated, when combined with traditional British ethnocentric attitudes towards the Irish, were to be influential in determining perceptions of the role that monarchy could perform in the Irish context.

However, although Burke's defence of the Protestant constitution appeared to legitimise British nativist sentiment, and was used as such by opponents of Catholic emancipation,[23] he never intended his arguments to apply to Ireland, which he regarded as a distinctive national entity culturally riven by fiercely antagonistic traditions, made worse by the enforcement of penal laws against Catholics. It was with Ireland in mind that he explicitly rejected the coronation oath argument on which royal opposition to Catholic emancipation was based: '[In] that oath itself, as it is settled in the Act of William and Mary ... I do not find one word to preclude His Majesty from consenting to any arrangement which Parliament may make with regard to the civil privileges of any of his subjects.'[24] The maintenance of the penal laws merely perpetuated a deep chasm of values between Britain and Ireland. While in Britain dynastic and constitutional amendments were framed in the context of traditions and a culture which legitimised those changes, in Ireland the Protestant Ascendancy had kept alive the memory of conquest and expropriation on which its power was based, ensuring that a trans-sectarian, state-supportive, culture did not develop.[25] Whereas the traditions of Britain acted as a cement for the constitutional order, those of Ireland were subversive of it.[26] Ireland was not simply another region of the United Kingdom like Wales and Scotland whose local patriotic traditions were being overlaid in the early nineteenth century by a British cultural palimpsest acting to secure the state. In this context the failure to combine the Act of Union with the promised Catholic emancipation

---

[21] The Declaration is fully reproduced in Ernest Oldmeadow, *Francis Cardinal Bourne* (London, 1944), II, pp. 47–8.

[22] Harold Nicolson, *King George the Fifth: His Life and Reign* (London, 1953), pp. 162–3.

[23] See, for example, Lord Chancellor Eldon in the House of Lords, 17 May 1825, cited in Howard Twiss, *The Public and Private Life of Lord Chancellor Eldon* (London, 1844), II, p. 550.

[24] Burke to Sir Hercules Langrishe, 3 Jan. 1792, in Edmund Burke, *Letters, Speeches and Tracts on Irish Affairs*, ed. Matthew Arnold (London, 1881), p. 226.

[25] For a brilliant analysis of Burke's writings on Ireland, see Luke Gibbons, *Edmund Burke and Ireland: Aesthetics, Politics and the Colonial Sublime* (Cambridge, 2003), p. 164 and *passim*.

[26] On Catholic Ireland's historical persecution at the hands of alien Protestant oppressors, see Revd Thomas Burke, *Lectures on Faith and Fatherland* (Glasgow, n.d. [1870s]).

served only to reinforce ethno-cultural antagonism within the kingdom, and especially the moral illegitimacy the Act of Union immediately assumed for Irish nationalists.[27] A deep sense of betrayal was created that prepared the agitational ground for Daniel O'Connell's political career and with it the Irish constitutional tradition. That tradition, especially as it was informed by O'Connell's ideas, was to shape a multifaceted relationship between Catholic Ireland and the British monarchy, combining elements of opposition, attachment and indifference depending on context, and explicable in terms of neither undiluted allegiance or rejection.

I

At one level the refusal of emancipation belied the increasingly congenial relationship that had developed between the Hanoverian dynasty and the Catholic Church since the middle decades of the eighteenth century. On the death of the 'Old Pretender', James III, in 1766 Pope Clement XIII, hoping thereby to improve Anglo-papal relations and effect the removal of the penal laws, refused to recognise his son, Prince Charles Edward Stuart, as the rightful King of Britain and Ireland.[28] The progress of conciliation was enhanced enormously by the transforming effect of the French Revolution, which rendered obsolete the religiously framed conflicts of the previous century. Britain became a refuge for continental Catholic clergy; in Ireland the great seminary of Maynooth was established. Moreover, the French occupation of Rome in 1797 and capture of Pius VI led the pope to recognise George III formally as rightful King of Britain, and the King to confer on the economically straitened last Stuart heir to the British throne, Cardinal Henry, Duke of York, an annual pension of £4,000.[29] From 1804 to 1817 Pius VII facilitated the transfer of the Stuart archives from Rome to London.[30] A highly symbolic process, it served to confirm the Hanoverian regime as Britain's legitimate royal house at a time when, under the impetus of war, British patriotism was being shaped in the hegemonic monarchical mode it would

[27] See Gearóid Ó Tuathaigh, *Ireland before the Famine* (Dublin, 1972), pp. 34–41.

[28] Matthias Buschkühl, *Great Britain and the Holy See, 1746–1870* (Dublin, 1982), p. 19; Brendan O'Buchalla, '"James our True King": The Ideology of Irish Royalism in the Seventeenth Century' in D. G. Boyce et al. (eds.), *Political Thought in Ireland since the Seventeenth Century* (London and New York, 1993), pp. 1–35.

[29] Buschkühl, *Great Britain and the Holy See*, pp. 37–40.

[30] See Sir John Mackintosh to Colonel McMahon, 6 March 1813 in Arthur Aspinall (ed.), *The Letters of King George IV 1812–1830* (Cambridge 1938), I, p. 230; Prince Regent to Pope Pius VII, 6 Sept. 1817, ibid. II, p. 199 and footnote 1.

henceforth assume.[31] Indeed, the end of the Stuart claim to the throne with the death of the Cardinal Duke of York in 1807, and the disengagement of Jacobite symbolism and ideas from fears of dynastic destabilisation, left them available for exploitation as props and affectations to add glamour, an air of romance, and historical 'authenticity' to contemporary royal ceremonial.[32] George IV's coronation in July 1821, for instance, towards the cost of which Parliament authorised almost £243,000,[33] was modelled on that of James II.[34] His coronation visit to Scotland in 1822, choreographed by Sir Walter Scott, was a riot of tartanry, with the King disporting himself in the Stuart tartan the Young Pretender had devised on his arrival in Edinburgh in 1745.[35] At her coronation, Queen Victoria was impressed by aspects that connected it to that of James II,[36] and developed an illogical romantic attachment to her Stuart predecessors.[37] She had the sitting room in her 'medieval' Balmoral residence decorated in tartan.[38] In all of this it is possible to detect a desire for enhanced British rootedness – intuitively prescient given the monarchy's ancestral vulnerability during World War I – framed largely in the imaginative terrain sketched out in the works, and under the influence, of Sir Walter Scott. Scott was the ideal guide, for his selective appropriation of the Stuart period sidelined the Catholic question which was central to their demise and the 'Glorious Revolution' that established the less legitimate Protestant succession.

In Ireland, however, where the revolution of 1688–90 had served merely to consolidate problems of religious conflict, land ownership and state legitimacy, and where the historical passions that period had generated deeply informed contemporary political debate, the religious issue was a central political concern, and the place of the monarchy in popular opinion problematic. It was made more so by the crown's surrogate presence – the Irish Viceroyalty – the British state's constitutional and administrative apparatus.

---

[31] See Linda Colley, 'The Apotheosis of George III: Loyalty, Royalty and the British Nation 1760–1820', *Past and Present*, 102 (1984), 94–129.

[32] For the Scottish dimension see Colin Kidd, 'The Rehabilitation of Scottish Jacobitism', *Scottish Historical Review*, 78 (1998), 58–76.

[33] Christopher Hibbert, *George IV: Regent and King, 1811–1830* (London, 1974), p. 190.

[34] Roger Fulford, *George the Fourth* (London, 1935), p. 225.

[35] J. G. Lockhart, *Memoirs of Sir Walter Scott* (London, 1837), V, p. 204.

[36] Queen Victoria's Journal [QVJ], 28 June 1838, in Arthur Benson and Viscount Esher (eds.), *The Letters of Queen Victoria*, series one (London, 1907), I, pp. 157–8.

[37] Sidney Lee, *Queen Victoria: A Biography* (new edn, London, 1904), pp. 260, 574.

[38] See Adrienne Munich, *Queen Victoria's Secrets* (New York, 1995), pp. 40–5 for a stimulating discussion of 'Balmorality'.

II

Originating in the reign of Henry VI, the post of Lord Lieutenant increased in significance in the later eighteenth century, together with that of Chief Secretary to assist in handling Irish administration. It was a crucial office for the management of Government business during the period of Irish constitutional independence from 1782 to 1800, but the dissolution of the Irish Parliament on the enactment of the Union reduced its importance[39] and its abolition was repeatedly debated during the Union period. Its survival was due chiefly to inertia and, as nationalist Ireland showed little inclination to accept the Union, the need to have special provision for the direction of Irish affairs.[40] But while 'Lord Lieutenant' was the official description of the post, the term of office was known as a Viceroyalty, and 'Viceroy' is, in fact, a more appropriate description of the officeholder.[41] Centred in Dublin Castle and equipped with all the forms and ceremony of a court, the office was enhanced in 1783 when George III instituted, to accompany the Orders of the Rose and the Thistle, The Most Illustrious Order of St Patrick for 'the dignity and honour of Our Realm of Ireland'.[42] Moreover, just as the monarchy in Britain sat at the apex of a hierarchical social order, so in Ireland the Viceroyalty was supported by the landed aristocracy whose great houses provided staging posts for Viceroys on their tours of the Irish countryside.

More generally, the viceregal court functioned as a cohesive force in the Irish non-nationalist – though not entirely non-Catholic – world, setting a standard and pattern of social culture and manners.[43] It was a British world whose landscape, certainly in the urban thoroughfares of Dublin – Edward McParland has referred to the 'Englishness of Irish architecture'[44] in regard to the city's neo-classical public buildings – was signified through

---

[39] George III thought that, pending abolition, the Lord Lieutenant should consider himself 'a kind of President of the Council' whose chief function was to end Irish jobbery: King to Henry Addington, 11 Feb. 1801, in Pellew, *Sidmouth*, I, p. 303.

[40] For accounts, see Hiram Morgan and S. J. Connolly, 'Lord Deputy' and 'Lord Lieutenant' in S. J. Connolly (ed.), *The Oxford Companion to Irish History* (2nd edn, Oxford, 2002), pp. 343–4; Virginia Crossman, 'Chief Secretary', in ibid. pp. 85–6; Kieran Flanagan, 'The Chief Secretary's Office, 1853–1914', *Irish Historical Studies* [*IHS*], 24 (1984), 197–225; R. B. McDowell, *The Irish Administration 1800–1914* (London, 1964).

[41] The usage is illustrated in Charles O' Mahony, *The Viceroys of Ireland* (London, 1912).

[42] Peter Galloway, *The Most Illustrious Order of St Patrick 1783–1983* (Chichester, 1983), p. xiii.

[43] 'The Court of Dublin Castle' in R. B. McDowell, *Historical Essays, 1938–2001* (Dublin, 2003), p. 31; and for a general discussion, Joseph Robins, *Champagne and Silver Buckles: The Viceregal Court at Dublin Castle 1700–1922* (Dublin, 2001).

[44] McParland quoted in Alistair Rowan, 'The Irishness of Irish Architecture', *Journal of the Society of Architectural Historians of Great Britain*, 40 (1997), 16.

1 Viceregal Lodge, the Phoenix Park, 1890s.

naming and monuments. Dublin's synecdochal embodiment of loyal Ireland was marked topographically by street names, hospitals, bridges, monuments – contentiously in the case of the equestrian statue of William III in College Green and strikingly in the great memorials to Admiral Lord Nelson in Dublin's main thoroughfare, Sackville (now O'Connell) Street, and the Duke of Wellington in the Phoenix Park.[45]

The Phoenix Park was the location of the Viceregal Lodge (Fig. 1), the Viceroy's private residence, and underwent its own marking as a British landscape when, in common with royal palaces in Britain, it was renovated in the 1830s and 1840s.[46] But unlike in Britain, where such sites acted to reinforce a developing British nationality, in Ireland they represented an *assertion* of authority. Necessarily encoded in the Nelson and Wellington monuments was the message that Irish nationalists should not look for successful assistance to England's enemies. Moreover, in Ireland as a whole it is possible to read the residences of great landlords – Britain's 'garrison' in Ireland – as themselves identity statements[47] in an often hostile environment and outnumbered by many more historically

[45] McDowell, 'Court of Dublin Castle', p. 2; Paula Murphy, 'The Politics of the Street Monument', *Irish Arts Review*, 10 (1994), 202–4; Yvonne Whelan, *Reinventing Modern Dublin: Streetscape, Iconography and the Politics of Identity* (Dublin, 2003), chs. 2 and 3.

[46] Dana Arnold, 'Transplanting National Cultures: The Phoenix Park (1832–49), an Urban Hetertopia?' in Arnold (ed.), *Cultural Identities and the Aesthetics of Britishness* (Manchester, 2004), p. 71 and *passim*.

[47] For pertinent comment, see Sophia Cross, 'The Country House Is Just a Flag', in ibid. pp. 53–66.

resonant 'oppositional' structures. As Burke remarked, the ruins and monuments of native Ireland could encode effective counter-narratives to misleading victors' accounts.[48] In fact a relationship between architecture and environment in general has long been noted, especially a close connection between 'architectural strength and political disorder',[49] or in Ireland's case, more often, constitutional uncertainty. The Viceroyalty itself, structurally and constitutionally, embodied such uncertainty.

The Union may have established constitutional unity between Britain and Ireland, but the continued existence of the Viceroyalty suggested that Ireland's relationship to Britain was, in fact, colonial; an impression popular British attitudes to Ireland lent plausibility to. In Britain royalty developed massively its charity work in the nineteenth century to create a 'welfare monarchy'[50] that functioned to consolidate the status quo; so too – but with a more serious issue of legitimacy to address – can a viceregal dimension in Ireland to this practice be observed.[51] Certainly the differences between the monarchy and the Viceroyalty were more significant than the similarities. Whereas in Britain the monarchy increasingly was the master-symbol embodying state and nation, not only did the Viceroyalty denote ambiguity about Ireland's place in the expanded British state, but the relationship between 'monarch' and 'Prime Minister' in Ireland – Viceroy and Chief Secretary – was not permanently fixed. In a period of crisis a personally authoritative Viceroy could dominate his Chief Secretary and combine the powers of both offices, and with it the seat in Cabinet that was usually the Chief Secretary's preserve.[52] In this context, as we shall see, the elevated arena above party politics that the monarchy increasingly assumed in Britain from 1830 onwards was difficult to establish in Ireland and could easily disappear. This was due not merely to the dynamics of Irish politics, but to the fact that the Viceroy's assumption of a royal persona was undermined by the officeholder always being a political appointee whose term ended with that of the administration that appointed him. Accordingly, not only were the Viceroy's regal pretensions a subject of popular ridicule, but the officeholders were themselves often astounded at having to play royalty.[53]

---

[48] Gibbons, *Burke and Ireland*, p. 159.

[49] David Milne, 'Architecture, Politics and the Public Realm', *Canadian Journal of Political and Social Theory*, 5 (1981), 133–5.

[50] Frank Prochaska, *Royal Bounty: The Making of a Welfare Monarchy* (New Haven and London, 1995).

[51] For the period up to 1830, see Edward Brynn, *Crown and Castle: British Rule in Ireland 1800–1830* (Dublin, 1978), pp. 101–9.

[52] See below ch. 8.

[53] Lord Kimberley, Viceroy in the mid-1860s, described viceregal ceremonial as 'not only absurd but extravagantly costly': entry (19 Oct. 1864) in Angus Hawkins and John

2 Throne room, Dublin Castle.

Lack of regal authenticity also extended to the built environment of royal sites. While the great royal palaces in Britain could be seen increasingly as symbolic of the separation between the constitutionally representative and the politically functional (Westminster) in the nineteenth century, as the monarchy lost its direct political influence, this was not the case in Ireland. Dublin Castle housed both the throne room (Fig. 2) and offices dealing with the suppression of rebellion, agrarian crime and popular agitation. In 1893 an ADC to the Liberal Viceroy, Lord Houghton, remarked on the negative position of the symbolic 'figure of justice' above the gates of Dublin Castle: it was 'looking inward with *her back turned to the people*'.[54] Moreover, if a traditional function of royal magnificence has been to symbolise the physical well-being of the land and people of which the monarch is the embodiment,[55] it was a function

Powell (eds.), *The Journal of John Wodehouse Earl of Kimberley for 1862–1902* (Cambridge, 1997), p. 144; also *Earl Cowper* by his Wife (London, 1913), p. 363; A Native, *Recollections of Dublin Castle and Dublin Society* (London, 1902), p. 6.

[54] Trevelyan quoted in A. J. A. Morris, *C. P. Trevelyan: Portrait of a Radical 1870–1958* (Belfast, 1977), p. 14.

[55] See A. M. Hocart, *Kings and Councillors: An Essay in the Comparative Anatomy of Human Society*, ed. with Introduction by Rodney Needham (1936; Chicago and London, 1970), p. 202; Lucy Mair, *Primitive Government* (Harmondsworth, 1962), p. 220.

Dublin Castle signally failed to perform as the nineteenth century developed. With the loss of its Parliament in 1801 and the departure of the Irish governing class, Dublin entered on a period of increasing urban decay, and the Castle's location in one of the most deprived and poverty-ridden areas of the city – arising 'like an upas tree amid ruins and death'[56] – was noted. As such, it spoke metaphorical volumes about the relationship of the Castle with the mass of the Irish people. While popular and/or respected Viceroys can be identified – Marquess Wellesley, Marquess Anglesey (at times) and Lord Mulgrave, for instance, in the pre-famine period[57] – they were overshadowed by a much greater number of unpopular officeholders: twenty-seven of the thirty-seven Viceroyalties between 1800 and 1909 were, according to one estimate, out of sympathy with 'Irish national feeling'.[58]

In sum, the Viceroyalty's ability to embody the monarchic identity of the extended British state after 1800 suffered from serious weaknesses. Often lacking whole-hearted support from London, it combined regal pretensions with lack of authenticity, and in a deeply divided country functioned, especially during the early period of the Union, simply as a tool of the Protestant Ascendancy. As such, it was singularly ill-equipped to meet the challenge to British rule posed by popular agitations, especially that of Daniel O'Connell.

---

[56] George Moore, *Parnell and His Island* (London, 1887), p. 20.
[57] See O'Mahony, *Viceroys of Ireland*, for accounts of their periods of office.
[58] R. B. O'Brien, *Dublin Castle and the Irish People* (London, 1909), pp. 16–17.

Part I

The crown and O'Connellite Ireland

1   Legitimacy, authority and emancipation

The point of departure for O'Connell's career was the first Catholic petition to Parliament on emancipation on 25 March 1805. Informed by the increasingly supportive role the Catholic hierarchy was offering to the state, its language is instructive, declaring the petitioners' allegiance to the 'person, family and government of the King'.[1] Specifying the royal *family* as the focus of allegiance was in keeping with a development Linda Colley has noted in Britain as occurring during the second half of George III's reign.[2] The shift of allegiance from the public persona of the King to the family was significant, for it blurred the boundaries between the private/personal and the public/political, allowing monarchy to invest all spheres of life in a way suggested by Burke, and which Queen Victoria would make her own in her role as a model of middle-class values in the domestic realm. But despite offering assurances for the security of the existing (Cromwellian) land settlement in Ireland, the position of the established church, and the Protestant religion and government in Ireland, the petition was rejected in both houses of Parliament. That it was, reflected the anti-Catholic prejudices of British opinion, but no less widespread establishment fears about the constitutionally destabilising influence of Ireland that existed throughout the pre-famine period, especially in the Napoleonic era: 'Buonaparte is the Barometer by which we must judge and act in this country.'[3] The example of the United Irishmen's rebellion of 1798, and its 1803 addendum led by Robert Emmet, was a powerful influence in London, lending every significant upheaval in Britain thereafter a real or imagined Irish dimension.[4] To

---

[1] The petition is cited in full in Horace Twiss, *The Public and Private Life of Lord Chancellor Eldon* (London, 1844), I, pp. 490–2.

[2] Linda Colley, 'The Apotheosis of George III: Loyalty, Royalty and the British Nation 1760–1820', *Past and Present*, 102 (1984), 121–5.

[3] William Gregory to Secretary Peel, 23 March 1815, in Lady Gregory (ed.), *Mr Gregory's Letter Box, 1813–1835* (1898; Gerrards Cross, Bucks, 1981), pp. 62–3.

[4] On, respectively, the supposed Irish dimension to Colonel Despard's plot of 1802; the Peterloo gathering; the Cato Street conspiracy; Scottish disturbances in 1820; Irish and

imagine the British nation in this period, at least within establishment circles, was to envisage a tension between the state-consolidating influence of the monarchy and the destabilising forces of indigenous lower-class discontent infected by an Irish virus. And for most British politicians that virus was personified in Daniel O'Connell.

I

The most politically gifted and personally impressive politician in Ireland, O'Connell capitalised on the rejection of the 1805 petition to build his political career and shape the emancipation campaign. At this time, Irish supporters of emancipation in Parliament such as Henry Grattan and W. C. Plunket, together with their Whig and English Catholic supporters, were in favour of a qualified emancipation that would have allowed the sovereign a veto on the appointment of Catholic prelates, and an influence on the Catholic clergy through a subsidy for their upkeep. In 1808, however, O'Connell successfully urged the rejection of the veto, citing the freedom of the Catholic Church as 'the last remnant of national independence' untrammelled by British rule. But while this was an effective demonstration of O'Connell's power, a division was created in emancipist ranks that lasted almost ten years.[5]

The issues at stake were significant. Those supporting or accepting the veto were prepared to tolerate the Protestant constitution, though modified in such a way that Catholics had a place within it; and, by implication, were primarily British subjects freely owing allegiance to the King. O'Connell never rejected allegiance to the King, but his framing of the issue in terms of nationality shifted the ground of the issue from British citizenship to an emotively powerful Irish narrative of historical grievance, one which conceived it as an increment of freedom that would only be fully realised when Ireland regained her constitutional independence.

O'Connell's concept of freedom was of a piece with his wider political philosophy, which found expression in support for parliamentary reform, anti-slavery, the Aborigines Protection Society and individual rights in

English unrest attending the downfall of Charles X in France; and the Chartist movement: Duke of Buckingham and Chandos, *Memoirs of the Courts and Cabinets of George III* (London, 1855), III, pp. 216–18; Duke of Buckingham and Chandos, *Memoirs of the Court of England during the Regency 1811–1820* (London, 1856), II, p. 340; Duke of Buckingham and Chandos, *Memoirs of the Court of George IV* (London, 1856), I, p. 97; Duke of Buckingham and Chandos, *Court of England during the Regency*, II, p. 375; Duke of Buckingham and Chandos, *Memoirs of the Courts of William IV and Victoria* (London, 1861), I, pp. 182 and 113–15; James Loughlin, 'Allegiance and Illusion: Queen Victoria's Irish Visit of 1849', *History*, 87 (2002), 495.

5 Fergus O'Ferrall, *Daniel O'Connell* (Dublin, 1981), pp. 26–31.

general,[6] and which demonstrated his ability to enter imaginatively into the condition of others. In the same vein, he was acutely alive to how a subordinate relationship of the Catholic Church to the monarchy might produce corrupted mentalities. A royal veto on ecclesiastical appointments would be likely to produce clerical 'flunkeyism' while complete emancipation, on the other hand, would remove the alienating factor that prevented Irish Catholics and Protestants from uniting in the cause of Irish freedom.[7] And yet O'Connell was oddly unreflective about the nature of Irish nationality.

The subjective question of what it meant to be Irish, which vexed nationalists in the Young Ireland movement, and was to be the central motive of Gaelic revivalism from the end of the of the nineteenth century, did not concern him. Totally confident in his identity, he was indifferent to the issue of 'whether any of his attitudes or notions might be labelled British. It was simply not an issue.'[8] His concept of Irish nationality was basically locational, to be determined solely by Irish birth and residence, dwarfing every difference of class interest, culture, language – the Irish language he was quite prepared to see disappear in the cause of embracing English for 'all modern communications'[9] – or even religion. The great objective to be attained was 'that greatest of all political blessings, an Irish King, an Irish House of Lords and an Irish House of Commons',[10] creating an Ireland that would take its place in a dual monarchy with Britain and having its contribution to the British empire recognised.[11]

A problem arises almost immediately, however, with O'Connell's conception of King, Lords and Commons in Ireland. The latter two estates of the Irish realm might be depended upon to pursue the Irish national interest, but could that be assumed for an English King? For Ireland to realise its destiny under such a system implied the monarch always acting in accord with the wishes of his Irish ministers, merely giving constitutional legitimation to the Irish Government's decisions. Such a role became normal for the crown in a Commonwealth context in the twentieth century, but was highly unlikely in O'Connell's day. Certainly, before the accession of the eccentric William IV, whose uncertain normality, if not

---

[6] Oliver McDonagh, 'O'Connell's Ideology' in Laurence Brockless and David Eastwood (eds.), *A Union of Multiple Identities: The British Isles, c. 1750–c. 1850* (Manchester, 1997), pp. 148–9.

[7] W. J. O'Neill Daunt, *Ireland since the Union* (Dublin, 1889), pp. 63–7. Daunt had been a close political associate of O'Connell.

[8] McDonagh, 'O'Connell's Ideology', p. 152.

[9] O'Connell quoted in W. J. O'Neill Daunt, *Personal Recollections of O'Connell* (London, 1848), I, p. 15.

[10] McDonagh, 'O'Connell's Ideology', p. 156.   [11] Ibid. pp. 156–8.

actual madness – evident to O'Connell[12] – seriously weakened the political authority of the monarchical office, this was an important consideration, and could not be assumed. To a considerable extent, O'Connell's attitude to the monarchy is consistent with what Oliver McDonagh has described as his early nineteenth-century utilitarian philosophy,[13] which seems to have envisaged state institutions functioning objectively, or neutrally, to facilitate the ends of government. But like much in O'Connell's outlook, there seems to have been considerable wishful thinking on this subject. Certainly his reformist critics, such as the Ulster land reformer Sharman Crawford, did not share his confidence that the link of the monarch between Britain and Ireland could secure Irish political rights, given the inevitably hegemonic influence of British interests,[14] not to mention the likely anti-Irish animus of English monarchs rendering any desire to comply with a Dublin Parliament's decisions on contentious issues uncertain.[15]

O'Connell, however, seems to have believed that his ideas could work effectively if royal goodwill was cultivated. Sincerely loyal to the crown,[16] he did not see why his loyalty should not be taken at face value, especially as his protestations were supported by a historical narrative extolling Irish Catholic loyalty to William III and his Protestant successors and a corresponding rejection of James II and the Jacobite tradition – a rewriting of Irish history at the expense of a now redundant monarchical cause. O'Connell did play on Ireland's national grievances to sustain popular support, but he framed their solution – emancipation and repeal – within the historical carapace of the Glorious Revolution,[17] apparently recognising the increasing importance of the monarchy to British nationality and state identity. He was presented with a perfect opportunity for the cultivation of royal goodwill with the announcement that George IV would visit Ireland shortly after his coronation in July 1821.

---

[12] See O'Connell to P. V. Fitzpatrick, 22 May 1834, in Maurice O'Connell (ed.), *The Correspondence of Daniel O'Connell V: 1833–1836* (Dublin, 1977), p. 134. For later nationalists William IV's reign marked the end of the personal rule of the sovereign: Justin McCarthy, *A History of Our Own Times* (new edn, London, 1907), I, pp. 1–2.

[13] McDonagh, 'O'Connell's Ideology', pp. 148–9.

[14] B. A. Kennedy, 'Sharman Crawford's Federal Scheme for Ireland' in H. A. Cronne et al. (eds.), *Essays in British and Irish History in Honour of James Edie Todd* (London, 1949), pp. 244–5.

[15] For George III Ireland was 'that uncivilised land': Edward Brynn, *Crown and Castle: British Rule in Ireland 1800–1830* (Dublin, 1978), p. 25.

[16] Daunt, *Ireland since the Union*, p. 69.

[17] See speeches of O'Connell, 13 Jan. 1800, 18 Sept. 1810, 15 Dec. 1812, 29 May 1813, 4 March 1831: John O'Connell (ed.), *The Life and Speeches of Daniel O'Connell* (Dublin, 1846), I, pp. 31, 153, 266, 343–4; M. F. Cusack, *The Speeches and Public Letters of the Liberator* (Dublin, 1875), I, p. 106. On its 'principles' and demands for reform in general, see Jacqueline Hill, 'National Festivals, the State and "Protestant Ascendancy" in Ireland 1790–1829', *Irish Historical Studies*, 24 (1984), 33–4.

II

The visit was remarkable for a number of reasons. It initiated the tradition of royal visits that has grown to be a staple of the royal itinerary up to the present. It was a quite astounding and unexpected success, appearing to defy rational explanation, and puzzling to participants and historians alike given the troubled history of Anglo-Irish relations. A host of contemporary observers testified to the mass emotion stimulated by the King's presence in Dublin, and, not least, shame and indignation at the servile 'foot-licking idolatry' it appeared to exhibit.[18] The distinguished architectural historian Maurice Craig has suggested an explanation in the loss of Ireland's native parliament and associated sense of national cohesion: it was now 'an era of individuals, of occurrences apparently isolated and apparently without meaning ... How else but in isolation can we regard the fantastic scenes at the visit of George IV in 1821?'[19] This phenomenon can be logically explained, but to do so its context must be sought well beyond the environs of Dublin.

As the visit, which began on 12 August, followed so quickly on the coronation of George IV on 19 July, the two events tended to run together in popular consciousness, with the visit partaking of the majestic aura of the coronation and having the appearance of a special favour to Ireland. In itself the coronation was charged with popular interest and drama. George IV was widely regarded as a morally worthless individual who set standards of excess unequalled since the revolution of 1688.[20] His coronation, the most lavish of modern times, had a background of public controversy rooted in the King's efforts to prevent his estranged, rather vulgar wife, Queen Caroline, from assuming the throne as his Consort, and from participating in the coronation ceremony. In the process he alienated large swathes of British public opinion.[21]

---

[18] Diary (21 Sept. 1821), Lord John Russell (ed.), *Memoirs, Journal and Correspondence of Thomas Moore* (London, 1853), III, p. 176; Valentine Lord Cloncurry, *Personal Recollections* (Dublin, 1849), p. 277; Countess Glengall to Mrs Francis Taylor, 27 Aug. 1821, in John Gore (ed.), [Thomas] *Creevey* (London, 1949), pp. 218–19; Dorothy Howell-Thomas, *Duncannon: Reformer and Reconciler 1781–1847* (Norwich, 1987), p. 101.

[19] Maurice Craig, *Dublin 1660–1860* (Dublin, 1952), p. 307.

[20] J. H. Plumb, *The First Four Georges* (London, 1966), p. 151: 'Few monarchies have struggled under the weight of such ... self-indulgent vulgarity.'

[21] For these issues, ibid. ch. 5; Christopher Hibbert, *George IV: Regent and King* (London, 1973), chs. 11–13. There was even a fear that the challenge of the King's Champion to anyone contesting the King's right to the throne would be taken up: J. Tounson to the Earl of Harrowby, 10 July 1821, Coronation materials, National Archives [NA] (Kew), HO44/7. No challenger appeared on this, the last royal occasion, on which the King's Champion had a part.

In the event, the coronation, a neo-Gothic extravaganza[22] – *The Times* thought it inconsistent with the position of 'a constitutional King in a limited monarchy'[23] – and the public festivities associated with it, coincided with a turn in public opinion, serving to revive the King's public reputation.[24] In a specifically Irish context, moreover, the King was subject to a more positive interpretation than he often was in London, while the background to the visit had a congenial aspect.

In April 1821 a Catholic relief bill – containing qualifications and therefore lacking O'Connell's approval – had been passed by the House of Commons, and though rejected by the Lords it was still a significant landmark. It was the last time that quarrels over the veto complicated the emancipation struggle and it set the pattern for the 1820s, whereby a united non-vetoist emancipation campaign would deliver small majorities in the Commons only to be rejected by larger majorities in the upper House.[25] Recognising the advance, the bill's promoters, especially Henry Parnell – having erroneously interpreted the 150 Lords votes for the bill as indicating the King's support for the measure – advised Catholic prelates to encourage the presentation of non-contentious addresses welcoming the King to Ireland,[26] a policy endorsed by Daniel O'Connell,[27] whose support for the visit was vital for its success.

That Parnell should have misread the King's views was understandable, for in an Irish context he had something of a radical reputation. Unaware of his current opinions on emancipation – significantly, he had disallowed any Catholic or Irish representation in the coronation ceremony[28] – it was remembered that on the occasion of George III's first

---

[22] Roger Fulford, *King George the Fourth* (London, 1935), p. 231.

[23] *The Times* [*TT*], 23 July 1821.

[24] Prochaska has put the revival of his reputation, in part at least, down to his charitable activities: Frank Prochaska, *Royal Bounty: The Making of a Welfare Monarchy* (New Haven and London, 1995), pp. 45–7.

[25] G. I. T. Machin, *The Catholic Question in English Politics 1820–1830* (Oxford, 1964), pp. 31–2.

[26] See Parnell to Denis Scully, 19 April 1821, in Brian McDermott (ed.), *The Catholic Question in Ireland and England 1798–1822: The Papers of Denis Scully* (Dublin, 1988), p. 648.

[27] See The O'Conor Don to O'Connell, 18 June 1821, in Maurice O'Connell (ed.), *The Correspondence of Daniel O'Connell* II: *1818–1825* (Dublin, 1974), pp. 326–7; J. B. Sheil to O'Connell, 1 April 1821; *ibid.* pp. 311–12; O'Connell to O'Conor Don, 23 April 1821, in *ibid.* p. 319; *Dublin Evening Post* [*DEP*], 19, 21 July 1821.

[28] The application of Patrick O'Hanlon of Orier, to perform his family's role as hereditary Standard Bearer of Ireland at the ceremony, was refused, as was that of the Catholic Earl of Shrewsbury to perform the ancestral duties of Steward of All Ireland: Shane Leslie, *The Irish Tangle for English Readers* (London, 1947), p. 67; Lords of the Committee Appointed to Consider of His Majesty's Coronation, to George IV, 16 July 1821, in Arthur Aspinall (ed.), *The Letters of George IV* (Cambridge, 1938), III, p. 446.

bout of insanity in 1789 the Irish Parliament had considered the Prince of Wales such a friend to Ireland that, unlike the Westminster Parliament, it was prepared to offer him the Irish Regency without any limitation on his powers.[29] Having declared his sympathy for Catholic claims before his second period as Regent in 1811,[30] by which time he was a confirmed opponent,[31] he was known as the friend of pro-emancipation reformers such as Lord Moira, Marquess Wellesley, brother of the Duke of Wellington, and Charles James Fox. As Prince of Wales George IV had sought the Irish Viceroyalty in the 1790s, while his secret marriage to a Catholic, Mrs Fitzherbert, was public knowledge. Accordingly, the expectations of many Catholics, especially prelates with powerful influence among the laity, were high, made more so by the fact that George IV would be the first English monarch to visit Ireland as a friend and conciliator, and who had, moreover, ennobled nine Irishmen in his coronation honours.[32] Thus they readily gave a lead to the Catholic population through their participation in the events associated with the visit.[33] That genealogical inquiries had discovered a plausible connection between George IV and Ireland's ancient monarchs[34] added to the general atmosphere of good feeling.

As with the planning of his coronation, it would seem that the King was just as meticulous about the Irish arrangements, taking care not to cause offence to anyone expecting to be, but not, invited to royal events, by having it appear that the King himself 'may be supposed to be a guest' of the Viceroy, Lord Talbot.[35] Moreover, well before his arrival he had it made known in Ireland that he wished unity to prevail among the island's religious factions,[36] while a conciliatory gesture to the Catholic community was made with the news that Lord Forbes, son of the Catholic Earl of Granard, would be one of the King's aides-de-camp during his Irish sojourn.[37] But much more symbolically important was the news that

---

[29] J. C. Beckett, *The Making of Modern Ireland 1603–1923* (London, 1966), pp. 240–1.

[30] Daunt, *Ireland since the Union*, p. 67.

[31] Lord Greville to Buckingham, 8 April 1812 in Buckingham and Chandos, *Court of England during the Regency*, I, p. 274.

[32] *London Observer* cited in *Belfast News-Letter* [*BNL*], 10 Aug. 1821.

[33] W. J. Fitzpatrick, *The Life, Times and Correspondence of Dr Doyle, Bishop of Kildare and Leighlin* (Dublin, 1880), I, p. 181.

[34] *Newry Telegraph* reports reproduced in *BNL*, 17 Aug. 1821.

[35] Lord Whitworth to William Gregory, 19 March 1821 in Gregory (ed.), *Gregory's Letter Box*, p. 92.

[36] *TT*, 1 Aug. 1821; Anon, *The Royal Visit, containing A Full Circumstantial Account of Everything Connected with the King's Visit to Ireland* (Dublin, 1821), pp. 4–5. Thanks to the Orange Lord Mayor of Dublin, Alderman Bradley King, O'Connell and other Catholic leaders, his wishes were largely, though not entirely, complied with.

[37] *TT*, 4 Aug. 1821.

the Earl of Fingall would be the first Catholic to be installed as a member of the Order of St Patrick.[38] It would be the only installation in the history of the Order at which a monarch presided in person.[39] Furthermore, a 'Letter' addressed to the 'People of Ireland', and quite likely emanating from Dublin Castle, urged 'self-discipline' on the Dublin populace, the rejection of 'demagogues', but also specifically dissociated the King from any responsibility for the parliamentary defeat of the recent Catholic relief bill.[40] The economic context of the visit may not have been favourable,[41] but the proclamation announcing it provided a significant, if local, boost: a cheap commemorative medal of the occasion was produced for sale;[42] houses were let; services were engaged; while trade was given an 'extraordinary' stimulus by a request from the King that all his subjects approach him in Irish-made attire.[43] At the same time, interest and involvement in the activities associated with the visit were driven by the scramble for honours that this royal visit, like all its successors, generated.[44] In sum, the visit and the enthusiasm it engendered can be seen largely as driven by its own political and socio-economic dynamism. Moreover, just as the King was embarking for Ireland the tension of expectation that was building in Dublin was invested with a strain of acute anxiety on the news that Queen Caroline had fallen mortally ill, immediately raising the prospect that the visit might be called off.[45] The *Freeman's Journal* exclaimed: 'At no period within our recollection was the public mind wound up to so high a pitch of anxiety for intelligence from the other side of the Channel, as it was yesterday [8 Aug.].'[46] Her death on 7 August had brought the suspense and uncertainty to a pitch: bad weather had initially delayed the King at Holyhead, and the delay was extended while arrangements for the Queen's funeral were made. Accordingly, it was not until 12 August that the King arrived at Howth, north of Dublin,[47] and the tension dissipated. Nevertheless, it could only

---

[38] *Freeman's Journal* [*FJ*], 21 Aug. 1821.

[39] Patrick Galloway, *The Most Illustrious Order of St Patrick 1783–1983* (Chichester, 1983), p. 23.

[40] Anon., *The King's Visit to Ireland, in a Letter Addressed to the People of Ireland* (Dublin, 1821), *passim*.

[41] Geróid Ó Tuathaigh, *Ireland before the Famine 1748–1848* (Dublin, 1972), pp. 137–8.

[42] *FJ*, 4 Aug. 1821.

[43] *DEP*, 19 July 1821; *FJ*, 8 Aug. 1821; S. H. Burke, *Ireland Sixty Years Ago: Being an Account of a Visit to Ireland by H. M. King George IV in the Year 1821* (London, 1885), p. 29. The activity generated can be gauged from materials on the royal visit of 1849: NA (Kew), HO45/2522.

[44] Shivaun Lynam, *Humanity Dick Martin: 'King of Connemara'* (Dublin, 1989), p. 200.

[45] *TT*, 11 Aug. 1821.   [46] *FJ*, 9 Aug. 1821.

[47] George Pellew, *The Life and Correspondence of Henry Addington, Viscount Sidmouth* (London, 1847), III, p. 355.

have contributed significantly to the release of mass emotion that his presence in Dublin called forth. There was little concern for the fate of the Queen, as the King found to his great delight when he arrived in Dublin.[48] Certainly O'Connell seems to have had little interest in the scandal of the royal marriage, apart from taking pleasure in the discomfort it was causing in court circles;[49] to which end he had sought to have himself appointed Her Majesty's Attorney General in Ireland.[50]

If the events surrounding the death of the Queen brought popular opinion in Dublin to a pitch of expectation, the language depicting the relationship between monarch and people was such as to facilitate its expression by eliminating imaginative barriers between the personal and the public realms. The *Newry Telegraph*, for instance, recorded the King's arrival in Dublin as follows: 'we recognise the tenderness of an affectionate father for his children, and the princely solicitude of a great monarch for his people'.[51] It was a form of language widely employed, not least in the addresses of O'Connell and Catholic prelates[52] whose own religious discourse in general – 'Mary Queen of Heaven', 'the throne of God', 'Christ the King' – was easily adaptable to the earthly monarchical sphere. Certainly familiarity devoid of distance-asserting ritual characterises the meeting of monarch and subjects when George IV arrived at Howth.

With the necessity to be seen to acknowledge appropriately the Queen's passing, the intended landing at Dunleary, south of Dublin, complete with a reception and public entry into the city,[53] was abandoned in favour of a private arrival at Howth and journey to the Viceregal Lodge in the Phoenix Park.[54] However, owing to a state of intoxication – 'a state ... to double in sight even the numbers of his gracious subjects assembled on the pier'[55] – the King immediately thrust forward to mingle with a crowd, shaking hands indiscriminately, before setting off in the midst of a disorderly entourage for

[48] Press accounts of her fate, north and south, tended to be unemotionally factual: *BNL*, 8 Aug. 1821; *FJ*, 18 July 1821.

[49] See O'Connell to his Wife, 11 Oct. 1820, in O'Connell (ed.), *Correspondence of O'Connell*, II, p. 285.

[50] O'Connell to T. Spring Rice, 16 Nov. 1820, in ibid. pp. 287–8; also, Wife to O'Connell, 19 March 1821, in ibid. p. 309.

[51] *Newry Telegraph* cited in *BNL*, 17 Aug. 1821.   [52] See *BNL*, 24, 28 Aug. 1821.

[53] A printed copy of the intended proceedings at Dunleary, *Ceremonial to be Observed at the Reception of His Most Excellent Majesty King George the Fourth upon His Happy Arrival from England to Visit the Metropolis of Dublin* (Dublin, 1821), can be consulted: NA (Kew), HO45/2522.

[54] For the King's account of the changes, see George IV to Sir William Knighton, 10 Aug. 1821, in Lady Knighton (ed.), *Memoirs of Sir William Knighton* (London, 1838), I, pp. 144–8.

[55] W. H. Freemantle to the Duke of Buckingham, 26 Aug. 1821, in Buckingham and Chandos, *Memoirs of the Court of George IV*, II, p. 194.

the Viceregal Lodge.[56] On reaching the Phoenix Park the King insisted on the gates being thrown open so his following could accompany him right up to the door of the Lodge, whereupon he dispensed largess to a number of farmers and peasants, making an emotional speech acknowledging their welcome.[57] A sympathetic commentator described a remarkable scene: 'The greatest monarch in the world sails in a common steampacket, lands among his subjects, unaffected, unattended, unguarded, without any emblem of dignity, makes his way among a crowd mostly composed of peasantry.'[58] But a more critical commentary remarked on the King coming 'not like a sovereign ... in state and pomp to a part of his dominions' but 'like a popular candidate come down upon an electioneering trip'.[59]

Despite their differences, both accounts describe a spontaneous, immediate and direct – or 'liminal'[60] – relationship in which the mystified condition of awed loyalty that royal ritual is intended to produce[61] has been replaced by unregulated emotional identity. The King himself seems to have recognised the liminal nature of the occasion. In his brief speech to the crowd at the Viceregal Lodge, he declared: 'rank, station and honour are nothing; to feel that I live in the hearts of my Irish subjects, is to me the most exalted happiness'.[62]

In his discussion of the reformist Tsar, Alexander II, Richard Wortman argues that he set out to create a 'scenario of love': 'an image of the autocrat as a beloved national leader that both made possible his acceptance of reforms and established their limits'.[63] Up to a point this could also be said of George IV's approach to Ireland. A scenario of love he clearly wished to establish. And, to an extent, changes in the administration of Ireland following the visit gave some colour to Sir Benjamin Bloomfield's claim that only to their 'illustrious master' were the Irish people to look with confidence for 'benefits and kindness'.[64] However,

---

[56] Anon., *The Royal Visit*, pp. 12–13.   [57] Burke, *Ireland Sixty Years Ago*, pp. 5–7.
[58] Anon., *The Royal Visit*, p. 16. Correct as to specific details of the landing, this work erroneously has the King landing at his original destination of Dunleary.
[59] See Buckingham and Chandos, *Memoirs of the Court of George IV*, II, p. 207.
[60] Victor Turner, *Dramas, Fields and Metaphors: Symbolic Interaction in Human Society* (Ithaca, NY and London, 1974), pp. 273–4.
[61] See Erving Goffman, *The Presentation of Self in Everyday Life* (Harmondsworth, 1976), pp. 74–5.
[62] George IV cited in Anon., *The Royal Visit*, p. 14. Apparently he recognised in them qualities of 'warmth, impulsiveness, generosity, a degree of fecklessness, and intense personal charm' he himself possessed: E. A. Smith, *George IV* (New Haven and London, 1999), p. 193.
[63] Richard Wortman, *Scenarios of Power: Myth and Ceremony in Russian Monarchy, II: From Alexander II to the Abdication of Nicholas II* (Princeton, NJ, 2000), p. 20.
[64] *FJ*, 2 Aug. 1821; Anon., *The King's Visit*, p. 7. His agent in Ireland, Bloomfield spoke at a dinner in Dublin to celebrate the coronation on 1 August.

unlike Alexander II for whom defeat in the Crimean War made fundamental socio-economic reforms unavoidable, George IV, on the back of the defeat of Napoleonic France, was under no such imperative. The Protestant state had vindicated itself. The emancipatory reforms desired by the Catholic Irish were not driven by a crisis of the state; and as events would show, it was only when they produced such a crisis that emancipation would be conceded. So the site, as it were, for the coming together in harmony of the King and his Irish subjects in 1821 was a mutual misconception of what it was possible for the visit to achieve, what indeed it meant.

From the state perspective the visit was especially encouraging. The situational identity of Dublin was transformed. All the usual visual, architectural and sculptural signifiers of divisive political allegiance were overshadowed by arches, banners and illustrations expressing a hegemonic theme of British power and the constitutional integration of the nations of the United Kingdom around the central figure of the King. A depiction of George IV on his favourite white charger entering the city and being given the city keys by a female figure guiding a lion and an Irish wolfhound, with the scene wreathed in the national emblems of roses, thistles and shamrocks, went together with a plethora of associated symbols representing the coronation, empire, literature, architecture, justice, science, agriculture and industry. Daniel O'Connell's house had a rich transparency in the living room window inscribed: 'George IV, the only King that declared the Crown was held in trust for the good of the people.' Also, public buildings were illuminated, firework displays set off and fifteen large casks of porter – 'hogsheads' – supplied for the populace to drink the King's health.[65]

In sum, for the duration of the visit Dublin assumed a celebratory symbolic context that transcended the city's traditional ethno-sectarian divisions, the most remarkable aspect of which was the resignifying of Dublin Castle from the functional and symbolic centre of Ireland's coercion to a location for the holding of events in which mutual political alienation dissolved in common expressions of loyal allegiance. The two major barriers we have noted preventing Ireland's acceptance of the Union – the alienation of the Catholic population from state structures and the existence of deeply antagonistic ethno-national traditions – had apparently been neutralised by the presence of the King in Dublin. A veteran of the 1798 rebellion declared in his presence at the Viceregal Lodge: 'I was a rebel to ould King George in '98, and by G–d I'd now die

---

[65] Anon., *The King's Visit*, pp. 8–9, 45–59; *FJ*, 23 Aug. 1821.

3 George IV's official entry to Dublin, 1821.

a hundred deaths for his son';[66] and when Lord Sidmouth, the Home
Secretary, remarked on the loyalty of a people recently rebellious, the
King immediately put their former character down to 'misrule'.[67] The
most noteworthy demonstration of loyalty came from O'Connell, who
supported a proposal for an Irish royal palace, with the cost of construction being met not only by the donations of the prosperous, but by 'every
peasant' contributing 'his humble mite'; this being only appropriate as
'the joy of the [royal] occasion penetrated the humblest dwelling as well as
the most resplendent mansion'.[68] In supporting the proposal, O'Connell
stimulated a debate that would run through to the early twentieth century. During the royal visit the protestations of Irish loyalty made by
O'Connell and other Catholic leaders seemed amply demonstrated
when the King made his 'official' entry into Dublin on 17 August under
specially constructed 'city gates' at Sackville (now O'Connell) Street
(Fig. 3). Combining careful organisation with uncertain execution, the
occasion provides evidence to support David Cannadine's argument on

---

[66] Burke, *Ireland Sixty Years Ago*, p. 12. Even Lord Londonderry who, as Viscount
Castlereagh, was responsible for the carrying of the Act of Union was 'forgiven' by
bringing the King to Dublin: Lord Sidmouth to Earl Bathurst, 26 Aug. 1821, in
Historical Manuscripts Commission, *Report on the Manuscripts of Earl Bathurst*
(London, 1923), pp. 510–11. For further evidence of popular loyalty, see *FJ*, 23 Aug.
1821; *BNL*, 24 Aug. 1821.
[67] Shane Leslie, *George the Fourth* (2nd edn, London, 1930), pp. 138–9.
[68] *FJ*, 23 Aug. 1821.

the tendency to chaos of royal ceremonial in the early nineteenth century.[69]

Precise orders were given for the precedence of rank that was to characterise the procession of 200 carriages involved in the ceremony,[70] and for British visitors familiar only with the stereotype of the undisciplined Paddy the orderly cooperation of the massive crowds in the arrangements appeared remarkable.[71] For the event, the King was attired in full military uniform, decorated with the ribbon of the Order of St Patrick, while his hat was ornamented with a rosette 'more than twice the size of a military cockade', and he wore a crape of mourning on his right arm. The route was decorated with banners of welcome and the theatre of opening the 'gates' began with the Herald, Athlone Pursuivant, handing the keys to the King, who then returned them and made his 'entry', rising from his seat as he did so and showing 'the most lively feeling of gratification at his reception', repeatedly pointing to the shamrock at the front of his hat and with the crowd responding with 'the most deafening plaudits'. These the King stimulated by placing his hand 'upon his breast, in the most significant manner, [and] waving his hat, in order that the national emblem should be seen by all around him'.[72] In effect, the ceremony combined ordered ritual with a personal stimulus of popular emotion that threatened to destabilise the event. Encouraged by the King, the crowd pressed forward, bringing the procession to a standstill for nearly an hour:

it was in vain for the cavalry to extricate the sovereign's coach from the encompassing grasp of the populace. The horses of the dragoons were almost unmanageable; they were kept by the fluctuating pressure of the crowd in a state of constant motion, just as if swimming; the [King's] barouche was at times so shaken that the noblemen who sat opposite his Majesty were under the necessity of supporting the arms of the King, to enable him to stand in an erect position.[73]

Only Ulster loyalists fearful of emancipation, and for whom the Catholic Irish welcome for the King was unsettling, remained emotionally untouched by the proceedings.[74] Already in Ulster monarchical symbolism was being appropriated as a badge of regional loyalist

---

[69] David Cannadine, 'The Context, Meaning and Performance of Ritual: The British Monarchy and the "Invention of Tradition" in Eric Hobsbawm and Terence Ranger (eds.), *The Invention of Tradition* (Cambridge, 1983), pp. 116–17.

[70] Anon., *The Royal Visit*, pp. 18–23.

[71] Duke of Montrose to Lord Eldon, 30 Aug. 1821, in Twiss, *Eldon*, II, pp. 432–3.

[72] Anon., *The Royal Visit*, pp. 27–42. [73] Burke, *Ireland Sixty Years Ago*, p. 15.

[74] See the contemptuous description of the 'bloated' monarch by Lieut. Col. William Blacker, a founder of the Orange Order, in Appendix B: The Visit of George IV to Dublin in 1821 in Constantia Maxwell, *A History of Trinity College Dublin* (Dublin,

identity.[75] Northern loyalist exceptionalism, however, had no public presence as the community and the King combined to produce remarkable scenes of spectacle. And the King had other, strictly personal, reasons to be pleased with Dublin.

Throughout the visit he had the constant companionship of his current mistress, Lady Conyngham, of Slane Castle in County Meath – his chief excursions outside Dublin were pleasant trips to Slane and the Curragh race course;[76] he was free of the controversy and criticism he had recently been subject to in London; and Dublin showed no inclination to mourn the passing of the Queen. It is hardly surprising, therefore, that he should compare repeatedly the 'triumph of Dublin' with the 'horrors of London'.[77] Perhaps more significantly, those accompanying him could interpret the Dublin reception as a lesson to the disaffected of England,[78] and as a portent of the likely reception the King would receive if he ventured into parts of England such as Birmingham and the midlands[79] where, during the recent controversy over the Queen's constitutional position, he had not dared to go.[80] So impressed with the visit was the Scots poet Robert Fraser that he set about designing a commemorative medal for sale throughout Ireland 'at the trifling sum of ten pence each'.[81]

The popular reception for the King was not devoid of hope of municipal gain. Shortly before the royal visit, apparently well-founded press reports to the effect that the window tax in Ireland was soon to be abolished[82] ensured that calls for its abolition were heard more than once.[83] Also, sectional interests found expression in the addresses of the Anglican and Catholic churches, the former concerned for its established position, the latter hinting at emancipation.[84] Even the transparency in O'Connell's living room window could be easily decoded in terms of Catholic expectation. But more seriously, and controversially, sectarian identity found expression at the Corporation dinner in the King's honour

1946), pp. 276–7. Certainly the visit could be interpreted beyond Ulster as 'a blow to the Orange faction': Frederick Ponsonby to Viscount Milton, 3 Sept. 1821, in Machin, *Catholic Question in English Politics*, p. 32, fn. 4.

[75] See D. A. Chart (ed.), *The Drennan Letters 1776–1819* (Belfast, 1931), pp. 341, 350, for loyalist use of the national anthem and celebrations of British military victories to identify and attack perceived enemies.

[76] *FJ*, 25, 27, 29, 31 Aug., 1 Sept. 1821.

[77] Diary (17 Aug. 1821), Bernard Pool (ed.), *The Croker Papers, 1808–1857* (1884; abridged edn, London, 1967), p. 61; W. H. Freemantle to Duke of Buckingham, 26 Aug. 1821, in Buckingham and Chandos, *Court of George IV*, I, p. 194.

[78] Sir William Curtis at the Dublin Corporation dinner, 23 Aug. 1823: Anon., *The Royal Visit*, pp. 92–3.

[79] Robert Fraser to Sir Charles Grant, 29 Aug. 1821, NA (Kew), HO100/200.

[80] Henry Brougham to Thomas Creevey, 26 July 1821, in Gore (ed.), *Creevey*, p. 213.

[81] Fraser to Grant, 29 Aug. 1821, NA (Kew), HO100/200.

[82] *FJ*, 18 July 1821.   [83] Anon., *The Royal Visit*, p. 17.   [84] *BNL*, 29 Aug. 1821.

on 23 August, when, after his departure, Alderman Darley, the Chief Police Magistrate, proposed the controversial toast to 'The Glorious Memory' of William III, a toast participated in by the Viceroy, Lord Talbot, and which threatened to rupture the ecumenical relations between religious factions established just before the visit began. Only speedy assurances to Catholic leaders from Lord Sidmouth that the King would deal promptly with the issue retrieved the situation.[85]

Political tensions underlying the outward demonstration of municipal allegiance to the monarch were not unique to Dublin. But in Britain the ramifications of these tensions, even when involving national issues,[86] were usually easily containable within the local political and civic sphere. Dublin, as a capital city, was unique within the British Isles for the way in which powerful mobilising and antagonistic national ideologies invested the municipal arena, with issues of state allegiance and stability being of far greater moment.

The King apparently made only one *faux pas*, when, at a banquet, he told those assembled that they had made a great mistake at the time of the Union: 'You should have made terms as the Scotch did.'[87] This declaration, given the betrayed promise of emancipation, must have struck many of those present as deeply offensive. Otherwise he was a master of civil interaction,[88] with Catholic prelates received in their ecclesiastical costumes, even though their dignity as prelates had never officially been recognised, and with the Catholic laity received on exactly the same terms as Protestants.[89] It is true, of course, that the King's conciliation of Irish Catholics never went much beyond symbolic gestures; nevertheless, their psychological importance should be recognised. O'Connell, indeed, was to defend the visit on precisely these symbolic grounds: Catholics had been raised to a position of equality with Protestants through the agency of the King's favour, and by joint participation in the events of the visit a basis would be laid, as he thought, to 'unite both communities in the single name of Irishmen'.[90]

[85] See the correspondence between O'Connell and Lord Donoughmore on the issue (25 Aug.–9 Sept.) in O'Connell (ed.), *Correspondence of O'Connell*, II, pp. 328–33.

[86] See, for example, James Vernon, *Politics and the People: A Study in English Political Culture, c. 1815–1867* (Cambridge, 1993), pp. 76–9.

[87] George IV, quoted in Leslie, *George the Fourth*, p. 139.

[88] Charles Kendal Bushe, Irish Solicitor General, to his Wife, 28 Aug. 1821, in Gregory (ed.), *Gregory's Letter Box*, pp. 100–1. For a more caustic assessment: Countess of Glengall to Mrs Francis Taylor, 10 Sept. 1821, in Gore (ed.), *Creevey*, p. 219.

[89] David Plunket, *The Life, Letters and Speeches of Lord Plunket* (London, 1867), I, pp. 80–1.

[90] T. C. Luby, *The Life and Times of Daniel O'Connell* (Glasgow, n.d.), p. 458; Robert Dunlop, *Daniel O'Connell and the Revival of National Life in Ireland* (London, 1900), pp. 113–14.

The success of the visit raised concerns among British opponents and supporters of emancipation. There was a danger of the King being carried away by emotion into 'expressions which discretion may lament' and Irish expectations of reforms being raised which 'can hardly be realised'.[91] Pro-emancipists concurred, seeing also the problems involved for any new Viceroy in trying to 'ingratiate' himself with the Catholic people.[92] The King himself would come to fear that he had gone too far in Ireland.[93] But this was a reflection in tranquillity. At the time, he was enveloped in the euphoria of the visit, which continued until its conclusion, when a massive concourse of people accompanied the royal party to Dunleary – henceforth named Kingstown – on 5 September. Highly charged with emotion, the occasion is noteworthy especially for a gesture by O'Connell, who led a Catholic deputation to see the King off, and, when in the royal presence, melodramatically knelt in homage, offering a laurel wreath as he did so.[94] Like the King, who loathed him, O'Connell would reflect soberly on the occasion, remembering the sovereign as personally 'a most hideous object'.[95] But the expectations and atmosphere of the time clearly lent the sovereign a different aspect. The Irish royal visit formally ended there; however, it had a contemporary influence beyond Ireland. Embryonic preparations for the Scottish royal visit of August 1822 were already under way and the enthusiastic reception of the Irish for the King was noted.[96]

In Scotland the end of the Jacobite tradition with the demise of the Cardinal Duke of York made possible a more fully national celebration than might otherwise have been the case.[97] Arrangements for the visit fell overwhelmingly to Sir Walter Scott, a friend of the King, who proceeded to reinvent Scotland in the highland image of his historical novels, with the King attired in the Stuart tartan of the Young Pretender.[98] As spectacle it was far grander than the Dublin visit, well organised and effectively

---

[91] Duke of Montrose to Lord Eldon, 30 Aug. 1821, in Twiss, *Eldon*, II, p. 433.

[92] Charles Wynn to Buckingham, 9 Sept. 1821; W. H. Freemantle to Buckingham, 16 Sept. 1821, in Buckingham and Chandos, *Court of George IV*, I, pp. 197–201.

[93] W. H. Freemantle to the Marquis of Buckingham, 21 Sept. 1821, in ibid. pp. 201–2.

[94] Burke, *Ireland Sixty Years Ago*, pp. 27–8.

[95] O'Connell quoted in Daunt, *Personal Recollections of O'Connell*, I, p. 131.

[96] See *Glasgow Herald* report quoted in *FJ*, 13 Sept. 1821.

[97] Lord Stowell to Sidmouth, 31 Aug. 1821, in Pellew, *Sidmouth*, III, pp. 363–5; J. G. Lockhart, *Memoirs of the Life of Sir Walter Scott* (London, 1837), V, p. 190.

[98] Ibid. p. 204. See also Hugh Trevor-Roper, 'The Invention of Tradition: The Highland Tradition of Scotland' in Hobsbawm and Ranger (eds.), *Invention of Tradition*, pp. 15–46. The whole exercise, however, was made to look rather ridiculous when the very portly London Alderman, Sir William Curtis, arrived in the same Stuart tartan.

executed.[99] But then there is reason to see the Irish visit as a point of comparison – and departure – for the Scottish events. Certainly it was with the Irish visit in mind that Scott made his preparations. He was concerned both that the Scottish occasion should be on a grander scale than the Dublin celebrations, and that the unrestrained passion of the Irish reception be avoided.[100] In this he was successful. Ireland had presented an example of undisciplined 'Celtic' behaviour in keeping with the stereotype of the Catholic Irishman. A Scotland that was now well integrated into the British state was keen to present a more sober version of Celtic identity, one that Scott would give the finishing touches to with his tartan pageantry.[101]

At the visit's conclusion, initial contrasts between the 'national characteristics' of Scotland and Ireland – sobriety, discipline and decorum, as against emotion, disorder and implied vulgarity – seemed fully justified.[102] *The Scotsman* put it bluntly:

Every effort was made to impress the citizens with the same wild enthusiasm, and to make them display the same frantic and extravagant demonstration of joy, as had been demonstrated by the citizens of Dublin: but the good sense of the Scottish public has completely disappointed the hopes of the ultra sycophants . . . The truth is that the purveyors of blarney and bombastic adulation completely overshot the mark.[103]

And the King was apparently more gratified with the Scottish visit than with the Irish.[104] Nevertheless, the three major public occasions of 1821–2 – the coronation, and the visits to Ireland and Scotland – were similar in one crucial respect: collectively they demonstrated the power of spectacle to mobilise public sentiment in support of the throne. The Irish visit initiated the tradition of royal visits precisely because it was so successful. However, to adequately account for its success a closer assessment of the occasion is necessary.

III

To do so it may be best to start with the often contemptuous reactions we have noted of external commentators far removed from Dublin. They were not affected by the conditions that facilitated the collective emotion

[99] For a sketch of the arrangements, see B. C. Skinner, 'Scott as Pageant-master – the Royal Visit of 1822' in Alan Bell (ed.), *Scott Bicentenary Essays* (Edinburgh, 1973), pp. 228–37.

[100] On the latter point, see Scott to his son Walter, ? Aug. 1822, in Lockhart, *Memoirs of Scott*, V, pp. 210–11.

[101] *TT*, 14 Aug. 1822.   [102] *TT*, 2 Sept. 1822.

[103] *The Scotsman* reproduced in *TT*, 4 Sept. 1822.

[104] W. H. Fremantle to Buckingham, 8 Sept. 1822, in Buckingham and Chandos, *Court of George IV*, I, pp. 372–3.

and mass persuasion the situation engendered; and there is reason to think that the personage for whom the arrangements were made – a King – came encoded with charisma and supra-natural properties given plausibility by the language of homage indulged in by both lay and clerical leaders of opinion. That a visit by the King was regarded as being of an exceptional order is indicated by the fact that the spot at which George IV alighted at Howth harbour was marked by 'the print of his sacred feet cut out in stone'.[105]

Arguably, monarchical charisma is a function more of the office than of the officeholder. Irrespective of personal qualities, the office inherently carries with it a connection with the sacred, the source of charisma. But it is relatively 'rational' in nature, functioning as a force for the legitimation of powerful institutions and individuals.[106] As a general statement this would certainly apply to George IV in 1821, but it is in need of development. It can be argued that George IV came to Ireland with royal charisma derived from what Clifford Geertz has described as the integration of symbolism and power, and which he argues is always likely to be most influential among those farthest away from the centre of power,[107] a condition that would apply psychologically to British Catholics in general, and geographically to Irish Catholics in particular. The King was not just symbolic of the constitutional order but, given the monarchy's institutional centrality in a pre-Bagehotian age, was an authentic embodiment of the power that order possessed and which, in the dynamic circumstances of the Irish visit, was highly likely to have a mesmeric effect.

With the successful passage of a Catholic relief bill in the Commons and Catholic belief about the pro-emancipist sentiments of the King, their expectations and emotions – encouraged by both prelates and O'Connell – were high, with an inevitable tendency to indulge the irrational. For southern loyalists anxious to defend the Protestant Ascendancy, a similar set of considerations could be said to apply. Bearing in mind that the King came to this, the most troubled part of his kingdom, generating expectations that properties traditionally associated with the kingly office – 'a source of justice and assistance to all members alike of a polity that in other contexts seems to be sharply

---

[105] Countess Glengall to Mrs Francis Taylor, 10 Sept. 1821, in Gore (ed.), *Creevey*, p. 219. The spot was later marked by a brass plate, apparently following a French precedent, on the occasion of the return of Louis XVIII after the final defeat of Napoleon: Anon., *The Royal Visit*, p. 16.
[106] Charles Lindholm, *Charisma* (Oxford, 1990), p. 24.
[107] Clifford Geertz, 'Centres, Kings and Charisma: Reflections on the Symbolics of Power' in Joseph Ben-David and T. N. Clark (eds.), *Culture and Its Creators: Essays in Honour of Edward Shils* (Chicago, 1975), p. 151.

divided'[108] – suggested the fulfilment of, the mass adulation of the populace is understandable. Thus that adulation – 'They clawed and pawed him all over, and called him his *Ethereal* Majesty'[109] – fundamentally was a function of the power of royal spectacle and charisma which, however temporarily, served to establish the social reality to validate the myth of national homogeneity that monarchy embodied. And even though of a temporary nature, the intensity of 'enchantment' that it exercised should not be underestimated, a source of which has been located in the mass concentration spectacle engenders.[110]

The focus of concentration was the King, the hegemonic emblem of the Kingdom, and the mesmeric effects of his presence apparently lasted until his departure at Dunleary, when, on entering the royal barge, he appeared to those on land to be 'walking on water'.[111] Nor was it merely the superficially minded and gullible who were prey to the visit's enchanting effects. The brilliant scientist Sir William Rowan Hamilton, Astronomer Royal of Ireland in the 1840s, was, as a youth, present during the royal visit and struggled to make sense of his own actions – 'were I to give free vent to my feelings, I might appear ridiculous and affected' – finding an explanation in the combined effects of the sacredness of the royal office, the (supposed) personal worth of the occupant and the qualities of Irish national character.[112]

The assessment of the royal visit presented here would support the view that monarchical ritual does not merely reflect the power of the state, but is itself 'a visible form of power'.[113] Certainly the power of the state was necessary to allow the ritual to take place, but it is clear that the ritual itself, despite being imperfectly executed, was a mechanism for the engagement of powerful sentiments acting to consolidate and enhance the authority of the throne.

The Burkean conception of the monarchy's relationship to state and society recognised no categories or forms of self that it could not inform and give meaning to. The royal visit, framed outside the party political context, appeared to demonstrate magnificently what was possible when the monarch and his people were brought into direct, personal,

---

[108] Lucy Mair, *Primitive Government* (Harmondsworth, 1962), p. 229.
[109] Glengall to Mrs Francis Taylor, 27 Aug. 1821, in Gore (ed.), *Creevey*, p. 218.
[110] Guy Debord, *Society of the Spectacle* (Detroit, 1983), p. 2.
[111] Anon., *The Royal Visit*, pp. 137–8.
[112] Hamilton to his sister Eliza, 15 Oct. 1821, in R. P. Graves, *Life of Sir William Rowan Hamilton* (Dublin and London, 1882), I, p. 93.
[113] David Cannadine, 'Introduction: Divine Right of Kings' in David Cannadine and Simon Price (eds.), *Rituals of Royalty: Power and Ceremonial in Traditional Society* (Cambridge, 1992), p. 17.

'authentic' contact. As such, the visit informed a highly influential, if flawed, interpretation of the Irish question, one that would be at the centre of Westminster's approach to the Irish problem throughout the nineteenth century; namely, that nationalist agitators did not represent the 'real' interests and opinions of ordinary Irish people who were naturally loyal to crown and constitution; and that the best way of mobilising that sentiment was to bring the monarch and the Irish people more often into close contact. It was a view the King himself seemed to endorse when, in 1823, he declared that the only way to 'quiet' the country would be to hold a parliament there every three years,[114] which he, presumably, would have opened. Accordingly, the mobilising power of nationalist narratives at certain points in the century – for instance, on Repeal in the 1840s and land and Home Rule in the 1880s – would be challenged by that of impressive royal spectacle. In sum, the visit of 1821 established the sphere of everyday life as the terrain on which the nationalist threat could be effectively challenged; one that the development of welfare monarchism could play a significant role in cultivating.

Of course, and as will be seen, the sentiment royal spectacle mobilised tended to be unstable and, accordingly, made difficult state attempts to exploit it. Nevertheless, efforts to do so would be continually pursued, something the example of Scotland, as a 'Celtic' country at war for centuries with England and at last brought into harmonious union, would be largely responsible for; and apparently given colour by the close proximity of the equally successful Irish and Scottish royal visits of the early 1820s at a time when the prevailing Irish claim was for Catholic relief and inclusion within the political nation of the British state. In this context the constitutionally integrative power of monarchical influence appeared impressive.

IV

The 'scenario of love' that the visit established created a perspective for the understanding of subsequent developments. On leaving Dunleary and apparently greatly affected by O'Connell's gesture of homage, the King declared: 'Whenever an opportunity offers, wherein I can serve Ireland, I will seize on it with eagerness.'[115] Also, an official letter of thanks from the King to the Viceroy urged the continued amity of inter-community relations based on the mutual forbearance and goodwill

---

[114] See Charles Wynn to the Duke of Buckingham, 18 Dec. 1823, in Buckingham and Chandos, *Court of George IV*, II, p. 20.
[115] King quoted in Anon., *The Royal Visit*, p. 136.

which characterised the visit.[116] Almost immediately arrangements were
made at a meeting of Dublin householders to have 10,000 copies of the
King's letter distributed throughout Ireland,[117] while O'Connell sought
to give effect to the King's sentiments through the establishment of a –
short-lived – 'Royal Georgian Club' in Dublin, for the express purpose of
cultivating goodwill and perpetuating that 'affectionate gratitude towards
His Majesty King George the Fourth (whom God preserve), which now
animates every Irish bosom'.[118] Even Thomas Moore, who expressed
disgust at the servility of the Irish greeting for the King, was inclined to
think that 'many good results' could result from the visit if the King
remained in the same frame of mind that he demonstrated when in
Dublin.[119] And while the plan for an Irish royal palace did not bear
fruit, owing to lack of sufficient subscriptions,[120] the funds gathered –
by 6 September alone almost £7,600 was donated[121] – were enough for
the construction of a memorial 'King's Bridge' across the Liffey,[122] the
first specifically monarchical signifier in nineteenth-century Dublin's
cityscape. Moreover, Dr Doyle, bishop of Kildare and Leighlin, echoing
O'Connell, sought to counteract an upsurge in the growth of agrarian
secret societies and disturbances that had followed the visit by reminding
the Catholic population of the need to 'establish ourselves in the high
situation to which his Majesty raised us'. His influential address to the
Catholics of his diocese in January 1822 intoned: 'Our gracious sovereign
had just visited us like a common father, quelling the tumult of the
passions, allaying the spirit of party and dissension, and dispensing
among every class of his people, the blessings of peace and goodwill.'
But most significantly, the visit presaged 'mighty changes ... just
approaching'. The address was translated into the 'language of Ireland',
Dublin Castle produced and distributed 300,000 copies, while
O'Connell credited it with great effect among the Catholic people.[123] In
sum, on a number of fronts, a collective attempt was made to establish the
visit as a defining moment in Anglo-Irish relations, a zeitgeistian moment
that would provide an interpretative framework for a new era of inter-
community harmony between Ireland's divided ethno-religious groups as
well as between Ireland and Britain. Administrative changes at Dublin
Castle following the visit lent credibility to the view.

---

[116] *BNL*, 7 Sept. 1821.   [117] Anon., *The Royal Visit*, pp. 141–2.
[118] Dunlop, *O'Connell*, p. 116.
[119] Diary (9 Sept. 1821), Russell (ed.), *Memoirs of Thomas Moore*, III, p. 275.
[120] The proposal, however, earned Lord Byron's contempt: Dunlop, *O'Connell*, pp. 117–18.
[121] *FJ*, 7 Sept. 1821.   [122] Dunlop, *O'Connell*, pp. 115–16.
[123] Fitzpatrick, *Life of Dr Doyle*, I, pp. 199–206; also p. 278, rebutting Orange claims of
Catholic disloyalty by emphasising their monarchical loyalty.

For instance, the egregious insult Viceroy Talbot had offered to Catholics at the Corporation dinner, and which they had been promised would be dealt with appropriately, met its just reward at the end of November 1821 when the Viceroy, to his great chagrin,[124] was abruptly dismissed from office. He was replaced by the pro-emancipist Marquess Wellesley, brother of the Duke of Wellington.[125] Wellesley had an Anglo-Irish pedigree going back to Edward II and, apparently, even family connections to the last Irish High King, Rory O'Conor.[126] During his Viceroyalty Wellesley married a Roman Catholic.[127] His accession to office saw other important changes in the administration, with the emancipation campaigner W. C. (later Lord) Plunket appointed Irish Attorney General to replace William Saurin, an ardent defender of the Protestant Ascendancy, and Charles Kendal Bushe, another liberal, as Solicitor General. The Dublin Castle administration, accordingly, took on a reformist cast with Wellesley's appointment. And Wellesley's reply to the Catholic prelates' address of welcome on his appointment referred to the royal visit, and himself as the conduit of the King's wishes;[128] a point repeated in a parliamentary debate on the state of Ireland by Plunket in April 1822, when he cited the visit as the point of departure for progressive developments in Ireland.[129]

Reformism, however, had more image than substance. The progressive cast of Wellesley's administration was undercut by the appointment of Henry Goulburn, an opponent of Catholic relief, to the crucial post of Irish Chief Secretary. Both the Prime Minister, Lord Liverpool, and the Home Secretary, Sir Robert Peel, were strongly opposed to emancipation and concerned to neutralise Wellesley's scope for reform. Clear as the line of causation from Talbot's Orange toast during the royal visit to his removal at the end of November was to Irish opinion, the reality was more complex. The Government, unpopular in Britain over the Queen Caroline affair[130] and domestic issues, had, even before the royal visit, sought to liberalise its *image* through changes to the Irish administration, in particular by the appointment of Plunket, an impressive parliamentary performer. Talbot, however, had opposed the appointment of so

---

[124] See Talbot to William Gregory, 1, 2, 10, 16, 19, 25 Jan., 28 March, 25 April 1822 in Gregory (ed.), *Gregory's Letter Box*, pp. 107–13.

[125] O'Mahony, *Viceroys of Ireland*, pp. 224–5.

[126] R. R. Pearce, *Memoirs and Correspondence of Richard, Marquess Wellesley* (London, 1846), I, pp. 2–9.

[127] O'Mahoney, *Viceroys of Ireland*, p. 227.   [128] Pearce, *Wellesley*, III, pp. 323–4.

[129] Plunket in the Commons, 22 April 1822 in J. C. Hoey (ed.), *Speeches of Lord Plunket* (Dublin, 1867), p. 243.

[130] The Government had badly mishandled her funeral.

prominent a liberal, leaving the Government seeking for an excuse to remove him. The occasion arose when the Irish administration had difficulties in responding to the upsurge of agrarian disorder that occurred in November 1821.[131] Accordingly, the Irish understanding of the Irish administrative changes, while plausible, was, it seems, largely a fiction useful to the Government in its relations with the Catholic community. Moreover, the obstacles to reform were clearly demonstrated when Wellesley sought at least to give symbolic effect to the new dispensation the royal visit appeared to inaugurate by formally banning Orange decorations of the controversial statue of William III on College Green.

Long a source of factional strife, the statue encoded the Protestant settlement on which the Ascendancy was based: its annual decoration was both a reaffirmation of Orange dominance and a reminder to Catholics of their constitutionally inferior position.[132] Wellesley's action was bound to inflame Orange opinion and he found that his position as the King's surrogate did not protect him from attempted assault at a Dublin theatre. Moreover, although the culprit was caught, he eluded punishment when a grand jury refused to convict. Nor did Plunket's argument that Wellesley was merely giving effect to the wishes of the King[133] deter Orange sympathisers who raised the issue in the Commons and who only narrowly failed in a motion of censure against the Viceroy.[134] The ban on Orange decorations of the statue was militarily enforced and ended the practice, but the controversy retarded progress on the emancipation issue, while Wellesley's judgement was called into question.[135] But for our purposes, the consequences of the affair went much further.

It glaringly exposed not only the progressive limitations of the Wellesley Viceroyalty, but also the hollowness of the King's rhetoric in Dublin and belief in monarchical influence as an agency of change. From this point, Catholics gradually realised that only a sustained popular campaign in Ireland would create the pressure to advance their interests. And yet while O'Connell later claimed that 'we' were not 'humbugged' in 1821,[136] well into the 1820s he was anxious to credit the King – on little or no evidence – with favourable intentions towards Irish reform.[137] In

[131] See Machin, *Catholic Question in English Politics*, pp. 31–3.
[132] Judith Hill, *Irish Public Sculpture* (Dublin, 1998), pp. 41–3.
[133] Hoey (ed.), *Speeches of Lord Plunket*, pp. 260–4.
[134] O'Mahoney, *Viceroys of Ireland*, p. 225.
[135] See Charles Wynn to Buckingham, 17 Feb. 1823, in Buckingham and Chandos, *Court of George IV*, I, pp. 431–2; Hill, 'National Festivals', 46–7.
[136] O'Connell cited in Daunt, *Personal Recollections of O'Connell*, I, p. 131.
[137] O'Connell to his Wife, 19 April 1825, in Maurice O'Connell (ed.), *The Correspondence of Daniel O'Connell* III: *1824–1828* (Dublin, 1974), p. 149.

March 1827, following a parliamentary defeat on a motion supporting emancipation, he suggested a petition to the King, claiming a 'deep debt of gratitude' was owed to Ireland for its acknowledgement of his kingly status in 1821 when he was reviled in England, and hoping that he would yet give Catholics 'cause to rejoice at our fidelity'.[138] On the death of the reactionary Duke of York in 1827 he cultivated the heir to the throne, the Duke of Clarence, later William IV, with the promise of Irish Catholic allegiance, 'heart, hand and soul', if only they get 'fair play'.[139] By mid-1827, however, the extent of royal opposition to emancipation was evident even to O'Connell, though he lamented this disposition becoming public knowledge, feeling that it 'ought to have been concealed'.[140]

The concession was made by the Wellington ministry in defiance of the King, to avert a major state crisis that followed O'Connell's mobilisation of a mass movement of priests and people organised by the Catholic Association he had formed in 1824.[141] Emancipation, however, was accompanied by the abolition of the forty shilling freeholder franchise – the franchise which enabled O'Connell to be elected to Parliament for County Clare in 1828, thereby initiating the constitutional crisis that made action on emancipation imperative. It was also hedged about with petty restrictions and conditions concerning Catholic allegiance and religious status and practice to conciliate diehard Protestant opinion. But more importantly for our purposes, a ban on Roman Catholics holding the office of Irish Viceroy was also enacted.[142] This would unnecessarily hamper the development of a conciliatory relationship between the Viceroyalty and the Irish people when popular nationalism and agrarian agitation threatened the administration of Ireland in the later nineteenth century. Of more immediate significance were the consequences of royal opposition to emancipation and the necessity of O'Connell forcing the issue. His success enormously enhanced his standing with the Irish people, offering an oppositional centre of allegiance to the sovereign.

---

[138] O'Connell to Edward Dwyer, 9 March 1827, in ibid. p. 298. His hopes were encouraged by the Knight of Kerry: Kerry to O'Connell, 14, 23 April 1827, in ibid. pp. 305, 309.

[139] O'Connell to R. N. Bennett, 15 Jan. 1827, in O'Connell (ed.), *Correspondence of O'Connell*, III, p. 288.

[140] O'Connell to Knight of Kerry, 9 June 1827, in ibid. pp. 323–4; Richard Lalor Sheil to O'Connell, 6 Aug. 1828, in ibid. pp. 399–400; O'Connell to his Wife, 3, 5 March 1829, in Maurice O'Connell (ed.), *The Correspondence of Daniel O'Connell* IV: *1829–1832* (Dublin, 1977), pp. 16, 19.

[141] For succinct coverage of the campaign, see O'Ferrall, *O'Connell*, ch. 3.

[142] Patrick Fagan, *Divided Loyalties: The Question of an Oath for Irish Catholics in the Eighteenth Century* (Dublin, 1997), epilogue.

2   Royalty and repeal

O'Connell's successful campaign for emancipation earned him the epithet 'Liberator'. It was a symbolically potent term, at once acknowledging his political achievement while at the same time suggesting that O'Connell himself was a focus of national allegiance. In fact emancipation had transformed O'Connell from Ireland's leading nationalist politician to a Geertzian figure 'of authority'; a leader with a neo-royal presence. In this period he was not unique. In Britain, the Duke of Wellington, the great hero of Waterloo, occupied an analogous position. Wellington, of whom 'the King stands completely in awe',[1] had demonstrated his authority by forcing through Catholic emancipation against the sovereign's will,[2] the 'royal' dimension of which was brilliantly captured in a contemporary political cartoon drawing on the ancient notion of the King as the centre of the universe, but with the royal presence of George IV eclipsed by the Duke (Fig. 4). The difference between Wellington and O'Connell, however, was that Wellington's motivation was the safety and consolidation of the existing constitution, O'Connell's its dissolution. But perhaps more importantly, in Britain Wellington would, and could, never aspire to be a neo-royal embodiment of the nation; in Ireland this is exactly what had happened to O'Connell by 1830, at least for many Irish Catholics.

I

O'Connell's regal presence was widely subscribed to: in praises sung to the tune of 'God Save the King'; at least one case of his hunting cap being applied to a swelling in the hope of relief – a variation on the royal touch;[3] pageants that had a significant royal aspect;[4] the fact that he gained three

---

[1] Entry (22 Feb. 1829), P. W. Wilson (ed.), *The Greville Diary, Including Passages Hitherto Withheld* (London, 1927), I, p. 188.

[2] Fergus O'Ferrell, *Daniel O'Connell* (Dublin, 1981), pp. 66–7.

[3] W. J. O'Neill Daunt, *Personal Recollections of O'Connell* (Dublin, 1848), I, p. 69.

[4] Ibid. pp. 98–9.

4 Eclipse of the King.

votes in the election for the King of Belgium in 1830;[5] anecdotes in which O'Connell and George IV are equal, if antagonistic – on the King's part – characters;[6] and the tendency of the Orange press to present him as someone who, in a self-governing Ireland, would not be a subject of, but a 'balance' to, the sovereign.[7] In this context it is noteworthy that an 'Irish Milesian Crown' was designed by the Young Ireland leader Charles Gavan Duffy and the painter Henry MacManus, in 1843, and presented to O'Connell at a monster meeting,[8] while his great meeting at Tara, the residence of Ireland's ancient High Kings, in August 1843, was used to

[5] Ibid. p. 108.   [6] Ibid. pp. 130–1.   [7] Ibid. II, pp. 152–3.
[8] See Jeanne Sheehy, *The Rediscovery of Ireland's Past: The Celtic Revival 1830–1930* (London, 1980), pp. 38–9.

MR. O'CONNELL, IN HIS TRIUMPHAL CAR.

5 O'Connell in royal triumph.

invoke the sanction of a native monarchical tradition on the contemporary Repeal campaign.[9] Certainly the reception which greeted O'Connell on release from prison in 1844[10] had all the character of a royal progress. Its centrepiece was an elaborate 'royal carriage' (Fig. 5), while the crowd assembled, estimated at 500,000, was of royal proportions and reportedly all sober.[11]

Accordingly, strenuously as O'Connell might declare his allegiance to the throne, the reality of his position in Ireland appeared to undervalue those protestations. By the late 1820s there is evidence that he was coming to personify the country. The action of a soldier in Ennis, County Clare, in breaking ranks to 'grasp the hand of the *father* [my italics] of my country'[12] is an individual example of his national

[9] For an insightful study of O'Connell's speech at Tara and other Repeal speeches, see W. E. White, 'Daniel O'Connell's Oratory on Repeal', unpublished PhD thesis, University of Wisconsin (1954), p. 252 and *passim*.

[10] O'Connell had been convicted on a charge of treason by a packed, anti-nationalist, jury, following the cancellation of the great monster meeting at Clontarf, which the Government had banned.

[11] See the detailed account of the proceedings in *Illustrated London News*, 14 Sept. 1844.

[12] Cited in R. B. O'Brien, *A Hundred Years of Irish History*, Intro. John Redmond (London, 1901), p. 75.

significance, which the Irish folk tradition – in which O'Connell has a much larger presence than other nationalist leaders such as Wolfe Tone, Thomas Davis or Parnell[13] – supplies a great body of evidence to support.

The folk interpretation of O'Connell, contrary to his own arguments, placed him in the company of the Young Pretender, Charles Edward Stuart, and Napoleon as saviours of Ireland.[14] The Tara meeting served to confirm his 'royal' status in the folk tradition,[15] while on his death in 1847 over a million copies of a ballad entitled 'Erin's King' were said to have been sold in Britain and Ireland.[16] In the Irish folk tradition O'Connell appears as a numinous entity, awe-inspiring, a neo-royal centre of the Irish universe. It was a position though that his British enemies were not slow to ridicule.[17] O'Connell had achieved 'royal' status at a significant landmark. Emancipation would allow him to build a parliamentary base from 1830, a year noteworthy for the death of George IV and the accession of the rather eccentric William IV.

II

There was nothing in the coronation ritual of William IV to allow a 'reading' of his attitude to Ireland. In fact, the King did not wish to have a formal coronation ceremony at all, and only agreed to one under pressure from Wellington, the Prime Minister.[18] He had been given robust advice on the practice of kingship by the outspoken Irish Viceroy, Lord Anglesey,[19] and had wanted to adopt the comparatively abbreviated ritual of viceregal installation.[20] It did not take place until July 1831 and, even then, in a greatly reduced form, ostensibly on the grounds that lavish pageantry would incur an expense incompatible with economic difficulties the country was facing at this time.[21] But in reality he considered the coronation a 'pointless piece of flummery, a compound

---

[13] Ríonach Uí Ógáin, *Immortal Dan: Daniel O'Connell in Irish Folk Tradition* (Dublin, 1996), p. 1; Story files, Department of Irish Folklore, University College Dublin.

[14] Ógáin, *Immortal Dan*, p. 87.   [15] Ibid. pp. 105–6.

[16] Diarmuid Ó Muirithe, 'O'Connell in the Irish Folk Tradition' in K. B. Nowlan and M. R. O'Connell (eds.), *Daniel O'Connell: Portrait of a Radical* (Belfast, 1984), p. 67.

[17] *Punch* (1843) presented 'King O'Connell' as an unscrupulous demagogue exploiting an impoverished people: cartoon reproduced in R. N. Lebow, *White Britain and Black Ireland: The Influence of Stereotypes on Colonial Policy* (Philadelphia, 1976), p. 54.

[18] See Wellington to Duke of Buckingham, 22 July 1831, in Duke of Buckingham and Chandos, *Memoirs of the Courts and Cabinets of William IV and Victoria* (London, 1861), I, pp. 333–4.

[19] See p. 45.

[20] Emily Crawford, *Victoria: Queen and Ruler* (London, 1903), p. 176.

[21] Henry Reeve (ed.), *The Greville Memoirs: A Journal of the Reigns of George IV and William IV* (London, 1875), II, pp. 165–6.

of superstition and sentimental antiquarianism which attempted to veil in mystery the perfectly straightforward relationship between a sovereign and his people'. Restricted to the service in Westminster Abbey, the coronation cost just over £30,000 compared to the near quarter million pounds expended by George IV.[22]

The King was largely an unknown quantity to O'Connell at this time, though he had, as we noted, sought to cultivate his goodwill when the Duke of Clarence became heir to the throne, and scanned his initial actions as King for evidence of sympathetic Irish intent. Thus, when, as one of the King's first acts, the Catholic Duke of Norfolk was made a Privy Councillor, O'Connell exulted: 'Long live King William!'[23] He was no doubt similarly encouraged when the Earl of Fingall was made Baron Fingall in the English peerage as one of a number of coronation honours in 1831.[24] O'Connell's goodwill was not reciprocated. The King had much earlier in life taken the view that force was the only way to deal with Ireland and his opinion had not significantly changed on accession to office. He warmly applauded the enactment of Irish coercion measures in the 1830s, while O'Connell's arrest and conviction in 1831 for defying a viceregal proclamation against the holding of political meetings report-edly threw him into 'perfect ecstasies'.[25] Moreover, maintenance of the Union occupied the same place in William IV's mindset as opposition to emancipation had in that of George IV. He came to regard O'Connell as virtually an antichrist for pressing Repeal, believing that any attempt to effect it should be made high treason and punished accordingly.[26] It was hardly unusual, then, that in 1831 a King with a reputation for behav-ioural eccentricity would express from the throne his personal 'surprise' and 'indignation' at Irish support for Repeal, an outburst O'Connell denounced as a declaration of war against Ireland.[27] The combination of emotional engagement and political calculation that characterised O'Connell's attitude to monarchy in general would find little outlet under the reign of William IV.

To some extent this was due to a decision by the King regarding his constitutional position and in accordance with developing political

[22] Philip Ziegler, *King William IV* (London, 1971), pp. 192–3.
[23] O'Connell to Richard Bennett, 28 June 1830, in W. J. Fitzpatrick (ed.), *Correspondence of Daniel O'Connell* (London, 1888), I, p. 206.
[24] Buckingham and Chandos, *Memoirs of the Courts of William IV and Victoria*, I, p. 357.
[25] Thomas Creevey to Miss Ord, 31 Jan. 1831, in John Gore (ed.), *Creevey* (London, 1949), p. 319. O'Connell escaped imprisonment because the act under which he was convicted expired in the interval between conviction and sentencing.
[26] Ziegler, *William IV*, pp. 241–2.
[27] W. J. O'Neill Daunt, *Ireland and Her Agitators* (Dublin, 1845), pp. 171–2.

realities following the passage of the Great Reform Act of 1832. He explicitly rejected the idea of 'Rights of the Sovereign', declaring that it was the monarch's duty to support his ministers, except when they were out of touch with national opinion. Philip Ziegler has argued that, with some exceptions, he held to these decisions and thus has earned the right to be considered the first constitutional monarch.[28] Indeed, the apparent reduction of the King to a cipher – much aided by his eccentric behaviour – created worries about the dignity of the crown.[29] However, the degree of William IV's political meddling in his short reign – three dismissed ministries, two prematurely dissolved Parliaments, three personal attempts at cross-party coalitions, and tolerance of his name being used to influence a House of Lords vote[30] – significantly undermines Ziegler's claim. In this context, the King's personal outburst against Repeal should be seen, not as an exception to a constitutional rule, but as of a piece with a tendency to arbitrary political interventionism. And yet, while the King's outburst against Repeal earned an equally robust response from O'Connell, the latter had no political advantage to gain by making a vendetta out of the incident, while his personal anger was considerably disarmed by knowledge of the King's mental instability: 'The King does occasionally strange things, and every effort . . . [is made] to keep his wildness secret. This, however, is to be treated gently; we must not quarrel with him unnecessarily.'[31] Accordingly, O'Connell's attitude to the King was akin to that of a carer for his charge. It was an attitude he could afford to indulge, as with the passage of emancipation he set about building up a parliamentary following, and thus political influence, in the Commons. This he used to give effect to his overmastering political authority in Catholic Ireland. Dr Doyle recorded that without O'Connell England could not govern Ireland,[32] a view the Viceroy, Lord Anglesey, seemed to endorse when he exclaimed: 'the question is whether O'Connell or I shall govern Ireland'.[33]

O'Connell cultivated this view, declaring in a debate on the Repeal of the Union in November 1830: 'I am not to be intimidated by you [government ministers]. I shall continue to stand by Ireland; for I represent her

---

[28] Zeigler, *William IV*, pp. 147–50.   [29] Reeve (ed.), *Greville Memoirs* III, pp. 276–7.

[30] Norman Gash, *Reaction and Reconstruction in English Politics, 1832–1852* (Oxford, 1965), cited in David Cannadine, 'The Context, Performance and Meaning of Ritual: The British Monarchy and the "Invention of Tradition"', in Eric Hobsbawm and Terence Ranger (eds.), *The Invention of Tradition* (Cambridge, 1983), pp. 108–9.

[31] O'Connell to Richard Barrett, 8 July 1830, in Maurice O'Connell (ed.), *The Correspondence of Daniel O'Connell*, IV: *1829–1832* (Dublin, 1977), p. 178.

[32] W. J. Fitzpatrick, *The Life, Times and Correspondence of Dr Doyle, Bishop of Kildare and Leighlin* (Dublin, 1880), II, pp. 334–6.

[33] Anglesey quoted in Fitzpatrick (ed.), *Correspondence of O'Connell*, I, p. 238.

wants, her wishes, and her grievances.'[34] He made the same, politically self-interested, point on another occasion, but rather differently and less bombastically: 'nothing but the effect of my advice and influence keeps the people from violent courses', but to avoid this he had to keep pursuing the question of the Union.[35] O'Connell's position as Ireland's national leader may well have inhibited any direct monarchical contact with Ireland.

The outspoken Lord Anglesey, who, remarkably for a royal surrogate, had the temerity to offer William IV lessons in kingship apparently on the basis of his first term as Irish Viceroy in the late 1820s, urged the King to 'hold Courts from time to time at Dublin & at Edinburgh'.[36] As we have noted, George IV had thought the holding of Parliaments in Ireland every three years would consolidate the Union, but, like that suggestion, Anglesey's advice was also not acted upon. Nor was the King and Queen's expressed desire in 1831 to visit Ireland,[37] in this or any other year of his reign. For his part, O'Connell, faced with an antagonistic monarch, lacked any particular need for royal contact. His success in returning thirty-nine committed Repeal MPs at the general election of 1832–3 gave him effective political influence. Melbourne's Whigs lost their overall majority at the election and, when an arrangement was made with O'Connell to keep them in office, a Whig–Repeal compact came into being.[38]

Substantive advantages accrued for Ireland during the six years of the alliance, especially under the reformist Viceroyalty of Lord Mulgrave (1835–9). With Lord Morpeth as Chief Secretary and Thomas Drummond as Undersecretary,[39] all were deeply committed to the improvement of Ireland and working in the interests of all the people, to the annoyance of Tories and Orangemen. Accordingly, in this period there was a close relationship between O'Connell and Dublin Castle. Effective action was taken in particular to ensure the fair operation of the administration of justice, and for the first time since the Union a Government went through its term without recourse to coercive

---

[34] O'Connell in the Commons, 8 Nov. 1830, cited in Buckingham and Chandos, *Courts of William IV and Victoria*, I, p. 124.

[35] O'Connell to R. N. Bennett, 31 Aug. 1830, in Fitzpatrick (ed.), *Correspondence of O'Connell*, I, p. 237.

[36] Anglesey quoted in Marquess of Anglesey, *One-Leg: The Life and Letters of Henry William Paget, First Marquess of Anglesey* (London, 1961), pp. 229 and 226–31.

[37] Royal response to accession address from Lord Mayor and civic dignitaries of Dublin: *Belfast News-Letter* [*BNL*], 2 Nov. 1830.

[38] O'Ferrall, *O'Connell*, pp. 88–9.

[39] Drummond's impressive contribution is detailed in R. B. O'Brien, *Thomas Drummond: Undersecretary for Ireland: Life and Letters* (London, 1889).

legislation to pacify Ireland, in a period of difficult economic circumstances, and with a substantial Irish legislative record: the Church Temporalities Act of 1833, replacing church taxes raised from Catholics and Protestants with a tax on clerical incomes; the end of the 'Tithe war' by the Tithe Rentcharge Act of 1838, converting tithe as a tax on occupiers to a charge payable by landlords; and municipal reform in 1840, which ended the Protestant monopoly of corporations and the administration of justice. These were thus opened up to nationalist influence and control,[40] epitomised by O'Connell's election as Lord Mayor of Dublin in 1840.[41]

Nationalist Ireland's relationship with the state in the 1830s, thus, was markedly different from the 1820s, when the King was seen as a central political as well as constitutional figure, and great hopes were pinned on monarchical influence as a source of change. Now nationalist influence in the Commons directly translated into reforms in Ireland. Accordingly, as determined by O'Connell, the Repeal party could afford to treat William IV generally with the utmost respect. Moreover, his death in 1837 appeared to offer the prospect of combining political power with a congenial royal relationship.

III

In fact, the accession of Queen Victoria in 1837 was to initiate a 'scenario of love' for O'Connell far more intense than that occasioned by George IV's Irish visit of 1821. Personally inclined to revere monarchy against a background in which it seemed that the alienation of Britain and Ireland was at last being overcome through Irish government administered in the interests of the people, O'Connell's highly sentimental and emotional nature was vulnerable to monarchical charisma, especially of a feminine nature. There were strong personal as well as political reasons for this.

In 1836 his wife, to whom he was devoted and who was an intelligent and perceptive confidante,[42] died, leaving O'Connell emotionally bereft and in need of a substitute focus of affection. The heir to the throne, the young and attractive Victoria, was an almost irresistible candidate for his attentions, especially given the antagonism between William IV and her mother the Duchess of Kent. The King disliked both her self-promotion as a Princess Dowager for her daughter and her Whig associations. The mutual antagonism led the Duchess into ever closer association with the

[40] See O'Ferrall, *O'Connell*, pp. 92–4.
[41] W. J. O'Neill Daunt, *Ireland since the Union* (London, 1885), pp. 121–3.
[42] O'Ferrall, *O'Connell*, pp. 21–3.

Whigs and their allies, among whom was O'Connell.[43] Her donation of £20 towards the building of Tuam Catholic cathedral in 1836[44] was indicative of her political sympathies. O'Connell, moreover, had a close association with John Conroy, an Irishman, the Duchess of Kent's supposed lover and, effectively, Victoria's guardian. Accordingly, O'Connell saw an heir to the throne coming to maturity under a benign Irish influence and trained up to sympathy with Irish grievances.[45] Thus from March 1837, before William IV's death, he set about conditioning Irish opinion in loyalty to the future sovereign and her family, successfully urging the submission of an address from the Repeal Association to Victoria, and, though unsuccessfully, requesting that she pay a visit to Ireland.[46]

O'Connell was further reassured about the future Queen as she was known to be strongly influenced in her political education by the Prime Minister, Lord Melbourne, with whom he was in alliance. As William IV's demise became certain – he died on 20 June 1837 – O'Connell was happy that Victoria 'is at present in excellent [Melbourne's] hands'.[47] A favourable result in a parliamentary debate on a Church Rent-charge bill a few days later was regarded as a 'hint to the young coming Queen that Lord Melbourne's Government, *aided by the Court*, will be all powerful'.[48] On the day that Victoria's accession was announced at St James's Palace O'Connell played a conspicuous part, acting as a sort of fugleman to the multitude, 'regulating their acclamations'.[49] A week after the Queen's accession he was urging the unqualified and enthusiastic allegiance of the Catholic Irish for the Queen and her 'benevolent intentions' for Ireland, to be expressed through a society entitled 'The Friends of the Queen':

We have on the Throne a monarch educated to cherish the rights and liberties of all of the people, free from preoccupations and prejudice, and ready to do justice to all, without distinction of sect or persuasion. We have surrounding her Majesty a Ministry ... desirous to promote the interests and protect the franchises of every part of the empire. For the first time Ireland may raise her head in hope ... Ireland is now ready to amalgamate with the entire empire. We are prepared for full and perpetual conciliation. Let Cork County and Yorkshire be put on a footing – let Ireland and England be identified ... To make the Union real and effectual we have the benevolent wishes of the fine-minded Sovereign; we have the full

[43] Crawford, *Victoria*, pp. 82–3.   [44] *Dublin Evening Post* [*DEP*], 21 June 1836.
[45] Crawford, *Victoria*, p. 120. Crawford had a family connection to the Conroys.
[46] Ibid. pp. 120–1, 130–1.
[47] O'Connell to P. V. Fitzpatrick, 9 June 1837, in Fitzpatrick (ed.), *Correspondence of O'Connell*, II, p. 95.
[48] O'Connell to P. V. Fitzpatrick, 13 June 1837, in ibid. pp. 96–7.
[49] From 'Diaries and Recollections' of Lord Broughton, cited in Fitzpatrick (ed.), *Correspondence of O'Connell*, II, p. 100, footnote 8.

assistance of the Ministry; we have the voice of all that is liberal and enlightened in England and Scotland;[50] we have the giant strength of the Irish nation.[51]

O'Connell specified absolute equality of treatment for Ireland if the Union was to work; nevertheless, he now redirected his political objectives towards equality for Ireland *within* the United Kingdom of Great Britain and Ireland. This dimension to his politics is often regarded as a temporary distraction indulged 'for political reasons', given his 'real' objective of legislative independence.[52]

This view, however, greatly underplays the emotional intensity of O'Connell's commitment at the time and, no less, tends to miss much of the personal reason for it. At the time, it registered unmistakably with Irish popular opinion, reflected in folk stories of the Liberator defending the Queen's honour;[53] or, as a figure possessed of enormous sexual prowess, having the young Queen as a mistress.[54]

In February 1838 he excitedly confided to P. V. Fitzpatrick: 'the Queen has expressed a wish to see me. She is determined to conciliate Ireland.'[55] O'Connell's unbridled loyalty undoubtedly had a massive influence on Irish Catholic responses to the Queen's coronation at the end of June 1838. The ceremony, which followed the more restricted example of William IV rather than the lavish ceremony of George IV,[56] was lacking any symbolic representation of Catholic Ireland.[57] But Ireland united in enthusiastic celebration of the event. In a manner unthinkable at the end of the century, and certainly not repeated for the coronation of Edward VII in 1902, Dublin was brilliantly illuminated and joined with Belfast, Cork, Wexford, Waterford, Limerick, Sligo and almost every town of any size in the country in joyously marking the occasion.[58] Indeed, what was significant about occasional instances of pointed refusal to join in the celebrations, at least as reported by the liberal *Freeman's Journal*, was that these came, not from diehard Irish nationalists or republicans, but from Tories.

[50] O'Connell had made a triumphal 'rabble' tour of Scotland in 1835: Journal (27 Sept. 1835), Reeve, *The Greville Memoirs*, III, p. 316.

[51] O'Connell to Arthur French, 28 June 1837, in Fitzpatrick (ed.), *Correspondence of O'Connell*, II, pp. 103–5.

[52] See, for example, O'Ferrall, *O'Connell*, p. 111.

[53] See for instance, 'The Counsellor and Queen Victoria', IFC 1146, Department of Irish Folklore, University College Dublin. I am grateful to Professor A. O'Corrain, Dept of Irish, Magee campus, University of Ulster, for translating the story from the Irish.

[54] Ó Muirithe, 'O'Connell in the Irish Folk Tradition', p. 59.

[55] O'Connell to P. V. Fitzpatrick, 15 Feb. 1838, in Fitzpatrick (ed.), *Correspondence of O'Connell*, II, p. 128.

[56] *Gentleman's Magazine*, 10 (1838), 188. The expense involved was £70,000.

[57] *FJ*, 2 July 1838.

[58] 'Celebrations of Her Majesty's Coronation in the Provinces' in *FJ*, 6 July 1838.

They were deeply disaffected by a parliamentary onslaught on the Orange Order in 1836, amid rumours of a conspiracy, probably unfounded,[59] but widely believed, to the effect that the Order's Grand Master, the Queen's uncle, the Duke of Cumberland, was hatching a plot to prevent her ascending the throne.[60] The parliamentary investigation occasioned the dissolution of the Order's central governing body, the Grand Lodge, and the Order's influence in Britain rapidly declined. Understandably, in Ulster, Orangemen deprived of the prospect of a monarch of their own ilk reacted with sullen suspicion to Victoria's accession.[61] In Ireland, Undersecretary Drummond launched a highly effective assault on the orders.[62]

Few developments would have been as emotionally satisfying to O'Connell than this, and his enthusiasm for the Melbourne administration, expressed in demonstrations of allegiance to the monarch with whom it was so closely associated in his mind, abounded accordingly. In May 1839 he exulted at the defeat of the short-lived Tory ministry in the 'Bedchamber crisis' and the return of Melbourne to office: 'Hurrah for the darling little Queen!'[63] Shortly after, he was wishing for an Irish royal visit, not least to discomfort an Orange faction forced to behold the harmony between the court and the 'popular party'.[64] In August 1839 he was speculating that the Queen, 'full of intellect', might not marry for years, 'as she wishes to enjoy *her* power'.[65] But when, in October, the news of Victoria's engagement to Prince Albert was announced, O'Connell was no less enthusiastic, giving a quite remarkable public demonstration of the extent of his personal attachment to the Queen during a mass demonstration at Bandon, County Cork:

'God bless the Queen! ... in the face of heaven I pray with as much honesty and fervency for Queen Victoria as I do for any one of my own progeny ... Oh! if I be not greatly mistaken, I'd get in one day 500,000 brave Irishmen to defend the life, the honour, and the person of the beloved young lady by whom England's throne is now filled! [*Exulting and protracted cheers.*] Let every man in the vast and multitudinous assembly stretched out before me, who is loyal to the Queen and would defend her to the last, lift up his right hand! [*The entire assembly responded to the appeal.*][66]

---

[59] See Duke of Wellington to Sir Robert Peel, 11 Feb. 1836, describing Cumberland and his Orange activities as a nuisance, in L. S. Parker (ed.), *Sir Robert Peel from His Private Papers* (London, 1899), II, pp. 323–4.

[60] Report from Wexford, *FJ*, 6 July 1838.   [61] Crawford, *Victoria*, p. 130.

[62] Beckett, *Making of Modern Ireland*, pp. 316–17.

[63] O'Connell to P. V. Fitzpatrick, 10 May 1939, in Fitzpatrick (ed.), *Correspondence of O'Connell*, II, p. 178.

[64] O'Connell to P. V. Fitzpatrick, 16 May 1839, in ibid. p. 185.

[65] O'Connell to P. V. Fitzpatrick, 5 Aug. 1839, in ibid. p. 192.

[66] *Annual Register* (London, 1839), p. 314; Sir Sidney Lee, *Queen Victoria: A Biography* (revised edn, London, 1904), pp. 110–11, footnote 2.

When Victoria gave birth to Princess Victoria in November 1840 O'Connell declared: "Blessed be God! ... the young mother is safe. God preserve the dear little lady! We must illuminate the house next Sunday night, and burn tar-barrels."[67] And even when the Tories were in power in 1842, O'Connell was sure she remained 'as firm as a rock'.[68] Once he returned to the Repeal issue,[69] she continued to be a central figure in his conception of how it might be brought to a successful conclusion. His *A Memoir of Ireland Native and Saxon* (London, 1842), a historical litany of the evils England inflicted on Ireland, was dedicated to the Queen, but it was also literally intended for the enlightenment of a sovereign O'Connell viewed as open to persuasion on nationalist claims; a sovereign he had in fact 'constructed' according to his own needs.

Throughout the period of the Melbourne–Repeal administration, during which she ascended the throne, and after, O'Connell, always subject to all-embracing enthusiasms, was consumed by a romantic attachment to the Queen,[70] having married his emotional engagement to her person with his political objectives. His refusal physically to confront the Tory government over the banned Clontarf meeting in 1843 produced accusations that he never really desired Repeal and did not expect to succeed in pursuit of it.[71] However, O'Neill Daunt, his close associate, argued persuasively enough that O'Connell did have a strategy, if a rather loose one, to secure legislative independence. It seems he looked, as was the case with the emancipation issue in 1828–9, to creating, legally, a crisis of the state that might be resolved by an act of the Imperial Parliament establishing an Irish legislature, or, as he clearly personally preferred, a direct call from the Queen summoning her faithful Peers and Commons on College Green. This was not quite as fanciful as it seems. Both Prince Albert and Victoria, it has been argued,[72] saw themselves as representing the true national interest, above and distinct from the narrow interests of party politics, a

---

[67] O'Connell quoted in Daunt, *Personal Recollections of O'Connell*, I, p. 195.

[68] O'Connell to P. V. Fitzpatrick, 26 Feb. 1842, in Fitzpatrick (ed.), *Correspondence of O'Connell*, II, pp. 281–2.

[69] O'Connell found that the absence of mass agitation had a detrimental effect on his popular and financial support, together with his party's cohesion: O'Ferrall, *O'Connell*, pp. 101–3; Angus Macintyre, *The Liberator: Daniel O'Connell and the Irish Party 1830–1847* (London, 1965), pp. 262–4.

[70] He formed a no less romantic attachment to Mary Queen of Scots, having consulted 'her manuscript' in the Advocates' Library in Edinburgh: 'I kissed the writing and pressed it to my heart!': Daunt, *Personal Recollections of O'Connell*, I, p. 84.

[71] Ibid. II, p. 173.

[72] David Cannadine, 'The Last Hanoverian Sovereign? The Victorian Monarchy in Historical Perspective 1688–1988' in A. L. Beier and J. M. Rosenheim (eds.), *The First Modern Society: Essays in English History in Honour of Laurence Stone* (Cambridge, 1989), pp. 139–41.

view transmitted to the Queen by William IV. Indeed, there was support for such a role in British radical circles, which saw the realisation of their hopes as best effected by an autonomous sovereign capable of taking a disinterested national view of political affairs.[73] In general this was also characteristic of O'Connell, but in his case it was given greater specificity by his personal and political contacts with the court and Government.

A specifically political calculation has been discerned in O'Connell's ultra loyalty: it was a card that could be employed to exclude militarily inclined rivals from the Repeal movement.[74] Certainly this seems plausible, but if so it was far from being the only, or the chief, consideration. The evidence of O'Connell's personal attachment to the sovereign, especially in the late 1830s and early 1840s, is abundant. There was, of course, a large degree of wishful thinking in O'Connell's speculations on how the monarchy might be used to effect legislative independence. There were enormous differences between the emancipation and Repeal issues. Britain was divided on the former, which was about Catholic rights *within* the state; it was united on the latter, an issue involving the breaking of it. But even assuming that the issue could have been resolved by the Queen acting alone – just about plausible in what was still a pre-Bagehotian age – what was the likelihood of her acting as O'Connell wished?

In fact, there were signals that she would not, signals that O'Connell chose to ignore. For example, he received a very public rebuff at her hands, when – in the company of the Lord Mayor of London and in his capacity of Lord Mayor of Dublin – he presented addresses on the birth of the Prince of Wales in 1841. The Lord Mayor of London was rewarded with a baronetcy, O'Connell not at all. It was a perceived public insult that his supporters in Ireland were in the process of raising an agitation on until O'Connell dismissed the issue as unimportant.[75] More significantly, when the Irish Lord Chancellor, Edward Sugden, emphatically stated the Queen's firm opposition to Repeal,[76] O'Connell declared his 'most utter and inexpressible astonishment. You *must* know ... when you made that assertion – that it was utterly unfounded.'[77] But Sugden was correct.[78]

---

[73] Alex Tyrrell and Yvonne Ward, ' "God Bless Her Little Majesty": The Popularising of Monarchy in the 1840s', *National Identities*, 2 (2000), 117–18.

[74] See Richard Davis, *The Young Ireland Movement* (Dublin, 1987), pp. 92–3.

[75] Daunt, *Personal Recollections of O'Connell*, II, pp. 64–6.

[76] Lord Chancellor to the Viceroy, Lord French, 22 May 1843, citing the grounds for O'Connell being removed as a justice of the peace for Kerry, in ibid. pp. 158–9.

[77] O'Connell to Edward Sugden, 27 May 1843, replying to the Lord Chancellor's arguments, cited in ibid. pp. 159–61. See also James Murphy, *Abject Loyalty: Nationalism and Monarchy in Ireland during the Reign of Queen Victoria* (Cork, 2001), pp. 38–40.

[78] Sir Robert Peel to Sir Edward Sugden, 1 June 1843, in Parker (ed.), *Peel*, III, pp. 51–2.

The young Victoria was not, as O'Connell thought, a *tabula rasa* on which Irish national rights might be inscribed. It was true that his political ally, Lord Melbourne, had shaped the Queen's political education, but O'Connell was wrong in thinking she was being educated in the justness of Irish claims which the Government's reformist legislation seemed to validate. Together with lessons in the arts of government, Melbourne also imbued her with a contemptuous regard for the rebellious 'low Irish' and their supposedly fabricated grievances.[79] Just as seriously, and contrary to O'Connell's understanding, the presence of Conroy in her family circle meant that Ireland had impacted very directly and negatively on the Queen's domestic life. Conroy seems to have had royal pretensions of his own, having traced his lineage back to courtiers of the Irish High Kings at Tara. His relationship with her mother was a great offence to Victoria's sense of propriety, to which his abrasive attempts to control the future Queen added personal animus at the same time as it created divisions in her family.[80] As for her personal attitude to O'Connell, imbued with traditional British anti-papal prejudices, she found his mobilisation of priests and people in pursuit of an abhorrent cause deeply threatening,[81] especially in a period when Chartism, under its Irish leaders Fergus O'Connor and James Bronterre O'Brien, was giving more credibility than usual to establishment fears of Irish inspired revolution in Britain.[82] In fact, Victoria came to regard the Irish as largely responsible for popular discontent that appeared to be bringing the whole country to the verge of revolution.[83]

As the Repeal crisis developed in Ireland in the summer of 1843, Victoria and Albert responded to reports by the Home Secretary, Sir James Graham, of 'foreign interference' – in the form of 'several Frenchmen, appearing in different parts of Ireland'[84] – by undertaking a visit to the French King, Louis Philippe, to signal publicly that O'Connell could expect no help from that quarter. Following the

---

[79] Elizabeth Longford, *Victoria R.I.* (London, 1964), pp. 67–9.

[80] Cecil Woodham-Smith, *Queen Victoria: Her Life and Times 1819–1861* (London, 1972), p. 70. Conroy's involvement with the royal family is dealt with thoroughly in Katherine Hudson, *A Royal Conflict: Sir John Conroy and the Young Victoria* (London, 1994).

[81] *Annual Register: 1839* (London, 1840), p. 314; Lee, *Victoria*, pp. 110–11; Oliver McDonagh, *Daniel O'Connell, 1830–1847* (London, 1989), pp. 179–85; Longford, *Victoria*, p. 181.

[82] For brief accounts, see Juliet Gardner and Neal Wenbourn, *The History Today Companion to British History* (London, 1995), p. 562; Asa Briggs, 'Fergus O'Connor and James Bronterre O'Brien' in J. W. Boyle (ed.), *Leaders and Workers* (Cork, n.d. [1967]), pp. 27–36.

[83] Melbourne to the Queen, 17 Aug. 1842, in Arthur Benson and Viscount Esher (eds.), *The Letters of Queen Victoria*, first series (London, 1907), I, pp. 532–3.

[84] Graham to the Queen, 23 June 1843, in ibid. p. 606.

Government's success in facing down O'Connell at Clontarf the Queen exulted in his arrest, interpreting 'abuse' O'Connell expressed of the French King as due to the fact that 'our visit to [Château de] Eu [Louis Philippe's residence near Trefort] has put an end to any hope of assistance from France, which he pretended there would be'.[85] Baron Stockmar, a friend of the Belgian King and a seminal educational influence on Prince Albert, congratulated him on the 'perfect success' of their strategy: 'the plan was *adhered to to the letter*'.[86]

Despite O'Connell's hopes for cultivating a close relationship between the Queen and Ireland, by 1842 the Queen's Celtic preferences were becoming clear. With the purchase of the Balmoral estate in Scotland, the building of a castle in the medieval style, and the Queen and Prince Albert disporting themselves in tartan and affecting the lifestyle of Highland lairds,[87] Scotland's membership of the United Kingdom was being invested with a subjective personal dimension that was lacking in regard to either Ireland or Wales. Politically volatile Ireland held no such attractions. In the sixty-four years of her reign, less than five weeks was spent in Ireland as compared to almost seven years in Scotland,[88] though the effusively loyal Welsh were accorded only seven *nights*. The only parts of Wales the Queen found attractive were those that most resembled the Scottish Highlands.[89]

By 1844 the Queen's opposition to Repeal was accepted even by O'Connell, and with all the anger of a betrayed lover he declared, on hearing that a royal visit to Ireland was being planned, that if she came she would find the word 'Repeal' written up wherever she went.[90] This discouraged an Irish visit until after his death. The only Irish constitutional reform Victoria favoured, to which he was firmly opposed,[91] was abolition of the Irish Viceroyalty so that the Union would be consolidated and Ireland governed like her beloved Scotland.[92] But fundamentally what made a meeting of minds between the Queen and O'Connell

---

[85] Victoria to Leopold, King of the Belgians, 17 Oct. 1843, in ibid. p. 621.

[86] Stockmar to the Prince Consort, 27 Nov. 1843, in Theodore Martin, *Life of the Prince Consort* (London, 1975), I, pp. 191–2.

[87] For stimulating discussion, see Adrienne Munich, *Queen Victoria's Secrets* (New York, 1996), ch. 2.

[88] Hector Bolitho, *Victoria: The Widow and Her Son* (London, 1934), p. 69.

[89] John Davies, 'Victoria and Victorian Wales' in G. H. Jenkins and J. B. Smith (eds.), *Politics and Society in Wales: Essays in Honour of Ieuan Gwynedd* (Cardiff, 1988), pp. 7, 10.

[90] Longford, *Victoria*, p. 181.

[91] This was confirmed decades later by O'Neill Daunt. See Daunt to the editor, *Nation*, 7 July 1883.

[92] Lee, *Victoria*, pp. 157–8.

unlikely was that incompatible views on Ireland's constitutional status fed *similar* notions of personal betrayal.

The Queen's conception of allegiance was not one that recognised the subject owing fealty *symbolically* to the crown through the parliamentary institutions of the state; rather, it was owed directly and personally to the sovereign. Indeed, it was observed during her reign that her conception of her constitutional role was one determined, not historically by the play of politics, but by divine will:

> she was the anointed of the Lord, called by the most solemn warrant to rule a great nation in the fear of God ... When the Queen spoke of her subjects as 'loyal' she meant it in the *medieval* [my italics] sense. The relationship was not, in her eyes, voluntary or sentimental but imperative ... Subjects must be 'loyal'; if they loved their sovereign, so much the better for them and for her, but affection was not essential. In her phraseology this constantly peeped out – 'I, the Queen', 'my people', 'my soldiers'. She regarded herself ... as the pivot round which the whole machinery of state revolves.[93]

She held forth precisely in this vein to Lord John Russell during a heated discussion on revolutions in early August 1848: 'Obedience to the laws & to the Sovereign, is obedience to a higher Power, divinely instituted for the good of the people, not of the Sovereign, who has equal duties and obligations.'[94] It was in this light that she viewed the Irish. However, it was an attitude that was only too likely to result in disappointment. When the Irish were perceived to act treasonably the 'insult' would be felt personally and directly, rather than symbolically, and with quite profound implications for the monarchy's relationship with Ireland.

IV

The Clontarf fiasco of 1843, when the Government successfully faced down O'Connell's militaristic attempt to compel the concession of Repeal through force of numbers, resulted in his imprisonment. But despite the verdict being overturned, imprisonment, abetted by ailing health, marked both the decline of O'Connell's career and the failure of the Repeal project. Yet O'Connell was a major influence on Irish and British politics. As a figure of central authority for the nationalist people of Ireland he established loyalty to the throne as a core element of the Irish constitutional tradition. It would remain so until – and arguably beyond – the demise of that tradition in 1918.

---

[93] Edmund Gosse, 'The Character of Queen Victoria', *Quarterly Review*, 3 (1901), 337.
[94] Victoria quoted in Longford, *Victoria*, p. 198.

Part II

Victorian values

3   Allegiance and illusion in the famine era

The collapse of the Repeal project had quite profound consequences. The political organisation shaping nationalist Ireland's relationship with the state disintegrated, thereby opening an era of localism – politics focused around personal, familial and regional interests. Not until the rise of Parnell in the late 1870s would Ireland see a national and nationalist movement to compare with O'Connell's. The new era was one which seemed to provide an ideal opportunity for the monarchy to establish itself – and state loyalty – in the affections of the Irish people. The legacy of O'Connell was not the least significant element in this scenario. His later reservations about the Queen's attitude to Ireland was preceded by sustained promotion of loyalty to the throne delivered to the massive crowds gathered at his 'monster' meetings – at least forty-five of which were held during the Repeal campaign[1] – and made a deep impression on Irish Catholic opinion. It is difficult to assess Irish public opinion accurately in this period but, as we have noted, a fairly adequate idea of the popular significance of O'Connell, and the Queen, can be gleaned from the Irish folk tradition. O'Connell in his prime was often seen to embody Ireland, and unlike the Queen, whom very few Irish people could have seen in the flesh, was personally known to many thousands. The great abundance of stories about O'Connell in the files of the Irish Folklore Commission testifies to his dominance of the Irish popular imagination. It would seem that the Queen only, or chiefly, entered that tradition in roles relative to, though not necessarily subordinate to, O'Connell, with her authority affected by his presence, suggesting ambiguity about the degree of allegiance she was due. Ambiguity about allegiance that the folk tradition suggests was mirrored in the oaths sworn by branches of the Ribbon movement, a secret society existing to defend the interests of lower-class Catholics, often by violent means. The oaths tended to vary somewhat according to locality, with some groups 'pledging the most

[1] W. J. O'Neill Daunt, *Ireland and Her Agitators* (Dublin, 1845), p. 277.

devoted fealty to the Queen; others ... swearing allegiance to "Daniel O'Connell, real King of Ireland and his eldest son, Maurice O'Connell as Chief Commander"".[2] Loyalty to, and identity with, the Queen was nevertheless a core value of nationalist ideology; and with his political and physical demise that ideology remained, lacking the direction that O'Connell gave it and available for exploitation in the state's interest. O'Connell's demise, however, was not an unmixed blessing. While his overmastering influence in Ireland was resented at Westminster, he had interpreted the historical narrative of Irish nationalism, not entirely authentically, but consistently in a constitutional and monarchical mode. He may often have had veterans of the 1798 Rebellion on his platforms and exploited the visual symbolism of the Volunteers of 1782,[3] but his abhorrence of political violence determined the suppression of that element of the national narrative.

The waning of O'Connell's political career, however, coincided with the discovery and rededication of Wolfe Tone's grave. This was conducted in private so as not to embarrass the Liberator. Nevertheless, this event and the emergence of historical and poetic works dealing with the 1798 Rebellion[4] was a signal that the kind of narrative manipulation O'Connell freely indulged in could be more difficult to effect in the future, especially after the Young Ireland revolt of 1848 – though farcical – established a point of continuity, and a stimulus, to the militant strand in the national memory. Yet the task facing Young Ireland propagandists such as Charles Gavan Duffy was formidable.[5] O'Connell's historical inventiveness itself indicated the absence of an authoritative and coherent national understanding of the Irish past, while the lack of a tradition of nationalistic art in nineteenth-century Ireland, apparently because there was no substantial public – that is, middle-class – demand for it, indicated a corresponding lack of interest.[6] The dominant visual presence in

---

[2] Quoted in A. M. Sullivan, *New Ireland: Political Sketches and Personal Reminiscences of Thirty Years of Irish Public Life* (1st edn 1877; 10th edn Glasgow, n.d. [1880s]), p. 136. See also Michael Beames, *Peasants and Power: The Whiteboy Movement and Their Control in Pre-Famine Ireland* (Brighton, 1983), pp. 144–5.

[3] Tom Garvin, *The Evolution of Irish Nationalist Politics* (Dublin, 1981), p. 47.

[4] Kevin Whelan, *The Tree of Liberty: Radicalism, Catholicism and the Construction of Irish Identity 1760–1830* (Cork, 1996), p. 168; Luke Gibbons, "'Where Wolfe Tone's Statue Was Not": Joyce, Monuments and Memory' in Ian McBride (ed.), *History and Memory in Ireland* (Cambridge, 2001), p. 145, footnote 18.

[5] C. G. Duffy, *A Short Life of Thomas Davis* (London, 1895), pp. 112–13.

[6] Cyril Barrett, 'Irish Nationalism and Art 1880–1921', *Studies* (Winter, 1975), 408; Fintan Cullen, 'Union and Display in Nineteenth-Century Ireland' in Dana Arnold (ed.), *Cultural Identities and the Aesthetics of Britishness* (Manchester, 2004), pp. 120–1; Jeanne Sheehy, *The Rediscovery of Ireland's Past: The Cultural Revival 1830–1930* (London, 1980), pp. 7–8.

Irish art was 'British – English, at that'. It would seem that prosperous Catholics who benefited from emancipation in 1829 were inclined to demonstrate that they were 'as good as any Englishman by imitating that Englishman as closely as possible'.[7] In this context, then, to note the re-emergence of a militant strand to the Irish national myth in the 1840s is not to suggest a foreclosure of progress on inculcating loyal allegiance to the monarch in mid-nineteenth-century Ireland; but to remark that while a period of opportunity for the enterprise existed, it was one that needed to be resolutely grasped.

I

The prospects for the success of such an enterprise, however, were conditioned, among other things, by the negative attitude to the Irish of a Queen who came to regard them as largely responsible for popular discontent that appeared to be bringing the state to the verge of revolution. There might be a case for reform in Ireland, but she was chiefly concerned with the repression of 'violence and disorder' and was reassured to some extent in 1843 when the Government took a firm line against Rebecca rioters in Wales, not least 'for the effect it may have in Ireland'.[8]

Alienated from constitutionally destabilising nationalist Ireland, Victoria and Albert in this period were developing their life-long infatuation with the now constitutionally secure Scottish Highlands. In Scotland perceived threats to the social order, such as the so-called 'radical war' of 1820, seemed only to encourage mass demonstrations of loyalty; indeed the enthusiastic embracing of a wider British patriotism that characterised the country from the late eighteenth century found one of its most significant forms of mass expression in popular, if rowdy, celebrations of the monarch's birthday.[9] The close personal identity of the monarch with the Highlands, however, would act in conjunction with ethnocentric discourses on Ireland to reinforce the credibility of the flawed idea that Scotland – another 'Celtic' country with a long history of conflict with England – was a model for Irish integration into the British state. An inappropriate model was, in itself, no determinant of failure, but it was complemented by alienating policies pursued by the

---

[7] Cullen, 'Union and Display', p. 119; Sheehy, *Rediscovery of Ireland's Past*, p. 7.

[8] Victoria to Sir James Graham, Home Secretary, 23 June 1843, in Arthur Benson and Viscount Esher (eds.), *The Letters of Queen Victoria*, first series (London, 1907), I, p. 605.

[9] Christopher Whatley, 'Royal Day, People's Day: The Monarch's Day in Scotland, c.1660–1860' in Roger Mason and Norman McDougall (eds.), *People and Power in Scotland: Essays in Honour of T. C. Smout* (Edinburgh, 1992), pp. 170–88.

Irish Viceroyalty, whose responsibility it was, in the first instance, to cultivate popular loyalty.

The prospects for doing so were rather better than they might have appeared. Not only was the Repeal campaign effectively at an end, but the theatre of political entertainment it had provided for the masses had tended to conceal class discontent. Alexis de Tocqueville apparently had little difficulty in finding a peasant class grievance against O'Connell and rich Catholics, who could now sit in Parliament while 'we starve just the same'.[10] A national struggle could easily leave more immediate and fundamental grievances unaddressed, while the absence of such struggle could expose the weakness of ties binding leader and led, as O'Connell found in the late 1830s. From 1843 an opportunity to cultivate Irish loyalty through good government existed, but how well could it be carried through?

This subject has a number of dimensions. For instance, a metaphorical statement of good government has been found in the remodelling of the Phoenix Park, the location of the Viceregal Lodge and the Wellington monument, in common with royal parks in Britain in this period, 'linking key monuments to national greatness, the nation's heroes and impressive government offices and residences'.[11] In Dublin the transformation of a landscape characterised by indeterminate boundaries, hilly aspects, boggy lands and ramshackle buildings into one smoothed and ordered duplicated that transformation. Unlike the settled constitutional environment of Britain, however, it did so in a contested 'colonial' environment.[12] In other words, what was a symbolic *affirmation* of good government in Britain was merely a metaphorical *assertion* of enlightened rule in Dublin. But most importantly, the improved landscape of the Phoenix Park was only one – if significant – element of the municipal realm of the Irish capital, of which the Viceroyalty was the hegemonic emblem, and as a locational metaphor of good government was undermined by the impact in Britain and Ireland of its image as a somewhat absurd, inauthentic imitation of its parent. W. M. Thackeray's visceral critique of the institution in the crisis year of 1843, with its ridicule of the 'basest Dublinites' going 'in long trains to a sham court . . . playing sham aristocracy before a sham sovereign . . . [in] that old humbug of a

---

[10] Alexis de Tocqueville cited in K. T. Hoppen, *The Mid-Victorian Generation 1846–1886* (Oxford, 1998), p. 560, footnote 2.

[11] Dana Arnold, 'Trans-planting National Cultures: The Phoenix Park, Dublin (1832–49), an Urban Heterotopia?' in Arnold (ed.), *Cultural Identities and the Aesthetics of Britishness*, p. 171.

[12] Ibid. *passim*.

[Dublin] Castle! ... the greatest sham of all the shams in Ireland',[13] expressed a widespread opinion in a manner that ensured it would endure. Moreover, the Viceroyalty seemed incapable of compensating for its monarchical inauthenticity by taking a large enough view of state interests.

Well before the Repeal campaign was faced down, Prime Minister Peel was concerned that in the conflict with O'Connell the Dublin Castle authorities were failing to provide an effective pole of counter-allegiance, with unwise prosecutions for seditious language at meetings at which 'studious loyalty to the Queen was expressed'; the folly of the Irish Lord Chancellor, Sir Edward Sugden, bringing the Queen personally and publicly into the Repeal controversy by declaring that she was determined to thwart it; while disagreement between the Viceroy, Lord de Grey, and the Chief Secretary, Edward Lord Eliot, risked a paralysis of government that might compel reform resulting in the abolition of the viceregal system.[14] The weakness of the Viceroyalty was its view that 'only two classes ... divide the country: determined enemies and zealous friends', when in fact, 'We must look for respectable Roman Catholics for office.'[15]

The great difficulty facing the state lay in the combination of the popish clergy and popular movements. It was a problem, however, which Peel realised could not be met by force alone. The threat of force had successfully faced down O'Connell, but that merely created a basis on which to tackle the fundamental problem and which only 'a just, kind and conciliatory policy' with the purpose of disuniting the Roman Catholic body and thus breaking it up could adequately meet.[16] It was to this end that his reform programme, especially charitable bequests and the Maynooth grant, was directed. Significantly, Peel found a template for his Irish policy in how his Government was dealing – through sensible legislation to attract the support of 'moderate men' – with the crisis in the Church of Scotland, which experienced the great 'disruption' in 1843.[17] He

---

[13] 'The Irish Sketchbook' in W. M. Thackeray, *Sketchbooks* (1843; London, 1902), pp. 577–8.

[14] Peel to Sugden, 1 June 1843, in L. S. Parker, *Sir Robert Peel from His Private Papers* (London, 1899), III, pp. 51–2.

[15] Peel to Sir James Graham, 16 June 1843; Peel to the Irish Viceroy, Lord de Grey, 24 July 1843, in ibid. pp. 53–5.

[16] Peel to Lord Heytesbury, 8 Aug. 1844, in ibid. p. 120; Peel to Lord Lincoln, [n.d.] March 1846, in Donal Kerr, *Peel, Priests and Politics: Sir Robert Peel's Administration and the Roman Catholic Church in Ireland, 1841–1846* (Oxford, 1982), p. 121.

[17] The disruption between moderates and evangelicals involved the seccession of about 40 per cent of the church's membership: Juliet Gardner and Neal Wenborn (eds.), *The History Today Companion to British History* (London, 1995), p. 238.

informed the Home Secretary: 'You must act on the same principle in Ireland.'[18] It was a policy that had the wholehearted support of the Queen and Prince Albert.[19] However, as de Grey persisted in a 'startling' policy of exclusively Protestant appointments with the prospect of Catholics viewing emancipation a 'dead letter', and being impelled towards demagoguery,[20] a change of viceregal personnel was necessary.

And yet how far reformist legislation could inculcate loyalty was uncertain. The Scottish template may have been adequate for a problem *within* the Scottish Protestant family but the religious division in Ireland was more fundamental. Indeed the legislative ban on Catholics holding the post of Viceroy, and which Peel did not intend to repeal, could be read as indicating constitutional approval for sectarianism. At one level the ban merely mirrored the Act of Settlement's ban on Catholics holding the monarchical office, but in the Irish context it was a profoundly negative state symbol. In fact, not just the post of Viceroy, but the whole viceregal household was still staffed entirely by Protestants almost twenty years after Peel expressed his anxieties about sectarian exclusivity in official appointments.[21] Moreover, although Peel replaced de Grey with Lord Heytesbury in 1844 the onset of the Great Famine in 1845 radically redirected Government concerns.

The famine was a development which, to many commentators, offered a unique opportunity for a new start for British policy in Ireland, at a time when its effect on the Queen's reputation among Irish nationalists, at home and abroad, could not be forseen. Leaving over one million dead from starvation and millions more as forced emigrants, the famine would enter Irish nationalist mythology as a great atrocity perpetrated by a callous English Government. The reality was more complex. The nationalist myth of a deliberately enacted policy aimed at exterminating the native population was untrue, but there is, nevertheless, enough evidence to show that anti-Irish prejudice – expressed in a tendency to blame the famine on supposed Irish character faults[22] – played a significant role in the determination of policies which made the sufferings of the famine-striken greater than they need have been.[23]

---

[18] Peel to Sir James Graham, 16 June 1843, in Parker, *Peel*, III, pp. 53–4.

[19] Queen to Peel, ? Sept. 1844, in ibid. p. 108.

[20] Peel to de Grey, 22 Aug. 1843, in ibid. pp. 56–7.

[21] See Gerald McElroy, 'Employment of Catholics in the Public Service in Ireland, 1859–1921: A Broad Overview' in Alan O'Day (ed.), *Government and Institutions in the Post-1832 United Kingdom* (Lampeter, 1995), p. 311.

[22] See for example, 'Paddy and Mr Punch' in R. F. Foster, *Paddy and Mr Punch: Connections in Irish and English History* (London, 1994), pp. 176–82.

[23] For an effective recent assessment, see G. L. Bernstein, 'Liberals, the Irish Famine and the Role of the State', *Irish Historical Studies* [*IHS*], 19 (Nov. 1995), 513–36.

It was almost inevitable that the blame cast upon the Government for the famine would attach itself to the Queen. A myth about Victoria's miserly attitude to famine relief would gradually emerge that can easily be read as a variation on the theme of Government-facilitated genocide,[24] and which still exerts an influence on Irish opinion today.[25] The myth became fully developed only during the nationalist struggles of the later nineteenth century, but its origins entered the Catholic Irish popular imagination during the famine itself,[26] in fact at the same time as preparations were being made for a visit to Ireland by the Queen. The backdrop was provided by events in Britain and Ireland during 1848, events given a revolutionary edge by the abdication of King Louis Philippe of France in February.

II

Chartism, Irish nationalism and the events in Paris combined to unsettle the royal family deeply, with Prince Albert urging on the Prime Minister, Lord John Russell, any feasible plan of Irish reform for immediate implementation to forestall revolution,[27] and a distraught Victoria praying that if the worst came to the worst she and Albert would at least be allowed to remain together.[28] In the event, however, London was not Paris: 10 April – the date of an expected revolt on the occasion of a Chartist petition to Parliament – came and went with relatively little revolutionary activity,[29] while in Ireland a revolt by the Young Ireland movement in July was a wholly ineffectual affair. With the revolutionary tide clearly subsiding, the Government began to think of a new era in Anglo-Irish relations.

Capitalising on the effects of the famine, the Encumbered Estates Act, enacted in 1849, would remove the most indebted landlords and give

---

[24] It was claimed that she donated only £5 to famine relief. In fact she personally contributed £2,500, while a royal appeal for funds raised, in conjunction with other appeals, £435,000: Peter Gray, *Famine, Land and Politics: British Government and Irish Society 1843–1850* (Dublin, 1999), p. 259.

[25] See controversies over proposed restorations of statues of Queen Victoria at University College Cork and Belfast: *The Times* [*TT*], 25 June 1994; *Belfast Telegraph*, 2 Nov. 2000.

[26] For instance, Michael Slattery, Catholic archbishop of Cashel, complained of Victoria's 'indifference' to the famine: Donal Kerr, *'A Nation of Beggars?' Priests, People, and Politics in Famine Ireland 1846–1852* (Oxford, 1994), p. 203.

[27] Prince Albert to Lord John Russell, 5 April 1848, in Frank Eyck, *The Prince Consort: A Political Biography* (2nd edn, Bath, 1975), p. 166.

[28] Elizabeth Longford, *Victoria R.I.* (London, 1964), pp. 195–6.

[29] Donald McRaild, *Irish Migrants in Modern Britain 1750–1922* (Basingstoke, 1999), pp. 136–8; Theodore Martin, *Life of the Prince Consort* (London, 1876), II, pp. 41–2.

hope that a new beginning on the land question could be made,[30] while the Government also attempted to conciliate through endowment the Irish Catholic clergy – a body of men that, given popular British religio-national prejudices, was viewed as being almost as threatening to the constitutional order as revolutionists.[31] The initiative failed. Nevertheless, it was an indication of official reforming intent at a time when the Government and the administration in Ireland were growing confident once again of their ability to secure Irish allegiance to the Union. Prince Albert's prescription for Ireland's ills at the end of the year contrasted with his earlier, rather panic-striken, advice. Now he discounted a rush to legislate, advising instead a combination of Malthusian and Smilesian remedies – a regulation of population in accordance with food supply, the cultivation of habits of industry and self-reliance, the exploitation of the country's natural resources and the spread of 'sound knowledge' – as the best means of countering 'the malign influence of those who inflamed the people with mad dreams of old wrongs to be avenged, and of the blessings of a separate nationality'.[32] The Queen's presence in Ireland was intended to encourage the development of that process and provide a focus for the loyalty to the state it would produce.

Conditions for such a visit hardly seemed ideal given the still prevailing famine conditions.[33] But the Queen was determined to go, partly because it was a region of her kingdom she had never visited before, but also because she feared that since a visit had been openly bruited for at least six years, the impression might be created among her Irish subjects that she was afraid to come.[34] Moreover, the Irish Viceroy, Lord Clarendon, was keen to promote it. Clarendon, though he shared with the Prime Minister, Lord Russell, a concern about how the Queen would be received in Ireland,[35] thought that no time since Victoria had ascended the throne was more propitious:

Agitation is extinct, Repeal is forgotten – the seditious associations are closed – the priests are frightened and the people are tranquil. Everything tends to secure for the Queen an enthusiastic reception, and the one drawback, which is the general

---

[30] John Prest, *Lord John Russell* (London, 1972), pp. 296–8

[31] See Lord Lansdowne to Russell, 29 Oct. 1848, in G. P. Gooch (ed.), *The Later Correspondence of Lord John Russell 1840–1878* (London, 1925), I, pp. 231–2; Memo by Lord Palmerston, 31 March 1848, in ibid. p. 225; Lord Clarendon to G. L. Lewis, 10 Oct. 1849, in Sir Herbert Maxwell, *The Life and Letters of George William Frederick, Fourth Earl of Clarendon* (London, 1913), I, p. 298.

[32] Prince Albert, Memo on Ireland, 30 Oct. 1848, in Martin, *Prince Consort*, II, pp. 135–6: Albert to the Home Secretary, Sir George Grey, 22 Dec. 1848, in ibid. pp. 138–9.

[33] Stanley Weintraub, *Albert: Uncrowned King* (London, 1997), p. 221.

[34] Longford, *Victoria*, p. 188; Prest, *Russell*, p. 300.   [35] Prest, *Russell*, p. 300.

distress of all classes, has its advantages, for it will enable the Queen to do what is kind and considerate to those who are suffering.[36]

The representative organ of British middle-class opinion, *Illustrated London News*, put it more succinctly: 'famine and plague have taught all classes that the real evils of Ireland are social and not political'.[37] The famine, it seems, had served to validate the Union. Moreover, the royal party, Lord Palmerston claimed, could depend on the effusive nature of the Irish character to ensure a good popular reception.[38] The Government sought to facilitate this end by rushing a bill through Parliament commuting death sentences passed on the insurgents of 1848.[39]

Alive to the impropriety of ostentation in famine conditions, Prince Albert suggested a yachting excursion, taking in Cork, Waterford, Dublin and Belfast before proceeding onwards to Scotland, a suggestion accepted following Lord Russell's insistence that it run over several days.[40] For his part, Clarendon, who only accepted the post of Viceroy on the understanding that it would be abolished on his retirement, and saw this royal visit as signalling a new beginning, went to considerable personal expense to make it a success.[41]

Nevertheless, the preparations proved controversial. A decision to keep the royal progress to the main Dublin thoroughfares to avoid scenes of desolation provoked criticism from both nationalist and Tory sources that the real Ireland was being hidden: a 'great lie', it seemed, was about to be enacted, and this impression moved some who might have been expected to attend Dublin Castle functions, such as Lords Montegle and Fitzwilliam, to abstain.[42] When the Lord Mayor of Dublin, Timothy O'Leary, suggested making municipal funds available to furnish street illuminations, it was met with a chorus of protest demanding that any such funds should be directed to the relief of the starving.[43] Among Dublin tradespeople opinion was divided between those doubtful about the morality of the visit in the still prevailing famine conditions, and those

[36] Martin, *Prince Consort*, II, p. 192.   [37] *Illustrated London News*, 4 Aug. 1849.

[38] Palmerston to Russell, 5 Aug. 1849, in Gooch (ed.), *Letters of Russell*, I, p. 235.

[39] Lee, *Victoria*, pp. 202–3.

[40] Russell to Clarendon, 23 June 1849, in Benson and Esher (eds.), *Letters of Victoria*, first series, II, pp. 223–4; Prest, *Russell*, p. 300.

[41] Clarendon to Henry Reeve, 17 Dec. 1848, in Maxwell, *Clarendon*, I, pp. 292–4; Clarendon to Sir George Grey, 29 June 1849: Royal Visit file, National Archives, [NA], Kew, HO45/052522.

[42] Cecil Woodham-Smith, *The Great Hunger: Ireland 1845–49* (London, 1964), pp. 384–5; *Freeman's Journal [FJ]*, 29 June 1849.

[43] See Thomas Webb to Sir George Grey, 20 July 1849, Royal Visit file, NA (Kew), HO45/052522; Woodham-Smith, *Great Hunger*, p. 385.

conscious of its possible stimulus to trade.[44] It was a signal of the way in which popular opinion was moving that the latter view proved persuasive. It was reflected in the failure of Dublin Corporation, a Repeal-dominated body, to pass a resolution calling for an Irish Parliament, even one coupled with protestations of loyalty to the Queen;[45] though it seems that the authorities took the precaution of incarcerating anyone suspected of posing a threat to the visit's success.[46] In sum, the situational reconstruction of the Dublin cityscape as a royal domain involved tension between local concerns that the plight of the country be acknowledged and an increasingly accepted need that the city provide a fitting environment for the monarch, whose presence as its hegemonic emblem, anywhere in the state, arguably designated that location as its symbolic centre.

Thus although the visit was not to be a state occasion, a special coach was built in Dublin to convey the sovereign through the city, while the royal couple expressed their concern that the visit should be 'well done' by declaring themselves ready to receive 'any declarations of loyalty the people of Dublin may wish to display'. Also, the royal party itself was to be large – thirty-six people, including four royal children – while despite the financial constraints, at the end of July triumphal arches, platforms and 'devices' were erected. Dublin Castle was given a facelift, the Four Courts being illuminated by gas on the night of the royal arrival, and Nelson's Pillar by electric light[47] – the latter associating the royal presence with modernity. In fact, the arrangements for the visit, as with those of 1821, served socio-economically to energise the urban context into a state of heightened expectation.[48] For her part, the Queen signalled her concern to conciliate Irish Catholic opinion by letting it be known that she had refused to make a donation to a Protestant charitable institution, precisely because it was 'exclusively Protestant'.[49]

The Queen's visit to Ireland was not, as she stated, undertaken without some personal cost. A bad sailor, she suffered 'dreadfully' on the trip over to Ireland on the royal yacht, *Victoria and Albert*, while it was known that Dublin suffered a cholera outbreak during the period of the visit.[50] The first port of call was Cobh, County Cork, on 2 August, where the Queen briefly stopped so that the people could have the satisfaction of renaming it 'Queenstown', in honour of its being 'the first spot on which I set foot

---

[44] Clarendon was of the latter view: Maxwell, *Clarendon*, I, p. 303.
[45] *TT*, 9, 14, 24 July 1849.   [46] See *FJ*, 25 July 1849; *TT*, 26 July 1849.
[47] *TT*, 30 July 1849; Woodham-Smith, *Great Hunger*, pp. 387–90.
[48] For an overall impression, see Royal Visit file, NA (Kew), HO45/052522.
[49] *TT*, 1 Aug. 1849.   [50] Woodham-Smith, *Great Hunger*, pp. 382–3.

upon Irish ground', thus following the precedent set by George IV in September 1821.[51] The royal party then immediately re-embarked and proceeded up the River Lee to Cork city.[52]

The significance of the occasion, the beauty of the young Queen, the situational preparations[53] and popular expectations ensured the visit would exhibit all the characteristics of 'organic' harmony between monarch and subjects. Thus the popular reception of the royal party by the people of both Cobh and Cork city was highly enthusiastic, with parliamentary, political and ecclesiastical dignitaries paying homage.[54] At the city's University College a statue of the Queen that would cause controversy in the 1990s was erected. To mark the success of the Cork dimension to the visit, the Mayor was knighted on the deck of the royal yacht. Of her progress through the city the Queen recorded: 'it took two hours ... The crowd ... noisy, excitable, but a very good-natured one, running and pushing about, and laughing, talking and shrieking.'[55] Victoria's account of her Irish visit reveals a sharp eye for human and topographical detail. While the visit was structured in such a way as to disguise evidence of famine and destitution, the fact that in Cork, and later Dublin, 'the men are very poorly, often raggedly dressed' did not escape her attention.[56] The journals also reveal – especially where her Stuart predecessors were concerned, to whom she had a rather illogical romantic attachment[57] – her knowledge of Irish history.[58] From Waterford the royal party proceeded to Kingstown and another ecstatic reception: 'it was really very striking'.[59] Nor did Dublin disappoint Victoria: 'It was a wonderful and striking scene, such masses of human beings, so enthusiastic, so excited, yet such perfect order maintained ... a never-to-be-forgotten scene; when one reflected how lately the country had been in open revolt and under martial law.'[60] Delighted at her reception by the populace, Victoria was well conditioned to be impressed by Dublin as a city, praising its layout and public

---

[51] Lee, *Victoria*, p. 203; W. M. Drew to Sir George Grey, 14 July 1849, NA (Kew), HO45/052522.

[52] Queen Victoria [QV], *Leaves from the Journal of Our Life in the Highland*, ed. Arthur Helps (London, 1868), p. 249.

[53] Prince George, the Queen's first cousin, was in charge of militia arrangements during the visit and earned the applause of the royal couple, Clarendon and Sir George Grey for a flawless operation: Giles St Aubyn, *The Royal George: 1819–1904: The Life of H.R.H. Prince George Duke of Cambridge* (London, 1963), pp. 44–5.

[54] QV, *Leaves*, p. 250. In Cork, as in Dublin, initial attempts to include political aspirations in the address to the Queen were abandoned in favour of an uncontentious loyal welcome: *TT*, 6 Aug. 1849.

[55] QV, *Leaves*, p. 251.   [56] Ibid. pp. 251, 261, 262.   [57] Lee, *Victoria*, pp. 260, 574.

[58] QV, *Leaves*, p. 252.   [59] Ibid. p. 254.

[60] Ibid. pp. 254–5; also *FJ*, 7 Aug. 1849; *TT*, 8 Aug. 1849.

6 Queen Victoria's official entry to Dublin, 1849.

buildings, while the care taken by the city authorities to ensure the visit was a success is reflected in her account of her official entry to the city (Fig. 6): 'There are no gates to the town, but temporary ones were erected under an arch; and here we stopped, and the Mayor presented me with the keys with some appropriate words. At the last triumphal arch a poor little dove was let down into my lap, with an olive branch round its neck, alive and very tame.'[61]

The routine of the first four days of the royal stay in Dublin was taken up with visits to public institutions, and meetings with, and the receiving of addresses from, leading personages, political, civic and religious, the latter including Dr Murray, the Roman Catholic bishop of Dublin. In addition, there were drawing rooms, balls and levees held at Dublin Castle. The last day of the Dublin stay was mainly given over to a visit to Carton, the residence of the Duke of Leinster, a visit which impressed the Queen especially by the evidently harmonious hierarchical relationship that existed between the Duke and his tenantry: 'the Duke is so kind to them, that a word from him will make them do anything'.[62] It was reported, moreover, that a display of Irish dancing provided by the Duke's tenantry for the Queen's benefit was performed by disciples – of 'neat and comfortable appearance' – of Father Mathew's temperance

[61] QV, *Leaves*, pp. 255–6.   [62] Ibid. pp. 258–63.

movement:[63] representatives, in fact, of the more respectable Ireland that, it was hoped, the royal visit would promote, and the values of which, in Ireland as in Britain, the Queen was already coming to personify.[64]

From Dublin the royal party proceeded to Belfast. Passing Carrickfergus, the Queen noted its significance as the place where William III landed in Ireland. At Belfast the same popular delight that was occasioned by the royal round of public engagements in Dublin was evident, but more impressive given the fierce antagonism that normally existed between the province's religious and political groups,[65] and despite the fact that the Queen, as she had in Dublin, refused to visit exclusively Protestant charitable institutions. But at most, Belfast was a brief staging point on the royal progress from Dublin to the monarch's beloved Scottish Highlands. She rounded off her journal record of the Irish visit with a tribute to the Irish Constabulary, 'all Irish, and chiefly Roman Catholics; and not one of whom, during the trying times last year, fraternised with the rebels'.[66]

Victoria's delight at the success of the Irish visit is evident not only in her journals, but also in the correspondence of the royal couple,[67] and the conferring of the title 'Earl of Dublin' on Albert Edward, the young Prince of Wales.[68] She also complied with the pleading of a woman – who assured her that if she 'made' one of her children 'Prince Patrick' all Ireland 'would die for you'[69] – by giving Prince Arthur, born in 1850, the secondary name 'Patrick'.[70] The Queen's delight at her reception in Ireland was based on beliefs about what that reception seemed to imply about Irish loyalty to the crown and constitution. Prince Albert,

---

[63] *Illustrated London News* [*ILN*], 4 Aug. 1849.

[64] See High Sheriff of County Down to Sir George Grey, 27 July 1849, enclosing an Address from the people of the county thanking God 'for the gracious example set by Your Majesty of private and domestic virtues', Royal Visit file, NA (Kew), HO45/052522.

[65] Shortly before the visit possibly thirty Catholics were killed in a riot in County Down. Potential for disorder existed in the presence among the royal party of Lady Fanny Jocelyn, daughter of Lord Roden, the Orange leader on whose property the riot took place: Kevin Nowlan, *The Politics of Repeal: A Study in the Relations between Great Britain and Ireland 1841–50* (London, 1965), p. 228; *FJ*, 3 Aug. 1849; James Murphy, *Abject Loyalty: Nationalism and Monarchy in Ireland during the Reign of Queen Victoria* (Cork, 2001), pp. 96–7.

[66] See *TT*, 13, 16 Aug. 1849; QV, *Leaves*, pp. 264–8. Following the visit the Queen made a donation of £300 for the relief of the poor of Belfast communicated in terms intended to discourage sectarianism: *TT*, 30 Aug. 1849.

[67] See, for example, Victoria to King Leopold of the Belgians, 6 Aug. 1849 in Benson and Esher (eds.), *Letters of Victoria*, first series, II, pp. 224–6; Victoria to Clarendon, 18 Aug. 1849, in Maxwell, *Clarendon*, I, pp. 303–4.

[68] QV, *Leaves*, p. 269.   [69] Martin, *Prince Consort*, II, p. 207.

[70] Sir George Aston, *His Royal Highness the Duke of Connaught and Strathearn* (London, 1929), p. 35.

Lord Lansdowne and Viceroy Clarendon exulted and marvelled at the apparent transformation from treason to loyalty the royal couple's presence and conduct facilitated.[71] For Clarendon, the visit's secret lay in how the royal presence had elevated the self-estimation of the populace:

the people are not only enchanted with the Queen and the gracious kindness of her manner, and the confidence she has shown in them, but they are pleased with themselves for their own good feelings and behaviour, which they consider have removed the barriers that hitherto existed between the Sovereign and themselves, and that they now occupy a higher position in the eyes of the world.[72]

And enough evidence seemed to exist to justify these observations. Victoria's first cousin, the Duke of Cambridge, a very young Edward Carpenter, later bishop of Ripon, and Lord Dufferin, later Viceroy of Canada and of India, were among the crowds that greeted the Queen in Dublin, and testified to their often hysterical enthusiasm,[73] while nationalist and Tory opinion which had been unfavourable to the visit at the outset, whether for political or moral reasons, swung around to support it as it proceeded.[74] Moreover, the unity between antagonistic religious and political groups that the visit appeared to call forth also seemed to persist after it was over, most surprisingly, in Belfast, though the tendency of Ulster loyalists to appropriate the monarchy to assert a binary opposition between loyal Ulster and supposedly disloyal southern Ireland was also evident.[75] In Kingstown, one of the most popular actions of the Queen was made just before her departure, when she stepped down from the royal yacht on to the paddle-box that was used to travel between the yacht and the shore, and lowered the royal standard three times in acknowledgement of the great reception she had been given. Clarendon remarked: 'there is not an individual who does not take it as a personal compliment to himself'. Even the separatists, he enthused, were now, according to police reports, among the Queen's

---

[71] Martin, *Prince Consort*, II, pp. 205–6, 209; Lansdowne to Lord Russell, 9 Aug. 1849 in Gooch (ed.), *Letters of Russell*, I, p. 235; Clarendon to Sir George Grey, 15 Aug. 1849, in Maxwell, *Clarendon*, I, p. 303. The Dublin Metropolitan Police declined to prosecute English pickpockets arrested in Dublin, on the grounds that the disclosure of their nationality would have mortified the Queen: Crawford, *Victoria*, pp. 304–5.

[72] Clarendon to Sir George Grey, 14 Aug. 1849, in Benson and Esher (eds.), *Letters of Victoria*, first series, II, p. 226.

[73] St Aubyn, *Royal George*, pp. 44–5; Revd W. Boyd Carpenter, *Some Pages from My Life* (London, 1911), pp. 274–5; Sir Alfred Lyall, *The Life of the Marquis of Dufferin and Ava* (2nd edn in 1 vol., London, n.d.), p. 69.

[74] Woodham-Smith, *Great Hunger*, p. 397. For a grudging acceptance of the warm popular reception for the Queen, see *FJ*, 6 Aug. 1849.

[75] See *BNL*, 17, 21 Aug. 1849; *Londonderry Sentinel*, 17, 24 Aug. 1849.

most loyal subjects.[76] If he was aware of it, Clarendon was undoubtedly gratified by the fact that 'God Save the Queen', a frequent accompaniment to royal events in Dublin, had been sung in honour of the Catholic James II[77] and was now being sung by the descendants of his Irish supporters in honour of a Protestant Queen. He would have been even more gratified had he known of the demoralising effect the Irish reception for the Queen had upon the most dangerous of the revolutionary leaders of 1848, John Mitchel: 'the debased nation set its neck under her feet in a paroxysm of fictitious "loyalty". It is painful to relate, but it is the disgraceful fact.'[78] Indeed, so fulsome was the Irish reception for the Queen that it is tempting to apply Richard Wortman's description of the nationally epitomatic function of royal ceremonial in the Russia of Victoria's contemporary, Tsar Nicholas I,[79] in the Irish context: Victoria and Albert, the 'signifiers' of an apparently loyal Irish people, symbolically engulfed the 'signified', Ireland. Given his anxieties for the success of the visit, Clarendon's evident wish to read into the Queen's reception the elimination of Irish disloyalty is understandable. It symbolised a new beginning for the Irish people, 'a turn in the tide of their affairs after four years of suffering, with an unprecedented influx of strangers and expenditure of money, and as they will contrast this year with the last, their conclusion must be unfavourable to political agitation'.[80] Undoubtedly the visit was a great success.[81]

Set against the background of the highly troubled Anglo-Irish relationship in general, and the Great Famine in particular, it appears as an almost unreal occasion divorced from the environment in which it took place. In fact, it took place at a transitional, or liminal, moment in Irish history, in which that environment was changing. The famine was destroying the old rural social order, while the new one, consisting of the substantial tenant-farmer class that would develop over the twenty-five years from 1850, and whose interests a substantially anti-monarchical

---

[76] Clarendon to Sir George Grey, 14 Aug. 1849, in Benson and Esher (eds.), *Letters of Victoria*, first series, II, p. 226. Reflecting this sentiment *The Times* (9 Aug. 1849) exclaimed: 'The Queen's visit to Ireland is the concluding chapter of the history of the Irish rebellion [of 1848].'

[77] Charles Dimot, 'God Save the Queen: The History of the National Anthem', *History Today*, 3 (May 1953), 361–2.

[78] John Mitchel, *Jail Journal* (1854; new edn, Dublin, n.d.[1961]), p. 6, footnote.

[79] Richard Wortman, *Scenarios of Power: Myth and Ceremony in Russian Monarchy*, I. *From Peter the Great to the Death of Nicholas I* (Princeton, NJ, 1995), p. 298.

[80] Clarendon to Sir George Grey, 15 Aug. 1849, in Maxwell, *Clarendon*, I, p. 303.

[81] The denials of the Fenian leader, John O'Leary (*Recollections of Fenians and Fenianism* (London, 1896), I, p. 61), are so at variance with a wealth of oppositional evidence that they can be safely disregarded.

Parnellite nationalism would mobilise for its own purposes from 1879,[82] had yet to develop. Moreover, in this context, with both revolutionary and constitutional nationalism in disarray, the royal visitors not only faced no significant movement opposed to monarchy, but could actually capitalise on strands of O'Connell's monarchical propaganda that now lacked organisational direction. Moreover, communication between sovereign and people, visual and verbal, was an instrumental channel for the expressions of loyalty it facilitated.

The Queen was a pretty young woman whose pleasant personality and attire, which usually sported an appropriate Irish motif, were well calculated to appeal to a people only too ready to be pleased, while the giving and acknowledging of homage were conducted in language at once simplistic, abbreviated, non-contentious and essentially celebratory. It was a highly formalised kind of public interaction, consisting of very limited personal contact which was yet potent in its ability to foster expressions of loyalty. In fact, evidence exists that techniques of regulated contact, designed to maximise awe of the royal presence, had been employed by British monarchs throughout the nineteenth century.[83] Certainly Victoria's activities in Dublin demonstrate a refined skill in the art of public interaction. An insightful assessment, noting her 'distinct theatrical instinct', remarks that she 'was unrivalled in her sense of the proper *mise en scène* of a formal ceremonial'.[84] In the 1840s she had an avid interest in the theatre, both as patron and participant in family amateur productions.[85] Accordingly, it would not be implausible to see her acknowledging of the crowds at Kingstown by lowering the royal standard three times as a piece of royal theatre timed for maximum effect.[86]

The factors which facilitated harmony between monarch and subjects also facilitated what might be described as the mesmerising effects of royal charisma. As we have seen, Geertz located the source of charisma in the relationship between symbolism and power and considered it most influential among those farthest away from the centre of power. As with

---

[82] There is a substantial literature dealing with these developments. See, for example, F. S. L. Lyons, *Ireland since the Famine* (2nd edn, London, 1973); K. T. Hoppen, *Ireland since 1800* (2nd edn, London, 2000); Tom Garvin, *The Evolution of Irish Nationalist Politics* (Dublin, 1981).

[83] Linda Colley, *Britons: Forging the Nation 1707–1837* (New Haven and London, 1992), pp. 233–5; Sir Frederick Ponsonby, *Recollections of Three Reigns* (London, 1951), p. 194.

[84] Edmund Gosse, 'The Character of Queen Victoria', *Quarterly Review*, 3 (1901), 314.

[85] George Rowell, *Queen Victoria Goes to the Theatre* (London, 1978), *passim*; Magdalen Ponsonby (ed.), *Mary Ponsonby: A Memoir, Some Letters and a Journal* (London, 1927), p. xi.

[86] It was a talent she would draw on to great effect during the later years of her reign: Richard Williams, *The Contentious Crown: Public Discussion of the British Monarchy in the Reign of Queen Victoria* (Aldershot, 1997), pp. 216–18.

George IV, her presence was not just symbolic of the constitutional order but, given the institutional centrality of the monarchy in what was still a pre-Bagehotian age – as evidenced not least in O'Connell's own marrying of monarchy and Whig politics – an authentic embodiment of the power that order possessed. Symbolism in itself clearly would have been insufficient to invoke charisma effectively. The Viceroy may have been the monarch's substitute in Ireland, but the fact that he was a Government appointee engaged in pursuing often controversial policies undermined the claims of his office authentically to embody the majesty of monarchy and the authority of the constitution.

In the presence of the Queen, however, and as Clarendon suggested, the Dublin crowds could have a sense of their acknowledgement by the most powerful symbolic and authoritative source in the British state. Moreover, there is some evidence that this conception of the Queen set her apart from Governments responsible for the mass deaths of the famine and – in regard to the monarchical office as a source of justice and assistance – made her an authority whom the people could address, both to bring those politicians to account and for material relief.[87] However, care needs to be taken in assessing the visit, especially in regard to the extent and durability of the loyalty demonstrated.

Despite his initial delight at its success, Clarendon, on reflection, was less euphoric about its lasting effects and concluded that, if the beneficial effects of the visit were to be capitalised on, stern coercion measures would be needed to 'protect the people from themselves and those by whom they have been so long deceived'. The royal visit alone could not produce a social revolution 'nor at once remove evils that are the growth of ages'.[88] Accordingly, he could not go the 'length' of the prophets who were now springing up and predicting 'all manner of permanent good from the temporary presence of our gracious Mistress'.[89] Nor could important organs of opinion in Britain such as the *Quarterly Review* and *Punch*, which, removed from the intoxicating atmosphere of Dublin, were more likely to view the visit in a critical light.[90] Their scepticism about the visit's beneficial effects was based on a belief that the mass loyalty the Queen's presence called forth in Dublin, if not merely

---

[87] See 'An Irishman' to Sir George Grey, 16 July 1849; Patrick Lynagh and Patrick McGuire, on behalf of the Inhabitants of Drogheda, to Sir George Grey, 7 Aug. 1849; William O'Hara, Alderman, enclosing 'Address of Citizens of Limerick Meeting in Public', to Sir George Grey, 6 Aug. 1849: Royal Visit file, NA (Kew), HO45/052522.

[88] Clarendon to G. L. Lewis, 27 Aug. 1849, in Maxwell, *Clarendon*, II, p. 304.

[89] Ibid.

[90] See the commentary in Joseph Hone, 'Queen Victoria in Ireland', *History Today* 3 (1953), 501.

ephemeral, was at best *aspirational* in nature. The visit indicated the Ireland that it might be possible to create, but concealed the range of complex problems in the way of firmly establishing it.

In his discussions of crowds, John Berger argues that when such gatherings occupy public spaces in defiance of constituted authority they are asserting symbolically a power they have yet fully to possess: 'Demonstrations express political ambitions before the political means necessary to realise them have been created.'[91] This insight has been tellingly applied to O'Connell's 'monster meetings'.[92] It can, however, also be usefully applied to the royal visit of 1849. Despite the fact that the Queen was the pre-eminent embodiment of constituted order, in Ireland the period since the Union had demonstrated the extent to which that order lacked popular legitimacy. In this context, and as Clarendon's more reflective assessment of the visit's significance indicates, the unity of sovereign and people that it demonstrated was symbolic and unstable. No less than O'Connell's mass meetings, it expressed a political ambition before the actual means necessary to realise it had been created. That the visit appeared much more successful than it was is largely explicable in terms of the forms of concealment that royal ceremony often embodies,[93] and which Bagehot defined as the 'greatest' function of the British monarchy.[94] Certainly John Mitchel, who was appalled by the Irish reception for the Queen, denied, on reflection, that authentic allegiance could be inferred from it, citing the natural courtesy of the people, the attraction of a pageant, viceregal largess to the Catholic middle class and hope that Victoria would pardon the 1848 insurgents.[95] Whatever the merits of Mitchel's argument, the royal visit of 1849 did entail a large element of concealment.

As we have noted, the ambitions of those anxious for a successful visit even went so far as the – unrealistic – concealment of the effects of famine. Other forms of concealment, however, were more successful. At state level, for instance, there was a refusal to acknowledge controversial

---

[91] 'The Nature of Mass Demonstrations' in John Berger, *Selected Essays and Articles: The Look of Things* (Harmondsworth, 1972), p. 249.

[92] See Gary Owens, 'Nationalism without Words: Symbolism and Ritual Behaviour in the Repeal "Monster Meetings" of 1843–5' in J. S. Donnelly Jr and K. A. Miller (eds.), *Irish Popular Culture 1650–1850* (Dublin, 1998), pp. 256–7.

[93] For a succinct and relevant discussion, see B. C. Alexander, 'Ceremony' in Mircea Eliade (eds.), *The Encyclopedia of Religion* (New York, 1987), pp. 179–83. The concealment function of royal ritual is also a major theme of David Cannadine and Simon Price (eds.), *Rituals of Royalty: Power and Ceremonial in Traditional Societies* (Cambridge, 1992), p. 15.

[94] Walter Bagehot, *The English Constitution*, Intro. R. H. S. Crossman (1867; London, 1971), p. 97.

[95] Mitchel, *Jail Journal*, pp. 202–3.

addresses in the official publication, the *Dublin Gazette*.[96] But the process went much further, especially in masking profoundly deep religious and political divisions within the country, no less than fundamental problems complicating the Anglo-Irish relationship. Most significantly, the visit masked the continued existence of nationalism. One pressman, presumably nationalist, was said to have been sacked for a misprint in his coverage of the visit that was considered deliberate: 'The Queen *pissed* over the bridge.'[97] More seriously, not all separatists had abandoned their activities. Rebellion may have failed in 1848, but the farcical nature of that revolt left many radical nationalists ashamed and keen for another attempt to obliterate its memory: the Queen's visit appeared to offer an appropriate opportunity to redeem Irish revolutionary honour. Accordingly plans were made to effect a major propagandist coup involving the capture of Dublin Castle and the kidnapping of the Queen. It was a foolhardy plan, but was called off only at the last moment owing to lack of adequate support.[98] In the event, the revolutionary apparatus that had been assembled in 1849 soon disintegrated, with nothing more to show for its efforts than an assault upon the constabulary barracks at Cappoquin, County Waterford, on 16 September,[99] one month after the Queen's departure. As such it fell outside the context of the royal visit and thus did not mar the close relationship that apparently existed between the sovereign and her Irish subjects.

Another area of concealment lay in the homage paid by the Irish Catholic clergy to the Queen. This was less comprehensive than it appeared. In fact, the clergy's address was signed by only thirteen of twenty-seven prelates, reflecting divisions between the archbishops of Tuam, Cashel and Dublin.[100] Dr MacHale of Tuam, the spokesman of the radical wing of the hierarchy, demanded, unsuccessfully, that it arrange a meeting with the monarch to explain the real state of the country. Again, unsuccessfully, he urged that any address by the hierarchy to the Queen should indict the Government for the deaths of thousands of his flock. In the hands of the compliant Daniel Murray of Dublin, however, the

---

[96] See notes to addresses submitted by citizens of Drogheda and Limerick, and Catholic clergy and people of Barony of Upper Colonoe, County Limerick, Royal Visit file, NA (Kew), HO45/052522.

[97] David Thompson and Moya McGusty (eds.), *The Irish Journals of Elizabeth Smith 1840–1850* (Oxford, 1980), p. 225, footnote 1.

[98] Marcus Burke, *John O'Leary: A Study in Irish Separatism* (Tralee, 1967), pp. 25–6; Sir Charles Gavan Duffy, *Four Years of Irish History 1845–1849* (London, 1883), pp. 759–63.

[99] R. V. Comerford, *The Fenians in Context: Irish Politics and Society 1848–82* (Dublin, 1985), p. 18.

[100] The see of Armagh was vacant owing to the death of Archbishop Crolly.

hierarchy's address was devoid of contentious issues.[101] Moreover, the unity of religious denominations that the visit seemed to call forth belied the anger of some sections of Ulster Protestant opinion at an apparently more enthusiastic royal response to the Roman Catholic address, than to the address submitted by the Presbyterian clergy.[102]

This reaction may have been hypersensitive, and it missed a more important point; namely, that among the representatives of the Roman Catholic and Protestant communities who paid homage to the sovereign significant differences, in the degrees of allegiance offered and legitimacy accepted, existed. The royal visit, as with many such visits,[103] partook of a divine, no less than a secular, dimension. The Queen was not only head of state but also head of the established church of England and Ireland. For Anglicans, the divine dimension was inescapable from the homage offered, something that applied, in a wider Protestant sense, we may assume, to Presbyterians also. For Roman Catholics, however, it could not have been present. The homage offered was to the Queen as head of state only; and a religio-political crisis over Catholic ecclesiastical jurisdiction – the 'papal aggression' of 1850 – would soon arise in Britain and Ireland that would make this clear, as well as stimulate the still influential anti-Irish and anti-Catholic prejudices that coloured popular British attitudes to Ireland. These were prejudices that the Queen herself, to a significant extent, shared. They would have been reinforced, moreover, in May 1849 when the first of a number of attempts on the lives of members of the royal family by Irishmen took place. William Hamilton 'fired' on the Queen at Constitution Hill as she was returning from her official birthday celebrations. Hamilton was transported for seven years, although he was deranged and his gun unloaded. Victoria, however, was more conscious of the fact that he was Irish than that he was insane.[104] In sum, the success of the royal visit was more limited than it outwardly seemed. However, that is not to suggest the inevitable failure of the state project in Ireland, rather to indicate the dimensions of the task it faced.

III

The visit of 1849 invites comparison with that of George IV in 1821, and while there were similarities there were also differences. The effects of contextual scene-setting, spectacle and charisma were broadly the same; even the pre-visit anxieties of 1821 were repeated when reports of

[101] Kerr, 'A Nation of Beggars?', pp. 203–4.   [102] BNL, 17 Aug. 1849.
[103] Alexander, 'Ceremony', pp. 182–3.   [104] Longford, Victoria, p. 192.

Victoria's arrival at Cork fuelled wild rumours in Dublin that she was already at Kingstown and would proceed secretly to Dublin Castle, thus denying the people the opportunity to offer her a public welcome.[105] But the differences were more significant. For instance, the background of political agitation and expectation of reform that provided the context for the visit of 1821 was absent in 1849; and while the enthusiasm George IV engendered in 1821 owed much to intoxicated camaraderie and quite reckless populism, that of 1849 depended much more on the formal execution of royal ceremonial. In this context the very different personalities of the two monarchs have relevance. Respect and devotion to George IV was largely a function of his monarchical office; as a person he was widely regarded as disreputable. Victoria, however, not only had the devotion due her constitutional position, but personally still had the attractions of youth and was also the central figure of a royal family that was rapidly becoming the embodiment of a zeitgeist of middle-class respectability that appealed as much to the Irish middle class as to the British – even among Fenians.[106] In this context it is worth noting that the 'Famine Queen' myth that developed as part of nationalist propaganda in the late nineteenth century appears not to have impaired the Queen's reputation as a model of those values. Relatedly, and probably most importantly, whereas the attempt in the 1820s to identify George IV's visit as a defining moment in Irish politics – a conceptual point of departure for the development of harmonious Anglo-Irish relations – collapsed in the face of O'Connellite agitation and loyalist reaction, Victoria emblematised values that spoke to the spirit of the age at a time when Ireland was entering an era of localism in which those values could have a much better opportunity to shape popular mentalities. And there could hardly have been a better socio-economic environment for the project, as Ireland and Britain entered the period of mid-century prosperity.

[105] *TT*, 7 Aug. 1849.
[106] John O'Leary described Victoria as 'a highly respectable foreign lady, apparently with the merits and demerits of the English *bourgeoisie* ... she could not well help being English and a Queen, or rather the English Queen of Ireland': O'Leary, *Recollections of Fenians and Fenianism*, I, p. 131.

4   Loyalty and localism

The Ireland that emerged from the famine was untroubled not only by organised nationalism, but apparently even by the desire for self-government. Rather, it was characterised by 'a sense of embarrassment and inadequacy'.[1] Moreover, the recent social upheavals in Europe and at home had impressed upon Albert and Victoria the necessity of the monarchy positioning itself much more centrally in the life of the nation, especially the need to stabilise the social order by addressing the concerns of the poor.[2] And while Prince Albert may have baulked at the suggestion that he take a superintending role – as Chancellor of the Queen's University – in the affairs of the religiously and politically controversial Queen's colleges,[3] nevertheless, while avoiding contentious issues, an enhanced social dimension to the monarchy's role in Ireland was accepted.

The state would not have a monopoly on ideas of how post-famine Ireland should be reconstructed. The Irish landlord class – the social support-base of the Viceroyalty – came under attack in the early 1850s from a range of agrarian interests united under the banner of 'Tenant Right',[4] a movement whose theorist, James Fintan Lawlor, argued that while the famine had *dissolved* Irish society, this could only be remade on the basis of the tenant farmer interest,[5] a social group the Parnellite movement would mobilise effectively for its own nationalist ends from 1879. But the mid-nineteenth century – 1850s to the mid-1870s – was an era of 'deeply pervasive and enduring localist traditions',[6] in which Irish nationalism was but one ideology on offer to the Irish population in competition with that of the state. Indeed, despite the Fenian rising of

---

[1] Vincent Comerford quoted in R. F. Foster, *Modern Ireland 1600–1972* (London, 1989), p. 373.
[2] Frank Prochaska, *Royal Bounty: The Making of a Welfare Monarchy* (New Haven and London, 1995), pp. 84–5.
[3] See Theodore Martin, *Life of the Prince Consort* (London, 1875), II, p. 221.
[4] Foster, *Modern Ireland*, pp. 380–1.   [5] Ibid. p. 381.
[6] K. T. Hoppen, *Elections, Politics and Society in Ireland 1832–1885* (Oxford, 1984), p. viii.

1867, Ireland, as indicated by its parliamentary representation at the general election of 1868, appeared to share the assumptions of Britain, given the predominance of Liberals and Tories returned.[7] The impression of British assimilation this conveyed was enhanced by the absence of hegemonic nationalist symbols in this period.

While the green flag was recognised as a nationalist emblem in general since the beginning of the nineteenth century, only from the end of the 1870s, with the development of Parnellism, did it transmute from a political emblem to the 'Irish national flag'.[8] At the same time, only in 1867 was what would later be an emotively powerful nationalist anthem penned: 'God Save Ireland'.[9] Also, while the date of the Fenian executions, 23 November, would give rise to an annual festival that served to register opposition to the Union,[10] the significance of this, as with the other symbols, would not develop until the 1870s. In fact, even when moderate nationalists succeeded in marking the cityscape of Dublin with statues of O'Connell, Grattan, William Smith O'Brien and John Gray, editor of the influential *Freeman's Journal*, the sculptural form 'was easily comprehensible to the English', giving the impression of a desire for acceptance on largely English terms: 'there was less an implication that Ireland should have a separate distinctive existence than that Ireland be considered equivalent to England'.[11] This tendency was also visually discernible in the images displayed at exhibitions in Dublin and Cork in the 1850s and 1860s – overwhelmingly of a non-Irish, largely imperial character.[12] Moreover, the Irish provincial press in the 1850s largely abjured encouragement of constitutional agitation in favour of moral and economic regeneration achieved through education and the development of industrial enterprise, exactly the values promoted by the welfare monarchism of Albert and Victoria. The development of the press was integral to the modernisation process – 'the development of towns,

---

[7] H. J. Hanham, *Elections and Party Management: Politics in the Age of Disraeli and Gladstone* (Hassocks, Sussex, 1978), p. 179.

[8] Peter Alter, 'Symbols of Irish Nationalism' in Alan O'Day (ed.), *Reactions to Irish Nationalism* (London, 1987), p. 4.

[9] Ibid. pp. 6–7; T. D. Sullivan, *Troubled Times in Irish Politics* (Dublin, 1905), ch. 19. Sullivan, editor of the *Nation*, used the last words from the scaffold – 'God save Ireland' – of the Fenian 'martyrs', Allen, Larkin and O'Brien, hanged for the accidental killing of a policeman in an attempt to rescue a colleague from a prison van in Manchester.

[10] Alter, 'Symbols of Irish Nationalism', pp. 8–9.

[11] Catherine Hill, 'Ideology and Cultural Production: Nationalism and the Public Monument in Mid-Nineteenth Century Ireland' in Tadhg Foley and Sean Ryder (eds.), *Ideology and Ireland in the Nineteenth Century* (Dublin, 1998), pp. 67–8.

[12] See Louis Cullen, 'Union and Display in Ireland' in Dana Arnold (ed.), *Cultural Identities and the Aesthetics of Britishness* (Manchester, 2004), pp. 121–3.

with markets, shops, roads and railway stations'[13] – the anti-nationalist impetus of which was aided by Government suppression of the reading rooms of the Repeal movement. The popular imagination was thus 'being no longer deceived by delusive expectations (and seductive and poisonous doctrine)'.[14]

In the 1850s and 1860s 'nationalist' was an ill-defined term, and attempts to found constitutional nationalist organisations in these years failed to attract significant support.[15] With the symbolic universe of late nineteenth-century nationalism still to be established, in this period Ireland was conducive to a sustained exercise of royal influence. Changes affecting the monarchy, however, would complicate the exercise.

I

The relatively moderate attitude of the Queen to Catholicism up to 1850, for instance, underwent a transformation from that year. It was due partly to the 'papal aggression' provoked by Pope Pius IX's creation of a hierarchy of bishops for England and Wales, which, triumphantly heralded in Britain by the new archbishop of Westminster, Cardinal Nicholas Wiseman, revived age-old nativist fears of papal domination;[16] and partly to the death of Victoria's beloved aunt Louise, the Catholic Queen of King Leopold of the Belgians, whose influence on the young Victoria had hitherto conditioned a conciliatory attitude to Catholicism.[17] Affronted by what was widely regarded at the time as a papal 'invasion of the royal supremacy',[18] the Queen inspired the ill-advised Ecclesiastical Titles Bill enacted in June 1851, designed to outlaw the assumption of English territorial titles by Catholic prelates.[19] This was an 'evil', Prince Albert

---

[13] Marie-Louise Legg, *Newspapers and Nationalism: The Irish Provincial Press 1850–1892* (Dublin, 1999), pp. 25–8.

[14] Cork Resident Magistrate quoted in ibid. p. 64.

[15] Hill, 'Ideology and Cultural Production', p. 56.

[16] See John Wolffe, *God and Greater Britain: Religion and National Life in Britain and Ireland 1843–1945* (London, 1994), pp. 111–15. Papal aggression sentiment affected the Irish Viceroy, Clarendon, as well as Victoria and Albert.

[17] Walter Arnstein, 'Queen Victoria and the Challenge of Roman Catholicism', *The Historian*, 58 (1996), 300–1.

[18] Martin, *Prince Consort*, II, p. 338.

[19] Walter Arnstein, *Queen Victoria* (Basingstoke, 2003), pp. 93–4. The Ecclesiastical Titles Act, however, was almost immediately a dead letter, having been denuded of its most stringent clauses. It was quietly repealed by Gladstone in 1868.

argued unfairly,[20] 'which the Pope has brought upon us', and which 'will have to be set right by the Protestant body'.[21]

The crisis, however, was a litmus test not just of British national feeling at mid-century, but of Anglo-Irish tensions. Indicative of anxieties about the growth of Catholicism in Britain, it was also informed by developments in Ireland, where the Ecclesiastical Titles Act caused great offence. At the Synod of Thurles in 1850 – the first canonical synod of the Irish church since the twelfth century – the reforming archbishop of Armagh, Paul Cullen, had galvanised the church in opposition to government policies on primary and university education, and developed a process of pastoral, administrative and disciplinary reforms that would shape the church in Ireland until the 1980s.[22] But from a British perspective, and, it seems, especially from that of the Government and the royal family, the synod provided alarming evidence of a papal intent to assert Catholic independence of state control, especially when it appeared to marry denunciation of Government policies on Irish education with pronouncements on the land question[23] supportive of tenant rights. Lord John Russell informed the Irish Viceroy, Clarendon: 'I fear an angel from heaven would have little effect at Rome if he brought credentials from our Queen.'[24]

The timing of the 'papal aggression' crisis was significant. It came just a few months before the projection of a modernising Britain in the Great Exhibition and registered the vibrancy of traditional British Protestant patriotism.[25] Proposed and erected under Prince Albert's direction, and funded by public subscription rather than government subvention, the exhibition was seen as truly representative of British national character, and national Protestantism strongly coloured its character,[26] something reflected in the storm of protest provoked by Augustin Pugin's medieval 'Popish chapel'.[27] The testimony to British industrial pre-eminence

[20] The pope's intention to re-establish a hierarchy in England had been well advertised since 1847, and with apparent British acceptance: Matthias Buschkühl, *Great Britain and the Holy See 1746–1870* (Dublin, 1982), pp. 88–92.

[21] Albert to Prince William of Prussia, 24 Dec. 1850, in Kurt Jagow (ed.), *Letters of the Prince Consort 1831–1861* (London, 1938), p. 175.

[22] Thomas O'Connor, 'Paul Cullen' in S. J. Connolly (ed.), *The Oxford Companion to Irish History* (2nd edn, Oxford, 2002), p. 137.

[23] Martin, *Prince Consort*, II, p. 336.

[24] Russell to Clarendon, 1 Oct. 1850, cited in John Prest, *Lord John Russell* (London, 1972), p. 320.

[25] Wolffe, *God and Greater Britain*, pp. 113–14.

[26] Jeffrey Auerbach, *The Great Exhibition of 1851: A Nation on Display* (New Haven and London, 1999), p. 169. See Prince Albert's speech explicitly sourcing England's achievements and leading world role to the Reformation: *Belfast News-Letter* [BNL], 20 June 1851.

[27] Auerbach, *Great Exhibition*, pp. 170–1.

that the exhibition evidenced was directly sourced to the particular qualities of self-reliance, personal judgement, peace and prosperity that Protestantism encouraged, as opposed to the enervating, retrograde, despotic characteristics associated with Romanism and which seemed to be evidenced by a number of Catholic states in Europe, and, closer to home, Ireland. Here the rapidly industrialising Protestant north-east in an otherwise rural Ireland provided a useful domestic object lesson to make the point.[28]

As mediated to the British public in the *Illustrated London News*,[29] and judged by the standard of industrialising Britain, Ireland's presence in the exhibition registered as a backward, underdeveloped region: 'There are, accordingly, not many objects in the Exhibition sent from Ireland which attract or deserve much attention.'[30] Ireland's contribution was much more favourably assessed by the *Illustrated Exhibitor*, a magazine founded to commemorate the exhibition,[31] and the Irish *Freeman's Journal*.[32] But neither had the impact in Britain of the *Illustrated London News*, which explained Ireland in a neo-colonialist discourse that served to distance it as foreign to British experience. This experience – especially that of Scotland – had set a model for Ireland to follow, something the famine and the royal visit of 1849 had created the conditions for.[33] To an extent, the attitude of the *Freeman's Journal* exhibited the desired attitude with its pride in Irish manufactures; but even for this, the most respectable of Irish liberal prints, such patriotic pride was merely part of a larger conception of Irish national identity. And while at one level north-east Ulster appeared to demonstrate the qualities praised by the *Illustrated London News*, Ulster loyalism framed Irish involvement in the exhibition with its own interests very much in mind.[34] In fact, 'Certain are we, that the beneficial effects of so prompt and cordial a response to the behest of the Queen's Consort [for subscriptions] will react in the most favourable manner upon the welfare of this province.'[35] Moreover, for a region that was already in the process of mythicising its industrial development in terms of regional 'character' – it was in this period that the stereotype of the archetypal hard-headed 'Ulsterman' first began to

[28] Ibid. pp. 171, 173.
[29] Leon Litvack, 'Exhibiting Ireland 1851–3: Colonial Mimicry in London, Cork and Dublin' in Leon Litvack and Glenn Hooper (eds.), *Ireland in the Nineteenth Century: Regional Identity* (Dublin, 2000), p. 18.
[30] 'Ireland in the Exhibition', *Exhibition Supplement to the Illustrated London News* [*ILN*], 4 Oct. 1851.
[31] Litvack, 'Exhibiting Ireland', pp. 23–4.   [32] *Freeman's Journal* [FJ], 8, 14 May 1851.
[33] 'Ireland in the Exhibition', *ILN*, 4 Oct. 1851.   [34] *BNL*, 5 May 1851.
[35] *BNL*, 7 May 1851.

develop[36] – Prince Albert's concern to establish an 'aristocracy of merit', as against one of birth,[37] was an element of the Victorian self-improving zeitgeist of which he was the most emblematic figure and which Ulster loyalists could feel that they were fully subscribing to; especially so, as it sustained a commonality of identity already reinforced by opposition to 'papal aggression'.[38]

For our purposes, given its royal origins, values and execution, the exhibition's significance is as a site wherein the project of integrating Ireland into the United Kingdom – and the difficulties involved – could be outlined. The anti-Catholic protests over Pugin's 'chapel', the ethno-centric perspective within which Ireland was explained, and different interpretations of the exhibition within Ireland, all indicated that the task would not be easy. At a time when the prospects for engendering Irish allegiance to the throne seemed positive, it is clear there was no conception in the royal or governmental mindset that a rethinking of the nature of Britishness as a national identity to accommodate Ireland's approximate 6,500,000 Catholic people – not to mention the greatly increasing Catholic population of Britain – might be necessary. A Protestant and Anglo-Saxon racial definition of the nation was an exclusionary specification that, in Ireland, could easily leave welfare monarchism ideologically weakened, lacking essential supports that might have assisted governmental and royal purposes. This point is worth emphasising, because the exhibition did have an important influence in Ireland.

II

Given 'southern Ireland's' undistinguished contribution to the Great Exhibition, news that an industrial exhibition would be held in Cork in 1852 was a source of surprise in Britain.[39] Nevertheless, the Cork exhibition drew significant support, with Prince Albert donating £100,

---

[36] It's 'scientific' origins can be traced to the congress in Belfast in 1852 of the British Association for the Advancement of Science: A. C. Hume, 'Origin and Characteristics of the Population in the Counties of Down and Antrim', *Journal of the Ethnological Society of London*, 2, reprinted in *Ulster Journal of Archaeology*, first series, 1 (1852), 9–26, 120–9, 246–54; 2nd edn, *BNL*, 1872.

[37] Albert's speech to the Royal Academy of Art during the first week of the Great Exhibition (*BNL*, 12 May 1851) expounded on this subject and was a particular instance of his general outlook; also Prochaska (*Royal Bounty*, p. 91), for the Exhibition as an expression of Prince Albert's social philosophy based on Smilesian values.

[38] Editorials, *BNL*, 21 May, 1 Oct. 1851.

[39] A. C. Davies, 'The First Irish Industrial Exhibition: Cork 1852', *Irish Economic and Social History*, 2 (1975), 46.

Viceroy Clarendon £50, and altogether £3,000 being raised. It soon developed from a local event to assume national proportions.[40]

To a significant extent, the decision to hold the Cork exhibition was an index of Irish modernisation, especially the growth of Irish railways, essential to the transportation of visitors, especially British visitors, the facilitation of which the railway companies attempted by special rates.[41] But for our purposes, one of the exhibition's most significant aspects was the way in which it followed the precedent of the London exhibition in its royal connections. Viceroy Clarendon performed the opening ceremony 'in all the pomp and circumstance of majesty',[42] his presence signifying state endorsement for an enterprise at once intrinsically praiseworthy, but which also identified intended material benefit for the Irish people with the pre-eminent symbol of state and British national identity.

The authorities, however, could not either claim ideological ownership of the exhibition or monopolise credit for its staging. Certainly the objectives of J. F. Maguire, the moving spirit of the enterprise,[43] supporter of tenant right and MP for Dungarvan as a leading member of the 'Pope's brass band' – the Irish Catholic electoral response to the papal aggression controversy – were not synonymous with those of the Viceroy. Like many commentators, Maguire believed that the famine had marked a crucial turning point in Irish history, one that demonstrated the need to move beyond a reliance on agriculture; however, manufacturing industry was to be called upon, not as a developmental aid to constitutional assimilation,[44] but "if this people is to be rescued from destruction and this ancient nation saved from utter exhaustion". In fact the Cork exhibition was not a great success: attendance at around 140,000 was small and exhibits demonstrated the dominance of British products in the Irish market. Yet its very limitations encouraged the railway magnate, William Dargan, to finance and organise the much more ambitious Dublin Exhibition of 1853.[45]

This was a much more important undertaking, signified by the presence of Albert and Victoria. While the Viceroy could embody monarchy for functional purposes, the presence of the monarch in rarely visited Ireland, had, as we have noted in respect of the royal visits of 1821 and 1849, the power to shape perspectives and expectations on the Irish question. In this context it might be noted that the minutely detailed reportage of royal actions pioneered by the *Illustrated London News* in the

[40] Ibid. p. 47.   [41] Ibid. p. 49.   [42] *Athenaeum*, quoted ibid. p. 49.   [43] Ibid. p. 47.
[44] *ILN*, 19 June 1852, for the exhibition's contribution to enabling Ireland to become an 'integral part of Great Britain'.
[45] Davies, 'First Irish Industrial Exhibition', pp. 50–4, 58–9.

1840s – a *textual* version of the public concentration royal personages attracted – was, it seems, now being copied by the press in general.[46] But more significantly, in a period when the mobilising power of nationalist myths was greatly diminished, the royal visit of 1853 would become a central focus in a meta-narrative serving the interests of Irish and British loyalism.

As expounded by the Conservative organ, the *Daily Express*, on the occasion of Albert and Victoria's short visit to Ireland in 1861 – a reference point from which to view Irish progress during the 1850s[47] – the narrative had its point of origin in 1849 when the royal visit diverted the Irish imagination away from 'gloomy and dismal meditations' to focus hopefully on the future. In 1853 the Queen facilitated 'the first, great, united effort Ireland ever made to show the extent of her native resources, to prove what her sons and daughters are capable of'.[48] Moreover, a national leader evocative of the new Ireland that was developing was found in the non-political Dargan, a Catholic self-made man – 'the O'Connell of industry' – the moving spirit behind the Dublin Exhibition and its sole financial supporter (Fig. 7).[49] Out of the wreckage of failed political agitation he 'stepped forward and pointed out to a long-deluded people the true path that would lead to prosperity and happiness'.[50]

Dargan had made an enormous contribution to Irish modernisation in general, and was especially attractive to constitutionalists given his background: several uncles had been executed for their part in the United Irishmen's rising of 1798,[51] and seen in a familial and generational context – born in 1799 – he represented an ideal example of the new Ireland modernisation would hopefully bring about. From the loyalist perspective of 1861, therefore, the Dublin Exhibition of 1853 was a central event in the narrative of an Ireland in which nationalism had been abandoned. It was undoubtedly of major significance. The Cork exhibition applied the model of the Great Exhibition to Ireland, but the

---

[46] See for instance the report of the royal family making their fourth visit to the Dublin Exhibition of 1853: *FJ*, 3 Sept. 1853.

[47] The Queen came in 1853 'to inaugurate [prosperity], she comes now to witness': *Daily Express* [DE], 8 July 1861.

[48] *DE*, 8 July 1861; press cuttings, Thomas Larcom papers, National Library of Ireland [NLI], MS 7484.

[49] 'Memoir of William Dargan' in John Sproule (ed.), *The Irish Industrial Exhibition of 1853* (Dublin, 1854), p. xiv.

[50] *DE*, 8 July 1861; newspaper cuttings, Larcom papers, NLI, MS 7484; also *ILN*, 14 May 1853.

[51] A. J. Saris, 'Imagining Ireland in the Great Exhibition of 1853' in Litvack and Cooper (eds.), *Ireland in the Nineteenth Century*, p. 75.

7 William Dargan, the O'Connell of Irish industry.

Dublin Exhibition consecrated the practice in 1853, in terms of both its scale and the royal imprimatur it occasioned. Accordingly, as a display of Irish enterprise and a site of identity it deserves close attention.

Like the Cork exhibition, Dublin attracted the same diversity of support. Moderate nationalism as exemplified in the *Freeman's Journal*, while loyal to the throne and respectful of the Viceroyalty, had it own perspective. It positioned Dargan – a massive statue of whom was authorised by Dublin Corporation in early April 1853 – not in opposition to nationalist heroes but in the pantheon of Irish patriots: 'the statue [would stand] . . . side by side with those of Lucas, of Grattan, and of O'Connell . . . [taking] its place among Ireland's most cherished ones'.[52]

[52] *FJ*, 5 April 1853.

Differing perspectives on Dargan were reflective of the differences in motives of those who would cooperate in Irish industrial exhibitions until the early 1880s: industrial development as a way of addressing Ireland's 'real' problems, as against industrial development to enable an autonomous Ireland to prosper. Both perspectives were framed within a monarchical context. But for Irish loyalism, economic prosperity and the removal of Ireland's 'real' grievances would allow monarchy to *shape* Irish identity, as it seemed to be increasingly doing in Britain, while for respectable nationalist opinion loyalty would be a function of the constitutional carapace monarchy provided for a future self-governing and prosperous Ireland. Under these conditions an O'Connellite dual British–Irish national identity would develop, with the monarch as its focus. Whether agricultural Ireland could be brought up to British levels of prosperity to make the project feasible, however, was doubtful. Certainly, as will be seen, economic crises would provide a stimulus to the exacerbation of antagonistic national traditions. Nevertheless, in 1853 the prospects for Ireland's constitutional integration on the state's terms seemed bright, and the diversity of meaning and ambiguity of identity evident in the Dublin Exhibition itself posed no apparent threat to its realisation.

The *Freeman's Journal* saw the exhibition – 'As the Romans date their annals from the "Building of that city" so shall we date ours from [its] opening'[53] – facilitating the education of a largely ignorant Irish people in Ireland's great national heroes, to be effected through the creation of a national gallery, but the definition of 'national' was eclectic. No narrow association existed between the definition of hero and the struggle for, or defence of, independence. The roster included Anglo-Irish literary luminaries, philosophers, loyal Viceroys and British national heroes such as Wellington, together with Robert Emmet and O'Connell. The gallery proposal created a lively debate about the terms of inclusion, but the *Freeman's Journal*, concerned to provide several stimulating 'models' of Irish identity, settled on birth as the requirement: 'something which colours the stream of man's life, and which no foreign discipline can wholly obliterate'.[54] No less than for loyalists, moderate nationalism was alive to the fact that in an era when Ireland appeared about to undergo modernisation and economically prosper, the process would entail imaginative as well as material transformation: a struggle whose terrain was the nature of the 'imagined community' the Irish should identify was in train.

---

[53] *FJ*, 13 May 1851.   [54] *FJ*, 15 April 1853.

Perhaps most significantly, for the Viceroyalty, whose ability to engage with Irish popular sentiment was often limited and highly problematic, the exhibition, which the Viceroy inaugurated amid 'a pomp and ceremony exceeding anything of the kind ever before witnessed in Ireland',[55] provided it with the opportunity to occupy a central place in Irish public life.[56] It was a site of identity wherein royal and viceregal encouragement of industry and 'those habits of order, of foresight, and of frugality, without which wealth itself is of little use'[57] was extolled. These were sentiments which Ulster loyalist opinion, priding itself on having already put the lessons of industry into practice for the evident benefit of the northeast, heartily endorsed.[58] Inevitably less impressive than the Crystal Palace, the exhibition building was, nevertheless, the most impressive Irish structural edifice of its kind in the nineteenth century.

Architecturally of 'singular beauty and adaptation ... to the ends for which it was designed',[59] it was erected on grounds belonging to the Royal Dublin Society near Merrion Square, and divided into one large central and two smaller halls: 'the former 425 feet long, 100 feet wide, and 105 feet high; the latter, each 355 feet long, 50 feet wide, and 65 feet high. The whole occupies an area of 210,000 square feet.'[60] As in the Crystal Palace there was a medieval court and a fine arts and antiquities section,[61] but unlike the London exhibition, and reflecting the *Freeman's Journal*'s campaign for a national gallery as part of the exhibition, paintings were included in the fine arts section, though they were not arranged in such a way as to delineate clearly an Irish national tradition in the way the paper suggested; rather 'Irish and English works [were] all mixed together as "The British School".'[62]

Portraits of O'Connell, for instance, the most obvious signifier of the struggle for national independence, managed to depict a great national leader without reference to the campaigns on which his greatness was

[55] Editorial, *FJ*, 13 May 1853.
[56] Nationalist opinion was favourably influenced towards the Viceroy by the Aberdeen Government's – now including two members of the 'Irish Brigade' – pursuit of a 'conciliation' policy in Ireland, evident in its decision not to abolish the Viceroyalty.
[57] *FJ*, 13 May 1853.   [58] Editorial, *BNL*, 18 July 1853.   [59] *FJ*, 14 May 1853.
[60] *Annual Register, 1853* (London, 1854), p. 60. Exhibits were divided into thirty classes, covering many aspects of manufacturing industry, agriculture, chemicals, foodstuffs, defence, mining and precious metals, and included 'minerals, silk and wool, general hardware, naval and railway machinery, agricultural machinery, exhibits from India ... France, Belgium and the [German] Zollverein'.
[61] John Turpin, 'Exhibitions of Arts and Industries in Victorian Ireland: The Irish Arts and Industrial Exhibition Movement 1834–1864', *Dublin Historical Record* 35 (1981–2), 7.
[62] Ibid. p. 8.

based.[63] In the exhibition the specification of what was national and what was national*ist* remained ambiguous. And yet, arguably, this merely reflected the lack of a distinctive national movement in Ireland at this time. Certainly news that Albert and Victoria would visit the exhibition at some point before its closure stirred the *Freeman's Journal* to exuberant expectations of a state visit that would place the Dublin Exhibition on a par with the Great Exhibition, and also enhance the popular authority of the Irish Viceroyalty.[64] In the context of the national symbolism evident in the exhibition, the popular significance attaching to viceregal/royal emblems and spectacle greatly overshadowed the uncertain assertions of Irish national identity. An example of Irish woodwork in the exhibition, supplied by Arthur Jones of Dublin in the form of a statuette of Queen Victoria freighted with English and Irish symbolism, illustrated the dominance of the monarchy in the Anglo-Irish context. Moreover, given that for British political opinion the monarchy could not be construed – as O'Connell had sought to do – as amenable to constitutional diversity in the Kingdom, its symbolism in the exhibition was a powerful affirmation of the status quo, and the crowds drawn by royal spectacle were deemed to be affirming that order.

As with all the visits made by the royal couple to Ireland, their ultimate destination was Scotland, which set the ideal standard of constitutional loyalty for Ireland to aspire to. The royal progress through the city would follow the same route as that of the visit of 1849 and the city thoroughfares were decorated in anticipation.[65] But this visit was to be unlike that of 1849; there were to be no formal deputations,[66] presentations and levees. The focus, apart from a few other visitations, was specifically on the exhibition, the lack of pomp and ceremony being declared by *The Times* as more in keeping with 'the true spirit of industry'.[67]

Indicative of the societal significance Albert and Victoria placed on the exhibition as a harbinger of the new Ireland was the inclusion of Dargan in the royal entourage. He rode in the Viceroy's carriage to Kingstown to greet the Queen, and on her arrival was immediately introduced to the

---

[63] See Litvack, 'Exhibiting Ireland', pp. 51–6.

[64] *FJ*, 25 May 1853. Saris, 'Imagining Ireland', p. 85. Using attendance statistics of the Crystal Palace exhibition as a relative guide, the total for Dublin, at 1,149,369, was deemed satisfactory; however, the exhibition failed to draw the attendance of the Irish masses: Sproule, *Irish Industrial Exhibition*, p. 26; Editorial, *FJ*, 2 June 1853; Saris, 'Imagining Ireland', pp. 81–3. The Times [*TT*], 31 Aug. 1853, claimed that when the royal party ventured out to other locations the central hall was deserted.

[65] *TT*, 22 Aug. 1853.

[66] See Henry Ponsonby, viceregal secretary, to Joseph Murphy, 25 Aug. 1853, in *TT*, 26 Aug. 1853.

[67] *TT*, 29 Aug. 1853.

royal party,[68] before it proceeded into Dublin and to a popular reception characterised by an enthusiasm 'almost beyond that which had greeted them four years before'.[69] The close personal identity of the royal couple with Dargan continued throughout the visit. The Dargans were visited at their home, and publicly – and symbolically – at the exhibition, which the royal couple visited every day of their stay.[70] The Queen not only was impressed with Dargan's public role as a leader of the new Ireland, but found his 'personal history' and modesty of conduct 'very satisfactory': Dargan politely refused the offer of a baronetcy but agreed to accept from the Queen a present of marble busts of Prince Albert and himself.[71]

The Queen not only was an enthusiastic patron of exhibition goods, but had made significant indications of her support for the exhibition, especially a 'dress coach' ordered from a highly regarded Dublin firm earlier in the year, and which the present Queen, Elizabeth II, would use to drive to her wedding in 1947.[72] So impressed was Albert with the progress of the new Ireland the exhibition seemed to evidence that he indulged the –unsupported – belief that the Catholic clergy had opposed the exhibition and that their failure to prevent it had broken the hold of superstition they formerly held over the Catholic people. The people were now amenable to 'liberal' education, and he saw it as another indicator of social progress that when O'Connell's possessions came up for auction there was an apparent lack of public interest.[73] In the same vein, Ulster loyalists interpreted a conclave of the Catholic hierarchy at Thurles, County Tipperary, as a failed attempt to divert the attention of the Irish people from the royal visit – 'the most unequivocal proof of her Majesty's popularity in this part of her dominions' (see Fig. 8).[74]

The suggestion that one million people greeted the Queen on her arrival at Kingstown[75] seems exaggerated; nevertheless, the visit was a great success. Nothing of significance occurred to mar it. The action of a church organist who threw a paper into the Queen's carriage – a petition for the Queen's assistance in recovering an outstanding debt – created momentary alarm.[76] But there was no harmful intent. In fact,

---

[68] Joseph Hone, 'Queen Victoria in Ireland, 1853', *History Today*, 3 (1953), 502.

[69] Martin, *Prince Consort*, II, p. 504.   [70] *TT*, 31 Aug. 1853.

[71] Queen Victoria's Journal (31 Aug. 1853), cited in Martin, *Prince Consort*, II, pp. 504–5; Hone, 'Queen Victoria in Ireland', p. 504.

[72] Ibid. p. 503.

[73] Prince Albert, Memo 28 Sept. 1853, cited in James Murphy, *Abject Loyalty: Nationalism and Monarchy in Ireland during the Reign of Queen Victoria* (Cork, 2001), p. 118.

[74] *BNL*, 7 Sept. 1853.

[75] Sir Sidney Lee, *Queen Victoria: A Biography* (rev. edn, London, 1904), p. 236.

[76] *FJ*, 5 Sept. 1853.

8 Albert and Victoria at the Dublin Exhibition, 1853.

it could be regarded merely as an expression of the age-old belief
that the monarch was the ultimate source of honour and justice, and
was a well-established practice in Britain.[77] Difficulties could have
emerged had the Catholic priesthood presented an address, given

[77] See Metropolitan Police report, 'Insane Persons and Others who have come under the
Cognisance of the Police for Offences against Her Majesty Queen Victoria, 1837–1852',
Metropolitan Police file, NA (Kew), MEPO/2/44.

the resentment over the papal aggression controversy, but divisions within the hierarchy deterred Archbishop Cullen, who wished to present one.[78]

The success of the visit in a context where both constitutional and revolutionary nationalism were in disarray, and where the Catholic Church had no official presence, allowed the 'Queen in Ireland' to be defined as a moment of national epiphany with the exhibition as its location:

She has not come in state, because it is not the pomp and circumstance of Royalty we sigh for, but the earnest, cordial countenance of our Queen, smiling upon her Irish subjects, *as a mother upon her children – a sincere sharer of our honest joys and our honest hopes* [my italics] ... The Great Exhibition, which is now a symbol of the heart of Ireland ... pointed as plainly to the existence of a manly self-reliant spirit in the bosoms of Irishmen, as patriot could desire, or philanthropist applaud. The history of this Royal Visit, and its cause and result, will constitute one of the brightest pages in our national annals.[79]

The unity of monarchy and people envisaged here, and the expectations for the future it exhibited, was informed not only by the disarray of organised nationalism, but by an intellectual zeitgeist among Irish classical economists imbued with the belief that the country was now on a wave of prosperity based on, and validating, free market principles[80] – principles Prince Albert championed and which a consensus of economic opinion was convinced the future of Ireland depended on.

The latter 1850s, moreover, were to see the tenure of popular Viceroys, Lords Eglinton and Carlisle, while the decade was also notable in this context for the creation of an Irish viceregal flag – the only *officially* recognised flag of Ireland in the Union period and suggestive of official confidence about Ireland's constitutional position (Fig. 9).[81]

---

[78] Paul Cullen to Tobias Kirby, 18 Aug. 1853, in Emmet Larkin, *The Making of the Roman Catholic Church in Ireland 1850–1860* (Chapel Hill, NC, 1980), p. 207.

[79] Editorial, *BNL*, 31 Aug. 1853.

[80] On this subject, see Peter Gray, 'The Making of Mid-Victorian Ireland? Political Economy and the Memory of the Great Famine' in Peter Gray (ed.), *Victoria's Ireland? Irishness and Britishness* (Dublin, 2004), pp. 151–8.

[81] W. J. Gordon, *Flags of the World: Past and Present* (London, 1926), p. 101. The Viceroy's flag was the model for that of the Indian Viceroyalty.

9 Flag of the Irish Viceroy, 1850s.

III

The Industrial Exhibition of 1853 appears as both an impressive material prospectus of Ireland's engagement with modernity, and a metaphor of the Irish people as they engaged with the project. As such, its central place in the loyalist meta-narrative of Irish development framed in terms of monarchy is understandable. When Albert and Victoria visited Ireland for the last time in 1861, the perspective on the 1850s which foregrounded the Dublin Exhibition and the royal presence as indicative of the development of a new loyal Ireland[82] was still just about plausible, and validated by the relative freedom the royal visitors had in deciding where to reside without overwhelming security. For the *Morning Post* the fact that the Prince of Wales – then posted with the army in Ireland – was being billeted in an open tent was evidence of Irish loyalty, as was the fact that the Queen would stay in a lodge that in 1803, the year of the Emmet rebellion, was 'barricaded'.[83] The general view underpinning these comments was widely shared by the press.[84]

---

[82] *DE*, 8 July 1861; press cuttings, Larcom papers, NLI, MS 7484.

[83] *Morning Post*, 8 Aug. 1861.

[84] *TT*, 8, 20, 21 Aug. 1861; *DE*, 14, 27 Aug. 1861; *Dublin Evening Mail [DEM]*, 22 Aug. 1861; S. C. Hall, 'Something of What the Queen Will See and Will Not See in Ireland', *St. James Gazette* (Sept. 1861), 242 and *passim*; *FJ*, 23 Aug. 1861.

Although the visit was a private one, devoid of pomp and splendour and the public ritual characteristic of a state visit,[85] the intense media focus on the royal progress to Dublin served to index socio-economic developments: 'every portion of her route has been marked by some improvement'.[86] Perhaps surprisingly, the *Freeman's Journal* declared: 'The highest honours and proudest offices of the state are, under our Constitutional Monarch, open to all irrespective of rank.'[87] As it proceeded, the *Dublin Evening Mail* averred that if George IV's visit in 1821 demonstrated that rebel chiefs and agitators reigned in Ireland, it was only due to the absence of the sovereign.[88]

Although it was a family visit, almost immediately Albert began a round of public engagements in addition to visiting the Prince of Wales at the Curragh, while Victoria received an address from Dublin Corporation. A royal procession through the city was well received,[89] while a visit to Killarney and a meeting with a loyalist brother of O'Connell led the Queen to see the area through a Scottish lens: 'The hills ... often reminded me of the dear *Highlands*.'[90] Of the evident Irish improvement, Albert later exulted: 'The country has visibly made great progress in the last eight years, and is conscious of the fact. We had a most hearty reception everywhere that we went, and returned here [Balmoral] yesterday rather tired.'[91] As meta-narrative, however, the story of an industrially developing and increasingly loyal Ireland suffered from significant weaknesses.

IV

This is best illustrated by comparison with the O'Connellite narrative, its oppositional point of departure. O'Connellite myth – a *mobilising* myth – served the objectives of a movement organised on a nation-wide basis towards the realisation of the specific objectives of emancipation and Repeal. The monarchical-framed loyalist narrative, however, had no politically *specific* objectives and directing organisation. An assumption

---

[85] See Undersecretary Larcom to Lord Mayor of Dublin, 4 Aug. 1861, Larcom papers, NLI, MS 7484.

[86] *DE*, 23 Aug. 1861. The Queen remarked: 'There were great numbers of people in the streets, all most friendly and enthusiastic': QVJ (22 Aug. 1861), Martin, *Prince Consort*, V, p. 377.

[87] *FJ*, 23 Aug. 1861.   [88] *DEM*, 27 Aug. 1861.

[89] QVJ (23 Aug. 1861), Martin, *Prince Consort*, V, p. 378.

[90] Queen Victoria, *Leaves from the Journal of Our Life in the Highlands*, ed. Sir Arthur Helps (London, 1868), p. 311; also p. 314; Martin, *Prince Consort*, V, pp. 379–82.

[91] Albert to William I of Prussia, 1 Sept. 1861, in Jagow (ed.), *Letters of the Prince Consort*, p. 367.

was made that a functional relationship existed between socio-economic progress, modernity and constitutional loyalty, with the monarch an inevitable pole of attraction and loyalty for the Catholic Irish 'Celt'. As the Irish Lord Chancellor (1858–9) Sir Joseph Napier put it: 'Let religious dissensions cease, suppress all organised sedition against constituted authority, enlighten ignorance, and imitate the self-reliance, intelligence, and industry of the English people, and it would soon be found that there was no more an Irish difficulty than an English one.'[92] The difficulty with this assumption, however, was that it failed to account for how political and personal factors – variables – could complicate royal and Government expectations.

For example, the recurring issue of abolition of the Irish Viceroyalty, which Lord John Russell conceived as part of an extensive plan of Irish reforms in the mid-1840s to consolidate the Union of Britain and Ireland,[93] appeared to be settled by progress in transport and communications: 'separate government within fifteen hours of London appears unnecessary – the separate court a mockery'.[94] But when Russell introduced a bill to effect abolition in May 1850 – pithily stating that *Bradshaw's Railway Guide* had disposed of the question[95] – the opposition of the Duke of Wellington, the only figure of authority in Britain comparable to the Queen, determined its defeat.[96] By 1861, abolition was a more difficult proposition: 'there is an organised agitation on the subject, and the country would be up in arms'.[97] Moreover, while popular Viceroys held office in the 1850s this was not capitalised upon. A combination of complacency – arguably encouraged by the impressive Irish popular response to the royal visit of 1853 – and divisions within British parties producing unstable government made the development of a 'coherent programme for Ireland' a low priority: 'The Chief Secretaryship was held by eight different men between 1852 and 1868, most of whom had neither the time or the inclination to leave any mark

---

[92] A. C. Ewald, *The Life of Sir Joseph Napier* (London, 1887), p. 280. For a similar argument framed more specifically in racial terms, see George Ellis, *Irish Ethnology Socially and Politically Considered: Embracing a General Outline of the Celtic and Saxon Races* (Dublin, 1852), pp. 101–3.

[93] Prest, *Russell*, pp. 236–7.

[94] Russell quoted in R. B. McDowell, 'The Irish Executive in the Nineteenth Century', *Irish Historical Studies*, 11 (Sept. 1954), 275. See the theory of progress argument justifying abolition in editorial, *TT*, 18 May 1850.

[95] Ibid.

[96] Entry (18 April 1861), John Vincent (ed.), *Disraeli, Derby and the Conservative Party: Journals and Memoirs of Edward Henry, Lord Stanley 1849–1869* (Hassocks, Sussex, 1978), p. 169.

[97] Ibid. The Viceroyalty's significance as an Irish national institution was not entirely the preserve of nationalists. See Ewald, *Sir Joseph Napier*, pp. 72–6.

on the office or the country.'[98] The zero-sum assumption that the collapse of organised nationalism inevitably translated into loyalty to the constitution offered no correction to this state of affairs. Moreover, the Viceroyalty, and the administrative system it embodied, was far from being as nationally unproblematic as even liberal nationalists like to claim.

Despite the *Freeman's Journal* assertion that all Irish public offices were now open to all on the basis of merit, the findings of the first Irish census in 1861 painted a different picture. The office of Viceroy, of course, had been barred to Catholics by a law of 1829, but, as we have noted, there were no Catholics employed in the Viceroy's household; and while they were fairly well represented in the lower levels of the Irish civil service, there were none at its highest echelons, a situation that would remain unchanged until the twentieth century.[99] The view that Irish 'enlightenment' would inevitably undermine 'popish superstition' was an alienating factor that would constitute a mental block vitiating British policy in Ireland almost until the end of the Union in 1921. At the same time, this belief was part of a wider – and erroneous – conception of the Irish 'Celt' informed by influential racial discourses in the period from the 1850s to the 1890s.[100] In this context the Catholic Irish were deemed to be especially susceptible to the appeal of personal, and therefore royal, leadership as opposed to the Saxon allegiance to institutions. Furthermore, the exhibition of 1853 itself was interpreted in a way that showed scant awareness of how modernity might serve interests incompatible with those of the state. Exhibits on rail, photography – daguerreotype portraits of O'Connell and Young Ireland leaders had been made in the 1840s[101] – the electrical telegraph, and printing and publishing all showcased developments that would function to enhance the Home Rule movement as a national organisation from the late 1870s.[102]

Even in the immediate term, state complacency about Irish loyalty led to an underestimation of nationalism's influence. Thus while nationally organised nationalism may have been absent, it can be argued that

[98] Virginia Crossman, *Politics, Law and Order in Nineteenth Century Ireland* (Dublin, 1996), p. 92.

[99] Gerald McElroy, 'Employment of Catholics in the Public Service in Ireland, 1859–1921: A Broad Overview' in Alan O'Day (ed.), *Government and Institutions in the Post-1832 United Kingdom* (Lampeter, 1995), pp. 310–11.

[100] See L. P. Curtis Jr, *Anglo-Saxons and Celts* (Bridgeport, Conn., 1968), *passim*.

[101] Edward Chandler, *Photography in Ireland: The Nineteenth Century* (Dublin, 2001), pp. 22–5.

[102] See James Loughlin, 'Constructing the Political Spectacle: Parnell, the Press and National Leadership 1879–1885' in D. G. Boyce and Alan O'Day (eds.), *Parnell in Perspective* (London, 1991), pp. 221–41.

political conflict merely shifted from the national public sphere to the local, with struggles taking place to identify landscape politically and control territory. In Limerick in 1857, for example, a mobilisation of priests and local nationalists succeeded in erecting the first statue to O'Connell in Ireland, defeating a counter-proposal to claim the urban space for the Union through a memorial to Viscount Fitzgibbon, a casualty of the Crimean War.[103] A similar motivation and circumstances surrounded the erection of a statue to O'Connell in Ennis, County Clare, a year later.[104] But far more significantly, in 1860 the *Nation*, long contemptuous of Irish royal visits and associated 'flunkeyism', initiated a dramatic intervention that enabled nationalism to make the transition from the local to the national arena, one directed specifically at allegiance to the throne.

A national petition to the Queen appealing for the restoration of Irish self-rule was inaugurated. Provoked to do so by widespread British political and press support for plebiscites in Italian territories annexed from the papacy by the kingdom of Piedmont-Sardinia,[105] the petition – a popular option in a period when petition mania was in vogue in Britain – quickly caught the popular mood in nationalist Ireland.[106] In part, its popularity was a function of the modernising process lauded by Prince Albert: petitions 'appealed particularly to those who had attained the proud accomplishment of writing their names but were denied the satisfaction of the franchise'.[107] The petition's popularity surprised both its promoters and its opponents. By the deadline of April 1861, 423,026 signatures had been appended. It was then transported to London where The O'Donoghue, the head of an old Gaelic family and a grand-nephew of O'Connell, requested a personal audience with the Queen to submit it, before accepting the usual route of submission through the Home Secretary.

There is reason to query the national representativeness of the petition, as to the number of signatures, their authenticity and where they had been gathered at a time when the Irish Catholic community was divided on the merits of self-government.[108] Nevertheless, in Ireland it succeeded as a propaganda exercise to embarrass the Government and

---

[103] Hill, *Irish Public Sculpture*. pp. 90–1.   [104] Ibid. pp. 91–2.

[105] The Queen was ambivalent about Italian reunification, encouraged by the development of a liberal state modelled on Britain, but discomfited by the violation of ancient treaties and dispossession of hereditary rulers: Arnstein, 'Queen Victoria and the Challenge of Roman Catholicism', 305.

[106] R. V. Comerford, *The Fenians in Context: Irish Politics and Society 1848–82* (Dublin, 1998), p. 63; A. M. Sullivan, *New Ireland* (10th edn, Glasgow, 1878), pp. 240–2.

[107] Comerford, *Fenians in Context*, p. 63.   [108] Ibid. pp. 64–5.

especially the Queen: 'The fate of the National Petition was pointed to; the contemptuous silence of the Sovereign was called disdain for a people who would not clutch the arms whereby alone their right to chose their own government could be secured.'[109]

The persuasiveness of the Victorian monarchy as an institution giving meaning to, or 'colonising', the sphere of everyday life derived from the representation of the royal family, especially in the developing photographic and print media, as symbiotically combining majestic and domestic signification, not least the familial values that identified the Queen as 'mother' of the people. She was a 'mother', the organisers of the National Petition implied, who had rejected her Irish 'children'. Moreover, many of the parish branches established as part of the National Petition Movement remained in existence after the petition had been gathered, some being later absorbed into the Fenian organisation.[110]

This movement had been in progress since 1858 and would emphasise the revival of nationalism through the impressive public spectacle involved in the Dublin funeral of the Young Irelander Terence Bellew McManus, in November 1861, just two months after the royal visit.[111] As with royal spectacle, it would be rash to equate popular attendance at, or observance of, the funeral with active support for Fenianism. The 'elite of Irish nationalist ideologues found in the late 1850s that even in a time of international crisis they could evoke no more than very muted responses from within Irish society'.[112] Nevertheless, the funeral, planned to include streets in which incidents connected with the 1798 rebellion and that of Robert Emmet in 1803 took place, was a physical traversal of space signalling revolutionary ambition.[113] As such, it was a clear indication that the state's dominance of the Irish public arena would come under its most significant challenge since the days of O'Connell. Moreover, at the same time as the revival of nationalist sentiment was developing, and months before the royal visit of 1861, Prince Albert's reputation in Ireland was damaged when some disparaging comments he made in the 1840s about the Irish and the Poles were exploited by

[109] Sullivan, *New Ireland*, p. 243.

[110] Tom Garvin, *Evolution of Irish Nationalist Politics* (Dublin, 1983), p. 60. On Fenianism's investment of local issues and grievances with a national perspective, see Joseph Lee, *The Modernisation of Irish Society 1848–1918* (Dublin, 1973), pp. 57–8.

[111] Comerford, *Fenians in Context*, pp. 77–9.   [112] Ibid. p. 66.

[113] See Luke Gibbons, '"Where Wolfe Tone's Statue Was Not": Joyce, Monuments and Memory' in Ian McBride (ed.), *History and Memory in Ireland* (Cambridge, 2001), pp. 151–2.

radical nationalists.[114] In this context, despite the laudatory accounts of the visit in loyalist prints and those penned by Albert and Victoria, some press reports – pro- and anti-royal – detected a lukewarm public engagement.[115] Moreover, unlike the wholehearted engagement of the Queen with Ireland in 1853, her personal attitude to the country was now becoming distinctly negative, reflected in a concern to avoid personal contact with the population, and an insistence on being accompanied by an unnecessarily large detachment of troops on her trip to Kilarney.[116] Also, the attraction Victoria expressed to Killarney – its Scottish aspect suggesting the location for a possible royal residence – was checked by information that the area was residence to a wholly Catholic population, nunneries, Catholic brotherhoods and monks.[117]

At this time Victoria was still depressed by the death in late March of her mother, the Duchess of Kent,[118] and her mood would not have been improved by the information that the Prince of Wales's commitment to his soldierly duties in Ireland left much to be desired. His tryst with an 'actress', Nellie Clifden – afterwards nicknamed the 'Princess of Wales' – during his time at the Curragh threatened to destroy the royal reputation for familial respectability built up over twenty years. In Victoria's mind it was the real cause of the illness that ended Albert's life in December.[119] In sum, at the same time as organised nationalism was reviving in Ireland, the country, in both personal and public aspects, impacted negatively on the Queen. It is from this period that her profound alienation from Irish Catholicism and nationalism can be dated.[120]

[114] See *Nation*, 29 June 1861. They had originally appeared in the published letters of Alexander Von Humboldt in 1860. Albert denied having made the comments. See Albert to his daughter Victoria, the Princess Royal, 21 March 1860, in Jagow (ed.), *Letters of the Prince Consort*, p. 346.

[115] See, for example, *Nation*, 31 Aug. 1861; *Irish Times*, 28 Aug. 1861.

[116] Sir Charles Phipps, Queen Victoria's Private Secretary, to Lord Carlisle, 18 Aug. 1861, Larcom papers NLI, MS 7484. Viscount Castlerosse to Carlisle, 18 Aug. 1861, ibid.; Note, 19 Aug. 1861, ibid.

[117] For insightful comment on the Killarney dimension to the royal visit, see Murphy, *Abject Loyalty*, pp. 129–32.

[118] QVJ (24 Aug. 1861), Martin, *Prince Consort*, V, p. 379; also Christopher Hibbert (ed.), *Queen Victoria in Her Letters and Journals* (Harmondsworth, 1985), pp. 118–19.

[119] Kinley Roby, *The King, the Press and the People: A Study of Edward VII* (London, 1975), pp. 92–3; Giles St Aubyn, *Edward VII: Prince and King* (New York, 1979), pp. 50–3. The actual cause was typhoid fever, sourced to the drains at Windsor Castle.

[120] See Victoria to Crown Princess Victoria, 23 Dec. 1865, 16 Nov. 1867, 18 Aug. 1869, in Roger Fulford (ed.), *Your Dear Letter: Private Correspondence of Queen Victoria and the Crown Princess of Prussia 1865–71* (London, 1971), pp. 50, 160–1, 245–6.

V

The 1850s provided the state with the best opportunity under the Union to engender loyalty to the Union, but the project suffered from fundamental conceptual and practical weaknesses. Its greatest failing lay in the simplistic relationship assumed between modernity, loyalty and monarchy, leading those in power to fail to engage effectively with the complexity of the Irish question. The replication of great royal successes from 1821 to 1853, which provided the underpinning for the credibility of the loyalist narrative, misleadingly suggested a fundamental core of popular loyalty easily cultivated by the royal presence. But as we have seen, explanations for these occasions have to be sought fundamentally in the contextual, and especially *situational*, factors that facilitated them: their 'enchanting' effects could not be extrapolated beyond their time and place. It was a mistake to assume that, as in Britain, they were indicative of an intense popular attachment to the Queen, instead of being singular. Unlike monarchism in Britain they were not underpinned and validated by a deeply entrenched ethno-national myth. In this context, as a basis for generalisation about Irish popular loyalty in the 1850s the royal visit of 1853 served only to deceive. Moreover, there is reason to think that the Queen, the source of royal charisma, was herself no less misled about monarchy's persuasive influence on the Irish populace. There is a sense of betrayal in her attitude to Ireland as the revival of nationalism at the end of the 1850s made royal hopes and efforts towards the development of constitutional loyalty seem just so much wasted effort. Bereft of Prince Albert's guidance in political affairs and deeply alienated from the Catholic Irish, she would give free reign to her prejudices in an area she regarded as outside that which politicians had a right to determine. In particular, she would prove highly resistant to governmental initiatives that sought to engage the monarchy more closely with Ireland.

5 Nationalist revival and royal responses

It was perhaps unfortunate that Queen Victoria's alienation from Ireland was synonymous with, and stimulated by, the revival of nationalism, for the loyalist sense of constitutional urgency that Fenianism provoked was expressed in an increased concern to bring the monarchy and Ireland into closer contact than infrequent royal visits allowed. The favoured method of doing so was through the creation of an Irish royal residence. This proposal, though around at least since George IV's Irish visit of 1821, only really took off from the royal visit of 1861.[1] An expanded royal family and the increasing availability of royal personages other than the Queen for public service was largely responsible for giving life to the issue, aided by communicative developments, especially photographic processes that allowed royal imagery to be widely distributed in the form of *cartes de visite*.

The Prince of Wales's public activities in Ireland, from his military training in 1861 through visits of 1865 and 1868, together with his marriage to Princess Alexandra of Denmark in 1863, would be the subject of widespread illustrative dissemination,[2] a process, moreover, coincident with his mother's retreat from public engagements. Thus, in a period of greatly developing modernisation in transport, literacy – the transatlantic electric telegraph was laid in the early 1860s – and illustration, the United Kingdom of Great Britain and Ireland was becoming, communicatively, an ever more integrated public realm. It was one in which the struggle for allegiance between a reviving militant nationalism and the state would become acute, and with a demand for a royal residence in Ireland pressed with increasing urgency. That challenge was evident in the increasingly nationalist preoccupations of the Irish press, building on rising literacy levels.[3] In a period of widening democracy, when Ireland's

---

[1] *Daily Express* [*DE*], 30 Aug. 1861.
[2] See Peadar Slattery, 'The Uses of Photography in Ireland 1839–1900', unpublished PhD thesis, University of Dublin (1991), I, pp. 103–6.
[3] Marie-Louise Legg, *Newspapers and Nationalism: The Irish Provincial Press 1850–1892* (Dublin, 1999), ch. 5.

distinctive problems and exceptionalism within the state would be aired at Westminster with greater effect than hitherto, the task of national and state representation facing the monarchy became correspondingly difficult.

The issue of an Irish royal residence was more significant than it might seem. With reference to Tsarist Russia, Richard Wortman has argued: given that in a monarchy 'the locus of the monarch is the political center', the fact that there were two such loci – Moscow and St Petersburg – betrayed 'the Tsar's own ambivalence about the heritage, nature and goals of the state, creating ambiguity about what exactly the monarchy signified'.[4] With some adjustment of context and perspective this state-ment could well apply to Anglo-Irish relations. Deeply imbued with the idea of Ireland as an inalienable part of her kingdom, Victoria's inability to concede 'true belonging' to Catholic Irish membership of the British nation left the monarchy's status as an institution representative of the whole United Kingdom problematic. As the national myth underpinning the monarchy was not coextensive with the state, and with the expect-ations of the 1850s that Ireland would follow the Scottish model of integration failing to materialise, a combination of Irish political events – especially a controversy over the Albert statue in Dublin – the Queen's own anti-Catholic and anti-nationalist prejudices, together with concerns about the suitability of the Prince of Wales for the purpose, presented a serious impediment to the realisation of the residency project. Nevertheless, despite the difficulties involved, as an emphatic situational statement of royal identity in Ireland a regal residence had attractions to varying degrees across the political spectrum.

I

The wider context of Victoria's problematic relationship with Ireland in the 1860s was public criticism in Britain of her apparent abandonment of her public role following the death of Albert.[5] The absence of the monarch as a focus of popular affection threatened both the security of the monarchy and the stability of the state.[6] But while such concerns were of a general nature in Britain, the Irish question entailed a specificity of anxiety and criticism of Victoria.

[4] Richard Wortman, 'Moscow and Petersburg: The Problem of Political Center in Tsarist Russia, 1881–1914' in Sean Wilenz (ed.), *Rites of Power: Symbolism, Ritualism and Politics since the Middle Ages* (Philadelphia, 1985), p. 268.
[5] For a recent discussion, see Richard Williams, *The Contentious Crown: Public Discussion of the British Monarchy in the Reign of Queen Victoria* (Aldershot, 1997), ch. 3.
[6] *Saturday Review* [*SR*], 26 March 1864.

By 1864 her close association with the Scottish Highlands was twenty years old, well established in the public consciousness, and, as Ireland faced a resurgence of radical nationalism, it provided an increasingly seductive – and misleading – paradigm of the efficacy of monarchy for the inculcation of loyalty 'among so sensitive a people as the Irish'.[7] The reference to a people so 'sensitive' was indicative of the way in which Victorian race-theorising would foreground 'national character' as one of the central terms of debate on the Irish question. This was almost inevitable given Victorian society's obsession with 'character' as essential to success in life, no less than to British national success on the world stage.[8] The first important 'site' of debate was provided by the marriage of Albert Edward, Prince of Wales to Princess Alexandra of Denmark in 1863.

It was indicative of the developing conflictual character of the Irish political arena that this event, which in the 1850s would have been the occasion of unproblematic celebration, was now a source of public disorder. At one level, in the context of the development of the illustrative press, the civic celebrations organised by Dublin Corporation could be reported and visually integrated into a montage of similar images of celebrations mounted by cities in Britain to create a holistic impression of a state 'organically' united in loyal celebration.[9] It was a misleading impression. The corporation's decision to stage illuminations and a firework display to celebrate the royal marriage provoked popular disturbances, accompanying disorder in Cork, Tipperary and Ballina, County Mayo. In Dublin 146 people were arrested, while an illumination erected on the building of the Catholic University by the Rector was torn down by the institution's students.[10] A proposed address from the Catholic Church became mired in controversy as some prelates sought to emphasise 'the duty of princes to protect the poor' while the outright hostility of others prevented its submission.[11]

To a large extent the antagonism surrounding the Irish response to the royal wedding was a product of the modernisation of communications. This had not only served to establish the British state as a more integrated

---

[7] Robert Cecil, later Lord Salisbury in *SR*, 3 Dec. 1864.

[8] See Stefan Collini, 'The Idea of "Character" in Victorian Thought', *Transactions of the Royal Historical Society*, fifth series, 35 (1985), *passim*.

[9] See Richard Holmes, *Edward VII: His Life and Times* (London, 1911), I, p. 179.

[10] *Irish Times* [*IT*], 12, 17 March 1863; *Dublin Evening Mail* [*DEM*], 14 March 1863; *Nation*, 14 March 1863; *Freeman's Journal* [*FJ*], 21 March 1863; also James Murphy, *Abject Loyalty: Nationalism and Monarchy in Ireland during the Reign of Queen Victoria* (Cork, 2001), pp. 138–9.

[11] Cullen to Bishop Gilloly 12, 17 March 1863; Cullen to Tobias Kirby, 27 March 1863 in Peadar Mac Suibhne (ed.), *Paul Cullen and His Contemporaries with Their Letters from 1820–1902* (Naas, Co. Kildare, 1974), IV, pp. 137–9.

communicative arena, but had also extended to Europe the imaginative context in which the Irish question had meaning. The Polish revolt against Russian rule in 1863, especially, provided a stimulus to Irish nationalists,[12] reviving in nationalist minds the disparaging association between Ireland and Poland made by 'Albert the Good-for-Nothing', while also inspiring the formation of an Irish relief fund and praise of Pius IX as the only true defender of Poland.[13] The insurrection alarmed the Queen, mindful of Albert's concern about the seriousness of the Polish question[14] – and like him, regarding the Poles, like the Irish, as 'quite unfit to govern themselves'.[15] It was another encouragement to the anti-Irish animus that increasingly informed her outlook at a time when anti-monarchism in various forms was the nexus of a range of grievances affecting Irish Catholic society, not least in the Dublin municipal sphere.

In 1863 an ongoing controversy erupted over a requirement for Catholic local government – especially Dublin – councillors to swear an oath of allegiance to the Queen on assuming office, when no oath was required of non-Catholic councillors,[16] while a proposal by Dublin Corporation to provide a civic welcome for the British fleet provoked argument over both its role during the famine and the contribution of the Queen to famine relief.[17] If not quite the 'Famine Queen' myth that would develop later in the century, it was nevertheless a clear indication of its germination. For the loyalist press and British prints, however, anxiety about Irish politics made a monarchical initiative in Ireland imperative.[18]

For those for whom the monarchy was a central focus of allegiance, the sense of being slighted by the monarch's preference for Scotland was enhanced by the belief, in the run-up to the royal wedding, that Edinburgh had been favoured in the presentation of addresses at

---

[12] See Sir Robert Peel, Irish Chief Secretary to Undersecretary Larcom, 21 March 1863, Larcom papers, National Library of Ireland [NLI], MS 7487; *DE*, 18 March 1863; *Nation*, 21 March 1863.

[13] *Nation*, 26 Sept., 3, 10 Oct. 1863.

[14] Victoria to Lord Granville, 23 Feb. 1863, in G. E. Buckle (ed.), *Letters of Queen Victoria 1862–1878*, second series (London, 1926), I, pp. 66–7.

[15] Victoria to Crown Princess Victoria, 8 July 1865, in Roger Fulford (ed.), *Your Dear Letter: Private Correspondence between Queen Victoria and the Crown Princess of Prussia 1865–1871* (London, 1971), p. 34.

[16] See *DE*, 25, 29, 30 Sept., 3 Oct. 1863; *Nation*, 3 Oct. 1863; Lord Carlisle, Viceroy, to Sir Charles Grey, Queen Victoria's Private Secretary, 6, 10, 18 Oct. 1863, Larcom papers, NLI, MS 7585; Grey to Carlisle, 7 Oct. 1863, ibid.; entry (19 March 1865), in Angus Hawkins and John Powell (eds.), *The Journal of John Wodehouse First Earl of Kimberley* (Cambridge, 1997), p. 155.

[17] *FJ*, 21, 25 Sept. 1863; *Nation*, 3 Oct. 1863; also, issue of 3 Nov. 1863.

[18] *IT*, 23 March 1863.

Dublin's expense. It was an issue that involved a wide spectrum of Irish nationalist and loyalist opinion, from the contemptuous to the deeply engaged, and ran in the columns of the Irish press for nearly a year,[19] with Ireland's chief herald, Ulster King of Arms Sir Bernard Burke, claiming that a Viceroyalty determined a region and capital next in place to the sovereign, thus giving Dublin precedence.[20] But the issue was only resolved when the Queen referred the matter to the Judicial Committee of the Privy Council, and a decision was arrived at which determined that neither city was to have precedence, the first address to arrive having right of 'pre-audience'.[21]

Insubstantial as the issue seems, it nevertheless was carefully monitored by Dublin Castle,[22] and is reflective of the anxieties of the Irish authorities and loyalist opinion at a time when Fenianism was posing a challenge to the state, and with the upshot yet to be determined. In this context the precedence issue, however thinly, allowed nationality to be reframed in a way that appeared to establish a unity of interest and identity between the Viceroyalty and the people. But it could only be of significance in this respect if part of a more substantial undertaking, and this was not the case.

Indeed, the Carlisle Viceroyalty presented an almost outlandish example of the inability, already noted, of Irish administrations to devise coherent and relevant Irish policies up to 1868. Viceroy from 1855 to 1858 and from 1859 to 1864, Lord Carlisle was apparently incapable of even maintaining the dignity of an office all too easy to satirise, as Thackeray demonstrated. Of unfortunate facial aspect himself,[23] Carlisle's conception of Irish character was distinctly stage Irish and he acted accordingly, indulging in ceremonial buffoonery demeaning both his office and the destitute residents of the district in which Dublin Castle was located. A celebration of the Queen's birthday included Carlisle throwing 'cakes, bread, &c ... down to the mob ... who struggled and fought for the morsels. This humiliating scene went on for a long time.'[24]

Carlisle was popular in this crucial period, but chiefly because he was ridiculous. More seriously, Sir George Peel, the Chief Secretary and head

[19] See, for example, *IT*, 29 April 1863; *Galway Vindicator*, 1 May 1863; *FJ*, 1 June 1863; *Nation*, 6 June 1863; *Dublin Evening Post* [*DEP*], 30 June 1863; *DE*, 3 July 1863.

[20] *DE*, 3 Aug. 1863.

[21] *IT*, 29 Jan. 1864; *DE*, 26 Feb. 1864; *FJ*, 29 Feb. 1864. *Nation* (26 March 1863), predictably, thought the whole issue laughable.

[22] For files of newspaper clippings on the issue: Larcom papers, NLI, MS 7585.

[23] A Native, *Recollections of Dublin Castle and of Dublin Society* (London, 1902), pp. 60–1 'what an extraordinary face it was! – rubicund cheeks, an enormous mouth, perpetually kept open'.

[24] Ibid. pp. 61–2.

of the Irish administration, added to Carlisle's ceremonial degradations a tendency to offensive utterances about the character and religion of Irish Catholics.[25] Much more than Carlisle's buffoonery, Peel's indiscretions left the viceregal system unnecessarily vulnerable to attack at a time when nationalist grievances tended to exhibit royal dimensions. Increasingly throughout the 1860s, the associations of monarchical references with sporting or public dinners were seen not, as in the 1850s, as uncontroversial expressions of allegiance, but as investing such occasions with overt political significance; and their contestation as an indicator of the challenge the loyal associations that promoted them were being faced with.[26] The politicisation of monarchy was demonstrated dramatically in the conflict over a proposal to construct a memorial to Prince Albert in Dublin.

II

The controversy can be seen as another index of the way in which specifically nationalist concerns had moved from 'submerged' local contexts in the later 1850s to register in the national public sphere. The project was initiated at a meeting of the officially recognised Dublin Prince Albert Statue Committee in the Mansion House on 15 March 1862. By October around £6,000 had been promised. The initial plan was to erect the monument on St Stephen's Green, which would then be opened to the public as the Albert Park, but a parliamentary bill to effect the project was defeated.[27] The Albert Statue project stimulated the organisation of others commemorating the nationalist heroes O'Connell and Henry Grattan, together with controversies over appropriate sites among supporters of the various memorials. The most contentious was the historically resonant College Green, location of the Bank of Ireland, formerly Ireland's parliament house.

The memorialists, however, soon found themselves in disorderly conflict with Fenians, eager to diminish the influence of constitutionalism and believing that the *Nation* had reported Fenian activities in such a way as to leave their members vulnerable to arrest.[28] Convinced that the hour of revolutionary liberation was almost at hand, Fenians had little interest in public monuments to either Albert or Grattan: 'What matter about statues

[25] Entry (6 Dec. 1865), in Hawkins and Powell (eds.), *Kimberley Journal*, p. 180.
[26] Tom Hayes, 'God Save the Green, God Save the Queen and the Usual Loyal Toasts': Sporting and Dining for Ireland and/or the Queen' in Peter Gray (ed.), *Victoria's Ireland? Irishness and Britishness 1837–1901* (Dublin, 2004), p. 85.
[27] Elizabeth Darby and Nicola Smith, *The Cult of the Prince Consort* (New Haven and London, 1983), p. 70; Judith Hill, *Irish Public Sculpture: A History* (Dublin, 1998), p. 100.
[28] Murphy, *Abject Loyalty*, pp. 136–8, 140–5; John Devoy, *Recollections of an Irish Rebel* (New York, 1929), pp. 37–40; A. M. Sullivan, *New Ireland* (10th edn, Glasgow, 1878), pp. 250–4.

10 Albert Statue, Dublin.

of Grattan or Prince Albert? In the coming days of revolutionary conflict if
an Albert statue should cumber the ground in College Green it could easily
be pulled down, and the bronze would come in handy for the casting of
bullets or cannon for the patriot army.'[29] The upshot of the controversy
was that the site was barred, and not until the early 1870s was a rather
obscure location found for the Albert memorial: situated on government property, it is the only royal monument still standing in Dublin
(Fig. 10). Victoria, obsessed with grief over Albert's death throughout
the 1860s, perceived an insult she would not forget.[30]

---

[29] Fenian opinion expressed to T. D. Sullivan: Sullivan, *Troubled Times in Irish Politics*
(Dublin, 1905), pp. 96–7.
[30] She often referred to the paucity of Albert memorials in Ireland: David Duff, *Victoria
Travels: Journeys of Queen Victoria between 1830 and 1900* (London, 1970), p. 187.

11 Albert Memorial, Belfast.

By way of comparison, the construction of the Albert memorial clock on a prominent site in central Belfast in the same period (Fig. 11) may have been attended by a financial scandal,[31] but was otherwise the

[31] Darby and Smith, *Cult of the Prince Consort*, pp. 90–1.

respectful homage to the late prince of a loyal population. As such, it was both an appropriately functional monument and a useful investment in royal goodwill for a people busily engaged in building a loyal regional identity for north-east Ulster at a time when Anglo-Saxonist theorising allowed the civilising myth of the Ulster plantation to be integrated with that of British imperialism. Indicative of the popular Protestant engagement with the process was the reception in Belfast for *The Secret of England's Greatness* or *Queen Victoria Presenting a Bible in the Audience Chamber at Windsor* by Thomas Jones Barker.[32] The painting's integrated signification of monarchy and imperial greatness sourced to the Bible resonated powerfully with a community whose own industrial growth and prosperity were integrally linked to imperial expansion.[33] Unsurprisingly, it was, and remains, incorporated into the visual repertoire of loyalist iconography by the north's militant sectarian formation, the Orange Order (Fig. 12).

By the mid-1860s a significant change in attitudes to the monarchy in Ireland was taking place. In the north a developing era of British imperialism allowed Ulster loyalism to enhance its appropriation of the monarchy, while in the south royalty seemed increasingly a focus of alienation from the British state as Fenian and radical nationalist influence was progressively asserted. Nor was there any prospect of a Queen deeply disillusioned about the prospects of inculcating loyalty among the Catholic Irish, and resentful of demands for a sustained royal presence in Ireland, willingly acting to rectify this situation. Nor, as Viceroy from October 1864, would Lord Kimberley take the monarchical dimension to his duties seriously: viceregal ritual and ceremony were absurd 'mummeries' of an office deserving abolition.[34]

And yet, while himself entertaining anti-Irish prejudices, Kimberley had an acute appreciation of the very different conditions of Ireland and Britain, recognising the effects of past misgovernment and religious hatred in making Ireland ungovernable for the foreseeable future 'according to English principles ... A century is not too long for such an operation.'[35] Certainly there could hardly have been a more apt metaphor for the collapse of the loyalist hopes of the 1850s than the fate of William Dargan, the 'O'Connell of Irish industry'. An attempt to develop Irish

[32] Fintan Cullen, 'Union and Display in Nineteenth Century Ireland' in Dana Arnold (ed.), *Cultural Identities and the Aesthetics of Britishness* (Manchester, 2004), p. 122.
[33] See *BNL*, 30 April 1864.
[34] Entries (9 Oct., 1 Nov. 1864), in Hawkins and Powell (eds.), *Kimberley Journal*, p. 144.
[35] Kimberley to Raikes Currie, 2 Dec. 1864, in John Powell (ed.), *Liberal by Principle: The Politics of John Wodehouse 1st Earl of Kimberley, 1843–1902* (London, 1996), p. 99.

12 The Imperial Queen in Orange iconography.

textile manufactures in the early 1860s proved disastrous: he died penni-less in 1867.[36]

III

The Dublin of the mid-1860s was a very different place from the city that was the centrepiece of loyal Ireland a decade earlier. Kimberley recorded a city often gripped by panic and wild rumours, extending to the south and west of Ireland in general as the progress of the Fenian movement was

---

[36] Neal Garnham, 'William Dargan' in S. J. Connolly (ed.), *The Oxford Companion to Irish History* (2nd edn, Oxford, 2002), p. 144.

charted, and rising almost to paranoid levels in Ulster where ancestral fears fuelled contemporary anxieties that the movement represented a threat of Catholic-inspired massacres.[37] The year 1865 drew to an end with a public panic about 'a great rebellion' and the proclaiming of Dublin city and county, together with the cities of Tipperary and Waterford as areas subject to coercive measures such as curfews and other civic restrictions, together with detention without trial.[38] This state of affairs, with its frequent alarms, continued until the Fenians took the field in a significant, but ultimately unsuccessful, rising in early March 1867, defeated by bad weather, informers, a well-prepared Government and a disciplined army.[39] Before this eventuality, the British mindset, which conceived the Irish as inevitably pulled between the opposing poles of loyalty to the monarch and separatism, regarded another royal visit an effective counter to the Fenian menace.[40] The focus was provided by an International Exhibition of Arts and Manufactures in Dublin that the Prince of Wales would open on 8 May 1865. The public reaction to the Prince ranged from tepid to outright antagonistic,[41] though he was, apparently, not disillusioned. Edward 'spoke sensibly of Ireland, & seems to wish to conciliate the Irish'.[42]

That the visit was not a ringing success is not surprising: 1865 saw the Fenian movement at its strongest, especially in Dublin, and was the optimum year for a rising. A royal presence in the Irish capital to counter its influence was ill considered. The great royal successes of 1821, 1849 and 1853 had supportive contexts as essential conditions. That was not the case in 1865. As against the demonstration of a loyal Ireland that royal ceremonial in Dublin sought unsuccessfully to engineer, Fenianism was well organised and could demonstrate multiple centres of oppositional activity. And while it was the case that relatively few were prepared eventually to take the field militarily in the Fenian cause, the movement was much more effective in colonising the Irish imagination: the plight of Fenian prisoners after the rising struck a chord of sympathy with wide sections of the people.[43]

---

[37] Entry (14 Oct. 1865), in Hawkins and Powell (eds.), *Kimberley Journal*, p. 176.
[38] Wodehouse to Raikes Currie, 23 Dec. 1865, 31 Jan. 1866, in Powell (ed.), *Liberal by Principle*, p. 108; entries (25 Dec. 1865; 13 Jan. 1866), in Hawkins and Powell (eds.), *Kimberley Journal*, pp. 180, 182.
[39] James Loughlin, 'Fenianism' in Connolly (ed.), *Oxford Companion to Irish History*, p. 199.
[40] See Palmerston to Victoria, 17 Feb. 1865, in Buckle (ed.), *Letters of Queen Victoria*, I, pp. 250–1.
[41] Entries (8–9 May 1865), in Hawkins and Powell (eds.), *Kimberley Journal*, p. 159.
[42] Entry (12 May 1865), in ibid. p. 160.
[43] Lord Naas thought it alarming: entry (14 June 1867), in John Vincent (ed.), *Disraeli, Derby and the Conservative Party: Journals and Memoirs of Edward Henry, Lord Stanley 1849–1869* (London, 1978), p. 311.

Public demonstrations across the south and west of Ireland followed the execution on 23 November 1867 of the 'Manchester martyrs', William Philip Allen, Michael Larkin and Michael O'Brien.[44] Their execution was pressed by a vexed Queen.[45] In Dublin, 8 December 1867 saw a demonstration of approximately 50,000 people in the form of a mock funeral in sympathy with the martyrs,[46] presaging the shift in Irish public opinion that would take place following the execution of the leaders of the Easter Rebellion in 1916. It was at this level – popular imagination – that the loyalty-inducing role of monarchy in the Irish context was failing. Moreover, despite Fenianism's military failure, anxieties about its influence persisted. Public anxiety extended even to Windsor Castle, where a rumour that the Fenians intended to kidnap the Queen led to what she described as 'a good deal of nonsense and foolish panic'.[47] There was, however, good reason for royal concern. Just two months after her dismissal of the Fenian threat, her son Alfred, Duke of Edinburgh, was shot in the back and badly wounded by a Fenian sympathiser, Henry James O'Farrell, at a place called Clontarf in the vicinity of Sydney, Australia. The assassination attempt, probably intended as revenge for the Manchester executions, was made on 12 March 1868: O'Farrell was promptly tried, convicted and executed by 21 April 1868.[48] The Queen grieved that a Fenian 'or an Irishman' had been moved to pursue 'the vile and atrocious purpose intended'.[49]

IV

The real significance of the Fenian rising of 1867 was, arguably, less its military and imaginative effects in Ireland than its effect on parliamentary opinion. This was reflected, for instance, in an unsuccessful attempt to open the Irish Viceroyalty to Roman Catholics,[50] and a less wise parliamentary question by the Irish Liberal MP, Denis Reardan, as to whether

---

[44] Owen McGee, '"God Save Ireland": Manchester Martyr Demonstrations in Dublin, 1867–1916', *Eire–Ireland*, 36 (fall/winter 2001), 39–42; Vincent Comerford, *The Fenians in Context* (Dublin, 1998), pp. 148–9.

[45] Murphy, *Abject Loyalty*, pp. 156–7.   [46] McGee, '"God Save Ireland"', p. 43.

[47] Victoria to Crown Princess Victoria, 11 Jan. 1868, in Fulford (ed.), *Your Dear Letter*, p. 169.

[48] Sullivan, *Troubled Times in Irish Politics*, pp. 103–4.

[49] Victoria to Crown Princess Victoria, 25, 29 April 1868, in Fulford (ed.), *Your Dear Letter*, p. 185.

[50] Entry (11 July 1867), in Hawkins and Powell (eds.), *Kimberley Journal*, p. 205. It was defeated by anti-Catholic prejudice.

the Queen's inability to perform her public duties required her abdication.[51] These took place in a context where Disraeli's Tory Government was moved to consider a Roman Catholic university for Ireland, but which Gladstone trumped by the passage of a motion, on 3 April 1868, in favour of disestablishing the Irish Anglican Church, thus initiating a campaign in the country on the issue. This was seen as indicative of a future radical Gladstonian plan of Irish reforms. That the Fenian rising had made him alive to Irish grievances is clear.[52] But most importantly, with Fenianism militarily defeated, the British zero-sum scenario in which the struggle for Irish loyalty was framed determined that Fenianism's defeat would be consolidated by the royal presence in Ireland. Unlike the 1865 event, the royal visit of 1868 by the Prince of Wales would take advantage of Westminster's apparent reforming intent to create a congenial context. Indeed, as preparations for it were underway, the *Irish Times* was already assuming that royal visits would now be more frequent and of longer duration.[53]

The visit had been formally requested by the Viceroy, Lord Abercorn, and pressed on the Queen by the obsequious Disraeli on the basis of the 'highly advantageous' consequences to be expected from it. Given the political context and the expectations with which it was freighted, the preparations were as thoroughgoing as those for the visit of 1849. A ball to be attended by 3,500 people was prepared for, with much effort made in ensuring that the committee set up to organise it had the *appearance* of a spontaneous nature; while Lord Abercorn, a personal friend of the Prince, ensured that an opulence of ceremony characterised the Prince's stay, complete with a display of ironclad ships in Dublin Bay, intended to distract attention away from a 'harangue' the atheist republican Charles Bradlaugh was to make in the city. The Chief Secretary, Lord Mayo, curried popular favour by virtually clearing out the prisons (presumably of non-dangerous offenders) before the arrival of the royal party.

The ostensible focus of the visit was the installation of the Prince of Wales as a Knight of the Order of St Patrick, and the commander of crown forces in Ireland, Lord Strathnairn, was so concerned that the inauguration in the Anglican Christ Church cathedral might offend Catholic opinion that he suggested moving the ceremony to the Catholic cathedral. This could not be done, but Catholic sensibilities were addressed by a profuse supply of tickets and by a decision that no

---

[51] Entry (29 May 1868), in ibid. p. 220. Kimberley considered the idea a reasonable thought but an unwise utterance. Reardan was howled down.

[52] J. L. Hammond, *Gladstone and the Irish Nation* (London, 1938), pp. 79–81.

[53] *IT*, 19 March 1868.

Protestant religious service would take place in association with the inauguration.[54] For their part, the royal couple did their best to conciliate Irish opinion. Unlike his mother, the Prince relished ceremonial occasions, and had a keen interest in viceregal processions.[55] On the occasion of the visit, Edward, who had an almost perfect sense of how to balance the social distance and informality essential to the effectiveness of public performance, took pains to ensure that royal apparel included garments of Irish manufacture and motifs of national signification, especially fresh shamrock. Also, the royal entry to Dublin was effected to give the greatest popular 'pleasure',[56] while his public exposure was greatly enhanced by the inclusion of Punchestown racecourse in his itinerary.[57]

The Prince's presence in Dublin lived up to the administration's hopes. Edward demonstrated his political nous by making a point, when visiting the Catholic university, of warmly shaking hands with the Rector, Cardinal Cullen, much to the gratification of the crowd and the consternation of Tory and Protestant opinion, which, detecting an insult to the Anglican bishop of Dublin, had the issue raised in Parliament.[58] But this was of little consequence. As with the decision to hold his installation as a Knight of St Patrick devoid of a Protestant religious service – Sir Bernard Burke described the ceremony, which he performed, as 'ever memorable as the most brilliant pageant in Irish courtly annals'[59] – so too was Edward's warm greeting of Cullen an important acknowledgement of the increasing moral and social influence of the Catholic Church. He was so impressed by the royal party's reception in Dublin that he assured his mother she would have been 'astounded' had she witnessed it.[60] Viceroy Abercorn's claims of 100,000 people attending Punchestown races and 150,000 at the Phoenix Park to see the royal couple[61] provided supporting evidence.

The impression the royal couple made moved the *Freeman's Journal* to marvel at the remarkable speed with which the phenomenon of Fenianism

---

[54] Leon O'Broin, *Fenian Fever: An Anglo-American Dilemma* (London, 1971), pp. 228–34.

[55] See Edward to Duchess of Abercorn, 24 Aug. 1866, requesting an account of the Duke's ceremonial entry to Dublin on taking up the post of Viceroy: Abercorn papers, Public Record Office of Northern Ireland [PRONI], D623/A/327/28.

[56] Edward to the Duke of Abercorn, Easter Sunday 1868, PRONI, D623/A/327/43.

[57] Edward to Victoria, 11 March 1868, in Buckle (ed.), *Letters of Queen Victoria*, I, p. 515.

[58] O'Broin, *Fenian Fever*, pp. 237–8. On Edward's diplomatic approach to Irish issues in general, see L. J. Jennings, 'The Public Life of the Prince of Wales', *Quarterly Review*, 168 (1889), 286–8.

[59] Sir Bernard Burke, *Reminiscences: Ancestral, Anecdotal and Historic* (London, n.d. [1882]), pp. 177–8.

[60] Edward to Victoria, 18 April 1868 in Buckle (ed.), *Letters of Queen Victoria*, I, pp. 522–3.

[61] Abercorn to Victoria, 25 April 1868, RA VIC/D 24/34.

had been lost in the outpouring of enthusiasm for 'our future Sovereign'.[62] 'While the Princess Alexandra lives', it opined, 'Ireland will never want for a friend at court.'[63] There was some truth in this. The visit was her first acquaintance with Ireland and she was delighted by the people and the country, which, significantly, she thought more beautiful than Scotland.[64] A native of Denmark, she found it easy to identify with a small country, and, more importantly, she came to Ireland with none of the political baggage that encumbered almost all British royal visitors. She was also eminently suited to an era of welfare monarchism: 'Capricious and feather-headed, she pursued charity to the point of recklessness ... [but] when aroused she could be a powerful advocate and fundraiser.'[65] As we shall see, she would become a supporter of Irish Home Rule and, by extension, gain her husband, quite unjustifiably, popularity in Ireland for his supposed pro-autonomy sympathies.

The visit was a great success and to account for it we should note again the kind of contextual dynamics that determined great public engagement on previous major royal occasions. But to this we could add factors specific to the political environment of 1868; for example, the development of photography which helped ensure the dissemination of the image, and therefore the public presence of the Prince, in the form of photographic *cartes de visite*, common in the Irish public sphere since the early 1860s.[66] Edward had sat for photographic portraits during his Dublin visit in 1865 that apparently proved highly profitable when reproduced in this format.[67] Moreover, the parliamentary context of the visit was one in which Irish reformist legislation was being prioritised, while the Prince's refusal to accommodate Canadian Orangemen in 1860 was well known in Ireland and a source of great satisfaction to Catholics.[68] A pro-Catholic image may well have informed hopes that the visit would occasion the release of Fenian prisoners.[69]

In sum, a favourable context, personal disposition, ceremonial expertise and his constitutional position as heir to the throne integrated

---

[62] *FJ*, 16 April 1868.   [63] *FJ*, 17 April 1868.

[64] Dean of Windsor [A. V. Baillie] and Hector Bolitho (eds.), *Later Letters of Augusta Stanley 1864–1876* (London, 1929), p. 77; Georgina Battiscombe, *Queen Alexandra* (London, 1969), p. 96.

[65] Frank Prochaska, *Royal Bounty: The Making of a Welfare Monarchy* (New Haven and London, 1995), pp. 124–6; Mark Urban, 'Leviathan', BBC 2, 1998, compares Alexandra to Princess Diana in her qualities of character and involvement in charitable causes.

[66] See Edward Chandler, *Photography in Ireland: The Nineteenth Century* (Dublin, 2001), pp. 45, 47.

[67] Ibid. p. 47.

[68] Sir Sidney Lee, *King Edward VII: A Biography* (London, 1925), I, pp. 93–5; *FJ*, 20–6 Sept. 1860.

[69] Murphy, *Abject Loyalty*, p. 164. Some releases preceded the visit.

powerfully to position the Prince of Wales as the conciliatory face of the British monarchy. Moreover, the significance of what the visit *appeared* to achieve undoubtedly drew heavily on the sharp contrast between its ability to engage popular emotions against the background of the dis-affection of the very recent past. Although 'contrast', to an extent, was a factor in the success of the royal visit of 1849, the Young Ireland revolt in 1848 was not nearly as significant as the Fenian rising of 1867, the culmination point of several years' of revolutionary threat. But there is another dimension to the 'contrast'[70] dimension of the 1868 visit. The popularity of the Prince of Wales developed in Ireland at a time when Queen Victoria – already perceived in Ireland as anti-Irish and whose negative association with the famine was beginning to develop – had abdicated her public role.

In assessing the significance of the visit, however, the concealment dimension of royal occasions especially merits attention. It has been rightly argued that the popularity of the 1868 visit should not be seen as representing the expression of any *definite* views on constitutional ques-tions, apart from the absence of a deep commitment to Fenianism.[71] But the ethnocentric prism of 'national character' which informed the state perception of the Irish question exercised a powerful influence both in simplifying its complexity and in overestimating the visit's achievements. In this context the state's objectives in Ireland would clearly be served by establishing a royal residence to allow the 'personal' disposition of the Irish character to be exploited. Thus the loyalist *Daily Express* opined: 'Of all forms of government the monarchy is most suited to the disposition of the Celt ... The Saxon is law-loving and the Celt king-loving.'[72] Augusta Stanley accounted for the visit's success in essentially the same terms: 'Many ... filled with the most hostile theories, gradually warmed and warmed, when the theoretical *abstractions* which they thought of at a distance with such bitter feelings, were brought face to face with them in the form of *Persons* whom they could look on and honour, and who were ready to appreciate them and their country.'[73] The Duke of Cambridge claimed: 'The fact is, that the Irish are a very impressionable people. They are very easily guided to mischief by bad and designing persons, but ... they are as easily directed to good if only the occasion offers.'[74]

---

[70] For its significance as an element of charismatic leadership, see Ann Ruth Willner, *The Spellbinders: Charismatic Political Leadership* (New Haven and London, 1984), pp. 93–4.

[71] Comerford, *Fenians in Context*, p. 154.

[72] *DE*, 26 May 1868.

[73] Augusta Stanley to Victoria, post-April 1868, in Dean of Windsor and Bolitho (eds.) *Later Letters of Augusta Stanley*, p. 96.

[74] Cambridge to Victoria, 21 April 1868, RA VIC/D 24/26.

The monarchical familialism that was so influential in Britain had an added relevance in the Irish context when framed through an ethnocentric lens: the royal presence in Dublin in 1868 had created a 'scenario of love' that brought the Kingdom's estranged Irish children back to the bosom of the British national family. Augusta Stanley urged on Victoria the necessity of building on the visit's success by the establishment of an Irish royal residence. Stanley emphasised the attractions of the Donegal Highlands – together with a visit by the Queen herself.[75] Against a background of expected Irish reforms and with the supposed efficacy of personal contact with the Irish people in mind, the Ulster liberal *Northern Whig* declared: all royals 'are called up to come here and do their part in the great work of Irish reform ... They are called upon not merely to unite Ireland to Great Britain by Act of Parliament, but by personal affection to the ruling dynasty.'[76] The establishment of an Irish royal residence as an essential requirement of the success of this project almost became received wisdom at this time.[77]

A motion on the subject was moved in the Commons in May 1868 by the leading Irish Catholic lawyer and MP for Clare, Sir Colman O'Loghlen. O'Loghlen, who also proposed an ill-fated bill to remove the offensive clauses in the coronation oath condemning transubstantiation,[78] posited a royal residence as a central mechanism in a strategy to place Ireland on a developmental trajectory to constitutional loyalty. Focusing on the widespread belief that absentee landlords were largely responsible for Ireland's economic weakness, he argued that the Queen was the greatest absentee of all: a royal residence would encourage absentees to return while also making the royal presence 'racy of the soil', thus aligning Ireland on the side of law and order in the same way as Scotland.[79] O'Loghlen's argument was part of an extensive debate on the Irish question at this time, provoked by the Fenian rising, stimulated by the highly successful Irish visit of the Prince and Princess of Wales, and which accepted that fundamental reforms were needed.[80] For the first time in the nineteenth century the monarchy's relationship with Ireland

---

[75] Stanley to Victoria, post-April 1868, in Dean of Windsor and Bolitho (eds.), *Later Letters of Augusta Stanley*, p. 96.

[76] *Northern Whig* [*NW*], 27 Aug. 1868.   [77] See 'The Irish Balmoral', *Punch*, 2 May 1868.

[78] See O'Loglen to editor, *Daily News*, 1 June 1869. The paper had claimed he wanted to open the monarchy to Catholics.

[79] *Hansard*, 3rd ser., 192 (15 May 1868), cols. 346–51.

[80] See, for instance, J. C. Morison, 'Ireland for the British', *Fortnightly Review* [*FR*], 3, n.s. (Jan.–June 1868), 93–4; T. E. Cliffe Leslie, 'Ireland in 1868', ibid. pp. 136–7, 140–4; James Godkin, 'Ireland and Scotland', ibid. 319–20, 326–9; W. T. Thornton, 'Critical Notices' [a generally approving review of J. S. Mill's historicist pamphlet, *England and Ireland*], ibid. 372–4.

was being articulated in the context of a fairly comprehensive plan of Irish reforms which Gladstone's successful motion on Irish church disestablishment in April had signalled. Ironically, given her opposition to the proposal, the popularity and credibility of an Irish royal residence was boosted unintentionally by the Queen when her personal reminiscences of the Scottish Highlands appeared at the height of this debate.

Leaves from the Journal of Our Life in the Highlands included, with her record of the royal family's Highland sojourns, the Irish visits of 1849 and 1853. It had originally been prepared for private circulation within the royal family in 1865 and was published at the beginning of 1868.[81] The first edition sold 18,000 copies in a week and was soon followed by a cheap edition which, by March 1868, had sold 35,000 copies, and by early May, 80,000.[82] The book provided a highly romanticised account of an 'organic' relationship between the monarch and her Scottish subjects, especially her 'loyal Highlanders', to whom the book was dedicated; and, if anything, the dedication could be read as an implied rebuke to the disloyal Irish. But the descriptions of the highly successful Irish visits appeared – something the Queen seems not to have appreciated – to validate the royal experience of Scotland as a precedent for Ireland, and the obvious conclusions could be critical of its royal author: 'So *nice* it [the book] is ... but ... if it had been Ireland she had visited and settled on, instead of Aberdeenshire – the ecstasies and interests that would have grown up would have been just as great – and fenianism would never have existed.'[83] The boost that Victoria's reminiscences gave to the belief in an enhanced royal presence in Ireland as an aid to constitutional loyalty, moreover, was greatly stimulated at the end of 1868 by W. S. Trench's *Realities of Irish Life*, the publishing sensation of the period.

V

The book was a brilliant example of writing to the moment. Appearing just as Gladstone took office, in little over a year it ran through five editions, Trench's landlord background enhancing enormously its appeal to British political and public opinion. A talented writer, Trench conveniently anecdotalised the Irish question in a series of stories dealing with particular aspects of Irish life – for example 'The Ribbon Code', 'The

[81] Fulford (ed.), *Your Dear Letter*, p. 51; Victoria to Crown Princess Victoria, 11 Jan. 1868, p. 169.
[82] Victoria to Crown Princess Victoria, 11 Jan. 1868, in ibid. p. 169; 18 Jan., 25 March, 13 May 1868, in ibid. pp. 171, 180, 189.
[83] Dean of Windsor and Bolitho (eds.), *Later Letters of Augusta Stanley*, p. 65.

Conspiracy', 'The Murder', etc. – the common denominator of which was the problematic Irish 'character' itself. But he reassured his readers that 'justice fully and firmly administered' would resolve the Irish difficulty.[84] Trench 'never for a moment' doubted the people's 'loyalty to the Queen ... their country [or] their respect for their landlord'.[85]

In a climate of political anxiety about the feasibility of retaining Ireland, Trench's work was enthusiastically received in Britain and loyalist Ireland[86] as a validating personal interpretation of the dominant British meta-narrative of the Irish question.[87] The radical nationalist John Martin wrote: 'All England, it seems, takes it for gospel. And takes Mr Trench for a Seer.'[88] But for our purposes it is important to note its influence among political leaders.

The ex-Prime Minister, Lord John Russell, for example, would cite several pages from the book in his reminiscences to validate both the Union in general, and Scotland in particular, as a model that Ireland could be eventually expected to follow.[89] The Queen instructed Crown Princess Victoria of Prussia: 'If you have not read that book on Ireland by Trench – you should do so, for it will make you understand the people and the real causes of the state of that unhappy country.'[90] Significantly, Gladstone – about to embark on an extensive Irish reform programme – read it in late January 1869[91] but apparently left no record of his impressions.

Realities of Irish Life made a quite profound impact on British attitudes to Ireland. At the end of a decade of revolutionary threat it offered reassurance that the country could be successfully integrated into the British state. The Queen, however, could appreciate Trench's argument while remaining adamantly resistant to the royal implications it facilitated. The most the clamour for an Irish royal residence gained from the monarch, to the fury of even her Private Secretary, General Sir Charles Grey,[92] was the concession of 'frequent visits (not State ones) of any of

---

[84] Ibid. pp. iv–vi.   [85] Ibid. p. 371.

[86] *Dublin Evening Mail* [*DEM*], 12 March 1869; *IT*, 23 Dec. 1868; *DEP*, 12 March 1869; *NW*, 22 Dec. 1868.

[87] See, for example, *TT*, 24 Dec. 1868; *Pall Mall Gazette*, 16 Dec. 1868; *Standard*, 30 Jan. 1869; *Westminster Gazette*, 26 Dec. 1868; *Vanity Fair*, 30 Jan. 1869; *St James' Chronicle*, 13 Feb. 1869; *The Economist*, 2 Jan. 1869; *Tablet*, 26 Dec. 1868; *SR*, 19 Dec. 1868. *Spectator* (30 Jan. 1869) was an exception.

[88] John Martin to W. J. O'Neill Daunt, 23 Jan. 1869, Daunt papers, NLI, MS 8047(2); also *Cork Examiner*, 5 Jan. 1869.

[89] John Earl Russell, *Recollections and Suggestions 1813–1873* (London, 1875), ch. ix.

[90] Victoria to Crown Princess Victoria, 17 March 1869, in Fulford (ed.), *Your Dear Letter*, p. 229.

[91] H. C. G. Matthew (ed.), *The Gladstone Diaries VII* (Oxford, 1982), p. 17.

[92] Dean of Windsor and Bolitho (eds.), *Later Letters of Augusta Stanley*, p. 111.

the Royal Family', but while these might be 'a good thing ... I cannot believe it will have any permanent effect.'[93] This was a verdict she had also passed on the visit of the Prince and Princess of Wales,[94] about which British political and public opinion enthused.

When, in the run-up to the Irish visit of 1868, Disraeli tentatively suggested the possibility of future stays of longer duration with the clear implication of a royal residence,[95] he was rebuked with the argument that if this was conceded in Ireland, 'Wales and the colonies even' might make similar claims; moreover, the personal character of the Prince of Wales made him unsuitable for the purpose. Short visits by various members of the royal family would be acceptable, 'if the Irish behaved themselves'. But going to Ireland, she argued, was bound to be an uncongenial task: 'For health and relaxation no one goes to Ireland, and people only go who have their estates to attend to. But for health and relaxation thousands go to Scotland.'[96]

Fortuitously supportive of state consolidation as the domestic persona of the Victorian monarchy was in Britain, Ireland exposed its limitations. Victoria's inability or unwillingness to distinguish between her private interests and those of the state left the Irish question subsumed within a subjective realm of personal prejudice and on a trajectory of developing estrangement as Disraeli came to influence her political outlook, blending anti-Catholic and anti-Irish prejudice with personal animus towards Gladstone, who was soon to assume office: he was a reckless politician dependent on the support of 'Radicals, Romanists and Irish Papists'[97] while Disraeli could 'only offer devotion'.[98] Insofar as Victoria's sense of her constitutional duty informed her relationship with Ireland, it was, as we have seen, framed within a divinely ordained, non-negotiable relationship between sovereign and subjects. In this context, loyalty – a bounden duty of the subject – as in Scotland, could earn the favour of a benign royal presence, but Irish disloyalty was a failing for which they were responsible, not her; and she owed them no special dispensation. From her long experience of the Irish question, indeed, she might have regarded the 1860s as a replay of the 1840s, with the Fenian movement a reincarnation of the Chartists, fears for the physical safety of members of the royal

[93] Victoria to Crown Princess Victoria, 29 April 1868 in Fulford (ed.), *Your Dear Letter*, pp. 187–8.
[94] Ibid. 22 April 1868, p. 185.
[95] Disraeli to Victoria, 6 March 1868, in Buckle (ed.), *Letters of Queen Victoria*, I, pp. 512–13.
[96] Victoria to General Grey, 7 March 1868, in ibid. pp. 513–14.
[97] Disraeli to Victoria, 23 March, 24 April 1868, in ibid. pp. 518–22.
[98] Disraeli to Victoria, 26 Feb. 1868, in ibid. p. 506.

family, and a conjunction of domestic problems and worrying foreign – the American Civil War and its Fenian ramifications – developments.[99]

The only Catholic Irishmen the Queen seemed now to approve of were those employed in the Irish constabulary, whose efforts in suppressing the Fenian revolt were rewarded with the term 'Royal' being added to the force's name (RIC).[100] Accordingly, at the very time Westminster was prepared holistically to address Irish problems, thereby creating a con-genial context for the exercise of royal influence in Ireland, the Queen was conditioned to take a negative view of the project's possibilities. But how the monarchy's relationship with Ireland was to be determined was also reflected in differing party stances

Although it was ultimately defeated by a majority of 44 in a House of 122,[101] it is possible to divine in the parliamentary debate on O'Loglen's motion for an Irish royal residence positions being taken that would shape the approaches of the major parties for the future. Disraeli, well aware of both the Queen's dislike of the Irish and her opposition to an Irish residence, justified her past absences from Ireland on the grounds of poor communications, coupled with a defence of the much-ridiculed Irish Viceroyalty. Claiming to be personally sympathetic to O'Loglen's motion, Disraeli was yet aware that it would not have a successful outcome and argued successfully for postponement on the grounds that it would be 'inconvenient' to press it to a vote in the prevailing circumstances.[102] Gladstone agreed.[103] Soon to take office, his time would be fully occupied with the highly complex disestablish-ment issue. But whereas Disraeli sought postponement as a means of putting off an issue on which no progress was likely, Gladstone did so in the belief that the best way to pursue O'Loglen's objectives, to which he was firmly committed, was privately and informally with the Queen, and in the context of thoroughgoing reformist legislation.

---

[99] For the Scottish dimension to the public mood of panic about Fenianism that charac-terised Britain as a whole, see Elaine McFarland, 'A Reality and yet Impalpable: The Fenian Panic in Mid-Victorian Scotland', *Scottish Historical Review*, 78 (Oct. 1998), 199–223.
[100] Lee, *King Edward*, I, p. 222.   [101] *Weekly Register*, 27 June 1868.
[102] *Hansard*, 3rd ser., 192 (15 May 1868), cols. 359–61.   [103] Ibid. cols. 361–2.

Part III

Gladstonian monarchism

6   Ireland and the crown: the Gladstonian perspective

Gladstone's accession to power in December 1868 entailed a distinctive perspective on Ireland. Sharing, up to a point, the popular view of the Irish as an 'unstable' people, he nevertheless sourced the Irish problem primarily to past misgovernment, something which entailed a moral obligation on contemporary politicians to remedy.[1] It was an obligation he felt personally as he came, by 1868, to accept the Irish as a distinctive nationality, though not yet a separatist people.[2] His was an outlook informed by Burke's strictures on alienating historical traditions but not yet Burke's constitutional conclusions. It was an outlook in gradual evolution and fraught with inconsistencies, illuminated by J. L. Hammond's comment that Gladstone 'combined Irish memory of the past with English institutions of the present'.[3] This faultline in his thinking would constitute one of the most serious weaknesses of his plan to integrate Ireland into the British state and, by extension, the monarchy as the mechanism through which Irish constitutional loyalty could find expression. The importance of the monarchy in that scheme derived from the significance Gladstone attached to it in British society in general.

I

The best insights into this subject are provided in the series of commentaries Gladstone made on the crown in the 1870s.[4] He was enormously

---

[1] Gladstone to Victoria/Victoria to Gladstone, 1 May 1869, in Philip Guedalla (ed.), *The Queen and Mr Gladstone* (London, 1933), I, pp. 172–3.

[2] Queen Victoria, Journal [QVJ] (24 Nov. 1866), cited in Elizabeth Longford, *Victoria R.I.* (London, 1964), p. 359; Asa Briggs (ed.), *Gladstone's Boswell: Late Victorian Conversations by Lionel A. Tollemache and Other Documents* (1898; Brighton, 1984), p. 102; Shane Leslie, *Henry Edward Manning: His Life and Labours* (London, 1921), pp. 203–4; J. L. Hammond, *Gladstone and the Irish Nation* (London, 1938), pp. 80–1.

[3] Hammond, *Gladstone*, p. 86.

[4] Mainly addresses on the death of the Prince Consort and reviews of Theodore Martin's biography of the Prince Consort (5 vols., London, 1875–80), reproduced in W. E. Gladstone, *Gleanings of Past Years, 1843–78*, 8 vols. (London, 1879).

impressed by the way that the blameless home life of Albert and Victoria, together with the social industry of the former, had set a societal example: 'they contributed perhaps no less than wise legislation, and conduct inflexibly constitutional, to draw close the ties between the people and the throne'.[5] It was a firmly Bagehotian interpretation of the monarchy's place in British society, and one that hardly accorded with reality,[6] as Gladstone already knew. But for the sake of the institution's wider societal and state utility it was important that the ideal of the Queen's constitutional propriety be maintained:[7] 'The Sovereign in England is the symbol of the nation's unity, and at the apex of the social structure ... the constitution would regard the default of the Monarch, with his [sic] heirs, as the chaos of the State.'[8] Moreover the nation of which the monarch was the symbol was not egalitarian, but hierarchical. The British people, he argued, were not apt to 'untune' the social degrees of society,[9] a view, as we shall see in regard to Home Rule, he would apply no less to Ireland in the 1880s. The question was, however, how far could Ireland be incorporated within such a conception of the monarchy's relationship to state and society? Gladstone's belief that it could, arguably, owes much to the hegemonic influence in British political discourse of 'constitutionalism' – an ideological field of multiple interpretation but characterised by an acceptance among all social groups of the existing constitution. Expressed in allegiance to the throne, constitutionalism as employed by the state involved attempts to define acceptably loyal political behaviour, at least up to 1867, in a public sphere coercively determined so that the influence of the socio-economically influential would predominate. A necessary corollary to this process was the creation of forms of civic ceremony and activities geared to generating support from sections of society excluded by official political culture.[10]

It takes only a little imaginative leap to validate Vernon's theory in the Irish context from 1800: in a region representing the most serious threat to the constitutional order, state power found expression in multiple coercion acts, a militarised police force, a restrictive franchise, and press censorship;[11] and in attempts to restrict the

[5] Ibid. I, pp. 22–3.

[6] See Frank Hardie, *The Political Influence of Queen Victoria 1861–1901* (2nd edn, Oxford, 1938).

[7] Gladstone, *Gleanings*, I, pp. 37, 41–6.   [8] Ibid. p. 227.   [9] Ibid. pp. 234–5.

[10] James Vernon, *Politics and the People: A Study in English Political Culture c. 1815–1867* (Cambridge, 1993), *passim*; also John Plunkett, *Queen Victoria: First Media Monarch* (Oxford, 2003), pp. 14–16.

[11] On this subject, see Brian Inglis, *The Freedom of the Press in Ireland 1784–1841* (London, 1954); Marie-Louise Legg, *Newspapers and Nationalism: The Irish Provincial Press 1852–1892* (Dublin, 1999), pp. 76, 95.

political arena to the constitutionally loyal, with the monarchy functioning at a popular level to neutralise 'seditious' sentiment. This approach also informed Gladstone's Irish policy during his first administration.

Gladstone admitted that the word 'constitution' had 'but a cold and hollow sound in the ears of the Irish people';[12] nevertheless, it had yet to be demonstrated that the Irish question could not be settled within the Union as it then existed. The task was to invest the term 'constitution' with meaning and belonging in an Irish context, a task in which the monarchy would have an important role, and something Gladstone undoubtedly sought to facilitate by adding an Irish dimension to the royal household with the appointment of the Liberal, Lord Lurgan, as one of the Queen's Lords-in-Waiting.[13] Gladstone envisaged the royal presence – embodying a powerful integration of state symbolism and authority with moral excellence – establishing an Irish context of moral engagement that would bring out the (loyal) best in the people in a context of reforms to address 'legitimate' Irish grievances. It was a position born of idealism informed by a knowledge of Ireland based not on personal experience,[14] but on correspondence with the Irish administration, political contacts, parliamentary inquiries, historical and political writings. In this respect it is worth noting that Gladstone's first administration lacked both Irish experience and membership.[15] John Morley later reflected that it was 'almost a point of honour … for British Cabinets to make Irish laws out of their own heads'.[16] Certainly Baron O'Hagan, whose appointment as Irish Lord Chancellor – the first Catholic to hold the post in 200 years – was intended as a signal of enlightened legislation, found that while a 'large portion of the Irish' assumed him to have political influence, his views were ignored.[17]

[12] Gladstone to C. S. P. Fortescue, Irish Chief Secretary, 16 Oct. 1869, in H. C. G. Matthew (ed.), *The Gladstone Diaries VII* (Oxford, 1982), p. 149.

[13] Lord Granville to Gladstone, 6 Jan. 1869, in Agatha Ramm (ed.), *The Political Correspondence of Mr Gladstone and Lord Granville 1868–1876* (London, 1952), I, p. 7.

[14] H. C. G. Matthew, *Gladstone 1809–1874* (Oxford, 1986), p. 192; Briggs (ed.), *Gladstone's Boswell*, pp. 59–60; also James Loughlin, *Gladstone, Home Rule and the Ulster Question 1882–93* (Dublin, 1986), pp. 287–9.

[15] Peter Gordon (ed.), *The Red Earl: The Papers of the Fifth Earl Spencer 1835–1910* (Northampton, 1986), I, p. 8.

[16] John Morley, *The Life of Gladstone* (London, 1903), II, p. 292.

[17] Granville to Gladstone, 31 March 1870, in Ramm (ed.), *Gladstone–Granville Correspondence*, I, p. 96.

II

Gladstone's land reform of 1870 drew on a sustained study of ancient Irish society to argue that the Irish peasant was deeply committed to customary rights in land that had long ceased to exist in England.[18] This understanding, while recognising the Irish peasant's 'backward' stage of civilisation, also legitimised, on the basis of an Irish reality that had to be addressed, the politically 'progressive' amendment to absolute rights in property contained in his land act. At the same time, it was an act that pertained merely to a specific region within the state. It was intended to remove a threat to the state's stability, and, being officially signed into law by the state's hegemonic signifier, the monarch, was thereby denuded of any possible 'revolutionary' implications. Moreover, as the beneficial effects of reformist legislation worked through, monarchical influence could be relied upon to guide Irish identity into safe constitutional channels. The central mechanism for both Gladstone and the Irish Viceroy, Lord Spencer – who regarded his office as the authentic embodiment of the monarchical presence in Ireland – was 'visible and sensible contact' between the Queen and her people.[19] Moreover, success in Ireland would benefit the Kingdom as a whole: '[civilised] society can hardly be such as to deserve that name, until the conditions of peace & order, & of mutual goodwill & confidence shall have been more firmly established in Ireland'.[20]

Gladstone's Irish reforms were to be quite specifically targeted. He entertained no real hope of bringing convinced Fenians into loyal allegiance; rather, 'our purpose and duty is to draw a line between the Fenians and the people of Ireland, & make the people of Ireland indisposed to cross it'.[21] The arbitrary distinction made between the Fenians and the people of Ireland indicated an ill-informed conception of Irish society; nevertheless, enough evidence could be pointed to in support of Gladstone's expectations. The sixty-six seats won by Irish Liberals at the general election of 1868 – up from fifty in 1859 – formed a significant element of the Liberal parliamentary party.[22] There was even a fleeting

---

[18] See E. D. Steele, *Irish Land and British Politics: Tenant Right and Nationality 1865–1870* (Cambridge, 1974), pp. 252–4.

[19] Freda Harcourt, 'Gladstone, Monarchism and the "New" Imperialism', *Journal of Imperial and Commonwealth History*, 14 (1985), 25–6.

[20] Gladstone to Bishop Samuel Wilberforce, 20 June 1870, in Matthew (ed.), *Gladstone Diaries VII*, p. 311.

[21] Gladstone to General Grey, 28 March 1869, in ibid. p. 45.

[22] K. T. Hoppen, *Elections, Politics and Society in Ireland 1832–1885* (Oxford, 1984), p. 273; Vincent Comerford, *The Fenians in Context* (Dublin, 1998), pp. 161–2.

Irish Reform League which favoured cross-channel cooperation.[23] Moreover, the apparent Irish loyalty attending the Prince of Wales's visit in April 1868 seemed to re-emerge when the new Irish Viceroy, Lord Spencer – approved of by a pro-reform Prince[24] – made his state entry into Dublin to receive a hearty welcome from the corporation and Cardinal Cullen.[25] Gladstone's understanding of how his reforms would serve the cause of Irish loyalty, however, failed to take account of several complicating factors.

First, it was not within his gift wholly to coordinate the pace with which the monarchy's relationship with Ireland would be harmonised with the implementation of reforms. The public debate on Ireland, especially in Parliament, proceeded under its own dynamic – Captain William Stacpoole, Liberal MP for Limerick, would, for instance, repeatedly press for an Irish royal residence – often expressed in terms of baffled exasperation and uncertainty about whether Ireland was likely to follow the Scottish route to constitutional loyalty.[26] Moreover, Gladstone's dealings with the monarch on Ireland were complicated somewhat by the dual responsibility of the Viceroy. The Viceroy was a Government appointee, but was usually not in the Cabinet and had a direct line of communication to the court, to which he was also accountable. Thus, in the first instance, the channel through which the Queen was made aware of the offer of an Irish royal residence in 1869 – when John La Touche of Harristown, County Kildare, offered his home[27] – was through Spencer, her proxy in Ireland. Even the offer of an Irish royal residence was problematic if, as was the case with the La Touche offer, it was premature.[28]

The belief that the Irish 'imagination' would respond enthusiastically to a resident royal presence was widespread, extending from members of the court, to the Government and the Irish administration.[29] And the

[23]   Hoppen, *Elections*, p. 274.
[24]   Prince of Wales to Gladstone, 26 Dec. 1868, 21 Jan. 1870, Gladstone papers, BL, Loan, 73/28.
[25]   Gordon (ed.), *Red Earl*, I, pp. 77–8.
[26]   See, for example, Antony Trollope, 'What Does Ireland Want?', *St Paul's Magazine of Arts and Sciences*, 5 (Dec. 1869), 301; J. C. Hoey, 'Is Ireland Irreconcilable?', *Dublin Review*, 14 (1870), 481; George Broderick, 'The Past and Future Relation of Ireland to Great Britain', *MacMillan's Magazine*, 24 (1870), 43.
[27]   H. C. G. Matthew (ed.), *The Gladstone Diaries VI* (Oxford, 1978), p. 652.
[28]   Ramm (ed.), *Gladstone–Granville Correspondence*, I, p. 7.
[29]   General Grey to Victoria, 23 Dec. 1868, RA VIC/D 24/63–4; Gladstone to Granville, 6 Jan. 1869, in Ramm (ed.), *Gladstone–Granville Correspondence*, I, p. 7; Grey to Victoria, 29 Dec. 1868, RA VIC/D 24/65.

Queen's inevitable rejection of the offer caused anger in court circles.[30] Going through an intense anti-Catholic phase and increasingly disliking Gladstone and his Irish reforms, she believed that Irish Catholics posed a threat to 'Protestant England' and that it was 'impossible' to treat them on terms of equality with Protestants.[31] As against Gladstone's promotion of a British civic nationality, even if flawed, the Queen, hegemonic emblem of the state, still conceived it through the prism of its Protestant origins, and the first of Gladstone's Irish legislative projects, disestablishment of the Anglican Church, exacerbated her prejudices.

The progress of the disestablishment bill in the Commons brought accusations that it would undermine the constitutional supremacy of the Queen in Ireland. Gladstone rejected the argument,[32] assuring the Queen that the reform would directly reap a proportional dividend in expressions of loyalty. But this theory was put to the test as the bill was on its parliamentary course, with disappointing results, when Prince Arthur undertook an Irish visit.

III

The Queen had agreed to the visit as a prelude to an extended period of military service in Canada for the Prince and had been assured about his safety by Gladstone and Spencer,[33] the latter pointing to the loyalty of the Catholic clergy and a pastoral letter from Cardinal Cullen condemning Fenianism.[34] It was clearly hoped that the visit would offer an alternative pole of loyal attraction in a period of rising nationalist consciousness

---

[30] Grey to Gladstone, 8 Jan. 1869, in G. E. Buckle (ed.), *The Letters of Queen Victoria*, second series (London, 1926), I, pp. 575–7 ; Guedalla (ed.), *Queen and Mr Gladstone*, I, pp. 150–1. Augusta Stanley thought she was 'so afraid lest any of them [members of the royal family] be taken up by, or take up the Irish so as to throw Balmoral into the shade': Dean of Windsor and Hector Bolitho (eds.), *Later Letters of Augusta Stanley* (London, 1929), p. 111.

[31] Victoria to Lord Granville, 24 Aug. 1869, in Guedalla (ed.), *Queen and Mr Gladstone*, I, pp. 200–1; also Victoria to Crown Princess Victoria, 18 Aug. 1869, in Roger Fulford (ed.), *Your Dear Letter: Private Correspondence of Queen Victoria and the Crown Princess of Prussia 1865–1871* (London, 1971), pp. 245–6. Victoria to Gladstone, 15 Oct. 1869, in Guedalla (ed.), *Queen and Mr Gladstone*, I, p. 204.

[32] See Commons report in *The Times* [*TT*], 26 March 1869; *Belfast News-Letter* [*BNL*], 26 March 1869; but also Manning to Cardinal Cullen (8 April 1868, in Leslie, *Manning*, p. 200), claiming it would bring down a whole wing of the 'royal supremacy'.

[33] Noble Frankland, *Witness of a Century: The Life and Times of Prince Arthur, Duke of Connaught* (no location, 1983), p. 31. General Grey to Gladstone, 26 March 1869, RA VIC/D 25/57; Spencer to Gladstone, 30 March 1869, RA VIC/D 25/59; Gladstone to the Queen, 2 April 1869, RA VIC/Add A/15/1374.

[34] Cullen, Lenten Pastoral Letter, 22 Feb. 1869, in P. F. Moran (ed.), *The Pastoral Letters and Other Writings of Cardinal Cullen* (Dublin, 1882), III, pp. 57–62.

energised by over forty monster meetings reminiscent of the O'Connell era. These were part of the Amnesty Campaign for Fenian prisoners, which had its own monarchical dimension in the form of a petition to the Queen of 250,000 signatures, while amnesty memorials to the monarch were presented from most of the corporations and town councils in southern Ireland.[35]

However, what must have seemed, against the background of the Prince of Wales's successful sojourn the previous year, a guaranteed mechanism for the expression of loyalty, was confounded almost as soon as the royal itinerary was published. The inclusion of a Masonic Order dinner provoked Cardinal Cullen to issue a pastoral reminder that Catholic attendance at such events entailed automatic excommunication.[36] Also, Cullen's letter provoked Ulster loyalist anger at the inclusion of a reference to an Ulster Anglican clergyman's claim that disestablishment would see Ulster kick the Queen's crown into the Boyne.[37] Cullen had used the pastoral letter to strike at two of his enemies, but by including the Ulster loyalists had heightened passions further on a subject already the source of fierce controversy. For a community that interpreted the monarch through the prism of its own community myths – not entirely inappropriately given the Queen's personal prejudices – the threat was uttered in the passion of frustration at her failure personally to reject the disestablishment bill.[38] Nationalists would remember the threat as an illustration of the hollowness of Ulster loyalty; but more immediately, the issue made it likely that the northern leg of the Prince's visit would be the occasion of civic disorder, which ensued as soon as he left Londonderry, with the consequence of two deaths and several injuries.[39]

The violence in Ulster, however, was overshadowed by a major dispute with a royal dimension in Cork, provoked by the Mayor, Daniel O'Sullivan, having praised the 'purity' of motive and 'heroism' of Henry James O'Farrell, executed in Australia for his attempt on the life of the Duke of Edinburgh in 1868.[40] The controversy was a gift to the

---

[35] David Thornley, *Isaac Butt and Home Rule* (London, 1964), pp. 65–7.
[36] Cullen, Pastoral Letter to the Dublin Clergy, 29 March 1869, in Moran (ed.), *Pastoral Letters*, III, p. 210.
[37] Ibid. p. 209; *BNL*, 5 April 1869.
[38] See *BNL*, 30 April 1869; Thomas McKnight, *Ulster As It Is: or Twenty-Eight Years' Experience as an Irish Editor* (London, 1896), I, pp. 183–5.
[39] *BNL*, 29 April 1869; *Londonderry Sentinel* [*LS*], 30 April 1869; *Londonderry Journal* [*LJ*], 1 May 1869. It also led to a heightening of the Prince's personal security and constraints on his public engagements in Belfast: Frankland, *Witness of a Century*, p. 33.
[40] *Daily News*, 30 April 1869; *TT*, 30 April 1869; *Daily Telegraph*, 30 April 1869; *LS*, 1 May 1869.

Tory opposition as a stick to beat Gladstone with, for his misguided Irish policies.[41] When faced with legislation to effect his removal, O'Sullivan resigned,[42] but Gladstone's claim that the episode, 'perhaps for the first time', illustrated the refusal of the Irish people to align themselves against the crown, did not find royal favour.[43] Nor did O'Sullivan's resignation end his capacity for controversy, telling a rally to elect his successor: 'Ireland should stand forward, free and unfettered, as she stood 200 years ago . . . as a nation under her lawful sovereign, James II.'[44]

Gladstone conceived the royal visit as a mechanism for the demonstration of loyal sentiment supposedly inherent in the Irish people. Instead it functioned to illustrate the limitations of Gladstone's conception of the royal relationship with Ireland. In particular, it demonstrated that the distinction he made between the benign, elevated sphere in which the monarchy related to the people, and the conflictual realm of politics, was flawed in the Irish context. Cardinal Cullen's warning to Catholics respecting Masonic events indicated clearly that what was a normal relationship between the monarchy and a respected institution of civil society in Protestant Britain had a very different complexion in Catholic Ireland. More generally, Gladstone did not fully appreciate how a royal presence in Ireland in a period of highly charged political passions could impact on the political arena. Freighted with hegemonic national and constitutional symbolism, royal personages, as we have noted, brought an intensity of public and media (press) attention capable of creating their own centres of political reference and activity, with, as in Prince Arthur's case, problematic consequences. Thus, while sectarian rivalry was endemic in Ulster's political environment, the visit of the Prince to Londonderry created a context which brought opposing factions into close proximity, making violent conflict virtually inevitable. At the same time, O'Sullivan's statements deserve close attention as a reflection of nationalist opinion.

The distinction he made, between the nobility of O'Farrell's motives and the depravity of his act, caused the uproar it did largely because the

---

[41] See, for instance, Lord Lifford in *TT*, 5 May 1869; *LJ*, 5 May 1869; Entry (3 May 1869), Angus Hawkins and John Powell (eds.), *The Journal of John Wodehouse First Earl of Kimberley* (Cambridge, 1997), p. 235; *LS*, 4 May 1869; Journal (8 May 1869), Daunt papers, NLI, MS 3041: W. J. O'Neill Daunt Journal, vol. II: 1868–79. Also Oliver McDonagh, 'The Last Bill of Pains and Penalties: The Case of Daniel O'Sullivan, 1869, *Irish Historical Studies*, 19 (Sept. 1974), 136–55.

[42] McDonagh, 'Last Bill of Pains and Penalties', 137–45, 152–3.

[43] Gladstone to Victoria, 11 May 1869, in Buckle (ed.), *Letters of Queen Victoria*, I, p. 599; Victoria, Crown Princess of Prussia, was more favourably disposed to Gladstone and his Irish plans: Fulford (ed.), *Your Dear Letter*, p. 234.

[44] *TT*, 25 May 1869.

subject of attack was a royal personage; but otherwise, O'Sullivan merely gave expression to what was, in fact, a central characteristic of the constitutional nationalist attitude to political violence in the nineteenth century: it could be *morally* justifiable, though usually impracticable, and therefore to be avoided.[45] The rigid division Gladstone made between Fenians and the rest of Irish society hardly reflected the complexity of Irish political attitudes. Even O'Sullivan's reference to James II as Ireland's legitimate monarch embodied a pointed question Gladstone never really addressed: to what extent could a Protestant sovereign truly give expression to the outlook and beliefs of a Catholic people? It was a relevant question given that Victoria's opposition to disestablishment was common knowledge in Ireland. As we shall see, this issue would recur up to, and beyond, the creation of the Irish Free State in 1921. Moreover, Gladstone's belief that Ireland's 'legitimate' religious grievances would be addressed by disestablishment reflected his own moral preoccupations rather than the extent to which disestablishment engaged Irish Catholic opinion. He was duly disappointed when the expected Irish appreciation for the measure failed to emerge,[46] while an irate Queen, angered by the incidents associated with Prince Arthur's visit, and also seeing no evidence of a change in Irish attitudes, abruptly rejected the petition in favour of releasing the forty remaining Fenian prisoners.[47]

IV

What sustained Gladstone's optimism, despite the disappointing results of disestablishment, was the belief that his proposed land bill for Ireland in 1870 – the centrepiece of his conciliation project – would thwart Fenianism,[48] while engaging the Queen's support in a way disestablishment had not: her 'own sympathies' would be 'in the same current as ours', especially as Ireland was the 'only real danger' to her 'noble empire'.[49]

It was a hopelessly misplaced belief. Early 1870 saw a significant rise in agrarian crime, especially murder;[50] the Queen's own anti-Catholicism

[45] See F. S. L. Lyons, 'The Two Faces of Home Rule', in K. B. Nowlan (ed.), *The Making of 1916: Studies in the History of the Rising* (Dublin, 1969), pp. 102–3.

[46] V. A. McClelland, *Cardinal Manning: His Public Life and Influence 1865–1892* (London, 1962), p. 173.

[47] Sir Thomas Biddulph to Gladstone, 29 Sept. 1869, in Buckle (ed.), *Letters of Queen Victoria*, I, pp. 628–9; Gladstone to the Queen, 16 Oct. 1869, in ibid. pp. 629–30.

[48] J. P. Parry, *Democracy and Religion: Gladstone and the Liberal Party 1867–1875* (Cambridge, 1989), p. 291.

[49] Gladstone to Granville, 16 Jan. 1870, in Ramm (ed.), *Gladstone–Granville Correspondence*, I, p. 85.

[50] Parry, *Democracy and Religion*, p. 292.

continued to frame her outlook on Ireland, especially the view that the Catholic bishops had only a negative influence on 'the passions of the people'.[51] But Gladstone's approach to the land issue was also flawed, combining positive engagement with personal ignorance of Irish conditions, ensuring unsatisfactory outcomes.[52] Thus while the land bill would succeed in marking a striking break with the idea of the sanctity of contract in land ownership by giving legal sanction to customary tenant right, it would fail to address effectively the areas it promised to, 'largely because the landlord's power to raise rent remained untouched and tenants evicted for non-payment of rent were beyond the power of the courts to help them'.[53] And to Gladstone's own limited ideas of how far it was proper to go in the bill must be added the pressures of British opinion opposed to measures believed 'calculated to produce a rupture of our social relations'.[54] Accordingly, Gladstone's Irish legislation in general was constrained by a combination of factors, including his own perceptual limitations, together with cabinet and public pressures as unsettling political and agrarian developments in Ireland unfolded.

Nevertheless, with land apparently being dealt with, more detailed consideration was given to how the monarchy's relationship with Ireland was to be reformed, an issue given added significance in conjunction with the possibility of Ireland providing a solution to the problem posed by the Prince of Wales, whose dissolute lifestyle contributed significantly to difficulties surrounding the public image of the monarchy in Britain. The problem, however, was that despite his personal affability and popularity, Prince Edward's character caused doubt about his ability to keep the crown out of party politics.[55]

Gladstone viewed Edward's character defects as a product of his existing position: 'acting as a mere cipher' with no 'exercise of his mind and intellect'. He envisaged a radical remodelling of the Irish administration, creating a consultative role for the Prince in which he would replace the Viceroy and, as such, perform the same duties – 'the shining influence' – in Ireland as the Queen in Britain. In this context, the Chief Secretary would take an enlarged role in Irish affairs and reside longer in the country. The plan would inevitably involve added royal expenditure which would provoke parliamentary objections, but both Gladstone and the Viceroy, Lord Spencer, believed these could be overcome. The only

---

[51] Victoria to Gladstone, 31 Jan. 1871, in Guedalla (ed.), *Queen and Mr Gladstone*, I, p. 219.
[52] Gladstone to Argyll, 5 Jan. 1870, in Matthew (ed.), *Gladstone Diaries VII*, p. 212.
[53] F. S. L. Lyons, *Ireland since the Famine* (2nd edn, London, 1973), p. 146.
[54] Gladstone quoted in Steele, *Irish Land and British Politics*, p. 300.
[55] Granville to Gladstone, 9 June 1870, in Ramm (ed.), *Gladstone–Granville Correspondence*, I, p. 101.

difference between them was one of emphasis. Gladstone envisaged a royal residence as part of a larger project, intended as much to resolve difficulties the royal family was having in Britain no less than in Ireland; Spencer, as Irish Viceroy, was naturally more narrowly concerned with a greater royal presence as a means of dispelling disloyal sentiment. In the meantime, however, both agreed that no effective action could be taken until a year after the land bill had been enacted and had a chance to eliminate the material basis of alienation.[56] At the same time, the issue of Ireland's relationship with the monarchy came to assume a significant place in the thinking of the founder of the Irish Home Rule movement, Isaac Butt.

V

Born in 1813, the son of an Anglican clergyman, Butt was educated at Trinity College Dublin, developing a conservative cast of mind that remained with him throughout his life. A former Orangeman, he had opposed O'Connell on Repeal in the 1840s and served as Tory MP for Youghal from 1853 to 1865. However, as a lawyer he developed professional links with nationalists, defending Young Irelanders in the 1840s and Fenians in the 1860s. Thereafter he became involved in nationalist politics, becoming president of the Amnesty Association in 1869 and founding the Home Government Association in 1870.[57]

The Home Government Association was historically of great significance. The Home Rule movement that grew out of it would define constitutional nationalist Ireland's relationship to the British state up to 1918. Butt originally conceived it less as an organised party, than as a pressure group for Home Rule, believing in the benign intentions of the British Parliament towards Ireland, and that Ireland's natural place in the political world was as a loyal, self-governing entity within a federal British state, an argument he rather naively believed the British Parliament would be persuaded by, through a respectful and loyal parliamentary campaign.[58]

The initial impact made by the Home Government Association was due to its ability to attract support from members of the Protestant landlord class alienated by disestablishment in 1869 and Britain's apparent

---

[56] See Spencer, 'Memorandum of a Conversation with Gladstone', 16 July 1870 in Gordon (ed.), *Red Earl*, I, pp. 84–6.
[57] James Loughlin, 'Isaac Butt' in S. J. Connolly (ed.), *Oxford Companion to Irish History* (2nd edn, Oxford, 2002), p. 69, and Thornley, *Isaac Butt and Home Rule*, for his career in depth.
[58] Loughlin, 'Isaac Butt', p. 69.

betrayal of their interests, no less than Liberals, nationalists and Fenians. This initial unity of political interests across the Irish political spectrum would not last, with the Protestant membership falling away as the Catholic lay and clerical membership increased, and as the incompatibility of these separate interests became clear. Nevertheless, the definition of federalism made by Butt in 1870[59] became the blueprint for Home Rule, and while its discussion of the monarchy's relationship with Ireland was intended especially to secure the support of Irish Protestants, it remained a crucial element of the programme, testifying to the movement's essential constitutional loyalty.

Butt fastened on the contemporary debate about the monarchy's relationship with Ireland – especially the advantage of an Irish royal residence – to attract Protestant support for the meeting in the Bilton Hotel, Dublin, on 19 May 1870, at which the Home Government Association was inaugurated. Of about sixty present at the meeting, about half were Protestant Conservatives and the proposal for an Irish parliament was carried by acclamation.[60] The Anglican Home Ruler, Revd J. A. Galbraith, who coined the term 'Home Rule', would, several years later, refer scornfully to some of the 'very foolish' speeches made at the first meeting, positing a royal residence and Viceroy as a solution for Ireland's ills,[61] but his comments do scant justice to the Irish political zeitgeist at this time. Prioritising the royal dimension to his plans was the most significant way Butt had of signposting the constitutional loyalty of the new movement, both to Irish Protestants and to British political opinion. In the explanation he provided of Irish federalism in 1870 the monarchy occupied an important place.

As a scheme of Irish autonomy Butt's federalist plan was designed to eliminate the weaknesses of the Irish parliament of 1782 – subject to Westminster manipulation – and improve on O'Connell's Repeal ideas. He proposed a parliament for Ireland to deal *only* with its domestic internal affairs, while reserving to Westminster control over all British and imperial issues. The plan was not without difficulties that would never be removed in the Home Rule period; especially, how was the difference between local and imperial matters to be made? And if Ireland was to be represented at Westminster for imperial purposes how was this to be arranged? Butt preferred to leave such questions aside until the case for Home Rule *in principle* had been won.[62]

---

[59] Isaac Butt, *Irish Federalism! Its Meaning, Its Objects and Its Hopes* (Dublin, 1870).
[60] Michael McDonagh, *The Irish Home Rule Movement* (Dublin, 1920), pp. 1–11.
[61] Galbraith in *Nation*, 10 Feb. 1877; Thornley, *Isaac Butt*, p. 93.
[62] See discussions in A. M. Sullivan, *New Ireland: Political Sketcher and Personal Reminiscences of Thirty Years of Public Life* (10th edn, Glasgow, [early 1880s], pp. 345–9; Thornley, *Isaac Butt*, pp. 98–104.

He was at pains to frame Home Rule within the existing constitution.[63] Statehood as expressed in his plan was twofold: the imperial Parliament and the monarchy embodied British statehood, including Ireland, in relation 'to other nations',[64] while internally Ireland's domestic Parliament embodied another. But the latter was no less a part of the British constitution than the former, which Butt illustrated by emphasising the crown's domestic authority in Ireland. Unlike the historically separate crowns of Scotland and England, united only in 1603, 'Ireland was always admitted to be one of the dominions of the British Crown.'[65] Moreover, whatever changes had been, and might be, made to the crown in England, under Home Rule Ireland would subscribe to existing constitutional enactments ensuring the Protestant succession.[66] Just as importantly, Butt's definition of the Irish Parliament as consisting of 'the Queen, Lords and Commons of Ireland' signalled its conservative character. The Viceroy would retain his existing authority and prerogatives, and be personally responsible to the Imperial Parliament.[67]

But Butt also added a further dimension to the role of monarchy by proposing the revival of royal prerogatives that had fallen into disuse in England, such as restoring references to the sovereign's commands on public documents and despatches, many of which now carried the relevant minister's name, and restoring to the monarch the right lost by the Act of Union of personally creating Irish life peers: 'men, distinguished in any field of intellectual advancement, as the Sovereign might think fit to associate with our hereditary nobility in the Upper House'.[68] With a view to the crown's difficulties in Britain, Butt remarked: 'It is in England, and not in Ireland that the elements which threaten danger to our monarchical institutions are to be found.'[69]

Butt's was the most sustained explanation and justification of the role of monarchy under Home Rule to be made during constitutional nationalism's long hegemony. Contemporaneously it was also astute. In a context where the monarchy in Britain was under 'infidel' and radical democratic attack, Ireland was presented to British and Irish loyalists as an environment where such threats did not exist. Far better for Ireland to have a Parliament and a Government that 'an English revolution could not touch'.[70]

Butt, thus, no less than Gladstone, envisaged a restructuring of Ireland's relationship with Britain in which the monarchy would have a significant role to play, but with it performing different functions. For

---

[63] Butt, *Federalism*, pp. 14–15.   [64] Ibid. pp. 15–16.   [65] Ibid. pp. 27–30.
[66] Ibid. pp. 29–30.   [67] Ibid. pp. 54–5.   [68] Ibid. p. 62.   [69] Ibid. p. 59.
[70] Ibid. p. 87.

Gladstone, it was the agency through which Irish loyalty to the existing constitutional arrangement between the two islands would be inculcated and expressed once the material sources of Irish alienation had been addressed, while at the same time providing a constitutionally and personally validating role for the Prince of Wales. For Butt, it was a means of authenticating an autonomous Ireland's membership of a restructured British state, accommodating the sentiment of Irish nationality with that of the wider British state patriotism. Both Gladstone and Butt, however, would find great difficulty in advancing their respective projects.

VI

Gladstone's difficulties with the Queen over Ireland would increase as she became aware of the extent of his proposals, while her dislike of Ireland was stimulated by the disclosure of an apparently Irish-sourced hoax involving the publication of forged letters purporting to be communications between members of the royal family.[71] Butt, however, clearly seems to have assumed the Queen would play a Bagehotian role in accommodating his Irish plans, if Westminster could be persuaded. Having no idea of the extent of her anti-Irish animus, he did not consider how the working of his federalist system might be complicated by the autonomous action of an ill-disposed monarch largely unconstrained by the conventions that applied in regard to the Westminster Parliament; especially so if she perceived, as was indeed the case at this time, that Home Rule lacked comprehensive popular support. Certainly the monarchical dimension did little to dissuade the Protestant membership of the Home Government Association from falling away as its Catholic membership increased. Moreover, some months after the circulation of Butt's plan the election of John Martin as Home Rule MP for County Meath was celebrated at a banquet where about half the guests refused to stand for the customary toast to the Queen's health,[72] an embarrassing occurrence given that each meeting of the Home Government Association opened with a declaration claiming an Irish parliament composed of the 'Queen, Lords and Commons of Ireland'.[73] Martin himself, an old Young Irelander carrying enormous authority in the nationalist community, strongly disagreed with some central elements of Butt's federalist case, preferring simple repeal of the Union and then an Irish Parliament

---

[71] See Victoria to Crown Princess Victoria, 8 June 1870, in Fulford (ed.), *Your Dear Letter*, pp. 281–2.
[72] *TT*, 7 Feb. 1871.   [73] *FJ*, 20 Sept., 4, 17 Nov., 14 Dec. 1870.

negotiating a federal arrangement with Westminster. Martin did envisage a symbolic role for the monarchy, but as the *only* connection between Britain and Ireland.[74] Martin would remain consistently 'off message'.

At the same time, Gladstone's hopes for a straightforward relationship between reform and the cultivation of Irish loyalty was complicated by continuing outbreaks of rural disorder requiring coercive legislation, and the outbreak of the Franco-Prussian War of 1870, which, given media advances, allowed the domestic mobilisation of support for the protagonists along sectarian lines.[75] But more seriously, Gladstone's hopes of capitalising on the enactment of his land act with the release of the remaining Fenian prisoners, thereby undermining the radical political mobilisation effected by the Amnesty Campaign, was thwarted by the Chief Secretary, Fortescue, and the Queen, intimidated by the declaration of a French Republic.[76]

The dynamics of the monarchy's relationship with Ireland, however, continued to fluctuate. The relentless Stacpoole kept the issue of an Irish royal residence before parliamentary and public attention,[77] while the Queen's attitude to Ireland was apparently mollified by a combination of Government coercion[78] and indications that the marriage of her daughter, Louise, to Lord Lorne, the son of the Duke of Argyll and technically a commoner – a novel departure for British royal marriages – was apparently as popular in Ireland as in the rest of the empire: 'it is quite marvellous'.[79] Against this background Gladstone sought again to promote his Irish royal project, suggesting that if the Prince of Wales replaced the Viceroy it would act powerfully to educate him in his future royal duties as sovereign, and allay present anxieties about the future of the monarchy, while at the same time having 'a very powerful effect on the public mind of Ireland'. The proposal for a royal residence in Ireland he regarded as supplementary to his plan and 'as valuable in itself compared to the present state of things'.[80] For Spencer, however, the residence issue had become an obsession, and

---

[74] Martin to W. J. O'Neill Daunt, 23 Sept. 1870, Daunt papers, NLI, MS 8047/2.

[75] Comerford, *Fenians in Context*, pp. 183–5.

[76] Gladstone to Spencer, 3 Sept. 1870, in Matthew (ed.), *Gladstone Diaries VII*, p. 352; Fortescue to Gladstone, 9 Sept. 1870, in ibid. p. 355, n.2; Victoria to Gladstone, 2 Oct. 1870, in Guedalla (ed.), *Queen and Mr Gladstone*, I, p. 256.

[77] See Stacpoole, Gladstone, *Hansard 3*, 203 (14 July 1870), col. 240; Stacpoole, Gladstone, ibid. 204 (20 Feb. 1871), cols. 490–1; Stacpoole, Gladstone, ibid. 207 (10 July 1871), col. 1341.

[78] Victoria to Gladstone, 23 April 1871, Gladstone papers, BL, Loan 73/10/720E.

[79] Victoria to Crown Princess Victoria, 1 Nov. 1870, in Fulford (ed.), *Your Dear Letter*, pp. 305–6.

[80] Gladstone to Granville, 3 Dec. 1870, in Ramm (ed.), *Gladstone–Granville Correspondence*, I, pp. 171–2.

his pressing of the issue in May 1871[81] presaged Cabinet discussion[82] and correspondence with the Queen on Ireland a month later.

The debate between Gladstone and the Queen, initially on the residency issue, matched, respectively, national duty as an issue going beyond the Irish question, on the one hand, with warnings about political uncertainty, unrealistic expectations and attendant disillusionment when these were not met, on the other.[83] In substance, the debate never got beyond this stage. The former Viceroy, Lord Kimberley, favoured viceregal abolition to secure the Union, but also because he feared the consequences of the Prince of Wales having a public role in Ireland.[84] Spencer, believing himself the embodiment of monarchy in Ireland, prioritised the retention of the Viceroyalty unless, and until, an enduring royal presence in Ireland was established.[85] However, despite continued public interest in the monarchy's relationship with Ireland[86] and apparent willingness on Gladstone's part to act,[87] the Queen's refusal to cooperate and his own reverence for her constitutional position inhibited Government inclination to compel her.[88] Nevertheless, with action on the royal project forestalled, options for defending the monarchy in a British context were desperately needed,[89] and Ireland still seemed to offer the best environment.

VII

Certainly there was no mention of a royal visit in the Cabinet discussions on Gladstone's Irish project, or in his communications with the Queen on

---

[81] Spencer to Gladstone, 28 May 1871, Gladstone papers, BL, Add. MS 44307.

[82] Cabinet notes, 24 June 1871 in Matthew (ed.), *Gladstone Diaries VII*, p. 513. The ministers were Kimberley, Spencer and Lord Hartington, who replaced Fortescue as Chief Secretary in December 1870.

[83] Gladstone, Memo. of a conversation with the Queen, 25 June 1871 in Matthew (ed.), *Gladstone Diaries VII*, pp. 514–16; Victoria, Memo. of conversation with Gladstone, 25 June 1871, RA VIC/D 27/74.

[84] Entry (24 June 1871), Hawkins and Powell (eds.), *Kimberley Journal*, p. 261; Kimberley to Gladstone, 28 June 1871, in Powell (ed.), *Liberal by Principle*, pp. 126–9.

[85] See Spencer to the Chief Secretary, Lord Hartington, 11 June 1871, in Gordon (ed.), *Red Earl*, I, p. 93; Spencer, 'Memo. on Royal Residence in Ireland: Position of the Lord Lieutenant', 4 July 1871, in ibid. I, pp. 93–5.

[86] *TT* (11 July 1871) duly picked up the issue, encouraging a greater role in Ireland for the large royal family.

[87] See H. C. G. Matthew (ed.), *The Gladstone Diaries VIII* (Oxford, 1982), p. 3 for a suggestion of Gladstone's encouragement of Stacpoole.

[88] Gladstone to the Queen, 5 July 1871, Gladstone papers, BL, Loan 73/10; Victoria to Gladstone, 5 July 1871, in Guedalla (ed.), *Queen and Mr Gladstone*, I, p. 285; Stacpoole, Gladstone, *Hansard 3*, 207 (10 July 1871), cols. 1341–3.

[89] See Williams, *Contentious Crown*, pp. 36–41, ch. 3, 166–8. Criticism of the royal family was largely republican in sentiment, focusing on the Queen's abdication of her public duties, royal dowries, aristocratic monopoly of land, the House of Lords and taxation.

the subject. That one was arranged to take place at the end of July 1871 speaks volumes about Government anxieties regarding the monarchy's difficulties in Britain no less than securing the Union in Ireland. State concerns in both these contexts also determined the membership of the royal party that would undertake the visit. The Prince of Wales was selected, clearly, because there was no prospect of persuading the Queen to undertake the journey; because of the manifest need to redeem his dissolute reputation in Britain; and because of the great success of his last Irish visit in 1868. The Duke of Edinburgh, the survivor of O'Farrell's assassination attempt in 1867, was included in the royal entourage and could be expected to garner some sympathy on that account, as well as remind the Irish people of the evil tendencies of Fenianism. Also included were the recently wed Marquis of Lorne and Princess Louise, members of the royal family whose dowries and allowances were the source of public controversy in Britain, and whose presence in Ireland as part of an expected successful tour would demonstrate the performance of public duties that justified their expense.

The itinerary of the visit, lasting a week from 31 July, was conventionally welfarist, while a ceremonial highlight was provided by the investiture in Dublin Castle of Lord Powerscourt as a Knight of the Order of St Patrick, a noteworthy choice given that he was a *resident* landlord and supposedly a good example to absentees. The investiture was also significant in marking a new departure for the Order. Anglican disestablishment had provided an opportunity for it to be permanently divested of its Protestant ceremonial. Together with the gradual elimination of its ecclesiastical officers, it would now be a national Order that all Irish people could identify with.[90]

Expectations for the visit were high given the Government's reformist legislation, but its context was not as favourable as that of 1868. Then militant nationalism had been defeated and a popular agitation on the Amnesty question had yet really to get underway. Now, however, the Irish political environment was very different, with agrarian strife ongoing; the Amnesty Campaign thriving and giving birth to a constitutional campaign for self-government; and Gladstone's land legislation falling far short of the 'three Fs'[91] that formed the substance of tenant demands. The Irish public arena, thus, was dynamically unsettled, lacking the conditions for the effective exercise of royal charisma and the consequent popular 'enchantment' evident on past major royal occasions. Moreover, expanding literacy levels and the impact of the

---

[90] *TT*, 19 July 1871.
[91] Fixity of tenure, fair rent, and free sale of the tenant's interest in his holding.

electric telegraph had established a single, communicative – and therefore imaginative – environment in the United Kingdom, ensuring that the crown's difficulties in Britain would be factors influencing how the royal party was received in Ireland. In this respect Irish opinion was now more aware of the ethnocentric condescension in British expectations of its success, and, accordingly, had a greater sense of awareness of what was appropriate and in keeping with 'national dignity' during the visit. In sum, it would be more difficult for metropolitan prints to 'spin' it for political effect in Britain than others in the past, though the attempt would be made to do so.[92] Though its lessons were ignored, the best indicator of this visit's success was that of Prince Arthur in 1869.

As it got underway the context-setting of the Irish press denied the hoped-for relationship between the royals and Irish Catholic opinion – uncomplicated and characterised by the enthusiastic paying of loyal homage and its acknowledgement. Even the *Freeman's Journal* settled for a sober statement of the constitutional utility of the monarchy in the Anglo-Irish context in recommending a respectful reception for the Prince.[93] Conscious of royal spectacle's ability to deceive through 'that fierce light that beats upon the throne',[94] it was especially concerned that moderate nationalism's position respecting the monarchy – as represented by the Home Government Association and Butt's *Federalism* – not be undermined.[95] More radical nationalist prints were less restrained. Both the *Nation* and the pro-Fenian *Flag of Ireland* found in the public controversy surrounding the monarchy in Britain ample material morally to discredit the royal party.[96]

Perhaps surprisingly, the Prince of Wales was not the chief focus of attention. As he was already well known in Ireland as 'the friend of Mrs Mordaunt'[97] the assumption may well have been made that, for a people undergoing a Catholic devotional revolution, he was already discredited, while detailed exploitation of the case would have been unseemly. Attention focused instead on Prince Arthur, and the recently wed Lord Lorne and Princess Louise. Prince Arthur was condemned for apparently disrespecting the tunic of a Fenian killed in raids on Canada the previous year,[98] Lord Lorne for anti-Irish statements reportedly made

[92] *TT* (24 July 1871) described it as 'the engrossing subject of the day' in Ireland, while ridiculing the activities of the Home Rule movement.
[93] *FJ*, 27 July 1871.   [94] Ibid.
[95] Ibid. For details of the Mordaunt scandal, see Kinley Roby, *The King, the Press and the People: A Biography of Edward VII* (London, 1975), ch. 7.
[96] *Nation*, 27 July 1871; *Flag of Ireland* [*FOI*], 22 July 1871.   [97] *FOI*, 29 July 1871.
[98] *FOI*, 29 July 1871. Three ineffectual incursions took place, in 1866, 1870 and 1871.

in a travel book on America.[99] The most serious attack, however, was on Princess Louise, excoriated for failing to respond, on the occasion of her wedding in March 1871, to an Irishwomen's petition organised by the Lord Mayoress of Dublin for the release of the remaining Fenian prisoners. It was only when they wrote a second time that an 'unfeeling and insulting' reply from a 'clerk' was received, to the effect that the Princess had no power to act in the matter.[100] It arrived on the eve of the royal visit, 27 July,[101] when its negative public effect would have been most intense.[102]

The attack on Princess Louise was politically astute. It was designed to undermine the welfarist credibility of the royal visit by illustrating royal contempt for Irish concerns pitched at the familial level. Inadequately prepared for and taking place in a politically charged environment by royal personages already morally and politically stigmatised,[103] it was unlikely that the visit could have achieved the results its organisers hoped for – something the *Freeman's Journal* ascribed to the 'democratic spirit' of the age: allegiance had now to be earned, unlike the 'blind King worship' of the Irish for George IV in 1821.[104] In particular, the failure to recognise that Britain and Ireland now constituted one communicative context instead of two meant that there was no real attempt to modify ethnocentric accounts of Irish attraction to royal personages. *The Times*'s expectation, that 'without attributing to Irish people a childish admiration for the great', the royal presence was 'likely to be more powerful with large numbers of them than the most cogent arguments in favour of the British connection',[105] was a validation of the sterotype it ostensibly denied. Virtually all strands of Dublin press opinion combined to refute it. The liberal loyalist *Irish Times* was surprised that London prints would attempt to 'make their glowing fictions go down with a public which has easy access nowadays to Irish journals'.[106] The Dublin press also united in opposition to a crude attempt at news management by anxious Dublin Castle authorities, who sought to subordinate it 'to a contemptible form of London worship'[107] by excluding from a Castle banquet reporters deemed

[99] *Nation*, 15 July 1871; *FOI*, 29 July 1871.   [100] *FOI*, 5 Aug. 1871.   [101] Ibid.

[102] *TT*, 2 Aug. 1871. Just as the visit was getting underway a meeting of the Amnesty Association took place in Dublin condemning the royal reply.

[103] See *Nation*, 5 Aug. 1871; *FOI*, 5 Aug. 1871.

[104] *FJ*, 1 Aug. 1871.   [105] Ibid.

[106] *IT*, 3 Aug. 1871. See also *DEM*, 4 Aug. 1871; *Nation*, 5 Aug. 1871. Only *DE* followed *TT*'s lead.

[107] *DEM*, 3–4 Aug. 1871; *FJ*, 3–4 Aug. 1871; *IT*, 4 Aug. 1871.

unsympathetic.[108] The Irish reception for this royal occasion, more-over, was influenced in a way none of its predecessors had been.

Having defined Ireland's relationship to the monarchy in the context of Butt's federal scheme, the leaders of the Home Government Association arranged a debate on Home Rule hosted by Dublin Corporation during the visit. It was not intended as an overt protest against the royal party, but in stating the framework in which Irish allegiance to the monarch could be freely given, it established a context for that relationship without precedent since the 1830s. Royal speeches that denied the reality of Irish conditions, public servants facilitating the royal visitors, and Irish MPs supporting a £15,000 annuity for Prince Arthur during the visit, were all subject to criticism.[109]

The perspective on the visit that the royal party reported to the Queen, however, was carefully screened to avoid its most contentious aspects, admitting some – unrepresentative – expressions of dissent,[110] but mainly upbeat about the Irish response,[111] and especially enthusiastic about the good effects of a royal residence, something the Prince of Wales was strongly assured of by Lord Spencer.[112] The Queen, however, drawing on her own long experience of the Irish question and deeply alienated from the Catholic Irish, was unimpressed: the visit was merely an unmerited reward for the 'troublesome, irreconcilable, and unchangeable behaviour of the Irish'.[113] A serious riot in the Phoenix Park at the end of the visit offered confirmation.

VIII

The riot had no direct or intended connection with the royal visit. A meeting of the Amnesty Association, calling for release of the remaining Fenian prisoners, was arranged to take place at the Wellington monument. It was banned on the day, but went ahead and was subject to a violent police over-reaction occasioning injuries to men, women and children. The meeting may have been in breach of a ban on public meetings, but the police action – condemned across the political

---

[108] See J. B. Hall, *Random Records of a Reporter* (London and Dublin, n.d. [1920s]), pp. 227–8.

[109] Entry (7 Aug. 1871), O'Neill Daunt Journal, NLI, MS 3041, vol.II: 1868–79; John Martin to Daunt, 5 Aug. 1871, O'Neill Daunt papers, NLI, MS 8047 (3); *Nation*, 5 Aug. 1871; *FOI*, 5 Aug. 1871; *FJ* simply gave a neutral account of the debate.

[110] Prince Arthur to the Queen, 3 Aug. 1871, RA VIC/Add A/15 1804.

[111] Lorne to Victoria, 5 Aug. 1871, RA VIC/D 27/91.

[112] Prince of Wales to Victoria, 3 Aug. 1871, RA VIC/D 27/89.

[113] Victoria to Lorne, 4 Aug. 1871, RA VIC/Add A/17/491; Victoria to Gladstone, 4, 5, Aug. 1871, Gladstone papers, BL, Loan 73/11.

spectrum[114] – was difficult for the Government to defend. In a context where it was anxious to demonstrate equality of treatment for Ireland, and where the right of public meeting in Hyde Park had recently been achieved amid much controversy, the Phoenix Park ban seemed to demonstrate that the Irish were accorded more limited political rights than the population of Britain.[115] Depressingly for Gladstone and his hopes of the monarchy's relationship with Ireland,[116] the riot occurred while the royal party was meeting with the Viceroy in the Park's Viceregal Lodge; and it was inevitable that negative associations between the two events would be made. The Amnesty Association cited the presence of the royal visitors in the park as the reason for the police violence, when in London communists, republicans and anarchists had freedom to 'assail the Crown, the Constitution and the Queen'.[117]

This last was telling. For despite the stream of British consciousness that easily ran Irish nationalism together with domestic 'threats' to the established order, unlike the 1840s there was little sympathy between British radicalism and Irish nationalism in this period.[118] Nor would nationalists have found anything to sympathise with in a British tradition which at this time apparently looked back to Cromwellian roots for inspiration.[119] The socially conservative nature of the nationalist mind-set, however, went unnoticed by authorities facing an enemy largely of their own construction. Refusing to accept that the police action in the Phoenix Park had destroyed the 'good effects' of the royal visit, Spencer blamed the Irish people themselves for the lack of 'moral courage' needed to 'put down disloyalty'.[120] In this context, the term 'Irish people' was a sign whose referent was an imaginative construct imposed on a complex – and perplexing – population. In fact, far from being an easily dismissed event, the Phoenix Park riot – establishing associations between royal personages and state brutality in a royal park – created the kind of popular indignation on which radical nationalism thrived. The incident would register deeply in local consciousness and be manipulated by nationalists when the Prince of Wales next visited Dublin in 1885, in far more

---

[114] Sullivan, *Troubled Times in Irish Politics*, pp. 138–42; British press citations in *LJ*, 16 Aug. 1871. Even the Ulster Orange leader, William 'Ballykilbeg' Johnston, condemned the police action: *LJ*, 19 Aug. 1871.

[115] John Martin to O'Neill Daunt, 8 Aug. 1871, Daunt papers, NLI, MS 8847 (3).

[116] Hartington to Spencer, 8 Aug. 1871, in Bernard Holland, *The Life of Spencer Compton Eighth Duke of Devonshire* (London, 1911), I, p. 87.

[117] Amnesty Association declaration reproduced in Sullivan, *Troubled Times in Irish Politics*, p. 140.

[118] See *Nation*, 16 Sept. 1871.   [119] Taylor, *'Down with the Crown'*, pp. 57–62.

[120] Spencer to the Queen, 8 Aug. 1871, in Gordon (ed.), *Red Earl*, I, pp. 95–6; also Lorne to Victoria, 7 Aug. 1871, RA VIC/D 27/92.

problematic circumstances. In the immediate term, moreover, it was seen to occasion a hurried and undignified exit of the royal party from Dublin[121] which conveyed the impression of failure.[122]

Negative consequences of the royal visit continued, with an attempt shortly afterwards to blow up the commemorative obelisk at Kingstown marking the departure of George IV in 1821.[123] And the visit seemed a failure not only in an Irish context. Gladstone's hopes that it might improve the image of the monarchy in Britain generally were also disappointed. As one of the institution's most forceful critics pointed out: it was a disaster with 'much public expense outlaid to no purpose'.[124] Moreover, despite an initially spirited defence of the police the administration eventually accepted responsibility for the riot and conceded the right of public meeting in the Park. Nationalists tested the right with a meeting on 3 September 1871.[125] Just as significantly, the Phoenix Park incident established an oppositional frame of reference for the reception of other high-profile visitors intended to reflect poorly on the royal party.

Thus, when, a fortnight after the visit, a French republican deputation visited Dublin to thank the Irish people for their support – in the form of an ambulance service – during the recent Franco-Prussian War, they were given a tumultuous reception that was only partly due to Francophile sentiment. The royal visitors may have been received 'cordially and respectfully' but, to Gladstone's great chagrin,[126] the reception for the French visitors was 'enthusiastic beyond measure'.[127] Probably the most serious consequence of the controversy in which the royal visit became mired, however, was its impact on the discussions Gladstone was having with the Queen on the restructuring of the Irish administration through a closer engagement by the royal family. The controversy effectively put an end to this round of negotiations.

IX

The royal visit, intended as an illustration of a hegemonic British theory of the Irish relationship to monarchy, instead strikingly exposed it failings. It was only plausible on the basis of Britain and Ireland remaining separate communicative arenas. The expansion of news, attendant upon a modernisation process in which the electric telegraph, rising literacy

---

[121] *The Universe*, 12 Aug. 1871.   [122] *FJ*, 8 Aug. 1871.   [123] *Nation*, 2 Sept. 1871.
[124] *Reynold's Newspaper*, 10 Sept. 1871.
[125] *Hansard 3*, 208 (17 Aug. 1871), cols. 1774–1837; Sullivan, *Troubled Times in Irish Politics*, p. 143.
[126] Gladstone to Spencer, 25 Aug. 1871, in Matthew (ed.), *Gladstone Diaries VIII*, pp. 26–7.
[127] *LS*, 19 Aug. 1871; also *Nation*, 19, 26 Aug. 1871.

levels and national self-respect were crucial factors, rendered it untenable. And yet, the need to deny the legitimacy of movements critical of the state and opposed to the Union militated against taking the visit's lessons on board. Drawing plausibility from the mass devotion to the Queen in Britain – 'In Victoria, a national idea finds its articulation through gender, race, class and ethnicity'[128] – faith in the monarchy as a quasi-mystical agency capable of eliminating Irish alienation from the state endured.

[128] Elizabeth Langford, 'Nation and Nationality: Queen Victoria in the Developing Narratives of Englishness' in Margaret Homans and Adrienne Munich (eds.), *Remaking Queen Victoria* (Cambridge, 1997), p. 13.

While unimpressive at the time, the progress of the Home Rule movement in the early 1870s indicated that the mid-nineteenth-century
period of nationalist ineffectiveness was drawing to an end. Of eleven
by-elections held in 1871–2, Home Rule candidates won seven. Of the
losses, Catholic clerical, no less than Liberal and Conservative, opposition was responsible.[1] Even so, it was progress that entailed the loss of
Protestant support for Home Rule as that of Catholics expanded, and for
our purposes this is of some significance. The place envisaged for the
monarch under Butt's Home Rule plan was informed very much by his
own Anglican conservative and cultural background. The loss of
Protestant support represented a weakening of connection with the
Irish tradition most wholeheartedly allegiant to the monarchy. At the
same time as these developments were in train, Gladstone was engaged
in the ongoing struggle with the Queen to thwart Home Rule by establishing a closer relationship between the monarchy and Ireland. He acknowledged the rising significance of the Home Rule movement in a major
speech at Aberdeen in September 1871, shortly after Butt's election to
Parliament.

Scorning Butt's attempts to square Irish autonomy with British constitutional integrity – unifying the kingdom by dividing the kingdom –
Gladstone argued that the central problem in Ireland was one of arrested
social and political development, which led the Irish from time to time 'to
become the victim ... of this or that political delusion'.[2] He instructed
his audience: 'Large allowance is to be made for our friends and fellow-
countrymen in Ireland ... the virtues of self-reliance and political energy ...
are not the creation of a day.'[3] Gladstone equated the development of
these virtues with the realisation by the Irish people that their legitimate

---

[1] Vincent Comerford, *The Fenians in Context* (Dublin, 1998), pp. 191–2; David Thornley,
Isaac Butt and Home Rule (London, 1964), ch. 3.
[2] Gladstone at Aberdeen in *The Times* [*TT*], 27 Sept. 1871.   [3] Ibid.

grievances were being addressed and that Home Rule was not in their interests. Nevertheless, while conciliation would be pursued, Westminster had a greater concern, 'and that was that it should do its duty'.[4] A determination to effect the state's 'duty' in Ireland almost inevitably foregrounded Irish 'character' as the fundamental problem to be dealt with, and by association the credibility of the royal presence as the means of its solution: 'What the [personal] selection of the Royal family gave to Scotland, reason of state policy make desirable in the case of Ireland.'[5] The political context – at home and abroad – in which Gladstone sought to engage the monarchy more closely with Ireland at this time, however, was unpropitious.

I

The European context in late 1871 included not only disquieting developments in France with 'revolutionary' British implications[6] – the fall of the second empire, the declaration of a republic and collapse into class war[7] – but also Bismarck's *Kulterkampf* with the Catholic Church and its excitement of the Queen's own anti-Catholic prejudices.[8] Against this background, Gladstone felt he could only persuade the Queen of the merits of his scheme if he had the backing of 'opinions of weight', such as that of the Viceroy, Spencer.

Both were agreed on associating the monarchy with Ireland in general. There was much agreement in their positions. Spencer had now taken on board some of the Queen's concerns, accepting that having the Prince of Wales as Viceroy would not do 'politically', given his character and the likely 'bad effect of a small [aristocratic and conservative] society like the Irish upon him'. But he was concerned that, if the Viceroyalty was to be abolished, whether an Irish residence would be established and royal ceremonial in Dublin revived. Gladstone saw the merit in this 'as a nucleus of society to encourage Art, etc.', but pointed up the weaknesses of the 'Irish Balmoral' proposal. This could not do for Ireland what the Scottish precedent achieved because of the Queen's very different

---

[4] Ibid.   [5] *Standard*, 1 July 1871; also *Illustrated London News* [*ILN*], 5 Aug. 1871.

[6] The Radical MP for Chelsea, Sir Charles Dilke, engaged in a speaking tour expressing strong republican sympathies: Stephen Gwynn and Gertrude Tuckwell, *Life of Sir Charles Dilke* (London, 1917), I, pp. 138–44. For the Queen's concerns about Dilke, see Philip Guedalla (ed.), *The Queen and Mr Gladstone 1845–1879* (London, 1933), I, pp. 308–9.

[7] Freda Harcourt, 'Gladstone, Monarchism and the "New" Imperialism 1868–74', *Journal of Imperial and Commonwealth History*, 14 (1985), 28.

[8] Walter Arnstein, 'Queen Victoria and the Challenge of Roman Catholicism', *The Historian* (Winter, 1996), 307–8.

attitudes to the two countries, and the fact that the expenses attending Balmoral were met, not by the state, but out of the Queen's own account. An Irish Balmoral acquired 'at the public cost' would entail stipulations as to residence that would be difficult to meet. Greater appreciation of the problems associated with an Irish royal residence left Spencer more concerned to defend the Viceroyalty: he accepted abolition of the institution 'in principle', but not in the near future.[9] Considerations of administrative reform led on to the question of Home Rule, which Gladstone was inclined to respond to by having 'joint committees of Lords and Commons' sitting in Ireland, Scotland and England to deal with private bills, and with powers to deal with other legislation when delegated to do so 'by special vote of the Two Houses'. This discussion, however, was speculative and not intended as a basis for immediate legislation.[10]

The discussion on the monarchy and Ireland in general reflected the difficulties royal obduracy had placed in the way of progress. The stimulus to more committed engagement with the subject would be a fortuitous result of the crisis that beset the royal family when the Prince of Wales fell dangerously ill at the end of November 1871. This would engage Irish popular sympathy despite awareness of the Queen's alienation from the Irish people – the 'Monarch never showed any personal liking for us whatever'; and aided largely by a distaste for 'infidel' developments in Britain together with a somewhat mistaken view of the monarch's political powerlessness which emotionally neutralised attitudes: 'We can hardly blame the Queen for making law of all the enactments that kept us subject to the English, since the royal prerogative to refuse assent is now the very deadest of dead letters.'[11] It was a constitutionally correct view apparently reinforced by Bagehot's recently published *The English Constitution*,[12] but took no account of the degree of the Queen's political influence.

The onset of the Prince of Wales's life-threatening illness, following on from an illness suffered by his mother, brought to a head the political controversy surrounding the monarchy, exposing its shallowness.[13] As a national phenomenon it is instructive. A domestic crisis of a monarchy defined largely through its embodiment of family values was made national and dramatic mainly through the effectiveness of the electric

---

[9] Spencer, 'Memo. of a conversation with Mr Gladstone', 14 Oct. 1871, in Peter Gordon (ed.), *The Red Earl: The Papers of the Fifth Earl Spencer* (Northampton, 1986), I, p. 98.
[10] Ibid.   [11] *Nation*, 14 Oct. 1871; also 11, 25 Nov. 1871.   [12] London, 1867.
[13] Philip Magnus, *King Edward the Seventh* (London, 1964), p. 114.

telegraph in speedily disseminating its ongoing developments across the country. The process was aptly caught in the appalling verse of the future Poet Laureate, Alfred Austin:

> Flash'd from his bed, the electric tidings came,
> He is no better; he is much the same.[14]

It functioned to facilitate the positing of the domestic realm of royal life – a nationally emblematic arena – as a devastating moral critique of nefarious republicans whose object of attack was the striken family.[15] Accordingly, the crisis seemed to offer dramatic proof of the ability of monarchy to cut through false and seditious ideologies to inform and shape identity among all social classes. In this way, a powerful, and inevitably misleading, lens was provided with which to interpret the Irish response to the crisis.

At one level that response blended with opinion across the state as a whole, illustrated especially in public acts of respect and sympathy by Isaac Butt and Cardinal Cullen, and easily interpreted as indicating loyalty to Queen and constitution.[16] The moral and familial example set by the Queen was well respected by the Irish middle class, and as an autonomous strand in Irish Catholic and nationalist attitudes undoubtedly found expression at this time. As the Prince's health deteriorated the natural concern for a *family* apparently about to face a great personal tragedy was clearly evident, and was undoubtedly stimulated, in the case of Cardinal Cullen at least, by the information that at the height of the Prince's illness the Lord Privy Seal, Lord Halifax, had sought, on behalf of the royal family, the prayers of the pope.[17] When the Radical MP for Nottingham, Auberon Herbert, sought to capitalise on the crisis by arguing that when Victoria died England would have a republic and Ireland Home Rule, the *Nation* condemned his utterances as morally offensive.[18] Certainly the leading nationalist papers united with loyalist prints in expressing concern for the royal family, with even the Fenian *Flag of Ireland* more restrained in its anti-monarchical sentiment

---

[14] Austin quoted in ibid.
[15] For the impact of the illness on public and political opinion, see Jeffrey Lant, *Insubstantial Pageant: Ceremony and Confusion at Queen Victoria's Court* (London, 1978), pp. 26–33; W. M. Kuhn, *Democratic Royalism: The Transformation of the British Monarchy 1861–1914* (Basingstoke and London, 1996), pp. 39–47.
[16] See the extensive reports from Ireland in *TT*, 1–17 Dec. 1871; also Irish reports of the English Catholic and anti-Home Rule *Tablet*, 2, 9, 16, 23 Dec. 1871.
[17] Shane Leslie, *Life of Cardinal Manning* (London, 1921), pp. 253–4.
[18] *Nation*, 9 Dec. 1871.

than usual.[19] On the evident recovery of the Prince of Wales the *Freeman's Journal* declared: 'having regard to the peculiar condition of things prevailing here we think the general anxiety was more marked than in Great Britain'.[20] But how exactly should the Irish response to the crisis be interpreted?

Unlike the apparently uncomplicated outpouring of sympathy and celebration in other parts of the state, the Irish dimension to the crisis was informed by some specific considerations. In particular, alive to the fact that the imaginative context of their participation in the thanksgiving celebration – the Thanksgiving Service for the Prince's recovery in St Paul's Cathedral on 28 February 1872 was a great public occasion[21] – was the United Kingdom as a whole rather than Ireland only, and conscious of how elements of the British press had sought to misrepresent the royal visit of 1871, there was a concern not to do anything capable of constitutional misinterpretation.[22] Officially, the Irish thanksgiving for the Prince's recovery consisted of a state procession by the Viceroy to the Anglican Christ Church cathedral accompanied by armed police;[23] and apart from the maverick nationalist J. G. Biggar, Chairman of Belfast Harbour Board, who abrasively condemned its 'servile' thanksgiving address to the Queen,[24] Catholic and nationalist leaders adopted an attitude of respectful acknowledgement. In Cardinal Cullen's case, it meant negotiating a fine line between respect for the heir to the throne and ensuring that the public perception of his opposition to Freemasonry – the Prince had caused offence during his recent Dublin visit by meeting the city's Orangemen and Freemasons – was maintained.[25] Also, the Irish response was hardly lacking ulterior motives

---

[19] *Freeman's Journal [FJ]*, 1, 4, 9, 11–16 Dec. 1871; *Daily Express [DE]*, 4, 9, 18 Dec. 1871; *Irish Times [IT]*, 11–12, 15, 18 Dec. 1871; *Nation*, 16 Dec. 1871; *Flag of Ireland [FOI]*, 16 Dec. 1871.

[20] *FJ*, 18 Dec. 1871. This paper's sister print in Belfast, the *Belfast Morning News* (13, 15 Dec. 1871), took the same view.

[21] Queen Victoria's Journal (29 Feb. 1872), G. E. Buckle (ed.), *The Letters of Queen Victoria* (London, 1926), 2nd series, II, pp. 145–6; Lant, *Insubstantial Pageant*, pp. 26–33; Kuhn, *Democratic Royalism*, pp. 39–47.

[22] *Nation*, 2 March 1872; *FJ*, 28 Feb. 1872; *FOI* (2 March 1872) expressed satisfaction at authoritative proof that Ireland 'is not and cannot be a mere province of the "United Kingdom"'. The liberal loyalist *Irish Times* (28 Feb. 1872) essentially agreed, though it pointed out that, unlike Britain, the day was not a public holiday in Ireland and the Dublin activities were ceremonially impoverished.

[23] *IT*, 28 Feb. 1872.

[24] T. P. O'Connor, *The Parnell Movement* (London, 1886), pp. 249–50.

[25] Cullen to Cardinal Manning, 15 Feb. 1872, in Peadar Mc Suibne (ed.), *Paul Cullen and His Contemporaries 1820–1902* (Naas, Co. Kildare, 1977), V, pp. 178–9; Leslie, *Manning*, p. 254.

given the significance of the monarchy in Isaac Butt's Home Rule scenario.

Instead of postponing a meeting of the Home Government Association set for 12 December by post, Butt thought it important actually to meet and express the 'heartfelt' sympathy of 'the whole Irish nation' with the royal family.[26] That the Fenian *Flag of Ireland*[27] condemned the postponement would not have been unwelcome. Even the *Freeman's Journal* made political capital out of the crisis, comparing closures of public businesses in the south and west of Ireland with the apparent absence of such marks of respect among Orangemen and landlords in Ulster.[28] However, nuances in the Catholic nationalist response to the Prince's illness were lost on a Viceroy only too ready to read Ireland as offering merely a regional dimension of a wider British experience. Spencer informed the Queen:

> It was remarkable to notice how the tone of the most Fenian and extreme papers ... was changed. When the Prince first became seriously ill these papers had articles stating that whatever the English and Scotch felt, the Irish were indifferent to the recovery of the Prince, but this evidently did not accord with the sentiments of the people who take low papers for the following week they altered the spirit of their writings and expressed sympathy for Your Majesty and the Prince of Wales.[29]

More generally, for Spencer the construction to be put upon the actions of Butt, Cardinal Cullen and the inhibition of the Fenians was that the Government's reform programme – the social engineering of Irish society – was effecting loyalty to the throne and acceptance of the constitutional status quo.[30] The illness of the Prince of Wales had opportunely created circumstances that allowed the policy's success to be demonstrated.

It may be doubted how far the Queen was persuaded by Spencer's argument; nevertheless, such interpretations undoubtedly revived proposals envisaging an Irish public role for the Prince of Wales. Ireland retained its salience due to a belief that Edward's character faults made him unsuitable for a career in areas such as foreign affairs, the army, India and arts and sciences,[31] and the fact that the one area in which he showed flair – philanthrophy – was considered by Gladstone as not forming a 'suitable plan for life'.[32]

---

[26] *FJ*, 13 Dec. 1871.   [27] *FOI*, 16 Dec. 1871.   [28] *FJ*, 13 Dec. 1871.
[29] Spencer to the Queen, 27 Dec. 1871, Althorp papers, British Library [BL] K1.
[30] Ibid.
[31] Arthur Ponsonby, *Henry Ponsonby: His Life from His Letters* (London, 1943), pp. 99–102.
[32] Frank Prochaska, *Royal Bounty: The Making of a Welfare Monarchy* (New Haven and London, 1995), pp. 107–8.

The issue of the Prince's public role arose as soon as the worst of his illness had passed. Gladstone had been encouraged by his household and several other members of the royal family in the autumn of the previous year, including the Queen's Private Secretary, Sir Henry Ponsonby.[33] Ponsonby now suggested appointing Edward Viceroy but with a 'responsible' adviser, while keeping separate the issue of a royal residence,[34] fearing, it would seem, that the latter might be doomed if tied too closely to the more ambitious plan which the Queen remained adamantly opposed to.[35] With a widespread belief in the Irish propensity for hero-worship, and Ireland an enduring headache for Westminster, the attraction of a scheme intended to assist both Edward's moral, and Ireland's constitutional, redemption simultaneously is understandable.

II

Confident of Irish loyalty – reinforced by a private assurance from Cullen[36] and some Irish Liberals[37] that Irish Catholics were not favourable to self-government – Spencer predicted that 'in a year or two it [Home Rule] will be as little thought of as the old Repeal cry of O'Connell'.[38] Gladstone, confident of the efficacy of his Irish reforms, concluded that 'the duties of citizenship' were being well learnt.[39] With Captain Stacpoole constantly pressing for an Irish royal residence,[40] Gladstone, supported by the Queen's Private Secretary, Ponsonby,[41] again broached the royal relationship with Ireland.[42] As against the influence of apparent Irish loyalty as well as court and Government support, however, has to be set not only the Queen's ingrained anti-Irish prejudices, but an apparent attempt on her life on the day following

---

[33] Philip Magnus, *King Edward the Seventh* (London, 1964), p. 115.

[34] Ponsonby to Gladstone, 23 Dec. 1871, in Guedalla (ed.), *Queen and Mr Gladstone*, I, pp. 322–3.

[35] Ponsonby, *Henry Ponsonby*, p. 101.

[36] Spencer, 'Memo. of a Conversation with Cardinal Cullen', 25 Feb. 1872, in Gordon (ed.), *Red Earl*, I, p. 106. The Catholic hierarchy, however, was deeply split on the issue: Emmet Larkin, *The Roman Catholic Church and the Home Rule Movement 1870–1874* (Dublin, 1990), p. 340.

[37] See, for instance, J. A. Dease to William Monsell, Baron Emly, 29 Sept. 1872, Monsell papers, NLI, MS 81373(3).

[38] Spencer to the Queen, 11 Feb. 1872, Althorp papers, BL, K1; Ponsonby to the Queen, 15 Feb. 1872, RA VIC/D 27/98.

[39] Gladstone replying to deputation of Ulster Liberals in *LS*, 12 April 1872.

[40] Stacpoole, Gladstone, *Hansard 3*, 209 (15 Feb. 1872), col. 467.

[41] Ponsonby to the Queen, 19 Feb. 1872, in Buckle (ed.), *Letters of Queen Victoria*, II, pp. 197–8.

[42] Gladstone to the Queen, 15 Feb. 1872, Gladstone papers, BL, Loan 73/12.

the Thanksgiving Service. A mentally unbalanced Irish youth jumped on to the royal coach at Constitution Hill brandishing a pistol and demanding that she authorise the release of the remaining Fenian prisoners. Arthur O'Connor – a great-nephew of Fergus O'Connor,[43] Chartist leader of the 1840s – was quickly overpowered and his gun found to be empty; nevertheless, the shock suffered by the royal party was severe.[44]

The O'Connor incident was a microcosm of the Irish problem as the Queen, a monarch lacking the ability to divorce personal sentiment from the constitutionally objective interests of the state, experienced it. She was incensed that he was sentenced only to expulsion from the United Kingdom despite evidence of his insanity and his empty gun.[45] Nor was her attitude to Ireland improved by the personal receipt of a letter threatening her life shortly afterwards and purporting to come from a brother of O'Connor.[46] These incidents provided the worst possible background for a revival of Gladstone's Irish proposals, exacerbated when the Prince of Wales expressed his determination not to go to Ireland unless at the Queen's explicit direction.[47] All the old arguments were mobilised against the proposal, together with Edward's objection, when in Ireland, to taking second place to the Viceroy, something which appeared to rule out even the prospect of a royal residence.[48] And yet, the differences between Gladstone and the Queen on the monarchy's relationship with Ireland belied a shared Protestant outlook that complicated the inculcation of Irish Catholic loyalty to the throne. Indeed, Gladstone's indignant reaction to the effrontery of Catholic bishops employing 'illegal' ecclesiastical titles when offering addresses to the sovereign on the recovery of the Prince of Wales[49] signalled the great failure of his Irish policy in 1873.

In a context where both were influenced – not to say intimidated – by the rise in British anti-Catholic feeling attendant upon the Vatican Council declaration of papal infallibility in 1870,[50] they agreed that royal personages publicly avoid any actions which might cause offence

[43] Entry (9 March 1872), W. J. O'Neill Daunt Journals, NLI, MS 3041, vol. II, 1868–79.
[44] See QVJ (29 Feb. 1872), Buckle (ed.), *Letters of Queen Victoria*, II, pp. 197–8.
[45] Guedalla (ed.), *Queen and Mr Gladstone*, I, pp. 338–48.
[46] Ponsonby to Algernon West, 6 March 1872, Gladstone papers, BL, Loan 72/12. The letter was of a type that would normally never have reached the monarch.
[47] Ponsonby to the Queen, 7 March 1872, in Buckle (ed.), *Letters of Queen Victoria*, II, p. 201.
[48] Guedalla (ed.), *Queen and Mr Gladstone*, I, pp. 340–1; Cabinet memo., 9 March 1872 in Matthew (ed.), *Gladstone Diaries VIII*, pp. 122–3.
[49] Gladstone to H. A. Bruce, Home Secretary, 28 Feb. 1872, in Matthew (ed.), *Gladstone Diaries VIII*, pp. 117–18.
[50] E. R. Norman, *The Catholic Church and Ireland in the Age of Rebellion 1859–1873* (London, 1965), pp. 414–15.

in Britain. Thus when the Prince of Wales was in Rome during Holy Week he was instructed not to attend Catholic religious services,[51] the kind of gesture that would have been well received in Ireland. When Edward did have a private audience with Pius IX questions were duly raised in Parliament about Britain's contacts with the papacy;[52] and when Sir Colman O'Loghlen again sought to remove the ban of Catholics holding the viceregal office, Gladstone thought 'the times are now greatly more unfavourable' than on previous occasions when it was tried.[53] So it proved.[54] Moreover, unexpected Irish developments contributed added difficulties, especially an explosive attack on the model of the statue of Prince Albert in June 1872 on the occasion of an inaugural visit by Prince Alfred, Duke of Edinburgh.[55]

Unproblematic in any other part of the United Kingdom, an Albert statue in Dublin with supporting figures representing art, science, manufacturing and agriculture encoded an injunction against nationalist agitation[56] – a structural and controversial statement in a contentious debate about Ireland's status in the United Kingdom.[57] Accordingly, Dublin Corporation, finding it impossible to agree a non-contentious address to Prince Alfred, offered none. In fact a popular reception for the Prince was unlikely once it became known that expectations that the visit would be the occasion for announcing the release of the remaining Fenian prisoners were unfounded, and that the Irish administration – in a gross piece of cack-handedness – determined on the implementation of a coercion act in districts of County Meath and King's County for the day he arrived in Ireland.[58] Thus despite the attempts of the *Freeman's Journal*[59] and the anti-nationalist press to present his reception otherwise,[60] neither the Prince's entry to Dublin nor the opening of an industrial exhibition – the ostensible reason for his presence in Dublin – drew great

---

[51] Gladstone to Ponsonby, 23 March 1872, in Guedalla (ed.), *Queen and Mr Gladstone*, I, p. 343.

[52] Gladstone to the Queen, 5 April 1872, Gladstone papers, BL, Loan 73/12.

[53] Gladstone to O'Loghlen, 20 April 1872, in Matthew (ed.), *Gladstone Diaries VIII*, p. 141.

[54] See cuttings from *Daily News*, 24 April 1872; *Globe*, 25 April 1872, O'Loghlen papers, NLI, N.292/P. 2542. But it is also likely that Gladstone regarded O'Loghlen's initiative as inopportune. A successful outcome would have complicated his own royal plans for Ireland.

[55] Elizabeth Darby and Nicola Smith, *The Cult of the Prince Consort* (New Haven and London, 1983), pp. 70–3. Spencer had sought to have the Queen perform the inauguration ceremony: Spencer to the Queen, 14 March 1872, RA VIC/D 27/99; Gordon (ed.), *Red Earl*, I, p. 100.

[56] See Fig. 10, p. 107.

[57] *Nation*, 1 June 1872. *FJ* (20 May 1872) had already praised the Albert statue and called for a warm welcome for Prince Alfred.

[58] *Nation*, 8 June 1871.   [59] *FJ*, 8–10 June 1872.   [60] See *Nation*, 8 June 1872.

crowds, something Prince Alfred did not disguise.[61] But the worst aspect of the affair for the Queen was the explosive attack on the night following the Prince's inspection of the model, though the actual damage to the structure was minimal.

In allowing Prince Alfred to inaugurate the Dublin memorial southern Ireland was being accorded a favour that was not granted to loyal north-east Ulster when the Albert memorial in Belfast was formally inaugurated during the Prince of Wales's Irish visit of 1871.[62] Moreover, given that the only real exception to the Queen's abdication of her public duties in the 1860s was her acts of dedication of Albert memorials throughout Britain,[63] a duty religiously adhered to and suggestive of melancholic obsession, her response to the Dublin attack was one of great offence and deep distress, occasioning 'more anxiety than ever' about Irish affairs.[64] The attack completely discredited an account of the inauguration ceremony given by Spencer, in which a large supportive crowd effectively smothered attempts by lower-class Fenians to make trouble.[65] Claims about the personal element over the Irish in instilling loyalty to the throne, and the Gladstonian case on England's responsibility to rectify the effects of past misgovernment,[66] carried little weight with a monarch immune to historicist excuses for individual wrong-doing. Nevertheless, political need and the Irish response to the Prince of Wales's illness energised another attempt to effect the royal project.

III

Singlemindedly committed to his royal scheme for Ireland, Gladstone was oblivious to the effect of the Dublin explosion on the Queen's already negative attitude to Irish issues. With Captain Stacpoole acting as the parliamentary outrider for a royal presence in Ireland,[67] the issue was not allowed to fall out of public view, while he had prepared a comprehensive memorandum making the case for an Irish role for the Prince of Wales.

---

[61] Col. Ponsonby to Mrs Ponsonby, 8 June 1872, RA VIC/Add A36427.
[62] On this subject see Courtney Boyle, Private Secretary to the Viceroy to Col. Ponsonby, 2 Aug. 1871, RA VIC/D 27/88.
[63] Margaret Homans, *Royal Representations: Queen Victoria and British Culture 1837–1876* (Chicago, 1998), pp. 157–65.
[64] Ponsonby to Spencer, 13 June 1872, RA VIC/D 27/110; Buckle (ed.), *Letters of Queen Victoria*, II, pp. 213–14.
[65] Spencer to the Queen, 6, 10 June 1872, Althorp papers, BL, K1.
[66] Spencer to the Queen, 15 June 1872, RA VIC/D 27/111. Gladstone thought Spencer had done his best to rectify a 'manifest twist' on Ireland in the Queen's mind: Matthew (ed.), *Gladstone Diaries VIII*, p. 168.
[67] Stacpoole, *Hansard 3*, 212 (1 July 1872), col. 432.

There was little to add on substance, but Gladstone emphasised that Ireland offered the only practical arena in which the Prince could acquire a training in kingship – 'In Scotland there is no regular centre of administration'[68] – and stressed the need for a royal presence following a proposed abolition of the Viceroyalty; the latter both an administrative necessity and constitutionally desirable given the office's party political connections. With the Viceroyalty abolished and a minister for Ireland appointed to deal with the practical business of the country, the conditions would be established for reproducing on a smaller scale the ideal model of the Queen's 'own relation to business'. In this context a royal residence would be needed for four to five months each year. Dublin would then have a 'Court ... placed upon a higher and broader ground than at any former period'.[69] Echoing Spencer's belief about the beneficial effect of the royal presence among the Irish – 'unless the best judges of Irish character are wholly at fault', Gladstone claimed – a new and very effective provision would be made 'for eliciting and training some of the best portions of that character' together with promoting a healthy tone in Irish public opinion.[70] In this submission and in a following letter some days later, he focused on both the positive and negative aspects of the Prince's character to support his case. Edward's 'social qualities' or common touch with the masses could be exploited to great effect in Ireland, while his presence there would insulate him from the corrosive effects of London social life for at least part of the year.[71]

The question, however, was whether Irish society could be regarded as a valid training ground for the arts of kingship. The Queen emphasised the societal differences between Ireland and Britain, together with the Prince's personal faults and the Irish expectation of 'power and influence' to claim that it wasn't; and if the experiment failed, the Irish would regard the Viceroyalty as having been abolished under false pretences and the Queen and the Prince as party to a 'deception'. Ireland, she concluded, was not ready for great changes in administration, being 'in a state of fermentation', needing a 'fair, steady and quiet' administration to enable it to settle down.[72]

These arguments had some weight and the Queen's objections compelled Gladstone to modify his ideas. He proposed *regular* consultation with the Prince on Irish business as a means of inculcating habits of

---

[68] Gladstone to the Queen, 5 July 1872, Gladstone papers, BL, Loan 73/13.
[69] Ibid.   [70] Ibid.
[71] Gladstone to Ponsonby, 10 July 1872, Gladstone papers, BL, Loan 73/18.
[72] Queen to Gladstone, 12 July 1872, in Guedalla (ed.), *Queen and Mr Gladstone*, I, pp. 359–60.

industry; making explicit the terms of the Prince's role in Ireland to
forestall expectations of patronage; and compromising on the abolition
of the Viceroyalty: it was desirable, but his plan did not 'of necessity'
require it, and it need not be associated with a royal residence, though the
latter was a long-standing issue which pressed for a solution. Nor was a
royal stay in Ireland absolutely necessary, while, as to the condition of the
country, it was now quieter than it was twenty years before when a
Viceroyalty abolition bill had actually been passed in the Commons.[73]
These compromises reflected Gladstone's self-denying ordinance when
in conflict with the monarch; and when he complied with her request not
to bring his proposals before Cabinet until she sounded out the Prince on
the matter she regarded them as '*definitely* abandoned'.[74] A final attempt
to effect his Irish plans motivated by a lack of alternatives – only 'mere
nothings'[75] – and reasonable doubts about the extent to which the Irish
people supported Home Rule[76] failed on the rock of royal obstinacy.
Henry Ponsonby put the epitaph to the matter by disclosing that
the Prince of Wales had expressed his own strong objections.[77] The
Prince's opposition was more personal and vehement than the mere
tactical acquiescence to the Queen's will suggested by his official biogra-
pher,[78] and this sits rather oddly with the impression Gladstone had that
he favoured his Irish proposals. But the difference can be explained.

It has been persuasively argued that the Prince and Princess of Wales
were concerned for the safety of the monarchy because of the rift that was
opening between the Queen and the Liberal Party, and, accordingly, took
care to balance her disdain with a conciliatory approach to Gladstone;
and that this sometimes led to compliant appearances disguising fundamental disagreement.[79] Thus Gladstone's persistence in his Irish royal
project becomes more understandable. Yet the cost to his relationship
with the Queen was high, greatly intensifying her personal dislike and
laying up problems for the future. And yet, perhaps relieved at the final

[73] Gladstone to the Queen, 17 July 1872, in Guedalla (ed.), *Queen and Mr Gladstone*, I,
pp. 361–6.
[74] Queen to Gladstone, 5 Aug. 1872, in ibid. In any event, she professed not to believe in the
idea of a training for kingship. She herself had no interest in public affairs before her
accession, and simply worked hard thereafter: Simon Heffer, *Power and Place: The
Political Consequences of Edward VII* (London, 1998), p. 24.
[75] Gladstone to His Wife, 7 Aug. 1872, in A. Tilney Bassett (ed.), *Gladstone to His Wife*
(London, 1936), p. 194.
[76] Gladstone to Manning, 26 Aug. 1872, in Matthew (ed.), *Gladstone Diaries VIII*,
pp. 200–1.
[77] Ponsonby to Gladstone, 21 Oct. 1872, in Guedalla (ed.), *Queen and Mr Gladstone*, I,
p. 381.
[78] Sir Sidney Lee, *King Edward VII: A Biography* (London, 1925), I, p. 220.
[79] Richard Shannon, *Gladstone: Heroic Minister 1865–1898* (London, 1999), p. 111.

abandonment of Gladstone's Irish scheme, she proved less opposed to the idea of an Irish royal residence *per se*. This question had predated Gladstone's plan and now that it was disposed of the residence issue re-emerged as a separate issue again.

IV

Spencer was assisted by the Chief Secretary, Hartington, who took on the task of preparing a specific plan for Cabinet consideration in early December 1872.[80] In fact, a possible royal residence had already been suggested in Emo, Lord Portarlington's house in Queen's County. Residence here, Ponsonby suggested to the Queen, should be short at first so as not to exhaust the Irish love of 'novelty'.[81] The case for a residence had been made many times by Spencer and he suggested it now as somewhere all of the Queen's children might make use of for short periods, not just the Prince of Wales.[82] With Emo, a specific and suitable property, available Spencer assured the Queen that Parliament would be willing to pay for its upkeep if purchase of the property was thought desirable. Moreover, to eliminate discomfort the Prince of Wales had expressed about according precedence to the Viceroy, Spencer suggested the simple remedy of reversing that order.[83] The Queen suggested that a residence be hired rather than purchased, and that no member of the royal family be pledged to a fixed term of residence – a lengthened stay would reduce the 'novelty' effect, while 'excitement' might be sought in attacking the royal resident.[84]

The success of the plan, however, depended on Gladstone's support, and he had only been prepared to *press* a royal residence in the context of his own scheme. With its rejection he was not prepared to put his weight behind the lesser plan, convinced, as he had earlier informed Spencer, that an 'Irish Balmoral' per se could not replicate the success of its Scottish parent. Accordingly, it was a surprise to the Prince's household when he failed to raise the issue with the heir to the throne who himself was 'quite ready and prepared for the subject'.[85] Thereafter, Gladstone was fully occupied with the last great legislative proposal for Ireland, his ill-fated

---

[80] Cabinet note, 10 Dec. 1872, in Matthew (ed.), *Gladstone Diaries VIII*, p. 256.

[81] Ponsonby to the Queen, 11 Dec. 1872, RA VIC/D 27/116.

[82] Memo., 'Earl Spencer on the Proposed Scheme for a Royal Residence in Ireland', 7 Nov. 1872, RA VIC/D 27/117.

[83] Ibid.

[84] Ponsonby to Gladstone, 11 Dec. 1872, in Guedalla (ed.), *Queen and Mr Gladstone*, I, pp. 387–8.

[85] Knollys to Ponsonby, 8 Dec. 1872, in Ponsonby, *Henry Ponsonby*, p. 103.

Irish University bill. For the remainder of his administration the residency proposal was not pursued. Cabinet approval for a royal residence in February 1873 did not translate into a parliamentary statement on the matter,[86] though in June Spencer still regarded the issue as one among others 'standing over for decision'.[87] The prospect of a favourable outcome, however, rapidly deteriorated as Gladstone's relations with the Catholic Irish, especially the hierarchy, worsened over his refusal to concede an Irish university with a Catholic ethos and under the influence of prelates.[88] The bill was narrowly defeated on its second reading: 278 to 284.

The issue produced feelings of mutual betrayal, on the hierarchy's part because of trust placed in Gladstone in 1868,[89] for the latter from an ultramontane 'stab in the back'.[90] The political consequences were evident at the general election of 1874, which saw the virtual demise of Irish Liberalism: fifty-five Home Rulers were returned for the three southern provinces, only five Liberals.[91] Spencer, however, remained convinced that, with time, fairness of treatment and just measures 'will eventually win the Irish as the Scotch to be contented with English rule'.[92] And yet, flawed as Spencer's understanding of the Irish question was, it drew plausibility from the uncertain progress of the Home Rule movement at this time. Certainly it had yet to be irrevocably demonstrated that Home Rule represented the unequivocal demand of the Irish people, while a parliamentary attempt to define the demand through a parliamentary motion in 1874 collapsed owing to Butt's ineffective leadership and indiscipline among the Home Rule MPs.[93]

Spencer and Gladstone had a broadly shared outlook on the Irish question, but the latter's was much the more subtle mind, one in which moral considerations of justice to Ireland and recognition of its people as a separate nationality sat in uneasy equilibrium with a perception of the security needs of the state. While opposed to Home Rule as a political option he was nevertheless interested in the forms it might take, and was even favourably disposed to a diversity of local institutions,[94] subject

---

[86] Cabinet notes, 22 Feb. 1873, in Matthew (ed.), *Gladstone Diaries VIII*, p. 308.

[87] Spencer to Hartington, 1 June 1873, in Gordon (ed.), *Red Earl*, I, p. 110.

[88] For the issue, see J. P. Parry, *Democracy and Religion: Gladstone and the Liberal Party 1867–1875* (Cambridge, 1989), pp. 359–68.

[89] Dermot Quinn, *Patronage and Piety: The Politics of English Roman Catholicism 1860–1900* (Stanford, 1993), pp. 26–31.

[90] H. C. G. Matthew, *Gladstone 1809–1874* (Oxford, 1986), p. 200.

[91] Hanham, *Elections and Party Management*, p. 185.

[92] Spencer to the Queen, 23 Feb. 1874, in Gordon (ed.), *Red Earl*, I, pp. 119–20.

[93] Thornley, *Isaac Butt and Home Rule*, p. 215.

[94] Gladstone to Lord Fermoy, 28 Jan. 1874, in Matthew (ed.), *Gladstone Diaries VIII*, p. 451.

only to the 'unquestioned control of Parliament',[95] even appearing more sympathetic at times to its supporters than to his Chief Secretary, Hartington, a proponent of strong coercive measures.[96]

Gladstone's attitude to Irish autonomy may have been influenced by Butt's prioritising the role of the Queen, and the belief he had whole-hearted support within the movement. However, in the same period as he seemed open in principle to a consideration of Home Rule, his Vatican pamphlets – 'war against the religion of the Irish people'[97] – illustrated the limitations of even the best intentioned English politician. His only con-cession to Irish Catholic sentiment was to avoid using Ireland as a case study to illustrate his arguments.[98] When he did make his only Irish visit in 1877 his sense of grievance against the hierarchy ensured that as a learning experience it had little value, while the Catholic attitude to him was understandably cool.[99]

Presumably concerned to assess to what extent his Irish reforms had inculcated sentiments of loyalty in Ireland, he visited a place where the Prince of Wales had planted a tree during his visit of 1871, only to be dismayed by finding that it 'has since been pulled up'.[100] Where he was given a good reception, the usual ethnocentric comments about Irish character being unusually susceptible to personal influence and the need to build upon this through a royal residence followed.[101] But for Gladstone personally the only result of his attempts to force his royal project for Ireland on the Queen was the intensification of her dislike in a period when his political rhetoric in the country also led her to view him as constitutionally threatening.

The origins of this concern have been dated to the early 1860s, when Gladstone's rhetorical ability earned him the popular description, 'The People's William', a name the Queen disliked. By the end of the 1870s, his agitation against the iniquities of Turkish rule in Bulgaria[102] had prepared the ground for the mass adulation that would sweep him back to power in 1880. His apparent rhetorical excesses, such as appealing beyond the wealthy and privileged classes to the 'nation', appeared to

[95] *TT*, 24 Jan. 1874.
[96] See Holland, *Devonshire*, I, pp. 94–5; Gladstone to the Queen, 2 May 1872, Gladstone papers, BL, Loan 73/12.
[97] Lord Emly to Gladstone, 10 Oct. 1874, cited in R. Shannon, *Gladstone: Heroic Minister 1865–1898* (London, 1999), p. 148.
[98] Ibid. pp. 150–1.   [99] Shannon, *Gladstone*, pp. 208–10.
[100] Gladstone to Lord Granville, 31 Oct. 1877, in Agatha Ramm (ed.), *The Political Correspondence of Mr Gladstone and Lord Granville 1868–1876* (London, 1952), I, p. 56.
[101] *TT*, 8, 9 Nov. 1877.
[102] The standard text is Richard Shannon, *Gladstone and the Bulgarian Agitation 1876* (London, 1963).

suggest the confusing of his role as a political leader with that of monarch, leaving Victoria faced with what appeared to be 'a Dictator'.[103]

Gladstone, in fact, should be considered as another figure of 'central authority', a category we noted that included the Duke of Wellington in Britain and O'Connell in Ireland, figures attracting great popular allegiance and with an authority bordering on the 'regal'. However, while both Wellington and O'Connell were great overmastering *national* figures in their respective contexts, Gladstone's authority was more narrowly, and politically, defined. Certainly he lacked the kind of national authority that allowed Wellington to overawe George IV on the emancipation issue in 1829, and saved the Irish Viceroyalty from abolition in 1850. Gladstone's was great authority politically demarcated – like that of Eamon de Valera in post-independence Ireland. In Victoria he had a monarch fiercely determined to assert her prerogatives, and whose influence would impact negatively on Ireland's relationship with the crown, in both its British and its viceregal dimension, when Gladstone returned to office in 1880.

V

The return of Disraeli to power in 1874 ensured that the proposal for an Irish royal residence or a public role in Ireland for the Prince of Wales would not be revived. The only parliamentary issue which had a significant Irish dimension involved the controversial Royal Titles bill of 1876 which would confer the title of Empress of India on Queen Victoria.[104] A measure opposed by Gladstone and the Liberal Party as well as much Irish opinion,[105] it provoked scholarly opponents of a title with obviously despotic connotations to argue for the Queen following the precedent of Henry VIII in the case of Ireland and have herself crowned simply Queen of India.[106]

As the bill proceeded to implementation, Home Rule MPs sought, unsuccessfully, to bargain Irish support for the measure in exchange for the release for the remaining Fenian prisoners. A petition signed by over a

[103] See Elizabeth Longford, *Victoria R.I.* (London, 1964), pp. 357–9, 427–9.
[104] Roundell Palmer, *Memorials, Part II: Personal and Political 1865–1895* (London, 1898), pp. 444–7; Stanley Weintraub, *Victoria: Biography of a Queen* (London, 1987), p. 418.
[105] See entries (10, 17, 24, 31 March; 4 April 1876), N. E. Johnson (ed.), *The Diary of Gathorne Hardy, Later Lord Clonbrook 1866–1892: Political Selections* (Oxford, 1981), pp. 265–9.
[106] James Bryce, Max Muller to the editor, *TT*, 13, 15 March 1876; *FJ*, 14 March 1876. Regional nationalist opinion largely followed the same line. See, for example, *Londonderry Journal*, 21 April 1876.

hundred MPs, including many Liberals, appealed to the Queen for an amnesty to mark the conferring of the title.[107] Disraeli, though tempted by a proposal that would have widened parliamentary support for the measure,[108] was no doubt mindful of the Queen's likely response in declaring against it on 22 May, provoking a hostile reaction from Radical and Home Rule members, and racial abuse of the Jewish Disraeli by J. G. Biggar.[109] Butt, together with eighteen others, including Parnell and Biggar, abstained from voting on the bill: twenty-three Home Rule MPs voted with the Liberal opposition and three with the Government.[110]

In Ireland itself opinion was divided. In loyalist north-east Ulster the bill's enactment was regarded with elation. In a region undergoing a process of self-identification as 'the Imperial province'[111] this addition to royal nomenclature, without acknowledgement of its constitutional qualification – it had reference only to India not to the empire in general – allowed self-identity and monarchical identity to be more completely homogenised. Attempts to define alternative, but less jingoistic, titular forms were absurd.[112]

The Liberal and Home Rule opposition to the measure, however, was taken to excess by Joseph Biggar. Biggar was a standing contradiction to Butt's conception of a monarchically allegiant Home Rule movement. A persistent critic of royalty, he acquired British notoriety in April 1875 when, observing the Prince of Wales in the public gallery, he had him ousted through the device of 'spying' strangers, a declaration which, according to parliamentary rules, necessitated the clearing of the gallery.[113] Biggar would soon, with Charles Stewart Parnell, be a leader of the Irish campaign of parliamentary obstruction, and undoubtedly did much to lend Parnellite agitation an anti-monarchist colouring.

The title of Empress imaginatively extended the popular conception of the monarchy, and when imperial practices were attacked by nationalists in Ireland they inevitably had an enhanced monarchical dimension. And yet, a coherent popular image of an imperial Queen, either negative

---

[107] Thornley, *Isaac Butt*, p. 278.
[108] Entry (10 May 1876), John Vincent (ed.), *The Diaries of Henry Edward Stanley, 15th Earl of Derby 1869–1878* (London, 1994), pp. 294–5.
[109] Thornley, *Isaac Butt*, p. 278.   [110] Ibid. pp. 278–9.
[111] James Loughlin, 'Parades and Politics: Liberal Governments and the Orange Order 1880–86' in T. G. Fraser (ed.), *The Irish Parading Tradition: Following the Drum* (Basingstoke, 1999), p. 35.
[112] *Belfast News-Letter*, 13, 24 April 1876.
[113] Henry Lucy, *A Diary of Two Parliaments: The Disraeli Parliament 1874–1880* (London, 1885), I, pp. 82–4; *TT*, 28–30 April 1875. Biggar's action led to a change in parliamentary rules.

or positive, failed to emerge, as nationalist attitudes to the empire tended
to reflect the country's ambiguous status – constitutionally integrated
into the United Kingdom, but with a colonial viceregal administration –
and with pro- and anti-imperial stances taken as the occasion
demanded.[114] The circumstances in which the latter would become
more likely were signalled by the agricultural crisis that hit Ireland in
the late 1870s.

VI

On his visit to Ireland in 1877 Gladstone assessed the state of the country
as socially satisfactory but politically without 'any daylight', by which he
apparently meant the failure of Liberalism to recover lost ground at a
time when the Home Rule cause was still relatively weak, and when an Irish
royal residence still retained its unwarranted credibility as a mechanism for
cultivating loyalty. Unfounded rumours on the subject circulated for the
rest of the decade. The monarchy's relationship with Ireland at this time,
however, was complicated by disputes between the Prince of Wales and the
Disraeli Government over viceregal appointments, with consequent royal
resentment and refusal of successive requests from the Duke of
Marlborough to visit the country during his Viceroyalty.[115] At the same
time, the Queen's alienation from nationalist and Catholic Ireland continued, encouraged especially by the trusted Theodore Martin.

Author of the royally sanctioned five-volume biography of Prince
Albert, Martin fed the Queen's Irish anxieties with misleading information about the supposed 'seditious' intentions of Parnell,[116] the rising star
of Irish nationalism.[117] Not only completely erroneous, Martin left out of
account the rising anxiety among all social classes as the agrarian crisis
developed. Somewhat incongruously – and coincident with uncertainty
in Dublin Castle about the future of the Viceroyalty, agricultural crisis
and the radicalisation of nationalist politics – the forms of viceregal
ceremonial and spectacle were undergoing a process of refinement and
elaboration.

---

[114] For useful relevant discussions on Ireland and the empire, see S. J. Potter, 'Introduction'
in S. J. Potter (ed.), *Newspapers and Empire in Ireland and Britain: Reporting the British
Empire c. 1857–1921* (Dublin, 2004), pp. 11–19, chs. 5–9; Keith Jeffrey (ed.), *'An Irish
Empire'? Aspects of Ireland and the British Empire* (Manchester, 1996).

[115] Lee, *King Edward VII*, I, p. 233.

[116] Martin to the Queen, 30 July 1877, RA VIC/D 28/19 C.

[117] R. A. Cross, the Home Secretary, put Parnell's growing influence down to his obstruction campaign in the Commons and to the Irish being 'a warm-hearted but excitable and
easily misled people': Cross to the Queen, 23 Nov. 1879, RA VIC/D 28/40.

They did so under the direction of the obsessional Chief Herald of Ireland, the Ulster King of Arms, Sir Bernard Burke,[118] son of the creator of *Burke's Peerage*,[119] and at a time when royal ceremonial in Britain began to develop from being 'inept, private and of limited appeal' to become 'splendid, public and popular'.[120] Owing to his expertise, Burke became a prominent and indispensable figure at the viceregal court and something of an authority on court procedure, nationally and internationally. Naturally, when guidance was needed as to how and when the Queen's new imperial title was to be used, it was to Burke that Irish, and other, inquirers turned for guidance.[121] In an Irish context, therefore, Burke played a role in the design and management of court procedure analogous to that of Viscount Esher, the pageantmeister of late Victorian and Edwardian royal ceremonial.[122] However, whereas Esher's ceremonial expertise capitalised on conditions that greatly facilitated the popularity of the monarchy in Britain, Burke's refinement and elaboration of vice-regal ceremonial took place on the eve of one of the most serious crises of the Viceroyalty in the nineteenth century.

VII

The Gladstonian project for the monarchy in Ireland deserves close attention. It was the only time during the Union that a Prime Minister undertook and pressed such an initiative – combining radical reforms to remove 'real' grievances and cultivate the goodwill that monarchical influence established in Ireland could translate into constitutional loyalty. It is thus striking in its ambition to create an 'organic' relationship between the crown and the Irish people. The obstacles to its success, however, were considerable. These included: an ethnocentric discourse on Ireland that served to mislead rather than enlighten; the opposition of the Queen; the limitations of the land and university reforms; and relatedly, and probably most importantly, an anti-Catholicism shared by both monarch and Prime Minister. Only on the dubious basis that modernity

---

[118] Susan Hood, *Royal Roots – Republican Inheritance: The Survival of the Office of Arms* (Dublin, 2002), pp. 18–19.

[119] John Burke (1787–1848), Sir Sidney Lee (ed.), *The Concise Dictionary of National Biography* (London, 1920), p. 171.

[120] David Cannadine, 'The Context, Performance and Meaning of Ritual: The British Monarchy and the "Invention of Tradition," c. 1820–1977' in Eric Hobsbawm and Terence Ranger (eds.), *The Invention of Tradition* (Cambridge, 1983), p. 120.

[121] See *TT*, 3 May 1876. An example of Burke's ceremonial expertise was the elaborate spectacle attending the Duke of Marlborough's leave-taking of Ireland in 1880: Hood, *Royal Roots*, pp. 17–19.

[122] On Esher, see Kuhn, *Democratic Royalism*, ch. 3.

would make such a supposedly primitive form of religious belief as Catholicism redundant does the misleading Scottish model of integration seem credible. Otherwise, the view – especially after the promulgation of papal infallibility in 1870 – that Roman Catholicism was inconsistent with true loyalty to the Queen made the kind of relationship between monarch and people that existed in Scotland impossible to realise. As *The Times* remarked during the controversy over the conversion of Lord Ripon: 'To become a Roman Catholic and remain a thorough Englishman are – it cannot be disguised – almost incompatible conditions.'[123] Accordingly, the limitations of the Government's approach to the Irish question prevented it from more effectively pursuing the state's constitutional interests at a time when the Home Rule movement was failing to mobilise *committed* popular support.

Of course, the Government could not have prevented the great agricultural depression of the late 1870s on which aggressive nationalism developed, but royal absence, it can be argued, ensured that no perceptible mediating force – such as, for instance, George V sought to provide during the third Home Rule crisis in 1914, and more significantly in 1921 – existed between the landlord and tenant interests. As it was, once the political consequences of the agricultural crisis began to be felt, the opportunities for resolving the Irish question on the state's terms became much more difficult.

---

[123] *TT*, 5 Sept. 1874; also Lucien Wolff, *Life of the First Marquis of Ripon* (London, 1920), I, pp. 119–20; Disraeli to Lady Chesterfield, 5 Oct. 1874 in Marquis of Zetland (ed.), *The Letters of Disraeli to Lady Bradford and Lady Chesterfield* (London, 1929), I, p. 156: 'Popish Peers cannot be construed, by any sleight of hand, into defenders of Church and State.'

8   The uncrowned king and national identity

It has been rightly said of the land war of 1879–82 that it was initiated from below; that when the masses became involved in agrarian struggle the leaders were swept along; and that in the case of Charles Stewart Parnell the land war 'turned him from a coming young man into the "uncrowned king of Ireland" '.[1] What the masses could not do effectively, however, was give coherent national meaning to events they were engaged in. The epithet 'uncrowned king' signified a focus of identity that transcended faction, and, in Parnell's case, was acutely attuned to the opportunities and pitfalls inherent in a complex and rapidly developing political environment. It was first employed spontaneously by Timothy Healy in the excitement generated during a fund-raising tour of North America in 1880,[2] as one of the more attention-getting aspects of a sustained campaign, both to enhance Parnell's leadership of Irish nationalism and to shape the nature of Irish national identity itself in one of the most formative periods of modern Irish history. As the pre-eminent symbol of Britishness, the monarchy was the most important institution against which an independent Irish national identity could be defined, and Parnell registered, in this period of crisis, as a countervailing figure of central authority and pole of loyalty. Accordingly, it is not surprising that the creation of a 'royal' persona for Parnell, legitimised by reference to Ireland's ancient High Kings[3] – with its cluster of associations evoking deference and allegiance – was identified as a significant element of the process of de-legitimising the authority of the British state in Ireland at the same time as it advanced the interests of nationalism. What made the process effective, however, was how the agricultural crisis of the late 1870s had functioned to effect a unity between the nationalist political class and the everyday, local interests of tenant-farmers, organisationally

---

[1] Paul Bew, *C. S. Parnell* (Dublin, 1980), p. 143.
[2] T. M. Healy, *Letters and Leaders of My Day* (London, 1928), I, p. 183.
[3] W. M. Murphy, *The Parnell Myth and Irish Politics 1891–1956* (New York, 1986), pp. 66–7 and *passim*.

united in the Land League for the purpose of protecting their interests and furthering their claims for reform of the land laws. The operational mechanism of the league was the 'new departure', an alliance of tenant-farmer groups, Fenians, and Parnell with his growing band of young enthusiastic 'lieutenants'. Unlike previous periods of agrarian unrest, what distinguished the years 1879–82 was the quality of political leadership provided by Parnellites. Their substantive achievement was Gladstone's Land Act of 1881, which conceded the 'Three Fs' – fair rent, fixity of tenure and free sale of the tenant's interest in his holding – and which effectively created dual ownership in Irish land.[4] Had they been conceded during Gladstone's first administration, the agricultural crisis of the late 1870s would have been less freighted with mass anxiety, the land agitation less significant, and the political rise of Parnell more problematic. As it was, the unification of the personal, everyday interests of the farming class with the nationalist interests of Parnellism served, for the period of the land war at least, largely to close off the non-political sphere of Irish life that Westminster administrations saw as that which monarchy could inform for the purpose of shaping Irish identity and undermining sedition. Nevertheless, the idea that a closer, more frequent, engagement of royal personages with the Irish people could successfully meet the Parnellite challenge was influential with Dublin Castle authorities.

I

The process of modernisation that many British politicians looked to as a means of facilitating Ireland's integration into the British state was no less central to the success of Parnellism as a national phenomenon. Along with the electric telegraph, an extensive railway system had been established in Ireland by the mid-1870s. In Britain, as we have noted, these developments functioned to facilitate the integration of the community generally – as the national reaction to the illness of the Prince of Wales demonstrated – but in Ireland during the land war they had a central role in assisting the mobilisation and integration of the agrarian agitation, and especially in facilitating Parnellism as the medium through which the political world was made comprehensible to the largely peasant

---

[4] For general coverage of the land war, see F. S. L. Lyons, *Ireland since the Famine* (2nd edn, London, 1973), pp. 160–202; R. F. Foster, *Modern Ireland 1600–1972* (London, 1989), ch. 17; and for specialised treatments, Sam Clark, *Social Origins of the Irish Land War* (Princeton, 1979); Paul Bew, *Land and the National Question in Ireland 1858–82* (Dublin, 1979).

population.[5] In the same way the nationalist press, which expanded by 25 per cent in the first half of the 1880s,[6] strengthened the ideological arena within which the national persona of Parnell was established.[7] This level of attention – greatly stimulated by the Parnell movement's own party organ, *United Ireland* – reflected the peculiar nature of Parnell's stature.

Another Irish leader of central authority, he was so in a more impressive way than O'Connell, whose historical project he claimed to be pursuing. His political rise was faster and the circumstances which facilitated it much more freighted with mass anxiety about living conditions, and therefore led to more intense investment in his leadership and expectations of it. His leadership credentials combined imposing stature and personal manner, a parliamentary record of uncompromising defence of Irish interests and acute political antennae that allowed him successfully to exploit to the full political opportunities as they arose.[8] Parnell's national standing, especially among the poorer, superstitious peasantry, is illustrated by the evidence of his speaking tours, during which he became a magnet for lucky charms, slipped unobtrusively into the pockets of his greatcoat,[9] and their reactions to coincidences between natural phenomena and threats to the uncrowned king.[10] Of course Parnell's appeal extended beyond the poorer peasantry to the population at large. The simple fact was that readers of Parnell's exploits at Westminster in Irish newspapers were following a dramatic serial which touched their own lives, especially as it affected their material interests. But while an authority figure in the tradition of O'Connell, Parnell differed from previous nationalist leaders in the constitutional tradition in a very important respect. Unlike both O'Connell and Butt, who were anxious to stress the loyalty of the Irish to the monarch, Parnell's alienation from the British political establishment was such that he set no limits, royal or otherwise, to his critique of British rule in

---

[5] M. J. F. McCarthy, *The Irish Revolution*, I: *the Murdering Time* ([only one vol. published] London, 1912), p. 129.

[6] James Loughlin, *Gladstone, Home Rule and the Ulster Question 1882–93* (Dublin, 1986), p. 29.

[7] Ibid.

[8] For more developed coverage of Parnell's leadership, see James Loughlin, 'Constructing the Political Spectacle: Parnell, the Press and National Leadership 1879–1885' in D. G. Boyce and Alan O'Day (eds.), *Parnell in Perspective* (London, 1991), pp. 221–41.

[9] Katherine O'Shea, *Charles Stewart Parnell: His Love Story and Political Life* (London, 1914), I, pp. 185–7. On charms in rural Ireland, see Sean O' Suilleabhain, *Irish Folk Custom and Belief* (1967; 2nd edn, Cork, 1977), ch. 8.

[10] On the connection made between Parnell's arrest in October 1881 and a destructive storm, see Healy, *Letters and Leaders*, I, p. 138; *Irish Times* [*IT*], 15, 18 Oct. 1881.

Ireland.[11] Thus as he pursued the interests of the Land League during his North American tour in the early months of 1880 he had no qualms about attacking the personal character of the Queen.

The temptation to do so in the American context was considerable. Parnell was appealing for funds chiefly from a post-famine Catholic Irish immigrant community fed on the myth that the famine had been, to say the least, exploited by British administrations for the purpose of ridding Ireland of its troublesome 'Celtic' community, and against a background in which the initial autonomous mobilisation of peasants had taken place in impoverished Mayo, where fear of famine was widespread.[12] Accordingly, the promotion of the 'Famine Queen' myth was a tempting mechanism by which to refocus popular indignation at British policy in the 1840s on to that of the existing Disraeli Government; especially so, as it struck at the credibility of the welfare monarchism that characterised royalty's social engagements in Ireland no less than in Britain.

The personal respect for the Queen in Ireland – which Anthony Trollope succinctly caught in his novel of the land war when the republican agitator Gerald O'Mahoney declares his 'worship' of the best Queen in history[13] – suggested limits on the extent to which alienation could be taken. That Parnell should attempt to crush it is not surprising, especially given that the developing conflict between the Land League and the viceregal system in Ireland had still the character of a zero-sum game: what was lost by one appeared to be gained by the other. Also, such attacks enhanced his radical nationalist credentials at a time when he was in competition for funds with other relief organisations – including one organised by the Vicereine, Lady Marlborough, an example of welfare monarchism by proxy.[14] Moreover, having already criticised the Queen for contributing nothing to famine relief in the 1840s, the opportunity to keep this theme before the public was occasioned when the Viceroy's son, Lord Randolph Churchill, contradicted his accusation.[15]

---

[11] The best general study of Parnell's political career is F. S. L. Lyons, *Charles Stewart Parnell* (London, 1977); and of his personal life, R. F. Foster, *Parnell: The Man and His Family* (Hassocks, 1976).

[12] See peasant testimony to the Special Commission into the Parnellite movement in the late 1880s: *Report of the Special Commission 1888 . . .; Reprint of the Shorthand Notes of the Speeches* (London, 1890) [*Spec. Comm. 1888 Proc.*], I, pp. 408, 434.

[13] Anthony Trollope, *The Land Leaguers* (London, 1883), I, p. 79.

[14] Its advantage for the Irish executive, however, was limited as relations with even moderate nationalism deteriorated at this time. See Marlborough to Gray, 26 Jan. 1880 in Healy, *Letters and Leaders*, I, p. 79.

[15] R. F. Foster, *Randolph Churchill: A Political Life* (Oxford, 1981), pp. 30–2). For Parnell's response, see Parnell to the editor, *New York Herald*, 1 Feb. 1880, in P. J. Tynan, *The Irish National Invincibles and Their Times* (London, 1894), pp. 147–8.

Parnell's attack on the Queen was propagandistically acute: it facilitated the reduction of debate about British rule in Ireland to a comparison of the respective personal merits of himself and Victoria, the former selflessly struggling in the service of his native land, the latter 'selfish, vain and vixenish'.[16] However, Parnell did less than justice not only to the Queen's contribution to famine relief in the 1840s but also to her response to the contemporary Irish crisis. Her contribution of £500[17] to the Vicereine's relief fund was not overly generous, given the scale of the crisis, and she queried whether 'the whole £500' should be given to Ireland as there was 'so much distress in England'.[18] But the size of the donation was determined largely by Ponsonby's advice as to an appropriate sum.

Parnell's tour was a great political success. He came back from America with his popular authority confirmed as Ireland's uncrowned king, and physically, as Healy noted, Parnell 'looked like a King'.[19] Thereafter the royal dimension to his public persona developed accordingly, sharpening the imperious edge to an already existing hauteur that could find expression in a tendency to excuse non-appearances at public meetings without explanation as part of 'the ethics of kingship'.[20] It was an act the nationalist population and press seemed only too willing to comply with. His return from America was recorded as 'royal', as were his travels in Ireland thereafter. Certainly the term describes the ornate ceremonial welcome prepared for him by Land League branches in Dublin on his entry to the city in September 1881.[21] By this time a popular cult of Parnell was well under way, one that reflected the integration of the political concerns of the Irish public sphere with that of everyday life. This was illustrated in the production of crockery and jewellery embellished with images of the uncrowned king, waltzes composed in his honour, and, especially resonant for a Catholic population, a 'Home Rule medal' with a bust of Parnell on one side and 'God Save Ireland' on the other. Appropriately enough, it was produced by J.J. Lalor of Dublin, a retailer of Catholic religious merchandise.[22] The cult of Parnell

[16] C. M. O'Keeffe, 'Queen Victoria and Mr Parnell', *Celtic Monthly* (June 1880), 512, cited in James Murphy, *Abject Loyalty: Nationalism, Monarchy and Ireland during the Reign of Queen Victoria* (Cork, 2001), pp. 200–1.

[17] Ponsonby to the Queen, 21 Dec. 1880, RA VIC/D 28/43.

[18] Queen to Ponsonby, 22 Dec. 1880, RA VIC/D 28/43a.

[19] Healy quoted in Frank Callanan, *T. M. Healy* (Cork, 1996), p. 34.

[20] Katherine O'Shea, *Charles Stewart Parnell: His Love Story and Political Life* (London, 1914), II, p. 160.

[21] See report of his 'royal' progress –'Here Comes the King of Ireland' – in *Freeman's Journal* [*FJ*], 26 Sept. 1881.

[22] Loughlin, 'Constructing the Political Spectacle', *passim*.

in Ireland was contemporaneous with the cult of Queen Victoria, the Queen-Empress, in Britain: a cult that was promoted in a similar fashion, with the marketing of household and personal goods and luxuries – crockery, cigars and tobacco, soap, postcards, tea, biscuits, etc.[23] – testimony to how well the appeal of both had reached beyond the sphere of public affairs to inform that of everyday life. At a time when popular devotion to the Queen was being promoted in Britain and helping to shape the image of the British as an imperial race, the cult of Parnell – the 'uncrowned king' – was functioning to counteract its appeal in Ireland; and not least because the Queen's monetary petitions to parliament could so easily be posited satirically as examples of royal greed against which authentic Irish distress could be counterpointed, as the journal *Pat* demonstrated in 1882 with reference to the Duke of Albany, the Queen's youngest son.[24]

II

The monarchical dimension of the Parnellite critique of British rule in Ireland was difficult for the Government to respond to effectively. Any explicit attempt to exploit the monarchy in defence of the state would have been unthinkable for politicians committed to the convention that the institution remain aloof from political conflict. Thus, although the Duke of Edinburgh had taken personal direction of the distribution of relief supplies to destitute people on the west coast of Ireland in March 1880, there was no obvious way the Viceroy could respond when Dublin Corporation, Ireland's unofficial 'national parliament', ignored the Duke's efforts and conferred the freedom of the city on the captain of an American ship also engaged in relief.[25] Nor could he when Parnell exploited a hunting visit to Ireland by the Empress Elizabeth of Austria-Hungary – with obvious negative reference to Queen Victoria – by assuring her London ambassador that the Empress would always be welcome in Ireland.[26]

For both Government and Viceroy the conviction that Parnellism posed a serious constitutional challenge to the state, rather than being a contextually explicable response to an acute socio-economic crisis, was

---

[23] See J. M. McKenzie, *Propaganda and Empire: The Manipulation of British Public Opinion 1880–1960* (Manchester, 1984), ch. 1.

[24] 'A Case of Real Distress', *Pat*, 18 March 1882.

[25] Murphy, *Abject Loyalty*, pp. 207–8. An attempt was made to redress the omission at the time of the Prince of Wales's Irish visit in 1885. See 'G. H. Y' to the editor, *FJ*, 9 April 1885.

[26] Murphy, *Abject Loyalty*, pp. 204–5.

strong. Playing the royal card against the Parnellite movement, however, required delicacy and circumspection. Ideally, the desired outcome was mass attendance at, or approval for, royal or viceregal occasions that could be interpreted publicly as satisfaction with the Union and rejection of nationalist demands for Home Rule. This would not prove to be an easy task, given the transformation in Irish social attitudes agrarian struggle was initiating.[27] The task was made more difficult by the sovereign in whose interest it was undertaken, deeply alienated from the Irish masses and fearful that Irish disorder could ignite social chaos in England unless firmly suppressed.[28] Moreover, her fears were sometimes expanded by the media. American Fenians, for instance, responded to the assassination of Tsar Alexander II in March 1881 by making threats against the lives of the Queen and the Prince of Wales,[29] while the 'respectful and loyal petition' on Home Rule for Ireland and the release of Parnellite 'political prisoners' by the Canadian Parliament in the spring of 1882[30] were undoubtedly regarded as well-intentioned blundering in court circles.

Irish agrarian agitation served greatly to intensify Victoria's dislike of the country, made more so by the return to power of Gladstone at the general election of April 1880. The combination of Gladstone and Ireland, resulting in policies she disapproved of, was only too likely to bring out the worst in her, but, frustratingly – the obsequious language of royal address misleadingly suggested her autocratic inclinations would be indulged[31] – policies she could do little to change. Only in the area of the monarchy's personal role in Ireland could she assert effective influence, and then nearly always negatively, though she was not entirely representative of the royal family. In fact, it was a common perception in Ireland at this time that the monarchy had a janus-faced attitude to the country, with the Queen's dislike alternating with the Prince of Wales's conciliation.[32]

In the event, the burden of cultivating Irish loyalty fell to the Queen's surrogate in Ireland, the Viceroy; and for Lord Cowper, a reluctant

---

[27] Loyalty assumed a stable social hierarchy, something the land war was destroying. See Michael Davitt, *The Fall of Feudalism in Ireland* (London, 1904), p. 466; Loughlin, *Gladstone*, pp. 105–6.

[28] Queen to Lord Hartington, 12 Dec. 1880, RA VIC/D 29/200. A Fenian bombing campaign in London began at this time: K. R. M. Short, *The Dynamite War: Fenian Bombers in Victorian London* (Dublin, 1980).

[29] See J. A. Godley to Ponsonby, 16 June 1881, RA VIC/D 28/74.

[30] A. B. Keith (ed.), *Selected Speeches and Documents on British Colonial Policy 1763–1917* (London, 1933), II, pp. 193–6.

[31] On this point, see entry (16 Dec. 1882) in John Vincent (ed.), *The Diaries of Edward Henry Stanley 15th Earl of Derby 1878–1893* (Oxford, 2003), p. 484.

[32] A. M. Sullivan, *Old Ireland: Reminiscences of an Irish K. C.* (London, 1927), p. 23.

occupant of the office when Gladstone returned to office, and who combined a public commitment to his duties with – as had many of his predecessors – a private sense of 'the absurdity of suddenly doing royalty to an immense crowd',[33] the task was complicated by a range of factors: the frequent public ridicule the 'mock' viceregal court was subjected to;[34] a campaign of vilification on the platform, in the press and in journals, emphasising Dublin Castle's historical role as a centre of Irish oppression;[35] the developing cult of the uncrowned king; and the fact that Cowper did not have the Queen's confidence, though his instincts were as coercionist as hers.[36] In sum, the period from 1879 to 1890 was to see the state apparatus in Ireland come under a hitherto unprecedented attack, the range including historical myth, location, personnel, policies and symbolism.

But perhaps most significantly, in emphasising the Castle's coercive role in Irish history and politics, its function as a royal site above party conflict was made largely untenable at a time when the great royal palaces in Britain were symbolic of the separation between the constitutionally representative and the politically functional (Westminster). In Dublin, however, as we have noted, the Castle, a 'third-rate barracks' (Fig. 13),[37] housed both the Throne Room and the offices dealing with the suppression of rebellion, agrarian crime and popular agitation, while its situation in a slum district, moving the novelist George Moore to describe it as 'arising like an upas tree amid ruins and death',[38] metaphorically, and strikingly, registered its place in nationalist opinion.

The exercise of viceregal pretensions, refined and elaborated by Sir Bernard Burke, was enhanced in the period 1882–5, when Lord Spencer had his second period as Viceroy. One of the relatively few occupants of the office who took his ritual and ceremonial functions as the monarch's surrogate literally, Spencer would nevertheless face the same royal obduracy on Ireland as he had a decade earlier, as had his immediate predecessor. Thus Cowper met a blank refusal when he attempted to exploit a lull in agrarian violence in the spring of 1881

---

[33] Cowper to his mother, Dowager Lady Cowper, 1 June 1880, in *Earl Cowper* by his Wife (London, 1913), p. 363.

[34] See, for example, Justin McCarthy, 'Dublin Castle', *Contemporary Review* [*CR*] (Feb. 1885), 47, 153–63; J. J. Clancy, 'The "Castle" System and Its Operation' in *Subjects of the Day*, 3 (1890), 81.

[35] Ibid; *Nation*, 2 Jan. 1886.

[36] See Cowper to Gladstone, 12 Dec. 1880; Forster to Cowper, 15 Dec. 1880 in *Cowper*, pp. 446–9. The Protection of Person and Property Act implemented in early 1881 was only enacted under threat of Cowper's resignation.

[37] 'Dublin Castle' in George Smalley, *London Letters* (London, 1890), II, pp. 140–1.

[38] See above, Introduction, pp. 11–12.

13 Dublin Castle, 1890s.

through a visit by the Duke and Duchess of Connaught; and also when he sought to have Prince Leopold, Duke of Albany, preside at the Social Science Congress in Dublin in October 1881.[39]

The congress took place at the same time as the Parnellite leadership was arrested, and when the Land Act of 1881 was implemented. Its President, Goldwin Smith, a former Cambridge tutor of the Prince of Wales, defined the congress's purpose as demonstrating opposition to 'any wild schemes [Home Rule] that could only end in ruin'. Also, W. E. Forster, the Irish Chief Secretary, made a connection between the congress proceedings and the Government's efforts to 'solve the great social problem of Ireland'.[40] However, when Smith's assessment of Ireland's 'disordered' state included royal neglect that only a royal residence could remedy, he succeeded only in outraging British opinion,

[39] Cowper to Lord Spencer, 30 March 1881, in *Cowper*, pp. 486–7; Ponsonby to Cowper, 28 Aug. 1881, *ibid.* p. 517.
[40] Congress report in *The Times* [*TT*], 10 Oct. 1881.

appalled at the apparent suggestion that the Queen take up residence in Ireland.[41] Smith's initiative was without practical effect, but not without importance. The publicity it generated helped ensure that the monarchy's relationship with Ireland remained a significant element of the debate on the Irish question in general. That question entered a new and highly dangerous phase with the imprisonment of the Parnellite leadership and the suppression of the Land League. Intended to establish conditions of normalcy,[42] that might, among other things, facilitate a royal role in cultivating Irish loyalty, the arrests only succeeded in removing a restraining hand on agrarian violence, while grievously damaging one of the few remaining linkages between the royal family and Irish Catholic opinion – trades exhibitions.

III

These exhibitions, as we have seen, had their origins in the Great Exhibition of 1851 and its Irish equivalent in 1853, graced by Albert and Victoria, and had the purpose of developing Ireland's commerce and industry with the hoped for effect of disabling nationalist agitation. With the imminent incarceration of the Parnellite leadership in the offing, such considerations informed Government thinking on the intended Dublin trades exhibition of 1882, preparations for which began in autumn 1881: it would be 'an excellent occasion on which the Prince and Princess [of Wales] might show themselves ... the absence of real royalty in Ireland is not one of her [Ireland's] least wants or political grievances'.[43] Nationalists, however, regarded these exhibitions as enabling the prosperity essential to the economic success of self-government.[44]

Government and opposition in Ireland thus cooperated in the organising of trade exhibitions with very different motives. In 1881, however, the fraught political atmosphere made such cooperation impossible, as hitherto muted antagonisms found public expression in the aftermath of the Parnellite arrests and when a loyalist-dominated Belfast Committee – formed to organise Ulster's contribution to the exhibition – withdrew when the exhibition's Executive Committee rejected royal patronage. The Dublin Committee's distinction between its admiration for the Queen 'as a woman, wife and mother' and its objection merely to the

---

[41] See Goldwin Smith, *Reminiscences*, ed. Arnold Haultain (New York, 1910), pp. 314–15; Arnold Haultain (ed.), *The Correspondence of Goldwin Smith* (New York, 1913), p. 99.

[42] See Lord Spencer to the Queen, 21 Dec. 1881, in Peter Gordon (ed.), *The Red Earl: The Papers of the Fifth Earl Spencer, 1835–1910* (Northampton, 1986), I, pp. 178–9.

[43] Hamilton to Ponsonby, 12 Dec. 1881, RA VIC/D 28/82.

[44] See Parnell at Cork, *FJ*, 3 Oct. 1881.

way in which 'her name had been attached to many things that had been done in this country' failed to dissuade the Ulstermen. Certainly not all nationalists endorsed Parnellite militancy on the issue, but the temper of popular opinion made compliance with their wishes unavoidable.[45]

A Dublin trades exhibition did eventually take place, in March 1882, without either royal or viceregal patronage. It was an explicitly nationalist event, being opened on the same day as the O'Connell monument was unveiled in Sackville Street. Designed to demonstrate the extent of popular alienation from the viceregal administration, the two events attracted the largest crowds ever seen in central Dublin in the nineteenth century.[46] From its initiation in the early 1860s, it took the heightened nationalist consciousness of the land war to deliver the funds to complete the O'Connell memorial. As such it can be seen as a culmination point to the process of asserting the nationalist identity of the Irish landscape through monumental signifiers that began in the later 1850s. Certainly its position in the main thoroughfare of the Irish capital represented a striking assertion of nationalist purpose. A viceregal procession taking a direct route from the Castle to Sackville Street was met on arrival by an imposing situational statement of nationalist ambition that relegated to a secondary position the monument to the hero of Trafalgar, Lord Nelson (Fig. 14). By this time the Parnell movement had asserted its dominance in Irish politics; and by this time also Viceroy Cowper had decided to resign, repelled, among other things, by the rituals of 'a mock court', but especially by the understanding between Gladstone and Parnell known as the 'Kilmainham Treaty', under which the nationalist leadership was released from prison.[47] The compact also provoked the resignation of W. E. Forster, who had planned to combine the offices of Viceroy and Chief Secretary – the symbolic/constitutional and the functional/administrative. In effect it would have meant the revival of a post that had been abolished in the late seventeenth century, Lord Deputy.[48]

Coercionist at a time when Gladstone was keen to abandon it, it is highly unlikely that he would have complied with Forster's wishes. Gladstone was,

---

[45] For comprehensive and fairly objective coverage, see *Belfast News-Letter* [*BNL*], 17, 23 Dec. 1881.

[46] See Gary Owens, 'Nationalist Movements in Ireland, c.1870–1914: Symbolism and Ritual' in Raymond Gillespie and Brian Kennedy (eds.), *Ireland: Art into History* (Dublin, 1994), p. 106. An attempt made on the life of the Queen at this time was erroneously assumed in Britain to be Irish-inspired. But as Cowper informed Victoria: the attempt was condemned 'even in this country [Ireland]': Cowper to the Queen, 3 March 1882, RA VIC/D 28/127.

[47] Cowper to Gladstone, 2 May 1882 in *Cowper*, pp. 579–80.

[48] On this office, see Hiram Morgan and S. J. Connolly, 'Lord Deputy' in S. J. Connolly (ed.), *The Oxford Companion to Irish History* (Oxford, 1998), pp. 328–9.

14 O'Connell Monument, Dublin.

though, happy to accept the proposal when made by Cowper's replacement, Lord Spencer, a respected former Viceroy who was prepared to
take up the reins again, together with the seat in Cabinet that was
normally the preserve of the Chief Secretary.[49] Spencer, accordingly,
would perform a role emblematic of the integration of coercive and
monarchical symbolism structurally embodied in Dublin Castle itself,
something he would later regret.

Spencer's personal powers and authority were further enhanced as
a result of the Phoenix Park murders – the killing of T. H. Burke,
Undersecretary at Dublin Castle, and Lord Frederick Cavendish, a newly
appointed Irish Chief Secretary.[50] Cavendish's replacement, George Otto

---

[49] Spencer, 'More Notes on the Functions of Lord Lieutenant and Chief Secretary',
22 April 1882 in Gordon (ed.), *Red Earl*, I, p. 186.
[50] See Lyons, *Parnell*, pp. 207–20, 231–4.

Trevelyan, was a well-meaning but overly sensitive, weak politician, who would find his office extremely stressful,[51] and thus, even had he wanted to, was incapable of acting as a restraining influence on Spencer. The murders provoked a radical reorganisation of the Castle administration and the Dublin Metropolitan Police, together with a coercion act that gave the Viceroy personal powers to deal with Irish crime and disorder, including the establishment of non-jury trials and virtually unlimited powers of search.[52] But for our purposes, Spencer is especially significant for his long-held commitment to the belief that a closer connection between the royal family and the Irish masses was an essential element in the consolidation of the Union. It was a belief not dented in the least by the rise of Parnellism. Indeed, the mass gatherings that Parnell attracted could be read as validating the perception of the Catholic Irish as peculiarly susceptible to personal authority: the task was, 'in an image worshipping country', to redirect, with some urgency, that attraction towards royal personages.[53]

The task, however, was not made easier by a Queen whose alienation from 'semi-savage' nationalist Ireland was greatly intensified by the Phoenix Park murders, for which she blamed 'Mr Gladstone and his violent, radical advisers'.[54] Moreover, though Spencer had determined to use the formidable coercive powers he acquired only in 'emergencies', he was faced with a Parnellite Party that was about to redirect its energies away from agrarian agitation towards Home Rule, and which would do so by keeping Ireland in a state of emergency through aggressive agitation against the Irish executive.[55] Accordingly, it would prove extremely difficult for Spencer to perform his specifically viceregal functions – the monarch's surrogate uncontaminated by involvement in party conflict – and which he took extremely seriously.

Convinced that when he received a good public reception it represented the failure of agitators to dissuade the natural loyalty of the people from finding expression, it yet took only a simple accident, such as a birdcage falling from an upstairs window during a viceregal procession in Dublin, for panic and confusion out of all proportion to the incident to prevail.[56] Viceregal ritual continued to be performed in very trying circumstances, and usually with the vicinity and the viceregal procession itself heavily invested with plain-clothes policemen.[57] And yet, hostile

---

[51] Trevelyan was appointed, apparently, because he was believed to have 'some genius and imagination', qualities believed to be 'useful' in dealing with the Irish: Lord Northcote to Spencer, 7 May 1882, in Gordon (ed.), *Red Earl*, I, p. 193.

[52] Ibid. p. 188.   [53] Spencer to Harcourt, 26 May 1882, ibid. p. 202.

[54] RA QVJ: 6 May 1882.   [55] See Loughlin, *Gladstone*, ch. 1.

[56] See Elizabeth, Countess of Fingall, *Seventy Years Young* (New York, 1939), p. 127.

[57] See, for example, entry (1, 2 July 1882), Lady Alice Howard Diary, NLI, MS 3604.

as the Parnellites were to Dublin Castle, nationalist attitudes to the Viceroyalty as a constitutional office were somewhat ambiguous.

IV

In large measure this was a function of Parnell's refusal to define specifically what Home Rule should entail, reasoning quite rightly that nationalist unity would be best maintained by support for the abstract slogan, while also allowing for changing political conditions to be best exploited. However, when Justin McCarthy introduced a bill in the Commons proposing the abolition of the office in 1883[58] it exposed fault lines within the broad nationalist family. Anti-Parnellites argued, as had O'Connell and Butt, for its retention as a national signifier, proposing instead abolition of the ban on Catholic officeholders together with a royal occupant to depoliticise the office.[59] Divided nationalist opinion was also evident in the nationalist press.

This was unremarkable, except for the participation of W. J. O'Neill Daunt, a veteran Repealer and associate of O'Connell, and who enlisted the Liberator in the ranks of the anti-abolitionists.[60] But as the debate developed, it moved beyond the practical merits of abolition to address the issue's metaphoric significance as one dividing elitists and popular democrats in the broad nationalist family. Replying to Daunt, John M'Grath argued:

His ideas are apparently those of Grattan. They suited a time when Ireland looked to the aristocracy and gentry as the great pioneers of her freedom, and a true source of national pride. But matters have been reversed since then, and Mr Daunt, with other leading politicians, should adopt their minds to existing combinations.[61]

It was an acute observation. Daunt would never have admitted it publicly, but privately he was appalled at the apparently 'revolutionary' aspects of Parnellism and the prospect of Home Rule under such a movement, much preferring the rule of a native aristocracy made alive to its national responsibilities and unquestionably loyal to the Queen.[62]

---

[58] Justin McCarthy, *Hansard Parliamentary Debates*, 3rd ser. [*Hansard 3*], 280 (20 June 1883), cols. 1076–83.

[59] See E. D. Gray, *Hansard 3*, 280 (20 June 1883), cols. 1089–90; Richard O'Shaugnessy, cols. 1091; F. H. O'Donnell, col. 1093; Philip Callan, cols. 1091–2.

[60] Daunt to the editor, *Nation*, 7 July 1883.

[61] M'Grath to the editor, *Nation*, 11 Aug. 1883.

[62] See Daunt to W. E. H. Lecky, 8 June 1882, MS 1827–36, Trinity College Dublin, Lecky Correspondence, 257. For similar elitist opinions, see also Augusta Goold to the editor, *Nation*, 18 Aug. 1883; Goold to Daunt, 21 July, 1 Aug. 1883, W. J. O'Neill Daunt papers, NLI, MS 8045.

The subtext to the debate on abolition of the Viceroyalty was the kind of people the Catholic Irish were, and the extent to which it was possible to shape their identity. But while the anti-abolitionists generally expressed many of the sentiments Spencer wished to cultivate, their brand of nationalism was not in the ascendant. Both Gladstone and Spencer, however, heartened by the Viceroyalty controversy,[63] remained confident of undermining Parnellism, even foolishly discounting the inevitable electoral consequences in Ireland of the great franchise reforms of 1884–5.[64] And yet, the Parnellite movement was much less radical than it appeared. The rhetorical violence of its campaign against Spencer disguised a social conservatism that characterised leader and led,[65] and whose politics were attuned to the kind of accommodations they could persuade the British Parliament to make. When Daunt made the case for retention of the Viceroyalty to Parnell in 1885, the latter, while expressing a preference for abolition, nevertheless readily agreed that the case had merit.[66]

As the focus of their vilification it is perhaps understandable that Spencer underestimated Parnellism; but he also remained blind to constraints on Government ability to conciliate Ireland's Catholic population, not least the need to retain the support of the state's problematic Orange supporters in Ulster.[67] Accordingly, when William Shaw, a leading anti-Parnellite MP, introduced a bill to remove the ban on Catholics holding the viceregal office, Gladstone could privately acknowledge Cabinet approval for the measure, while publicly refusing the support that would have ensured its enactment.[68]

V

The year 1885 was to see the climax of the struggle between Parnellites and the Spencer regime. It was a year in which a general election would have to be held following the radical franchise reforms of 1884–5 and, with this in mind, both the efforts of the Viceroy to thwart Parnellism and

---

[63] Spencer to the Queen, 17 Oct. 1883, Althorp papers, British Library [BL], K2.

[64] Gladstone to Hartington, 29 Dec. 1883, in H. C. G. Matthew (ed.), *Gladstone Diaries XI* (Oxford, 1990), pp. 86–7; Spencer to Hartington, 21 Oct. 1883, in Gordon (ed.), *Red Earl*, I, pp. 251–4, 260.

[65] See Loughlin, *Gladstone*, p. 20.

[66] Parnell to Daunt, 15 July 1885, C. S. Parnell papers, NLI, MS 5934.

[67] Spencer ruefully admitted that in a doomsday situation in Ireland they might well have to consider arming the Orangemen: James Loughlin, 'Parades and Politics: Liberal Governments and the Orange Order 1880–86' in T. G. Fraser (ed.), *The Irish Parading Tradition: Following the Drum* (London and Basingstoke, 2000), p. 38.

[68] Gladstone to Spencer, 8 April 1884, Matthew (ed.), *Gladstone Diaries XI*, pp. 91–2.

the latter's response were attended to with greater urgency. Convinced that he had made considerable progress in re-establishing the 'natural' social order of Ireland, Spencer yet feared an aggressive Parnellite movement seeking to alienate the Irish people, not just from the Irish executive, but from the royal family also.[69] Spencer regarded this development as partly his own fault, a product of the 'emergency' measures he had been forced to implement and of his merging of the symbolic and administrative functions of Viceroy and Chief Secretary, which had, by proxy, mired the royal family in political controversy.[70] The nationalist journal, *Pat*, had already addressed the issue in a political cartoon depicting Spencer as a Viceroy surrounded by police above a legend wittily punning on the words 'levy' and 'levee' to illustrate the impossibility of imposing loyalty on the Irish people,[71] while in April Parnell was reported as having been deprived of the Commission of the Peace for sitting silently at a banquet when the Queen's name was hissed.[72] Spencer believed this situation could only be effectively redressed by a major royal visit, preferably by the Prince of Wales, and in conjunction with an extensive Irish reform package, to include local government, and a Secretary of State to replace the Viceroy for administrative purposes, together with a permanent royal residence in Ireland. In this way, 'the growing feeling of coldness to the Crown in Ireland where the people are more easily moved to loyalty for the Queen and the Royal family than the English or the Scotch' would be checked.[73] Anxiously pleading the urgency of the case, he gradually overcame the objections of a Queen concerned that she not appear to be responding to terrorist acts.[74]

Whether Spencer's Cabinet colleagues had quite the same belief in the constitutional efficacy of the royal presence in Ireland is questionable. Responsibility for the Prince's safety was placed on his shoulders,[75] while, given the impassioned atmosphere of Irish politics at this time, the visit was guaranteed to generate controversy.

In part, this was due to Parnellite anxieties about the progress of their movement. Growth in local branches of the National League since 1882 – when agrarian struggle was abandoned in favour of Home

[69] See Parnell at Cork, *FJ*, 24 Jan. 1885; *TT* cutting, RA VIC/D 37/4. Describing monarchical rapacity in Ireland through history, he rejected any limits to 'the march of a nation'.
[70] Spencer to Ponsonby, 25 Jan. 1885, RA VIC/T 9/4.
[71] *Pat*, 10 Feb. 1883.   [72] See *DE*, 21 April 1885.
[73] Spencer to Gladstone, 26 Jan. 1885, Althorp papers, BL, K8.
[74] Spencer to Ponsonby, 28 Jan. 1885, RA VIC/T 9/7. Fenian bombers had attacked London Bridge and the Tower of London in late December and early January 1885: W. V. Harcourt, Home Secretary, to the Queen, 23 Dec. 1884, 3 February 1885, RA VIC/D 37/104/5.
[75] See Gladstone to Spencer, 22 Dec. 1884, 4, 7 Feb. 1885, Althorp papers, BL, K8.

Rule – had been unimpressive, while the party organ, *United Ireland,* had not made a profit until 1884.[76] In this context the royal visit had a threatening aspect that needed to be countered,[77] and the movement's most brilliant propagandist, William O'Brien, editor of the party organ, sprang forward to lead the anti-visit agitation.

Having engineered his own expulsion from the House of Commons O'Brien called a mass 'indignation' meeting in the Phoenix Park at which the forthcoming royal visit was the chief focus of condemnation. The choice of the Phoenix Park for the protest was inspired: it allowed O'Brien to revive popular memory of the police attack on a nationalist meeting during the Prince's last Irish visit in 1871 and refocus it onto the forthcoming royal visit, reinforced by the charge that Dublin Castle regarded the Irish people 'as if they were a nation of Negroes' made docile by royal 'glass beads and trinkets',[78] an interpretation that was not entirely wide of the mark given Spencer's hopes for the visit.[79]

However, important as it was for Parnellite purposes to create and sustain popular opposition to the visit, it yet required careful handling. The trick was to maintain popular feeling against the visit at white heat while ensuring the physical well-being of the royal visitors. Accordingly, O'Brien advised the avoidance of discourtesy to a Prince the victim of Dublin Castle manipulation.[80]

Events would show, however, that it was impossible to maintain the balance between indignation and respect that Parnellites sought to strike. The problem was that a nationalist boycott of the visit allowed press comment in Britain to be dominated by the addresses of loyalists and Orangemen, which were likely to be portrayed as representative of Irish opinion in general. How, in such circumstances, could the nationalist viewpoint be authentically communicated to British public opinion? Eventually the need to do so would lead to the abandonment of aloof disdain in favour of harassment of the royal party. By mid-March, three weeks before the beginning of the visit, a tone of personal abuse of the Prince was entering nationalist commentaries.[81] At the same time an unforeseen development added to the fraught political context of the visit.

---

[76] See Timothy Harrington, national organiser of the National League, in *Spec. Com. 1888 Proc.,* IX, pp. 202–3; William O'Brien, *ibid.* VIII, pp. 136, 200.

[77] *Nation,* 28 Feb. 1885.   [78] *Nation,* 7 March 1885.

[79] See also political cartoon, 'A Step in the Right Direction', *Punch,* 7 March 1885.

[80] *Nation,* 7 March 1885. *United Ireland [UI]* (28 Feb. 1885) absolved the Prince of any responsibility for a politically manipulated visit.

[81] *Nation,* 14 March 1885.

In February 1885 the pro-administration Cardinal McCabe, Archbishop of Dublin, died, thereby initiating a struggle for the succession of this most important See between, on the one hand, Spencer and the Castle, intriguing at Rome to have a successor of the same ilk appointed, while, on the other, the Parnellite leadership and press pushed the claims of the better-qualified and nationalist president of Maynooth College, Dr William Walsh, who was eventually successful.[82] Spencer's belief that a public declaration by Gladstone to the effect that 'a message of condolence had been received from the Queen' would do much to cultivate popular opinion in Ireland tells us more about Spencer's mindset than about Irish Catholic opinion. But a more important factor enhancing the drift to aggressive opposition to the visit was the ability of royal issues to open fissures in nationalist ranks.[83]

As the royal visitors' first port of call would be Dublin, it was important that the city corporation be brought into line with Parnellite designs. Accordingly Parnell advised a policy of 'reserve' to demonstrate inalienable nationalist commitment and opposition to Spencer's suppression of constitutional principles.[84] However, the unreliable Lord Mayor, John O'Connor,[85] veered between extremes of hostility and conciliation on the visit, vehemently attacking it at O'Brien's 'indignation' meeting in the Phoenix Park, only to apologise then abjectly for his actions, occasioning consternation among the party leadership and comfort to Unionists.[86] O'Connor's action stimulated others with similar reservations to express them. E. D. Gray, editor of the *Freeman's Journal* and a friend of the Prince of Wales, recommended a respectful reception for a royal personage whose presence in Dublin, he erroneously stated, primarily concerned the work of the Royal Commission on the Housing of the Working Classes, of which both he and the Prince were members.[87] Again, at a meeting of ratepayers of Dublin's North Ward, Alfred Webb, a former treasurer of the National League and leading Protestant nationalist, invoked the authority of 'Grattan, O'Connell, Butt, and other patriots' to endorse the Lord Mayor's apology and a respectful reception for the royal visitors.[88] But such were the emotions aroused that he only got

[82] For the controversy, see C. J. Woods, 'Ireland and Anglo–Papal Relations 1880–85', *Irish Historical Studies [IHS]*, 18 (1972–3), 57–60.

[83] Spencer to Ponsonby, 11 Feb. 1885, RA VIC/D 37/23.

[84] Resolution reproduced in T. D. Sullivan, *Troubled Times in Irish Politics* (Dublin, 1905), p. 223.

[85] Murphy, *Abject Loyalty*, pp. 228–9.

[86] See *TT*, 5 March 1885; *DE*, 5 March 1885; *UI*, 14 March 1885.

[87] *FJ*, 6–7 March 1885. Knollys to Ponsonby, 24 Feb. 1885, RA VIC/T 9/17.

[88] Press cutting, 6 March 1885, Alfred Webb papers, NLI, MS 1745 (50).

home safely with the aid of police protection.[89] *United Ireland* sought
to dissuade dissenters by claiming their activities were 'debilitating to
the psychological welfare of Nationalists';[90] nevertheless, despite the
Parnellite majority on the corporation – now in possession of a florid,
overblown, 'royal' declaration from the party leadership advising
boycott[91] – ensuring its will would prevail, opposition, especially loyalist
opposition, continued.

It was not that it was individually very significant, rather that for a
Parnellite leadership acutely concerned about how Irish affairs were
reported/distorted in Britain, they could easily be made to appear indicative of nationalist weakness,[92] especially as public bodies in the rest of
Ireland divided for and against the visit.[93] In this context the temptation
to maximise Catholic opposition to it by smearing the Prince of Wales
with sectarianism was too great to resist.[94]

The difficulties besetting Parnellites gave some satisfaction to Spencer,
but were tempered by concern about the rising political temperature.
Accordingly, a forthcoming renewal of the Crimes Act of 1882 was
postponed until after the visit; addresses to the Prince from Orange lodges
were restricted to formal, non-contentious greetings;[95] and the Queen
was persuaded to invest the excursion with a family dimension through
the inclusion of the Wales's children[96] – a signifier of the domestic values
the monarchy embodied which might deter hostility. However, his hopes
of ensuring the visit's success by associating it with an extensive reform
programme soon ran into difficulties.

Spencer pressed his case in Cabinet,[97] while favourable public debate
was encouraged by the appearance in the *Fortnightly Review* of two

---

[89] Spencer to the Chief Secretary, Henry Campbell-Bannerman, 6 March 1885, Althorp
papers, BL, K10.

[90] *UI*, 14 March 1885.

[91] The declaration invited ridicule and suggested coercion, a charge Parnell rejected:
Parnell to the editor, *FJ*, reproduced in *UI*, 21 March 1885.

[92] The loyalist section of Dublin Corporation responded to their defeat by organising a
'Citizens Committee' to present an address: *DE*, 23 March 1885.

[93] See *Nation*, 21, 28 March 1885; *UI*, 21 March 1885.

[94] *UI* (28 March 1885) highlighted his recently assumed presidency of the 'anti-Catholic'
English Freemasons.

[95] See Spencer–Campbell-Bannerman correspondence, 10, 12, 15 March 1885, Althorp
papers, BL, K10.

[96] Spencer to the Queen, 26 March 1885, Althorp papers, BL, K10. He did, however, warn
the Prince of possible nationalist protests: Spencer to the Prince of Wales, 6 April 1885,
RA VIC/T 9/24.

[97] Spencer, 'Memo. for the Cabinet on Irish Legislation', 25 March 1885, Gladstone
papers, BL, MS 44312.

supportive articles.[98] Cabinet attention, however, was currently occupied with Joseph Chamberlain's ill-fated 'Central Board' scheme for Ireland, a plan that demanded attention owing to the somewhat misleading assurance of Cardinal Manning and a number of the Irish Catholic hierarchy that it would 'pacify' Ireland and enable them to oppose Home Rule.[99]

Spencer's and Chamberlain's reform plans were not entirely incompatible, and Chamberlain would later add abolition of the Viceroyalty to his scheme.[100] Nevertheless, division in the Cabinet on the nature and scope of Irish reforms meant that it was not possible to associate the royal visit to Ireland with an announcement of an extensive plan as a congenial context. As it was, the visit proceeded with only the certainty of a forthcoming renewal of coercion. The only conciliatory act was a proclamation in the official organ, the *Dublin Gazette*, announcing that in future prelates and bishops of the Catholic Church would, in Ireland, share 'the precedence' which belonged to such dignitaries of the Church of Ireland before disestablishment.[101] Even then it was not an entirely voluntary act, following in the wake of nationalist protests in Parliament.[102] Nor did the administration gain much from the gesture. Popular Protestant opinion was irritated,[103] while it did nothing to persuade the Catholic hierarchy to participate in the visit. The church had made a compact with Parnell in 1884 which it did not want to endanger, though the hierarchy was not unanimous. In fact, for some members of the Catholic clergy with memories of the patronage and protection the Prince had apparently offered Catholic institutions in Rome during political upheavals in Italy in the early 1870s, the idea of a boycott was repugnant.[104] In any event, as an influential institution of Irish Catholic society it had to be conciliated, which including the Catholic seminary, Maynooth, in the Prince's itinerary was intended to do.[105]

---

[98] See Henry Jephson, 'Royalty and Viceroyalty in Ireland: I: The Irish Viceroyalty', *Fortnightly Review*, 37 (April 1885), 500–11; R. O'Hara, 'Royalty and Viceroyalty in Ireland: II: A New Era for Ireland', *ibid.* 512–18. Jephson had, it seems, recently been a Dublin Castle employee.

[99] In its final form the scheme included an elected 'National Council' to deal administratively with education and communications, together with an overhaul of county government that would facilitate land purchase: C. H. D. Howard, 'Joseph Chamberlain, Parnell and the Irish "Central Board" Scheme 1884–5', *IHS*, 8 (1953), 329–61.

[100] Joseph Chamberlain, *A Political Memoir*, ed. C. H. D. Howard (London, 1953), pp. 144–5.

[101] Copy of '"The Prelates" Precedence', 26 March 1885, Archbishop William Walsh papers, Dublin Diocesan Archives [DDA], WP.1885, 357/1, II.

[102] *TT*, 4 March 1885.

[103] Walter Walsh, *The Religious Life of Queen Victoria* (London, 1902), pp. 195–7.

[104] See *TT* report cited in *DE*, 7 April 1885; *Nation*, 4 April 1885; *UI*, 4 April 1885.

[105] Campbell-Bannerman to Spencer, 22 March 1885, Althorp papers, BL, K10.

Nationalist difficulties in finding the most appropriate stance on the visit continued. Not only were loyalists getting their addresses prepared, but divisions continued to surface within nationalist ranks, producing somewhat schizoid commentaries, in which assurances that the Prince would be 'as safe in Ireland as he would be at Sandringham' went together with contempt for the 'fat middle-aged ... electioneering carpet-bagger' coming to Ireland to consolidate Spencer's coercion regime.[106]

VI

No royal visit to Ireland since 1849 had begun with such trepidation as that surrounding the visit of 1885. But it got off to an excellent start. The arrival at Kingstown and entry into Dublin on 8 April was a great success.[107] And from the beginning Edward struck the welfarist note that would characterise his activities thereafter, visiting the spring cattle show at the Royal Dublin Society, explaining the activities of the Royal Commission on the Housing of the Working Classes, and visiting a slum area where he reportedly declared his earnest intention to 'do all in my power' to improve their conditions.[108] Moreover, an attempt to expand the visual impact of the visit was made with the Chancellor studio of Dublin appointed as official photographers to record the visit for the purpose of sale to the public.[109]

The successful start to the visit came as an enormous relief to Spencer and Campbell-Bannerman, impressed by 'the vast crowds eager to demonstrate their loyalty' and inclined to read into it an endorsement of Spencer's 'conduct as Viceroy'.[110] The remaining engagements of the first week proved highly satisfactory. A levee at Dublin Castle attracted seventy peers, raising loyalist hopes for the reversal of landlord absenteeism and the establishment of an Irish royal residence.[111] Concerned that 'neutrality' was leaving the public sphere in the hands of the loyalist population, the *Nation* stressed the ephemerality of the emotions the royal visit aroused,[112] but it was William O'Brien, as editor of *United Ireland*, who produced the most impressive nationalist response.

---

[106] *UI*, 4 April 1885; *Nation*, 11 April 1885.
[107] *IT*, 9 April 1885. See also *DE*, 9 April 1885; Prince of Wales to the Queen, Telegram, 8 April 1885, RA VIC/Z 460/67: 'just arrived, most enthusiastic reception'.
[108] *Daily Telegraph* [*DT*], 10 April 1885; *Belfast Morning News* [*BMN*], 10 April 1885.
[109] Peadar Slattery, 'The Uses of Photography in Ireland 1839–1900', unpublished PhD thesis, University of Dublin (1991), I, pp. 107–9.
[110] Spencer to the Queen, 9 April 1885, in Gordon (ed.), *Red Earl*, I, p. 296; Campbell-Bannerman to Spencer, 8 April 1885, Althorp papers, BL, K10.
[111] *DE*, 13 April 1885.   [112] *Nation*, 11 April 1885.

To register Catholic and nationalist opposition, O'Brien produced the results of a massive survey of Irish opinion he had organised. In the days before opinion polls this was a truly impressive exercise, based on requests from local boards, National League branches, journals and individuals all over Ireland for expressions of opposition condensed into 'one sentence'. Produced as a supplement to *United Ireland* in the first week of the visit, the results disclosed that in the whole of the three southern provinces only three boards of Town Commissioners and Sligo Corporation would present addresses to the Prince. By contrast, the corporations of Dublin, Cork, Limerick, Waterford, Clonmel, Kilkenny, Wexford and Drogheda, together with 84 boards of Town Commissioners, and around 160 boards of Poor Law Guardians were boycotting the royal visit. They were following in the van of the Parnellite Party MPs, together with 800 local National League branches representing 'close on 200,000 members'. Of leading public figures, Archbishop Thomas Croke of Cashel and the bishops of Clonfert and Down and Connor, together with many more of the local clergy, supported the 'dignified reserve' and the 'charity' of the people's silence. Finally, O'Brien added to the main body of his survey as many private individual replies as he could find space for.[113]

There could hardly have been a more impressive mobilisation of nationalist opinion. And yet, it was not enough for Parnellite purposes. The exercise was undertaken, not to persuade committed nationalists of what they already knew, but to counteract the expected effects of the anti-nationalist press in Britain reporting congenial receptions for the royal party as representative of Irish opinion in general. So it proved. Not only did this occur, but, provokingly, the loyalist reception for the royal visitors was presented in zero-sum terms as indicating the weakness of Parnellism,[114] especially by *Punch* (Fig. 15). Thus, what had originally seemed a dignified and highly effective means of registering nationalist Ireland's protest against the coercive administration it laboured under, now appeared a major propagandist blunder. Accordingly, a decision was taken to repair the mistakes of the first week of the visit by aggressive opposition in the second.

On Sunday 12 April twelve major nationalist demonstrations took place at venues across the south and west of Ireland at which anti-royal and anti-imperial themes were integrated, and expressed in a focus on the

---

[113] 'A Salute to the Prince', supplement to *UI*, 11 April 1885.

[114] The triumphant chorus was led by *TT*, 11 April 1885 and included prints throughout Britain: survey of British press opinion in *BMN*, 16 April 1885. See also Sir Arthur Ellis to the Queen, 9 April 1885, RA VIC/Z 455/7.

PUNCH, OR THE LONDON CHARIVARI.—April 11, 1885.

"CEÀD MÌLE FÀILTHI"!!!

Erin. "BEHAVE NOW, YE MISCHIEVOUS LITTLE DIVIL! WOULD YE DISGRACE THE FAMILY?"

15 A British view of the royal visit, 1885.

'Famine Queen' myth, Disraeli's supposed enthusiasm for the effects of the Great Famine, and a re-enactment of the Madhi's defeat of British forces in the Sudan in 1884.[115] But it was O'Brien – convinced that the counter-productive effects of the previous week could only be effaced by being as 'relentless and disagreeable as the law will allow'[116] – who engineered the *coup de théâtre* that shaped nationalist reactions to the visit thereafter.

As MP for Mallow he staged a mass demonstration at Mallow railway station when the Prince alighted briefly to receive an address from the Town Commissioners on 13 April,[117] an action which ensured disorder and a strong police reaction, consequent nationalist indignation, and questions in Parliament about police brutality and sobriety, while

---

[115] See *UI*, 18 April 1885; *Nation*, 18 April 1885.   [116] *Nation*, 18 April 1885.
[117] Spencer was prepared to allow O'Brien a 'respectful' meeting with the Prince, without the presence of 'a mob': Spencer to County Inspector, Captain Plunkett, 12 April 1885, Chief Secretary's Office, Registered Papers [CSORP], National Archives of Ireland [NAI], CSORP/1885/8059; *DT*, 16 April 1885; *UI*, 18 April 1885.

British public opinion was left under no illusions about nationalist feeling on the visit.[118]

The emotions aroused at Mallow carried over to Cork City, the chief southern destination of the royal party. Houses displaying royal emblems had their windows smashed and reports circulated that the police and resident magistrates of the city had thrown upon the Lord Mayor personal responsibility for keeping the peace.[119] Appeals for calm were duly made and when the royal couple arrived they were able to carry out several of their duties. Nevertheless, at certain points they were subject to quite serious abuse, including threatening behaviour at close quarters, the firing of missiles and, most unpleasantly, the throwing of 'a miniature wooden coffin ... with accurate aim into the royal carriage, landing on the Princess's knees'.[120] A similar reception met the royal party in Limerick;[121] and it was surely with relief that they made the return journey to Dublin where a ball attended by 6,000 people awaited.[122] No less would the royal couple have been relieved when their itinerary took them northwards into Ulster – as was Spencer[123] – for the final stage of the visit. Here their round of engagements had the character of a triumphant progress of greetings and celebration, attracting saturated photographic coverage.[124] It was also here, during a speech at Belfast, that the Prince allowed himself an oblique expression of distaste at his southern reception by pointedly praising north-east Ulster as a model of industry and progress for the rest of Ireland to emulate.[125] At the height of north-east Ulster's industrial development, with its 'imperial' identity fully developed, the Prince's presence and commentary was a crowning moment. Significantly, in its characteristically detailed account of the visit, the *Illustrated London News*[126] highlighted the northern dimension.[127] From Belfast the royal party proceeded to Baronscourt, County Tyrone, the seat of the Prince's old friend the Duke of Abercorn. The trip drew a crowd of 7,000, which, the Duchess of Abercorn assured the Queen, included Catholics who 'came from distant

[118] For the Mallow fracas, see *DT*, 14, 16 April 1885; also *UI*, 18 April 1885.

[119] Ibid.

[120] Prince of Wales to the Queen, 19 April 1885, RA VIC/Z 455/20. On the Cork events, see also Lord Ernest Hamilton, *Forty Years On* (London, 1922), pp. 19–20.

[121] Resident Magistrate Irwin to Chief Secretary, 13–14 April 1885, CSORP, NAI, CSORP/1885/3142/85555; Irwin to Spencer, 20 April 1885, CSORP/1885/8011.

[122] *IT*, 20, 23 April 1885.

[123] Spencer to Campbell-Bannerman, 23 April 1885, Althorp papers, BL, K10.

[124] Slattery, 'Uses of Photography in Ireland', I, pp. 107–9.

[125] James Loughlin, *Ulster Unionism and British National Identity since 1885* (London, 1995), pp. 42–3.

[126] *ILN*, 18, 25 April, 2 May 1885.   [127] ILN, 2 May 1885.

mountainous districts'.[128] Only at Derry did disturbances occur, occasioned by a tableau displayed at the city's Opera House depicting the Queen and the Prince of Wales, but not Ireland's uncrowned king. But this did not occur until after the royal party had left Ireland.[129]

While the Parnellite reaction to the royal visit dominated the press accounts of its later stages, it was not the only variety of Irish nationalism to find expression. Just as the controversy over viceregal abolition drew out anti-Parnellite nationalism, so too did the royal visit of 1885, if more discreetly. For a strand of nationalism increasingly deemed elitist, it was perhaps entirely appropriate that the agency for its expression was the formidable Lady Florence Dixie,[130] a close friend of the Prince of Wales who was godfather to one of her children. Dixie used her royal access before and during the royal visit, attempting to enlist Edward's support for Daunt's anti-Parnellite idea of a Home Rule settlement that would undo the socially destabilising effects of the land war by restoring to political power the Irish nobility.[131] Daunt had not expected much to come of Dixie's efforts,[132] and when this proved to be the case she released her correspondence with the Prince to the press in the hope of encouraging public support for the project.[133]

Another personal approach made to the Prince of Wales during the visit came from his old tutor, Goldwin Smith, who pressed on Edward its value as a blow against Parnellism, which could effectively be built upon by an extensive reform programme to include a royal residence and parliamentary sittings in Dublin: 'they [the Irish] ought to see both the Sovereign and the Parliament'.[134] Whatever their differences, and despite the pronouncements of Bagehot's *English Constitution* on the apolitical position of the monarchy, all parties concerned with the royal visit of 1885 believed that, where Ireland was concerned, the monarchy was much too important an institution to be regarded as politically neutral.

---

[128] Louise, Duchess of Abercorn to the Queen, 29 April 1885, RA VIC/Z 460/79; *IT*, 27 April 1885.

[129] *UI*, 2 May 1885. Robert McVicker to the Chief Secretary, 22 April 1885, CSORP, NAI, CSORP/1885/8133.

[130] Dixie, Lady Florence Caroline (1857–1905), authoress and traveller: Sir Sydney Lee (ed.), *DNB*, 2nd suppl.: Index and Epitome (London, 1920), p. 33.

[131] See Dixie to Daunt, 13; 21, 25 April 1885; Dixie to the Prince of Wales, 25 April 1885, O'Neill Daunt Letters, NLI, MS 8045 (4).

[132] Entries (15, 16 April 1885), O'Neill Daunt Journals, vol. II, 1877–88, NLI, MS 3042.

[133] Ibid. 30 April, 5 May 1885.

[134] Goldwin Smith, 'The Administration of Ireland', *CR*, 48 (July 1885), 1–9. Smith supplied the Prince with a copy before his departure for Ireland: Arnold Haultain (ed.), *Goldwin Smith's Correspondence* (New York, 1913), p. 169.

VII

If it is a central function of public ritual to reflect and reinforce national integration,[135] then there could hardly be a worse illustrative example than the royal visit of 1885. The essential requirement of ritual effectiveness – a high level of societal integration[136] – was noteworthy by its absence. Not only were there deep national, cultural and religious differences dividing the societies of Britain and Ireland that royal ritual effected simultaneously to embody, but unlike the relatively simple native societies that anthropologists often focus on, the political arena of the visit of 1885 was dysfunctionally dynamic rather than stable, conflictual rather than harmonious, and complicated by a media variable widely recognised as crucial to perceptions of success and failure.

That Spencer was moved to arrange a royal visit in such unfavourable circumstances and that Parnellites were disposed to react to it with such unprecedented hostility was determined by their anxieties about the extent to which their policies in recent years had succeeded in mobilising the newly enfranchised Irish masses – bound to go to the polls in a matter of months – for their respective conceptions of national identity. Spencer's decision to arrange the visit represented, to say the least, the triumph of hope over experience, fuelled by his personal sense of guilt about implicating the monarchy in political controversy; by a conviction that the 'image worshipping' Catholic Irish were more susceptible to the royal presence than the Scots or English; and by the apparent success of the monarchy in Britain in stabilising the existing social and constitutional order in this period of democratic change.[137]

The evidential basis for the influence of the monarchy in Britain at this time, however, at least among the working class, is not substantial: there is reason to believe the existing constitutional and social order was accepted, but did not really influence working-class culture and values.[138] Irish Catholic attitudes to the monarchy were even more problematic. Emblematic of an accepted constitutional order in Britain, in Ireland it was compromised by the coercive and unpopular administrative system

---

[135] Steven Lukes, 'Political Ritual and Social Integration' in Lukes, *Essays in Social Theory* (London and Basingstoke, 1977), pp. 56–7.

[136] Victor Turner, *Dramas, Fields and Metaphors: Symbolic Action in Human Society* (Ithaca, NY, 1975), p. 56.

[137] See Frederick Engels quoted in Tom Nairn, *The Enchanted Glass: Britain and Its Monarchy* (London, 1988), p. 204 on the English constitution as an 'inverted pyramid': 'the apex is at the same time the base . . . Nowhere is a non-ruling personage more revered than in England.'

[138] See P. S. Baker, 'The Sociological and Ideological Role of the Monarchy in Late Victorian Britain', unpublished MA thesis, University of Lancaster (1978), p. 5.

based in Dublin Castle. Certainly it failed to achieve the ambitious objectives Spencer set in 1885. But while British press reporting of the first week of the Irish visit of 1885 provided the trigger for Parnellite opposition, of itself that hardly accounts for its vehemence. In fact, its legitimising context can be traced back at least to Parnell's north American tour of 1880, when he sought to undermine the moral credibility of the monarchy by establishing a 'Famine Queen' myth – significantly earlier than has recently been claimed.[139]

Accordingly, the effects of Spencer's amalgamation of viceregal and administrative functions, it can be argued, merely enhanced and sharpened antagonism that already had a fruitful soil in which to grow. At the same time, that he was not accountable to the Commons, and thus not personally available for Parnellites to vent their anger at, made it only too likely that they would do so by proxy in 1885, a time when anti-Spencerian agitation was deemed essential to sustaining popular support for the National League; something that could not be assumed.

Theodore Hoppen's argument on the significance of localism in Irish life is an important consideration when assessing Irish attitudes to politics and, by extension, royal occasions[140] at this time, as at others. Arguably, it was the fundamental obstacle in the way of both Parnellite and Spencerian campaigns for public support. The former's shift of policy from agrarian issues to Home Rule in 1882 entailed a change from substantive interests that affected the material lives of the tenant population to a national, but arguably sentimental, and psychological grievance. Thus while it was certainly the case that Spencer's hopes of thwarting Parnellism failed – and he could only have been further discomfited by the disclosure, shortly after the royal visit, that the 'uncrowned king' was apparently in direct genealogical descent from Edward I[141] – there is also reason to believe that the non-Unionist population were not as engaged with the Parnellite project as the party leadership would have wished. Parnellite success at the general election of 1885 was more likely due to a reputation for effective constituency representation than undiluted nationalism.

And yet, at the same time, James Murphy's argument that 'the Irish Party had to marshal all its resources in order to turn public opinion against the visit'[142] both fails to appreciate the complexity of Irish

---

[139] Murphy, *Abject Loyalty* (p. 291) first dated its emergence to the late 1890s; and more recently to the Golden Jubilee of 1887: 'Fashioning the Famine Queen' in Peter Gray (ed.), *Victoria's Ireland? Irishness and Britishness, 1837–1901* (Dublin, 2004), p. 24.

[140] K. T. Hoppen, *Elections, Politics and Society in Ireland 1832–1885* (Oxford, 1984), p. 484.

[141] This was a finding of a study of the genealogy of political leaders, reported in *DE*, 11 May 1885.

[142] Murphy, *Abject Loyalty*, p. 240.

Catholic attitudes and overstates the extent of public support for it. In the latter respect, he fails to take account of the substantial Protestant and loyalist community in the greater Dublin area – not to mention ease of railway access from Belfast – which could be relied upon to give the royal visitors an enthusiastic welcome even if no nationalists were present, and whose opinions Parnellite opposition would not have affected.

Parnellite gains from the royal visit of 1885 were highly questionable. It is by no means clear that their aggressive opposition increased popular support for the National League, while their activities hardly provided a supportive context for Gladstone's claim, some months later, that Home Rule would be accompanied by a growing sentiment of loyalty to crown and constitution.[143] It was clearly with the costs to the Home Rule campaign in mind – it also established a precedent of nationalist non-involvement in Irish royal occasions – that in his memoirs William O'Brien justified his actions by claiming that they had converted the Prince of Wales to Home Rule.[144] Rumours to this effect did circulate occasionally, but were totally without foundation, and undoubtedly due to the expressed sympathy for Irish autonomy of his wife, Princess Alexandra.[145] O'Brien's claim reflected a somewhat misguided tendency to assume a greater power for political rhetoric and action than was realistic.

[143] Loughlin, *Gladstone*, p. 66.
[144] William O'Brien, *Evening Memories* (Dublin and London, 1920), p. 240.
[145] See Reginald Viscount Esher, *Journals and Letters* ed. M. V. Brett (London, 1934), I, p. 161.

9   The first Home Rule bill: the monarchical
      dimension

The controversy surrounding the royal visit of 1885 was productive, less of enlightenment on the nature of the Irish question, than of self-deception. William O'Brien's delusions about the effects on the Prince of Wales of aggressive protest were matched by a countervailing misconception in Government and court circles that nationalist agitators had largely failed to mobilise 'the lowest classes' against the will of a people whose loyalty would be greatly stimulated by closer contact with royal personages.[1] Its plausibility is explicable largely by reference to a royal narrative of Irish visits.

Previous successful visits had occurred in the absence of hegemonic nationalist movements. In this context tensions within the broad nationalist family caused by Edward's visit, and the Parnellite protests themselves, could be read, misleadingly, as signs of *fundamental* weakness, especially given that a desperate need existed to think so: a general election was due in months, with the prospect of parliamentary chaos if Parnellites won a landslide of Irish seats. However, the Parnellite movement had, outside north-east Ulster, established a virtual monopoly of political mobilisation. There was no countervailing agency or organisation capable of effecting popular demonstrations supportive of the status quo from across the population as a whole. Spencer's claim – encouraged by the loyalist press[2] and requests for a royal residence contained in most of the addresses presented to the Prince[3] – that the visit demonstrated

---

[1] Spencer to Campbell-Bannerman, Gladstone, 23, 24 April 1885, Althorp papers, BL, K10, K8; Ponsonby to Courtney Boyle, Private Secretary to the Prince of Wales, 17 April 1885, Althorp papers, BL, K2; Prince of Wales to the Queen, 26 April 1885, RA VIC/Z 455/22; Gladstone to Prince of Wales, 27 April 1885, RA VIC/T 9/28; Lord Granville to Prince of Wales, 28 April 1885, RA VIC/T 9/29; Lord Lansdowne to Queen Victoria, 4 May 1885, RA VIC/P 26/117; also entry (28 April 1885), D. W. R. Bahlmann (ed.), *The Diary of Sir Edward Walter Hamilton 1880–1885* (Oxford, 1972), I, p. 851.
[2] See *Daily Express* [*DE*], 3 April 1885; letter to the editor, *DE*, 16 April 1885; editorials, *DE*, 21, 24 April 1885; letters to the editor, *DE*, 28 April, 11 May 1885; *Irish Times* [*IT*], 27 April 1885.
[3] Sir Digby Probyn to the Queen, 12 April 1885, RA VIC/Z 4455/22.

that if the 'loyal classes' combined at the next general election Parnellism could be vanquished,[4] was a wild flight of fancy. Nevertheless, notwithstanding misconceptions about its lessons, the royal visit served to energise the ongoing debate on the monarchy and Irish reform.

With the visit over, Spencer made the residency and reform case again to a Queen fundamentally opposed, but ostensibly concerned merely with finding the right location: she preferred the Viceregal Lodge, which Spencer thought unsuitable.[5] Spencer's preference was for a royal residence outside Dublin, and quite probably motivated by a desire to create as great a spatial distance as possible between royal personages and Dublin Castle, an administrative/royal site that had been the focus of unprecedented nationalist vilification since 1879. Sir Henry Ponsonby sought a solution by suggesting not one royal residence but several, depending on the occasion, and by mid-May was convinced, erroneously, that the issue had been virtually settled with the Prince of Wales's agreement.[6] Moreover, with progress on a royal residence stalling, Spencer's hopes for land and local government reforms to forestall radical constitutional change were also frustrated.

The main lines of debate on Irish reform had been established before the visit, chiefly around the schemes promoted by Spencer and Chamberlain. Political developments at the end of April, however, clarified the situation in a way detrimental to Chamberlain's hopes. Parnell specified that the Central Board plan could only be an instalment on, not a settlement of, the autonomy issue.[7] For his part, Spencer feared a Central Board would lead to administrative confusion and a division of authority in Dublin that would make effective government impossible, together with the closer relationship between the monarchy and Ireland he desired. Again, there was Ulster, which might well violently oppose the change.[8] Gladstone, moreover, now envisaged the possibility of Parnellite success at a forthcoming election and subsequent withdrawal from Parliament on the basis of speaking for Ireland: 'I look upon this as probable and much more formidable than the antic of a Central Board.'[9]

---

[4] Spencer to Edward Hamilton, 27 April 1885, Gladstone papers, BL, Add. MS 44312.
[5] Queen to Spencer, 6 May 1885, in Peter Gordon (ed.), *The Red Earl: The Papers of the Fifth Earl Spencer* (Northampton, 1986), I, p. 299; Spencer to the Queen, 6 May 1885, RA VIC/ D 37/40; Gordon (ed.), *Red Earl*, I, p. 299.
[6] Ponsonby to Spencer, 13 May 1885, Althorp papers, BL, K10; Ponsonby to Courtney Boyle, 14 May 1885, ibid.
[7] F. S. L. Lyons, *Charles Stewart Parnell* (London, 1978), pp. 140–1.
[8] Spencer, 'Notes of What Passed re. Crimes Act in May 1885' in Gordon (ed.), *Red Earl*, I, p. 301.
[9] Gladstone to Spencer, 6 May 1885, Gladstone papers, BL, Add. MS 44312.

Thus, as opposed to the difficulties expected from Chamberlain's scheme, Gladstone presented a much more problematic scenario.

Although having vastly more personal experience of Ireland than Gladstone, Spencer's outlook on the country was unduly framed through a Dublin Castle lens and was only too inclined to see that perspective validated in the mesmerising effects of royal spectacle. Thus he pressed his proposals on an uncooperative Queen[10] as the Government staggered on, deeply divided, for another month, sending out confused signals to Parliament about the coercive and remedial elements of its Irish policy.[11] Moreover, it would gradually become clear that with the failure to make progress on the royal project in mid-1885 the best opportunity for action was lost. When Gladstone committed the Liberal Party to Home Rule at the end of the year, a very different scenario emerged. The Home Rule plan produced by Gladstone retained the Viceroyalty, a provision the Parnellites accepted without demur, despite Parnell's preference for dealing 'directly with the Crown rather than with a nominee in Ireland of the English government of the day'.[12]

I

The collapse of Gladstone's second administration led, to the Queen's delight,[13] to a brief Tory interlude (Lord Salisbury's first government, June 1885 to January 1886), but not to a transformation of political realities. Salisbury only formed a Government on the understanding that Gladstone would not attempt to bring it down, and its scope for independent action was therefore circumscribed: its chief legislative enactment was the modestly financed Ashbourne Act which made a realistic advance in the process of Irish land purchase, together with the abandonment of coercion. The impending reality of a Parnellite controlled Ireland had still to be contended with, and how to meet that reality an enduring concern. The central issue remained whether Ireland was to have some form of self-government, how extensive it was to be, and which party was to concede it. Gladstone took steps to ensure the debate on the

---

[10] Spencer to Gladstone 13 May 1885, Gladstone papers, BL, MS 44312; Gladstone to Spencer, 15 May 1885, Althorp papers, BL, K8; Queen to Gladstone, 18 May 1885, in Philip Guedalla (ed.), *The Queen and Mr Gladstone* (London, 1933), II, p. 353.

[11] Lyons, *Parnell*, pp. 273–4.

[12] Parnell to O'Neill Daunt, 15 July 1885, Charles Stewart Parnell papers, NLI, MS5934. He included abolition in a Home Rule scheme submitted to Gladstone through Mrs O'Shea in October 1885: Katherine O'Shea, *Charles Stewart Parnell: His Love Story and Political Life* (London, 1914), II, p. 19. O'Shea erroneously gives the date of submission as early 1884.

[13] Entries (8 July, 1 Aug. 1885), N. E. Johnson (ed.), *The Diary of Gathorne Hardy, Later Lord Clonbrook 1866–1892: Political Selections* (Oxford, 1981), pp. 567, 573.

Irish question was maintained by engineering a series of articles in the *Nineteenth Century*,[14] while Salisbury combined limited but effective reform on land purchase with conciliation of Parnellites and misleading hints that his party would be prepared to embrace Home Rule.

Salisbury and Gladstone shared a similar belief as to the significance of the monarchy in British society and the state, the Queen's public appearance and ritual being central to the cultivation of mass loyalty, something the office alone was incapable of.[15] Salisbury also shared, as we have seen, the widespread establishment view that, 'among a people so sensitive as the Irish', the absence of the Queen was bound to be deeply felt.[16] But there were also differences.

While Gladstone was concerned primarily with the objective role of the monarchy in British society, Salisbury not only shared that concern, but sympathised with her belief in autonomous Queenship.[17] Their differences, however, were greatest on Ireland. Untroubled by a sense of Westminster's historical responsibility for past misgovernment, for all his intellectual brilliance Salisbury's understanding never got beyond the crudities of British ethnocentrism. Lacking positive engagement, insight and empathy with Ireland, apart from its loyalist minority – 'landholding, Protestant, loyalist'[18] – his recipe for the country's ills in the late 1880s would be twenty years of 'resolute government'.[19] His only Irish visit was in 1892, when he travelled to Ulster to encourage an already aggressive Unionist opposition to the second Home Rule bill.[20]

On his accession to office, and despite his earlier lament about the absence of monarchy in Ireland, he entertained no proposals of a Spencerian kind for bringing the royal family and the Irish into closer personal contact. However, he envisaged an important role for the Viceroy – a personage he had long regarded as a 'polite dummy who sits in the Viceregal chair',[21] at 'the centre of a mimic court'.[22] His appointee in 1885, Lord Carnarvon, had, like Spencer, a seat in Cabinet, and, as a

[14] Gladstone to J. R. Knowles, editor, 5 Aug. 1885, in H. C. G. Matthew (ed.), *The Gladstone Diaries XI* (Oxford, 1990), pp. 380–1.

[15] See 'The Queen', *Saturday Review* [*SR*], 26 March 1864.

[16] 'The Dublin Banquet [on Lord Kimberley's appointment as Viceroy]', *SR*, 3 Dec. 1864.

[17] See Lady Gwendolen Cecil, *Life of Robert, Marquis of Salisbury* (London, 1931), III, pp. 187–8.

[18] Ibid. II, pp. 150–1.

[19] Michael McDonagh, *The Home Rule Movement* (Dublin, 1920), p. 171.

[20] James Loughlin, *Gladstone, Home Rule and the Ulster Question 1882–93* (Dublin, 1986), p. 279.

[21] Salisbury, 'The Dublin Banquet', *SR*, 3 Dec. 1864.

[22] Salisbury in *SR*, 1881 quoted in Andrew Roberts, *Salisbury: Victorian Titan* (London, 1999), p. 348.

known Home Ruler[23] – he only accepted the Dublin post on the understanding that the Government would consider the whole question of Irish government[24] – had the task of conciliating Parnellites. With coercion abandoned and the Viceroy and Vicereine vigorously pursuing welfare monarchism,[25] the Irish dimension to the Government had a distinctly pro-nationalist complexion, with Carnarvon's Cabinet membership lending credibility to the impression that his views on Ireland had Government endorsement. In this context, much greater credibility was lent to Salisbury's pro-autonomy hints than they deserved. In fact, it is clear that all Salisbury wanted Carnarvon to do was to keep the Parnellites on side until the general election.

Carnarvon, however, went much further than it would seem Salisbury intended. In contact with the former Young Ireland leader and imperial statesman Sir Charles Gavan Duffy, Carnarvon was won over to Duffy's plan for an Irish Home Rule constitution dealing with purely internal affairs, with safeguards for the integrity of the United Kingdom and for Protestant interests in Ireland.[26] In his first communication with the Queen from Dublin he exuded hope of reconciliation, detailing how, on his arrival, he had dispensed with his armed escort and received an enthusiastic reception from the people,[27] a microcosm, given the royal proxy of his office, of Irish loyalty to the Queen.

Reassurances on this score had been conveyed by both Justin McCarthy and Parnell.[28] Subsequent reports from Carnarvon to the Queen on his tours of the Irish countryside emphasised an already existing Irish loyalty that was the seedbed for a much stronger monarchical sentiment 'if circumstances favour'. Nationalism existed 'almost universally' in the country, he admitted, but separatist sentiment was entertained by very few. In this context he emphasised the loyalty of the Catholic clergy and nuns.[29]

Against this background Carnarvon sought to engineer an appropriate public debate on the kind of autonomy he favoured.[30] Accordingly, a letter to the press on self-government was arranged with Duffy. It was a substantial argument for Home Rule on the colonial model and a significant contribution to public awareness of the issue. At the same time,

---

[23] Sir Arthur Hardinge, *The Life of H. H. Molyneux Herbert, Fourth Earl Carnarvon* (Oxford, 1925), III, p. 156.
[24] Ibid. pp. 157–8, 161.
[25] Sir Henry Robinson, *Memories: Wise and Otherwise* (London, 1924), ch. 8.
[26] Ibid. pp. 146–53.   [27] Carnarvon to the Queen, 6–8 July 1885, RA VIC/D 37/67–8.
[28] Hardinge, *Carnarvon*, III, pp. 164, 179–80; also Carnarvon to Archbishop William Walsh, 29 July 1885, in P. J. Walsh, *William J. Walsh: Archbishop of Dublin* (London, 1929), p. 199.
[29] Carnarvon to the Queen, 26 Aug. 1885, RA VIC/D 37/62.
[30] R. B. O'Brien, *The Life of Charles Stewart Parnell* (London, 1899), II, pp. 78–80. Duffy wrote the chapter dealing with the Carnarvon Viceroyalty.

impressed by the Irish popular reception he received, Carnarvon urged on the Queen the desirability of an Irish royal residence. In a rapidly developing political environment where an impending general election meant that both major parties were having to – or be seen to – seriously address the autonomy issue, a royal residence now took on greater significance. It could be easily imagined that a royal resident in Ireland acting as a focus for demonstrations of popular loyalty, at a time when the British Parliament was deciding the fate of an autonomy measure, could be a significant factor in undermining rejectionist sentiment.

Raising this issue, however, brought back into play associated considerations such as abolition of the Viceroyalty, and at this Carnarvon baulked. Reflecting the influence of the non-Parnellite nationalist sentiment he had been exposed to through Duffy, he opined: 'as far as [I] can understand Irish feeling, it must under all circumstances be retained'.[31] In addition to Irish sentiment, as a former Secretary of State for the Colonies Carnarvon recognised distinctly British state interests to consider, such as a possible future need to pursue coercion. In Ireland under Home Rule 'a Vice Roy would be as indispensable as in the large colonies'.[32] Carnarvon's argument reinforces the peculiarity of the Irish Viceroyalty: for many nationalists a symbolic representation of Ireland's national distinctiveness under the Union, and at the same time an instrument for the possible repression of those who so regarded it. Nevertheless, Carnarvon argued for Home Rule in present circumstances, when Ireland was relatively quiet, thus avoiding the appearance of it being extorted, a situation that might not pertain for long.[33]

The influence of Carnarvon's arguments are difficult to assess. Certainly when Salisbury declared against Home Rule the Queen was delighted. But before party battle lines on the issue had clarified, her journals suggest some open-mindedness on Irish legislative options. Her responses to Carnarvon's arguments, for instance, are devoid of the negative emotions often associated with Gladstone's policies.[34] Certainly Parnell at this time was doing his utmost to reassure British opinion that there was nothing to fear from Home Rule, and, like Carnarvon, was not above media manipulation for the purpose.[35]

The role of the press in shaping contexts and perceived realities, especially between the very different national arenas of Britain and Ireland, was long evident, as we have seen, and in regard to the Irish royal visit of 1885 had a serious impact on how it progressed. Carnarvon remained alert to the

---

[31] Carnarvon to the Queen, 26 Nov. 1885, RA VIC/D 37/99.   [32] Ibid.
[33] Ibid.   [34] RA VIC/QVJ: 23 Nov. 1885.
[35] See T. M. Healy, *Letters and Leaders of My Day* (London, 1928), I, p. 97.

need constructively to manage the monarchy's relationship with the Irish public. Thus when the Curtin controversy[36] broke in November 1885 and Lady Kenmare proposed that the Queen send a 'present' to the Curtin family to demonstrate her support, Carnarvon strongly advised keeping 'the Queen's name out of all connection with the matter'.[37]

The period of ambiguity on Home Rule that had sustained the Parnellite–Tory understanding from June until the election in November, however, was soon to end. The election result gave the Parnellite Party 85 MPs in Ireland and one in the Scotland division of Liverpool, gained by T. P. O'Connor. Parnell had directed Irish voters in Britain to vote for the Tories, but as only 249 Tory seats were gained to the Liberals' 335, it was clear that the Parnellites could not provide them with a parliamentary majority, and there was thus little to be gained for the latter by maintaining the informal alliance. The party was thus free to give expression to its anti-Home Rule sentiments. The understanding was probably doomed in any event. Salisbury was resolutely opposed to Home Rule, and opinion in the constituencies would have baulked at the prospect. As Carnarvon put it: what the Tories would gain in Ireland from supporting Home Rule would be outweighed by losses in England.[38]

The efforts of Parnellites to persuade British opinion that England had nothing to fear from Home Rule were of no avail. This is not surprising. Had the party been characterised by a Buttite reverence for British parliamentary institutions, then assurances about the authority of the crown and loyalty to the Queen might have had some effect. But the Parnellites' aggressive opposition to the Prince of Wales in April was too recent. In any assessment of Irish loyalty in 1885, it was the memorable experience. When Salisbury came out publicly against Home Rule in January 1886 the Tory press, which had feared an unacceptable policy turn, was heartened by the welcome affirmation of party principle.[39] And there was also little doubt about the Queen's personal preferences. Unsympathetic to the idea of Home Rule *per se*, she had, nevertheless, been reasoned in her response when Carnarvon had broached the issue, with the implication of Government sympathy. But when well-founded speculation on Gladstone's conversion to Irish autonomy appeared in the Tory *Standard*, her detestation of the politician was extended to the

---

[36] A Kerry farmer, John O'Connor Curtin was shot dead by moonlighters searching his house for arms. Curtin, however, killed one of his assailants and the rest of the gang was arrested on the evidence of Curtin family members: Marie-Louise Legg (ed.), *Alfred Webb: The Autobiography of a Quaker Nationalist* (Cork, 1999), p. 127.

[37] Carnarvon to Ponsonby, 23 Dec. 1885, RA VIC/D 37/106.

[38] Duffy in O'Brien, *Parnell*, II, p. 90.

[39] J. L. Hammond, *Gladstone and the Irish Nation* (London, 1938), pp. 386–7.

16 The Queen and Home Rule.

proposal.[40] Reinforced by the perception that her own opposition mirrored that of a large swathe of British public opinion,[41] it was something she made no secret of,[42] and signalled publicly through ritual.

Having refused to open Parliament during the five years of Gladstone's second administration, her decision to do so for the doomed Salisbury administration in January 1886, an administration lacking a parliamentary majority, could not have been more indicative of personal preference.[43] It also demonstrated that royal ritual was not necessarily, or always, an instrument of national cohesion. Indeed, she would willingly connive with Lord Salisbury to confound the Home Rule policy of her Prime Minister, and in fact only called on Gladstone to form a Government when pressed to do so by Unionists fearful of her constitutional position if she refused.[44] Nationalist awareness of her anti-Home Rule sentiments is clear (Fig. 16).

---

[40] RA VIC/QVJ: 18 Dec. 1885.
[41] Queen to Ponsonby, 19 Dec. 1885, in Arthur Ponsonby, *Henry Ponsonby: His Life from His Letters* (London, 1942), p. 201.
[42] Entry (30 Dec. 1885), Johnson (ed.), *Gathorne-Hardy Diary*, p. 587.
[43] Entry (21 Jan. 1886), D. W. R. Bahlmann (ed.), *The Diary of Sir Edward Walter Hamilton 1885–1906* (Hull, 1993), p. 16.
[44] See correspondence of Salisbury and George Goschen with the Queen, and her own memoranda for January 1886, in G. E. Buckle (ed.), *The Letters of Queen Victoria*, 3rd series (London, 1932), I, pp. 1–30.

II

A considerable literature exists on Gladstone's conversion to Home Rule, but for the purposes of this study it is enough to note that the causes were multiple: fear for the stability of the British political system if the Parnellite party were not conciliated; a moral view that the extended franchise on which the general election had been fought clearly demonstrated that Home Rule was the preference of the Irish *nation*; an undoubted consideration of political advantage – rationalised by the moral argument and hardly recognised as such; and a belief that intimations of unrest in Ireland dictated immediate action. Gladstone, however, took office, claiming to be considering merely the *feasibility* of Home Rule, and thus a wider debate on Irish reform continued, but it remained framed within the ethnocentric prejudices that prioritised a royal residence in Ireland with or without retention of the Viceroyalty.

Lord Randolph Churchill argued for the former, with the Prince of Wales as resident.[45] The former Viceroy, Lord Cowper, lamented the Irish 'tendency to place themselves blindly in the hands of a leader',[46] but his real complaint was that they followed the *wrong* leader. A royal resident in Ireland was intended, as we have seen, to capitalise on this perceived aspect, or weakness, of Irish national character. It also underlay the debate on the Viceroyalty at the end of January in the House of Lords, which emphasised its abolition.[47] Support for administrative reform along these lines was widespread among Irish loyalists.[48] Salisbury, however, repeated the Queen's opinion – without declaring that it was so – that so great a change could not be hurriedly made, and recommended successfully that the proposal be withdrawn.[49] Ironically, a consequence of the debate was to persuade Gladstone that an upper House prepared to consider radical options of this nature should have no difficulty accepting Home Rule.[50]

The Irish Protestant nationalist C. H. Oldham succinctly described the significance of Gladstone's Home Rule scheme thus: it 'did one great irrevocable service to the cause of Irish nationality: it defined it.'[51] The bill gave concrete form to the proposal Parnell had left unspecified. But

[45] Entry (5 Jan. 1886), *Earl Cowper: Memoir*, by his Wife (London, 1913), pp. 626–7.
[46] Cowper to the editor, *The Times [TT]*, 5 Jan. 1886.   [47] Ibid.
[48] Evidence collected by the Liberal intellectual, James Bryce, on an Irish fact-finding tour in autumn 1885: Bryce, 'Irish Opinions on the Irish Problem', Gladstone papers, BL, Add. MS 44700.
[49] Salisbury, *TT*, 26 Jan. 1886.
[50] Gladstone to the Duke of Argyll, 27 Jan. 1886, Gladstone papers, BL, Add. MS 56447.
[51] C. H. Oldham, 'The Prospects of Irish Nationality' in *Dublin University Review* (June 1886), cited Loughlin, *Gladstone*, p. 53.

for our purposes it also has a wider significance. Not only did it undermine the credibility of the Scottish model of constitutional integration,
but Gladstone saw Home Rule as possibly being extended to Scotland
and Wales. The making of the scheme has been dealt with elsewhere.[52]
The concern here is how the scheme was to function as the agency
through which Irish loyalty to the throne would be cultivated.

The proposed constitutional adjustments involved in the concession of
Home Rule were largely unproblematic. The remit of self-government
was restricted to Irish *internal* affairs. A Home Rule Ireland would have
had no presence in the international state system, no official national flag,
no army, no separate currency. British troops would be stationed in
Ireland as before, only very limited control over the police (at least at
first) was to be conceded, restrictions would be placed on the Irish
legislature's ability to legislate on religious questions, while the major
areas of taxation would also remain under Westminster's control.
Moreover, Ireland would also be liable to a substantial charge for imperial
expenses as a first commitment on its revenue.[53] In sum, the Home Rule
scheme proposed that the Union be *amended*, not ended. The scheme
certainly did not validate the account of Irish autonomy given by
Salisbury to the Queen in November 1885, when he claimed it would
reduce the connection between Britain and Ireland to 'a personal union
expressed in Her Majesty's sovereignty',[54] and which was a recurrent
element of Unionist propaganda.[55] But constitutional limitations did not
really address the need for a symbiotic relationship between Irish national
identity and the British state. Gladstone realised that issues of deep
historical alienation had to be addressed, and it is in its historicist ambitions that his Home Rule scheme impresses.

On the nature of Anglo-Irish alienation, Gladstone took Edmund
Burke as his guide: 'What a magazine of wisdom on Ireland and
America'; 'Made many extracts from Burke – *sometimes almost divine.*'[56]
And with Burke in mind he conceived Home Rule as a restorative,
not a radical measure, framed historically on the landlord-dominated
'Grattan's Parliament' of the period 1782–1800. O'Connell, in particu-
lar, with his emphasis on self-government combined with effusive loyalty

---

[52] Ibid. ch. 3; and for a brief account, see James Loughlin, 'Home Rule' in S. J. Connolly
(ed.), *The Oxford Companion to Irish History* (2nd edn, Oxford, 2002), pp. 257–8.
[53] Ibid.
[54] Salisbury to the Queen, 29 Nov. 1885, in Ponsonby, *Henry Ponsonby*, pp. 199–200.
[55] See, for instance, 'The Gladstone–Morley Administration', *Quarterly Review*, 162 (April
1886), 572–3.
[56] Gladstone diary (18 Dec. 1885, 9 Jan. 1886) cited in Loughlin, *Gladstone*, p. 179.

to the crown, exemplified the kind of mentality he wished to cultivate. Parnell, like O'Connell a landlord and his successor as nationalist leader, would 'guarantee' the prominence of Ireland's 'natural' social leaders in the conduct of an Irish parliament's affairs. They would also provide an essential link in the social gradations of society that led downwards from the monarch at its apex, ensuring that a 'natural' social hierarchy remained in place.[57] This hierarchical order, moreover, would be under-pinned by a massive land purchase scheme to address the agrarian prob-lem, thereby removing class alienation in the countryside. Gladstone's Home Rule and land schemes were the successor of his previous attempt to engineer Irish loyalty to the throne in the 1870s, but this time more on Irish terms. Nevertheless, it was misconceived. The nationalism of the aristocratic Irish parliament of 1782–1800 and the similarly elite nation-alism of O'Connell had been superseded in an increasingly democratic age by a Catholic political class representing tenant interests. That the landlord, Parnell, led this movement served merely to mislead.[58] Indeed the land scheme had to be temporarily withdrawn – so it was intended – early in the parliamentary session because of timetabling difficulties. But another difficulty lay in the position of the monarch, whom Gladstone seems to have assumed, despite his own personal difficulties with her, would act as a model of constitutional propriety.

In fact she took undisguised delight in the difficulties he experienced in filling places in the royal household owing to his Irish policy,[59] suggested they be openly communicated to the press,[60] and refused to accept that Parnellites represented the Irish people.[61] The view of Gladstone in royal circles was a lesson in demonisation fed by fears for Unionist interests in Britain and Ireland.[62] There were some exceptions, and especially the Prince of Wales[63]. As on previous issues, and despite being opposed to Home Rule, the Prince took care to observe constitutional proprieties,

---

[57] For the major texts of the crusade, see W. E. Gladstone, *Special Aspects of the Irish Question* (London, 1892).

[58] For discussion see Loughlin, *Gladstone*, ch. 7.

[59] Entry (17 Feb. 1886), D. W. R. Bahlmann (ed.), *The Diary of Sir Edward Walter Hamilton Diary 1880–1885* (Oxford, 1972), II, p. 27.

[60] Victoria to the Dowager Duchess of Roxburghe, 11 Feb. 1886, in Buckle (ed.), *Letters of Queen Victoria*, I, p. 51.

[61] See diary (11 April 1886), Ponsonby, *Henry Ponsonby*, p. 209.

[62] See Giles St Aubyn, *The Royal George 1819–1904: The Life of H.R.H. Prince George Duke of Cambridge* (London, 1963), p. 227; Lord Lansdowne to the Queen, 31 Jan. 1886, RA VIC/D 38/1A; Lady Arnott to the Queen, 9 March 1886, RA VIC/D 38/20.

[63] RA VIC/D 38/72; Entry (17 Feb. 1886), Bahlmann, *Hamilton Diary*, II, pp. 227–8; Richard Shannon, *Gladstone: Heroic Leader 1865–1898* (London, 1999), p. 415.

assisting Gladstone with the royal household and refusing to become a pawn of his mother. Indeed, an unfounded but apparently well-sourced rumour circulated that he had quarrelled with her over Home Rule.[64] The rumour would persist to the advantage of the Prince's reputation in nationalist circles.

The monarch's prejudices, however, became increasingly inflamed under Salisbury's influence: 'The grant of Home Rule appeared to be a concession to the forces of disorder' and in particular 'a betrayal of the loyalists of Ulster'.[65] This was a somewhat unusual concern for a group whose excesses of bigotry and violence in the past had earned her strong disapproval, but reflected Salisbury's perception of the developing importance of northern Ireland to the anti-Home Rule struggle. He claimed that to betray Ulster loyalists was actually 'inconsistent with the honour of an English Sovereign'.[66] That Ulster was the only region of Ireland that both appeared to honour loyally the memory of Prince Albert, and had enthusiastically greeted the Prince of Wales in April 1885, would have enhanced the credibility of his argument.

In fact, Salisbury manipulated the Queen's prejudices to feed her sense of centrality to the stability of the state – 'one of the few bonds of cohesion remaining to the community' – and the constitutional validity of her taking autonomous action, while, at the same time, restraining her from *publicly* exceeding her authority and thus endangering the crown.[67] Her partisanship grew as Gladstone set about the construction of his Home Rule scheme, exacerbated by his reluctance to inform her of what exactly he had in mind, and on being informed that, even in the Cabinet, there were deep reservations about Home Rule.[68]

Gladstone presented the bill as a solution to a centuries-old conflict, but had to contend with the apparently countervailing evidence of recent years – the massive disorder of the land war, and associated evidence of Irish disloyalty, of which nationalist protests during the royal visit of 1885 were the most egregious example. In August 1885 Parnell himself had declared that the only question was one not of Irish self-government, but of how much self-government the English could cheat them out of.[69] In this context, it was much easier for Salisbury to whip up traditional British

---

[64] See commentary for 13 May 1886 in W.S. Blunt, *The Land War in Ireland* (London, 1912), p. 87.
[65] Lee, *Victoria*, pp. 492–3.
[66] Salisbury to the Queen, 29 Nov. 1885, in Ponsonby, *Henry Ponsonby*, pp. 199–200.
[67] Salisbury to the Queen, 15 May 1886, RA VIC/D 44/35.
[68] Entry (11 May 1886), Vincent (ed.), *Derby Diaries 1878–93*, p. 834.
[69] *FJ*, 25 Aug. 1885.

ethno-national hatred of the Catholic Irish,[70] especially with reference to the Ulster issue which both Parnell and Gladstone had failed to address.

More generally, Gladstone's claim that Irish nationality resided historically in the constitutional tradition represented by the colonial Parliament that had existed until 1800 – ignoring the many bloody struggles against English rule – was simply not credible.[71] In this context, and given that an overt and explicit signifier of Ireland's continued membership of the United Kingdom was needed, the Viceroyalty, both as its role was determined in the Home Rule bill and in the Irish response to the occupant of the office he had appointed on assuming office, took on crucial significance.

As specified in the Home Rule bill, the definition of powers the Viceroy would exercise was extremely brief and general:

> The executive government of Ireland shall continue vested in Her Majesty and shall be carried on by the Lord Lieutenant on behalf of Her Majesty, with the aid of such officers and councils as to Her Majesty may from time to time seem fit.[72]

Gladstone argued that the Viceroyalty would only be altered by statute, the principal changes being the disconnection between the office and Government, and the removal of the ban on Roman Catholic occupants.[73] These provisions were welcomed by nationalist opinion in Ireland, where it was thought a Viceroy, especially a Catholic one – though this change was strongly objected to by Ulster Unionists[74] – would choose whether to exercise his veto powers by a consideration of Irish feeling on the spot. This was much preferable to abolition of the Viceroyalty with a veto being exercised by the Queen in London, where there would be 'less hesitation and more ignorance in affronting Irish feeling'.[75]

It is reasonable to assume, however, that Gladstone envisaged the constitutional practice of the white colonies – whereby the Viceroy represented the interests of the colonial parliament in the same manner in which the Queen gave constitutional expression to the legislative enactments of Westminster – would, in the Irish case, be reached only very gradually. He argued that while it was important that a legislative body

---

[70] Salisbury at the Crystal Palace in *Cork Constitution*, 5 March 1886; W. C. Lubenow, *Parliamentary Politics and the Home Rule Crisis: The British House of Commons in 1886* (Oxford, 1988), pp. 268–9.

[71] See Loughlin, *Gladstone*, ch. 7.   [72] Cited in ibid. p. 60.

[73] Hutton and Cohen (eds.), *Gladstone's Speeches 1886–8*, pp. 36–7.

[74] William 'Ballykilbeg' Johnston, *Hansard 3*, 304 (8 April 1886), col. 1232.

[75] See *UI*, 16 April 1886; also *Nation*, 9 April 1886.

should be established 'by a single stroke', the executive transition 'must necessarily be gradual'. By degrees and mutual trust the 'old state of things shall be adjusted to the new'.[76] In the immediate term, the Viceroy would, it seems, function to give effect to the wishes of the Westminster Government and/or the monarch, who might, or might not, endorse the legislative enactments of a Dublin parliament. As a later critic of the 1886 scheme argued: the freedom given to the Queen effectively to determine what powers the Viceroy should possess and ambiguity as to the terms and conditions of the office laid open the possibility of an ill-disposed Westminster Government retaining executive authority in its own hands 'without breach of statuary obligations'.[77]

The Home Rule scheme was informed to a large extent by colonial precedent, especially Canada. But the colonial precedent only fitted the Anglo-Irish case very imperfectly. The factor of distance alone made impractical any Westminster interference in colonial governmental affairs. Ireland, however, was not only close at hand, but, through imperial taxation and the necessary Westminster representation, would continue to be closely engaged in British affairs, not to mention the potential for trouble presented by the vociferously Unionist Irish landlord and Ulster Protestant communities.

On any estimation, the freedom proposed for the autonomous Irish Parliament under Home Rule was greatly circumscribed, but this was ignored by Unionists in favour of Gladstone's supposed failure effectively to secure the authority of the crown.[78] In 1886, however, these were hypothetical weaknesses, only likely to emerge, if at all, when the scheme was implemented. In the immediate term the task was to persuade British political opinion to accept Home Rule, and in this context the Irish Viceroy, Lord Aberdeen, was to have a central role.

III

When it was clear that he intended to retain the Viceroyalty, Gladstone's influential adviser, the Radical, Henry Labouchere, suggested a 'King Log' – a royal representative who could be relied upon not to use his powers – with Timothy Healy suggesting the Prince of Wales's son,

---

[76] Gladstone in the Commons, 8 April 1886 in Hutton and Cohen (eds.), *Gladstone's Speeches 1886–8*, p. 35.

[77] J. H. Morgan, 'The Constitution: A Commentary' in J. H. Morgan (ed.), *The New Irish Constitution: An Exposition and Some Arguments* (London, 1912), pp. 32–3.

[78] See, for example, Henry Chaplin, *Hansard 3*, 305 (18 May 1886), cols. 1327–8; Sir Henry James, ibid. (13 May 1886), cols. 928–9; Mr Boyd-Kinnear, ibid., col. 977.

Albert Victor, for the post.[79] Such a figure, however, would clearly have
been inadequate for Gladstone's purposes. Two tasks needed to be
accomplished if the scenario of love he envisaged between the sovereign
and her Irish subjects was to be established: first, repair of the damage
done to the relationship between the Viceroyalty and Irish public opinion
during Lord Spencer's period in office: second, the neutralising of the
negative effects in Ireland of the Queen's publicly perceived dislike of
Irish nationalists.

In the first instance, Gladstone considered the Catholic convert Lord
Ripon, but the difficulty of removing the ban on Catholic occupants[80] in a
parliamentary session that Home Rule would make highly controversial
deterred him. He next sought to address this issue, and, to some extent,
that of a royal residence, by having the Queen's son-in-law, Lord Lorne,
appointed.[81] Victoria, however, was determined that no member of her
family be associated with his Irish plan, though Gladstone was told the
problem was financial.[82] In the event, he offered the post to Lord
Aberdeen, considered a suitable appointment as the amiable, rather
nervous Viceroy was also unlikely to interfere with John Morley's role as
Chief Secretary.

The Vicereine, Lady Aberdeen, has recorded that their official arrival
in Dublin was not greeted with unbounded enthusiasm. It was known
that a Home Rule bill was to be prepared, but until its exact nature
was known 'the prevalent attitude was, though by no means unfriendly,
somewhat that of reserve'.[83] Certainly their reception was lukewarm
compared to that of Lord Carnarvon, Aberdeen's Tory predecessor.[84]
But while, as a Liberal Viceroy, Aberdeen clearly inherited some of the
negative backwash to the Spencer regime, that would soon change, for
both Lord and Lady Aberdeen – a more formidable character, intelligent
and with a strong social conscience – were enthusiastic promoters of
welfare monarchism.[85] In sum, if welfare monarchism was the most
effective means by which royalty could establish and strengthen the
bonds of popular allegiance, then the Aberdeens were ideally suited to

---

[79] See Labouchere to Joseph Chamberlain, 23 Dec. 1885, in Algar Thorold, *The Life of
Henry Labouchere* (London, 1913), pp. 255–7; Frank Callanan, *T. M. Healy* (Cork,
1996), pp. 139–40.

[80] Dermot Quinn, *Patronage and Piety: The Politics of English Roman Catholicism 1850–1900*
(Stanford, 1993), pp. 148–9.

[81] See Gladstone to the Queen, 4 Feb. 1886, in Buckle (ed.), *Letters of Queen Victoria*, I, p. 44.

[82] Victoria, note to ibid. The Prince of Wales more reasonably objected on the grounds of
the office's political connection with the Government: Edward to Ponsonby, 2 Feb.
1886, in Buckle (ed.), *Letters of Queen Victoria*, I, pp. 39–40.

[83] Lord and Lady Aberdeen, *'We Twa': Reminiscences* (2nd edn, London, 1927), I, p. 253.

[84] Ibid. pp. 252–3.   [85] Ibid. p. 248.

Gladstone's purposes in 1886, and certainly to mend the damage Spencer believed had been inflicted in Ireland through his own fusion of the duties of Chief Secretary and Viceroy. Untroubled by the detail and responsibilities of administrative policy in a period of Irish nationalist goodwill, Aberdeen was free to deploy his conciliatory gifts.

This was very effectively done. Popular opinion turned decidedly in the Viceroy's favour when the viceregal couple made an overture to T. D. Sullivan, Lord Mayor of Dublin and editor of the radical *Nation*, for a meeting to address the 'alleviation of public distress'. It was quickly responded to and generated significant funds. The importance Aberdeen attached to the meeting – held in the Lord Mayor's official residence, the Mansion House, a symbolic nationalist location – was evident in *how* he attended. Aberdeen arrived in state, 'in an open carriage, drawn by four horses, with postilions and outriders, and attended by some members of the [viceregal] staff'.[86]

The gesture's importance was immense given the political apartheid that had existed between the Mansion House and Dublin Castle during the Spencer years, but the most significant aspect of the visit was Aberdeen's initiating a personal meeting with Michael Davitt, the father of the Land League, who also was present. Given Aberdeen's viceregal status as simultaneously the representative of the Government and the embodiment of the monarchical presence in Ireland, the meeting, widely witnessed, was freighted with profound symbolism about the change in the British state's approach to Ireland. That the 'simple interchange of courtesy which took place had an instant and extraordinary effect'[87] is hardly surprising. Thereafter, the active engagement of the viceregal couple in the promotion of Irish manufactures and industries, and their evident goodwill towards the Irish people, was rewarded with hearty popular receptions and enthusiastic, if not always successful, attempts of local bands to render 'God Save the Queen'.

The priority of welfare monarchism in viceregal policy was evident in the formation of a Mansion House Ladies' Committee for the Relief of Distress and, especially, the inauguration of the Irish Industries Association, marked by a large garden party at the Viceregal Lodge at which guests were requested to come in 'garments of genuine Irish manufacture'.[88] In the Vicereine's case, her appearance as Aoife the Irish bride of Strongbow, in a dress heavily embroidered with Celtic motifs, was an impressive bodily display of 'aristocratic pleasure' and

---

[86] Ibid. p. 255; Sullivan, *Troubled Times in Irish Politics*, pp. 210–11.
[87] Aberdeen, *'We Twa'*, I, p. 257.   [88] Ibid. p. 259.

'Celtic revival' in the interests of Irish industry,[89] while in a wider sense symbolising the new era of Anglo-Irish amity to be opened up by Home Rule. It was to be one of the most successful enterprises of its kind.

At the end of the Aberdeen Viceroyalty in August, following the Liberal defeat at the general election held the previous month, their public send-off was one of the largest public processions Dublin had ever seen, and with the obvious intent of signalling Irish loyalty under Home Rule.[90] Only from Irish America did occasional cries of 'disgrace' erupt that Irishmen should embrace any representative of English rule in Ireland.[91]

IV

Though its duration was short, the Aberdeen Viceroyalty was an almost brilliant example of what welfare monarchism could achieve in Ireland if the political circumstances were right; and the Irish attitude to Aberdeen was duly exploited in Parliament to lend credibility to Gladstone's claim for Home Rule as a mechanism for the symbiotic development of loyalty to the monarch and Irish nationality.[92] The recent Irish past of course could easily be exploited no less for evidence of disloyalty,[93] and certainly for a Queen with a long experience of the Irish question this was more significant than the apparently fabricated loyalty now exhibited; and far less than with Irish Unionists, Aberdeen's real difficulties existed in his relations with the Queen.

He lacked the courage to acquaint her with his activities in Ireland, especially his congenial relations with nationalists. When, for instance, it came to conveying a message from Lord Mayor Sullivan to the Queen, looking forward to her inaugurating a Dublin Parliament, Aberdeen could not do so, opting instead to submit it through Ponsonby, 'in case Your Majesty may desire to be acquainted with the actual observations of the Lord Mayor'.[94] When he could not avoid seeing the Queen in person he was grateful for a hint from Ponsonby not to speak of his departure from Dublin, as he 'was far too nervous to have thought of touching on this topic'.[95] Thus whereas there is a quite substantial correspondence

---

[89] See Janice Helland, 'Embrodiered Spectacle: Celtic Revival as Aristocratic Display' in B. T. FitzSimon and J. H. Murphy (eds.), *The Celtic Revival Reappraised* (Dublin, 2004), p. 95.

[90] Aberdeen, *'We Twa'*, I, pp. 267–8.   [91] Sullivan, *Troubled Times in Irish Politics*, p. 213.

[92] See Thomas Sexton, *Hansard 3*, 306 (1 June 1886), cols. 722–3; T. D. Sullivan, ibid. 305 (18 May 1886), cols. 1353–4; William O'Brien, ibid. (21 May 1886), col. 1712.

[93] See for example, Robert Hanbury, ibid. 305 (18 May 1886), cols. 360–1.

[94] Aberdeen to the Queen, 5 Aug. 1886, RA VIC/D 38/139.

[95] Ponsonby to the Queen, 20 Aug. 1886, RA VIC/D 38/141.

between the Queen and his predecessors, no such correspondence exists for the Aberdeen Viceroyalty. Of a more courageous disposition, Lady Aberdeen impressed on Ponsonby the loyal intentions of the crowds attending their Dublin departure, and their own contribution to cultivating loyalty.[96] Prince Edward of Saxe-Weimar, Commander of Crown Forces in Ireland, however, painted a very different picture: 'rabble' celebrated the occasion with rebel tunes and '*not a single* British flag'. That the Aberdeens thought otherwise was due to their seeing everything 'in a rosy hue'.[97] Deeply distrustful of attempts to instil loyalty in the Catholic Irish, there can be little doubt which account the Queen found most persuasive.

V

The Home Rule crisis of 1886 had a profound impact on British and Irish politics, dividing and weakening the Liberal Party, and providing it, if not with a new ideology, then with a new legislative priority that overrode all others at least while Gladstone was party leader, and lay in wait for the party thereafter whenever Irish nationalist MPs held the balance of power at Westminster. By the same token, the crisis served to revive the fortunes of the Conservative Party, now the major partner in a Unionist political coalition that, apart from the brief Gladstonian interlude of 1892–5, would hold power from 1886 to 1905. But 1886 can also be seen as a culmination point in the debate over Ireland's relationship with the monarchy. If not closing debate on this subject, the Liberal conversion to Home Rule narrowed it significantly.

The perception of the monarchy as a factor in the Irish question shared essentially by both British parties hitherto – a British pole of attraction in a zero-sum game between loyalty and sedition – was transformed by Gladstone's promotion of nationality and loyalty. For Liberals and nationalists the position of the Viceroyalty would be settled as the agency through which that relationship would largely be mediated. But most importantly for our purposes, although the scheme of 1886 was defeated, the Parnellite–Liberal alliance it effected entailed a significant change in Irish nationalist attitudes to the crown.

The freedom Parnell had during the land war to attack not just the Government, but the moral credibility of the Queen, no longer existed. An essential part of the campaign for Home Rule would be the demonstration of Irish loyalty to an, albeit antagonistic, monarch. More

---

[96] Ibid.   [97] Saxe-Weimar to Ponsonby, 11 Aug. 1886, RA VIC/D 38/142.

generally, the Liberal conversion to Home Rule largely foreclosed the feasibility of lesser plans of administrative autonomy, as the fate of the devolution proposal of 1904–5 and the Irish Councils bill of 1908 would demonstrate. From 1886 the only real alternatives were either the existing Union or legislative autonomy. Demonstrating loyalty, however, would be fraught with tension as a Unionist administration took office and acted on Salisbury's prescription of twenty years of firm government.

Part IV

Constructive Unionism and the crown

10   Allegiance and agrarian struggle

Had the Home Rule bill of 1886 been enacted, the basic conditions envisaged by Gladstone for the symbiotic development in Ireland of loyalty to the monarchy and the British state together with Irish nationality would have been established. As it was, its rejection, the election of a Tory-dominated Unionist administration committed to 'resolute government', and the onset of an agricultural crisis entailing tenant agitation for rent reductions,[1] set the scene for conflict rather than conciliation, energising the kind of nationalist narrative a developing Anglo-Irish patriotism was intended to neutralise. At the same time, the Home Rule crisis of 1886 had functioned to clarify publicly the anti-Home Rule sentiment of the Queen, complementing the 'non-political' Primrose League's promotion of monarcho-imperial patriotism that all too clearly encoded a jingoistic political agenda.[2] Moreover, the neo-regal status of Parnell in Ireland made it easy for Unionists to deny the possibility of him ever being a simple 'subject' of the British monarch: 'Queen Victoria cannot wear the crown while Parnell holds the sceptre. He would as soon knock the crown off her head and put it on his own.'[3] In sum, Gladstone's imaginative reconstruction of the Anglo-Irish relationship, entailing a fusion of Irish national and British patriotisms focused on the monarchy, was now much more problematic than it had been just a few months earlier.

I

Salisbury's administration came to office pledged to a 'resolute' approach to Irish government – redress of 'real' grievances combined with stern application of the law to repress illegality – but some attempt was made to conciliate Irish Catholic opinion. Salisbury thought the appointment of

---

[1] For the campaign see Laurence Geary, *The Plan of Campaign 1886–91* (Cork, 1987).
[2] See Martin Pugh, *The Tories and the People 1880–1935* (Oxford, 1985), pp. 72–80.
[3] J. Townshend Trench, 'Irish Interests', *Fortnightly Review* [*FR*], 39, n.s. (1886), 861–2.

Henry Matthews, a Roman Catholic, as Home Secretary – the first since the Glorious Revolution – would 'favourably influence moderate Roman Catholics in Ireland'.[4] This gesture, however, was insignificant compared to the changed relationship that took place between the Viceroyalty and large sections of the Irish people.

Whereas the Aberdeen Viceroyalty had functioned as a solvent of nationalist alienation, that of Lord Londonderry – chosen because of his wealth, background, opinions and 'family connections'[5] – was intended to conciliate, primarily, the virulently Unionist Ulster Protestant and Irish landlord communities. Where previously a close functional relationship existed between viceregal ceremonial, Government policy and Irish public engagement, state ritual under Londonderry functioned chiefly to illustrate state power. As Viceroy, Londonderry was expected to be little more than the 'King Log' envisaged by Henry Labouchere.[6] Needless to say, he did not have a seat in the Cabinet.

It is true that the Government's Irish policy included reform no less than coercion, but reforms were largely a sop to the Tories' Liberal Unionist allies, especially their leader, Joseph Chamberlain, anxious to demonstrate to his followers that Unionism was not inconsistent with progress. It has been plausibly argued that the Tory leadership subscribed to no such conception of the Irish question.[7] Electorally, a majority of Irish opinion may have expressed itself in favour of Home Rule, but Salisbury and the Chief Secretary Arthur Balfour were simply prepared to ignore that in the wider interests of a jingoistic conception of kingdom and empire. Such a stance was astute in the context of British opinion, for the Parnellite party now lacked the freedom to attack *all* aspects of the British presence in Ireland. A fine line between aggressive pursuit of tenant farmer interests and loyalty had to be drawn, but the pressure of events all too easily made this impossible as the Plan of Campaign for lower rents was met with a more effectively organised landlord reaction than during the land war.

---

[4] Salisbury to the Queen, 29 July 1886, in G. E. Buckle (ed.), *The Letters of Queen Victoria* (London, 1932), 3rd ser., I, pp. 167–8.

[5] Salisbury to the Prince of Wales, 27 July 1886, in Sir Sidney Lee, *King Edward VII: A Biography* (London, 1925), I, p. 243.

[6] See Balfour to Salisbury, 31 Jan. 1888, in R. H. Williams (ed.), *Balfour–Salisbury Correspondence: Letters Exchanged between the Third Marquis of Salisbury and His Nephew Arthur James Balfour 1869–1892* ([Hertfordshire], 1988), p. 235. Virginia Crossman, *Politics, Land and Order in Nineteenth Century Ireland* (Dublin, 1996), pp. 164–5.

[7] For coverage of Unionist policies in this period, see L. P. Curtis Jr., *Conflict and Conciliation in Ireland 1880–1892* (Princeton, 1963); Andrew Gailey, *Ireland and the Death of Kindness 1895–1905* (Cork, 1987).

The nature of the Home Rule crusade had, fundamentally, been established by the arguments Gladstone had made in favour of the bill of 1886. Strongly historicist in focus, these had framed the bill in the context of Ireland's *constitutional* tradition with the landlord-dominated patriot Parliament of 1782–1800 as a model. The agricultural crisis of late 1886, however, seriously complicated the credibility of Gladstone's case,[8] with landlords the focus of nationalists attack and the aggression of agrarian struggle almost inevitably finding voice in anti-royal expressions, especially in 1887, the year of the Queen's Golden Jubilee.[9] Thus a fundamental disjuncture existed between the narrative content and ambition of the Home Rule crusade in Britain and the dynamics of the Irish political environment. Aware of the damage that unrestrained rhetoric could present for the Home Rule cause in Britain, the more emotionally neutral Irish Protestant Home Rule Association warned against repeating the mistake of 1885, when the Prince of Wales was unfairly made to carry the responsibility for Spencer's coercion policy:

The royal initials, the Crown, and similar symbols of the sovereign have been thoughtlessly accepted as party insignia … The enemy have done well [in manoeuvring nationalists into this position], but the Nationalists have done foolishly in accepting such an issue … The Queen is our Queen, the empire is our empire.[10]

Plan leaders were not altogether unmindful of Gladstone's difficulties, but attempts to adjust agrarian objectives in Ireland with the needs of the Home Rule crusade[11] assumed an appreciation of Irish affairs that was largely beyond British public opinion. In this context Parnell emphatically rejected the Plan to consolidate his alliance with Gladstone. Nevertheless, the turbulence associated with agrarian agitation provided a problematic Irish background to the major royal occasion of the period.[12]

II

In as much as the Golden Jubilee of Queen Victoria's reign was a celebration of personal service to the country it was no less an exercise in

---

[8] T. M. Healy, 'Jubilee Time in Ireland', *Contemporary Review* [*CR*], 51 (1887), 130; John Dillon at Castlerea, County Roscommon in *Freeman's Journal* [*FJ*], 6 Dec. 1886; R. U. Penrose Fitzgerald, 'Home Rule and the Forces Behind It' in George Baden-Powell (ed.), *The Truth about Home Rule* (London, 1888), p. 126.

[9] See John Bright to Joseph Chamberlain, 30 May 1887, in H. J. Leech (ed.), *The Public Letters of John Bright* (London, 1895), pp. 142–5.

[10] 'The Link of the Crown', *North and South*, 28 May 1887.

[11] W. S. Blunt, *The Land War in Ireland* (London, 1912), pp. 291–3.

[12] F. S. L. Lyons, *Charles Stewart Parnell* (London, 1978), pp. 379–80.

monarcho-imperial mythology, a crucial landmark in the developing imperial identity of the British 'race'. The process entailed the mythicising not only of Victoria's reign – fifty years of unalloyed progress – but of the person of the Queen herself: the fallible, partisan and prejudiced human being was apotheosised in a flood of published Jubilee slush as an abstract model of moral and national rectitude.[13] And despite the millions of Catholics within its boundaries, for the Queen and much of British public opinion the empire, which she emblematised, had a fundamentally Protestant identity. She was quite ready to discard D.F. (defender of the faith) – an unnecessary designation of popish origin – to make room for her imperial title on Jubilee coins.[14] The 350 bonfires that blazed throughout the land on Jubilee night evoked images of those organised on the defeat of the Spanish Armada and were freighted with a lesson of national awareness for the future.[15] In this context, it was almost inevitable that the recent controversy over Home Rule would inform the Jubilee celebrations as the Unionist press conflated the national interest and 'non-political' celebration of the Queen's reign with a rejection of Gladstone's bill,[16] allowing a blending of contemporary 'national' anxieties with historicist sectarian prejudices. Certainly in Britain Catholicism had an inescapably destabilising – and Irish – persona, one conveniently scapegoated,[17] while the political atmosphere of the time raised establishment anxieties that Ireland, in its militant revolutionary no less than its agitational aspects, would find expression during the Jubilee,[18] pointing up the unresolvedness of national identity within the United Kingdom in the midst of celebrations emphasising ideological coherence and unity.[19] As an exception to the base of economic prosperity on which the Jubilee celebrations were largely grounded, at a time when the sovereign was increasingly perceived as the 'Famine Queen', Ireland could not easily be accommodated to the Jubilee experience.

---

[13] See Jeffrey Lant, *Insubstantial Pageant: Ceremony and Confusion at Queen Victoria's Court* (London, 1979), pp. 169–71.

[14] Ibid. pp. 183–4.

[15] Lant, *Insubstantial Pageant*, pp. 175–6. In the event D.F. remained: H.N. Cole, *Coronation and Royal Commemorative Medals 1887–1977* (London, 1977), p. 7.

[16] Richard Williams, *The Contentious Crown: Public Discussion of the British Monarchy in the Reign of Queen Victoria* (Aldershot, 1997), pp. 136–8.

[17] On Salisbury in this respect, see Lant, *Insubstantial Pageant*, pp. 172–3.

[18] For establishement fears of Fenian attacks in London on Jubilee, see Christy Campbell, *Fenian Fire: The British Government Plot to Assassinate Queen Victoria* (London, 2002), pp. 240–1.

[19] Jan Ruger, 'Nation, Empire and Navy: Identity Politics in the United Kingdom 1887–1914', *Past and Present*, 184 (Nov. 2004), 163.

Attempts to do so occurred at a number of levels but with uneven results. In particular, an attempt to incorporate Ireland within a Unionist narrative of progress during the Queen's reign was met, predictably enough, with a vigorous nationalist counter-narrative,[20] while a range of activities took place: criticism of the Jubilee estimates and the boycotting of official Jubilee activities in Britain, together with coercion, violence, boycotting, the flaunting of anti-Unionist symbols, and the commemoration of the famine as the defining experience of Victoria's reign in Ireland.[21]

Some signs of a nationalist willingness to embrace an Anglo-Irish identity were evident during the Jubilee, however, such as two banners displayed in Derry, consisting of 'green flags with the Union cross in the corner',[22] and which appeared to have a wider currency.[23] And despite the nationalist sense of alienation, it would not be accurate to describe it generally as the '*republican* [my italics] nationalist community'.[24] In fact, one Parnellite MP, the veteran Protestant nationalist Samuel Young, even attended a royal garden party, though he refused a personal meeting with the Queen.[25] The *Derry Journal*, an Ulster regional version of the *Freeman's Journal*, congratulated the Irish people on their attitude to the Jubilee, taking care to distinguish opposition to Government policies from loyalty to the monarch.[26]

The nationalist protests, nevertheless, served Unionist interests in Britain, contradicting Gladstone's Home Rule arguments and highlighting Ulster Unionist loyalty: ninety-nine occasions of Jubilee celebration, not including Belfast, took place in the north.[27] The Irish Chief Secretary, Arthur Balfour, remarked: 'I see no harm in this, rather the reverse.'[28] At the same time, however, it was necessary, at least for the public credibility of the Unionist argument about the *unrepresentativeness* of nationalist

---

[20] Sir Rowland Blennerhasset, 'Ireland' in T. H. Ward (ed.), *The Reign of Queen Victoria: Fifty Years of Progress* (London, 1887); 'Ireland in the Reign of Queen Victoria', *FJ*, 7 July 1887.

[21] Lant, *Insubstantial Pageant*, pp. 10, 76, 77; coverage of events in *United Ireland [UI]*, 25 June 1887. The 'loyal citizens of Dublin' presented the Queen with a silver casket engraved with a round tower, harp and wolfhound: *FJ*, 24 June 1887; *Standard*, 22 June 1887.

[22] *Derry* [formerly *Londonderry*] *Journal [DJ]*, 22 June 1887.

[23] See Lord Spencer to John Morley, 21 Aug. 1890, in Peter Gordon (ed.), *The Red Earl: The Papers of the Fifth Earl Spencer 1885–1910* (Northampton, 1986), II, pp. 163–4.

[24] Antony Taylor, *'Down with the Crown': British Anti-Monarchism and Debates about Royalty since 1790* (London, 1999), p. 140.

[25] J. G. Swift MacNeill, *What I Have Seen and Heard* (London, 1925), p. 280.

[26] *DJ*, 22 June 1887.   [27] See *Belfast News-Letter [BNL]*, 21–7 June 1887.

[28] Quoted ibid.

claims, that Ireland in general demonstrate evidence of a different national persona. For the purposes of the formal Jubilee Thanksgiving Service the problem was solved by simply filling the vacant places in St Paul's rejected by nationalist public officials with Irish loyalists,[29] while the Tory house journal, the *Standard*, could be relied upon to massage Irish events for its English readers so as to conform to the myth of state-wide expressions of national celebration.[30] The problem, nevertheless, was formidable.

The Undersecretary for Ireland, Major-General Sir Redvers Buller, acknowledged that it was 'hopeless' attempting to govern Ireland against the will of the people and saw in the priesthood the only possible intermediaries given that the Government had 'no mouthpiece in Ireland'. Buller speculated: 'Think what a social revolution would be effected if all the priests were suddenly to take in the "Irish Times," instead of the "Freeman" and instruct their flocks accordingly.'[31] It was a revealing comment, both on the construction of imaginative arenas and on British perceptions of the Irish question, one that accorded the Vatican undue influence.[32] The Jubilee was a tempting occasion on which to enlist its assistance.

In fact, 1887 was the Golden Jubilee, not only of Victoria's reign but also of Pope Leo XIII's ordination as a priest, and both the Vatican and the British Government were drawn to attempt a form of rapprochement, driven on the part of the former by a desire for formal diplomatic relations with the Court of St James's, and on the latter by the desire for Vatican support in the government of Ireland. These ambitions were complicated, however, both by British Protestant – especially the increasingly important Ulster Protestant – antagonism to anything resembling formal relations between the papacy and the United Kingdom, and at the Vatican by the Irish Catholic hierarchy, ever on the alert to any infringement of their prerogatives by the British Government, and anxious to prevent a repeat of the counter-productive papal rescript against Parnell in 1883.[33] Accordingly, while an exchange of gifts did take place, no

[29] Lant, *Insubstantial Pageant*, p. 77.   [30] *Standard*, 22 June 1887.

[31] Buller to Arthur Balfour, 8 April 1887, in Emmet Larkin, *The Roman Catholic Church and the Plan of Campaign 1886–1888* (Naas, Co. Kildare, 1978), pp. 84–5.

[32] Ibid. p. 85. See also Marie-Louise Legg, *Newspapers and Nationalism: The Irish Provincial Press 1850–1892* (Dublin, 1999), ch. 10, on the expansion of the newspaper industry and its political effects in the 1880s.

[33] On this issue, see James Loughlin, 'Constructing the Political Spectacle: Parnell, the Press and National Leadership 1879–1885' in D. G. Boyce and Alan O'Day (eds.), *Parnell in Perspective* (London, 1991), p. 232.

'substantive' relations followed from it.[34] A papal rescript against the Plan was obtained in 1888, and was as ineffective as that of 1883, serving only to weaken Vatican influence in Ireland.[35] But at the time of the Queen's Jubilee and in the context of a forthcoming Irish royal visit, the Pope hoped that a conciliatory attitude by Archbishop Walsh and the Irish hierarchy – focusing on the respect due the Queen as a woman, the embodiment of moral values, and the representative 'of the principle of authority which comes from God, devoid of all political considerations' – would assist his objectives.[36]

The problem, however, was that the Queen's political prejudices had been made so explicitly clear that an apolitical conception of her was difficult to maintain. As *United Ireland* succinctly put it: 'loyalty to her sacred person can be best testified by the unquestioning support of a Tory Government'.[37] The flag that flew outside Michael Davitt's cottage on Jubilee day – a black strip with the word 'Evictoria' worked in white[38] – cleverly framed that sentiment in the contemporary agrarian context. The kind of initiative the Pope wished Archbishop Walsh to take would have been not only repugnant to Walsh's own preferences, but politically unwise.

Ireland was not alone in the experience of domestic agrarian discontent impairing a readiness to enter into the wider national Jubilee celebrations. In Wales, experiencing a tithe agitation at this time, a similar pattern of non-compliance occurred in places.[39] Only in Ireland, however, was the pattern of alienation coextensive with such a large proportion of the population and drawing on wells of historical memory and myth capable of sustaining mass agitation. That an Irish royal visit by the Prince of Wales's sons, Princes Albert Victor and the future George V, was arranged for 27 to 30 June is perhaps surprising.

III

A royal visit may have been deemed necessary in any event, but it was pressed for strongly by the Viceroy, Londonderry,[40] under whom welfare

---

[34] Larkin, *Catholic Church and the Plan of Campaign*, pp. 85–100; Lant, *Insubstantial Pageant*, pp. 105–11. For a flavour of the kind of popular Protestant opinion that intimidated the Government, see Walter Walsh, *The Religious Life of Queen Victoria* (London, 1903), pp. 109–25.

[35] Geary, *Plan of Campaign*, p. 88.

[36] Tobias Kirby to Walsh, 17 June 1887, in P. J. Walsh, *William J. Walsh: Archbishop of Dublin* (London, 1928), pp. 265–6.

[37] *United Ireland* [*UI*], 2 July 1887.   [38] Blunt, *Land War in Ireland*, pp. 277–8.   [39] Ibid.

[40] Lee, *Edward VII*, I, p. 244; Queen to Londonderry, 5 March 1887, in Buckle (ed.), *Letters of Queen Victora*, I, p. 282.

monarchism was pursued in highly unpropitious circumstances:[41] vigorous coercion merely intensified the popular demonising of Ireland's
most important administrative/royal site, Dublin Castle. Apparently
ignorant of the ridicule often attending viceregal ritual,[42] Londonderry
boasted of the improbable success of his ceremonial duties: 'I cannot
conceal from myself a feeling of satisfaction that I have been able to
awaken feelings of loyalty and respect to Our Sovereign which ... have
been long dormant, and which I do not think anyone else could have
aroused.'[43] In the event, Victoria and the Prince of Wales did agree to his
sons making the trip, but only after the enactment of the Criminal Law
Amendment (Ireland) bill of 1887.[44]

The disorder surrounding the visit of 1885 clearly produced fears of a
similar outcome in 1887 and the itinerary of the latter visit was planned
with 1885 in mind. Arrival at Kingstown was to be followed by the
journey to Dublin, and a ball at Leinster Hall, while thereafter the usual
round of ritual and social engagements common to royal visits were to be
undertaken – the most significant being the investiture of the Prince
Albert Victor as a Knight of St Patrick – together with a number of
welfarist duties in and around the city before a return to Britain aboard
the *Ireland* on 30 June.[45] In sum, the visit was to, and did, follow closely
the itinerary of the successful *first* week of the 1885 visit, and was clearly a
condition of royal permission.[46] Of course, if the exercise of royal ritual is
seen as indicative of the remit of state authority, then that of 1887 could
be seen as an admission of state weakness. For the purpose of Jubilee
objectives, however, the itinerary served its purpose. Londonderry and
Ulster Unionists would declare a great success that had confounded the
nefarious designs of Parnellism.[47] The reality was different.

---

[41] The Vicereine, Lady Londonderry, enthusiastically took up the kind of socio-economic
work pursued by Lady Aberdeen: Elizabeth Countess of Fingall, *Seventy Years Young*
(New York, 1939), p. 164.

[42] MacNeill, *What I Have Seen and Heard*, p. 66.

[43] Londonderry to Lord Salisbury, 7 Feb. 1887, RA VIC/D 39/2; also, Londonderry to the
Queen, 16 Feb. 1887, RA VIC/D 39/4. This delusion earned a sharp royal rebuke: Queen
to Londonderry, 5 March 1887, RA VIC/D 39/5.

[44] The Act empowered the administration to proclaim and suppress any association as
dangerous, together with the institution of non-jury trials to prosecute offenders: Geary,
Plan of Campaign, p. 76; Queen to Londonderry, 5 March 1887, RA VIC/D 39/5;
Salisbury to the Queen, 11 May 1887, in Buckle (ed.), *Letters of Queen Victoria*, I, p. 310.

[45] Itinerary details in *Standard*, 27 June 1887.

[46] Londonderry to Lord Ashbourne, 27 May 1887, in A. B. Cooke and A. P. W.
Malcolmson (eds.), *The Ashbourne Papers: A Calender of the Papers of Edward Gibson, 1st
Lord Ashbourne* (Belfast, 1974), p. 147.

[47] Londonderry to the Queen, 1 July 1887, RA VIC/D 39/20; Revd John Kinnear, *The
Queen's Jubilee: The Joy of Her Subjects* (Londonderry, 1887), p. 11. BNL, 28, 30 June
1887.

Vatican attempts to persuade Archbishop Walsh to facilitate the visit were no more successful than on the matter of Jubilee celebrations.[48] In fact, Walsh moved to neutralise its impact by a letter to the laity in the *Freeman's Journal* on the day it began, urging a special collection for the Pope and the presentation of addresses in honour of his Golden Jubilee.[49] It reminded Catholics of an allegiance that, in a period of evangelical Catholic revival, was far closer to their hearts than that to British royalty. Certainly papal addresses had their own 'royal' connotations. Such deft discounting of the royal presence, however, was less easy for the Parnellite leadership, struggling to strike a balance between the needs of the Home Rule campaign in Britain and aggressive pursuit of agrarian interests against the Irish executive.

The observance of the Queen's Jubilee could, with difficulty, be managed without irreparable damage to the former. Protesting the presence of royalty in Ireland, however, raised the prospect of highly damaging publicity. But like the planners of the royal visit, nationalists also learned from the mistakes of 1885. Confrontation was avoided and they could congratulate themselves on avoiding any action that their enemies could exploit as treason to throne and empire.[50] While the restricted geographic scope of the visit and the discipline of the alliance with Gladstone facilitated this end, so too did the fact that British press organs had also learned from the negative experiences of 1885. On this royal occasion *The Times* fairly recorded the reception for the Princes as favourable by one section of the community 'and without disrespect by the other'.[51] Unionists could still claim that a boycott of Jubilee celebrations and the royal visit indicated that nationalists 'cherish designs very different from that which they openly avow',[52] but with 1885 as the example of what to avoid, a disaster had been averted. This kind of event management, however, was not always within nationalist control. Thus when a band at an exhibition of Irish industrial goods at Olympia in 1888 incurred public hostility by refusing to play *God Save the Queen* – 'they dared not go back to

---

[48] Walsh, *William Walsh*, pp. 286–7.

[49] 'Letter from His Grace the Archbishop of Dublin to the Clergy and Laity of the Diocese', *FJ*, 27 June 1887.

[50] *UI*, 2 July 1887.

[51] *The Times [TT]*, 28 May – 3 June 1887; also, *Daily Telegraph*, 28 June 1887; *Standard*, 27–30 June, 1 July 1887. For acknowledgement of responsible reporting by the English press, see *FJ*, 1 July 1887.

[52] See, for instance, the *Graphic*, 2 July 1887.

Ireland' if they did[53] – evidence of nationalist disloyalty[54] could easily be construed. The exhibition was a failure.

The national anthem was extremely potent as a national/constitutional symbol. Universally recognised, a refusal to play it registered immediately with British public opinion as disloyalty, while greatly embarrassing the Parnellite Party's allies, the Gladstonian Liberals.[55] Attempting to contain the damage to the Home Rule crusade, W. J. O'Neill Daunt argued that the band did not display 'disloyalty to Queen Victoria', as the Irish were loyal to the Queen as Queen of *Ireland*, not of England, and suggested the composition of a specifically Irish *God save the Queen*.[56] It was an unconvincing claim. The Queen had become so closely identified with the anti-Home Rule cause that the Royal Standard – surely with her approval – was being explicitly incorporated into Unionist propaganda (Fig. 17). It was a clever propaganda ploy. The omission of the Irish quartering left a distinct impression of constitutional imbalance.

Concerned about the difficulties facing the Home Rule campaign, Parnell responded with unambiguous public declarations of Irish loyalty under Home Rule, even publicly accepting a substantial donation from the great imperialist, Cecil Rhodes – whose brother was an ADC to the Irish Viceroy, Lord Londonderry – a donation made on the condition of Home Rule being a *final* settlement of the Irish question.[57] And when the Government failed in its attempt to smear him with complicity in crime through the Special Commission inquiry,[58] the resultant public vindication in Britain allowed the Irish leader to press home the message of an Ireland self-governing and enthusiastically loyal to the empire.[59] In sum, if, as Benedict Anderson has argued, the nation is primarily an 'imagined community',[60] then in this period of the Liberal–nationalist 'union of hearts' Parnell sought energetically to widen the imaginative parameters of the Irish nation to include a British monarcho-imperial dimension.

---

[53] *Pall Mall Gazette*, 22 Aug. 1888; *Musical Times* quoted in P. A. Scholes, *God Save the Queen: The History and Romance of the World's First National Anthem* (London, 1954), p. 222.

[54] W. J. O'Neill Daunt, *Ireland since the Union* (Dublin, 1888), p. 279. This work had originated in contributions to the British *Liberal Home Ruler*.

[55] Ibid.   [56] Ibid. pp. 279–80.

[57] McNeill, *What I Have Seen and Heard*, pp. 260–6, 39. *Pall Mall Gazette*, 10 July 1888. Parnell to Rhodes, 23 June 1888, in Katherine O'Shea, *Charles Stewart Parnell: His Love Story and Political Life* (London, 1914), II, pp. 155–7.

[58] The inquiry was established to investigate charges implicating Parnell in crime in forged letters that appeared in *The Times*, the credibility of which was damaged by the resulting scandal: F. S. Lyons, *Charles Stewart Parnell* (London, 1978), pp. 417–24.

[59] Ibid. p. 445.   [60] Benedict Anderson, *Imagined Communities* (London, 1983).

17 The Royal Standard as Unionist propaganda.

The initiative in managing Ireland's relationship with the crown, however, remained with the Government, and it was compelled to address it in 1889 when Lord Londonderry, believing he had seen the Irish administration through the worst of the agrarian trouble,[61] wished to resign. Finding a replacement was not easy. The office was expensive to

[61] Londonderry to the Queen, 21 Feb., 13 March 1889, RA VIC/D 40/20, 24.

maintain, requiring substantial private means, while the struggle with the Plan of Campaign ruled out the oft-rumoured royal personage for the post – 'the *last* idea for consideration':[62] an elevated royal arena above politics would have been virtually impossible to establish.[63] At the same time difficulties in finding a suitable viceregal candidate stimulated debate about the abolition of the office. The traditional argument based on consolidating the Union was now augmented by the significance attached to the Viceroyalty in the Home Rule scheme. Its abolition would create a major problem for Gladstone: 'Either he must recreate the Lord Lieutenancy, or he must reproduce a measure in which the separatist nature of his scheme, so artistically concealed in the Bill of 1886, will stand out in its full nakedness.'[64]

Strachey's argument was effective enough as propaganda. It focused on a significant aspect of the Home Rule scheme and gave it a seductively crucial significance. But while it was true that the Viceroyalty would be the constitutional form through which royal symbolism and British polit-ical authority was to be expressed, it was hardly the most substantive element determining Ireland's status under Home Rule. That was speci-fied in the very limited range of powers a Dublin parliament would wield as a governing institution. The definitive statement of the anti-Home Rule case, A. V. Dicey's *England's Case against Home Rule*,[65] could not have been more explicit: 'Home Rule does not mean National Independence. This proposition needs no elaboration.'[66] Nor from their own perspective did nationalists regard the office of substantive administrative importance: 'Under responsible government it is of little more importance who is Viceroy than who is Lord Mayor of Dublin.'[67] It was rather the channel the office provided for harmonising the Anglo-Irish relationship that gave it significance – as the Aberdeen Viceroyalty had so effectively demonstrated in 1886. On receiving the freedom of Edinburgh in 1889, Parnell invoked that loyal scenario: Aberdeen's recall in August 1886 was 'a dagger planted in the heart of Ireland ... It was a misfortune to us, but it was a misfortune that would not last long.'[68] This

---

[62] Balfour to Salisbury, 21 April 1889, in Williams, *Salisbury–Balfour Correspondence*, p. 286.

[63] See *Nation*, 18 May 1889. For rumours about the Prince of Wales and the Viceroyalty, see Edward Legge, *More about King Edward* (London, 1913), pp. 66–9.

[64] St. Loe Strachey, 'Shall We Abolish the Lord Lieutenant?', *National Review*, 2 (Aug. 1888), 788–91.

[65] London, 1886.

[66] A. V. Dicey, *England's Case against Home Rule* (London, 1886), p. 32.

[67] Sir Charles Gavan Duffy, 'A Fair Constitution for Ireland', *CR*, 52 (Sept. 1887), 318.

[68] See *TT*, 22 July 1889. As the *Nation* (18 May 1889) put it: 'Lord Aberdeen set an example that will yet be followed.'

was a distinct likelihood as a Government already fully preoccupied with Irish issues had no inclination to add to its burdens by tackling the complex issue of abolition. Moreover, as agrarian agitation began to wind down in the late 1880s the circumstances for demonstrating Irish loyalty were more favourable.

IV

A significant gesture in this respect was the decision of the nationalist controlled Dublin Corporation in 1889 to restore and repair the statue of William III in College Green, an Orange sacred site and indisputably the most contentious royal monument in the city.[69] Something more significant, however, was needed to impress British public opinion, and Gladstone sought to provide this by bringing Parnell into membership of a parliamentary committee on royal grants. This was not altogether easy. He had greatly offended his leading lieutenants by opposing the Plan of Campaign[70] and a too hasty defence of royal allowances could have been politically risky. Parnell only came on board after persistent pressure. Having done so, it was no small feat for him to have persuaded many of his party to support the committee's conclusions;[71] none of Gladstone's former Cabinet colleagues joined him and only thirteen Liberal MPs, the rest voting against. Certainly, viewed in the context of the 'Celtic regions', the contrast between Parnellite support and Scottish and Welsh opposition is noteworthy.[72] The majority was 355 to 134.[73] This was an issue, however, that the party leadership wished to restrict to the parliamentary domain. While Unionist prints supportively followed the Government line,[74] United Ireland ignored the subject.

The royal settlement was on Gladstone's terms, £36,000 per year for the Prince of Wales to provide for his children, on condition that the Queen waive demands for her other grandchildren. On such a controversial issue his proposals had to be accepted to contain controversy over the crown.[75] His central role was partly due to a deep sense of responsibility,[76] but also because the Prince of Wales took steps to ensure his

---

[69] R. J. Smith, *Ireland's Renaissance* (Dublin, 1903), p. 126.

[70] Geary, *Plan of Campaign*, pp. 122–6; Lyons, *Parnell*, pp. 381–9.

[71] Entry (6 July 1889), Bahlmann (ed.), *Hamilton Diary 1885–1906*, p. 99: 'It would be a great coup if he could secure it.'

[72] Davies, 'Victoria and Victorian Wales', pp. 21–2.   [73] *TT*, 29, 31 July 1889.

[74] See, for example, *Daily Express [DE]*, 5, 10, 12 July 1889.

[75] Williams, *Contentious Crown*, pp. 61–2.

[76] Entry (20 June 1889), Bahlmann (ed.), *Hamilton Diary, 1885–1906*, pp. 97–8. He had drawn up the Minute of 1860 providing for the Queen's children, but with the mistake of not having it submitted to a Parliamentary Committee.

involvement, concerned at a lack of 'straightforwardness' in the matter by Government.[77] Given the Queen's Unionist sentiments – she was appalled at the inclusion of 'that rebel Parnell' on the committee[78] – Gladstone hoped to use the issue to create a countervailing base of royal support around the Prince of Wales, with whom nationalists could align.[79] His claim that 'the Prince of Wales owed his allowance to the support Parnell had given him on that Committee'[80] was certainly an exaggeration, but explicable in terms of an Anglo-Irish union of hearts with the monarchy as a common pole of attraction. Certainly the Prince of Wales was the most appropriate royal personage for the purpose. He was widely, if wrongly, believed in Ireland to be sympathetic to nationalist aims,[81] and realised the need to conciliate Roman Catholicism: in 1889 he reportedly attended two Catholic religious services, reputedly the first heir-apparent to do so since James II as Duke of York.[82] But to what extent, if at all, did Parnellite displays of imperial loyalty further the Home Rule cause?

It was easy for opponents to be cynical. While the Special Commission exonerated Parnell personally of involvement in crime, it did unearth an uncomfortably close association between the land agitation in general and illegality. Thus *The Times* could claim: 'The Parnellites have special reasons of their own just at the moment for making a display of loyalty to the SOVEREIGN.'[83] For her part the Queen regarded the compromise on the royal grants as insulting, and it certainly did not mitigate her hostility to either Parnellites or Gladstonian Liberalism.[84] Nor would Parnell's engagement in mainland British politics in August 1889, when he lent strong nationalist support to Welsh Nonconformist attempts to obstruct a Government bill on tithe rent charge.[85]

---

[77] Entry (18 June 1889), ibid. p. 97.

[78] Queen to Salisbury, 9 July 1889, in Christopher Hibbert (ed.), *Queen Victoria in Her Diaries and Letters* (London, 1985), p. 316.

[79] Entry (6 July 1889), Bahlmann (ed.), *Hamilton Diary 1885–1906*, p. 99.

[80] Entry (10 Jan. 1891), H. G. Hutchinson (ed.), *The Private Diaries of Sir Algernon West* (London, 1922), pp. 13–14.

[81] Ibid. p. 13. Gladstone assured Parnell the Prince bore no ill-will to Ireland and would do nothing to obstruct 'her wishes'. The *Nation* (27 July 1889) referred to Edward's 'attitude to the Irish question, which is an open secret'; also Justin McCarthy and Mrs Campbell Praed, *Our Book of Memories: Letters of Justin McCarthy to Mrs Campbell Praed* (London, 1912), p. 225.

[82] See Legge, *King Edward*, pp. 216–17.   [83] *TT*, 24, 25 July 1889.

[84] Certainly a tendency Salisbury could be relied upon to exacerbate: Andrew Roberts, *Salisbury: Victorian Titan* (London, 1999), p. 539.

[85] See *TT*, 13, 14, 16 Aug. 1889. Roy Douglas, *Land, People and Politics: The Land Question in the United Kingdom 1878–1952* (London, 1976), p. 102; Viscount Chilston, *W. H. Smith* (London, 1965), p. 23.

V

The issue of nationalist allegiance to the monarch retained its salience as a test of the advisability of Home Rule as the Salisbury administration drew to a close, with royal or viceregal questions of recurring importance in a context where Gladstone's hopes for a decisive initiative that would convincingly validate the loyalty claims of the Home Rule crusade proved elusive. Lord Zetland replaced Londonderry as Viceroy in 1889, an appointment in the same mould – ridiculed as such by nationalists[86] – and reflecting consistency in a Unionist policy approach to Ireland which, at best, regarded the office's regal functions as a mere formality. Gladstone's mind, however, was turning to viceregal reform as a site for incremental advances facilitating the eventual enactment of Home Rule. Thus the opening of the office to Catholic occupants entailed in the Home Rule bill of 1886 was now taken up as a separate measure for enactment,[87] in conjunction with removal of a similar ban on Catholics holding the office of English Lord Chancellor.[88]

The environment seemed congenial given a 'kite' on the issue of a Catholic university that Arthur Balfour had flown at this time,[89] and with a Roman Catholic Home Secretary, Henry Matthews, suggesting Government amenability.[90] In the event, the university issue acted as a litmus test of the parliamentary strength of anti-Catholic sentiment in the Liberal no less than the Tory Party.[91] Gladstone failed to bring Presbyterian and Nonconformist sentiment with him on the issue.[92] Less publicly, but no less effectively, anti-Catholicism was a crucial weapon used by Salisbury to prevent the wedding of the Duke of Clarence and Princess Hélène, daughter of the Comte de Paris, despite her willingness to convert to Protestantism.[93] In the event, no action on the Viceroyalty emerged at this time. The eruption of the Parnell divorce

[86] 'Who is Lord Zetland?', Nation, 1 June 1889.
[87] Gladstone to Spencer, 9 Nov. 1889, in Gordon (ed.), Red Earl, II, p. 162.
[88] Entry (8 Feb. 1890), Angela Hawkins and John Powell (eds.), The Journal of John Wodehouse, First Earl of Kimberley (Cambridge, 1997), pp. 390–1.
[89] Walsh, William Walsh, pp. 490–1. Heirachical pressure on Parnell to advance the university issue was exerted at this time.
[90] H. C. G. Matthew (ed.), The Gladstone Diaries XIII (Oxford, 1994), p. 310.
[91] Williams (ed.), Salisbury–Balfour Correspondence, pp. 293–4. Ulster Unionist opposition was a central consideration.
[92] Gladstone to Parnell, 30 Aug. 1889, in J. L. Hammond, Gladstone and the Irish Nation (London, 1938), pp. 644–6.
[93] See correspondence of Balfour and Salisbury together with communications to, and from, the Queen, 30 Aug.–16 Sept., in Williams (ed.), Salisbury–Balfour Correspondence, pp. 317–30; Kenneth Young, Arthur James Balfour (London, 1963), pp. 122–4, 465–8; Entry (28 Dec. 1890), Bahlmann (ed.), Hamilton Diary 1885–1906, pp. 132–3.

crisis[94] dramatically effected a change of priorities. The same
Nonconformist conscience that refused support for a university with a
Catholic ethos was one of the most influential factors pushing Gladstone
to present the Irish Party with the ultimatum of either Parnell as leader or
Home Rule.[95] Nationalist politics over the course of 1891 crystallised
around an anti-Parnellite movement strongly influenced by the bishops,
and a significantly smaller Parnellite force, with its base in Dublin, and
with Parnell himself adopting ever more radical nationalist, neo-Fenian
and anti-Liberal positions. A desperate struggle to regain his national
authority ended with his death in October 1891.

The Parnellite crisis lacked an overt royal dimension, but attracted
royal attention. The Queen's tendency to frame constitutional issues in
a subjective moral perspective was reflected in her judgement on Parnell's
political downfall: 'It is a just nemesis.'[96] Nor did his death mitigate her
animosity: 'He was a really bad and worthless man who had to answer for
many lives lost in Ireland!'[97] A morally discredited metaphor of the
destructive movement he led, his demise facilitated the excellent
Government policies that had 'done wonders in Ireland'. The only danger was the return to office of the Liberal 'Socialist Home-ruling party'.[98]

Parnell's death, however, greatly facilitated the dominance of Catholic
hierarchical influence in Irish life, giving a greater impetus to the case for
the removal of Catholic disabilities in public life, and may well have
refocused Gladstone's mind on a Catholic disabilities bill respecting the
Irish Viceroyalty in early February 1891. It was only the third occasion in
his long parliamentary career that he had proposed a private member's
bill, but it faced the usual block of anti-Catholic prejudice. W. H. Smith,
the Leader of the House, remarked: ' I cannot see how it is that the Lord
Lieutenant, who is ... the alter ego of the Sovereign, should be relieved
from ... what the right hon. gentleman regards as a disability.'[99] A
Catholic Viceroy, moreover, would make a supposedly slender constitutional link between Britain and Ireland under Home Rule even more

---

[94] For comprehensive and expert coverage, see Lyons, *Parnell*, chs. 15–20. Parnell's long-
standing affair with Mrs O'Shea was exposed when he was named as co-respondent in the
O'Shea divorce case.

[95] Ibid. pp. 487–92.

[96] Queen to Crown Princess Victoria of Prussia, 29 Nov. 1890, in Agatha Ramm (ed.),
*Beloved and Darling Child: Last Letters between Queen Victoria and Her Eldest Daughter
1886–1901* (Stroud, 1990), p. 117.

[97] Victoria to Smith, 8 Oct. 1891, in Viscount Chilston, *W. H. Smith*, pp. 357–8.

[98] QVJ (7 Feb. 1890) in Buckle (ed.), *Letters of Queen Victoria*, I, p. 563; Queen to Salisbury,
27 June 1890, in ibid. p. 617.

[99] *TT*, 5 Feb. 1891.

tenuous, an argument reinforced by Ulster Unionist laments that a Protestant Viceroy was the only real support for their interests in Ireland. Furthermore, for a sovereign convinced of the excellence of Unionist policy in Ireland, there would have seemed little reason for change as the new Viceroy, Zetland, reported back to the court on his travels in the Irish countryside and the enthusiastically loyal receptions he met with.[100] Ireland, it seemed, having experienced five years of resolute government, was at last showing the loyal fruits.[101] Despite Gladstone's support for the Government on the royal grants, there was no reciprocity: the bill was narrowly defeated on its second reading.[102] It was enough to encourage Gladstone to persist in pressing the issue, though without success, and also, it must be said, without much popular interest in an Ireland where political upheaval occasioned by the Parnellite Party split totally overshadowed everything else, something that should be borne in mind when considering Zetland's claims on Irish loyalty.

Occurring as the Plan of Campaign was in its final stages and when the Parnellite Party split would monopolise Irish attention, a political space was created for them to proceed uncontroversially. They were also facilitated by a Catholic clergy whose church was assuming an ascendant position in Irish life, and which, collectively, had no intrinsic commitment to Home Rule: Zetland recorded the parish priest in many locations leading the deputations of greeting. There were other consider-ations. Most significantly, 1891 saw the establishment of the Congested Districts Board, a Government agency charged with the promotion of agriculture and industry in areas likely to experience acute distress, and, being willing to spend money, it was extremely popular.[103] That Zetland's tours in the west of Ireland included areas that were the Board's concern was only too likely to make his reception enthusiastic in this period of great expectation. Furthermore, it is important to note that viceregal ceremonial in rural communities must be considered differently from that in great urban centres such as Dublin.

As we have seen, in the latter, the successful management of viceregal/royal processions depended chiefly upon effective ritual organisation and contextual dynamics. In rural areas, however, the scope for *determining* popular reactions by community leaders, both gentry and clerical, was more considerable, and peasantry compliance accorded with a keen eye

---

[100] Zetland to the Queen, 17 Dec. 1889, 21 Jan., 30 Aug. 1890, 29 Aug. 1891, 15 Aug. 1892, RA VIC/D 40/34, 36, 42, 61, 92.
[101] Goschen to the Queen, 22 May 1892, in Buckle (ed.), *Letters of Queen Victoria*, I, p. 33.
[102] Ibid.
[103] See Virginia Crossman, 'Congested Districts Board' in S. J. Connolly (ed.), *The Oxford Companion to Irish History* (2nd edn, Oxford, 2002), p. 117.

to the realities of local power relations.[104] The outward display of loyal allegiance Zetland observed, explicable for both Viceroy and monarch in terms of effective Government policy, disguised a much more complex reality. As the administration went into its final year, Zetland continued to dispatch 'satisfactory' reports to the Queen on the state of Ireland, with extremists watched and under control,[105] convincing a susceptible sovereign that at last a solution to the Irish question had been found: 'Ireland has recovered its quiet and prosperity so wonderfully that it is very wicked to try and upset everything again.'[106] Her reaction to the result of the general election of 1892, with Gladstone returning to office dependent on nationalist support, was predictable: an 'awful' outcome, all too likely to undo the good work in Ireland of the 'best one [government] of the century'.[107]

VI

Given his dependence on nationalist support, Gladstone's return to office necessitated the immediate preparation of a Home Rule bill. However, the relative failure of the project to cultivate a symbiotic nationalist–British identity and the effects of the Parnell crisis had together left Irish attitudes to the monarchy ambivalent rather than allegiant, as the intended marriage and then death of Albert Victor, Duke of Clarence, demonstrated.

The Duke's death was tragic, not only because of its abruptness – ill with a cold on 9 January, he rapidly developed pneumonia and died on the 13th[108] – but because it followed so soon on news of his impending marriage to Princess Mary of Teck, set for 27 February. News of the marriage acted as a stimulus to demonstrations of loyalty throughout the state, except in nationalist Ireland. Nationalist politics were more complex now, following the factionalising of the Parnellite movement, with the main division between a smallish section that had remained loyal to Parnell, led by John Redmond with Dublin as its stronghold; and a much larger group of seceders, now established as the National Federation. In this context, it was inevitable that royal issues would join others as foci of

---

[104] See the account of a County Galway estate being organised to greet the Zetlands in April 1891: Gifford Lewis (ed.), *Selected Letters of Somerville and Ross* (London, 1989), pp. 170–4.

[105] Zetland to the Queen, 29 Aug., 1 Nov., 28 Dec. 1891, RA VIC/D 40/61, 72a, 73.

[106] Victoria to Crown Princess Victoria of Prussia, 22 June 1892, in Ramm (ed.), *Beloved and Darling Child*, pp. 144–5.

[107] Victoria to Crown Princess Victoria of Prussia, 20 Aug. 1892, in ibid. pp. 146–7.

[108] Elizabeth Longford, *Victoria R. I.* (London, 1964), p. 515.

dispute. Accordingly, Dublin Corporation's refusal of a wedding gift was attacked as damaging to Home Rule, and countered with references to Federationist backing for English Liberals opposed to the royal grant in 1889.[109]

The criticism of the corporation was not without substance. Refusal of a wedding present simply provided Unionists – especially in Ulster[110] – with convenient propaganda. Indeed, it is worth noting that as Ulster Unionism increasingly manifested itself violently in the public sphere, especially through Orange demonstrations, royal occasions and respectable spectator involvement in royal ritual allowed them to redeem, at least temporarily, their reputation for bigotry and extremism.

The Parnellite action was politically unwise, but understandable. Their rejection of English 'dictation' of nationalist politics inevitably had an emotional anti-British dimension, which was only too likely to shade off into anti-monarchism, consequently colouring, in some cases, reactions to the Duke's death. Without pushing the case too far, it could be argued that some Parnellites found a form of emotional revenge in royal tragedy for the death of Ireland's uncrowned king, seen as the result of English pressure.[111] In the main, however, all nationalist factions responded sympathetically to the Duke's death – which occurred on the same day as that of Cardinal Manning – expressed in an unambiguous wave of public sympathy for his parents from across the country, especially Parnellite Dublin. All public entertainments and official buildings were closed for the funeral.[112] *The Times* commented on 'an improved state of feeling on the part of the great mass of the people and the leaders of public opinion, such as could hardly have been anticipated a year or two ago ... There is no longer a fear to avow a loyal sentiment and a kindly sentiment with the Royal Family in its hour of trial.'[113]

The Irish response to the Duke's death was impressive and calls for some comment. The differences between nationalist attitudes to the issue of the wedding present and that of the Duke's death is readily explicable: it was easier to sympathise with a family tragedy than with a gift for the immensely rich. But most importantly, a family tragedy was much more likely to engage the familial and welfarist frame of reference which allowed royalty most effectively to attract public sympathy. In Ireland that engagement was enhanced by the Prince of Wales's perceived

---

[109] See reports in *TT*, 13 Jan. 1892.   [110] *Derry Standard*, 13 Jan. 1892.

[111] See Lennox Robinson, Tom Robinson and Nora Dorman, *Three Homes* (Dublin, 1958), recording their family nurse's profound personal grief at the death of Parnell, followed by her 'savage delight' at the death of the Duke of Clarence (pp. 17, 45).

[112] *TT*, 15, 16, 21 Jan. 1892; *FJ*, 19 Jan. 1892; *BNL*, 15, 19, 22 Jan. 1892.

[113] *TT*, 22 Jan. 1892.

sympathy for Home Rule. Commentary surrounding the death of the Duke was informed by the myth that the Prince of Wales was 'carefully inducting' his dead son on the Irish question with a view to the 'estimate he was to form of Ireland as a factor in the Empire', and it was noted that the Prince's reply to Dublin Corporation on its condolences 'was among the warmest and least formal of the Royal acknowledgements'.[114] With the likelihood of Gladstone's return to office in the near future, though, political calculation in public condolences cannot be discounted.

VII

Affronted by the defeat of Salisbury's excellent administration, the Queen's Unionist sentiments became more entrenched. She called on Gladstone to form a Government only under pressure. Unwilling to accept Irish Catholic nationalists as authentic members of the British state, a Government based on their votes lacked validity.[115]

There is much in Queen Victoria's attitudes to Ireland at this time to support the view of her as an embodiment of the advanced 'upper-class paranoia ... which was to erupt with such violence in England between 1910 and 1914'.[116] It was a violence that might well have erupted in the 1890s had the House of Lords not still had the power to defeat Home Rule. And yet while the Queen perceived a threatening unity of 'anti-national' Gladstonian and Irish forces, the Parnellite split had effected a somewhat changed attitude by the Liberal leadership to their Irish allies. Having abandoned Parnell at Gladstone's dictation, nationalists were in a more subservient and weakened relationship to the Liberal Party. The Parnellite faction itself may have been independent of the Liberals, but all that this really amounted to was *truculent* compliance with Gladstonian wishes on Home Rule. The changed situation was reflected in the Irish Viceroyalty.

Whereas in 1886 an antidote to the alienation produced by the Spencer regime was needed and found to great effect in Lord Aberdeen, now a rather different concern was identified – the need to conciliate Ireland's non-nationalist community. In fact, Aberdeen was rather too successful; he had overwhelmingly identified a supposedly

---

[114] *DJ*, 22, 27 Jan. 1892. The Irish Catholic hierarchy's condolences to both the Queen and the bereaved parents drew a response of 'sincere thanks' from the former, but a distinctly friendlier 'warmest thanks' from the Waleses.

[115] Hutchinson (ed.), *West Diaries*, pp. 51–3, 67; Ponsonby to the Queen, 31 May 1892 in Buckle (ed.), *Letters of Queen Victoria*, 3rd ser., II, p. 121; Queen to Gladstone, 30 July 1893 in Guedalla (ed.), *Queen and Mr Gladstone*, II, p. 474.

[116] David Cannadine, *The Pleasures of the Past* (London, 1990), p. 29.

non-partisan constitutional office with one political faction. It was now necessary to redress the balance and establish a position of equidistance between the country's political groups.

Most significant, however, was the influence of John Morley, Chief Secretary in 1886, with a low opinion of Aberdeen's abilities and now both 'determined to have the entire responsibility for Irish affairs' and 'an *effective* Viceroy'.[117] Lord Houghton accepted the post. Unlike Aberdeen, Houghton was direct and forthright, concerned to follow strictly the official role of his office: 'clever, shrewd ... serviceable, and anxious for work', though 'not "hail fellow well met" ... too kingly'.[118] His official entry to Dublin was 'friendly and cordial, though not of an enthusiastic character' and while 'accompanied by all the respect due to Your Majesty's representative, without any mark of a political demonstration'.[119] It was almost a point of principle for Houghton to do things differently from Aberdeen.[120] His objective attitude, however, was not reflected by his royal mistress. His honesty in recording the fears of Irish Unionists, that they would not get the 'fair play of an Englishman' under Home Rule,[121] merely provided a weapon to attack Gladstone's scheme,[122] encouraging her to suggest that Irish constitutional rights be reduced, especially when an explosion at Dublin Castle at Christmas 1892 killed a passing detective.[123] Houghton's opinions on Ireland were not synonymous with those of the Queen. But they were informed by English prejudices and ill-comprehended the nature of Irish society; and with the Aberdeen Viceroyalty as the standard nationalists had come to expect from a Liberal Government a sense of alienation found expression. Timothy Healy – the future first Governor General of the Irish Free State – perceived a Viceroy compliant with the reactionary Castle establishment: 'If there is not sufficient "touch" to appoint the right Viceroy, what can be expected in administrative details?'[124] Thus

---

[117] Morley to Spencer, 28 July 1891 in Gordon (ed.), *Red Earl*, II, p. 174; entry (22 July 1892), Bahlmann (ed.), *Hamilton Diary 1885–1906*, p. 163
[118] Entry (17 Dec. 1892), Hutchinson (ed.), *West Diaries*, p. 93.
[119] Houghton to the Queen, 6 Oct. 1892, RA VIC/D 41/10.
[120] Sir Herbert Jekyll, Secretary to Houghton, to Algernon West, 29 Dec. 1892 in Hutchinson (ed.), *West Diaries*, pp. 102–4.
[121] Houghton to the Queen, 29 Oct. 1892, RA VIC/D 41/19; Queen to Gladstone, 15 Nov. 1892, RA VIC/D 41/25.
[122] Queen to Gladstone, 16 Nov. 1892, in Guedalla (ed.), *Queen and Mr Gladstone*, II, p. 454.
[123] See Morley to Ponsonby 25 Dec. 1892; Morley to the Queen, 25 Dec. 1892; Queen to Morley, 27 Dec. 1892, RA VIC/D 41/39, 40, 44; Gladstone to Morley, 2 Jan. 1893, in Matthew (ed.), *Gladstone Diaries XIII*, pp. 174–5.
[124] Healy to Morley, 14 Sept. 1892, in T. M. Healy, *Letters and Leaders of My Day* (London, 1928), II, p. 383.

the social distance maintained by Houghton – who, being unmarried, lacked a Vicereine to assist in promoting welfarist activities – helped ensure that Dublin Castle, despite being a royal site, remained ostracised by nationalists. For Gladstone, however, positive indicators on Home Rule came from within the royal family, including the Princess of Wales, who openly declared her support for the policy,[125] while her husband expressed a wish to be familiarised with Government business,[126] inevitably including the Home Rule bill, a personal interest Gladstone sought to cultivate.[127] The possibilities royal engagement might have provided to ease the Home Rule bill's legislative path, however, were quickly closed off by the Queen.

In particular, she thwarted Gladstone's hopes of engineering a great Irish demonstration of loyalty to the throne during an intended visit to Dublin by the Duke of York in June 1893. To take place around the time the Home Rule bill was being passed by the Commons – with rejection by the Lords bound to follow – such a demonstration could have had a powerful effect on British opinion at a subsequent general election on the issue, an option Gladstone intended to pursue. The Queen, however, strenuously opposed a royal visit to Ireland at any time during Gladstone's administration, opposition reinforced when, in late 1893, talk circulated about the Duke having a permanent Irish residence.[128] Henry Ponsonby admitted: 'We failed in our attempt to make the Duke of York an Irishman.'[129]

VIII

It its essentials, the second bill did not differ substantially from the first. A similar parsimonious financial arrangement was proposed, and similar related difficulties over Irish representation at Westminster were encountered. As to the significance of the monarchical dimension, it had a somewhat higher profile than in 1886 given the Unionist focus on the Viceroyalty, and the Queen's intensifying opposition.

---

[125] Entry (4 Sept. 1892), M. V. Brett (ed.), *Journals and Letters of Reginald Viscount Esher* (London, 1934), I, p. 161.

[126] See correspondence of Algernon West, with Henry Ponsonby and Francis Knollys, the Prince's Private Secretary, 2, 8, 13 Nov. 1892, in Hutchinson (ed.), *West Diaries*, p. 73; and the Queen's concern to limit his access: Salisbury to Ponsonby, 14 Nov. 1892; Victoria to Ponsonby, 15 Nov. 1892, in Buckle (ed.), *Letters of Queen Victoria*, II, p. 180–1.

[127] Entry (16 April 1893), Hutchinson (ed.), *West Diaries*, p. 152.

[128] See Ponsonby to Knollys, 22 Nov. 1893; Ponsonby to West, 24 Nov. 1893, ibid. p. 220.

[129] Ponsonby to West, 27 June 1893 in ibid. p. 170.

Gladstone sought to satisfy the demands of the bill's Irish supporters and Unionist critics by giving something to each. As determined by the bill, the Viceroyalty clause incorporated the provision of the defeated viceregal disabilities measure of February 1891: the office was opened to 'every subject of the Queen ... without reference to his religious belief'. The term of office was to be six years, subject to the Queen's approval. The Viceroy would, on the advice of the 'Executive Committee' – the term Cabinet was avoided to limit the separatist connotations of Home Rule – 'give or withhold the assent of Her Majesty to Bills passed by the two Houses of the Irish Legislature, subject nevertheless to any instructions given by H.M. in respect of any such Bill'.[130]

Thus while, unlike in 1886, the advice of the Irish Government was specified as the authority on which bills were to be enacted, the retention of the Queen's powers of intervention largely nullified this provision. More prejudiced against Irish autonomy than in 1886 – she refused to accept Gladstone's proposed title as a bill for the 'better government'[131] of Ireland – her hostile interference with a Home Rule Parliament would have been only too likely. Again, there was the difficulty that would be presented by a hostile Viceroy supported by an unsympathetic Unionist administration at Westminster, and facing opposition from a Dublin parliament.[132] For Unionists, however, these issues were less significant than the propagandistically attractive presentation of the Viceroyalty as the only tenuous and insubstantial link between Britain and Ireland.[133] Only ruthless use of the closure limited their exploitation of the issue in Parliament.[134]

The Home Rule bill, nevertheless, had a stormy parliamentary passage, with the strength of Unionist opposition reflected in the fact that opposition speeches outnumbered those of the Government in a proportion of 2 to 1 in number and 3 to 1 in time.[135] And a number of minor concessions were conceded.[136] But for our purposes one of the most noteworthy aspects of the debate was the example it provided of the Ulster Unionist understanding of monarchical power and how it should be used to defeat Home Rule.

---

[130] Clause 5: Executive Authority of Government of Ireland Bill, in A. V. Dicey, *A Leap in the Dark: A Criticism of the Principles of Home Rule as Illustrated by the Bill of 1893* (2nd edn, London, 1911), Appendix.

[131] Entry (30 Jan. 1893), Bahlmann (ed.), *Hamilton Diaries, 1885–1906*, p. 188.

[132] Ponsonby to the Queen, 12 Jan. 1893, RA VIC/D 41/50.

[133] A. V. Dicey, who discounted its significance in 1886, now reflected its importance in Unionist propaganda: Dicey, *A Leap in the Dark*, pp, 210, 70–1, 93.

[134] Entry (9 May 1893), Bahlmann (ed.), *Hamilton Diaries 1885–1906*, p. 200.

[135] Loughlin, *Gladstone*, p. 266.

[136] Entry (9 May 1893), Bahlmann (ed.), *Hamilton Diaries 1885–1906*, p. 200.

In 1893 the frontier – and anti-democratic – mentality of Ulster Unionists was expressed in a petition against Home Rule which their leader, Colonel Saunderson, insisted on delivering personally to an anti-nationalist Queen, for the purpose, effectively, of having her dismiss her disloyal ministers.[137] But such a meeting was only permissible if the same facility was allowed to Home Rulers, which the Queen was loathe to do.[138] The Ulster loyalist petition reflected the strength of community opposition to Home Rule, expressed also in a great Ulster convention at Belfast in 1892. Significantly, as Edward Hamilton noted, no great meetings in favour of Home Rule took place in southern Ireland.[139]

Passed by a small majority in the Commons, the Home Rule bill was overwhelmingly defeated in the Lords: 419 to 41. Gladstone wished to take the issue to the country on a platform of 'Peers versus People', but his Cabinet colleagues refused to comply.[140] Nor, it should be noted, was there a significant popular reaction to the defeat in nationalist Ireland. Home Rule would be revived in the future, but more immediately the end of the Gladstonian era was followed by the Unionist success at the general election of 1895 and a different context for the development of the monarchy's relationship with Ireland.

---

[137] See Ponsonby to Saunderson, 16 July 1893 in Reginald Lucas, *Colonel Saunderson M.P.* (London, 1908), pp. 203–4.
[138] Saunderson to Ponsonby, 26 July 1893, RA VIC/D 43/4; Asquith to Ponsonby, 11 Aug. 1893, RA VIC/D 43/7; Ponsonby to the Queen, 12 Aug. 1893, RA VIC/D 43/8, especially Victoria's note to the letter.
[139] Entry (7 April 1893), Bahlmann (ed.), *Hamilton Diaries 1885–1906*, p. 198.
[140] Ibid. p. 273.

11 Welfare monarchism and conciliation

The second period of Unionist rule was broadly coincident with socio-cultural developments that influenced perceptions of the Irish question. By the mid-1890s the credibility of mid-nineteenth-century Anglo-Saxonist race theorising about Irish 'character' had greatly diminished,[1] while In Ireland the disintegration of constitutional nationalism created a space for new ideas of Irish identity to be debated whose state-destabilising implications would take time to become apparent.[2] The debate within Irish nationalism that ensued between cultural and constitutional nationalists can be seen as differing ways of embracing modernity.[3] But it also signified a condition of liminality and flux which provided the state, with its own modernist agenda, with the most favourable context for success since the 'apolitical' 1850s. During the first phase of Unionist reformism in the years 1886–92, the policy was complicated by widespread agrarian strife, the need for stringent coercion measures, a Gladstonian campaign for Home Rule and a hegemonic nationalist movement. The absence of all these factors now provided an ideal context for the exercise of viceregal and royal ceremonial.[4] Between 1895 and 1905, the Duke of York, Queen Victoria and King Edward VII would all make successful trips to Ireland, attempting to coordinate the royal presence with reformist legislation

---

[1] See L. P. Curtis Jr, *Anglo-Saxons and Celts: A Study of Anti-Irish Prejudice in Victorian England* (Bridgeport, Conn., 1968), pp. 103–4; W. D. Babbington, *Fallacies of Race Theories as Applied to National Character* (London, 1895); J. M. Robertson, *The Saxon and the Celt* (London, 1897); and on the importance of empirical analysis, J. Urry, 'Englishmen, Celts and Iberians: The Ethnographic Survey of the United Kingdom 1892–99' in J. R. Stocking Jr (ed.), *Functionalism Historicised: Essays on British Social Anthropology* (Madison, Wis., 1984), pp. 83–103.

[2] The debate was effectively initiated by Douglas Hyde's seminal speech of 1892, 'The Importance of De-Anglicising Ireland'. As Curtis argues, it was a 'Celticist' response to Anglo-Saxonism: *Anglo-Saxons and Celts*, pp. 113–15.

[3] Senia Pašeta, *Nationalism, Social Change and Ireland's Catholic Elite 1879–1922* (Cork, 1999), pp. 130–2.

[4] Viceroy Cadogan to the Queen, 5 Oct. 1896, RA VIC/D 43/30. Cadogan claimed the Irish people were 'weary of political strife, and are turning their attention to social and remedial legislation'.

while the debate on mechanisms to synchronise the constitutional centrality of the monarchy in the life of the state with its imaginative centrality in
the life of the Irish people proceeded.

I

St Loe Strachey, acknowledging the negative symbolism of Dublin Castle
as a royal site, advised its abandonment, though to be kept as a 'national
monument'.[5] The less symbolically contaminated Viceregal Lodge, on
the other hand, could still function as a royal residence during the Dublin
social season.[6] These suggestions, however, were uninformed about the
reasons why such proposals had never previously come to fruition, especially the negative attitude of the Queen. Only too aware of royal opposition, British Governments sought instead to create the most effective
viceregal administrations. In 1895 the appointment of Lord Cadogan to
the Viceroyalty put the office in accord with the reformist tendencies of
the Chief Secretary, Gerald Balfour.

At one level, Cadogan falls into the same 'King Log' category as Lord
Londonderry in the later 1880s. Arthur Balfour had described both as
intellectually challenged in the same letter,[7] while Cadogan's own son
conceded that his father was 'not of nimble mind'.[8] However, while no
intellectual, Cadogan combined meticulous attention to detail and routine with 'a wise appreciation of reconciling old faiths with new, or
adjusting old systems to modern needs'.[9] Conscious of his dual role as
Government appointee and monarchical surrogate, Cadogan adopted a
flexible combination of regal formality and personal familiarity – 'as from
man to men' – as each situation seemed to require, thereby doing much to
conciliate moderate political opinion, nationalist and Unionist.[10]
Certainly Cadogan's practice as Viceroy struck a more responsive public
chord than that of his stiffly aloof Home Rule predecessor, Lord
Houghton, as was evident during his official entry to Dublin when 'some

---

[5] St Loe Strachey, 'A Royal Residence in Ireland', *National Review*, 25 (Aug. 1895), 746–9.
[6] Ibid. p. 747.
[7] Balfour to Salisbury, 31 Jan. 1888, in R. H. Williams (ed.), *The Salisbury–Balfour Correspondence 1869–1892* (Ware, 1988), pp. 235–6.
[8] Sir Edward Cadogan, *Before the Deluge: Memoirs and Reflections 1880–1914* (London, 1961), p. 4.
[9] Ibid. pp. 4–5.
[10] M. J. F. McCarthy, *Five Years in Ireland 1895–1900* (Dublin, 1901), pp. 53–4; *Freeman's Journal* [*FJ*], 18 Aug. 1895; *FJ* quoted ibid. p. 54; T. M. Healy, *Letters and Leaders of My Day* (London, 1928), II, pp. 375–6, 457–8.

seven or eight hundred of the populace' spontaneously intermingled with the viceregal procession.[11]

Acting in accordance with the spirit of Unionist conciliation, Cadogan sought, where possible, to appoint and promote Catholics, especially high-level prelates, to the public administration, law and several viceregal commissions for which his term of office was noted, even raising the prospect of a Catholic university.[12] At a time when nationalism was factionalised and weak, and when the prospects seemed good for removing the alienation created by the land issue and allowing the Ascendancy to establish a new societal role as the old class structure disintegrated,[13] Cadogan's cultivation of the hierarchy was astute.[14] Government reformism provoked nationalist concern about popular support for Home Rule across the nationalist spectrum. John Dillon would oppose the settlement of the land question precisely for this reason, while W. B. Yeats would argue that reform had so diminished 'misrule' that without the advent of a major war nationalism would have to be refounded on 'a partly intellectual and historical nationalism like that of Norway, with the language question as its lever'.[15] With Home Rule in abeyance, groups attempting to fill the national space created shifted to the Irish public arena, especially Dublin, where, no less than for the state, demonstrations constituted an important mechanism for gauging and cultivating support.

Political demonstrations fluctuated with the fortunes of the Home Rule cause in the 1890s, waning when the enactment of Gladstone's second bill seemed likely in 1892–3, waxing following its defeat and the Unionist accession to power, and despite tensions between different groups being well sustained until the Unionists left office in 1905.[16] They were given a crucial focus in the late 1890s – for constitutionalists no less than republicans – in the centenary commemorations for the 1798 Rebellion. As we have noted, constitutionalists only denied the practicality, not the morality, of armed insurrection: the mobilisation of Irish traditions of

---

[11] 'The Cadogans in Ireland', supplement to *The Gentlewoman* (31 Aug. 1895), vii.

[12] Sir John Ross, *Pilgrim Script: More Random Reminiscences* (London, 1924), p. 122. Ross was the last Irish Lord Chancellor; McCarthy, *Five Years in Ireland*, pp. 431, 244,

[13] For this ambition as reflected in the work of Horace Plunkett, see Paul Rempe, 'Sir Horace Plunkett and Irish Politics 1890–1914', *Eire-Ireland*, 13 (1978), 9–10, 14–15. The legislative record of the period was impressive, with, among others, measures dealing with land purchase, local government, and agricultural education and promotion: F. S. L. Lyons, *Ireland since the Famine* (2nd edn, London, 1973), pp. 116–17.

[14] Ibid. p. 514.

[15] Yeats to the Editor, *The Leader*, 26 Aug. 1900, in J. Gould et al. (eds.), *Collected Letters of W. B. Yeats* (Oxford, 1997), II, pp. 562–3.

[16] Owen McGee, ' "God Save Ireland": Manchester Martyr Demonstrations in Dublin 1867–1916', *Eire-Ireland*, 36 (2001), 47–50.

244 Constructive Unionism and the crown

struggle was a central strategy in the Home Rule campaign. They were no less important in the run-up to the centenary of the 1798 Rebellion in 1898, the commemoration of which would give powerful impetus to the signifying of the Irish landscape in a proliferation of national monuments. Nationalist determination to mark the centenary derived in part from the oppositional stimulus provided by the polished state ceremonial employed to celebrate Queen Victoria's Diamond Jubilee in 1897.[17]

The Jubilee celebrations, together with a royal visit by the Duke and Duchess of York following hard on the event, brought an intensity of British media attention to Ireland, with Jubilee and royal ceremonial offering seductive – and inevitably distorting – prisms through which the extent of Ireland's integration into the British state, and with it the success of Government policies, would be demonstrated. This had always been the case, but the 1897 events were arguably more persuasive in a context where the Home Rule project was in apparently terminal decline.

The means at the disposal of Cadogan to arrange Jubilee ceremonial, certainly in the cityscape of Dublin, were substantial, while the Protestant population of the greater Dublin area – large enough to return Sir Horace Plunkett as a Unionist MP in the 1890s[18] – could be guaranteed to participate in Jubilee events, suggesting greater popular support than was in fact the case, and encouraging an extension to Ireland of the British perspective in which a pro-Jubilee consensus among the population in general existed.[19] But in Dublin it was only at Protestant places of worship that Jubilee services were held and 'abnormally large' attendances recorded, accompanied by flag and bunting displays, and at which a reign of unparalleled prosperity was extolled.[20] That same Protestant population, the dominant group among Dublin's business community,[21] could be relied upon to close their businesses for the Jubilee and to facilitate the symbolic transformation of the cityscape with royal decorations and illuminations.

Effectively an exercise in royal mystification, the media focus on Dublin, the location of Ireland's only royal sites, disguised the diversity of opinion not only in Dublin but in the rest of the country. Lady Augusta

---

[17] T. J. O'Keeffe, 'The 1898 Efforts to Celebrate the United Irishmen: The '98 Centennial', *Eire-Ireland*, 23 (1988), 52–3.

[18] Sir Henry Robinson, *Memories: Wise and Otherwise* (London, 1924), p. 135.

[19] For a case study of Cambridge during the Diamond Jubilee, see Elizabeth Hammerton and David Cannadine, 'Conflict and Consensus on a Ceremonial Occasion: The Diamond Jubilee in Cambridge in 1897', *Historical Journal*, 24 (1981), 111–46.

[20] *Derry Journal* [*DJ*], 21 June 1897.

[21] Mary Daly, 'Late Nineteenth and Early Twentieth Century Dublin' in David Harkness and Mary O'Dowd (eds.), *The Town in Ireland: Historical Studies XIII* (Belfast, 1979), p. 226.

Gregory, Yeats's colleague in the Irish Literary Revival, noted that the bonfires arranged by her landlord neighbours to celebrate the Diamond Jubilee were ignored by the tenantry, unlike the celebration of the Catholic religious festival of St John's Eve on the following night: 'the mountains were alive with bonfires, & the people in crowds around them'.[22]

As with past royal occasions, the Diamond Jubilee celebrations illuminated fissures within the broad nationalist family, but the new cultural separatists could both reject the occasion and recognise that it had the positive function of allowing the identification of 'true' nationalism, as those engaged in Jubilee celebrations were exposed,[23] while the apparent failure of Ulster Unionists to raise enough funds for a statue of Queen Victoria in Belfast to commemorate the Jubilee[24] could be interpreted as lack of real commitment to the Union.

In fact, the Jubilee celebrations in Dublin acted as a catalyst for the coordination of the activities of various groups engaged in planning 1798 commemorations, and who chose Jubilee day, 21 June, as the occasion for a symbolic assertion of nationalist identity in the form of a congress in Dublin City Hall.[25] On Jubilee night oppositional demonstrations in a packed city centre were associated with disorder, conflict with the police, and the death of a bystander.[26] These events were effectively submerged in the primacy the press gave to the official Jubilee celebrations,[27] but they were not ignored by Cadogan as he prepared for the visit of the Duke and Duchess of York a week later.

II

Those preparations had both a long- and a short-term focus. For example, the shadow of the controversial visit of the Prince of Wales in 1885 continued to be cast over such occasions, with nationalists warning of the need to avoid giving them a political taint.[28] But it says much about the confidence of the Viceroyalty in this period that, unlike the Golden Jubilee visit of Prince Albert Victor in 1887, which merely followed the pattern of the successful *first* week of the 1885 visit, an extensive

---

[22] Entry (30 Nov. 1897) detailing Jubilee events of June 1897 in James Pethica (ed.), *Lady Gregory's Diaries 1892–1902* (Gerrards Cross, 1996), p. 148.

[23] *Shan Van Vocht*, [*SVV*], 8 Jan. 1897.

[24] *SVV*, 5 July 1897; also *DJ*, 25 June 1897.   [25] *SVV*, 5 July 1897.

[26] See reports in *Weekly Nation*, 3 July 1897; and for a not altogether reliable account by a leading participant, Maud Gonne, *A Servant of the Queen* (1938; Chicago, 1994), pp. 214–18.

[27] Ibid. p. 219.   [28] *DJ*, 28 June, 27 Aug. 1897.

country-wide tour was now planned. Dublin would be the initial arena for royal ceremony, but the royal visitors would then proceed to Kilkenny and the south, before turning up the west midlands towards Tyrone, Derry and Belfast.

The scene-setting for the visit had been in preparation throughout the year. Targeting Catholic opinion in particular, Cadogan had raised expectations of a Catholic university as a bait for clerical involvement,[29] together with a number of welfarist initiatives, while a viceregal Jubilee banquet included 252 'distinguished Irishmen' of all professions, all creeds and 'all parties'.[30] Cadogan also made known the Duke's refusal of an address from the Orange Order.[31]

A centrepiece to the visit was the investing of the Duke as a Knight of the Order of St Patrick, while an Exhibition of Irish Manufactures Cadogan had initiated earlier in the year provided a suitable occasion for the exercise of royal welfarism, when the Duke performed the official opening.[32] If the shadow of 1885 hung over Irish royal visits in this period, it also provided a standard of effectiveness against which the visit of 1897 compared favourably, occasioning effusive testimony to the Queen of Irish loyalty.[33]

Important to the occasion's success was the fact the lessons of 1885 were still being observed; in particular, British prints were careful not to overstate the nature of its success.[34] And yet, while it can be read as a successful defiance of extremist opponents, their activities, especially the disorder in Dublin on Jubilee night, may well have influenced its manifestation. While the state entry to Dublin and public duties in the city went off well, they were apparently conducted with rather less popular display and pomp than was usually associated with great state occasions,[35] and during the visit Cadogan frequently referred to the Duke, not as a royal personage and likely future King of Ireland, but merely as a 'tourist' and stranger travelling to see the country. It was a ploy to deter hostility by framing the occasion as personal, rather than constitutional, in character. Republicans, not unreasonably, thought the practice 'remarkable' and an inhibiting result of the Dublin protests.[36]

---

[29] McCarthy, *Five Years in Ireland*, p. 244.   [30] Ibid. pp. 245–6.

[31] *FJ* in *DJ*, 27 Aug. 1897.

[32] For details of the visit, see *DJ*, 30 Aug. 1897; McCarthy, *Five Years in Ireland*, pp. 260–2.

[33] Duke of York to the Queen, 16 Sept. 1897, RA GV/AA 12/64. Cadogan to the Queen, 1 Sept. 1897, RA VIC/Z 477/261; Salisbury to the Queen, 9 Sept. 1897, in George Buckle (ed.), *Letters of Queen Victoria*, 3rd ser., III, (London, 1932), p. 198, footnote; Knight of Kerry to the Queen, 31 Aug. 1897; Marquis of Dufferin to the Queen, 2 Sept. 1897, RA VIC/Z 477/260, 263.

[34] *Standard* cited in *DJ*, 18 Aug. 1897.   [35] *DJ*, 20 Aug. 1897.   [36] *SVV*, 6 Sept. 1897.

Accordingly, while the visit was successfully executed, the nature of its significance was ambiguous.

Arguably, Cadogan's presentation of the Duke as merely a tourist reduced royal ritual and ceremony to mere non-signifying public entertainment. But more substantive consequences can be suggested. As the first Irish visit by the Duke of York as an adult, it clearly made a very favourable personal impression, and can reasonably be regarded as a significant influence determining his attitude to Ireland as King – which was decidedly conciliatory during the troubled period from 1910 to 1922. More immediately, he was impressed by repeated requests for an Irish royal residence, which he regarded as necessary to cultivating the loyalty already existing.[37] Such appeals had also been conveyed to the Queen by Cadogan.

The royal visit of 1897 thus served to stimulate another round of debate on the issue of the viceroyalty/royalty in Ireland, within well-established parameters of, on the one hand, Unionist desires for viceregal abolition, a royal resident and a more effective Anglo-Irish Union;[38] and, on the other, nationalist – on this occasion Protestant nationalist – arguments for a more effective Viceroyalty through a royal appointment to the office.[39] Cultural nationalists, still marginal voices however individually impressive, insisted on the irrelevance of the royal presence to the question of Irish interests.[40] But it was a debate without practical effect, in the face of monarchical opposition, expected complications affecting Irish administration, and the necessary *pressure* for change strong enough to overcome the Queen's opposition. For nationalists it was not a burning issue. Certainly for constitutionalists looking forward to Home Rule the Gladstonian schemes had fundamentally settled the Viceroyalty question; the issue of a royal officeholder could be left until then. Thus, successful as the royal visit was in sustaining the royal dimension to the Irish question, it did so in a context that foreclosed immediate results. Moreover, while the royal visit was the highlight of Ireland's Jubilee celebrations, these were not the only festive activities.

The year 1897 was one of multiple jubilees in Ireland, a great many of them organised by the Catholic clergy. The thirteenth centennial anniversary of the birth of St Columba, for instance, was celebrated on a

---

[37] Duke of York to the Queen, 25 Aug., 16 Sept. 1897, RA GV/AA 12/63, 64.
[38] Lord Charles Beresford in *The Times* [*TT*], 24 July 1897; Beresford, *Memoirs* (London, 1914), pp. 412–14.
[39] J. G. Swift McNeill, 'The Lord-Lieutenancy and a Royal Residence', *Fortnightly Review*, 64, n.s. (Oct. 1897), 504–12.
[40] Yeats reported in *Irish Daily Independent* [*IDI*], 4 Oct. 1897, cited in Gould et al. (eds.), *Letters of Yeats*, II, pp. 133–4, footnote 3.

similar scale to the Queen's Jubilee, in June, in the presence of enormous crowds and by High Mass, Benediction and Te Deum.[41] But the most politically significant was the commemoration of the Golden Jubilee of O'Connell's death, monopolised by priests and celebrated with High Masses. It can be seen as indicative of the church's own political stance, positioned between monarchical allegiance and the Union on the one hand and nationalist claims on the other, and, as it were, open to offers. This was something the authorities were clearly aware of in the run-up to the 1798 commemoration.

III

While the commemoration was clearly viewed with viceregal disfavour, it was not without possible advantage. Given the disparate groups involved, from constitutional nationalists to socialist republicans, there was for a while every likelihood that the enterprise would self-destruct in conflict and disorder and the authorities made no attempt to interfere with the preparations, only too conscious of the danger of creating unity in opposition.[42] In fact, only the prospect of the 'appalling public spectacle' of nationalist groups vilifying each other in honour of the United Irishmen brought enforced unity.[43] Commemorative preparations proceeded across the country, culminating in a ceremony to inaugurate a foundation stone for a Wolfe Tone memorial in Dublin. Taking place on the same day as Ireland's most important Catholic religious festival, Our Lady's Day, 15 August – thereby enhancing the celebratory atmosphere – the ceremony involved an impressive exercise in the stimulation of national and revolutionary memory. A vast procession traversed every important site associated with the rebellion, together with those associated with the 1803 attempt by Robert Emmet, thus symbolically identifying the capital in opposition to the Jubilee celebrations of the previous year. Across the country commemorative ceremonies and the monuments that were their focus took on the character of 'sacred objects and were the focus for ritual'.[44]

Symbolic intent without the means to deliver on it, however, merely required vigilance on the part of the authorities. As one commentator noted, the commemorations 'did not in the least interfere with the other business of the country'[45] and were not necessarily evidence of a

[41] Ibid. pp. 246–58.   [42] McCarthy, *Five Years in Ireland*, p. 393.
[43] O'Keeffe, 'The 1898 Efforts to Celebrate the United Irishmen', pp. 64–72.
[44] Judith Hill, *Irish Public Sculpture* (Dublin, 1998), p. 134.
[45] McCarthy, *Five Years in Ireland*, p. 398.

mass radical consciousness. Certainly if monument building and ritual were an index of consciousness and commitment, the activities undertaken, and structures erected, by both constitutional or revolutionary nationalists were greatly overshadowed by those associated with religion.[46] Moreover, a decision of leading city Unionists to raise a subscription for a monument to Queen Victoria on Leinster Lawn evidenced their readiness to contest the nationalist signifying of the cityscape.[47] Viceregal satisfaction with the state of the country was evident in the return visit to Ireland of the Duke and Duchess of York in April 1899, less formal than that of 1897 and taking in a number of racing and recreational locations around the country.[48] Both visits by the Duke of York can be seen as useful experience for the preparation of the Queen's visit to Ireland in April 1900, which was apparently suggested by the Duke, encouraged by his own congenial receptions.[49]

The visit was prompted primarily by her appreciation of the bravery of Irish troops in the South African War,[50] though there were other contributing factors. The Home Rule threat seemed to have disappeared and her virulent anti-Catholic and anti-Irish prejudice was dissipating accordingly,[51] while both the Prince of Wales and Cadogan provided strong encouragement.[52] Against a background of police reports from across the country describing anti-recruitment sentiment falling as public opinion apparently took pride in Irish military valour,[53] with disloyal feeling 'lacking depth' when 'tested by demands for action to give it emphasis',

[46] At least twenty-four cathedrals and over 3,000 substantial churches were erected in the century following emancipation: T. P. Kennedy, 'Church Building' in Patrick Corish (ed.), *A History of Irish Catholicism*, V: *The Church since Emancipation* (Dublin, 1970), p. 8.

[47] *TT*, 16 April 1900; Alan Denson (ed.), *John Hughes Sculptor: A Documentary Biography* (Kendal, Westmorland, 1969), pp. 101–2.

[48] McCarthy, *Five Years in Ireland*, pp. 440–1.

[49] Sir Frederick Ponsonby, *Recollections of Three Reigns* (London, 1951), p. 62.

[50] Buckle (ed.), *Letters of Queen Victoria*, III, pp. 490, 498; Lord Wolseley to Sir Arthur Bigge, 20 Feb., 1 March 1900, in ibid. p. 501. It was marked by the creation of a new regiment, the Irish Guards, and permission for all Irish soldiers to wear shamrock on St Patrick's Day; Gould et al. (eds.), *Letters of Yeats*, II, p. 477. Lasting from 1899 to 1902, the war arose out of British annexation of the Transvaal in 1877: Juliet Gardner and Neil Wenborn (eds.), *History Today Companion to British History* (London, 1995), p. 89.

[51] See Buckle (ed.), *Letters of Queen Victoria*, III, pp. 227–8, 232–5. She had Lord Denbeigh accompany her, hoping his presence would soften religious antagonism: Lord Denbeigh in *The Universe*, cited in *ibid.* p. 531, footnote 1.

[52] Ibid. pp. 499–502.

[53] Terence Denman, 'The Campaign against Army Recruitment in Ireland 1899–1914', *Irish Historical Studies*, 29 (1994), 116–17.

and with 'people in general . . . prosperous and contented'[54] the omens for the visit seemed excellent. It is important, however, to see these reports in the context of the Unionist project of conciliation and the substantive Government reforms associated with it. Accordingly, while the visit was primarily a personal acknowledgement by the Queen of Irish military valour, it was also, to a significant extent, a mechanism to gauge the success of those policies in consolidating the Union.

The political environment of Dublin, however, was the most dysfunctionally dynamic for any royal occasion since 1885. The visit brought accusations of a recruiting exercise for a war deeply unpopular with the nationalist population,[55] with Republicans who had raised 'brigades' for service with the Boers[56] bound to protest.[57] James Connolly – the future leader of the 1916 rebels – even had hopes for a national insurgency in this period.[58] Constitutional nationalists, newly reunited as one party under John Redmond's leadership,[59] but internally schismatic, would exhibit a variety of responses to the occasion, as personal respect due an aged monarch and professed allegiance to the empire[60] coexisted uneasily with instinctive sympathy for the Boers. Redmond's initial suggestion of a chivalrous and respectful greeting for the Queen caused leadership dissension and had to be qualified,[61] and yet no nationalist MP opposed recruiting for the war in the Commons.[62]

It was indicative of the ability of royal associations with Ireland to stimulate oppositional associations that the date on which the Queen left Windsor, 2 April, was noted as the centenary of the day on which

---

[54] N. Reed, Inspector General of RIC, to Undersecretary, Dublin Castle, 9 March 1900, Report of the County Inspectors for February 1900, Harvester Press Microfilm, *The British in Ireland: CO904* (Brighton, 1984), Series One, Part Three: Police Reports 1899–1913, Reel 36 [Harvester, *British in Ireland*, Reel]. N. Reed to Undersecretary, 9 April 1900, 'Reports of the County Inspectors for the Month of March 1900': Harvester, *British in Ireland*, Reel 36.

[55] Gonne, *Servant of the Queen*, p. 268 ; Yeats to editor, *FJ*, 20 March 1900.

[56] Keith Jeffrey, 'Boer War' in S. J. Connolly, *The Oxford Companion to Irish History* (Oxford, 2002), p. 50.

[57] Yeats to the editor, *DE*, 30 March 1900; Yeats to editor, *FJ*, 3 April 1900; also Gould et al. (eds.), *Letters of Yeats*, II, pp. 507–9.

[58] Ibid. p. 477.

[59] Factional unity was compelled by the dramatic rise of William O'Brien's agrarian organisation, the United Irish League, which threatened to sideline the other nationalist groups: A. C. Hepburn, 'United Irish League' in Connolly (ed.), *Oxford Companion to Irish History*, p. 567.

[60] Denman, 'The Campaign against Army Recruitment in Ireland', p. 212.

[61] See Healy, *Letters and Leaders*, II, pp. 447–9; *TT*, 9 March 1900; *FJ*, 14 March 1900; O'Brien in *Irish People*, 17 March 1900; Dillon in *Daily Nation*, 19 March 1900; Gould et al. (eds.), *Letters of Yeats*, II, pp. 503–4.

[62] Denman, 'The Campaign against Army Recruitment in Ireland', pp. 214–17.

the Irish Act of Union was introduced into the Westminster Parliament,[63] and coincided with the burial in New York of Grace Georgina Maxwell, a grand-daughter of Wolfe Tone.[64] For the Viceroy, who took a leading role in organising the visit, it required careful handling. The disorder in Dublin on Jubilee night in 1897 illustrated how easily the cityscape could be reduced to a chaotic state. Cadogan, thus, no less than Redmond, faced a problem of some delicacy. But the visit cannot be considered only on the plane of national identity and allegiance.

Disputes about how the Queen should be regarded entailed a complex interrelationship between national and municipal issues. At the centre of these disputes was Thomas Pile, Lord Mayor of Dublin, a Protestant fishmonger and recent convert to nationalism, proof of which was apparently demonstrated by a donation of £10,000 to the '98 Centenary Committee.[65] The Queen's visit, however, placed Pile's new-found nationalist sympathies under severe strain, as, to the consternation of fellow nationalists on the corporation, he proved only too ready to cooperate in facilitating the visit arrangements:[66] a misleading signal was being sent out to other Irish local authorities from Ireland's unofficial national parliament.[67] Pile's 'betrayal' was underlaid by municipal conflicts: a firm temperance advocate, he had vowed to drive the substantial publican element from the corporation chamber. The result was hostility verging on physical conflict between Pile, his supporters and the larger publican element on the corporation. During a St Patrick's Day procession shortly before it began the Lord Mayor's coach was attacked, raising fears of violence during the royal visit.[68]

The viceregal response was to establish a clampdown of the cityscape for the duration of the Queen's sojourn, threatening tradespeople inclined to protest with loss of their business licences and pressurising bill posting organisations and the press not to handle opposition material: 'None of the newspapers except the *Daily Nation* will report on any of their [Transvaal Committee's] proceedings.'[69] Anti-royal symbols were removed, while members of the Transvaal and '98 committees suspected of planning hostile demonstrations were closely watched.[70] An attempt

[63] Yeats to the editor, *FJ*, 20 March 1900.
[64] *New York Sun* reproduced in *IDI*, 21 April 1900.
[65] Gonne, *Servant of the Queen*, p. 269.
[66] See, for instance, Pile to Cadogan, 15 March 1900, Chief Secretary's Office, Registered Papers, CSORP, NAI, CSORP/1900/15355.
[67] For the spread of the 'Pile epidemic' to Listowel, County Cork, see *IDI*, 19 April 1900.
[68] J. J. Jones, Commissioner of Dublin Metropolitan Police, to the Undersecretary, Dublin Castle, 22 March 1900, CSORP, NIA, CSORP/1900/15355.
[69] Jones to Undersecretary, 1, 2 April 1900, ibid.
[70] J. J. Jones to Undersecretary, 30, 31 March 1900, ibid.

to hold a torchlight procession on the night of the Queen's arrival was hampered by police action, occasioning accusations of brutality serious enough to require an official response.[71] Arthur Griffith's *United Irishman*, a forum of anti-visit comment, was suppressed, an act prompted primarily by an article by Maud Gonne describing Victoria as the 'Famine Queen'.[72] Cadogan, moreover, combined situational coercion with news management: organised and privileged access to the Dublin press[73] reporting royal events was provided while a weak attempt at establishing an Irish royal narrative for the visit was made by the journalist Michael McDonagh.[74]

IV

As with the Duke of York's visit in 1897, Cadogan presented the 1900 occasion as being of a personal, rather than a 'state', nature,[75] but as he was well aware, constitutionality was inherent in any public appearance by the Queen and loyalty an inevitable interpretative perspective. And despite Castle anxieties the visit got off to an excellent start, with the Queen seeking to maximise Irish goodwill by ordering that a declaration establishing the Irish Guards not be announced until she was actually in Ireland.[76] She recorded a magnificent reception in Dublin, even noting without apparent alarm the addition of a substantial reinforcement of mounted troops and officials as the royal entourage reached Ballsbridge on the city outskirts.[77]

The official entry took place via 'gates' at Leeson Street in brilliant sunshine and with Lord Mayor Pile and several members of the corporation in attendance, including John Parnell, brother of the uncrowned king, in his capacity as City Marshal, holding a cushion on which lay the keys of the city.[78] A Catholic prelate remarked: 'the streets are transformed out of all recognition by the Decorations. The crowds are

---

[71] Jones to Irish Attorney General, 3, 9 April 1900, CSORP, NIA, CSORP/1900/15355. For the accusations, see *United Irishman* [*UI*], 7 April 1900.

[72] 3,500 copies were confiscated because it was 'calculated to produce discontent and disaffection among supporters of Her Majesty the Queen': J. J. Jones, Commissioner of the DMP to Irish Attorney General, 9 April 1900, CSORP, NIA, CSORP/1900/15355. It was the first of three occasions in 1900 when it was suppressed: R. M. Henry, *The Evolution of Sinn Fein* (Dublin, n.d. [1920s]), p. 54.

[73] Cadogan, *Before the Deluge*, p. 80: 'No one was a more resourceful or a more thorough organiser.'

[74] Michael McDonagh, 'An Irish Royal Visit', *FR*, 67, n.s. (1900), 649–59.

[75] Cadogan, *Before the Deluge*, p. 80.   [76] Ponsonby, *Recollections of Three Reigns*, p. 63.

[77] QVJ (4 April 1900), in Buckle (ed.), *Letters of Queen Victoria*, III, p. 521.

[78] McCarthy, *Five Years in Ireland*, pp. 469, 476–8.

enormous.'[79] Thus as with George IV's visit in 1821 and her own previous visits of 1849 and 1853, the usually divisive and conflictual cityscape was submerged in a suffusion of monarchical signification and celebration. Indeed Victoria was even persuaded that nationalists at the City Hall had come out to cheer her arrival.[80] The only cause of momentary worry was occasioned by a report of an assassination attempt on the Prince of Wales in Belgium, from which he emerged wholly unscathed.[81]

The evident age of the Queen and her black, non-regal attire, played to Cadogan's portrayal of the visit as purely personal. Indeed, one spectator declared bluntly: 'Sure, she is only an old body like ourselves!'[82] At the same time, the celebratory atmosphere of the visit belied the massive security operation in train to sustain it – a police report recorded that during her stay the Queen took fifteen drives totalling 297 miles.[83] Dublin's chief of detectives, John Mallon, exclaimed: 'I wish to God she was out of the country.'[84] Nothing untoward, however, occurred during the visit. Addresses were presented in accordance with established practice, the only noteworthy aspect of the process being an ostentatious address from Belfast Corporation delivered in a gold casket enclosing a narrative of Ulster's progress since the royal visit of 1849,[85] and very much in keeping with the northern Unionist tendency to frame monarchy in the context of Ulster rather than of Ireland. After three weeks of welfarist activities in which displays of spontaneous harmony between monarch and subjects were exhibited, the Queen left Ireland on 26 April with regret.[86] The visit, the *Irish Daily Independent* opined, was a great success: the Queen had been greeted with enthusiasm by Unionists, and nationalists had offered no disrespect.[87]

As this visit was clearly the last the Queen would make to Ireland, it naturally posited her first visit of 1849 as its point of comparative departure. Certain changes were now very obvious. The Queen had lost the charms of youth and was no longer the *tabula rasa* on which Irish hopes might be inscribed; nor indeed was Ireland itself the *tabula rasa* it appeared to be after the famine – a land and people ready to be remade in a loyalist British image. The relationship between the Queen and Catholic Ireland

---

[79] Bishop Donnelly to Walsh, 5 April 1900, Archbishop Walsh papers, Dublin Diocesan Archives [DDA], WP/1900/371/I.

[80] RA QVJ: 4 April 1900.   [81] Ibid.

[82] Cited in Elizabeth Countess of Fingall, *Seventy Years Young* (New York, 1939), p. 252.

[83] 'Royal Visit', CSORP, NIA, CSORP/1900/15355.

[84] Mallon cited in Ramsay Colles, *In Castle and Court House* (London, n.d), pp. 53–4.

[85] *IDI*, 19 April 1900.

[86] QVJ (26 April 1900), in Buckle (ed.), *Letters of Queen Victoria*, III, p. 544.

[87] Editorial, 'The Queen's Visit', *IDI*, 27 April 1900.

had matured since the 1840s in a far from congenial manner: the legacy of popular loyalty left by O'Connell had dissipated and the 'Famine Queen' epithet was taking root. The *Irish Times*'s description of Dublin having 'awakened after a vivid and delightful dream'[88] would have reflected the Protestant and Unionist experience of royal enchantment accurately enough, but the *Irish Daily Independent*'s reference to such comments as 'comic drivel'[89] registered the gap that separated the nationalist and Unionist communities.

That gap can also be gauged by incidents the visit's micro-management disguised. The dissent of the city's offical Sword Bearer, James Egan, who refused to participate in the official entry of the Queen, was covered by simply appointing a replacement.[90] More significant was the refusal of the Catholic clergy to participate, dramatically expressed in condemnation as political 'souperism' of a viceregal banquet for 50,000 Dublin children, at which they would meet the Queen. The reference was to a reputed famine practice of Protestant evangelists offering soup for religious conversion and inevitably reinforced the credibility of the 'Famine Queen' epithet. The Catholic boycott of the banquet which ensued[91] was an impressive demonstration of clerical influence, energised by indignation at attempts to mobilise Catholic schoolchildren under the Protestant and Unionist auspices of the Band of Hope and the Union Jack for a show of constitutional loyalty at a time when serious problems remained unaddressed – the refusal of a Catholic university, Irish over-taxation, the continued state proclaiming of Catholic religious orders, the denial of Home Rule[92] – together with opposition to the South African War. The banquet boycott proved effective because of the way the religious grievances of the clergy intersected with wider Irish complaints. The controversy would also allow republican groups the opportunity for a propaganda event through the organising of a great 'Patriotic' children's treat, catering for about 30,000 children.[93] A recent view, that the organisers of the royal visit 'managed brilliantly' to wrong-foot its opponents by focusing it on children,[94] is wide of the mark. The undoubtedly strong turn-out for the Queen from the substantial Protestant and Unionist community of the greater Dublin area could be taken for granted and

[88] *IT*, 26 April 1900.   [89] *IDI*, 27 April 1900.
[90] McCarthy, *Five Years in Ireland*, p. 477.   [91] Ibid. pp. 482–6.
[92] *FJ*, 28 March 1900; *Evening Telegraph*, 27–31 March 1900; *Nation*, 31 March 1900; also *IDI*, 27 April 1900 for list of Irish grievances; McCarthy, *Five Years in Ireland*, pp. 533–40.
[93] Margaret Ward, *Women in Irish Nationalism* (London, 1995), pp. 47–9.
[94] James Murphy, *Abject Loyalty: Nationalism and Monarchy in Ireland during the Reign of Queen Victoria* (Cork, 2001), p. 287.

hardly registers the visit a great success. Nor should the testimony of the royal party itself, possibly the most deceived by enthusiastic appearances.[95] That historians still register the visit as a success is testimony to Cadogan's effective event management.

Embarrassing enough as the Phoenix Park event was, it might have been less obvious had the Catholic hierarchy been prepared to offer an address, but none was forthcoming, and Archbishop Walsh's absence from Dublin could hardly have been more indicative of hierarchical aloofness.[96] A number of Catholic gentry retrieved the situation somewhat by persuading the impressionable Cardinal Logue, Primate of All Ireland, to attend a viceregal banquet, on the misleading premise that the Queen would thereby facilitate the establishment of a Catholic university: Logue's intimations of Catholic grievances to the monarch, however, were 'hardly noticed'.[97] But from the Castle's perspective the public impression was conveyed that the royal visit had the church's imprimatur.

The royal visit of 1900 was clearly a *personal* success for the aged Queen, in that nothing occurred to cause her distress – she seems to have been unaware of its problematic dimensions. But it no less offered a snapshot of serious Anglo-Irish difficulties even in a period of sustained legislative reformism. Moreover, while Cadogan's effective stage-management curtailed the activities of militant cultural and republican protestors, the visit nevertheless provided these groups with an opportunity to enhance their ideological coherence and organisational effectiveness.[98] It is doubtful, however, how far the limitations of royal spectacle were acknowledged by the Castle authorities.

The distorting prism provided by the RIC of opinion in the country registered an Ireland in which only one anti-visit act of vandalism was reported: the royal presence was nullifying pro-Boer sentiment and the United Irish League was effectively inoperative.[99] Accordingly, the high degree of coercive manipulation that attended the visit could well have seemed justified, insofar as it merely served to bring the capital into true representative alignment with Ireland as a whole. As such, the visit facilitated Government complacency about how successful their Irish

---

[95] See the fulsome account in Sir Frederick Ponsonby, *Recollections of Three Reigns* (London, 1951), pp. 62–6.

[96] Sir Gerald Dease to Walsh, 11 March 1900, Walsh papers, DDA, WP/1900/371/II; Walsh to Cadogan, Good Friday, April 1900, ibid.; Walsh to Dease, 22 April 1900, ibid.

[97] Logue to Walsh, 9 April 1900, Walsh papers, DDA, WP/1900/371/I; Logue to Father Petit, 'Friday Evening', April 1900, Walsh papers, DDA, WP/1900/371/I.

[98] Senia Pašeta, 'Nationalist Reactions to Two Royal Visits, 1900 and 1903', *Irish Historical Studies* 31 (1999), 488–505.

[99] A. Reed, Inspector General, RIC to Undersecretary, Dublin Castle, Confidential Report on the State of Ireland for April 1900, 11 May 1900: Harvester, *British in Ireland*, Reel 36.

policies really were, while also encouraging Unionist efforts to contest the nationalist marking of the Dublin cityscape.

Thus the construction of a statue to Queen Victoria, initiated by the RDS in 1897, was given a boost when, on the day the Queen left Ireland, the project was opened up to public subscription, thus fulfilling a necessary condition of acquiring the desired site, Leinster Lawn. However, a decision to augment the monument with supporting figures representing 'her Irish soldiers'[100] was an addition guaranteed to restrict support to the Protestant and Unionist community, especially when a proclamation rashly assuming Archbishop Walsh's support for the project earned a public rebuke.[101] This was virtually guaranteed when, on the death of the Queen in January 1901, a decision was taken to widen the signification of the monument to include a celebration of the Queen's entire reign, with committees of 'Ladies and Gentlemen' being established throughout the country for the purpose.[102]

This decision may well have been informed by a misunderstanding of Irish reactions to Victoria's demise. Police reports, inevitably reflecting the Dublin Castle mindset, read respectful acknowledgement of the event as 'profound feeling' that would have 'the good effect in keeping alive that strong sentiment of loyalty to the Crown which was evoked at the time of the Queen's visit last summer'.[103] That a nationalist decision to hold aloof from official expressions of condolence was far from wholly observed by party MPs[104] would not have gone unnoticed.

Victoria's passing and the accession of Edward VII marked a significant turning point in the monarchy's relationship with Ireland. It immediately distanced the throne from the Great Famine and provided a congenial Irish context for a monarch already popular in the country. Certainly his accession was not marked by any explicit protest in Ireland: the police reported enthusiastic crowds marking the occasion in the politically volatile cities of Cork and Limerick.[105] This was of some significance.

---

[100] *TT*, 30 April, 16 May 1900. See also leaflet 'Statue of Her Majesty the Queen', Walsh papers, DDA, WP/1900/371/II.

[101] John Joly and R. R. Kane to Walsh, 15 May 1900, ibid.; newspaper cutting, 'Proposed Statue to the Queen in Dublin', attached to letter of J. Alletson to Walsh, 9 July 1900, ibid.; also Thomas Pile, Lord Mayor, to Walsh, 1 July 1900 (ibid.), disclaiming any responsibility in the affair.

[102] *TT*, 19 Feb. 1901; Denson (ed.), *John Hughes*, p. 203.

[103] Col. N. Chamberlain, Inspector General, RIC to Undersecretary, Report on the Condition of Ireland for January 1901, 12 Feb. 1901: Harvester, *British in Ireland*, Reel 38.

[104] J. R. R. McConnel, 'The View from the Backbench: Irish Nationalist MPs and Their Work, 1910–1914', unpublished PhD thesis, University of Durham (2002), p. 66.

[105] Chamberlain to Undersecretary, 'Report on the Condition of Ireland for January 1901', 12 Feb. 1901: Harvester, *British in Ireland*, Reel 38.

Edward's accession inevitably brought into the public realm the deeply offensive anti-Catholic Declaration of Accession.[106] It should have been a gift for republican elements anxious to discredit the crown,[107] but their efforts had little political effect; and though Timothy Healy, a spokesman for clerical interests, together with Cardinal Logue,[108] led a chorus of Catholic protest across the country[109] none of the indignation raised was directed personally against the King. Not only was he perceived as sympathetic to Home Rule, but his personal excesses were reflective of general human failings that many in Ireland found easy to forgive. James Joyce made the point in his short story 'Ivy Day in the Committee Room', but to illustrate hypocrisy in nationalist public attitudes: 'Do you think after what he did Parnell was a fit man to lead us? Why then would we ... [welcome] Edward VII?'[110] Almost coincident with the accession of the new King, the context of Anglo-Irish relations changed significantly.

V

First, Earl Cadogan resigned the Viceroyalty in August 1902. At his best organising public display and ceremony, Cadogan flourished in the relative political and agrarian peace from 1895, but when a phase of agrarian agitation and strife took off from late 1901 he became the spokesman of Irish Unionist opinion, demanding coercive measures and in conflict with a new Chief Secretary, George Wyndham, keen to sustain conciliation and a settlement of the land and university questions.[111] He was replaced by Lord Dudley, one of the richest men in England, who rapidly developed pro-Irish sympathies.

With Dudley's appointment the viceregal system assumed its most pronationalist and pro-Catholic complexion since 1886, at the same time as a new King with a favourable reputation in Ireland and in close sympathy

---

[106] For the controversy it raised in Britain, see Roy Strong, *Coronation: A History of Kingship and the British Monarchy* (London, 2005), p. 471.
[107] See for instance, *The Irish People*, 28 Feb. 1901.
[108] Oldmeadow, *Bourne*, II, pp. 49–50.
[109] Col. N. Chamberlain to Undersecretary, Report on the Condition of Ireland for March 1901: Harvester, *British in Ireland*, Reel 38.
[110] James Joyce, *Dubliners* (1914; Mineola, NY, 1991), p. 88.
[111] Wyndham was a direct descendant of the United Irishmen leader, Lord Edward Fitzgerald, and even admitted to being 'theoretically' a Home Ruler, though it was not yet practical politics: Sir Charles Petrie, *Walter Long and His Times* (London, 1936), pp. 78–9; Entry (30 March 1903), W. S. Blunt, *My Diaries, Being a Personal Record of Events 1888–1914* (London, 1932), p. 461.

with the Irish administration[112] had assumed the throne. Indeed it was a convinced belief of nationalists and others that the appointment of the Catholic A. P. McDonnell as Undersecretary at this time was 'entirely down to the King'.[113]

The monarch had been keen to visit Ireland as soon as possible after his coronation in 1902, but was deterred by the exultant response of nationalist MPs to British set-backs in South Africa,[114] and by a rising level of agrarian agitation.[115] Illness led to the postponement of the coronation until August 1902, but despite agrarian unrest the coronation celebrations in Ireland went off almost entirely without incident,[116] thereby sending favourable signals. It was true that nationalists in Parliament and in the new local councils refused to participate in coronation celebrations, but it was recognised that this was a long-standing formality. Indeed the nationalist position that the monarch could not be officially recognised until Home Rule was conceded was not a rejection of royal authority, merely suspended endorsement; and despite the official party boycott of the coronation ceremony in Westminster Abbey, at least five nationalist MPs, and possibly nine, attended anyway.[117]

The coronation, in fact, can be seen as the symbolic starting point of the new phase of enhanced conciliation. The ceremony took place on 9 August; Dudley was installed as Viceroy on 16 August,[118] and was so impressed by the popular response to his official entry to Dublin that he apparently set about considering immediately ideas for the improvement of the country and the lives of its people.[119] Just three months after the coronation George Wyndham was preparing to add a royal residence in conjunction with abolition of the Viceroyalty to reforms he was already planning:[120] it would 'appeal to the sentiment of the Irish and ... sever, in Ireland as in Great Britain any connection ... between the Crown and Party Politics'.[121]

---

[112] Certainly when, during a Cabinet crisis in 1903, Wyndham was proposed for the War Office, the King opposed his removal from Ireland: Viscount Chilston, *Chief Whip: The Political Life and Times of Aretas Akers-Douglas* (London, 1961), p. 314.

[113] Healy to his father, 10 March 1903 in Healy, *Letters and Leaders*, II, p. 461; Fingall, *Seventy Years Young*, p. 277.

[114] See Salisbury to the King, 11 March 1902, RA VIC/R 22/73.

[115] Cadogan to the King, 16 March 1902, RA VIC/W 74/02.

[116] Col. Chamberlain to Undersecretary, Report on the Condition of Ireland for August 1902: Harvester, *British in Ireland*, Reel 41.

[117] McConnel, 'The View from the Backbench', p. 67; *TT*, 14 Aug. 1902

[118] *TT*, 18 Aug. 1902.   [119] Fingall, *Seventy Years Young*, p. 278.

[120] Wyndham, 'A Policy for Ireland', 14 Nov. 1902, RA VIC/W 74/11.

[121] Ibid.

This would be the last occasion on which the issue would be seriously considered, and merits attention because there was now no royal impediment to its implementation. Certainly the King took the issue seriously. The eminent Irish historian W. E. H. Lecky, much admired by Edward and one of the first recipients of the new Order of Merit which he inaugurated on his accession, was commissioned to draw up a report on the proposal. But Lecky, although he had long left behind youthful nationalist leanings, made a robust patriotic case against abolition, arguing for the 'general' popularity of Viceroys and the enhanced status Dublin derived from their presence; the affront to 'national feeling' transcending party boundaries that abolition would entail; the economic advantage and welfarism it facilitated; the social leadership Viceroys provided and the likelihood that in their absence 'every important social and industrial movement for the benefit of Ireland which is started in Dublin' would have a nationalist Lord Mayor or Archbishop as its patron. Lecky cautioned against attempting to diminish national feeling; rather, it should be 'safely' encouraged, though he rejected the now largely discredited Scottish model of constitutional integration in the Irish context. Moreover, he dismissed the notion that viceregal abolition could effect the defeat of Home Rule nationalism; rather a developing weariness with agitation and the growth of land ownership was contributing largely to this end. Abolition would only stimulate a 'flagging' movement, without 'any clear and definite improvements'.[122]

Lecky's verdict, the inherent difficulties associated with the proposal and a crowded parliamentary timetable effectively ruled out action on the issue, though the King remained sympathetic to the idea. At the same time, the new Viceroy and the massive wealth he could draw on in the service of his office fortuitously demonstrated its utility[123] when Wyndham was making preparations for the King's coronation visit to Ireland.

VI

Aware of the importance of the press in framing the interpretative context of the occasion, Wyndham emphasised the King's welfarist interests and privately speculated on how a major fire or accident entailing loss of life – 'which we must hope may not be' – would create a profoundly human and non-political environment the King could exploit.[124] Nevertheless, with

---

[122] W. E. H. Lecky, 'Memorandum on the Proposed Abolition of the Viceroyalty in Ireland', n.d. [1902], RA VIC/W 74/6.

[123] For an example of viceregal largess for a Cork industrial exhibition, see Wyndham to Knollys, 17 Dec. 1902, RA VIC/W 74/12.

[124] Wyndham to Knollys, 17 Feb. 1903, RA VIC/W 74/14.

both the Viceroy and the Chief Secretary at one in pushing forward a reformist agenda[125] which had the King's endorsement, Wyndham believed that there was now a 'more favourable opportunity [for the state] in Ireland than has occurred for a century'.[126] Moreover, while Wyndham worked to condition Irish public opinion for the visit, the King made his own contribution in spring 1903 by a visit to Italy that inevitably – and in the face of much Protestant resistance in the Government and British public opinion[127] – included a visit to the Vatican,[128] the view of the 'English in Rome' apparently being that 'as the King wanted to go to Ireland it was a necessity for him to go to the Pope'.[129]

The popularity of the King in Ireland was unsettling for nationalists, who feared a popular reception for the King would give a misleading impression of Irish opinion in Britain: how he was to be received was fraught with 'the weightiest political significance'.[130] Such anxieties also preoccupied republican and cultural nationalist groups, which influenced Dublin Corporation to vote narrowly against the presentation of an address.[131] The *Freeman's Journal* sought to deter hostility by stressing the welfarist nature of the visit[132] but what did much to ensure a good reception for the monarch was the widespread, and well-founded, belief that he actively facilitated the enactment of the Wyndham land act, then going through its parliamentary stages, and which would effectively solve the Irish agrarian question.[133] Moreover, Edward, 'very anxious that special prominence be given to his visit to Ireland', instructed that it not

---

[125] See Dudley to Lord Ashbourne, Irish Lord Chancellor, 22 Nov. 1902, in A. P. W. Malcolmson (ed.), *The Ashbourne Papers 1869–1914: A Calender of the Papers of Edward Gibson, 1st Lord Ashbourne* (Belfast, 1974), p. 108.

[126] Wyndham to Knollys, 17 Feb. 1903, RA EDVII/W74/14.

[127] Balfour to the King, 8, 10, 12 April 1903, John Sandars papers, Bodleian Library [Bod. L.], C715/22, 23, 36.

[128] King to Balfour, 13 April 1903, Sandars papers, Bod. L., C715/38.

[129] W. H. Murphy, Irish College, Rome, to Archbishop Walsh, 1 May 1903, Walsh papers, DDA, WP/1903/365/I. For the diplomatic agreement on an unoffical visit, see Gordon Brook-Shepherd, *Uncle of Europe: The Social and Political Life of Edward VII* (London, 1975), pp. 184–5.

[130] Alfred Webb to Editor, 'A Royal Address', *FJ*, 15 May 1903 (press cutting), Webb papers, NLI, MS1747.

[131] See Yeats to the editor, *United Irishman* [*UI*], 20 May 1903, in John Kelly and Ronald Schuchard (eds.), *The Collected Letters of W. B. Yeats* I, II: *1901–1904* (Oxford, 1994), pp. 377–8, footnote 1.

[132] Editorial, 'Loyal Addresses', *FJ*, 2 July 1903.

[133] The product of a conference of tenants representatives, led by William O'Brien and landlord representatives, of whom the most prominent was Lord Dunraven. See Earl of Dunraven, *Past Times and Pastimes* (London, n.d. [1920s]), II, ch. 1; *IDI*, 20 July 1903. For circumstantial evidence of the King's role, see William O'Brien, *An Olive Branch in Ireland* (London, 1910), pp. 242–3. The King placed his Irish landed interests at the disposal of Parliament: Arthur Balfour in *ILN*, 25 July 1903.

be 'classed with his visit to Scotland, as if one had no more significance than the other': 'he very properly insisted upon a paragraph [in the *London Gazette*] describing the whole itinerary relating to Ireland'.[134] For their part, constitutionalist nationalists, having made the ritual observance of an official boycott, collaborated with Wyndham to ensure that his required presence in Ireland during the visit did not hinder the enactment of Irish legislation.[135] Siren voices warning of a repeat of the false hopes aroused by George IV's visit in 1821[136] had little effect. Moreover, a considerable degree of luck attended the scene-setting for the visit.

As the royal yacht proceeded to Ireland it became known that Pope Leo XIII had died. The King, though personally unaffected,[137] responded as though he was, making a number of very public gestures of acknowledgement.[138] On arrival at Kingstown he made a point of mentioning his recent visit to the Vatican, acknowledged Irish sorrow at the pontiff's death and claimed to share it himself.[139] In a period of greatly developing Catholic piety, the King's actions resonated powerfully with Irish opinion, reflected in a child's remark: 'I am so glad that we may love the King now because he spoke so nicely about the Pope.'[140] A radical nationalist intention to turn Catholics against the King by circulating copies of the the crudely anti-Catholic sections of the Declaration of Accession[141] had little impact on public opinion.[142] The impression conveyed was of personal grief publicly objectified by a monarch widely believed to have Home Rule sympathies, and whose response to addresses of welcome focused on his welfarist commitment to Ireland's social, economic, scientific and artistic life, responses so well pitched to his popular image

---

[134] Sir Almeric Fitzroy, *Memoirs* (London, n.d.), I, p. 146. Fitzroy was Clerk of the Privy Council.

[135] See Wyndham to Redmond, 18 July 1903, Redmond papers, NLI, MS 15233(2).

[136] Yeats to the Editor, *FJ*, 13 July 1903. See also *Irish People*, 25 July 1903.

[137] George Wyndham to his sister Pamela, 25 July 1903, in J. W. Mackail and Guy Wyndham (eds.), *Life and Letters of George Wyndham* (London, n.d.), II, p. 461.

[138] Fingall, *Seventy Years Young*, p. 284; *ILN*, 25 July 1903; Sidney Lee, *King Edward VII: A Biography* (London, 1927), II, pp. 161–3. The flag of his yacht was lowered to half-mast; a well-publicised telegram of condolence was sent to the Irish Primate, Cardinal Logue; a planned visit to the theatre was cancelled.

[139] *FJ*, 22 July 1903.

[140] Wyndham to Arthur Balfour, 26 July 1903, in Mackail and Wyndham (eds.), *Wyndham*, II, p. 466.

[141] Maud Gonne's organisation, the Inghinidhe na hEireann (Daughters of Erin) had plastered central Dublin with well in excess of 10,000 leaflets detailing the Declaration by the eve of the visit: Ward, *Unmanageable Revolutionaries*, p. 63.

[142] The claims of one recent commentator that Maud Gonne's anti-royal campaign had 'succeeded in capturing the [popular?] imagination' is hardly credible. See Ward, *Unmanageable Revolutionaries*, p. 63.

in Ireland that support for Home Rule was easily inferred.[143] Dublin Corporation may have refused an official address of welcome and none of the more than eighty addresses submitted to the King in southern Ireland came from a publicly elected body.[144] Rather, they came from professional, ecclesiastical, mercantile and scientific associations.[145] But of course anti-Home Rule opinion in Britain was more inclined to find the authentic expression of Irish opinion in these institutions of civil society.[146] It was clear that the sixty-three Special Constables sworn in by the Dublin Metropolitan Police to help keep order in the event of a rumoured 'tumult' to be organised during the Dublin stage of the visit[147] would not be needed.

Edward's action did much to ensure the compliance of the Catholic hierarchy, especially Archbishop Walsh, who attended a levee and was instrumental in facilitating the very successful royal call at the Maynooth seminary,[148] 'statesmanlike' action which, it was argued, strengthened the Home Rule and education arguments by showing that self-government would not mean separation.[149] Certainly the popular welcome for Edward provided a stark contrast to his reception in 1885. Yet it served to frame even that visit in a favourable light. It could now be seen as an index of Irish alienation which conciliatory legislation since then had successfully removed. Moreover, unlike 1885, nationalist Ireland now had no uncrowned king acting as an oppositional source of 'royal' allegiance. Pointing up the way in which welfare monarchism defined the context of the visit at the expense of nationalism, the *Illustrated London News* exclaimed: 'When the Irish bard tunes his lyre, which will he find the more inspiring theme, the King's visit to the carpenters and cobblers in their tenements, or the Lord Mayor's refusal to bid him welcome?'[150] Nor was its success merely a Dublin phenomenon. It was no less successful in the country at large, especially in the impoverished west of Ireland,[151] a stage of the visit organised by Horace Plunkett and which offered an excellent arena for the exercise of welfare monarchism in conditions of

---

[143] *FJ*, 23 July 1903.   [144] Pašeta, 'Nationalist Responses to Two Royal Visits', 501.

[145] Earl of Meath, *Memories of the Twentieth Century* (London, 1924), p. 67.

[146] They were indicative of the 'spontaneous good-will of the Irish people': *ILN*, 3 Aug. 1903.

[147] J. Wall, Chief Magistrate to Undersecretary, Dublin Castle, 18 July 1903, CSORP, INA, CSORP/1903/14162.

[148] See Revd D. Dargan to Walsh, 25 July 1903; Walsh to Lord Primate of Church of Ireland, 23 July 1903, Walsh papers, DDA, WP/365/I.

[149] William Delany to Walsh, 22 July 1903, ibid.   [150] *ILN*, 1 Aug. 1903.

[151] The effect of Edward's acknowledgement of the Pope's death was reflected in the banner 'Friend of Our Pope': Sir Henry Robinson, *Memories: Wise and Otherwise* (London, 1924), p. 154.

personal engagement not seen since George IV's disorderly journey from Howth to the Viceregal Lodge in 1821, but without the alcoholic stimulant present then. Lady Clonbrook evidenced the enchantment the King's presence engendered: 'It seemed strangely like a dream to see the Head of the great Empire standing there before us and to hear him refer to our "Citie of the Tribes" [Galway] as though it were quite a familiar name to him.'[152]

The success of the southern dimension to the visit created resentment among Ulster loyalists used to localising the royal presence, expressed in derisive references to the King as 'Popish Ned'.[153] However, these never entered public discourse. Instead the Ulster Unionist press presented the southern success as a vindication of the example Ulster set for the rest of Ireland in 1885: Irish Catholics might now settle down and 'make the best of their heritage as British subjects', thus demonstrating that 'the United Kingdom is really one'.[154] Instructed by the King to construct an appropriate 'manifesto' he could deliver on leaving Ireland, Wyndham, with a keen eye to the 'organic' relationship between monarch and subjects the visit apparently established, advised abandoning the 'third person' form of communication preferred by Queen Victoria, in favour of the first person singular. This was in keeping with the form of the King's replies to addresses and 'brings him into closer touch with the country'.[155]

Edward VII's Irish visit of 1903 was the most successful since 1849. It took place when constitutional nationalism was relatively weak; when newer forms of cultural nationalism had yet to develop significantly; when the state had entered upon the most sustained phase of remedial legislation under the Union; when the scene-setting for the visit – deliberate and accidental – was brilliantly exploited by a monarch of impressive diplomatic skill and with a reputation of goodwill towards Ireland, who genuinely liked the country and its people and enthusiastically engaged with the visit; and when the Irish Viceroyalty itself had a 'nationalist' persona. A verdict on the visit penned by Horace Plunkett, a leading contributor to Irish socio-economic reform, concluded:

What I now find among the people is the feeling that the King recognises that he is . . . not only the people's leader, but that he is in real sympathy with them: that he

---

[152] 'Reminiscences of the Royal Visit to Galway by a Galway Woman [Lady Clonbrook]', Clonbrook papers, NLI, MS 19668.

[153] Shane Leslie, *Long Shadows* (London, 1966), p. 130.

[154] *BNL*, 22, 23, 27 July 1903; also, *Banbridge Chronicle*, 1 April, 22, 25 July 1903; *Ulster Gazette*, 25 July, 1 Aug. 1903; *Tyrone Constitution*, 25 July 1903; *Weekly Northern Whig* [*WNW*], 25 July 1903.

[155] Wyndham to Knollys, 28 July 1903, RA VIC/W74/33.

felt for them in their sorrow when they lost the head of their church, and that he went to extraordinary exertions to see for himself the darker side of their poverty.

No King had been as popular among the mass of the Irish 'since the days of James II., and there is this great difference between the two cases, that the affection for James II soon came to lack the element of respect'.[156] Police reports for Ireland over the next year described a country largely tranquil,[157] as the King made another satisfactory visit.[158] Sir Anthony McDonnell could assure the court that the Gaelic League in Ireland – the seedbed of the governing elite that would assume power in the Irish Free State from 1922 – was 'social and literary & not political',[159] as indeed it largely then was, inspiring an unsuccessful royal attempt to patronise the Irish Literary Theatre. It was rebuffed by Yeats and Lady Gregory, concerned to use Irish culture as a means of shaping a national identity in opposition to that of imperial Britain.[160]

In fact, in this period the cultural movement had a diverse socio-political background that was reflected in a range of stances on the monarchy; for instance, a debate about its Irish identity with a focus on the origins of the Stone of Scone.[161] But most significantly, in 1904, the year of the King's second visit to Ireland, Arthur Griffith responded by publishing *The Resurrection of Hungary*.

VII

Griffith argued for the withdrawal of nationalist MPs from Westminster, as Hungarian deputies had been from the Austrian Imperial Diet in 1866, leading to the dual monarchy solution to the Austro-Hungarian problem in 1867; and for the establishment of a Council of Three Hundred to formulate national policies for implementation by the local councils and the already existing local boards controlled by Dublin Castle. With 'Grattan's Parliament' as an (imperfect) model, Griffith envisaged Ireland establishing a form of internal Home Rule under the British monarchy which could unite nationalists and Unionists, until events

---

[156] Plunkett to Knollys, 30 Nov. 1903, RA VIC/W74/37.
[157] See, for instance, McDonnell to Knollys, 16, 25 March, 11 May 1904. RA VIC/W74/42, 44, 51.
[158] Sir Sidney Lee, *King Edward VII: A Biography* (London, 1927), II, p. 172.
[159] McDonnell to Knollys, 7 May 1904, RA VIC/W74/46.
[160] See Yeats to John Quinn, 16 Jan., 1 Feb. 1904, in Kelly and Schuchard (eds.), *Letters of Yeats*, III, pp. 519, 540–1.
[161] The pro-imperialist T. W. Rolleston asserted the authenticity of the monarchy's Irish links: *The Myths and Legends of the Celtic Race* (London, 1905), p. 105; William Bulfin (*Rambles in Eirinn*, Dublin, 1907, pp. 100–2) regarded such arguments as mere inventions 'for the high purpose of reconciling the Irish people to the blessings of English rule'.

favoured the establishment of greater independence.[162] These ideas were not completely original, as previous Irish leaders from O'Connell to Parnell had toyed with the idea of withdrawal from Westminster.[163] The timing of Griffith's proposals, however, calls for comment.

The argument unfolded gradually over the period from January to June 1904, within a monarchical carapace provided by the recent visit and the planning and execution of the King's forthcoming return.[164] Moreover, while Griffith was a radical nationalist, a suggestion of his own monarchical inclinations has been found in the 'lengthy, detailed and indulgent descriptions of Franz Joseph's coronation and Hungarian "enthusiasm" for it'.[165] As the signatory of a treaty that conceded dominion status for Ireland under the crown in 1921, it is quite possible that Griffith accepted that Irish enthusiasm for the Edwardian monarchy – which he may have shared – had a depth that had to be effectively negotiated, especially so at a time when state initiatives driven by a progressive dynamic had yet to run their course and might condition the Irish people to accept something less than full independence.

Thus the devolution scheme of 1904–5, proposing a *via media* between the Union and Home Rule, was a follow-on to the Wyndham conference that produced a solution to the agrarian issue in 1903. Its failure, a product of Ulster and backbench Unionist opposition, was not foreseen as inevitable in 1904: it produced a backlash that forced Wyndham's resignation, a largely sectarian, though unsuccessful, campaign against Sir Anthony McDonnell, and condemnation of Dudley, the 'nationalist' Viceroy.[166] Constitutional nationalists, anxious about popular support for Home Rule, also turned on the Viceroy: 'The English monarchy is the embodiment of English nationality; the Irish Viceroyalty is the very negation of Irish national sentiment ... the people are not behind you.'[167] Yet despite the political furore, there is no evidence of the King's opposition to the devolution proposals, while he intimated clearly

---

[162] See the insightful discussion in Virginia Glandon, *Arthur Griffith and the Advanced-Nationalist Press in Ireland 1900–1922* (New York, 1985), pp. 15–17.

[163] Ibid. p. 16.

[164] On the visit's success see Prince Arthur to his sister Louise, 1 May 1904, RA VIC/Add A/17/1020.

[165] See Andrew Gibson, *Joyce's Revenge: History, Politics and Aesthetics in Ulysses* (Oxford, 2002), p. 193, footnote 43.

[166] For a short account, see A. C. Hepburn, 'Devolution Crisis' in Connolly (ed.), *Oxford Companion to Irish History*, pp. 144–5; for a clear narrative of the issue, see Earl of Dunraven, *Past Times and Pastimes* (London, n. d.), ch. 1; and the Ulster Unionist response in Reginald Lucas, *Colonel Saunderson MP* (London, 1908), pp. 334–6.

[167] R. B. O'Brien, *England's Title in Ireland: A Letter Addressed to His Excellency the Lord Lieutenant of Ireland* (London, 1905), pp. 3–4.

to the Government a disapproval of Dudley leaving Ireland because of the crisis.[168] Following on from a failed attempt to solve the university question,[169] however, the crisis registered the limits of constructive Unionism and a determination to drive the Irish administration in a traditionalist direction. Wyndham was replaced by Walter Long, whose appointment initiated conflict at the heart of Irish government as Long's coercive tendencies – supported by Edward Carson who even then was adopting the somewhat paranoid Ulster loyalist mindset[170] – met fierce resistance from Dudley, putting the issue of the relative primacy of the offices of Chief Secretary and Viceroy in contention.[171] Yet progressive as the Irish administration's policies had been, they did not constitute governing Ireland according to 'Irish ideas', but rather governing Ireland according to the interests and mindset of the administration. A political cost lay in too public an exposition of that mindset. That became clear when Horace Plunkett published *Ireland in the New Century* in 1904.

VIII

Intending to encourage the development of Irish 'character', Plunkett described that character as 'economically paralysing', a weakness sourced to Roman Catholicism which deterred the spirit of scientific and indus-trial progress, and encouraged a lack of moral fibre and a non-analytical mindset prone to inconsequential fancies.[172] Plunkett's was a grossly inept contribution to the state's conciliationist project. It reflected the demise of explicit racism in British popular discourse on Ireland, but no less the durability of the mindset that produced it. His condemnation of great architectural edifices raised in recent times to glorify the Catholic faith as shocking to 'the economic sense' brought an inevitable response citing the multiplicity of state, civic and landlord structures which, on a 'utilitarian' basis, provided more egregious examples of economic 'shock'; while references to needless expense exposed the target of royal

---

[168] See Knollys to Sandars, 21 Feb. 1905, BL, Add. MS 49684. Together with sympathy for a reformist administration, Edward still hoped to abolish the Viceroyalty in con-junction with the establishment of a royal residence. See also Field Marshal Lord Grenfell, *Memoirs* (London, n.d.), p. 176.

[169] Eunan O'Halpin, *The Decline of the Union: British Government in Ireland 1892–1920* (Dublin, 1987), pp. 35–6.

[170] Dudley–Carson correspondence, *BNL*, 19–20 March 1906.

[171] Dudley to Long, 8 July 1905, in Petrie, *Walter Long*, pp. 89–90; Dudley–Long corres-pondence, May–Aug. 1905, ibid., pp. 86–97

[172] *Ireland in the New Century* (London, 1904), *passim*; also see commentary in Gibson, *Joyce's Revenge*, pp. 238–9.

ceremonial: 'about £400,000 was spent in connection with the King's coronation ... but I have not heard that any economist has been scandalised at the cost'.[173]

Plunkett had blundered seriously. His provocative publication did much to unite the two forces in Irish Catholic society the Viceroyalty had sought so hard to keep apart, and especially lent venom to nationalist assessments of Unionist policy. These could point to continued economic depression despite the range of reforms enacted, and with the problem sourced to a British determination to focus on individuals whereas the Irish saw the Anglo-Irish difficulty as a 'State grievance between the two islands as separate kingdoms'.[174] The controversy was a major setback to the development of a common narrative which could transcend antagonistic British and Irish traditions and which was necessary if the monarchy's relationship with the Irish people was to mirror that of Britain.

As the period of Unionist rule ended, state policy was weakened by reaction from within the Unionist camp and self-inflicted wounds which enormously strengthened its nationalist critics. They no less accepted the monarchy's role in Ireland as a source of allegiance and identity, but in a reshaped constitutional order.

---

[173] Revd M. Riordan, *Catholicity and Progress in Ireland* (London, 1906), pp. 19–20.
[174] Thomas Lough, 'Ten Years Tory Rule in Ireland', *CR*, 87 (1905), 783–8.

Part V

Royalty and revolution

12   Home Rule, crisis and the crown

The return of the Liberal Party to power in 1906 on the back of a landslide majority heralded a period of extensive legislative reforms, but no immediate appetite to implement Home Rule. Party leader Henry Campbell-Bannerman was committed to the policy, but led a party lacking a Gladstonian commitment to prioritising the issue. The commitment remained, but British interests took priority. Instead, and as outlined during the election campaign, the Government's immediate Irish policy would consist of Wyndham-style reformism and the Dunraven–McDonnell ideas of governing Ireland 'according to Irish ideas'.[1] But reformism proceeded now in a context which transformed its meaning and how the monarchy related to the Irish people: no longer a substitute for Home Rule, it now registered acceptable and incremental instalments on the path to constitutional autonomy.

I

Contextual transformation was registered at once with the appointment of Lord Aberdeen to the Viceroyalty.[2] In the absence of immediate legislation to implement Home Rule, Aberdeen's appointment was the most convincing statement of Liberal good faith. Lacking the constraints that prevented Wyndham from dealing with the university issue, the Liberal Government would embark on a series of reforms that provided the basis for viceregal cultivation of Irish loyalty. Unlike their previous viceregal term in 1886, however, the Aberdeens, in what promised to be a long viceregal sojourn, were now concerned to be as politically centrist as possible, especially with an Ulster Unionist community in mind whose opposition to Home Rule was recognised as a more significant obstacle

---

[1] Anon, 'The Real Needs of Ireland', *Quarterly Review*, 205 (1906), 561–3.
[2] Healy to Maurice Healy, 12 Dec. 1905, in T. M. Healy, *Letters and Leaders of My Day* (London, 1928), II, p. 475: Healy described Aberdeen as 'the "decoy" duck for the Irish [who] carries no guns'.

now than it had been in the mid-1880s.[3] They were also, however, somewhat anxious about their viceregal roles.

A previous posting in Canada had brought a degree of ridicule on the Viceregal office,[4] leaving Aberdeen's dignity as the embodiment of the monarchical presence in Ireland somewhat problematic. And initial false steps were made. Rumours of unorthodox social intercourse between the viceregal couple and their household servants may have been unfounded, but ill-advised sartorial changes to Castle staff and mishandling of viceregal ritual were noted.[5] Fastidious about ceremonial dignity, Edward VII developed a fraught, unhappy relationship with his Irish surrogates, consolidated by unfortunate developments, of which the theft in 1907 of the insignia of the Grand Master of the Order of St Patrick, the 'Irish Crown Jewels', was the most significant.

The theft was discovered as preparations were in hand for the arrival of the King on his last Irish visit, to inaugurate an Irish Exhibition promoted by the Aberdeens. It was a crime with, at its outer edges, homosexual connotations involving members of the royal and viceregal families. They were not suspected of the theft, but any public exposure of indictable practices concerning royal personages, and for which there was widespread public abhorrence, had to be avoided. Accordingly, when a convenient culprit presented himself in the form of the unfortunate Sir Arthur Vicars, Ulster King of Arms, who had *formal* responsibility for the jewels, the opportunity was taken effectively to close the investigation. The jewels were never recovered, Vicars vigorously and persistently pressed his innocence, while the failure publicly to prosecute the matter fed unfounded rumours of royal and viceregal involvement, occasionally requiring recourse to the courts.[6]

Outwardly the royal visit proceeded and was a public success, with the King endorsing the social legislation of the Liberal Government.[7] But it was not a happy experience, with probably unfounded concerns about the

---

[3] Lady Aberdeen cited in Lord Grenfell, *Memoirs* (London, n.d.), p. 178.

[4] The contrast between Lady Aberdeen's physical and psychological robustness and the lack of these attributes in the Viceroy had been a source of mockery. See Marjorie Pentland, *A Bonnie Fechter: The Life of Ishbel Marjoribanks, Marchioness of Aberdeen and Temair* (London, 1952), p. 152; Healy, *Letters and Leaders*, II, p. 475.

[5] See Nevile Wilkinson, *To All and Singular* (London, n.d.), pp. 195–7. Wilkinson would succeed Sir Arthur Vicars as Ulster King of Arms.

[6] The topic has been well worked over, but the most authoritative work remains Francis Bamford and Viola Banks, *Vicious Circle: The Case of the Missing Irish Crown Jewels* (London, 1965). For a brief assessment, see Tomas O'Riordan, 'The Theft of the Irish Crown Jewels, 1907', *History Ireland* (Winter, 2001), 23–8.

[7] See for example, *The Times* [*TT*], 11 July 1907; *Londonderry Sentinel* [*LS*], 11 July 1907; *Belfast News-Letter* [*BNL*], 11, 12 July 1907; 'Seeing the King and Queen', *LS*, 16 July 1907.

King's safety, and incompetence attending a proposed knighthood for William Martin Murphy, a leading nationalist and the exhibition's most important benefactor: the King moved to confer the honour on a candidate who had no wish to receive it.[8] Accordingly, despite the enthusiastic promotion of welfare monarchism that united both Viceroy and monarch and the care Aberdeen took in appraising the King of incidents demonstrating popular loyalty to the crown, the latter became irredeemably alienated from his Irish Viceroy from mid-1907,[9] though this remained unknown to the public.

In the Irish public realm the Aberdeens were a significant presence, one of the most effective agencies of crown and state in harmonising the problematic Anglo-Irish relationship and, especially, in transforming the profoundly negative image of Dublin Castle as an emblem of oppression. Enthusiastic in their engagement with the Irish public across a wide area, including the promotion of Gaelic culture,[10] employment, public housing and slum clearance, and especially an all-Ireland programme of treatment to combat tuberculosis,[11] they successfully cultivated Irish goodwill. The only complication occurred when Redmond and other nationalist leaders initially approved the Irish Council bill of 1908.

A measure of *administrative* devolution that would have placed the vast majority of Dublin Castle's responsibilities – though not the police – within the domain of elected popular control under the headship of the Viceroy, this could have transformed perceptions of Dublin Castle's place in the life of the Irish people, allowing it to be regarded more authentically as a royal site and placing the Viceroy in a more direct line of allegiance and responsibility in the relationship between the Irish people and the monarchy. A party convention, however, voted to reject the measure, fearing implications it might have for progress towards Home Rule.[12] But if a significant defeat for Redmond personally, the devolution issue was a minor hiccup in the context of a broad range of substantive legislative

---

[8] For the Aberdeens' version, see Lord and Lady Aberdeen, *'We Twa': Reminiscences* (London, 1927), II, pp. 140–1.

[9] As Ireland experienced agrarian strife in early 1909, the 'childish' Aberdeens seemed merely to engage in 'masquerading and dancing': Lord Crewe to Knollys, 20 Feb. 1909; Aberdeen to Knollys and the King, 7 March 1909, RA VIC/W 75/64, 66.

[10] See Pentland, *A Bonnie Fechter*, pp. 154–5; Brendán Mac Oadha, 'Was This a Social Revolution?' in Sean O'Tuama (ed.), *The Gaelic League Idea* (Cork and Dublin, 1972), pp. 22–3.

[11] Maureen Keane, *Ishbel: Lady Aberdeen in Ireland* (Newtownards, Co. Down, 1999), *passim*.

[12] Denis Gwynn, *The Life of John Redmond* (Dublin, 1932), pp. 142–8; A. C. Hepburn, 'Irish Council Bill' in S. J. Connolly (ed.), *Oxford Companion to Irish History* (2nd edn, Oxford, 2002), p. 279.

18 Queen Victoria monument, Leinster Lawn.

enactments that included the Irish Universities Act of 1908,[13] Old Age
Pensions in 1909, together with measures to remove difficulties in the
operation of the Wyndham Act – a fundamental source of agrarian
agitation in the period 1907–9 – the repeal of Unionist coercion acts,
and measures to improve public health, working-class housing and school
conditions. Between 1907 and 1912 an impressive total of fifty-six remedial measures were enacted, all of them due to the energy and political
skill of the Chief Secretary, Augustine Birrell, the agency of nationalist
influence in the Cabinet,[14] and who had come to Dublin Castle pre-
disposed to view it through the scurrilous lens provided by Thackeray in
the 1840s.[15] In this congenial context the contentious statue to Queen
Victoria, planning for which began in 1897, was inaugurated by
Aberdeen in 1908 without public controversy (Fig. 18).

Positioned in the foreground of Leinster House – the site of the
Parliament of the Irish Free State just fourteen years later – the statue
was the last major British contribution to the state–nationalist conflict of

[13] *Derry Journal* [*DJ*], 2 Sept. 1908; also *Freeman's Journal* [*FJ*], 2 Sept. 1908.
[14] See Patricia Jalland, 'A Liberal Chief Secretary and the Irish Question: Augustine Birrell
1907–1914', *Historical Journal*, 16 (1976), 425–51.
[15] Augustine Birrell, *Things Past Redress* (London, 1937), p. 198.

memorials that had marked periodically the Dublin cityscape since the mid-nineteenth century. With figures at its base commemorating the Irish contribution to the South African War, the monument was a monarchical statement of Irish integration – testified in blood – into the British state and identity.[16] With viceregal tours throughout Ireland – including up to 1911 Ulster[17] – greeted with widespread enthusiasm[18] and Home Rule a promise for the future, there seemed an abundance of evidence to justify the claim that the Aberdeens were doing great good, '*that best kind of good which is wrought on men's feelings and associations* [my italics]'.[19] Nationalists pointed out that the party boycott of royal functions and ceremonial was now merely a formality, lacking any emotive or personal dimension on the part of the people. Marginal groups might disrupt the playing of 'God Save the King', but Unionists exaggerated their importance.[20] Accordingly, if, as we have noted, the revival of nationalism in the 1860s could be charted through controversies over toasts to the monarch and singing of the national anthem at social events, the approval of such gestures in the Edwardian period no less suggested an accommodation of nationalist with monarchical, and therefore state, identity. In this context it is worth noting that when Sinn Fein entered a candidate at a by-election in 1908 it was so effectively routed that it did not do so again until 1918,[21] while the apparent onset of Home Rule from 1911 served as a check both to its growth and to that of the language movement.[22] A harmonious relationship of state and people framed through the 'familial' perspective of welfare monarchism was being established. But in this respect, the intended result of the Aberdeens' activities should be noted: the containment of Irish national expectations within the limited constitutional constraints of the Gladstonian conception of self-government.

---

[16] For press accounts, see *FJ*, 17 Feb. 1908; *Irish Independent* [*II*], 17 Feb. 1908; *Irish Times* [*IT*], 17 Feb. 1908.

[17] Aberdeen, '*We Twa*', II, pp. 180–1; *BNL*, 29 March 1906; J. R. B. McMinn (ed.), *Against the Tide: A Calender of the Papers of Revd J. B. Armour, Presbyterian Minister and Home Ruler 1869–1914* (Belfast, 1985), p. lx.

[18] On the apparent evidence of increasing loyalty to the Queen see for example, Aberdeen to the King, 1 Oct. 1906, 3 Feb. 1908, RA PS/EDVII/W 75/14, 56.

[19] Sir James Bryce, Chief Secretary (1907) to Aberdeen, 14 Feb. 1907, in Aberdeen, '*We Twa*', II, pp. 174–5.

[20] See M. F. J. O'Donnell, *Ireland and the Home Rule Movement* (Dublin, 1908), p. 173–4. The book carried Redmond's imprimatur in a Preface.

[21] F. X. Martin, 'The Origins of the Irish Rising of 1916' in Desmond Williams (ed.), *The Irish Struggle 1916–1926* (London, 1966), p. 3.

[22] Earnen De Blaghd, 'Hyde in Conflict' in O'Tuama (ed.), *Gaelic League Idea*, p. 35.

II

In fact, popular commitment to Home Rule – something perceived to be at risk from the influence of familial and localist interests since at least the early 1880s – was an ongoing concern that had to be addressed. Tellingly, when the party leadership was criticised by younger members alleging compliance with Liberal inaction on Home Rule, Redmond replied: 'If Ireland does not choose to make the Irish question an urgent one by action in Ireland, in Parliament, and in England, then she herself is to blame.'[23] It was a view not without foundation. Tom Garvin's study of Irish popular opinion in the highly radicalised conditions of 1916 to 1922 concludes that only about 25 per cent of the total population were 'actually separatist' while 50 per cent were 'mildly nationalist, but not emotionally caught up in nationalism'.[24] Arguably, the percentage of the population in the latter category would have been larger in the conciliationist pre-war period. Redmond's concern in these circumstances was to balance encouragement of personal allegiance to the King with popular commitment to Home Rule based on a recognition of the *structural*, if no longer intentional, oppression of the Irish people by the state.

Certainly the transformation of Dublin Castle's identity under the Aberdeen Viceroyalty was threatening to deprive nationalists of a central mobilising symbol. Justin McCarthy remarked: 'Dublin Castle may be taken as the architectural emblem of England's rule over Ireland. [Or] . . . a local and comical version of the Athenian Acropolis or the Pyramids of Egypt . . . It has in our present time lost, or voluntarily surrendered, much of its oppressive political power.'[25] The archaeological reference is noteworthy. R. B. O'Brien's indictment of the Irish administration, *Dublin Castle and the Irish People*, was overwhelmingly historical in its citations of oppression, finding in religious discrimination – from which Birrell and the Aberdeens were absolved – the most significant *contemporary* example of popular grievance.[26] The indictment seems clearly intended to capitalise on the angry Irish reaction in September 1908 to the Government's refusal to allow the public display of the Host and religious vestments at

---

[23] Redmond cited in Gwynn, *Redmond*, p. 156.

[24] Tom Garvin, *Nationalist Revolutionaries in Ireland 1858–1928* (Oxford, 1987), p. 150.

[25] Justin McCarthy, *Irish Recollections* (London, n.d. [1909–10]), p. 155.

[26] R. B. O'Brien, *Dublin Castle and the Irish People* (London, 1909), pp. 78–80, 410. This was also true of the richly produced popular history by Revd E. A. D'Alton, *History of Ireland from the Earliest Times to the Day: Half-Volume VI 1879–1908* (London, n.d. [1911]), p. 469: 'From its doors honesty and public spirit were driven; within its walls virtue died.'

the Eucharistic Congress of that year in London,[27] action taken in response to British public opinion but nevertheless illustrating the socio-cultural gulf between Britain and Catholic Ireland. In the main, however, O'Brien's book functioned chiefly as a public reminder to the people of the nationalist case for Home Rule, rather than a call to action. The predominant spirit of Dublin was evident when the city prepared to receive George V in July 1911, shortly after his coronation.

III

The success of the visit is explicable largely in terms of reformist legislation and viceregal welfarism, but its causes went deeper. The new King had a recent history of congenial Irish experiences, reinforcing his tolerant attitude to Catholicism, which, it is reasonable to assume, shaped his belief that a special relationship existed between the monarch and the Irish people outside the political – and therefore in a more 'organic' – realm.[28] This belief, arguably, enabled George V to be, like his mother, more favourably disposed to Irish Home Rule than Edward VII, though he accepted his late father's position on the constitutional crisis over the powers of the House of Lords, into which he was immediately pitched on accession.

The focus of the crisis was the refusal by the Lords to enact the Liberal Budget of 1909, with its controversial taxation clauses. Two general elections – delivering Liberal Governments dependent on nationalist support – were necessary before the issue was resolved on the basis of the Lords' veto on Commons legislation being replaced by a suspensory power of two years.[29] Thereafter, Unionists promoted the idea of a Government driven to undermine the legitimate powers of the House of Lords: the 'constitution' had been disorganised at the behest of an Irish dictator,[30] or 'Leviathan' – one of Asquith's nicknames for Redmond.[31] Asquith, moreover, had insisted that Edward VII agree to create sufficient

---

[27] For coverage of the issue, see Simon Heffer, *Power and Place: The Political Consequences of Edward VII* (London, 1998), pp. 271–3; *BNL*, 31 Aug.–22 Sept. 1908; Ernest Oldmeadow, *Francis Cardinal Bourne* (London, 1940), I, ch. 47; Roy Jenkins, *Asquith* (London, 1964), pp. 191–2; *The Times* [*TT*], 10, 14, 21–4, 29 Sept. 1908; *FJ*, 14 Sept. 1908; *DJ*, 9, 14 Sept. 1908; Carol Devlin, 'The Eucharistic Procession of 1908: The Dilemmas of the Liberal Government', *Church History*, 63 (1994), 407–25.

[28] Nicolson, *King George V*, p. 148.

[29] The changed circumstances created a 'great sensation' affecting the Liberal press and Cabinet: Almeric Fitzroy, *Memoirs* (London, n.d.), I, p. 395.

[30] McDonagh, *Home Rule Movement*, pp. 252–3; *Punch*, 2 Feb. 1910.

[31] See Herbert Asquith to Venetia Stanley, 3 Feb. 1914, in Michael and Eleanor Brock (eds.), *H. H. Asquith: Letters to Venetia Stanley* (London, 1982), p. 44, note 1.

Peers to guarantee the enactment of Government legislation if the Lords remained recalcitrant, a condition the King agreed to, as did George V, reluctantly, when he succeeded to the throne.[32] Accordingly, the Irish coronation visit took place with the Irish public fully aware of the role the King was playing in a controversy that would create the conditions for the implementation of Home Rule. Already, the combination of Government reforms and viceregal welfarism had made the Dublin city-scape a safe environment for the ceremonial announcement by Ulster King of Arms of the accession of the new King in May 1910, something which had not occurred on the death of Queen Victoria for fear of political disruption.[33] Also, the coronation itself, which preceded the visit by merely three weeks, was freighted with congenial indicators.

The legitimacy of the British monarchy in an Irish context was symboli-cally asserted in the coronation ceremony by the presence of The O'Conor Don, a Catholic and direct lineal descendant of Ireland's last native High King, Rory O'Conor,[34] who carried the Standard of Ireland, though his legitimacy in this respect was contested by Sinn Fein.[35] But more importantly, the King had made it known publicly that he person-ally had insisted that the offensively anti-Catholic Declaration of Accession was amended before he would consent to open Parliament.[36]

This was an evident aggravation to Catholic opinion in the Kingdom as a consequence of the controversy surrounding the Eucharistic Congress in London in 1908, and against this background the King's amendment of the Declaration created a highly favourable impression in Ireland. Moreover, for an institution identified as living in fear of materialist modernisation in this period,[37] the monarch as an embodiment of social stability and tradition may well have had an additional appeal for senior Catholic prelates, who were perceived to be among the most honoured guests at coronation festivities.[38] In these circumstances the nationalist boycott of royal functions was difficult to maintain: some prominent public officials such as the Mayor of Limerick accepted their coronation invitations,[39] while Redmond himself successfully proposed, initially, an

[32] Ibid. pp. 117–24. While Edward VII had agreed to create the Peers, if required, in the event of the Liberals being returned to office, George V was asked to declare publicly in advance of the election his intention to do so, thereby possibly influencing its outcome.
[33] Wilkinson, *To All and Singular*, pp. 184–6.
[34] Mark Bence-Jones, *The British Aristocracy* (London, 1979), p. 148.
[35] *Sinn Fein*, 24 June 1911.   [36] Nicolson, *King George V*, p. 162.
[37] Garvin, *Nationalist Revolutionaries in Ireland*, pp. 58–66.
[38] See Oldmeadow, *Bourne*, II, pp. 54–5.
[39] See 'Limerick and Its Mayor', *Leader*, 8 July 1910.

abandonment of the boycott and was only deterred by the resulting prospect of intra-party conflict.[40]

The Mayor of Limerick's action, however, was reflective of a positive attitude to the royal family nationwide which pre-dated George V's accession. It was evidenced in police reports of countrywide mourning on the death of Edward VII, with 'blinds kept down in private houses in nearly every town in the country'.[41] Mourning was encouraged by the Catholic Church. Archbishop Walsh ordered a votive mass to be celebrated in the city's Pro-Cathedral at the hour of the funeral of a King who was 'a well-wisher of Ireland'.[42] Republicans daubed the steps of the cathedral with tar in protest[43] and an occasional radical newspaper expressed bemused comment on the mourning phenomenon,[44] but this was exceptional and unrepresentative.

The Inspector General's report did make the distinction between mourning for a *personally* popular King as opposed to loyalty to the throne as an institution. Nevertheless, as Bagehot recognised, the royal person and the institution were difficult to disengage symbolically. Certainly the King's death occasioned an impressive demonstration of how the localist and personal sentiment of Irish everyday life could be actively engaged by a great monarchical personage; and it was another royal occasion to which constitutional nationalism had difficulty in finding a unified response.[45] Redmond accepted that the King's coronation visit would have a good reception 'whatever we do'.[46]

Brief though it was – 8 to 12 July 1911 – it had some claim to be the most important Irish royal occasion since 1689. None since then had occurred in the midst of a major constitutional crisis, but more importantly, the visit itself was a crucial potential site of conflict, with the possibility of adverse consequences for the Home Rule project. While the Liberal Party was officially committed to the policy, there had been Cabinet

---

[40] J. R. R. McConnel, 'The View from the Backbench: Irish Nationalist MPs and Their Work 1910–1914', unpublished PhD thesis, University of Durham (2002), pp. 69–70. Redmond denied the accuracy of press reports of the issue.

[41] Inspector General of RIC's report on the state of Ireland for May 1910, to Undersecretary Dougherty, 13 June 1910: Harvester Press Microfilm, *The British in Ireland: CO904* (Brighton, 1984), Series One, Part Three: Police Reports 1899–1913, Reel 46 [Harvester, *British in Ireland*, Reel].

[42] Walsh quoted in Oldmeadow, *Bourne*, II, p. 44.

[43] Leon O'Broin, *The Chief Secretary: Augustine Birrell in Ireland* (London, 1969), p. 41.

[44] See, for example, '"Nationalist" Ireland & Its English King', *Midland Tribune*, 21 May 1910.

[45] For the variety of reactions among nationalist MPs, see McConnel, 'The View from the Backbench', pp. 68–9.

[46] Redmond to John Dillon, 29 Jan. 1911, in ibid. p. 70.

resentment at the way Redmond had forced Home Rule on the Government.[47] The Irish Chief Secretary, Augustine Birrell, saw a possible problem in getting the Liberal Party to accept a Home Rule plan: 'Much would depend on how the Irish received the King on the occasion of his visit to Dublin in the summer. If the King was not well received it would be difficult to pass a Home Rule Bill. The whole thing depended for its value ... on our getting the Irish to join with us in loyalty to the Empire.'[48] Moreover, although the King personally was supportive of Home Rule, he had a volatile temperament, was used to an environment in which his beliefs and opinions were not contradicted, and, in the Irish context, was highly pained by claims that he was betraying Irish loyalists.[49] A poor reception in Dublin could well serve to alienate the central personage in the constitutional crisis, one whose capacity for autonomous action was still significant.

The importance of the visit caused Redmond and other leading nationalists to emphasise the distinction between the formality of their royal boycott and personal enthusiasm for the monarch, which they encouraged.[50] This was part of the scene-setting for the visit, which began as soon as it was announced in February 1911. Another dimension was historicist in form. The propagandist R. B. O'Brien quickly set about producing a new edition of his *A Hundred Years of Irish History*.[51] The book had first appeared in the accession year of Edward VII as a reminder of the reasons for Ireland's alienation from the British state and at a time when there was little prospect of Home Rule. Now, however, the national narrative could be updated in the context of George V's Irish visit and with every prospect of a happy Home Rule ending. But at the same time, the socio-political context of the visit was not unproblematic. Evidence existed of Unionist readiness to exploit the monarchy in the run-up to the occasion.[52] In Dublin the urging of the *Irish Times* for a strong police presence in the city to restrain crowds during the visit appeared to nationalists a provocation.[53] Ironically, on this occasion nationalists had every political interest in seeing the visit succeed, Unionists in seeing it fail. Coronation day in Dublin gave some indication of how it could proceed.

---

[47] Fitzroy, *Memoirs*, I, p. 395.
[48] Record of conversation with Birrell, entry (28 Jan. 1911), W. S. Blunt, *My Diaries, Being a Personal Record of Events 1888–1914* (London, 1932), p. 750.
[49] Fitzroy, *Memoirs*, II, p. 458.   [50] See Gwynn, *Redmond*, pp. 188–9.
[51] London and Dublin, 1911; review in *FJ*, 6 June 1911.
[52] *FJ*, 6, 8 July 1911; Ulster Unionist Council, Leaflet no. 48: *Loyalty(?) in Limerick* (Belfast, 1912).
[53] *IT*, 6 July 1911; *FJ*, 7 July 1911.

The cityscape exhibited a complex picture, with the main thorough-fares flooded with people, making traffic impassable, and activated by motives ranging from intense loyalty, to curious non-political interest in the coronation illuminations, and, at the other extreme, intense opposi-tion to the occasion. As such, it represented a cross-section of attitudes to nationality – Irish and British – among the populace. The cityscape was a contested arena. Police maintained a vigorous presence to deter 'disor-der',[54] while republicans sought to organise a broad-based spectrum of nationalist opposition to the crown. The Parnell monument, initiated in 1899, was finally completed and erected at the top of the main city thoroughfare, Sackville Street. Like the Victoria monument on Leinster Lawn, it was the last major architectural statement in the capital's city-scape of an ideology that within a decade would be publicly discredited. On coronation day, however, it easily lent itself as a symbol of the dominant position that constitutional nationalism had established over the British parliamentary agenda. The events of coronation day indicated the variety of responses likely to the royal visit: all sides, recognising the latter's greater significance, prepared accordingly.

Republicans attempted to intimidate public officials;[55] Liberal prints raised fears about Unionist manipulation of the King's itinerary;[56] Castle elements detected Catholic intrigue in arrangements for the King to visit the seminary of Maynooth on the Orange anniversary of 12 July and made adjustments.[57] In the event, and despite mutual suspicion between London and Dublin, arrangements were skilfully handled, especially by the Undersecretary at Dublin Castle, Sir J. B. Dougherty, a northern Presbyterian Home Ruler and hyper-conscious of anything that might cause royal embarrassment[58] – such as a reference welcoming the amend-ment of the Declaration of Accession in an address from Cork Corporation.[59] The court was only too aware that the majority of Irish Protestants did not approve of the change.[60] On the other hand, a

---

[54] Two youths who snatched a Union Jack from a house in Merrion Street were sentenced to a month in jail, though released after ten days (*FJ*, 6 July 1911).

[55] *IT* (10 June 1911), press cutting and subsequent police investigations, 12, 13 June 1911: Irish National Archives, Chief Secretary's Office, Registered Papers [CSORP], National Archives of Ireland [NAI], CSORP /1911/10955.

[56] *Westminster Gazette* Irish report, reproduced in 'King George and Ireland', *FJ*, 16 June 1911.

[57] Wilkinson, *To All and Singular*, p. 198.

[58] Revd J. B. Armour to W. S. Armour, 20 July 1911, in J. R. B. McMinn (ed.), *Against the Tide: A Calender of the Papers of the Revd J. B. Armour 1869–1914* (Belfast, 1985). Dougherty was honoured with a KCVO for his efforts.

[59] Dougherty–Bigge correspondence, 10, 12, 14, 17 June 1911, RA PS/GV/PS 4246/39, 43, 47/VISUK.

[60] See Bigge to the King, 2 July 1911, RA PS/GEOV/PS 4246/76/VISUK.

suggestion from Lord Iveagh to renew the connection between the Order of St Patrick and the Anglican cathedral through the provision of a chapel was refused on advice from Birrell, partly at least because it would be virtually impossible for Catholic knights to attend.[61] At the same time, Nevile Wilkinson took care to craft a 'safe' ceremonial route through the city for the King's official entry, one designed to ensure demonstrations of loyal allegiance.[62]

The visit went according to plan, apart from a conflict originating in a decision of Dublin Corporation not to offer an official welcome to the King. The decision provoked the Lord Mayor, John J. Farrell, to plan his own personal address in defiance of party policy when the King made his official entry to the city. The prospect of public controversy and disorder caused this traditional feature of Irish royal visits to be cancelled.[63] Otherwise, the perceptibly pro-Home Rule King resided at Dublin Castle, thereby reinforcing its identity as a royal site,[64] while the four days of the royal sojourn, during which the King and Queen were accompanied by the Prince of Wales (the future Edward VIII) and Princess Mary, were taken up with a range of welfarist and civic activities. The most noteworthy was a visit to Maynooth, where the royal couple was enthusiastically received by the Lord Primate, Cardinal Logue, and the Irish hierarchy. Also included was the investiture of Lords Kitchener and Shaftesbury as Knights of the Order of St Patrick, while the King made a donation of £1,000 for relief of the city's poor.[65] Moreover, an Address of Welcome from the women of Ireland, instigated by the Vicereine and with 165,000 signatures attached, was presented,[66] one of 133 the King recorded receiving on 10 July in the throne room of Dublin Castle.[67] And while the corporation refused an official welcome, an unofficial one was nevertheless forthcoming from a 'Citizens Reception Committee'.[68] The visit was no less a success for the Aberdeens, whom the King, like his late father, had a rather low opinion of. The monarch would be fulsome in his

[61] Peter Galloway, *The Most Illustrious Order of St Patrick* (Chichester, 1983), pp. 48–9.
[62] Wilkinson, *To All and Singular*, p. 198.
[63] For the controversy, see ibid. p. 200; *FJ*, 6–8 July 1911; Dougherty, Sir Arthur Bigge, with associated letters from Frederick Ponsonby and V. V. Le Fanu, RA PS/GV/PS 4246/75–80, 82–3/VISUK; also Prince Arthur of Connaught to his sister Louise, 5 July 1911, RA VIC/Add A 17/1090.
[64] Royal residency was made possible through the agency of Lord Pirrie, who directed the renovation of the Castle's internal arrangements, especially its sanitary and drainage system: Lord and Lady Aberdeen, *More Cracks with 'We Twa'* (London, 1929), p. 144.
[65] 'Royal Programme', *FJ*, 8 July 1911, and issues of 8–12 July 1911.
[66] Aberdeen, *More Cracks with 'We Twa'*, p. 147.   [67] RA GV/GVD: 10 July 1911.
[68] See 'Public Notices', *FJ*, 13 July 1911.

19 George V and Queen Mary (centre) with their viceregal surrogates.

praise of their efforts in making it a success.[69] A group photograph
(Fig. 19) signified royal satisfaction. Moreover, the much abused Lord
Mayor eventually got to meet the King, who spotted him at a garden party
at the Viceregal Lodge and was introduced by the Vicereine.[70]

A collection of republican and socialist groups sought to assert a dissident presence in the city during royal events, but were ineffectual, not
least because one of the more significant republican organisations, the
Irish Republican Brotherhood, and for reasons that are unclear, decided
not to support anti-royal protests.[71] At the same time, goodwill for the
royal visitors was facilitated by the method chosen to report the visit by
Ireland's leading nationalist paper, the *Freeman's Journal*.

Exhaustive reporting in the most minute detail of the events associated
with the visit sat side by side with columns covering the crisis over the
House of Lords veto in Britain. The nationalist reader was thus reminded

[69] King to Aberdeen, 12 July 1911, reproduced ibid. p. 154.
[70] Aberdeen, *More Cracks with 'We Twa'*, pp. 145–6.
[71] See, for instance, Diana Norman, *Terrible Beauty: A Life of Constance Markievicz
1868–1927* (London, 1987), pp. 76–8; Ward, *Unmanageable Revolutionaries*, pp. 78–80.

of the King's role in facilitating the introduction of a future Home Rule bill. But the paper's exercise in opinion shaping went much further. Anxious to neutralise the kind of British press comment that had such a destructive impact on the royal visit of 1885, it claimed that British Unionist prints had 'completely dropped' their attempts politically to exploit George V's Irish visit.[72] It was not true.

Leading Unionist prints such as the *Daily Telegraph* and the *Standard*, which led the way for other Unionist journals, provocatively described the King's reception as 'mutiny' against nationalism, and a demonstration of the success of constructive Unionism. While these commentaries were characteristic of Unionist opinion generally on the visit, the influential *Illustrated London News* made the point brilliantly in a photograph depicting a vast throng of people on College Green – 'More Loyal than Some of their Municipal Governors' – with the statue of the nationalist hero Henry Grattan as a point of perspective and enveloped in a sea of Irish loyalty.[73] The *Freeman's Journal* did report these arguments, but not until the visit was over.[74]

Given the King's temperament, it was clearly important that the reception he received affirmed his belief in a special understanding with the Irish people – the royal party thought their reception possibly outdid that for Edward VII in 1903.[75] Compared to the mass enthusiasm of the Dublin crowds the formal boycott by constitutional nationalists would have been of little significance. But fully to appreciate the King's experience of Ireland, it should be contrasted with contemporary British urban society and the 'revolutionary' socialism – more exactly Labourism – it appeared to be giving rise to, developments highly worrying to the King and Queen as a threat to the established order.[76] In this context, and given the ease with which disloyal elements had been marginalised, Dublin could well have appeared a model of a loyal society. More so than for party politicians, the King would have had an acute sense of the United Kingdom as an imagined community and, arguably, with its internal differences very much in mind. If the King was the embodiment of British identity and the history that shaped it, his reception in Dublin offered reassurance that the alienation at the heart of Anglo-Irish relations for so long had been fundamentally dissolved. Self-government

[72] Editorial, *FJ*, 8 July 1911.
[73] 'Dublin as Enthusiastic as London over the Royal Visit', *ILN*, 15 July 1911.
[74] 'Unionists and the Royal Visit: The Old Story': *FJ*, 13 July 1911; also editorial, ibid.
[75] Prince Arthur to Louise, 8, 12 July 1911, RA VIC/Add A/15/8687, 8689; RA/GVJ: 8–10 July 1911.
[76] Frank Prochaska, *Royal Bounty: The Making of a Welfare Monarchy* (New Haven and London, 1995), pp. 170–2.

might have to be conceded, but Home Rule would not make Ireland an independent state and its Redmondite promoters were, in socio-political outlook, anything but revolutionary. And yet, while the visit was a great success, its limitations should not be overlooked.

Like previous successful visits, though to a possibly greater extent, that of 1911 served to create a distinctive body of sentiment, or 'constituency', from across – and outside – the political spectrum, unique to the moment and virtually impossible to mobilise for purposes beyond the special circumstances that created it. Certainly it did not constitute a solid phalanx of uncomplicatedly loyal anti-nationalist allegiance, as the Unionist press argued. Moreover, the ease with which radical nationalist and socialist opposition had been thwarted disguised tensions within Catholic society in this period, especially in Dublin, produced by a national identity struggling to negotiate Irishness and Britishness.[77] Such considerations, however, do not detract from the visit's political significance. Although brief, the visit had, as Augustine Birrell acknowledged, the potential to derail the Home Rule project. Instead, Dublin appeared a synecdoche of a contentedly loyal country. At the same time, the success of the visit, having deprived Unionists of a quick and satisfactory conclusion to the constitutional crisis, ensured it also played a part in assisting the latter's deepening and prolongation. Just two months later Edward Carson began the process of preparing to oppose Home Rule, by force of arms if necessary.

IV

The crisis that developed was to bring the British state to the brink of civil war by August 1914.[78] It did so precisely because of the way in which constitutional innovation appeared to have offended strongly entrenched elitist notions of national identity, especially the belief that the constitution – unwritten and evolving in a 'commonsense' way according to need – was a reflection of national character.[79] The belief was indicative

---

[77] For penetrating comment on this subject, see 'Am I in England or in Ireland?' in Senia Paseta, *Before the Revolution: Nationalism, Social Change and Ireland: Catholic Elites 1879–1922* (Cork, 1999), ch. 6.

[78] Of a wealth of material on the period 1910–14, the most succinct treatment on the Irish dimension is Michael Laffan, *The Partition of Ireland 1911–1925* (Dublin, 1983). For wider and more substantive treatments, George Dangerfield, *The Damnable Question: A Study in Anglo-Irish Relations* (London, 1977); Robert Blake, *The Unknown Prime Minister: The Life and Times of Andrew Bonar Law 1858–1923* (London, 1955); R. J. Q. Adams, *Bonar Law* (London, 1999); Jeremy Smith, *The Tories and Ireland 1910–1914: Conservative Party Politics and Ireland* (Dublin, 2000).

[79] A. F. Pollard, *The Evolution of Parliament* (London, 1920), pp. 4–5.

of the extent to which Burkean organicism had been normalised in historical and political discourse, making easy the destruction of the 'old constitution' as a metaphor for the decay of 'national character' and even 'war upon the manners and customs of the people'.[80] In sum, with the passage of the Parliament Act, 'the national will acting through Parliament'[81] no longer existed. The constitution was now in a disorganised state, with the country controlled by a dictatorial House of Commons under the grip of a small clique, the Cabinet, itself acting at the dictation of John Redmond. In this scenario the House of Lords represented, while the House of Commons misrepresented, 'the will of the nation'.[82] And as Irish nationalism had forced this crisis, Ireland would be the site of its resolution as the Tory Party – with Bonar Law, a leader with Ulster connections, at its helm from 1911 – and Willoughby de Broke, especially, mobilised to support Ulster Unionism militarily.[83]

Conservative ideology adjusted to this situation accordingly, with a more autonomous and powerful role for the monarch in politics being called for,[84] and constitutional authorities such as A. V. Dicey[85] and the Tory leaders, Arthur Balfour and Andrew Bonar Law, calling for the King to dismiss the Government and place the Home Rule issue before the electorate. The King was central to Unionist plans, not just because of the latent constitutional powers a crisis might permit him to exercise, but because he was the embodiment of the nation in a context where the United Kingdom as a state had failed to engender emotional attachment. Leo Amery lamented 'that not a soul throughout these [Home Rule] debates ever says anything to suggest that he feels the United Kingdom is really a nation and that Irish nationalism in any shape or form means the end of United Kingdom nationalism'. The source of the problem lay in the double failure to invent 'a single name for the United Kingdom in

[80] Lord Willoughby de Broke, 'The Unionist Party and the General Election', *National Review*, 63 (1914), 776–7.

[81] Lord Willoughby de Broke, 'The Constitutional and the Individual' in *Rights of Citizenship: A Survey of Safeguards for the People* (London, 1912), p. 46. This publication was a manifesto by leading Unionist politicians and intellectuals.

[82] A. V. Dicey, in ibid. p. 86. For extended discussion on the Unionist contribution to the crisis, see James Loughlin, *Ulster Unionism and British National Identity since 1885* (London, 1995), ch. 3; and for the third Home Rule crisis in general, Jeremy Smith, *The Tories and Ireland 1910–1914* (Dublin, 2000).

[83] Willoughby de Broke to Bonar Law, 11 Sept. 1913, Bonar Law papers, House of Lords Record Office [HLRO], Box 27/30/2/10.

[84] Lord Hugh Cecil, *Conservatism* (1912; London, 1929), p. 226.

[85] R. A. Cosgrove, *The Rule of Law: Albert Venn Dicey, Victorian Jurist* (London, 1980), pp. 241, 249–51, 255.

1800' and to abolish the Irish Viceroyalty.[86] Most seriously, this lack of state national consciousness was strikingly illustrated in the failure of one of the chief strategies through which Unionists sought to convince the King to act: a national petition. Drawing only 2 million signatures, less than a third of English electors, it could not be presented as the will of the 'people'.[87] While a national referendum was theoretically attractive, in practice it was ill-understood by an English people apathetic about Home Rule[88] – reports from localities across the country, from Bristol to Newcastle-upon-Tyne, provided irrefutable evidence.[89]

In fact, Unionists found themselves faced with an acute version of the problem that, to varying degrees, had faced Irish nationalists since the 1880s – how far the engaged commitment of the political class resonated with, and informed, the sphere of everyday life. As difficult as the problem was for Irish nationalists, Britain was a more complex society and the task of making an indifferent people alive to the 'destruction' of the 'constitution' much more difficult.[90]

The hysteria of Unionist politics during the third Home Rule crisis is largely explicable in terms of trying to remedy this situation, but in only one part of the Kingdom – north-east Ulster – was it successfully achieved. Only there did a community exist imbued with a powerful historical myth of persistent threat from an ever-present enemy, and for whom the constitutional crisis functioned to dissolve the already fragile boundary between the public sphere of politics and that of everyday experience, as first the Ulster Unionists,[91] and then nationalists, armed and drilled for the possible resolution of the Irish question by armed conflict.

---

[86] Entry (15 Jan. 1913), John Barnes and David Nicholson (eds.), *The Leo Amery Diaries*, I: *1896–1929* (London, 1980), p. 92. On the state and 'emotional associations', see also Graham Wallas, *Human Nature in Politics* (London, 1908), p. 80.

[87] For a politically informed construction of 'the people' according to J. L. Garvin, editor of the *Observer* and the Unionist movement's most influential propagandist, see R. J. Scally, *The Origins of the Lloyd George Coalition: The Politics of Social Imperialism 1900–1918* (Princeton, NJ, 1975), pp. 371–4; also Edmund Talbot to Law, 2 Sept. 1913, Law papers, HLRO, Box 27/30/2/3.

[88] Fred Wrench to Law, 20 Oct. 1913, HLRO, Box 27/30/3/47.

[89] See Walter Long to Bonar Law, n.d. [1912], HLRO, Box 26/1/23; also entry (19 June 1912), John Ramsden (ed.), *Real Old Tory Politics: The Political Diaries of Sir Robert Sandars, Lord Bayard 1910–1935* (London, 1984), p. 47: 'the country is lethargic about home rule'.

[90] For compelling evidence of the influence of localist factors in the outcome of elections in this period, see Henry Pelling, *The Social Geography of British Elections 1885–1914* (London, 1967).

[91] See J. B. Armour to W. S. Armour, 2 Feb. 1911, in McMinn (ed.), *Against the Tide*, pp. 86–7.

V

The crisis demanded the controlling hands of the Prime Minister and Cabinet, and thereby inevitably sidelined Dublin Castle and the Viceroyalty. For the latter to have retained its primacy would have required a Viceroy of the calibre, and with the powers, accorded Lord Spencer in the 1880s. Aberdeen, however, was a Viceroy for untroubled times and lacked the will and ability, while Birrell, no less marginalised than Aberdeen, wanted out of Ireland and remained only at Asquith's insistence.[92] At the same time as it was being politically sidelined, moreover, the Viceroyalty was also seen to fail in its welfarist dimension. The efforts of the Vicereine appeared highly inadequate to the suffering of workers' families during the Dublin lockout of 1913,[93] while the Viceroy's inept attempts to mediate between employers and labour leaders brought ridicule on his office and awkward inquiries from the King.[94]

By 1914 the significance of the Aberdeen presence in Dublin was purely symbolic. At a time when the Home Rule crisis was reaching a climax and nationalists feared compromises they never expected having to make, the Aberdeen Viceroyalty reassured them that the Government remained committed to the Home Rule project. The Aberdeens' removal, Redmond warned Asquith, 'would most certainly be regarded as a triumph by Irish Unionists'.[95] In fact, Aberdeen's resignation, much to his chagrin, had already been compelled, though it was not to take public effect until February 1915. Even then gross misjudgement marked his going.

Convinced that a harmonious fusion of Irish and British identities had been effected, Aberdeen took the occasion of the conferring of a marquisate to request that he be known as 'Aberdeen and Tara' – Lady Aberdeen had requested an Irish Dukedom for Aberdeen and a place in a future Irish Senate.[96] This appropriation of one of Ireland's most sacred cultural sites for a Scottish title, however, created uproar among Irish Unionists and nationalists alike, with even Redmond regarding it as the 'extreme

[92] Jalland, 'A Liberal Chief Secretary and the Irish Question', 449–51.

[93] The most serious labour dispute of the period, it was initiated by employers attempting to break the Irish Transport and General Workers Union. The Vicereine was compromised by close association with the employers' leader, W. M. Murphy, a leading Nationalist Party member.

[94] Keane, *Ishbel*, pp. 206–9; J. B. Armour to Jennie Armour, n.d. Sept? 1913, detailing his conversation with Aberdeen on the subject in McMinn (ed.), *Against the Tide*, p. 130.

[95] Redmond to Asquith, 31 Oct. 1914, in Brock (ed.), *Asquith –Stanley Letters*, p. 304; also J. B. Armour to W. S. Armour, n.d. 1914, in McMinn (ed.), *Against the Tide*, p. 140.

[96] See Brock (ed.), *Asquith–Stanley Letters*, pp. 321, 381–2.

height of folly'.[97] It was an unfortunate end to a viceregal term that
probably had done as much as could have been to remove the alienation
of the Irish people from the state. Although he would not be the last
Viceroy, Aberdeen's resignation effectively marked the end of the office
in the ritual and ceremonial form that had traditionally characterised
it. By then political attention had long been distracted from the official
seat of the monarchy in Ireland to Ulster and the activities of 'King
Carson'.

VI

Carson responded to the crisis of the state as it developed from 1909 by an
imaginative and emotive submersion of the self in the story of a nation
apparently suffering terminal decay under a weak Prime Minister: political complexities were simplified and the crisis was seen as resolvable only
by a triumph of will – 'the nation (like women) loves a strong man'.[98]
Consumed by feelings of intensifying rage,[99] as 1911 unfolded with the
Lords acquiescing in the destruction of their constitutional powers before
a Government having forced its will on the King, Carson at last prepared
'to lead for myself this time. The whole country is in a shocking state . . .
[it] is calling out for a *strong man* [my italics].'[100] He resolved to fight
Home Rule 'to the finish'.[101] Despite his Dublin, Liberal Unionist background, Carson shared with Ulster Unionists the 'frontier' patriot's sim-
plicity of outlook, inclined to regard the compromises of democratic
politics as treachery, apocalyptically justifying a resort to arms. Indeed,
there was much in Carson's outlook to connect it with a proto-Fascistic
development of the radical Right across Europe at this time, of those who
despaired of the conservative establishment and craved the simple solution of the national dictator.[102]

---

[97] Asquith to Venetia Stanley, 6 Feb. 1915, ibid. p. 416. For the Aberdeen account of the
issue, see *'We Twa'*, II, pp. 270–5; also Keane, *Ishbel*, pp. 219–24. Tara was changed to
Temair, the Scottish form of the word.

[98] Carson to Lady Londonderry, n.d., [1909?], Lady Londonderry papers, Public Records
Office of Northern Ireland [PRONI], D2846/I/1/40.

[99] Carson to Lady Londonderry, 13 Jan. 1911, PRONI, D2846/I/1/60; also letter of 6 June
1909, PRONI, D2846/I/1/29.

[100] Carson to Lady Londonderry, 29 Aug. 1911, PRONI, D2846/1/1/68. See also letters
of 3 June, n.d. [June], 30 July 1911. For Carson's career: H. Montgomery Hyde, *Carson*
(London, 1953); Alvin Jackson, *Sir Edward Carson* (Dublin, 1993).

[101] *TT*, 25 Sept. 1911.

[102] W. Fest, 'Jingoism and Xenophobia in the Electioneering Strategies of British Ruling
Elites before 1914' in Paul Kennedy and Anthony Nicholls (eds.), *Nationalist and
Racialist Movements in Britain and Germany before 1914* (Basingstoke, 1991), pp. 171–89.

In early 1912 Carson recognised in Bonar law a leader with 'great powers of development',[103] but by this time, for Ulster Unionists, Carson himself was coming to assume the role of a political saviour personifying community values in a time of acute crisis. In this respect his role was analogous to that of Parnell in the 1880s; and just as political deification for Parnell entailed the epithet 'uncrowned King', so too did 'King' Carson attract 'regal' signification, satirised by *Punch*.[104] Redmond, as we have seen, attracted the epithet 'dictator', but in his case it referred to his dominance of the Liberal parliamentary agenda, not to his relationship with nationalist Ireland. Redmond's leadership remained mainly managerial in character rather than inspirational. Certainly the support of the nationalist people in general for Home Rule, as demonstrated in the public realm, was less emotionally engaged than that of Ulster Unionists against it, while it was only in reaction to paramilitary mobilisation in the north that a similar nationalist response emerged.

During the period 1912–14 Carson, supported by the Tory leadership, Willoughby de Broke and leading Unionist prints, shaped the Ulster Unionist community's involvement in the crisis. Carson constructed a set of rituals and validating stratagems: a 'compact' with the Ulster people; the appointment of a 'committee' to construct a 'constitution' for Ulster; the formation of a paramilitary Ulster Volunteer Force; and the writing and signing of a sacral document, the Solemn League and Covenant, to legitimise the formation of a Provisional Government and an ultimate resort to arms against the state, if necessary.[105] In sum, Ulster Unionist opposition to Home Rule was conducted in terms of legitimising rituals intended to persuade the monarch, ultimately, of the validity of the objective they were intended to serve.[106] Carson's leadership, objectively considered, may well have been primarily concerned with adjusting the Ulster Unionist response to the practicalities of a rapidly developing political environment,[107] but a possible resort to arms with himself as leader and legitimising agent was clearly envisaged. Almost inevitably

---

[103] Carson to Lady Londonderry, 12 March 1912, Londonderry papers, PRONI, D2846/1/1/85.

[104] Political cartoon, 'The Ulster King-at-Arms', *Punch*, 6 May 1911.

[105] For a contemporary Liberal account playing on Carson's 'royal' pretensions, see George Peel, *The Reign of Edward Carson* (London, 1914), *passim*; Laffan, *Partition of Ireland*, chs. 1–2.

[106] In his communications with the court, Bonar Law sought to impress the monarch with the dignity of 'the military order, the solemnity, the absolute silence' of Unionist protests: Lord Stamfordham to the King, 14 Dec. 1912, RA PS/GEOV/2553(1)/1.

[107] Andrew Gailey, 'King Carson: An Essay on the Invention of Political Leadership', *IHS*, 30 (1996), 66–87.

Carson's position as an authority figure had implications for the Ulster Unionist attitude to King George V.

The monarchical dimension of the crisis had an additional aspect for Unionists that did not apply in Britain. Having subsumed the monarch as a source of identity and loyalty within Ulster loyalist myth, they could not, for instance, accommodate the notion of a British King personally or willingly forcing the amendment of the Declaration of Accession as George V had done. The villains had to be found elsewhere, with nationalists identified as pressing the change on the nation as the price of their support for the Government.[108] However, Ulster Unionist frustrations were inevitably, if mutedly, directed at the King as the constitutional crisis developed and he failed to act in accordance with their wishes. Carson wrote: 'I am told he [the King] is saturated with "constitutional-ism" which he translates into doing everything his P.M. tells him – What a good King!'[109] Certainly, for someone whose model of a British monarch was the stridently Unionist Queen Empress Victoria, George V was a sovereign whose actions failed to match up to 'the greatness of his office'.[110] It was a view with wide currency in the Ulster Unionist com-munity: 'the King is no good. He is not loyal.'[111] Ulster Unionist frus-trations were enhanced, moreover, by the singularity of their position within the state.

Lacking the kind of ethno-national identity which allowed state patrio-tism to be locally balanced, as in Wales and Scotland, Ulster Unionists identified primarily with the state as a single entity, and with their own community values as the standard for Britain, and the monarch, to subscribe to. But as neither Britain, nor the monarch, seemed prepared to follow their lead a rationalisation was required to justify their para-military activities. Accordingly, the King was viewed as effectively a prisoner of a nationally unrepresentative Government, and their actions as merely a necessity intended to allow him to assume his legitimate constitutional role. The more strongly determined Ulster was, literally and figuratively, to stick to its guns, 'the easier it became for His Majesty to refuse to sign the [Home Rule] Bill until it had been submitted to the

---

[108] See *Weekly Northern Whig*, 16, 23 July 1910. In this context even a Liberal Prime Minister was defined by his Protestantism, and as agreeing to the amendment with a keen sense of the 'shame and disgrace of the act'.

[109] Carson to Lady Londonderry, 27 March 1912, Londonderry papers, PRONI, D2846/1/1/86.

[110] Carson to Lady Londonderry, 12 March 1912, Londonderry papers, PRONI, D2846/1/1/85.

[111] See Nora Robertson, *Crowned Harp: Memories of the Last Years of the Crown in Ireland* (Dublin, 1960), p. 83.

people'.[112] This scenario, however, still presupposed a substantial proportion of the British people coming to support the Ulster Unionist case.
But the community mobilisation characteristic of Unionist Ulster never
materialised in Britain. Carson found the experience of returning to an
apathetic Britain from an energetically engaged Ulster highly dispiriting:
'No one cares here and everyone does there – that is the whole difference.'
It was a disjuncture that remained throughout the crisis,[113] except for
unrepresentative pockets such as Liverpool.

The Unionist campaign, nevertheless, was not without success. As the
Government mishandling of the 'Curragh Mutiny' in March 1914 demonstrated, army officers were, quite unnecessarily, allowed to express
their opinion not to serve in Ulster.[114] Moreover, while the King personally was proving difficult to convince of Unionist arguments, the monarch
as a *symbol* had an autonomous significance that could serve Unionist
ends. Lord Roberts, Chief of the General Staff, was convinced that the
national anthem, 'God Save the King', had an independent influence on
the public mind, and in the Ulster context the army was unlikely to fire on
people singing it: 'if blood was shed in Ulster it would have a disastrous
effect on the army'.[115]

British Unionists were alive to the disastrous consequences this might
have for the national interest in general at a time of international tension.
Nevertheless, the dynamic of political extremism they had encouraged
since 1910, including a significant role in the arming of the UVF,[116] was
self-sustaining by early 1914, especially as the King had made clear that
he would not depart from the constitutional practice of acting on the
advice of his ministers. His position in this regard had been settled in
October 1913, following a meeting with Asquith in which it was pointed
out that Ulster Unionists were determined to resist Home Rule regardless
of what the electorate decided, while even if Unionists won an election
the Home Rule problem would still remain.[117]

At the same time, however, the Curragh Mutiny in March 1914 and the
Larne gun-running the following month, had raised the political stakes
enormously. Together with an apparent Unionist Party threat to vote

[112] Sir George Armstrong to Stamfordham, 30 June 1913, detailing a conversation with
Carson, who almost certainly had transmission to the court in mind, RA PS/GV/K
2553(1)/35.
[113] Carson to Lady Londonderry, 13 Aug. 1912, 3 Feb. 1914, Londonderry papers,
PRONI, D2846/1/1/88, 115.
[114] Patrick Buckland, *A History of Northern Ireland* (Dublin, 1989), pp. 13–14.
[115] Roberts to Law, 5 Jan. 1914, Law papers, HLRO, Box 27/31/2/16.
[116] See Smith, *Tories and Ireland*, pp. 78–81.
[117] Stamfordham to Lord Lansdowne, 9 Oct. 1913, Law papers, HLRO, Box, 30/3/17.

against army estimates in Parliament, thereby putting its very existence at risk, the possibility of coercing Ulster to accept Home Rule virtually disappeared and the pressure for political compromise grew. The Ulster Unionist position itself had moved, from opposition to Home Rule in general, to partition for the nine counties of Ulster, and then to the six north-eastern counties they felt they could control. Accordingly, by the spring of 1914 the question became one of deciding what area the excluded region of Ulster should cover, and for how long exclusion should last.

Over this period the King was fraught with anxiety, or 'blue funk' as Asquith described it.[118] In part, this was due to Asquith's method of dealing with the crisis. Asquith was phlegmatic and kept his strategy to himself, while the King was the recipient of a stream of Unionist advice – especially Ulster Unionist advice from within the royal household on their determination to reject Home Rule that was at variance with Asquith's complacency.[119] Unionists combined warnings about the dangers of an 'interim' constitution with claims that the Irish did not really want Home Rule, only more money and continued prosperity.[120] Certainly it was a fact that the most impressive demonstration of public feeling in Dublin in recent times had not been for Home Rule, but for the King himself on the occasion of his coronation visit of 1911, though the two were not entirely unrelated.

These concerns were on his mind when, in December 1913, he spoke to Birrell. Birrell strongly countered the Unionist advice the King had received,[121] and from this point on he seems to have been satisfied that both Ulster Unionists and Home Rulers were in earnest. Accordingly, when the political and paramilitary developments of spring 1914 effectively ruled out coercion to enforce Home Rule on Ulster, he saw the opportunity to pursue more effectively the role of conciliator between the contending parties than had attended his efforts in this regard in 1913.[122]

---

[118] Entry (13 Sept. 1913), Mark Bonham Carter and Mark Pottle (eds.), *Lantern Slides: The Diaries and Letters of Violet Bonham Carter 1904–1914* (London, 1996), p. 391.

[119] Asquith, second memo. to the King on Home Rule, Sept. 1913, in Spender and Asquith, *Life of Lord Oxford*, II, pp. 31–3; George V quoted (13 Sept. 1913) in Reginald Viscount Esher, *Journals and Letters*, ed. Oliver Viscount Esher (London, 1938), III, p. 133.

[120] Lord Stamfordham, Memo. on his discussion with Lord Lansdowne on Home Rule, stating this as a universal Unionist view, 1 July 1913, RA PS/GV/2553(1)/36; Jenkins, *Asquith*, p. 283.

[121] Stamfordham, Memo. on Birrell's audience with the King, 24 Dec. 1913, RA PS/GEOV/K 2553/(1)/45.

[122] The King's conciliation initiatives are covered in J. D. Fair, 'The King, the Constitution and Ulster: The Interparty Negotiations of 1913 and 1914', *Eire-Ireland*, 6 (1971), 35–52.

As Stamfordham was to record, throughout the crisis the King's view was that while it was for the politicians to decide whether Home Rule was enacted, his concern was the prevention of civil war.[123] Theirs were primarily political concerns, his national; and as the crisis worsened in early 1914, the King informed Asquith that, if necessary to avoid civil war, 'he should feel it his duty to do what in his own judgment was best for his people generally'.[124] To obviate this outcome he promoted negotiations between the nationalist and Unionist party leaders.

Meetings prompted by the King on 2 May produced a decision to introduce an amending bill with the purpose of excluding Ulster from the operation of the Home Rule bill while a final settlement was arranged, a development which convinced him that the party leaders recognised now that they were dealing with a great national and constitutional, rather than party, question.[125] It was to effect a settlement upon national lines that he sought to convene a formal conference of all parties at Buckingham Palace in July 1914. It was a role that only the King could play, as party leaders could claim that they were only attending at the King's command and so no weakening of their positions was entailed.[126]

For Ulster Unionists the King's initiative re-established his role as a focus of *true* national identity following the uncertainties of the recent past. If his action was unprecedented, it was because there was 'no precedent to the situation in which the Government now stands to the King and to the country in seeking to pass the Home Rule Bill into law'. And when, in a speech to the conference, the King referred to the danger of 'civil war' it was taken as an endorsement of the Unionist view of the crisis.[127] Thus for Ulster Unionists the King's initiative allowed him to be firmly reintegrated into their own community myths and frontier version of Britishness. Nor would the stability of the relationship depend on the actual success of the conference. As the Speaker of the House of Commons would chair the conference meetings, the King was absolved from compromise in any, likely, failure. When the conference did fail, on the question of what area of Ulster should be excluded from the Home Rule bill,[128] Sir James Craig responded to a royal request for advice on his future course of action by indicating that the King take instruction from his ministers, but adding that he would still have to advise his community

[123] Stamfordham, memo. on the Home Rule crisis, 17 Sept. 1914, RA PS/GV/K 2553/(6)/103.
[124] King cited in Nicolson, *King George V*, p. 223.   [125] Ibid. pp. 40–7.
[126] Ibid. pp. 48–50.   [127] See *BNL*, 21–2 July 1914.   [128] Gwynn, *Redmond*, pp. 334–42.

to oppose Home Rule. The King was thus reminded of the danger that following Asquith's advice could entail.[129]

For nationalists their relationship with the monarch was much less problematic. His reputation as being favourable to Home Rule had long shaped their view of the sovereign. The resolution of the Irish question was a party issue that did not substantively involve the head of state, as indeed the King impressed upon Redmond during a private meeting at the conference's conclusion. The meeting was of some importance. The King's conversation disclosed the impression that his reception during the visit of 1911 had made and his view of Ireland as having a natural place within a constitutionally modified United Kingdom. Redmond, having his first meeting with the sovereign, was 'deeply impressed by the friendliness and sympathy for his position he had received',[130] and it may well have influenced his enthusiasm for the British war effort when hostilities began at the end of July. Certainly Asquith thought him easily impressed by monarchical connections.

It was chiefly at the level of personal engagement and conciliation by the King that the conference registered success. The constitutional crisis endured, with the position of the Liberal Party especially problematic. Asquith feared the parliamentary failure of an amending bill to the Home Rule measure excluding the six Ulster counties of Antrim, Down, Londonderry, Armagh, Fermanagh and Tyrone from its operation, with the King insisting on a dissolution before the royal assent to Home Rule was given: 'and ... if we are unable to agree to this ... he will politely dismiss us & send for Ministers who will agree. A general election under such conditions would be one of the worst things that cd. happen to the country, or (I suspect) to the Liberal Party.'[131] This is a clear enough approximation of the King's view, as he had suggested as much to Lord Crewe: surely the Government would not expect the King 'to put his name to a Bill which they themselves believed would result in civil war',[132] which he understood to mean 'bloodshed among his loyal subjects in any part of his Dominion'.[133] The important point for our purposes, however, is Asquith's acceptance of the possibility of autonomous action by the monarch in a way that had not occurred since the reign of William IV.

[129] Entry (22 July 1914), Lady Craigavon diary, PRONI, 1415/B/38.
[130] Gwynn, *Redmond*, p. 342.
[131] Asquith to Venetia Stanley, 26 July 1914, in Brock (ed.), *Asquith–Stanley Letters*, p. 125.
[132] Stamfordham, memo. of conversation between the King and Lord Crewe on Home Rule, 6 June 1914, RA PS/GV/K 2553/(5)/46.
[133] King cited in Nicolson, *King George V*, p. 233.

VII

George V's compliance with Government wishes throughout the crisis of 1910–14 had never been unquestioned, but was rather a product of both stable and variable factors: Bagehotian prescription, historically recent constitutional practice, and a personal perception of the national interest in extreme circumstances. In this context, the King's experience of Ireland and its apparent attitude to the throne was a significant consideration in shaping his responses as the crisis unfolded. And when the Home Rule bill was passed in September 1914, together with a bill suspending its operation for the duration of the war – thus allowing for negotiations on the position of the excluded Ulster counties – he regarded it with dislike, but as a formality: in the future Home Rule would not come into effect without a settlement on Ulster and a general election taking place.[134] However, an electoral verdict decided mainly on domestic British issues – as all were, even if Home Rule was to be the formal issue before the electorate – left every prospect of the return of a Unionist administration, one that might repeal the Home Rule Act, with consequent violence in Ireland on a scale possibly greater than that envisaged up to 1914.

---

[134] Bogdanor, *Monarchy and the Constitution*, pp. 130–2.

13   War and national transformation

Nationalist Ireland's engagement with the Great War was registered emphatically in John Redmond's famous Woodenbridge speech in August 1914 committing it to the British war effort. With the benefit of hindsight an act of political or national effrontery, in the context of the narrow time-set of late 1914 to mid-1915 – when the idea of a short war prevailed – it appears much less so. A calculated investment of short-term commitment to an apparently ethical conflict might deliver an emphatic British commitment to the nationalist perspective on Home Rule.[1] At the same time, in accounting for Redmond's initiative we have to take account of his own imperialist sentiments, reinforced undoubtedly by the favourable impression made by his personal meeting with George V following the Buckingham Palace conference. But a wider social context is needed.

In large measure, the popular response to Redmond's call to arms – total Irish recruitment may have exceeded 200,000 with Catholics constituting around 60,000[2] and which largely occurred from 1914 to 1916 – was also a function of the extent to which Catholic Ireland had been conciliated by the Liberal Government and Irish Viceroyalty since 1906, of which the formal enactment of Home Rule, at the time, seemed an appropriate culmination. Certainly an Irish rush to the colours in a period of state coercion would have been inconceivable. Irish engagement in the British war effort, moreover, was of major significance in engaging popular interest in national issues, with the public and private spheres of life becoming enmeshed.

---

[1] Nicholas Mansergh, 'John Redmond' in C. C. O'Brien (ed.), *The Shaping of Modern Ireland* (London, 1960), pp. 44–6.

[2] James Loughlin, 'Mobilising the Sacred Dead: Ulster Unionists, the Great War and the Politics of Remembrance' in Adrian Gregory and Senia Pašeta (eds.), *Ireland and the Great War: 'A War to Unite Us All'?* (Manchester, 2002), p. 137.

I

The outbreak of war was to transform relations, radically and symbolically, between the administration and the populace. Emblematic of the new era was the conversion of Dublin Castle into a Red Cross hospital, a proposal originating with the Viceroy, attracting the personal and financial support of the King, and wholeheartedly endorsed by the Lord Mayor.[3] It was the most outstanding example of symbolic change in a city where the traditional architectural and party signifiers of national antagonism were submerged in a sea of British patriotic symbolism, with theatres hosting British patriotic spectacles to the accompaniment of 'God Save the King' and 'Rule Britannia', and 'with nothing to distinguish the Irish capital from any other British city'.[4] In the Irish countryside also, 'King and Country' posters adorned public houses and separatist verse was modified to address new common Anglo-Irish concerns:

> Sound the bugles to advance, says the Shan Van Vocht,
> For the Germans are in France, says the Shan Van Vocht.[5]

In the first months of the war it seemed that, apart from the minority of the Irish National Volunteers (reconstituted as the Irish Volunteers) who refused Redmond's call for enlistment, Anglo-Irish conflict had been resolved: 'It was a revelation, indeed, and most astonishing to those who knew Ireland best – her constant brooding over her past wrongs, and her feeling against England as the cause of them all.'[6] That a radical transformation in Anglo-Irish relations had apparently occurred was brought home to the King – the recipient of a 'remarkable' document from the strongly nationalist Town Council of Drogheda, pledging ardent loyalty to the crown and the British connection.[7] A state-sponsored press organisation charged, effectively, with establishing a communcative network committed to the war effort[8] sought, among other things, to consolidate this condition of Anglo-Irish amity.

---

[3] Lord and Lady Aberdeen, 'We Twa': Reminiscences (London, 1927), II, pp. 234–7.

[4] Wilmot Irwin, Betrayal in Ireland (Belfast, n.d. [1969]), p. 17. See also Percy Scholes, God Save the Queen! The History and Romance of the World's First National Anthem (London, 1954), pp. 222–3.

[5] See Lionel Fleming, Head or Harp (London, 1965), pp. 53, 55; Irwin, Betrayal in Ireland, p. 19.

[6] Michael McDonagh, The Home Rule Movement (Dublin, 1920), p. 282; Winston Churchill to Bonar Law, 14 Sept. 1914, in Martin Gilbert, Winston S. Churchill III: 1914–1916 (London, 1971), p. 79; also Darrell Figgis, Recollections of the Irish War (London, 1927), p. 60. Figgis was involved in the Howth gun-running of 1914 and would later draw up the constitution of the Irish Free State.

[7] Almeric Fitzroy, Memoirs, II (6 Aug. 1914), p. 562.

[8] Lord Riddell, War Diary 1914–1918 (London, n.d. [1933]), pp. 18–19, 87.

Certainly in the early months of the war the engagement of nationalist Ireland was wholehearted. Michael McDonagh's account of an occasion in 1915 when Redmond, in the company of the King, took the salute of Irish regiments about to embark for France, 'with bands of pipers wearing the saffron kilts of the ancient Gaels, playing national airs, and carrying green flags',[9] reads as a moment of Anglo-Irish epiphany: a revelation of fundamental, harmonious common interests heralding a new Anglo-Irish era.

And yet, such parades were no less a form of public ritual acting to disguise and mislead in a way ritual almost invariably does. For instance, it masked growing nationalist unhappiness with the enlistment 'bargain' Redmond had made in return for the mere placing of Home Rule on the statute book: 'Our people are not pro-German, but think the price too high for the kind of Home Rule that has been "granted".'[10] Moreover, it appeared to, but did not, eliminate the sense among nationalists of a British state that during the Home Rule crisis was seen to connive with Ulster paramilitarism while responding violently to similar activities by nationalists.[11] It was a sense reinforced at the outbreak of war, when the formation of regiments from the Irish National Volunteers was resisted, at the same time as the creation of the 36th Ulster Division from the ranks of the Ulster Volunteer Force proceeded unproblematically.[12] These sentiments were only of *contingent* import: had the war ended before 1916 with Home Rule rapidly implemented, they would have had no political significance. As it was, it factored into Irish disillusionment with the cost of the war from late 1915 and was capitalised upon by separatists from July 1916. Furthermore, while the impressiveness of the public communion of the King and his Irish subjects in 1915 recorded by McDonagh could well have seemed a positive augury for the monarch's future relationship with Ireland, it was not to be. There would be no further royal visits to Dublin. While the war would stimulate an unprecedented exercise of welfare monarchism in Britain by the King and Queen throughout the 1914–18 period,[13] both the actual monarchical presence and that of its viceregal surrogate would be virtually absent from the Irish public arena.

---

[9] McDonagh, *Home Rule Movement*, p. 283. The King had already presented shamrock to the Irish Guards on St Patrick's Day: Stephen Gwynn, *The Life of John Redmond* (London, 1932), pp. 468–9.

[10] Healy to Maurice Healy, 19 Dec. 1914, in T. M. Healy, *Letters and Leaders of My Days* (London, 1928), II, p. 552.

[11] Maurice Headlam, *Irish Reminiscences* (London, 1947), p. 188, note 1. Treasury Remembrancer and Deputy Paymaster for Ireland, Headlam was also a Unionist.

[12] James Loughlin, *Ulster Unionism and British National Identity* (London, 1995), pp. 76–7.

[13] Frank Prochaska, *Royal Bounty: The Making of a Welfare Monarchy* (New Haven and London, 1995), pp. 176–8.

The public reception for Lord Wimborne in Dublin in April 1915 as Aberdeen's successor was in marked contrast to the latter's leave-taking: 'The crowd was small and apathetic, but not hostile.'[14] In truth, it would have been impossible for any successor to have received the public approbation the Aberdeens were regularly accorded. Moreover, in the context of the redesignation of Dublin Castle for hospital uses, viceregal ceremonial was attenuated virtually to the point of non-existence. The only ceremonial occasion involving Wimborne, and that a perfunctory private affair devoid of pomp and splendour, was his installation as a Knight of the Order of St Patrick.[15] There was, accordingly, and irritatingly for a Viceroy of Curzonian pretensions,[16] little opportunity for Wimborne to establish a public presence as the monarchical embodiment in the Irish public sphere. He found himself in the shadow of Aberdeen in other ways, as Birrell jealously maintained the existing separation of administrative and ceremonial functions accruing to the Chief Secretary and the Viceroy respectively. Despite Birrell's wish to retire, Redmond, watching the pre-war certainties of his party's relationship with the Liberal Government dissolve as the latter proceeded towards coalition with the Tories, insisted that he be retained.[17]

Wimborne's viceregal ambition, nevertheless, remained unconstrained, not to say unrealistic: he boasted of how well he was governing Ireland and entertained plans for talks with nationalist leaders at the Viceregal Lodge,[18] when, in reality, his scope for action was restricted to the promotion of recruiting. And yet, from his arrival as Viceroy up to the Easter Rising of 1916, Wimborne was more alive to the possible danger of a separatist revolt than other leading officials of the administration, and of the need to take effective measures to prevent it.[19] Certainly, as 1915 unfolded, both hopes of an early end to the war and the fortunes of constitutional nationalism deteriorated.

Nationalist influence at Westminster, and in Government especially, diminished when Asquith formed a coalition Government in May 1915 that included Sir Edward Carson and Tory leaders but not Redmond, who was bound by the party policy of distance from British parties until

---

[14] Headlam, *Irish Reminiscences*, p. 73.   [15] Ibid. pp. 73–4.
[16] See Lady Cynthia Asquith, *Diaries 1915–1918* (London, 1968), pp. 125–31.
[17] Charles Townshend, *Easter 1916: The Irish Rebellion* (London, 2005), p. 147; Asquith to Venetia Stanley, 17 March 1915, in Michael and Eleanor Brock (eds.), *H. H. Asquith: Letters to Venetia Stanley* (Oxford, 1982), p. 485.
[18] Headlam, *Irish Reminscences*, p. 74; Asquith to Venetia Stanley, 23 Dec. 1914, 13 Jan. 1915, in Brock (ed.), *Asquith–Stanley Letters*, pp. 337, 377.
[19] Townshend, *Easter 1916*, pp. 145–51.

Home Rule was established.[20] In Ireland, the appalling cost of the war in human lives set against the achievement of a Home Rule scheme that was on the statute book, but inoperative, seemed grossly disproportionate, and, with fears of conscription in the future, acted powerfully to enhance the influence of separatist propaganda at a time when the Nationalist Party was subdued. Furthermore, the Castle administration, owing to a combination of complacency, organisational ineffectiveness, and anxiety not to alienate Irish public opinion, left separatists to dominate the Dublin cityscape at a time when viceregal ritual was attenuated and the mass enlistment of Redmondites meant that no countervailing body of public influence could be mobilised.[21] Accordingly, Dublin was available as an arena in which the Irish Volunteers could attempt to seduce, through public ritual, popular sentiment from a position still, if uneasily, supportive of Redmond and the National Volunteers. The opportunity arose in June 1915, when Jeremiah O'Donovan Rossa, a Fenian leader of 1867, died in the USA and arrangements were made for his burial in Dublin.

It proved a brilliant propagandist exercise, engaging public sympathy for a hero of a *past* revolt while at the same time inescapably associating the population with contemporary dissident nationalism.[22] The exercise effected 'a remarkable transfiguration', one that excluded the parliamentary leaders. Popular sentiment was marshalled in mourning by men whose design was the political downfall of those leaders, and treated to a lecture by Padraig Pearse on the folly of state authorities whose great mistake was to 'have left us our Fenian dead, and while Ireland holds these graves Ireland unfree shall never be at peace'.[23] Uncomplicated national homage was demonstrated that spoke to a growing disillusion with constitutional nationalism while appearing to signal the trajectory of nationalist opinion over the next six years.

Yet the opposition the funeral seemingly illustrated between principled nationalist devotion and compromising constitutionalism was more apparent than real. As we have noted, the *morality* of violent rebellion in Irish history had been a central element of constitutional nationalist rhetoric. Attendance at O'Rossa's funeral, therefore, could be regarded as wholly consistent with it. There was no necessary connection between doing so and the success of separatist nationalism in Ireland four years later. Militant republicanism would remain a minority sentiment, and the

---

[20] Loughlin, 'Mobilising the Sacred Dead', p. 134; also Figgis, *Recollections*, pp. 99–100.

[21] For a concise assessment, see Eunan O'Halpin, *Decline of the Union: British Government in Ireland 1892–1920* (Dublin, 1987), pp. 106–14; also Townshend, *Easter 1916*, pp. 142–6.

[22] Figgis, *Recollections*, pp. 100–2.   [23] Ibid. pp. 102–3.

degree of its success dependent largely on a combination of state indulgence and repression.

II

Our concern is not with accounting for the Easter Rising of 1916, which has been fully explored by historians. Apart from noting how it radically resignified the architectural environment of Dublin city centre, registering the General Post Office in Sackville Street – the headquarters of the insurgents – as a sacred site for post-independence Ireland; it is attempting rather to assess the Rising's impact on Irish attitudes to the monarchy and the latter's significance in the political developments that would eventuate in the constitutional settlement of December 1921.

To judge by the evidence of his private diaries, the King initially attached little significance to the Rising, having been reassured about troop levels and measures taken to suppress it.[24] This was natural in a context where the initial response of the Dublin populace was hostile to a revolt which had occasioned 426 deaths (230 of which were civilian), reduced the centre of the city to rubble, and caused food shortages and delays in the payment of old age pensions.[25] The immediate reaction, however, soon gave way to gradual support as the rebel leaders, with heroic bearing, were executed, as mass arrests took place across the country,[26] and as fear of conscription in 'England's war' spread in a country 'with a rural economy experiencing a boom and absence of emigration'.[27] While in 1915 Irish local and familial interests still seemed best served by constitutional nationalism, by the end of 1916 support was dwindling, hastened by Lloyd George's rather duplicitous attempt to implement Home Rule,[28] at the same time as Sinn Fein reformed and expanded organisationally throughout the country.

This period was one in which nationalist press organs throughout the country effectively brought Redmondism to book before the court of Anglo-Irish relations since the Union, pointing up the folly of Irish dependency upon the goodwill of British parties and how only coercive pressure had brought redress of grievances.[29] Reports in April 1918 that

[24] RA GV/GVD: 26, 28 April, 3 May 1916.   [25] Figgis, *Recollections*, 49–50.
[26] Ibid. pp. 151–2.
[27] Tom Garvin, *The Evolution of Irish Nationalist Politics* (Dublin, 1982), p. 115.
[28] Redmond was promised the temporary, and Carson the permanent, exclusion of Ulster from the remit of a Home Rule parliament. Once the inconsistency was exposed the initiative collapsed.
[29] For illustrative quotations from the provincial press, see Thomas Hennessy, *Dividing Ireland: World War 1 and Partition* (London, 1998), pp. 160–5.

the Government intended to impose conscription in Ireland were a crucial development, serving to confirm the lessons of history and provoking the Catholic Church to enter officially into alliance with Sinn Fein and other parties to oppose it.[30] The most influential organisation in Irish Catholic society straddling the local and public spheres, it acted powerfully to further Sinn Fein's growing political dominance; especially as, at its October Convention of 1917, Sinn Fein had established a national organisation across the country based on Catholic Church parishes and 'therefore, entered as nearly, as any political organisation may, into the communal life of the people'.[31] Inevitably, political developments in this period affected significantly the monarchy's relationship with the Irish people, north and south, and how it was imagined.

This was perhaps most significant in Ulster. The King's acquiescence in Government policy during the late Home Rule crisis was, as we have seen, deeply unsettling to a community which had long constructed British monarchs in its own image. Moreover, the transformation in Anglo-Irish relations at the outbreak of war did not extend to the Ulster Unionist mindset.[32] The 1916 Rising, however, re-established the political order as Ulster Unionists preferred to understand it, establishing a clear line of division between the loyal and the disloyal, between 'King's men' and traitors,[33] the former consisting of the British public and Ulster loyalists, who would pledge their loyalty in the slaughter of the Somme on 1 July 1916. As the *Larne Times* accurately forecast: 'To Ulstermen henceforth 1st July will be a day of sacred memories; a day when the blood of her sons was poured out like water for the defence of Britain's honour and freedom.'[34] Moreover, as Redmond argued against the execution of the leaders of the Rising so as to forestall a swing of Irish opinion in their favour, from an Ulster Unionist perspective what already seemed a dubious distinction between constitutional and separatist nationalism disappeared.[35] Nevertheless, Ulster Unionist interests were affected by the Rising in rather complex ways, not always favourably.

From his inclusion in the Coalition Government in May 1915 Carson's enthusiasm for the war effort had enabled him to establish a following of

---

[30] Garvin, *Evolution of Irish Nationalist Politics*, pp. 114–18.

[31] Figgis, *Recollections*, pp. 172, 173–5.

[32] The Ulster Division carried loyalist sectarianism into the ranks: ibid. p. 129.

[33] *Ulster Gazzette*, 29 April 1916; *Larne Times*, 29 April, 6 May 1916; *Tyrone Constitution*, 28 April 1916; *Fermanagh Times*, 4 May 1916; *Cookstown News*, 13 May 1916.

[34] *Larne Times*, 15 July 1916. Also *Witness*, 21 July 1916; *Banbridge Chronicle*, 29 April 1916; *Tyrone Constitution*, 14 July 1916; *Fermanagh Times*, 13 July 1916.

[35] *Banbridge Chronicle*, 17 May 1916; *Tyrone Constitution*, 12 May 1916; *Fermanagh Times*, 11, 18 May, 1 June 1916; *Ballymena Observer*, 26 May 1916.

about a hundred MPs, and with Lloyd George and Alfred Milner he had sought compulsory powers to establish, under the mantle of patriotism and efficiency, a social imperialist order to nullify the threat of post-war socialism.[36] Carson's influence was at its height in the spring of 1916, when calls for a Government of 'National Unity' to prosecute the war more effectively were at their height – suggesting that the figure of central authority for Ulster Unionists might be about to assume the same mantle for Britain. The Rising and the manner in which it brought the Home Rule issue back to the centre of British concerns, however, forced Carson to reposition himself as an Ulster sectional, as opposed to a British national, leader.[37] From a position at the centre of Government where he could have *guaranteed* the constitutional position of Ulster Unionism, he was now once more a leader fighting for sectional interests, in competition with others and in an increasingly unfavourable political context.

The onward rise of Sinn Fein from 1916 made a resolution of the Irish question both more difficult and also more urgent, at a time when American involvement in the war effort was being arranged and consolidated. In this context the Irish-American community became an influential factor, the addressing of which functioned to sideline Ulster Unionism. Thus while in Ulster the Easter Rising served to identify Unionists as 'King and Empire' men, an identity that was enhanced by separatist propaganda that portrayed the war as 'King George's war',[38] their actual position in terms of the British national interest deteriorated.

It was galling to those protesting loyalty to the crown, and urging ever stronger coercion to suppress disloyalty, to be apparently ignored while those vilifying the monarch appeared to be indulged. Conciliation was pursued, effectively in so far as the administration succeeded 'in keeping Ireland peaceful between August 1916 and April 1918'.[39] Moreover, following the reappointment of Wimborne as Viceroy in 1916 – he had resigned after the Rising – and with H. E. Duke to replace Birrell as Chief Secretary, the Castle took on a decidedly Catholic air as Romanists, two of whom were Irish, filled the posts of Inspector General of the RIC, Undersecretary at Dublin Castle and army commander in Ireland.[40] Government policies and the administration, however, failed to find a

---

[36] J. J. Scally, *The Origins of the Lloyd George Coalition: The Politics of Social Imperialism* (Princeton, 1975), pp. 276–9.

[37] Ibid. pp. 284, 295.

[38] Ben Novick, *Conceiving Revolution: Irish Nationalist Propaganda during the First World War* (Dublin, 2001), p. 201.

[39] Eunan O'Halpin, 'H. E. Duke and the Irish Administration 1916–1918', *Irish Historical Studies*, 20 (1981), 362.

[40] Ibid. pp. 363–4.

solution to the Home Rule issue – the collapse of Lloyd George's initiative
in the wake of the Rising was followed by the failure of the Irish
Convention in 1917–18 – as a Cabinet preoccupied with the war was
unable to force Ulster Unionists, who had made their blood sacrifice for
Britain at the Somme, to accept a settlement designed to satisfy
nationalists.

III

As Sinn Fein grew in strength and the Irish crisis grew in intensity,
constitutional options became more seriously debated within the movement, with the monarchy a significant factor in the discussion. Bagehot
claimed a virtue of the institution that it made Government easily comprehensible to the 'vacant many'.[41] In post-1916 Ireland, however, as we
have seen, it no less served the propagandist purposes of Sinn Fein by
simplifying and reducing Anglo-Irish relations to a struggle between
Ireland's true defenders and the oppressive propagators of 'King
George's war'. Moreover, while a xenophobic public mood in Britain
forced George V to abandon his German heritage and titles in 1917 and
the redesignation of the royal family as the House of Windsor,[42] for many
Irish separatists it merely reinforced the monarchy's British identity and
therefore alien character. De Valera claimed that even if a monarchy was
accepted by the Irish people, it could not be the House of Windsor.[43] Yet
attitudes to the monarchy within the movement were more complex than
propaganda might suggest.

   In this period it was a broad church reflecting a variety of nationalist
opinion across the political spectrum, and while the ideal of an Irish
republic was enshrined in the 1916 Proclamation, already a sacral document, it by no means foreclosed debate on a possible role for the monarchy in a constitutional settlement. As the struggle gradually reached a
climax it brought a greater clarity of focus on options, with a central
theme of debate the relative merits of Ireland as a dominion acknowledging the King as head of the empire, or Ireland restored to the king-
domhood it possessed until the passage of the Act of Union, the basis of
the 'dual monarchy' Arthur Griffith articulated in the early years of the
century. Griffith rejected dominion status primarily on the basis of

[41] Walter Bagehot, *English Constitution*, ed. Richard Crossman (1867; London, 1971),
   p. 85.
[42] Kenneth Rose, *King George V* (London, 1983), pp. 174–5; Fitzroy, *Memoirs*, II,
   pp. 652–4.
[43] Hennessy, *Dividing Ireland*, p. 168

Ireland's historic nationality: 'We have a past – a glorious past – the Colonies have no past.'[44]

Ireland under a dual monarchy, according to Griffith, would have the same powers as a republic, a view he was encouraged in by the Imperial Conference of 1917, which appeared to suggest a position of equality between the Dominions and England at war's end. In this context Ireland could accept a position of equality with other states in the British imperial order. Griffith's argument was open to criticism on the grounds of the historical debasement of Ireland's status by English monarchs, and of being a disguise for continued subjection given the transformation in the role of the monarch over the nineteenth century. Nevertheless, a dual monarchy found substantial support within the Sinn Fein movement. Edward MacLysaght, an unofficial observer for Sinn Fein at the Irish Convention in 1917, in fact proposed it to the forum as a view endorsed by 'the great bulk' of the movement.[45] Thus while the Sinn Fein convention of October 1917 declared a preference for an Irish republic, it was accompanied by a statement proposing a referendum to settle Ireland's final constitutional form.[46]

From outside the movement, a politically weakening Nationalist Party argued for ideological support and engagement with the imperial project – the only means by which Ulster Unionists could accept constitutional independence – based on acceptance of Ireland's historic links with the crown, and the monarchy as an inherent ingredient of an Irish national self.[47] But this was a position that had lost significant credibility since the reformist pre-war period, and since the state's response to the Rising had served to revive the militant tradition in nationalist ideology. The only source from which the constitutionalists gained support was from southern Irish Unionists who had largely come to accept that in any settlement they would remain under nationalist rule, and for whom the unashamed imperial patriotisn and enthusiastic engagement of Redmondites in the war effort undoubtedly helped to sweeten the pill.

The position on Ireland's future constitutional status as defined at the Sinn Fein conference of October 1917 was not to endure. The selection of Sinn Fein candidates for the general election of 1918 was an affair manipulated by the Irish Republican Brotherhood, headed by Michael Collins and facilitated by Government arrests of more moderate Sinn Fein members.[48] Accordingly, the great sweep of nationalist Ireland achieved by Sinn Fein at the election produced a result that Griffith,

---

[44] Griffith's paper, *Irish Nation*, 6 Jan. l917 quoted in ibid. p. 169.
[45] MacLysaght quoted in ibid. pp. 173–5.   [46] Ibid. p. 168.
[47] Moore and Gwynn, quoted in ibid. pp. 177–8.   [48] Figgis, *Recollections*, pp. 216–22.

whose stance on the national question was amenable to a solution that might include the monarchy, had sought to avert: 'It meant a contest less for liberty than for a name [republic]; it meant rigidity; and it meant the shock of violence where violence might have been avoided.'[49] The Sinn Fein representatives who assembled in Dublin on 21 January 1919 at the Lord Mayor's residence declared Ireland an independent republic and promulgated a temporary constitution with Eamon de Valera as President.[50]

IV

The tactics of separatist opposition to the state, as the Rossa funeral in 1915 so effectively demonstrated, included public ritual as well as armed revolt and electoral contests. Now in the aftermath of electoral success and the establishment of the first Dáil, public ritual was again resorted to to enhance the claim to independence. In March 1919 it was decided to mark the public emergence of Eamon de Valera, who had been in hiding since escaping from Lincoln prison before the general election, with a 'state' entry to Dublin.

While the British monarchy was rejected, it was clear that the ritual envisaged was framed in terms of more recent royal visits to Dublin, and in particular that of Queen Victoria in 1900:[51]

Not since Queen Victoria had paid her State visit to Dublin in 1900 had such a State entry at the gates been made. The ... announcement therefore compelled a comparison with that event. It meant, of course, that de Valera would enter as the official head of an established and independent State.'[52]

The aping of royal ceremonial was clearly intended as a constitutional challenge to the Dublin Castle authorities. But while the Irish administration had tolerated separatist dominance of the Dublin cityscape when they had seemed a minor political force, the proposed challenge to the Viceroyalty now was such that a subsequent proclamation of public demonstrations in the city was widely expected, duly effected, and de Valera's 'state' entry was cancelled. It transpired that the ritual had been arranged by Michael Collins with the intention of provoking the authorities into a violent reaction and the consequent resolution of the

[49] Ibid. p. 229.
[50] Ibid. pp. 234–5; J. M. Regan, *The Irish Counter-Revolution 1921–36: Treatyite Politics and Settlement in Independent Ireland* (Dublin, 1999), p. 40; Deirdre McMahon, 'Eamon de Valera' in S. J. Connolly (ed.), *The Oxford Companion to Irish History* (2nd edn, Oxford, 2002), pp. 607–8.
[51] Public announcement quoted in Figgis, *Recollections*, p. 241.   [52] Ibid. pp. 241–2.

independence struggle by violent means.[53] Thwarted in this regard, a new National Executive of Sinn Fein was elected and manipulated to secure a majority for the purpose.[54] At the same time, a process of public acclimatisation for armed struggle was begun with a campaign of social isolation, and then violence, against the RIC.[55]

V

The period 1919–21 would see a partial resolution of the Irish question, following an IRA campaign of violence that was met by an administration reaction that effectively restored Dublin Castle to its pre-Aberdeen configuration in nationalist myth as an emblem of oppression. At the centre of the process was an adjustment to the relationship between the posts of Chief Secretary – the new Chief Secretary was a Liberal, Edward Shortt – and Viceroy, following Lord French's appointment to the post in May 1918: 'administrative power was partially shifted from the chief secretary to the lord lieutenant, under whom three councils were established to co-ordinate business, handle military affairs and ascertain from representative Irishmen what government economic and social policy should be'.[56]

French appeared a good choice in some respects, being Irish and an apparent Home Ruler, but he had been the author of the disastrous advice to extend conscription to Ireland, and, as Sir Almeric Fitzroy disquietingly remarked, was determined to treat the Irish problem as a military question:[57] 'even if the attempt to enforce conscription was to deluge the country with blood – a regrettable necessity which he seemed to think might have to be faced'. By comparison, the new Chief Secretary had much sounder judgement.[58] Fitzroy's assessment was perceptive. During his term of office which, effectively though not formally, ended in May 1920, French's practice as Viceroy lacked consistency and foresight. Denied the military man's preferred clear field of action, he veered from an initial Home Rule stance to Balfourian authoritarianism, as the administration gradually came under the control of die-hards. French, accordingly, came to regard the Sinn Fein success at the general election of 1918 as unrepresentative of 'real' Irish opinion, and to believe that Catholic members of the Irish administration were 'dirty elements' that needed to be weeded out. Thereafter, socio-economic development combined with firm government would solve the Irish question.[59] It was a knee-jerk, late

---

[53] Ibid. pp. 242–5.   [54] Ibid. pp. 246–7, 260–1.   [55] Ibid. pp. 261–4.
[56] O'Halpin, *Decline of the Union*, p. 157.   [57] Ibid. p. 158.
[58] Fitzroy, *Memoirs*, II (8 May 1918), pp. 674–5.
[59] French Memorandum, 17 Dec. 1919, cited in O'Halpin, *Decline of the Union*, pp. 193–4.

nineteenth-century, reaction to the Irish difficulty with no hope of success. Ironically, in his authoritarianism French mirrored militant republicanism in its claim to represent the real spirit of the Irish people as against a debased electorate with a 'slave mentality'.[60]

In the event, French's plans for Irish government in general were sacrificed to his obsession with a coercive security policy, which further alienated the nationalist population: Sinn Fein became ever more popular while the authority of an administration riven by internal disputes diminished daily.[61] Needless to say, the reports of the appalling state of Ireland Viceroy French conveyed to a King increasingly disenchanted with Government coercion[62] did not include his own contribution to this state of affairs.

As the monarchical embodiment in Ireland, the nature of the French Viceroyalty helped to reinforce republican arguments and a refusal to consider an Irish settlement with an imperial dimension. Moreover, it made easy the decision to attempt his assassination in late 1919, attractive as much for constitutionally symbolic reasons as for military, with the preferred site for the act, the Phoenix Park. The import of the intended assassination was described by a leading member of the assassination group: 'The Phoenix Park was as well known to the world as Hyde Park. Think then of the sensation that would be created when this man, a Field Marshal of the British Army, and Head of the Government in Ireland, was shot dead at ... [its] gates ... in the capital of the country he was supposed to rule.'[63] The killing of the Viceroy at a symbolic site of British authority in Ireland – a royal park – would simultaneously strike mortally at the idea of the King as a constitutional and imaginative emblem of Ireland.

The attack went ahead and French narrowly escaped with his life, though one attacker was killed and two policemen wounded.[64] He remained in his viceregal post until May 1921, but effectively lost control of administrative affairs a year earlier when a committee under Sir Warren Fisher produced a devastating report on the Castle administration that led to its complete reorganisation.[65]

---

[60] Bill Kissane, *The Politics of the Irish Civil War* (Oxford, 2005), pp. 44, 59–60.
[61] O'Halpin, *Decline of the Union*, p. 192, and chs. 6–7, *passim*.
[62] RA GV/GVD: 18 March, 15 May 1920.
[63] Dan Breen, *My Fight for Irish Freedom* (1924; Dublin, 1950), p. 125.
[64] Ibid. ch. 15; National Archives (Kew), 'Attempt to Assassinate Lord French', HO45/10974; also *Evening Telegraph*, 20 Dec. 1919; *Sunday Independent*, 21 Dec. 1919.
[65] O'Halpin, *Decline of the Union*, pp. 203, 209: also Michael Hopkinson (ed.), *The Last Days of Dublin Castle: The Mark Sturgis Diaries* (Dublin, 1999), pp. 2–3.

Reorganisation of the Castle, however, went together with a Cabinet policy of trying to defeat Irish separatism by force; and an intensification of violence by the IRA at the same time meant that the civil administration had little meaningful control over crown forces.[66] It was a politically unpromising environment, especially so as the implementation of the Government of Ireland Act of 1920, while satisfying the Ulster Unionist demand for permanent exclusion from Dublin rule, was rejected by Sinn Fein; a rejection intensified undoubtedly by reports in leading Dublin papers that the Government was planning a scheme of dominion status for Ireland.[67] At the same time, Government efforts in the period 1920–21 to defeat the IRA through the agency of the Black and Tans was both morally and politically counter-productive as both the King and British public opinion rejected their methods.[68] By mid-1921 a stalemate had been reached: the Government could only secure their objectives by morally and politically unacceptable means, while the IRA had the capacity to make large parts of the country ungovernable, but not to defeat crown forces.

It was not that the manpower in nationalist Ireland did not exist, but rather, as Tom Garvin suggests, that the segment of the population committed enough to put their lives at risk in military struggle was a distinct minority. Indeed, Mark Sturgis was to remark on the apparently contradictory attitude to the state of those whom the IRA claimed to represent: 'while it is their proudest boast that they repudiate British authority and that they are fighting the tyrant [,] no sooner is any one of 'em caught than the prayers that he may be let off pour in without shame usually addressed in most completely respectful tones to HE The Lord Lieutenant. Strange anomaly.'[69] The anomaly, however, derived chiefly from Dublin Castle's simplistic and undifferentiated view of the 'people', and especially how the republican struggle inevitably entailed involvement by the apolitical and less nationally committed. In this context, it can be argued, the dual identity of the Viceroy, simultaneously both a political figure and the embodiment of the non-political monarchical presence, allowed an approach to be made on a relatively non-political plane. In fact, in mid-1921 it was through the agency of the Viceroy that

[66] O'Halpin, *Decline of the Union*, p. 210.

[67] See, for example, Hopkinson (ed.), *Sturgis Diaries* (15 Aug. 1920), pp. 20–2.

[68] D. G. Boyce, *Englishmen and Irish Troubles: British Public Opinion and the Making of Irish Policy 1918–22* (Cambridge, Mass., 1972), pp. 56–9; Erskine Childers, President of Ireland to author, 31 Aug. 1973, in Elizabeth Longford, *Elizabeth R: A Biography* (London, 1983), p. 19.

[69] Entry (28 Feb. 1921), Hopkinson (ed.), *Sturgis Diaries*, pp. 134–5.

the scene-setting for an attempt to find a way out of the politico-military impasse was made.

VI

Preparation for this initiative took the form of the well-publicised appointment to the viceregal office of the Catholic Edmund Talbot, Lord FitzAlan, to succeed Lord French in April.[70] A former Tory politician, FitzAlan was personable, a leading Catholic layman influential at the Vatican,[71] and as such was clearly seen as an appropriate choice for a period in which a new departure in the Irish question was being contemplated, though even moderate nationalist opinion was struck more by the fact that he was English and a Tory.[72] And it was indicative of the changed position of the Catholic Church, which until quite recently would have welcomed a Catholic Viceroy, that FitzAlan faced 'immense' difficulties in 'finding a priest to undertake religious services'.[73] When the veteran Archbishop of Dublin, William Walsh, died in April 1921, his chaplain requested that the Viceroy not be represented at the funeral.[74]

And yet, despite the difficulties of his position, the significance of FitzAlan's appointment could hardly be ignored. The first – and albeit the last – Catholic appointment to the viceregal office was objectively an important conciliatory gesture given the history of the office, and the conciliatory context was further signalled through the appointment 'of six Lord Justices . . . including for the first time three Roman Catholics'.[75] Certainly Warren Fisher regarded FitzAlan's appointment as the first Catholic Viceroy as a harbinger of peace and the appropriate channel for a truce to be announced.[76] The fact that de Valera and the Ulster Unionist leader, James Craig, had a meeting at the same time as he took office – something the Castle engineered a positive Dublin press reception for – had the added bonus of FitzAlan being given 'the lion's share of the credit. This is no bad thing.'[77] Almost until the eve of the King's peace initiative at the inauguration of the Belfast Parliament on 21 June, hope

---

[70] 'A Reconciler in Ireland: Viceroy at a "Grave Moment"', *ILN*, 18 June 1921.
[71] Entry (31 March 1921), Hopkinson (ed.), *Sturgis Diaries*, p. 151.
[72] *FJ*, 2 April 1921; *II*, 2 April 1921; Entry (2 April 1921), Hopkinson (ed.), *Sturgis Diaries*, p. 152.
[73] Fitzroy, *Memoirs* (19 June 1921), II, p. 753: eventually a man was found willing to undertake 'the barest performance of the sacred rites'.
[74] Entry (14 April 1921), Hopkinson (ed.), *Sturgis Diaries*, p. 157.
[75] Entry (5 May 1921), ibid. p. 172.
[76] Thomas Jones, *Whitehall Diary III: Ireland 1918–1925* ed. Keith Middlemas (London, 1971), p. 66.
[77] Entries (5, 6 May 1921), Hopkinson (ed.), *Sturgis Diaries*, pp. 170–3.

existed in Dublin Castle for a meeting between de Valera, Craig and FitzAlan 'which is to bring peace'.[78] As the embodiment of the monarchical presence in Ireland, however, FitzAlan's real significance was as a harbinger for the King in creating such circumstances.

As a constitutional monarch George V would undoubtedly have done the bidding of the Prime Minister in this context in any event, but the King was no less personally committed to a peace initiative. As the hegemonic state symbol and self-conscious bearer of British values and national identity, he strongly deprecated the Government's coercion policy, and especially the Black and Tans; that he made his views known forcibly, and personally, to his viceregal surrogate[79] clearly indicated that he wished FitzAlan to exemplify that mindset.[80] This was not altogether easy for FitzAlan to do, given the dual source of his legitimacy and the fact that to the inflamed mindset of the Prime Minister the King's approach to the Irish question betokened nothing less than cowardice.[81] But George V's understanding of his relationship to the population of the United Kingdom was, as we have seen, more attuned to the sphere of everyday life, leaving him very much alive to the negative consequences of Government callousness, as his criticism of Lloyd George's attitude to the hunger strike in September 1920 of Terence MacSwiney, Lord Mayor of Cork, demonstrated.[82] MacSwiney's death and public funeral were a republican propaganda exercise similar to that of O'Rossa's in 1915. Accordingly, while the King's visit to Belfast to inaugurate the Northern Ireland Parliament in June 1921 was intended to create the conditions for peace negotiations, it was not entirely with the Prime Minister's goodwill. Though not discounting the possibility of media manipulation for political ends, reports in the American press shortly after the Belfast occasion detailing the King's outrage with Lloyd George at his reprisal policy – 'This thing cannot go on. I cannot have my people killed in this manner'[83] – has the ring of authenticity.

Encouraged by Sir Edward Grigg, Lloyd George's Private Secretary, Wickham Steed, editor of *The Times*, Lionel Curtis, editor of the *Round Table*, and Lord Stamfordham, the King's Private Secretary, among others,[84] a speech drawn up by Grigg and endorsed by the King – after

---

[78] Entry (13 June 1921), ibid. p. 188.
[79] Entry (11 May 1921), ibid. p. 176, recording a lunch the viceregal couple had with the King.
[80] FitzAlan approved either peace or war forcefully pursued: entry (29 May 1921), ibid. p. 183.
[81] Rose, *King George V*, p. 238.   [82] Ibid.   [83] Ibid. pp. 240–1.
[84] Jones, *Whitehall Diary III*, pp. 77–8.

he had inserted a statement of his own personal desire for peace[85] – was prepared. Its substance was largely shaped by General Smuts of South Africa, whose outlook on the Irish situation[86] was virtually identical to the King's own. Smuts regarded the Ulster visit as justified only if made the occasion of 'a really important declaration on the whole question', which he envisaged as leading to dominion status for Ireland. It was something only the King, occupying a plane above politics, could do: 'The promise of Dominion status *by the King* would create a new and definite situation which would crystallise opinion favourably both in Ireland and elsewhere.'[87] There was a wider British context to the hopes invested in the monarch. Intelligence reports on 'Revolutionary Organisations in the United Kingdom' in this period of industrial and social disorder – many British politicians regarded Sinn Fein as a closely related manifestation – identified the monarchy as one of the most important bonds of national cohesion.[88]

Initially, however, the decision for the King to perform the inauguration was far from unproblematic. Fears were expressed for his personal safety, fuelled by civil conflict in Belfast, together with concern about damage to 'the prestige of the monarch in Ireland and in the Empire' from his being used in a 'sectional interest'.[89] The crisis in which the state was embroiled, however, determined that strict constitutional propriety had to be sacrificed for the sake of peace,[90] though the usual care was taken with arrangements for the visit. To assist the Viceroy in drafting the monarch's reply to the Address from the City of Belfast, Stamfordham appraised FitzAlan of 'what is uppermost in the King's mind',[91] and the only disquieting accompaniments to the visit were belligerent speeches in the Lords and Commons on Irish policy from Winston Churchill and Lord Birkenhead, both Government ministers and probably engineered

---

[85] Rose, *King George V*, p. 238.

[86] Smuts to the Prime Minister, 14 June 1921, RA PS/GV/PS C32977/A/MAIN.

[87] Ibid. Costello's discussion of the King's Belfast speech as motivated by a British desire to enforce partition and for peace on their terms alone is debatable and lacking in nuance: Francis Costello, 'King George V's Speech at Stormont [*sic*] (1921): Prelude to the Anglo-Irish Truce', *Eire-Ireland*, 22 (1987), 43–57. The speech was delivered at Belfast City Hall. Construction of the Stormont parliament building began in the late 1920s. It was opened in 1932.

[88] See Directorate of Intelligence, *A Survey of Revolutionasry Feeling in the Year 1919*, National Archives (Kew) [NA], CAB24/96/CP462, pp. 4–5; Report no. 48: 'Report on Revolutionary Organisations in the United Kingdom', 30 March 1920, NA (Kew), CAB24/103/CP1009.

[89] Bishop of Chelmsford to Stamfordham, 15 June 1921; Una Pope-Hennessy to Stamfordham, 9 April 1921, RA PS/GV/PS 32977D/6,9/MAIN Fitzroy, *Memoirs* (19 June 1921), II, p. 753; also *Westminster Gazette*, 8 June 1921; Rose, *King George V*, p. 238.

[90] Ibid.   [91] Stamfordham to FitzAlan, 12 June 1921, RA PS/GV/PS 32977C/1/MAIN.

by Lloyd George, who believed that in dealing with the Irish an aggressive stance had to be adopted.[92]

FitzAlan, however, already had the delicate task as a Catholic Viceroy – the appointment of which Ulster Unionists had always opposed – of visiting Belfast and swearing in vigorously Protestant members of the Northern Ireland Parliament as Privy Councillors. This he effected with great diplomacy,[93] while during the royal visit itself the Vicereine, Lady FitzAlan, made their Catholicism palatable to their Orange hosts by describing their religious difficulties as English Roman Catholics among the southern Irish: 'It was a relief to them to leave Dublin and spend a few days in bigoted Orange Belfast!'[94]

Appeals for a royal inauguration had also come from Belfast, encouraged initially by the apparent augury for peace presented by the Craig–de Valera meeting of early May,[95] followed by moral blackmail focusing on the royal absence from Belfast during a war which saw every other ship-building region graced by the royal presence.[96] Initially Stamfordham argued that to inaugurate the Belfast Parliament would mean having to do the same in Dublin,[97] something clearly impossible given political conditions in the south. The way was cleared for the Belfast occasion, however, by Sinn Fein's boycott of the Dublin assembly and its permanent adjournment thereafter.

VII

The ritual of the Belfast visit was conditioned to a large extent by considerations of the King's safety. The route from Belfast docks to the city hall, and the buildings along it, were saturated with police and troops;[98] only very limited engagements, especially military inspections, were undertaken; and only forty addresses of the hundred submitted were accepted for presentation.[99] The intention was to effect the formal inaugural purpose of the visit, and more especially the King's peace initiative, and

---

[92] See Lloyd George's disingenuous explanation to an irate King for the speeches in Rose, *King George V*, p. 239.
[93] See Wilkinson, *To All and Singular*, p. 265.
[94] St. John Ervine, *Craigavon: Ulsterman* (London, 1949), p. 420.
[95] Stamfordham, Memo. of a meeting with the Lord Mayor of Belfast, 7 May 1921, RA PS/ GV/PS 32977/A/MAIN.
[96] Stamfordham, Memo. of a meeting with Lord Londonderry, 26 May 1921, ibid.
[97] Ibid.
[98] Entry (22 June 1921), Lady Craigavon diary, PRONI, D1415/B/38.
[99] Dawson Bates to Stamfordham, 15 June 1921; Sir James Craig to Stamfordham, 26 June 1921; Carrickfergus District Council, Telegram to Stamfordham, 20 July 1921, RA GV/ PS/32977/C/2,3/MAIN.

be out of the city as soon as possible: he was only ashore 'for about seven hours'.[100] And yet despite – perhaps because of – the fraught socio-political circumstances that surrounded the visit, for those who were its beneficiaries the occasion evinced elements of enchantment character-istic of previous royal occasions.

The Lord Mayor of Belfast, Sir Frederick Moneypenny, for instance, at whose official home, Belfast City Hall, the inauguration ceremony would take place, reported the sun shining brilliantly at the moment of the King's arrival at Donegal Quay – 'just as if the veil had been drawn aside by an invisible hand at the auspicious moment'.[101] It was an instance of an age-old association of monarchy with the elements and which A. M. Hocart noted as a tradition surviving in Britain denoted by the term 'King's weather'.[102] Nevile Wilkinson's account of the occasion also is infused with a sense of the magic of majesty: 'My great regret is that no painter was present who could perpetuate the fairy-like scene which greeted Their Majesties.'[103] In fact, the inaugural scene was captured in a photograph that was later the basis of a painting by the distinguished Ulster artist William Conor (Fig. 20).[104] These accounts of the inauguration cannot be divorced from the conditions of constitutional uncertainty that sur-rounded the occasion. David Cannadine comments on the importance placed on ceremonial suggesting stability and order in constitutionally uncertain conditions.[105] Political conditions in Belfast at this time, and the ongoing IRA struggle with crown forces, had established just this kind of background for the King's visit. Not until the Boundary Commission, set up under the Anglo-Irish Treaty of December 1921 to determine finally the borders between Northern Ireland and the Irish Free State – the culmination of the peace process set in train by the King's visit – was wound up in 1925, would Northern Ireland's constitutional position be secured for the foreseeable future. In this context, Moneypenny's sugges-tion of deital complicity in the inaugural ceremony in Belfast – fantasy underpinned by anxiety – is hardly surprising. Certainly Unionists emphas-ised the constitutional security a royal inauguration appeared to offer.[106]

---

[100] Wilkinson, *To All and Singular*, p. 265.
[101] Moneypenny to Stamfordham, 25 June 1921, RA PS/GV/PS 32977/E/MAIN.
[102] A. M. Hocart, *Kings and Councillors: An Essay in the Comparative Anatomy of Human Society* (Chicago, 1970), p. 146.
[103] Wilkinson, *To All and Singular*, p. 267.
[104] See Marquis of Dufferin and Ava to Conor in Judith Wilson, *Conor 1881–1968: The Life and Work of an Ulster Artist* (Belfast, 1981), p. 19.
[105] David Cannadine, 'Introduction' in David Cannadine and Simon Price (eds.), *Rituals of Royalty: Power and Ceremonial in Traditional Societies* (Cambridge, 1992), p. 8.
[106] See *Weekly Northern Whig*, 25 June 1921; Ian Colvin, *The Life of Carson* (London, 1936), III, p. 283; *Belfast Telegraph*, 22, 23 June 1921.

20 King George V inaugurating the Northern Ireland Parliament.

In a revealing editorial on the day after the visit, the *Belfast News-Letter*
admitted the factors had long led Ulster Unionists to interpret the monarch according to their own needs: the 'frontier' mentality of Ulster
Unionists, derived from a 'sense of detachment from the centre of
national life and government, and ... this feeling engenders in us a fonder
and keener appreciation of what the Sovereign stands for as the binding
link in the nation and the Empire'.[107] And the significance of the monarch for Ulster Unionists in this respect became enhanced in 1921 as
Lloyd George, in an effort to satisfy nationalist demands for a unified Irish
state, sought to persuade them to accept an all-Ireland settlement
whereby Ireland would retain her imperial membership, and Northern
Ireland her local autonomy.[108] For Ulster Unionists, however, British
identity as represented by allegiance to the monarch could only be valid as
part of a community that willingly demonstrated its allegiance, something

[107] *BNL*, 22 June 1921.
[108] On this episode, see D. G. Boyce, *Englishmen and Irish Troubles: British Public Opinion
and the Making of Irish Policy 1918–1922* (Cambridge, Mass., 1972), pp. 157–62.

they noted as conspicuously absent in nationalist Ireland. More importantly, since the development of the British nation had historically been a state-directed enterprise, the idea that British identity could be authentically experienced if one's community lay outside the constitutional framework of the United Kingdom was not likely to be convincing. And yet immensely reassuring to Unionists as the King's presence in Belfast was – he was also delighted by the inauguration[109] – this royal occasion no less functioned to mystify and mislead.

The sovereign was the hegemonic signifier of British national identity, but the form of national integration monarchy offered was 'vertical' – allegiance was directed 'upwards' as distinct from the *horizontal* identity that lent credibility to the idea of the people of Britain as one 'organic' national community. Accordingly, as we have seen, an assumed revision of state boundaries to exclude Ulster Unionists – something Tories argued Home Rule would do – entailed no protest by the mass of the British people. Thus despite the reassuring royal spectacle attending the inauguration ceremony in June 1921 Ulster Unionists remained vulnerable to British Government 'treachery' and anti-partitionist threats from the south – as Lloyd George's attempt to convince them of the merits of an all-Ireland settlement demonstrated.

In fact, the inaugural occasion itself was complex, freighted no less with implicitly destabilising, than with congenial and reassuring, dimensions. At the same time as it encouraged Unionists, for instance, it deeply alienated Catholics caught against their will in the new northern statelet: no Catholic clerical or nationalist representative was present at the event.[110] Subject to successive waves of pogroms from loyalists actively encouraged by many leading Unionists,[111] they could only regard the King's speech as a betrayal and evidence of a Government having abandoned them to their fate.

Their situation had been brought to the attention of the court. Concerned about the concealing capacity of royal ritual, the editor of the *Catholic Herald* urged that the King's ceremonial route in Belfast should not avoid 'streets where the homes of large numbers of Catholics had been destroyed, simply because they were Catholics'. Stamfordham, however, seems not to have familiarised the King with the letter and its inconvenient advice, but, describing it as 'rather disloyal', passed it on to the Ulster Unionist leader, Sir James Craig.[112]

---

[109] Entry (22 June 1921), Lady Craigavon Diary, PRONI, D1415/B/38.

[110] Ervine, *Craigavon*, p. 420.

[111] See Paul Canning, *British Policy towards Ireland 1921–1941* (Oxford, 1985), ch. 5.

[112] Stamfordham to Craig, 17 June 1921, RA PS/GV/PS 32977/D/5/MAIN; C.J. O'Donnell to Stamfordham, 12 June 1921, RA PS/GV/PS 32977/D/24/MAIN, also expressing fears for Ulster Catholics.

But the language of the King's speech during the inauguration itself was freighted with constitutional uncertainties Unionists failed to acknowledge.

While it received an 'inspiring reception by the *Imperial Province* [my italics]'[113] because it appeared to affirm partition – symbolically consolidated soon after by the construction of a Great Seal of Northern Ireland and coat of arms for the region designed by Nevile Wilkinson[114] – the national identity the King's speech encouraged was primarily Irish, not British, and was even ambiguous about whether a separate northern state would endure: 'May this historic gathering be the prelude of a day in which the Irish people, North and South, *under one Parliament or two* [my italics], as those Parliaments may themselves decide, shall work together in common love for Ireland.'[115] The celebratory atmosphere of the royal visit, moreover, did not extend far beyond Belfast; a troop train carrying soldiers and horses that had taken part in the visit was blown up in south Armagh on their way back to Dublin, killing three soldiers and a railway guard together with sixty horses.[116] Nevertheless, the King's speech succeeded in its purpose in creating an environment in which negotiations with separatists could begin, the latter encouraged by the prospects of Northern Ireland's early demise.[117]

VIII

While historicist ideology had always been important to Irish nationalists, it had greater salience for separatists anxious both to validate and to redeem it.[118] Michael Collins's plan for a 'state entry' to Dublin for Eamon de Valera in March 1919, for instance, was, when opposed within Sinn Fein, defended by calling up the national humiliation of O'Connell at Clontarf in 1843, having been faced down by the Government.[119] As the crisis over Ireland's constitutional future reached its climax – and impacted on large sectors of the population – the separatist engagement with Irish history became ever more intense, facilitating a blend of familial, regional and local experiences in ways which gave the country's

---

[113] *Londonderry Sentinel*, 23 June 1921.
[114] See James Loughlin, 'Consolidating "Ulster": Regime Propaganda and Architecture in the Inter-War Period', *National Identities*, 1 (1999), pp. 156–7.
[115] King's speech in Jones, *Whitehall Diary III*, pp. 78–9.
[116] See A.J. Sylvester to Stamfordham, 23 June 1921; Lt. Col. A. Seymour to Stamfordham, 29 June 1921; Stamfordham to Seymour, 30 June 1921, RA/PS/GEOV/37977E.
[117] Jones, *Whitehall Diary III*, p. 79.
[118] Garvin, *Nationalist Revolutionaries in Ireland*, p. 110.   [119] Figgis, *Recollections*, p. 244.

national narrative(s) an intense personal inflexion.[120] Accordingly, the characteristic noted by Lloyd George and General Smuts of de Valera – his tendency to concentrate on Ireland's historical suffering and grievances[121] – was hardly exceptional, rather merely reflective of the generation of separatists responsible for subverting Redmond's control of the nationalist agenda. Lloyd George would seek to turn this historicism to his own advantage by citing O'Connell and other constitutional leaders on their loyalty to the monarch,[122] but without success. History was also a crucial site of debate in arguments between pragmatists and purists – pro- and anti-Treatyites – on the acceptability of the controversial dominion status settlement that Arthur Griffith and Michael Collins took back to Dublin from their negotiations with Lloyd George in early December 1921.

Essentially the difference between the two sides came down to inter-pretations. On the one hand, there were those who regarded history as bestowing a purist legacy of independence and sovereignty that the mass of the people had never willingly abandoned, and which therefore still continued to exist – one which the present generation had the duty to further despite the risk of defeat. On the other side were those who, while they read history for proof of the authenticity of Ireland's ancient national lineage and lessons to apply in the pursuit of independence, were pre-pared to accept dominion status as an instalment of that complete inde-pendence which the future would bring.[123] This appealed especially to Arthur Griffith, for whom monarchy was an already established element of his conception of Irish national imagining, and whom, together with Collins, Lloyd George had interpreted – unlike de Valera – as amenable to a dominion settlement during his contacts with nationalist leaders in July 1921.

The anti-Treatyite outlook was essentially elitist, anti-democratic and profoundly distrustful of Irish popular democracy – to a large extent 'West Britonised' – as a repository of national identity.[124] Moreover, their understanding of nationality, based on Irish history as a singular island-based experience essentially shaped by opposition to, and coercion by, England, defined the Treatyite conception of Ireland as a member of the empire as an affront to the authenticity of Irish historical experience, while pointing up all too clearly the reality of Ireland's subordinate power relationship with Britain.[125]

---

[120] Garvin, *Nationalist Revolutionaries in Ireland,* pp. 110–11.
[121] Jones, *Whitehall Diary III,* p. 83, 90.   [122] Ibid. p. 103.
[123] See Kissane, *Politics of the Irish Civil War,* pp. 33–5.   [124] Ibid. p. 33.
[125] Ibid. pp. 35–6.

However, de Valera's attempt to square the dictates of political principle with the reality of a war that could not be won by the notion of external association – Ireland having the status of a republic but in association with the empire – was not something Collins and Griffith were prepared to insist upon as a final position in their negotiations with Lloyd George.[126] Already amenable to a dominion solution, they accepted the Government's terms when given the ultimatum of either dominion status or a resumption of war. For Treatyites, and especially Collins, 'membership of the Commonwealth would guarantee Irish independence since any loss of Ireland's legislative power would be opposed by the other dominions'. Moreover, taking the view that the Anglo-Irish relationship could work to Irish advantage, pro-Treatyites adjusted their historical perspective to incorporate the constitutionalist tradition, citing Parnell as an example of a nationalist leader who had taken an oath of allegiance to the King to further the nationalist cause;[127] though it should be noted that Griffith was citing Parnell as an example of principled nationalism as early as, and in the context of, the royal visit of 1911.[128] For purists, however, imperial membership entailed colonial status, and to accept the British King and the authority of the British Government over Ireland at the expense of principle was simply 'a denial of history'.[129] As these differences became clarified during the Treaty debates, which resulted in a narrow majority of 64 to 57 for acceptance in early January 1922, the chances of resolving them peacefully withered.

It is important, however, to register the limited extent to which these arguments engaged the interests of the Irish people as a whole. Garvin's suggestion that at this time – supposedly one of intense nationalist consciousness – only about a quarter of the Irish people were commitedly nationalist, one quarter Unionist and the rest mildly nationalist and concerned chiefly to get the IRA and the British off their backs,[130] provides useful perspective. His argument is given some support in the comments of a diarist recording the recovery of Irish independence: 'We heard tonight Ireland is a Free State ... Not a flag, not a bonfire, not a hurrah.'[131] Moreover, contemporary assessments of public opinion likewise registered apathy about constitutional principles and a practical

---

[126] Ibid. p. 54.   [127] Ibid. p. 62.
[128] 'Irishmen and British Honours', Sinn Fein, 24 June 1911.
[129] Kissane, Politics of the Irish Civil War, pp. 58–9, 63.
[130] Garvin, Nationalist Revolutionaries in Ireland, p. 150.
[131] Entry (Dec. 1921), Celia Shaw diary cited in Michael Hopkinson, Green against Green (Dublin, 1988), p. 35.

wish for the new Free State Government to govern.[132] That the Irish Civil War, as a military conflict, lasted only a few months also is instructive in this respect. That conflict, however, would have a profound effect on the Irish party system that developed from the mid-1920s, while during its parliamentary and military phases it included a symbolic dimension in which monarchic emblems had a significant role.

In this context, the always important Dublin Castle registered the beginning of a new era. Just three days after the Dáil voted to support the Treaty, Mark Sturgis noted: 'The Castle makes a good propaganda appearance with its gates standing open for the first time for at least two years and soldiers busy removing barbed wire.'[133] For their part, however, the new state authorities, alive to its negative symbolism, marked their possession of the Castle by failing to attend for a formal greeting by FitzAlan, and when deigning to appear signalled their contemptuous attitude to the site through sartorial and presentational disregard: 'a motley assemblage: some in tweed caps and unpolished boots; others with the beard of yester-eve still fresh on their chins; others with long lanky hair, collars and ties *au peintre*'.[134]

As a collective statement of distance from the old Castle regime, it should be seen in the context of assessments of Irish popular opinion which indicated a preference for the Castle's demolition,[135] and against the background of the recent military struggle in which symbolic violence against prominent buildings associated with the regime was common. The most spectacular example was the destruction of the Four Courts complex by Free State forces that inaugurated the Irish Civil War in 1922.[136] But while demolition of the Castle would have emphatically rubbed 'into the people here and everywhere that the new Government is not going to be Castle Government in any shape or form', it was not really practical. For the same reason, desirable as it was that the Viceregal Lodge should not fall into the hands of the new Governor General and that the officeholder should be a plain 'Mr', rather than a titled person, so as to give anti-Treatyites fewer weapons of attack,[137] it was a proposal only partially delivered on. The Viceregal Lodge *was* designated as the

[132] See 'Public Opinion on the Treaty' accumulating press extracts and popular opinion from Jan. to June 1922, Registered Files, Department of the Taoiseach [DT], National Archives of Ireland [NAI], TAOIS/S26.
[133] Entry (10 Jan. 1922), Hopkinson (ed.), *Sturgis Diaries*, p. 227.
[134] Periscope, 'The Last Days of Dublin Castle', *Blackwoods Magazine*, 212 (Aug. 1922), 188.
[135] 'Public Opinion on the Treaty', INA/Department of the President/TAOIS/S26.
[136] Garvin, *Nationalist Revolutionaries in Ireland*, p. 161.
[137] 'Copy no. 1: The Views of the Man in the Street', 16 Jan. 1922, Registered Files, DT, NAI, TAOIS/S26.

official residence of the Governor General, but the advice regarding non-titled officeholders was followed. In an interview with *The Times*, the first occupant of the office, Timothy Healy, was emphatic that he would concern himself only with essential duties totally devoid of all pomp and ceremony.[138] In other words, the role of Governor General would give effect to a merely functional relationship between Ireland and the crown. Concerned to deny the legitimacy of the new state, there was a note of desperation in republican attempts to smear Collins's reputation through claims that he had been seduced by the British aristocracy, and an incredible rumour of 'offers of marriage to a royal'.[139]

In the final analysis, however, both the new Government's concern to divest itself of all monarchical symbolism and anti-Treatyite attempts to besmirch it by association with the old regime counted far less with the Irish public in general than war weariness. Great majorities for the Treaty settlement were recorded at the general elections of 1922 and 1923,[140] indicating relief at a settlement with the British having been made, not enthusiasm for its particular form.[141] Popular ambivalence about constitutional forms would leave room for dispute in the future about Ireland's relationship with the crown.

---

[138] *TT*, 6 Dec. 1922.   [139] Garvin, *Nationalist Revolutionaries in Ireland*, p. 143.
[140] Kissane, *Politics of the Irish Civil War*, p. 73; Garvin, *Nationalist Revolutionaries in Ireland*, p. 149.
[141] Ibid. pp. 142, 145.

Part VI

The crown and independent Ireland

14   The monarchy and Ireland in the Free State era

A constitutional compromise between British and Irish interests, the Irish Free State, apart from the monarchical dimension, lacked historical and cultural underpinning. As a proclaimed basis from which to achieve more complete freedom, its supporters were impelled almost immediately to attempt to supersede its limitations, while republicans, defeated in the civil war, embarked on a sustained campaign, chiefly through propaganda, but also including coercion and violence, to undermine it. For both groups, if by different means and to different degrees, the aim was to establish an Irish identity for the state as distinct from Britain as possible.

I

Given their common origins in the cultural nationalism of the early years of the century, how the state embodied the nation as an imagined community was a central concern; accordingly, symbolic and institutional representations of monarchy in Ireland – especially the misnamed Oath of Allegiance to the Crown[1] and the Governor General – became central issues of controversy in a comprehensive field of debate that also included Ireland's urban and rural landscape and history. The latter continued to be highly important for republicans as a malleable site on which to establish a court of indictment for those who had betrayed the nation in 1921.

Thus while the separatist attempts to disrupt the King's coronation visit of 1911 were, as we have seen, completely ineffectual, they were now retold and magnified as heroic incidents in the struggle against an oppressive monarchical regime of which the Irish Free State was merely the latest manifestation, and with the office of the Governor General its central emblem of national degradation.[2] As the successor to the

---

[1] The Oath was one of allegiance to the Irish constitution and faithfulness to the King.
[2] See Countess Markiewicz in *Eire*, 16 June, 14, 21, 28 July, 4 Aug. 1923.

Viceroyalty, the shadow of the viceregal court hung over the office in the early years, incurring fears that the officeholder might be assassinated,[3] inhibiting the Government's scope for exploiting the office,[4] while, as Beatrice Webb remarked, the Governor General was largely treated with indifference by the public.[5] To the negative historical baggage the office attracted, moreover, could be added its expense. Unlike the Irish Viceroys, whose salaries were paid by the British exchequer and who were expected to fund a large part of their official duties from their own purse, the Free State paid the salary of the Governor General, thus allowing republicans to combine attacks on the office as emblematic of continued British subjection of Ireland with accusations of an oppressive financial exaction of £37,863 per year[6] at a time of severe economic depression (Fig. 21). That the Governor General's *pension* was to be paid by the British exchequer reinforced the view that he would be the mere puppet of the British Government rather than the guardian of Irish rights.[7] The appointment of Timothy Healy as the first Governor General, at the instigation of the Free State Government,[8] tended to lend colour to republican claims.

A former constitutional nationalist and spokesman for Catholic Church interests at Westminster, Healy was acceptable to Lloyd George because of his conservatism – 'the strongest Tory imaginable' – and pro-British sympathies.[9] However, no diplomat, Healy, despite his initial minimalist intentions for his office, was given to controversial utterances. He publicly disparaged the constitutional convention that relegated the King to the position of a mere mouthpiece of the Government without power of initiative, and with a clear suggestion that he would not be following it in regard to Free State ministers.[10] It

---

[3] The Viceregal Lodge came under intense gunfire in January 1923: Brendan Sexton, *Ireland and the Crown 1922–1936: The Governor-Generalship of the Irish Free State* (Dublin, 1989), pp. 98–9; G. F. Torsney, 'The Monarchy in the Irish Free State 1922–32', unpublished MA Thesis, University College Dublin (1980), p. 71–2.

[4] Ibid. p. 71.

[5] Entry (6 Sept. 1930), Beatrice Webb, *Diaries, 1924–1932*, ed. M. Cole (London, 1956), pp. 250–1.

[6] *Eire*, 16 June 1923, drawn from figures in the Government publication *Estimate for the Public Services for the Year Ending March 31, 1924.*

[7] 'The Governor-General's pension', *Eire*, 8 Sept. 1923.

[8] Torsney, 'Monarchy in the Irish Free State', p. 73.

[9] Almeric Fitzroy, *Memoirs* (London, n.d.), II, p. 790. See also Donal Lowry, 'New Ireland, Old Empire and the Outside World, 1922–1949: The Strange Evolution of a "Dictionary Republic"' in Mike Cronin and J. M. Regan (eds.), *Ireland: The Politics of Independence 1922–1949* (Basingstoke, 2000), p. 194; Paul Canning, *British Policy towards Ireland 1921–1941* (Oxford, 1985), p. 75; Thomas Jones, *Whitehall Diary III: Ireland 1918–1925* (London, 1971), p. 218.

[10] Sexton, *Ireland and the Crown*, p. 101.

THIS FREEDOM !

(" *The amount being paid by the people for the support of our Governor-General in the ' Free ' State would support 2,000 families in Connacht!* ")

21 Tyranny of the Governor General.

was a deliberate provocation to republicans, and especially de Valera, whom he repeatedly abused until his retirement in 1928.[11] In the process, however, he did much to validate republican attacks on his office, the Free State constitution and the place of the monarchy within it.[12]

In fact, Healy's overt anti-republicanism tended to obscure the real progress the Free State Government made in the 1920s in augmenting the independence achieved in 1921 under the monarchical and imperial

[11] Ibid. pp. 102–5; Torsney, 'Monarchy in the Irish Free State', pp. 86–92.
[12] His passing in 1931 was marked by fulsome condolences from the King, who had offered none on the death of Michael Collins in 1922: see Stamfordham to Earl of Desart, 2 Sept. 1922, RA PS/GV/O 1805/2; on Healy's Illness and Death, 1931, Registered Files, Department of the Taoiseach [DT], National Archives of Ireland [NAI], TAOIS/S5620.

carapace, especially through the issuing of Irish passports without reference to Britain,[13] and enhancing Dominion independence through action at the Imperial Conference of 1926 specifying their coequality: 'united by common allegiance to the Crown, and freely associated as members of the British Commonwealth of Nations'.[14] Perhaps most significantly, the conference redefined the status of the office of Governor General: he would no longer represent the British Government – to be represented in future by High Commissioners in the dominions – but would act in the Dominions in the same manner as the King in the British constitution. The right of the British Government to advise the King to disallow Dominion legislation, moreover, was declared to be at an end.[15] A further conference of 1930 formally defined United Kingdom–Dominion relations for the first time, conferring 'unlimited legislative power upon the Irish Free State and upon such of the other Dominions as wished to take advantage of it'.[16] It was a radical departure from the position of 1921 and claimed as a fulfilment of an Irish state objective to remove British influence from Irish governance: 'He is a King who functions entirely, so far as Irish affairs are concerned, at the will of the Irish Government.'[17] It was an impressive record, and it is important to see it as informed by a quite specific ideological project – Arthur Griffith's idea of Ireland as an independent Kingdom.

Within an ongoing process of imperial evolution, Kevin O'Higgins, leader of the Irish delegation to the Imperial Conference of 1926, envisaged the proposal being given ideological and symbolic form through the monarch being crowned in Dublin together with other national/emblematic changes. These included the substitution of the Irish Tricolour with a flag embodying the crown and the Irish harp on a blue background – in fact the centrepiece of the Viceroy's flag under the Union – and the monarch's head on Irish coins. By this means, he believed, the British identity of northern Protestants could also be catered for and Irish unity made more likely.[18] But perhaps most significantly, a crucial act of constitutional change would be effected, with the Free State, an existential

---

[13] D. W. Harkness, *The Restless Dominion: The Irish Free State and the British Commonwealth of Nations 1921–1931* (New York, 1970), p. 70.

[14] Quoted in Vincent Grogan, 'Irish Constitutional Development', *Studies*, 40 (1951), 391.

[15] Ibid. p. 392.

[16] Ibid. See also Canning, *British Policy towards Ireland*, pp. 111–12.

[17] P. McGilligan, *Dáil Debates*, 29 (16 July 1931), col. 2307; Grogan, 'Irish Constitutional Development', pp. 292–3.

[18] See Terence de Vere White, *Kevin O'Higgins* (2nd edn, Tralee, 1965), pp. 215–23; John Barnes and David Nicholson (eds.), *The Leo Amery Diaries* I: *1896–1929*, intro. Julian Amery (London, 1980), pp. 483–4, 515; Amery to Stanley Baldwin, 13 Dec. 1926, Stanley Baldwin papers, Cambridge University Library [CUL], vol. 101; Torsney, 'Monarchy in the Irish Free State', pp. 282–7.

form without roots in Irish history and traditions, being transformed into an authentic objectification of the historic Irish national personality.

O'Higgins was a leading member of W. T. Cosgrave's Government, but his assassination by republicans in 1927 was a major setback for the project. Nevertheless, the idea of ideologically aligning the monarchy with Irish sentiment proceeded. When George V fell seriously ill in the winter of 1928–9,[19] the Government highlighted his peacemaking role in creating the circumstances for the Truce and the subsequent peace settlement of 1921 that followed.[20] Also, on the centenary of Catholic emancipation in 1929 the state issued a stamp with a bust of O'Connell,[21] thus officially incorporating within its pantheon of national heroes the founder of a constitutional tradition combining self-government with allegiance to the crown; 1929 was also the year in which the General Post Office, the central structural signifier of contemporary republicanism, was rebuilt. But the occasion was marked in a low-key ceremony which barely mentioned the Easter Rising.[22] Moreover, the practice – still continued – of painting pre-independence post boxes green, but with the monarchical symbolism still clearly visible,[23] suggested the absence of popular anti-monarchical feeling.

The project of aligning the state with the monarchy, however, faced significant problems. The state's promotion of a pro-monarchist zeitgeist in a context of Commonwealth evolution encouraged Revd R. S. Devane to raise publicly the issue of the ban on Roman Catholics holding the monarchical office, a ban clearly inconsistent with civil rights accorded by the Irish constitution;[24] and with the hope that the issue might be put on the agenda of the Imperial Conference due in 1930. The initial Government response offered some hope of success;[25] however, close investigation of the subject brought the fundamental obstacles of British national, and wider Protestant, opposition in the empire clearly into

---

[19] Kenneth Rose, *King George V* (London, 1983), pp. 355–8.

[20] See the furious republican reaction: 'A Slave's Chorus', 'New Use for a Sick King', 'Your King and Cant Need You', *Honesty*, 16 Feb. 1929.

[21] See M. D. Buchalter (ed.), *Hibernian: Specialised Catalogue of the Postage Stamps of Ireland, 1922–1972* (Dublin, 1972), p. 45.

[22] Paul Gillespie, 'Reading 1916 Politics via Official Acts of Memory', *Irish Times* [*IT*], 8 April 2006.

[23] Fearghal McGarry, '"Too Damned Tolerant": Republicans and Imperialism in the Irish Free State' in F. McGarry (ed.), *Republicanism in Modern Ireland* (Dublin, 2003), p. 61.

[24] R. S. Devane, 'A Constitutional Anomaly', *Irish Ecclesiastical Record* (Aug. 1929), 113–40.

[25] See Devane to President Cosgrave, 30 Aug. 1929; Cosgrave to Devane, 19 Sept. 1929; Patrick McGilligan to Devane, 3 Oct. 1929, Registered Files, DT, NAI, TAOIS/S5927.

focus.[26] The upshot was determined attempts to silence Devane and close down debate on the subject.[27] The issue pointed up, as it had done in the pre-independence period, how religious differences could complicate the development of a common Anglo-Irish identity. Anti-Catholicism could still find British governmental expression: addresses from English Catholic prelates on the occasion of George V's Silver Jubilee in 1935 and George VI's coronation in 1937 were refused by the Home Office on the grounds that their ecclesiastical titles were unacceptable.[28] British anti-Catholicism would be a useful weapon for de Valera during his exercise in constitutional innovation in the 1930s. Yet the Cosgrave Government's own attitude to monarchical symbolism was inconsistent.

This was dramatically exposed in the controversy over the playing of 'God Save the King' in acknowledgement of the Governor General's attendance at Commencement celebrations in Trinity College in 1929. The Government's refusal to accept the British national anthem in preference to 'The Soldier's Song' led to acrimonious public debate which exposed continuing national divisions between ex-Unionists and former Home Rulers on the one hand, and both republicans and Free Staters on the other.[29] Moreover, a drive to eliminate symbols, and discredit rituals, of the British presence from the public arena of the state from 1922[30] left the Government bereft of ceremonial mechanisms that would allow popular engagement with monarchy. Nor would it have been easy to construct alternatives given the coercive pressure of an aggressive, often illegal and violent, republican campaign to the same end.

The campaign not only focused on opposition to the playing of 'God Save the King', but also included architecture, urban and rural landscape, cinematic coverage of royal events, and especially the Oath

---

[26] See D. A. Binchey, 'The Law Relating to the Sovereign and the Royal Family', 5 Oct. 1929, Registered Files, DT, NAI, TAOIS/S5927.

[27] McGilligan to Cosgrave, 21 Oct. 1929; Cosgrave to Father Hannon (Devane's superior), 29 Oct. 1929; Hannon to Cosgrave, 3 Nov. 1929; Cosgrave, 'Note on Opinion Regarding the King's Religion', 15 Nov. 1929, Registered Files, DT, NAI, TAOIS/S5927).

[28] *The Times* [*TT*], 21 May 1937; Lowry, 'Strange Evolution of a "Dictionary Republic"', p. 187.

[29] See Euan Morris, '"God Save the King" versus "The Soldier's Song": The 1929 Trinity College National Anthem Dispute and the Politics of the Irish Free State', *Irish Historical Studies*, 21 (May, 1998), 90 and *passim*.

[30] On the issue of Great War commemoration, see David Fitzpatrick, 'Commemoration in the Irish Free State: A Chronicle of Embarrassment' in Ian McBride (ed.), *History and Memory in Modern Ireland* (Cambridge, 2001), pp. 192–3. Only at the Cenotaph in London on Remembrance Day was the Free State represented.

of Allegiance.[31] Ostensibly expecting independence to herald architectural reconstruction emblematic of the new era, its failure to emerge provoked condemnation of the Free State authorities' architectural subservience to 'Anglo-Saxon influence'.[32] In fact straitened economic circumstances made any significant advance on this front difficult.[33]

Thus Dublin Castle, which popular sentiment seemed to be in favour of destroying in 1922, became the location of various Government departments and, by the late 1920s, was presented in official publications in terms approaching national neutrality.[34] Removal of the Oath of Allegiance would have to wait on the accession to power of Eamon de Valera in 1932, but from the mid-1920s republicans made their presence felt on Dublin's urban environment through a series of attacks on royal statuary, most dramatically on the formerly highly contentious monument to William III on College Green in 1927;[35] by preventing the flying of the Union Jack; and by attacks on cinemas showing factual and fictional accounts of royal subjects.[36] Both the authorities' inconsistencies of approach to monarchical symbolism and the aggressive opposition of republicans made impractical any hope that the institution might be a bridge to unity between north and south. Indeed, neither really understood the nature of the Ulster Unionist community's relationship with the crown.

II

While Northern Ireland's position as part of the United Kingdom had been consecrated by George V in 1921, continued Unionist anxieties about constitutional security put a primacy on an enhanced identity with the monarchy.

The direct institutional mechanism of that relationship was the office of the Governor, which was based, not on colonial precedent, but on the Irish Viceroyalty,[37] as was the flag of the Governor, with the area-specific designation forming a centre-piece to the Union flag. His residence,

---

[31] *Honesty*, 28 April 1926; 2, 16 April 1927.

[32] 'Our Addled Architecture: Ugly Dublin', *Honesty*, 28 April 1926.

[33] Yvonne Whelan, *Reinventing Modern Dublin: Streetscape, Iconography and the Politics of Identity* (Dublin, 2003), pp. 115–30.

[34] See, for example, H. G. Leask, *Caislean Baile Atha Claith: Dublin Castle* (Dublin, n.d. [late 1920s]).

[35] Whelan, *Reinventing Modern Dublin*, pp. 192–201.

[36] John Gibbons, *Ireland – the New Ally* (London, 1938), p. 214; McGarry, '"Too Damned Tolerant"', pp. 62–4.

[37] See correspondence of Stephen Tallents., Alan Lascelles, John Anderson and R. S. Meiklejohn, 1923–5, on Residence of Governor of Northern Ireland, National Archives [NA] (Kew), HO45/13010.

Hillsborough Castle, complete with a throne room, itself registered as an important situational marker of the region's constitutional identity.

The Governorship functioned like the Viceroyalty to combine constitutional membership with the suggestion of colonial status, but the separatist implications of the office were not noted by Unionists highly appreciative of the Governor's role as the King's representative. There was, however, little that was similar in the personalities of the first occupants of Ireland's respective monarchical offices. Whereas Healy was impetuous, sharp-tongued and controversial, the Duke of Abercorn (1922–45) served Ulster Unionist interests better through discretion and more strictly following official protocol.[38]

Certainly political sure-footedness was needed in a context where the existence of the northern state was theoretically – up to late 1925 – in contestation, when the Boundary Commission delivered its verdict and when, despite Unionist protests, the Free State authorities succeeded at the Imperial Conference of 1926 in having the King's title altered to reflect the constitutional changes of 1921: 'United Kingdom' was replaced with the geographical expression 'Britain and Ireland'.[39] Nor were they successful in their response to the change – having the regional singularity of the north highlighted through changing the designation 'Northern Ireland' to 'Ulster'.[40] Illuminating the mindset these concerns reflected, W. S. Armour remarked that in Northern Ireland 'the Crown, the Constitution, the Christian [Protestant] religion and the British Empire' were invested with 'mystic powers such as not possessed in any part of the Empire known to me',[41] while its sectarian inflexion is evidenced in Robert Harbinson's account of a Protestant childhood informed by a deification of monarchy framed through 'blood-curdling' Orange myth, in which the Catholic Duke of Norfolk's friendship with the royal family was regarded as 'a terrible betrayal'.[42] The Ulster Unionist outlook was starkly at odds with the spirit of the King's speech in Belfast in 1921, which assumed a primary love of, and commitment to, Ireland on their part, a belief which informed a communication with Craig in September 1924.[43] But as Armour remarked, if the language

---

[38] For the King's appreciation of his services, see correspondence of Sir John Gilmour, Sir C. Wigram, 2–4 July 1934, RA PS/GV/K 2149/2, 4.

[39] Harkness, *Restless Dominion*, pp. 104–5.

[40] Baldwin to Craigavon, 15 Feb. 1927, Stanley Baldwin papers, CUL/ vol. 101.

[41] W. S. Armour, *Facing the Irish Question* (London, 1935), p. 189.

[42] Robert Harbinson, *No Surrender: An Ulster Childhood* (1960; Belfast, 1989), pp. 131–3.

[43] Stamfordham to Craig, 17 Sept. 1924, Additional Craigavon papers, PRONI, T 3775/ 10/7; Ervine, *Craigavon*, p. 492.

the King employed had been used by one of his Ulster subjects it 'would have been regarded as treasonable. The very notion of a common love for Ireland Ascendancy ever regarded with abhorrence.'[44]

Unsurprisingly, the region was subject to territorial marking that outmatched nationalist efforts to denude the Free State of 'alien' emblems. The travel writer H. V. Morton declared: 'I seemed to be in England again.'[45] For a community whose collective mentality was so constructed, great royal occasions such as the Silver Jubilee celebrations of the reign of George V in 1935 offered the psychological reassurance of participation in state-wide rejoicing with the monarchical prism 'purifying' the region's recent history, stripping out unsettling developments and sectarian conflict.[46] It was virtually inevitable that efforts would be made to persuade the monarch and Westminster to relocate the Order of St Patrick to Northern Ireland from a ceremonially redundant Dublin.

III

With the monarch as its source and fount of honour the Order had placed pre-independence Ireland on a constitutional par in terms of status with Scotland and England, and the King, concerned to retain Ireland's connection with the crown, wanted to keep it in existence. While the Free State authorities might bar its citizens from accepting the honour, this would not affect Northern Ireland or Irishmen living outside Ireland.[47] The discussion of the Order's fate arose at the beginning of 1922 in connection with that of the office of Chief Herald of Ireland, Ulster King of Arms, which Nevile Wilkinson sought to save through a redesignation reflecting the changed constitutional configuration of Ireland: 'Ireland King of Arms and Ulster Provincial Herald'.[48] Abercorn had been invested with the Order in 1922, but, unlike his viceregal predecessors, was bereft of the facilities for ceremonial inauguration.[49]

[44] W. S. Armour, *Ulster, Ireland, Britain: A Forgotten Trust* (London, 1938), p. 196.
[45] H. V. Morton, *In Search of Ireland* (London, 1930), p. 231; also Gibbons, *Ireland – the New Ally*, pp. 137–8.
[46] See, for example, the photographic review of royal occasions in Northern Ireland since 1924 in Jubilee Supplement to *Northern Whig [NW]*, 6 May 1935.
[47] Lord Stamfordham to Earl of Desart, 2 Sept. 1922, RA PS/GV/O 1805/2.
[48] See Viceroy FitzAlan–Stamfordham correspondence, 27, 30 Jan. 1922, RA PS/GVI/PS 05680/016–018/HON.
[49] *Belfast News-Letter [BNL]*, 9 Aug. 1924; Oscar Henderson to Wilkinson, 26 May 1927, Governor's papers, PRONI/ GOV3/Box18/M/18; Duke of Abercorn to Stamfordham, 7 July 1924, RA PS/GVI/PS 05680/037/HON. The intended home was the Anglican cathedral at Armagh.

The London Government and the King, however, were at this time still hopeful that the Free State authorities might come to accept the Order;[50] and with the Boundary Commission in mind, were not prepared to consider its transfer to Northern Ireland and thereby seem to foreclose on the commission's deliberations. Moreover, southern Irish Peers, hopeful of governmental compromise, were strongly opposed to the transfer.[51] Political developments, however, militated against their, and crown, ambitions, as republicans entered the Dáil in 1927 and with a general election in the offing. Cosgrave, believing erroneously that the Order had been created as a Union bribe in 1800,[52] and with his political position in the country progressively weakening,[53] decided against reviving the Order. Moreover, he regarded it as solely the preserve of the Irish State and considered that no action could be taken respecting it by any other authority, especially the northern regime: 'They [Ulster Unionists] have, of course, all the Orders of the British Empire open to them.'[54]

Cosgrave's attitude to the Order provoked royal fury, partly because his outlook contrasted with the King's own view of Ireland – 'it practically declines to recognise Northern Ireland as being Irish'[55] – partly because Cosgrave presumed to pontificate on an issue the King regarded as his own. But it increasingly came to be accepted in London that given the changes in Dominion relations agreed at the Imperial Conference of 1926, no progress on the issue could be made until the Free State became 'more tractable'.[56] The only appointments made to the Order after 1922 were members of the Royal Family – the Prince of Wales, the Duke of York and the Duke of Gloucester – who as 'supernumerary' members were appointments requiring only the King's authority.[57] When Eamon

---

[50] Correspondence of G. R. A. Buckland, Capt. A. Hardinge and Stamfordham, Jan. 1923; Minute by Sir John Anderson on conclusions to Conference on Order of St Patrick, 30 April 1923, RA PS/GVI/PS 05680/022, 023, 029/HON.

[51] See correspondence of Sir Ronald Waterhouse, Stamfordham and Lord Granard, 14 July 1924–28 March 1927, RA PS/GVI/PS 05680/041, 043, 044, 046, 064, 066/HON.

[52] Granard to Stamfordham, 28 March, 1 April 1927, RA PS/GVI/PS 05680/066, 070/HON.

[53] Former Viceroy FitzAlan made this point to Stamfordham, 7 Oct. 1927, RA PS/GVI/PS 05680/081/HON.

[54] L. T. McC, Note by President on Order of St Patrick, 23 March 1927, Registered Files, DT, NAI, TAOIS/S5708A; Cosgrave, memo. on Order of St Patrick, 21 May 1928, RA PS/GVI/PS 05680/094/HON.

[55] Stamfordham to C. P. Duff, 17 Sept. 1930, RA PS/GVI/PS 05680/106/HON.

[56] C. P. Duff, 10 Downing Street, Résumé of Recent History Regarding the Order of St Patrick, 2, 4 Sept. 1930; Stamfordham to Duff, 17 Sept. 1930, RA PS/GVI/PS 05680/105,106/HON.

[57] Stamfordham to Waterhouse, 22 Feb. 1927, RA PS/GVI/PS 05680/061/HON; Peter Galloway, The Most Illustrious Order of St. Patrick 1783–1983 (Chichester, 1983), pp. 66–7; Torsney, 'Monarchy in the Irish Free State', pp. 158–67.

de Valera came to office in 1932 Anglo-Irish relations were preoccupied with difficulties compared to which the Order of St Patrick, and related matters concerning heraldic officers,[58] paled into insignificance.

IV

Denying the moral legitimacy of a Treaty imposed on the Irish people by threat of war,[59] de Valera approached Anglo-Irish relations by confrontation on two fronts: the withholding of Ireland's annuities due on the purchase of Irish land acts since the late nineteenth century, and which initiated a six-year trade war that entailed considerable damage to Anglo-Irish trade;[60] and a dismantling of the constitutional ties binding Ireland to Britain, beginning with the Oath of Allegiance.[61] De Valera's constitutional revisions proceeded with the downgrading and then abolition of the office of Governor General, and the redesignation of the Free State as Eire, a constitutional entity having a position of External Relation with the Empire and Commonwealth and acknowledging the monarch only for the purpose of authorising diplomatic representation.[62] The Governor General was replaced with an elected President whose official home was the Viceregal Lodge – the first occupant, Douglas Hyde, was inaugurated in Dublin Castle,[63] a profoundly symbolic act in what had been the centre of British rule. The accession and abdication of Edward VIII in 1936 offered de Valera opportunities to demonstrate Ireland's constitutional singularity.[64]

Unlike the Commonwealth, no official declaration of Edward VIII's accession was made in Dublin, and no offical Irish representation was present in London.[65] As the abdication crisis developed de Valera disclosed his own preference for the King – who undoubtedly gained his sympathy by a heartfelt letter of condolence on the accidental death of

---

[58] See Susan Hood, *Royal Roots – Republican Inheritance: The Survival of the Office of Arms* (Dublin, 2002), pp. 140–5.

[59] Despatch to British Government on 'Status of the Irish Free State', Nov. 1933, Registered Files, DI, NAI, TAOIS/S2242.

[60] D. McMahon, 'Economic War' in S. J. Connolly (ed.), The *Oxford Companion to Irish History* (2nd edn, Oxford, 2002), pp. 176–7.

[61] For the considerations that determined the British response and ultimate acquiescence to de Valera's actions, see Canning, *British Policy towards Ireland*, ch. 8.

[62] Donal O'Sullivan, *The Irish Free State and Its Senate: A Study in Contemporary Politics* (London, 1940), pp. 489–90; Sean O'Faolain, *De Valera* (Harmondsworth, 1939), p. 131.

[63] 'President of Eire', *TT*, 27 June 1938.

[64] An oft-told story; for a good account see Brian Inglis, *Abdication* (London, 1966).

[65] *IT*, 22 Jan. 1936; *Irish Independent*, 23 Jan. 1936; 'King Edward VIII: Accession to the Throne', 21 Jan. 1936, Registered Files, DT, NAI, TAOIS/S8520.

one of de Valera's sons[66] – retaining the crown with Mrs Simpson as consort but not Queen.[67] De Valera did engage in the process to effect the abdication, but in a way that distracted attention elsewhere: it was embodied, on 12 December 1936, in a sub-section of the External Relations Act in conjunction with a bill intending to abolish the office of Governor General and removing the King from the Irish constitution.[68]

And yet, while a triumph for de Valera, the referendum which confirmed his constitution was hardly a ringing national endorsement: 685,105 votes to 526,945.[69] It illustrated the limitations of republican rhetoric about national identity and the extent to which monarchical forms were regarded as alien by the population at large, and, no less, de Valera's status as a figure whose authority was, like Gladstone's, politically demarcated. Moreover, de Valera's belief that the retention of a tenuous royal link with the crown was necessary as an ideological bridge to the Ulster Unionist community failed to appreciate how the anti-monarchical campaign had merely served to facilitate its own exclusionary uses of the crown.

V

As under the Union, the significance of royal ceremonial and its effects in this period depended largely on the context in which it took place; but the Irish public arena available for such ceremonial was now greatly restricted, while the ongoing debate on the Irish question, especially partition, meant that the largely unproblematic public reception formerly common was no longer possible. The realms of politics and that of royal ceremonial and display were more closely enmeshed than in the past, especially so as self-government in Northern Ireland allowed the regime considerable initiative in the timing of royal occasions to suit its political interests. This was the case with the visit of the Duke and Duchess of York in 1924.

With the Boundary Commission about to convene and Ulster Unionists refusing cooperation and threatening violent resistance,[70] the regime, without consultation with the Home Office – which regarded it as politically

---

[66] John Gibbons, *Abroad in Ireland* (London, 1936), p. 101.
[67] File information on de Valera's attitude to the abdication; de Valera to Edward VIII, 5 Dec. 1936, NA (Kew), CAB21/4100/2. For British anxieties on de Valera's intentions, see Memo. in file on 'Abdication: Irish Free State', 28 Nov. 1936, NA (Kew), CAB21/4100/2.
[68] For a detailed discussion, see O'Sullivan, *Irish Free State*, pp. 482–7.
[69] McMahon, 'Constitution of Ireland', p. 118.
[70] See Dennis Kennedy, *The Widening Gulf: Northern Attitudes to the Independent Irish State 1919–1949* (Belfast, 1988), pp. 135–6.

inopportune[71] – issued an invitation directly to the Yorks with the obvious intention of impressing British public opinion with Northern Ireland's constitutional loyalty. The invitation to the Yorks which, given the King's close scrutiny of his children's royal duties,[72] he could only have agreed to as a goodwill measure, was undoubtedly intended to facilitate their cooperation with the commission. The King did not envisage the abrogation of self-government in Northern Ireland, rather agreement to a fairly innocuous All-Ireland Council with very limited powers, which was how the Westminster Government envisaged a solution to the issue in early 1924, but which the Unionists regarded as a stumbling block.[73] It was very much in this context that the Unionists regarded the royal visit.

It was a carefully constructed occasion, initiated by the Governor in a direct invitation in March 1924 – just after the Free State authorities had urged the London Government that the Boundary Commission be established 'forthwith' – and it met with a delighted and compliant response by the royal recipients.[74] And while the Home Secretary, Sir John Anderson, acted to ensure that none of the ninety-one addresses to be presented to the royal visitors was politically contentious,[75] what was important was what the Duke said when in Northern Ireland; and the content of his public utterances was largely shaped by Oscar Henderson, the Governor's Private Secretary. Henderson advised avoiding 'any question of Ireland as a whole, like the plague'[76] in favour of innocuous comments about the 'ruggedness' of Ulster and its loyalty to the King, together with a reference to the monarch's visit to the north in 1897.[77] In sum, Henderson was concerned that the royal visit (19–26 July), in a context where such a visit to the Free State was impossible, registered Northern Ireland as resolutely British, and that the Duke said nothing to suggest constitutional compromise, especially participation in the Boundary Commission.

But the royal visit should also be seen in a broader imaginative context, one in which Northern Ireland – unlike the Irish Free State[78] – was

---

[71] Waterhouse to Stamfordham, 14 July 1924, RA PS/GVI/PS 05680/041/HON.
[72] Frank Prochaska, *Royal Bounty: The Making of a Welfare Monarchy* (New Haven and London, 1995), p. 193.
[73] Thomas Jones, *Whitehall Diary III* (London, 1971), p. 226.
[74] Duke of Abercorn to their Royal Highnesses, the Duke and Duchess of York, 22 March 1924; Duke of York to Abercorn, 25 March 1924, RA ADYH/MAIN/102.
[75] Henderson to Anderson, 9 July 1924, NA (Kew), HO45/11773.
[76] Henderson to Capt. Brook, Secretary to the Duke of York, 19 June 1924, RA PS/Duke of York papers/Box 102.
[77] Ibid.
[78] An initial decision to participate was reversed owing to the 'condition of the country'. See Healy–Duke of Devonshire correspondence, 1923–4, Registered Files, DT, NAI, TAOIS/S1967.

represented at the British Empire exhibition at Wembley. Its presence was registered in an 'Ulster' Pavilion, complete with elaborate relief maps of the region, and in conjunction with which the Belfast authorities organised a tour of the border areas of Northern Ireland by over fifty British newspaper editors.[79] The royal visit would be the centre-piece of a highly ambitious exercise in British identity-shaping and consolidation in a context where it seemed to be under threat. Henderson remarked to the Duke's Private Secretary: 'As you may imagine, *the formation of a new State* [my italics] is no easy matter.'[80] And it undoubtedly served Unionist ends that the Yorks, still in their twenties, seem to have been naively unaware of the visit's wider political import and were 'astounded' by their reception in the north.[81] Only in their ambitions to use the visit to take possession of the Order of St Patrick, or to have appointments made to the Order in association with it,[82] were Unionists unsuccessful.

In the wider Irish context, however, the reputation of the monarchy suffered, as republicans detected evidence of Westminster treachery on the boundary issue, proving that the Anglo-Irish Treaty of 1921 had been a trap.[83] As Ulster Unionists became more rhetorically violent in their refusal to cooperate with the commission, so did the royal visit of 1924 assume ever greater significance as proof that the King and the British establishment were solidly behind them: 'In the Duke the Orangemen had a pledge which they regarded as making their future absolutely secure. It was little wonder that they took the princeling to their hearts.'[84] Pro-Government as well as republican opinion was also inclined to this view,[85] and it is just possible that it influenced Eoin McNeill, the Free State representative on the commission, whose passivity or fatalism was one factor in its decision to make only marginal changes to the existing border.

Accordingly, while there is no evidence that the Yorks willingly colluded in an Ulster Unionist strategem to thwart the commission, the representative function of monarchy in the context of Anglo-Irish relations at this time easily led to this reading. And the perceived royal association with the controversy lingered, inhibiting the southern

[79] James Loughlin, 'Creating "a Social and Geographical Fact": Regional Identity and the Ulster Question 1880s–1920s', *Past and Present*, forthcoming.

[80] Henderson to Capt. Brooke, Private Secretary to the Duke of York, 29 July 1924, RA ADYH/MAIN/102.

[81] Sir John Wheeler-Bennett, *King George VI* (London, 1958), p. 197.

[82] Waterhouse to Stamfordham, 14 July 1924, RA PS/GVI/PS/05680/041/HON.

[83] See 'Royalty and Orangeism', *Eire*, 28 June 1924; 'The Royal Word and Some Treachery', *Eire*, 26 July 1924.

[84] 'Royalty and Orangeism', *Eire*, 2 Aug. 1924.   [85] *Freeman's Journal*, reported ibid.

authorities' attempts to align the monarchy with Irish nationality, as pro-Government press opposition to a private visit to the Free State in 1928 by the King's daughter, Princess Mary, Viscountess Lascelles, indicated.[86]

It was a visit which Ulster Unionists had initiated for Northern Ireland from 12 to 15 October,[87] and they had little interest in the addition of a southern extension which might serve to blur the constitutional distinction between north and south in British minds. Accordingly, as the southern leg was to be undertaken first and to be private, Unionists arranged the northern dimension of the visit to be as public as possible. To this end the regime wanted the Princess to arrive in Northern Ireland 'by train'.[88]

It was in 1928 that the foundation stone of the impressive Stormont parliament building was laid with great ceremony. A visit by a prominent royal was seen as an occasion on which this important structural signifier of constitutional membership could be reinforced in the British public mind, especially so in a context where the strengthening republican presence in the south was expressed in anti-monarchism.[89] In Northern Ireland the Princess would alight at loyalist Portadown, and thereafter engage in an extensive round of welfarist engagements chiefly in the Belfast area, all safely Unionist.

The visit of 1928 was not of the same importance as that of 1924; nevertheless, it was significant as a stage in the developing Unionist tradition of using monarchy for the purpose of periodically emphasising Northern Ireland as loyally British in an often difficult Anglo-Irish context. The visits of the 1920s, however, tended to inculcate a complacent belief that royal visits would always work unproblematically to Unionist advantage, a belief those of the 1930s would confound.

The central factor in a successful visit was the willingness of the royal personage to comply with the wishes of the organisers, and this was demonstrably absent in the case of Edward, Prince of Wales – the most photogenic and publicity-attracting member of the royal family – who was virtually compelled by the King to undertake the official opening of the Stormont parliament building in November 1932. Efforts to engage his services going back to 1928 foundered upon an insistence that he would not visit the north unless the occasion involved engagements in the south;

[86] C. G. Markbreiter to Sir John Anderson, 28 July 1928, NA, HO45/20434.
[87] Henderson to Markbreiter, 23 July 1928, Markbreiter to Anderson, 28 July 1928, NA, HO45/20434.
[88] Henderson to Markbreiter, 26 Sept. 1928, NA (Kew), HO45/20434.
[89] See Henderson to Anderson, 11 Oct. 1928, NA (Kew), HO45/20434.

and he was supported in his stance at this time by the King, when the Free State Government was making conciliatory gestures to the crown.[90] By 1932, however, the Anglo-Irish context had changed radically. The accession of de Valera to power and the period of Anglo-Irish conflict it initiated effectively ruled out a royal visit to the south. And while he would develop a regard for de Valera's 'rare gift of natural good manners',[91] the abolition of the Oath of Allegiance and downgrading of the Governor General offended the King. Thus the arguments of 1928 had lost much of their credibility while de Valera's activities almost invited a royal riposte in the form of a high-profile Ulster visit, to which the King was now favourable. Edward, however, was an unfortunate choice.

Deeply disillusioned with his public role in general at this time, and resentful of his father's control of his activities, Edward was petulant and strongly opinionated.[92] Determined that the occasion be as minimalist as possible, he sternly lectured Abercorn on the need for economy at a time of great economic distress,[93] and resolutely rejected attempts to add to his duties. Moreover, in the run-up to the visit he was the recipient of information from nationalists flatly at odds with the protestations of undiluted loyalty conveyed by the northern regime and its press supporters.[94]

In an attempt to compel the Prince to accept addresses Abercorn claimed that some had come from Roman Catholics seeking to ameliorate sectarianism and not to receive them would be a rebuff to their efforts.[95] In fact, clerical and political leaders of the nationalist community boycotted the opening of a structure intended to house what Craigavon would later describe as 'a Protestant Parliament' in a 'Protestant State'.[96] And nationalists associated with the *Irish News* were quick to establish a negative and repressive historical narrative for the building to

---

[90] See Abercorn to Godfrey Thomas, 1 Feb. 1928; Thomas to Abercorn, 8 Feb 1928, RA EVIIIWH/MAIN/2596.

[91] Deirdre McMahon, 'Watching the March to War', *IT*, 9 Dec. 2006.

[92] See Francis Donaldson, *Edward VIII* (London, 1974), p. 131.

[93] J. Macnamara to Private Secretary, Prince of Wales, 13 Oct. 1932; Edward P. to the Duke of Abercorn, 17 Oct. 1932, RA EVIIIPH/MAIN/2596.

[94] *Irish News*, 3, 31 Oct. 1932, copy in file; Assist. Secretary to Abercorn, 8 Nov. 1932; Ancient Order of Hibernians, *Lord Craigavon and the Prince of Wales* (n.l., AOH, n.d. [1932]); 'Case of Ulster Editor: False Reports Charge', *Belfast Weekly Telegraph* [*BWT*], 26 Nov. 1932: RA EVIIIPH/MAIN/2596.

[95] Abercorn to the Prince, 10 Nov. 1932; Abercorn to Sir Lionel Halsey, 10 Nov. 1932, ibid. For activities and correspondence regarding the inauguration, see Committee on 'Stormont Opening Ceremony', PRONI/CAB9H/131/1.

[96] Craigavon at Stormont, April 1934 cited in Sean O'Faolain, *An Irish Journey* (London, 1941), p. 244.

invoke.[97] In the event, the Prince relented and extended his duties to a very limited degree, agreeing to receive personally six addresses and to visit a number of businesses and hospitals.

As acutely conscious of the symbolism of royal activities as Unionists, nationalist press organs placed great significance on the Prince's attitude, much to the discomfort of the regime.[98] Moreover, their pressure seems to have had some effect, in that a visit to the Catholic Mater Hospital was included on the itinerary. It was a short sojourn of only fifteen minutes, but something long remembered by the Catholic community of the region, accurately or not, as an event Edward forced upon the regime. Certainly throughout the visit Edward evidenced his personal distaste for the occasion.[99] Pro-Unionist accounts of the visit told one story, but the photographs quite another,[100] something Lady Craigavon, put down to 'southern elements' in his entourage who had given him 'a completely wrong idea about everything'.[101] Edward's demeanour in Belfast, as we have noted, is explicable to some extent by a disillusionment with his public role in general at this time, but the context in which Unionists framed the visit allowed of no such wider perspective. And it would have long-term as well as short-term negative consequences. Orangemen at Hillsborough persuaded the Prince to make an attempt at playing a Lambeg drum[102] and then apparently used photographs of the event to taunt Catholics. The *Derry Journal* posed the question: 'The Prince of Wales played the big drum with the Orangemen. But what is his real opinion of their loyalty?'[103] It was a relevant question. Significantly, in his memoirs Edward disclosed that the fundamental determinant of Orange loyalty to the monarch, the declaration of fidelity to the Protestant faith, was something he regarded with repugnance.[104] Accordingly he came to view the Lambeg incident and the Ulster visit of 1932 in general as a Unionist plot to exploit him for their own political ends. When it came to planning his coronation tour in 1936 he wished to ignore Northern Ireland altogether, to avoid according it any significance 'in connection with the

---

[97] 'QX', *The Truth about Stormont* (Belfast, 1933), pp. 5–6.
[98] See Henderson to Sir Lionel Halsey, 10 Nov. 1932, RA PS/EVIIIWH/MAIN/2596.
[99] See for example, *BWT*, 26 Nov. 1932.
[100] See for example, *Derry Journal* [*DJ*], 18 Nov. 1932.
[101] Entry (16 Nov. 1932), Lady Craigavon Diary, PRONI, D1415/B/38.
[102] See *BNL*, 17 Nov. 1932; *NW*, 19 Nov. 1932; *BWT*, 26 Nov. 1932; *Illustrated London News*, 26 Nov. 1932; James Henderson (brother of Oscar, the Governor's Secretary) to Halsey, 20 April 1933, enclosing clipping from *BNL*, RA EVIIIWH/MAIN/2596.
[103] *DJ*, 18 Nov. 1932.   [104] Duke of Windsor, *A King's Story* (London, 1953), p. 298.

Coronation'.[105] Political exploitation of the incident was also attempted by Lord Craigavon, who, unsuccessfully, tried to have a book exposing his Government's sectarian practices banned, ostensibly on the ground that it contained a reference disrespectful to the Prince regarding the drum incident.[106]

As to the royal visit in general, though, it indicated that Northern Ireland's relationship with monarchy in the 1930s would not be as congenial or politically advantageous as in the previous decade. A visit to Northern Ireland by the Duke of Gloucester as part of the Silver Jubilee celebrations in 1935 took place against a background of Government stimulated pogroms against the Catholic community in Belfast.[107] That the Duke, one of whose titles was 'Earl of Ulster', made a ringing commitment to the regime merely lent a colour of royal partisanship to the occasion.[108] While outwardly the forms of Jubilee celebration in Northern Ireland were virtually identical to those in Britain,[109] in reality they were informed by the sectarian practices and mentality of local Orangeism, with attendant disorder.[110]

The Jubilee celebrations in Northern Ireland in 1935 were attended by a level of violence and civil upheaval unmatched by any Irish royal occasion under the Union. Only the royal visit of 1885 offered a parallel, and even then it did not match the violence and disorder in Northern Ireland in 1935, which ran on long after the royal visit and got worse.[111] In all, 430 Catholic houses were burned, 514 Catholic families (2,241 people) intimidated out of Protestant areas, while 95 per cent of compensation paid went to Catholics.[112] In Britain the monarch and the royal family constituted a model of respectability for national emulation; in Belfast during the pogroms monarchy functioned largely as an excuse to justify sectarian attacks on Catholics, blamed for the trouble because they

---

[105] See Memo. of discussion of proposed royal tours between the Home Secretary and the King (17 Oct. 1936) sent for the attention of the President of the Council, Ramsay McDonald, McDonald papers, NA (Kew), PRO 30/69/8.

[106] Gibbons, *Abroad in Ireland*, pp. 238–9; 'Reference to Edward VIII as POW in Book *Abroad in Ireland*,' 10 July 1936, NA (Kew), HO45/20299; Markbreiter to 'My Dear Gransden', 7 July 1936, NA (Kew), HO144/20299.

[107] 'Orders to Leave Homes under Pain of Death: Belfast Still "Celebrating"', *DJ*, 10 May 1935; also issues of 8, 13 May 1935; Gibbons, *Abroad in Ireland*, pp. 202–3, 283–4.

[108] See 'Ulster and King's Jubilee', *Londonderry Sentinel [LS]*, 7, 14 May 1935. Alone of records of royal visits to Northern Ireland in this period at Kew, those for the Duke's visit are still unavailable to the public.

[109] See for example, *TT*, 7, 10, 13, 14 May 1935; Jubilee supplement to *NW*, 6 May 1935.

[110] 'Gates Were Barred against Them', *DJ*, 13 May 1935.

[111] See for example, *DJ*, 1, 15, 17 July 1935.

[112] Ronnie Monck and Bill Rolston, *Belfast in the 1930s: An Oral History* (Belfast, 1987), pp. 54–5.

refused to join in Jubilee celebrations.[113] That the Lord Mayor of Belfast could express the hopes for a royal residence in Northern Ireland against such a background[114] suggests at the least a denial of reality.

The anti-Catholic campaign of 1935 would stimulate British interest in Northern Ireland, leading to a damning exposé by the National Council for Civil Liberties the following year,[115] and helped ensure that the kind of national integration with the population of Britain Unionists desired would not be achieved, leaving them only with the 'vertical', and constitutionally vulnerable, bond of national identity that royal allegiance and spectacle embodied. That would become apparent in the late 1930s, after the most important royal engagement in Northern Ireland of the inter-war period.

VI

While the national celebrations for the coronation of George VI on 12 May 1937 – uniquely caught in Mass Observation's national study of the event[116] – revealed a northern Irish experience that, at one level, reson-ated with the weave of British experience in general; at another, more important level, it was informed by a regional geographic location and Eirean responses to the occasion. De Valera cited partition and the coronation service's anti-Catholic dimension as a reason for not officially acknowledging it,[117] though British fears that he would create a constitu-tional incident over the roles in the coronation ceremony of the ancient offices of High Constable and High Steward of Ireland proved unfounded. De Valera regarded them merely as 'traditional'.[118] On the day preceding the coronation legislation finally abolishing the office of Governor General was enacted.[119] Republicans marked the coronation by blowing up the statue of George II in St Stephen's Green. Even in Dublin, though, some indication of a popular attitude, not unlike that of the United Kingdom, was indicated.[120]

Press reports from the Free State revealed a contrasting picture of official non-participation – as the King and Queen were returning from

---

[113] Ibid. pp. 46–54.
[114] 'English Royal Jubilee: Celebrations in Belfast', *DJ*, 13 May 1935.
[115] For a survey of the British press coverage, see *DJ*, 25, 27 May, 1 June 1936.
[116] Humphery Jennings and Charles Madge (eds.), *May 12 1937: Mass Observation Day Survey* (1937, London, 1987).
[117] *Dáil Debates*, 65 (24 Feb. 1937), col. 869.
[118] Deirdre McMahon, 'Watching the March to War', *IT*, 9 Dec. 2006.
[119] O'Sullivan, *Irish Free State*, p. 489.
[120] Ibid.; Whelan, *Reinventing Modern Dublin*, p. 194.

Westminster Abbey, de Valera was asking the Dáil to give a second reading to the bill establishing his new constitution[121] – and popular private engagement with the occasion, as a reported 30,000 people travelled to London and many thousands more listened in to radio broadcasts.[122] Radio allowed a more immediate and directly imaginative arena for the monarchy to influence than was the case in the nineteenth century. But it facilitated both popular identity with, and opposition to, the crown, and conflicts between royalists and republicans erupted north and south.[123] The coronation procession in London itself became momentarily an arena for republican protest as Lord Craigavon's carriage was met with a cry of 'Up Dev' at Constitution Hill.[124] The degree of protest the coronation occasioned in Ireland was an unsettling augury for the Northern Ireland coronation visit some months later.

VII

Craigavon's attitude to the abdication crisis of 1936 was encapsulated in the statement: 'Trust Baldwin.'[125] There is nothing to suggest that he would have taken an independent line on the matter, and certainly, given his attitude to the Stormont inauguration in 1932, not on Edward VIII's behalf.[126] By contrast, the Duke of York's willingness to comply with Unionist wishes in 1924 could only have made his accession to the throne a welcome development.

With their acute attention to any royal detail on which they could put significance, Craigavon's participation in the coronation procession was regarded as a 'signal honour to the Imperial people of this Imperial province',[127] and much was read into the fact that the coronation visit to Northern Ireland of the new King and Queen, not originally planned for but requested by Craigavon, came so soon after their coronation on 12 May – they arrived on 28 July. Although the King and Queen decided on a one-day sojourn and wanted the traditional formalities, as in Wales and Scotland, to be kept to a minimum,[128] Craigavon succeeded in having

---

[121] *Daily Express [DE]*, 13 May 1937.   [122] 'I.F.S. "Tunes In" to Abbey', ibid.

[123] 'Glare from Ulster's Bonfires Seen in Scotland: All-Night Revelry'; 'Telephone Wires Cut Down while Ulster Celebrates'; 'Villages Fly "Rival" Flags', ibid.

[124] 'Free State Ex-Soldiers See Parade', ibid.

[125] *LS*, 8 Dec. 1936.

[126] Edward VIII's image was booed in Belfast cinemas: *DJ*, 9 Dec. 1936.

[127] *LS*, 29 July 1937.

[128] 'Extract from Report of the Second Meeting of the Coronation Executive Sub-Committee' (Scotland, Wales and Northern Ireland); Hardinge to Henderson, 19 April 1937, RA PS/GVI/PS/01000/075/A/01, 17/COR.

a more elaborate occasion agreed.[129] Only in attempting to have the region's title 'Northern Ireland' changed to 'Ulster' in conjunction with the visit – giving the impression of royal support – did Craigavon fail.[130]

At one level the visit succeeded brilliantly, evoking happy memories of the 1924 occasion as the experience was repeated.[131] Certainly the carefully constructed and prepared route of the Belfast visit – confined to Unionist areas – allowed a relationship approaching immediacy of identity to be established between the monarch and his Unionist subjects: Catholic prelates and clergy had declined all invitations to events associated with the visit,[132] as had nationalists. But the occasion could not be divorced from its wider political and constitutional context. The IRA made it the setting for an organised operation of attacks on border posts and internal telephone lines in Northern Ireland, together with explosions in Belfast. And while Conservative prints in Britain such as the *Daily Mail* and *The Times* could be relied upon to give a favourably Unionist interpretation of the occasion,[133] even these, and many more, focused attention on the IRA activities and the apparent threat to the lives of the King and Queen.[134]

The regime's hopes that a public sphere framed by monarchy in which the north's British identity would have been unproblematically confirmed were frustrated. Rather, the King's presence established a media arena in which Northern Ireland's problematic and conflictual exceptionalism was crystallised, with British – and Empire and foreign[135] – fears for the

---

[129] Henderson to Hardinge, 22 April 1937; Vice-Admiral Dudley North to Hardinge, 8 May 1937, RA PS/GVI/PS 01000/075/A/19, 30/COR.

[130] See Memo. by Sir S. Scott, 9 July 1937; Note by Sir A. Maxwell, 13 July 1937; Note by 'H.F.B', 14 July 1937; Memo. by 'J.M.L.', 15 July 1937; Minutes to File by R.R.J., 18 July 1937, NA, HO45/202/2.

[131] *LS*, 29 July 1937; Viscount Templewood, *Nine Troubled Years* (London, 1954), p. 252. The telegram (28 July 1930), originally drafted by Hardinge, had referred to 'the' people of the region and was later changed to 'our' by the King: RA PS/GVI/PS 01000/075/A/84/COR.

[132] See Oscar Henderson to Sir Harry Boyd, Private Secretary to Northern Ireland Government, 15 July 1937, HO45/20567/698952.

[133] *Daily Mail [DM]*, 29 July 1937; *TT*, 29 July 1937.

[134] See 'Land Mine near Royal Route', *DE*, 27 July 1937; *II*, 29 July 1937; *News Chronicle*, 29 July 1937; *Birmingham Post*, 29 July 1937; *Liverpool Post*, 29 July 1937; *Daily Sketch*, 29 July 1937; *Daily Mirror*, 29 July, 4, 19 Aug. 1937; *Morning Post*, 29, 30 July, 24 Aug., 7, 19 Oct. 1937; *DM*, 29 July, 4 Aug. 1937; *Glasgow Herald*, 29 July 1937; *Star*, 29 July 1937; *Western Morning News*, 30 July 1937; *Daily Herald*, 30, 31 July 1937; *DE*, 30 July 1937; *Manchester Dispatch*, 30 July 1937; *Manchester Guardian*, 30 July 1937; *Yorkshire Post*, 4 Aug. 1937; *Irish Times*, 5, 12 Aug. 1937; *II*, 12, 19 Aug. 1937; *NW*, 19 Aug. 1937; *Daily Telegraph*, 19 Aug. 1937; *TT*, 24 Aug. 1937.

[135] See, for example, Suffragan Bishop of Los Angeles, Letter, Foreign Office, 14 Aug. 1937; Bhupiuderasingh, Maharaja of Patiala to 'His Imperial Majesty', Telegram, 3 Aug. 1937, RA PS/GVI/PS 01000/075/D/21, 22/COR.

safety of the royal couple indicating clearly that many regarded Northern Ireland as foreign territory. The response of Unionist politicians and press in over-reacting to 'lying and scandalous statements reflecting on the good name of Belfast' in Britain[136] merely emphasised the point. The Governor's Private Secretary, Henderson, and the King's, Hardinge, might agree that the press exaggerated the dangers of the visit,[137] but the damage was done.

Under optimum circumstances Unionist hopes of registering with British public opinion as an unproblematic region of the United Kingdom was hampered by the fact that, unlike Northern Ireland, national consciousness in Britain did not exist as a fixed element of the popular mindset, but usually required a major occasion like an imperial exhibition or a war to bring it clearly into focus. The vertical nature of allegiance to the monarch brought not a state-wide consciousness into focus but merely that of the community the King was visiting. Only if something of national concern occurred, such as the monarch's life being in danger, was a regional royal consciousness likely to take on state-wide dimensions. This is what occurred in 1937, and to Unionist detriment. Thus the real victory in 1937 was achieved by the IRA: their activities did nothing to end partition, but they did impress on British opinion that Northern Ireland could never be regarded as unproblematically British – a point reinforced in 1939 when an IRA declaration of hostilities against Britain caused a cancellation of a visit to the north by the Duke of Kent.[138]

And yet, having done much to condition the anti-royal atmosphere in which IRA activities took place, de Valera seemed to make a sham of the constitutional revisionism of previous years by participation in the Empire Exhibition of 1938 at Glasgow.[139] In fact the conditions for participation were favourable. The mutually damaging economic war had been in the process of resolution since mid-1937, especially as

---

[136] See *Yorkshire Post*, 4 Aug. 1937; *Daily Mirror*, 4 Aug. 1937; *Liverpool Post*, 14 Aug. 1937.

[137] Henderson to Hardinge, 3 Aug. 1937; Hardinge to Henderson, 9 Aug. 1937, RA PS/ GVI/PS 01000/075/A/94, 95/COR.

[138] Abercorn to Captain Lord Sidney Herbert, Equerry to the Duke of Kent, 8 Nov. 1938; J. A. Lowther to Abercorn, 16 Jan. 1939; Henderson to Lowther, 4 Feb. 1939; Abercorn to 'My Dear Sidney', 13 March 1939; Henderson to Lowther, 1 April 1939, RA GDKH/ENGT/10.

[139] See, for example, Donnach O'Brien to de Valera, 17 Feb. 1938, Registered Files, DI, NAI, AOIS/S10075. Moreover, de Valera had little difficulty in describing Eire as a constituent part of the empire when appealing, unsuccessfully, for a reprieve of the death sentences passed on two IRA men in 1940 as a result of the Coventry bombings in 1939: A. H. L. Harding to A. N. Rucker, 10 Downing Street, 6 Feb. 1940, conveying message from de Valera, RA PS/GVI/C 124/1–2.

London came to appreciate that de Valera's constitutional changes made little difference to Ireland's Commonwealth relations.[140] The exhibition, which had a hearty endorsement from the former Irish Vicereine, Lady Aberdeen,[141] allowed Eire to demonstrate its identity in an economically advantageous context, while the Irish Pavilion – with its 'Ireland' heading[142] – illustrated Eire's constitutional claim to represent the whole island of Ireland. Moroever, involvement in the exhibition could be construed as a monarchical and imperial bridge to Ulster Unionists, and eventual Irish unity.

Certainly from a London perspective Northern Ireland was regarded as expendable, though Irish unity, as considered by the Home Office at this time, was viewed only in the outdated and unrealistic terms of a restored Irish Viceroyalty.[143] Nevertheless, by the end of the Anglo-Irish economic war in 1938 Neville Chamberlain was convinced that a united Ireland would have to come, and sought to negotiate a settlement with de Valera, provoking the Stormont regime to a fury of opposition.[144] Nor, despite the congenial nature of the royal visits of 1924 and 1937, should an *identity* of outlook between the King and his Unionist subjects be assumed. George VI seems to have been personally equidistant in his attitude to the Irish people in general, congratulating Chamberlain on the successful conclusion of the Anglo-Irish negotiations, and looked forward to meeting de Valera, a former armed rebel against the crown.[145] He also responded warmly to de Valera's request for a reprieve of condemned IRA men in 1940, which the Government refused.[146] The outbreak of the Second World War, however, was to transform Westminster's relationship with the north.

---

[140] Deirdre McMahon, 'Economic War' in Connolly (ed.), *Oxford Companion to Irish History*, pp. 176–7.

[141] Ishbel Aberdeen and Temair, 'The Lesson of the Exhibition' in *Empire Exhibition: Scotland 1938* (Glasgow, 1938).

[142] Ibid.

[143] Martin Jones, 'Notes on de Valera on the Irish Question', 14 Jan. 1938, Governor's papers, PRONI/Gov 3/1/41. The historical content, especially the idea that Grattan's Parliament (1782–1800) had the same powers as Eire, was seriously flawed.

[144] See Loughlin, *Ulster Unionism and British National Identity*, pp. 94–5; Canning, *British Policy towards Ireland*, ch. 11; John Bowman, *De Valera and the Ulster Problem, 1917–1973* (Oxford, 1983).

[145] Wheeler-Bennett, *King George VI*, pp. 212–13.

[146] A. H. L. Hardinge to A. N. Rucker, 10 Downing Street, 6 Feb. 1940; Hardinge, Memo. on Meeting with Mr Dulanty, 6 Feb. 1940; Hardinge to the High Commissioner for Eire, 6 Feb. 1940, RA PS/GVI/124/1, 2, 3; Canning, *British Policy towards Ireland*, pp. 258–9.

VIII

In a context where Eire under de Valera remained neutral, Craigavon firmly pledged Northern Ireland's commitment to the British war effort with a broadcast to the people of Britain: Ulstermen were 'King's men, and we shall be with you to the end'.[147] It would be a commitment rewarded with over twenty years of resolute Westminster support for the northern regime, both as a reward for wartime allegiance and because the Cold War followed quickly thereafter, lending Northern Ireland a strategic importance hitherto absent.

The war brought into play all the factors likely to enhance the region's integration with Britain. Through a 'total' war fusing the sphere of everyday life and politics, a public realm was created in which the experiences of Northern Ireland could be regarded as representative of those in Britain to a large degree, if not completely. Moreover, the censorship of the press in wartime – it forbade mention of twenty-five things, among which was any mention of IRA activities[148] – functioned to create an impression of a region fully integrated into the war effort. *The Times* exhulted: 'On every front Northern Ireland is playing a full and worthy part in the struggle against Hitlerism.'[149] Accordingly, Northern Ireland shared a common experience with the British population in a period when national consciousness would reach levels not seen since 1918. Indeed Eire's neutrality even gave rise for a time to traditional British anti-Celticism and anti-Catholicism. It was, accordingly, an ideal circumstance in which the presence of monarchy in Northern Ireland might have a representative British function lacking in the inter-war period. Thus the cancelled visit by the Duke of Kent in 1939 took place in October 1940, in arguably more dangerous circumstances, during which, on the Londonderry leg, he found the citizens framing the Blitz experience of the 'mother' city in the context of the siege of 1689 and with plans to close Derry's gates again against the Nazi successors of the Jacobites, should they arrive.[150] Northern Ireland in general, and especially Londonderry, 'was not just a willing armourer, but a bastion in the battle of the Atlantic'.[151] And yet, the geographic position of Northern Ireland entailed certain realities that could not be ignored.

[147] See frontispiece to Ervine, *Craigavon*.   [148] Ibid.
[149] 'Ulster in Wartime', *TT*, 6 April 1940; Loughlin, *Ulster Unionism and British National Identity*, pp. 120–1.
[150] See *LS*, 26, 31 Oct. 1940. On the visit's supposed beneficial effects, see Abercorn to the King, 25 Oct. 1940, RA PS/GVI/PS 04129/36/NAVY.
[151] Robert Fisk, *In Time of War: Ireland, Ulster and the Price of Neutrality 1939–45* (London, 1975), p. 281.

Thus despite the urging of the regime to have British conscription extended to Northern Ireland, the determined opposition of northern Catholics, their clergy, and, not least, de Valera, deterred Westminster from doing so.[152] Moreover, as much as the war brought a unifying experience of Northern Ireland with Great Britain for Unionists, the area of engagement was most effective in the military sphere, the Government and monarchy; communities in Britain had a tendency to localise their war experience with the result that Northern Ireland's involvement was only imperfectly reciprocated at a popular level. This could be brought home, discomfortingly, as the Post Office and individual members of the armed forces persisted in viewing Northern Ireland as part of Eire. Moreover, Belfast's limited Blitz experience in 1941 necessitated an appeal to Dublin for assistance pointing up no less the inescapable exceptionalism of the north's position.[153] But perhaps most significant, given its monarchical import, was the negative result of Unionist attempts in this period to take possession of the Order of St Patrick.

The context could hardly have been more congenial, and Northern Ireland had finally received a form of heraldic recognition, when, on the death of the last Ulster King of Arms, Nevile Wilkinson, at the outbreak of war, 'the special relationship with Northern Ireland' was acknowledged by amending the office of Norry King of Arms to Norry and Ulster King of Arms.[154] Sir Basil Brooke, Northern Ireland Premier from 1943, made an apparently strong case for the conferring of the Order on generals Montgomery and Alexander, both of whom had northern Irish origins. But despite Churchill's initial support, concerns about punitive action in the south against Irish citizens awarded the honour, together with reluctance to antagonise de Valera unnecessarily, determined postponement of action.[155] Moreover, while a visit of the King and Queen to the north in 1942 was outwardly a harmonious demonstration of loyal allegiance and its acknowledgement,[156] it disguised tensions

[152] Canning, *British Policy towards Ireland*, pp. 233–8, 307–10.

[153] Loughlin, *Ulster Unionism and British National Identity*, pp. 127–32.

[154] Correspondence of J. J. Garner, Sir Alexander Hardinge and the Duke of Norfolk, 17 Dec. 1941–17 March 1943, RA PS/GVI/PS 05680/116, 117, 121, 122, 123/HON.

[155] J. J. Martin, 10 Downing St, to Hardinge, 17 May 1942; Minute by Attlee to Churchill, 25 May 1943; Committee on Grants of Honours, Decorations and Medals in Time of War, 1939–43: Provisional outline of Draft Report on the Order of St Patrick; Churchill, 19 July 1943, RA PS/GVI/PS 05680/02, 012, 014, 015/HON.

[156] *LS*, 27 June 1942. Correspondence of Churchill, Sir Alexander Hardinge, Oscar Henderson, Abercorn and Francis Williams, 22 Jan.–30 June 1942, RA PS/GVI/PS 05944/02, 17, 26, 27, 49/WARVIS. See also Home Intelligence, Weekly Report no. 91 in Paul Addison (ed.), *Home Intelligence [microfilm] Reports on Opinion and Morale 1940–1944* (Brighton, 1979), Reel, 2, p. 462.

between London and Belfast over Northern Ireland's contribution to the war effort.[157] These dissipated as the war turned decisively against the axis powers; and, arguably, Northern Ireland was subjectively the most loyal region of the United Kingdom.

Mass Observation reported a growing popular identity in Britain with Churchill as a national leader at the expense of privileged royals.[158] British opinion might appreciate George VI's attempts to share their experiences, especially when Buckingham Palace was bombed,[159] but wartime conditions served to identify Churchill as a figure of central authority usurping to a significant degree the usual role of the monarch in embodying the nation. This experience, however, did not extend to Northern Ireland, where there was, it seems, no popular diminishing in the monarch's national status. To a large extent this was due to the way in which Unionist myth framed both men. The Unionist experience of the King had been highly congenial from his first Ulster visit in 1924; Churchill, however, had been a Liberal minister supporting Home Rule in the pre-1914 period and had had the temerity to preach the 'separatist' message in Belfast. Moreover, while Belfast was severely bombed in 1941 the duration of this was brief, so the development of popular indifference to, or resentment of, privileged royals had much less opportunity to develop. The only local complication that royal visits to Northern Ireland in wartime gave rise to was some embarrassment to Catholics who had joined the local Civil Defence service.[160] As the war turned decisively in the allies' favour from 1943, with the tensions of the early years diminishing, the royal connection with Northern Ireland became consolidated.

There was a special dimension to this. The war years had been a formative experience for the young Princess Elizabeth, and against a socialising background in which she apparently, as Ben Pimlott suggests, imbibed the values of her parents uncomplicatedly,[161] their congenial experience of Northern Ireland was also likely to have been transmitted. Certainly she could hardly have been unaware of Northern Ireland's commitment to the war effort as against Eirean neutrality. In this context, it is worth noting that she personally took the initiative in making known

[157] Fisk, *In Time of War*, p. 455; P. Taylor, *Atlantic Bridgehead* [BBC documentary] (Belfast, 1991).
[158] Philip Ziegler, *Crown and People* (London, 1978), pp. 72–3; Tom Harrison, *Living through the Blitz* (Harmondsworth, 1990), p. 162.
[159] Wheeler-Bennett, *King George VI*, pp. 469–70.
[160] J. A. Oliver, *Working at Stormont* (Dublin, 1978), p. 68.
[161] Ben Pimlott, *The Queen: A Biography of Elizabeth II* (London, 1997), pp. 82–3.

to the Stormont authorities her wish to make a visit in 1945.[162] The King was glad to comply with the request,[163] while Brooke succeeded in having the occasion extended from the intended one day to three days, including an extensive tour of the six counties with the King honouring 'distinguished' people.[164] British goodwill was undoubtedly fuelled by de Valera offering his condolences to the German ambassador in Dublin on the death of Adolph Hitler in May 1945.[165]

That act, and de Valera's declaration that Eire was practically a republic,[166] emphasised the extent to which the war had functioned to create an imaginative British national arena that now unproblematically included Northern Ireland – at least among the British court and political class. The unity of court and people in Northern Ireland was emphasised when the King addressed both houses of Stormont on 18 July 1945, acknowledging the north's contribution to the war effort, and enthusiastically mingling with dignitaries and population thereafter.[167] More generally, the north's constitutional security registered in the four-day return trip made by Princess Elizabeth in 1946,[168] and visits in 1949 and 1950, the last in the company of the Queen and Princess Margaret,[169] who had also made her own visit to the province in 1947.[170] But what stands out in the five royal visits made to Northern Ireland in the period 1945–50 is the leading role and frequency of visits undertaken by the future Queen.

Ben Pimlott has noted disapprovingly how, during the 1946 visit, the Princess was used 'as a blatant political tool by one [Unionist] political faction . . . on some occasions crudely and disagreeably partisan'.[171] This was undoubtedly the case. As we have seen, it was something that had a long history. But the tone of Pimlott's comments reflects the history of the troubles since 1969, and may be misleading. Elizabeth was an intelligent young woman and someone whose own Protestant faith in the context of the war experience would have disposed her to sympathise with the local

---

[162] See Minute to File on the Royal Visit to Northern Ireland by 'R.H.', 12 March 1945, NA (Kew), PRO 45/20434/529400/1. The increasingly pro-Unionist Home Secretary, Herbert Morrison, was also supportive: Abercorn to Dear Home Secretary, 23 May 1945; Morrison to Abercorn, 25 May 1945, NA, HO45/698952.

[163] Alan Lascelles to Donald Somervill, Home Secretary, 15 June 1945; R. J. P. Hewison to Oscar Henderson, 18 June 1945, ibid.

[164] Brooke to Abercorn, 22 June 1945, ibid.

[165] Brian Kennedy, *The Widening Gulf: Northern Attitudes to the Independent Irish State 1919–49* (Belfast, 1988), pp. 234–5.

[166] See 'Royal Visit to Ulster', 'Eire and the Crown' in *TT*, 19 July 1945, p. 4.

[167] *TT*, 20, 21 July 1945.   [168] *TT*, 19–22 March 1946.

[169] *Ulster Year Book, 1953* (Belfast, 1953), p. xvi.

[170] See Lord Granville, Governor of Northern Ireland, to the King, 17 Oct. 1947, RA GVI/ PRIV/G/06.

[171] Pimlott, *The Queen*, pp. 83–4.

Protestant and Unionist outlook, especially so as nationalists in the north held aloof from royal occasions as a protest against partition. They were about to engage in an anti-partition campaign, which, together with Labour support at Westminster, stimulated activity in Eire.[172] In this context, the underbelly of loyalist bigotry might not have been as obvious, or as offensive, as it would be from the mid-1960s, when its paramilitary re-emegence was marked by the murder of a Roman Catholic. Certainly there is no reason to think she found the propaganda uses made of the visit by the Stormont regime in any way objectionable. Indeed, on the most significant visit made by the future Queen to Northern Ireland in this period – in May 1949 – she explicitly aligned the monarchy with the regime. The visit, made despite reservations about its appropriateness at a delicate time in Anglo-Irish relations,[173] took its significance from developments taking place in the south breaking Eire's remaining connection with the crown.

IX

The climate of anti-partitionism in nationalist Ireland rose significantly from 1945, beginning in the north and extending to the south with the accession of a coalition Government in 1948 that included a radical republican grouping with IRA connections, Clann na Poblachta. It expanded when de Valera, now in opposition, embarked on a world tour to promote Irish unity.[174] It found expression in a variety of ways; for instance, in a revival by the de Valera organ, *Irish Press*, of public interest in the theft of the Irish Crown Jewels in 1907 and their fate,[175] an issue reviving memories of the old discredited Dublin Castle regime and framing royalty in that context. Much more importantly, it found a focus, symbolically and practically, in the issue of the highly contentious statue of Queen Victoria on Leinster Lawn – calls for the removal of which having been made intermittently since 1922 – ostensibly to make way for a car park. Lord Rugby, the United Kingdom representative in Eire, largely accepted the merits of the argument, but 'no doubt they are quite glad to find an excuse for moving the statue'.[176] Its removal (Fig. 22), on Rugby's advice, occasioned no public British comment, in

---

[172] Kennedy, *The Widening Gulf*, p. 237.
[173] L. A. Nickolls, *Royal Cavalcade: A Diary of the Royal Year* (London, 1949), p. 66.
[174] Kennedy, *The Widening Gulf*, pp. 237–8.   [175] *Irish Press*, 8, 9, 11, 16 Oct. 1948.
[176] Rugby to Sir E. Machtig, 10 July 1948, Political and Constitutional Relations: Removal of Queen Victoria's Statue from Leinster House, NA (Kew), DO35/3957.

22 Victoria deposed.

case the Irish used it as an excuse to raise other issues, and to avoid giving the impression that Britain was cooperating in the matter: 'the Eire authorities should have sole responsibilities for their actions' and events should be allowed to take their course,[177] an argument the King agreed with.[178]

The statue, noted the *Irish Times*, cost £16,000 to execute in 1908 and £300 to take down and remove.[179] Its political and constitutional

---

[177] Machtig to A. Lascelles, 21 July 1948, ibid.
[178] Lascelles to Machtig, 27 July 1948, ibid.
[179] *IT*, 2 Aug. 1949. It remained in the obscurity of a Dublin Corporation yard until the mid-1980s, when it was presented to the city of Sydney: Whelan, *Reinventing Dublin*, pp. 200–1.

significance in 1948 was a reflection of the mindset that would occasion Ireland's departure from the Commonwealth in April 1949. The act to effect this had its first and second readings in the Dáil on 17 and 24 November 1948. With the act an inevitability, the crown and the British Government had to decide what their attitude should be. In this context the monarchy would have an important place.

The difficulty was to respond to the creation of the new republic in such a way that acknowledged its legitimacy while allowing existing Anglo-Irish relations to be pursued with as little disturbance as possible. Prime Minister Attlee was concerned that the insistence of the Irish Government in choosing Easter Monday, 18 April 1949, for the bill to take effect – the anniversary of the Easter Rising and with the ceremonies to include the hoisting of the Irish flag on the General Post Office – could mean that a message from the King to the President of the Irish Republic could make it difficult to defend the view that 'Eire is not foreign.' However, he was persuaded by Rugby's argument that, on the contrary, given the ability of the monarch to reach beyond the political sphere – to 'transcend all questions of politics' – and engage the personal realm of everyday life, a carefully constructed message 'will help to destroy the rebel significance of Easter Monday'.[180] Such a message, acknowledging the Irish contribution to victory in 1945, which Rugby found was highly appreciated by the Irish population,[181] would act subtly to undermine the republican nature of the Dublin ceremonies, ceremonies, Rugby added, which were the subject of much inter-party politicking.[182]

The King's message[183] proved to be inspired and was widely appreciated by both politicians and populace, the politicians especially being fulsome in their praise of its generous, conciliatory nature.[184] In fact, it was noted that the ceremonies chiefly involved politicians and the military; apparently the inauguration of a republic and the ceremonies associated with it failed to engage the enthusiastic support of the population in

---

[180] Attlee to Lascelles, 13 April 1949, RA PS/GVI/C 312/23. Rugby, Draft and recommendations for King's message to President of Irish Republic, RA PS/GVI/C 312/24.
[181] Ibid.
[182] Rugby to Lascelles, 18 April 1949, RA PS/GVI/C 312/36. The Northern Prime Minister, Basil Brooke, was allowed to scan the message before it was sent, and claimed to have considered sending his own message of congratulation: Lascelles, Note to draft of King's message to the Irish President, 15 April 1949 RA PS/GVI/C 312/30B.
[183] 'Eire a Republic from Today', *TT*, 18 April 1949.
[184] Sir Gilbert Laithwaite, UK Representative in Dublin, to Lascelles, 18 April 1949; Laithwaite to Leisching, 19 April 1949, RA PS/GVI/C 312/37, 44. For a more cool account of Eire's departure from the Commonwealth as described by a best-selling popular magazine, see 'Why Eire Wants To Leave Us', *Picture Post*, 27 Nov. 1948, 7–9.

general.[185] Rugby remarked that the King's message managed to delight southern Irish political and popular opinion while at the same time having 'sharply differentiated the Republic of Ireland from his Kingdom in Northern Ireland. This is a "milestone".'[186]

Certainly, against a background of some republican criticism in Eire,[187] the visit of Princess Elizabeth to Belfast just a few weeks later to receive the freedom of the city, and where in a heartfelt speech she affirmed the constitutional and *national* membership of the Unionist community in the British nation ('English, Scottish, Irish and Welsh – so different in origin and so well blended on the whole'[188]), was of great significance. It was a speech which mirrored the national identity of Unionist imagining, validated enthusiastically by the heir to the throne. A royal reporter recorded the speech as 'one of the most outstanding I have heard the Princess make'.[189] It would receive constitutional objectification in 1949 in the Ireland Act, which specified that in no event would any part of Northern Ireland cease to have membership of the United Kingdom without the consent of its Parliament.[190] And a monarchical readiness to endorse the Britishness of Northern Ireland was evident in other respects, such as awarding the prefix 'Royal' to northern societies where possible for the purpose of 'strengthening the link with the Crown and rewarding local patriotism'.[191] These were telling auguries for the monarchy's relationship with Ireland when Princess Elizabeth assumed the throne as Elizabeth II in 1952.

---

[185] 'Christening the Republic', *Round Table*, 39 (Dec. 1948–Sept. 1949), 219–20.
[186] Rugby to Lascelles, 26 April 1949, RA PS/GVI/C 312/57.   [187] *Irish Press*, 4 May 1949.
[188] Princess Elizabeth cited in Nickolls, *Royal Cavalcade*, pp. 66–7.   [189] Ibid.
[190] James Loughlin, *The Ulster Question since 1945* (2nd edn, Basingstoke, 2004), pp. 28–9.
[191] 'J.M.', Minute sheet to File on application for Royal prefix to name of Ulster Academy of Arts, 8 Sept. 1950, NA (Kew), HO45/25275/929354/2.

15   Ireland and the new Elizabethan age

The relationship between the monarchy and Ireland during the present Queen's reign has undergone a fundamental transformation, one that, to a significant extent, has duplicated that which obtained in the early decades of the Union. In that period the British state reacted to a period of external threat by offering solid and uncritical support to the loyalist interest in Ireland, only to be forced, under the pressure of political events, to adopt a position approaching equidistance between Irish political factions. A similar development has occurred since the 1950s, but unlike the nineteenth century, in a context where the long history of Anglo-Irish conflict may be coming to a close.

I

It would hardly be an exaggeration to say that the accession of Elizabeth II established a new British zeitgeist. The function of monarchy in encapsulating and embodying the nation's history made the era of the first Elizabeth an obvious conceptual reference point for the accession of the second. Similarities of national context seemed clear in regard to national bankruptcy, external wars and threats, but also a great 'revolution in ideas'.[1] The ascent of Everest almost at the moment of the Queen's coronation seemed a powerful augury for the new reign[2] at a time when 'the Crown was a truly sacred object, to be placed by a priest with ritual and infinite reverence upon the anointed head ... Just for a moment, on that day in June, the whole nation ... felt itself involved in a moment of epiphany.'[3]

That sense of participation extended perhaps more to the Ulster Unionist community than to the rest of the Kingdom. The historical reference period for the new reign was close to that of the Ulster

[1] Violet Markham, 'The New Elizabethan Age', *The Listener*, 28 May 1953, 863–4.
[2] *The Times* [*TT*], 2 June 1953.
[3] Jan Morris, 'On Top of the World', *The Times Magazine*, 15 May 1993, 9–11.

plantation and the latter could be imaginatively integrated into the new Elizabethan zeitgeist.[4] A bell which had been rung in St Patrick's Cathedral, Dublin, to inaugurate the reign of the first Elizabeth was brought to Belfast to ring in that of the second.[5] The coronation supplement of the *Belfast News-Letter*, for its part, carried an article on the anti-Catholic dimension of the first Elizabeth's coronation together with a history of the north's royal connections.[6] The war experience, the Ireland Act of 1949, and changes in the Queen's title explicitly specifying 'Northern Ireland' as part of her realm, were immensely reassuring; as also were southern anti-royalist protests, official and paramilitary.[7] Moreover, the effects of war in Britain had stimulated a nationwide revival of Protestant belief and practice, reinforcing the symbolic/emblematic function of monarchy as the embodiment of a Protestant nation,[8] and reflected in the monarch's own strong religious beliefs. In 1953 Ulster Unionist membership of the British nation was framed within a Protestant perspective that resonated politically – as it did historically – strongly across the state; and nowhere more so than in the coronation ceremony itself. The Duke of Norfolk, Earl Marshal and chief ceremonial organiser, could be seen as indicative of the extent to which the Catholic community of the state was represented,[9] but the degree of Ulster Protestant involvement was much more extensive, reflecting very much the personal preferences of the Queen. As John Grigg remarked, in all matters not covered by ministerial responsibility she has freedom of action.[10] On her accession to the throne in 1952 one of her first acts was to ennoble Sir Basil Brooke as Viscount Brookeborough. At the coronation, the generals who personally embodied Northern Ireland's contribution to the British war effort – Field Marshal Lord

[4] See R. N. Wilson, *Northern Ireland Parliamentary Debates* [*NIPD*], 36 (21 Feb. 1952), col. 87; William Le Hardy, *The Coronation Book: The History and Meaning of the Ceremonies at the Crowning of Her Majesty Queen Elizabeth II* (London, 1953), distributed to Northern Ireland schoolchildren; D. H. Christie, coronation letter to County Londonderry pupils, author's possession.

[5] Lisburn Camera Club, *A Royal Occasion: The Story of How the People of Ulster Celebrated Coronation Day 2 June 1953 and Later Welcomed Their New Queen* (Reconstructed, Belfast, BBC Northern Ireland, 1991).

[6] 'When Elizabeth Was Crowned: London Pageants Were Warning on Religion', 'Ulster's Part in Coronation', 'The Queen's Visits to Northern Ireland', 'Ulster's Royal Occasions', *Belfast News-Letter: Coronation Supplement*, 1 June 1953.

[7] Sean McBride, Eamon de Valera, *Dáil Debates*, 138 (21 May 1953), cols. 2205–6; 'Rights in Eire', *Londonderry Sentinel* [*LS*], 6 June 1953.

[8] Richard Weight, *Patriots: National Identity in Britain 1940–2000* (London, 2002), pp. 221–6.

[9] John Hall, 'Planning History', *Daily Mail: Coronation Souvenir* (London, 1953).

[10] John Grigg, 'The Making of a Monarch', *Spectator*, 5 Feb. 1977.

Alanbrooke, Viscount Montgomery of Alamein and Earl Alexander of Tunis – performed central coronation functions. Alanbrooke would command the 30,000 troops taking part in the procession and lining the route, and would also be a member of the Grand Procession in Westminster Abbey in his capacity of Lord High Constable of England. Viscount Montgomery would carry the Royal Standard, while Earl Alexander would bear the 'Orb, the Golden Globe surrounded by a cross, which is the symbol of the sovereignty of Christ'.[11] Lady Moyra, daughter of the Duke of Hamilton, would be one of the Queen's six Maids of Honour while Lord Brookeborough would attend and participate in the coronation procession in the first coach of the section carrying Prime Ministers[12] – something Sir Laurence Olivier would mention in his narration of a richly technicoloured cinematic production of the event.[13] Also in the Abbey would be the Speakers of the Senate and Commons, and the Lord Mayor and Lady Mayoress of Belfast, together with the late Lord Craigavon's son.[14] Reviewing the complete list, the *Northern Whig* could reasonably claim that 'in proportion to their numbers no section of the Queen's subjects will take a more active part in her crowning than the people of Northern Ireland'.[15] For Northern Ireland's coronation celebrations the Queen donated two swans to the people of deeply loyalist Portadown, which were promptly christened 'Charles and Anne', while the region also had a large number of recipients of the Queen's Coronation Medal.[16] British press reports of the region's coronation celebrations that ignored IRA bombs, nationalist and southern protests, and inter-community disputes about the celebrations,[17] reinforced the impression of British national membership. The celebrations at Dunmurray, on the outskirts of Belfast, were generalised as 'typical of all Northern Ireland'.[18] National integration, moreover, was made meaningful for the nation in a way not hitherto possible by the spread of television ownership, the popularity of which was growing in Northern Ireland as it was in Britain, and which the coronation created an

[11] *Northern Whig: Coronation Souvenir Edition*, 1 June 1953.

[12] King George's Jubilee Trust, *The Coronation of Her Majesty Queen Elizabeth II: Approved Souvenir Programme* (London, 1953), p. 18.

[13] General Film Distributors, *A Queen Is Crowned* (London, 1953), broadcast Channel 5, 2002.

[14] *Northern Whig: Coronation Souvenir Edition*, n.d.   [15] Ibid.

[16] See for instance, 'Queen's Coronation Medal: More North-West Recipients', *LS*, 9 June 1953.

[17] Ed Moloney and Andy Pollack, *Paisley* (Dublin, 1986), pp. 63–4; also, *TT*, 3 June 1953.

[18] *Time and Tide*, 6 June 1953. 'Covert Enthusiasm in Dublin: Informal Celebrations', *TT*, 3 June 1953.

enormous demand for.[19] The myth of Northern Ireland's royal integration persisted. It found expression in the only British feature film of the 1950s that took the region for its subject. Focusing on the coronation period, *Jacqueline* was a Unionist human interest story located in a Northern Ireland devoid of its nationalist community and political difficulties.[20] Furthermore, for Ulster Unionists British identity was devoid of the sense of diminishment attendant upon the gradual loss of empire taking place in this period.[21] The coronation symbolised membership of a great power. It was in this context that the Queen was received in Northern Ireland on the Ulster leg of her coronation tour of the United Kingdom, just a month after her crowning, and with the nationally unifying symbolism of the visit greatly facilitated by anti-partitionist boycotting.[22]

The visit entailed the usual round of welfarist and offical engagements common to royal visits in general, together with a high-profile visit to Stormont. Occasion was taken to emphasise the legitimacy of the Queen's rule in the north by a royal genealogy detailing her putative descent from the ancient Irish and Scottish Kings of Dalriada.[23] The unity of monarch and her Unionist subjects was perfectly caught in a photograph of Orange Lambeg drummers at Hillsborough Castle about to perform for the royal party (Fig. 23). And yet, the very success of the coronation celebrations was to be deceptively reassuring for both the royal party and the Unionist community.

While the coronation was an event which helped to define, not just royalty, but 'the British identity for the next generation',[24] it facilitated royal complacency about the need for adaptation to changing times, with the result that the monarchy missed an ideal opportunity to adjust to the modern age on its own terms, and instead had to be coerced to do so.[25] For Ulster Unionists, this was also the case, but with far more serious consequences. Ultimately the centrality of the monarchy to the British constitution ensured that the institution would adapt and survive. Ulster Unionism was in a much more problematic position. The coronation and the subsequent royal visit were seen to sanction and validate not just its

---

[19] 'Early Start to Ulster Gaiety', *TT*, 3 June 1953; 'A Dedicated Nation', *LS*, 9 June 1953.

[20] Rank Film Productions, *Jacqueline*, directed by Roy Baker (London, 1956).

[21] See for instance the debate on the significance of the Queen's Commonwealth tour of 1954 at Stormont, *NIPD*, 38 (13 May 1954), cols. 2042–50.

[22] 'Anti-Partitionists Issue a "Proclamation"', *LS*, 2 July 1953.

[23] Lisburn Camera Club, *A Royal Occasion*.

[24] Ben Pimlott, *The Queen: A Biography of Elizabeth II* (London, 1998), p. 217.

[25] Ibid. pp. 215–17.

23 An Orange greeting for Elizabeth II at Hillsborough.

British national identity but the Unionist *practice of government*, and this would only be changed at the cost of societal destabilisation.

In the decade from the coronation visit to Lord Brookeborough's resignation as Prime Minister of Northern Ireland in March 1963, a further eighteen visits by members of the royal family would take place to reassure Ulster Unionists about their status as British nationals.[26] Nationalists and republicans played a part in reinforcing Northern Ireland's constitutional security; the former through anti-partitionism and the latter, more significantly, through an ineffectual military campaign which failed to attract nationalist support within Northern Ireland,

---

[26] James Loughlin, *Ulster Unionism and British National Identity since 1885* (London, 1995), pp. 167–71.

serving merely to reinforce Westminster support for the regime, with leading Government figures such as Rab Butler and Prime Minister Harold Macmillan visiting the north to emphasise it.[27] The mass circulation *Picture Post* pithily expressed the Government position in its account of the IRA campaign: 'Assassins on Britain's Border'.[28] Ironically, the sense that the Northern Ireland border was a British border outside which lay foreign territory was facilitated by a continuation of the intermittent policy in the Irish Republic of destroying British monuments, with memorials to Lord Gough and Viceroy Carlisle in the Phoenix Park being blown up in 1955 and 1956.[29] Nevertheless, at the same time as Northern Ireland's constitutional position was being so roundly affirmed, change was taking place the effects of which would have profound consequences for the region.

II

The extension of the welfare state to Northern Ireland had greatly improved social welfare payments and the provision of social services, especially access to free university education. These were highly important factors determining the failure of northern Catholics to support the IRA campaign: socio-economic benefits were now so much better in Northern Ireland than anything the Irish Republic could promise. By 1959 signals were emerging of at least a middle-class Catholic desire to make an accommodation with the state,[30] and clearly an opportunity existed for the Unionist Party to encourage this; Orange influence, however, largely determined it was not pursued. At the same time, with massive sums available at the discretion of local councils for municipal purposes, much of this was misused in the politically vulnerable west of the province to discriminate against Catholics in jobs and housing. Free university education, however, facilitated the emergence of a group of talented Catholics unwilling to accept these conditions and who, significantly, campaigned, not for Irish unity, but 'British rights for British citizens'. When economic mismanagement led to Lord Brookeborough's resignation in 1963 his replacement was Terence

---

[27] Brian Faulkner, *Memoirs of a Statesman* (London, 1978), pp. 23–4. Ibid. pp. 22–3. Brookeborough, *NIPD*, 40 (18 Dec. 1956), col. 3209. *Derry Standard*, 19 Dec. 1958.

[28] *Picture Post*, 31 Dec. 1956, front cover, and pp. 40–3.

[29] Yvonne Whelan, *Reinventing Modern Dublin: Streetscape, Iconography and the Politics of Identity* (Dublin, 2003), p. 207.

[30] Patrick Buckland, *A History of Northern Ireland* (Dublin, 1989), pp. 89, 103; Cornelius O'Leary, 'Northern Ireland 1945–72' in J. J. Lee (ed.), *Ireland 1945–70* (Dublin, 1979), pp. 152–8.

O'Neill, a reformer who spoke a language of non-sectarianism offering hope for the redress of Catholic grievances.[31]

O'Neill had had a record of supporting liberal legislation since his maiden speech in 1946[32] and over the decade of the 1950s had developed a 'mainland' conception of Britishness framed on tolerance and compromise. His reformist ambitions, moreover, went beyond the domestic arena of Northern Ireland. He saw the region as forming one element in a framework of parliaments in the British Isles that would include the Irish Republic,[33] and which by implication would have some form of royal symbolism and identity.

O'Neill's conception of Britishness had been influenced by the coronation and the royal visit to Northern Ireland, during which he had briefly attended the Queen in his capacity as High Sheriff of County Antrim.[34] However, he was not elected to the post of premier; rather, following the model of the Tory party, where the Queen simply chose the most likely candidate, so O'Neill was the personal choice of the Queen's representative, Lord Wakehurst, Governor of Northern Ireland.[35]

He hoped that as his policies took effect the monarchy would play a fundamental part in consolidating the identity of the region. In particular, he had expectations that, as with British politicians pursuing constructive Unionism in the nineteenth century, a royal residence established in Northern Ireland would serve to centralise the monarch as a focus of identity in an integrated community. In fact, he was to claim that this proposal was under 'embryonic discussion' when the civil rights agitation arose and killed the project off.[36] Certainly a recurring concern to connect the region more closely with the monarchy can be detected. Thus when the Governorship of Northern Ireland became vacant in 1964, O'Neill successfully sought a Presbyterian replacement, Lord Erskine (1964–8), as this denomination was the most numerous in Northern Ireland;[37] and in his 'Crossroads' television broadcast to the Northern Irish people in December 1968, O'Neill's attack on extreme loyalists was framed in terms of allegiance to the Queen and constitution.[38] Moreover, whereas O'Neill's reformist scheme in many respects duplicated the constructive unionist policy of the late nineteenth century, it was, arguably, better placed initially to succeed.

---

[31] Ibid. pp. 159–62.
[32] See speech citation in Terence O'Neill, *Autobiography* (London, 1972), pp. 29–31.
[33] Ibid. p. 138; Frank Longford, *The Grain of Wheat* (London, 1974), p. 99.
[34] *LS*, 2 July 1953.   [35] O'Neill, *Autobiography*, pp. 42–3.   [36] Ibid. p. 4.
[37] Ibid. p. 66.   [38] Ibid. p. 147.

When Sean Lemass succeeded de Valera as Taoiseach in 1959 he abandoned anti-partitionism and in 1965 urged northern nationalists to accept their place in Northern Ireland and work to reform it: they were soon identifying with the institution and applauding O'Neill's gestural conciliationism.[39] Overly influenced by domestic media outlets that mirrored his own mentality in its concern to marginalise political fundamentalism,[40] however, O'Neill failed to perceive that the real danger to his project would come from within the Unionist community.

Traditional Unionism soon called forth a champion in Ian Paisley claiming to embody traditionalist values. A product of perceived crisis, Paisley, like Carson, whom he would often invoke the benediction of, was, and indeed is, a figure of central authority, claiming to be the authentic voice of the Unionist community, though more in the tradition of politically demarcated authority that included Gladstone and de Valera. His emergence as a political firebrand pointed up the disjuncture between the developing civic Britishness of the state and liberal Ulster Unionism, and that of local political traditions. This was no less British, but informed by an earlier age's commitment to Protestantism as its defining characteristic,[41] and accorded allegiance to the monarch, not automatically, but to the extent that she demonstrated the upholding of Protestantism that her coronation oath entailed.

Paisley and the growing band of working- and lower-middle-class Protestants attracted by his arguments scented 'treachery' in O'Neill's reformism which they met with aggressive street protests.[42] By 1966, a year of political commemorations in which the Queen would make, in July, her first major visit since 1953, the public arena of Northern Ireland was already characterised by emergent conflict, with a low-level campaign of violence against the Catholic community in the greater Belfast area, and the emergence of a Protestant parliamentary group calling itself the Ulster Volunteer Force and which marked its public presence by the murder of a Catholic barman. In Dublin, early March had seen the most noteworthy assault on a British monument since the attack on the statue of William III in 1927 when Nelson's Column was destroyed, while in

---

[39] James Loughlin, *The Ulster Question since 1945* (2nd edn, Basingstoke, 2004), p. 44.

[40] Cathcart, *Most Contrary Region*, pp. 201–2. See also the discussion of Robin Bryans, *Ulster: A Journey through the Six Counties* in Loughlin, *Ulster Unionism and British National Identity*, p. 177.

[41] See the following articles in Paisley's *Protestant Telegraph* [*PT*], 'Ramsey's Romeward Run' (18 June 1966; 'Protestants Awake: The Fight Is on in England' (30 July 1966); 'Cardinal Heenan: Britain's Mini-Pope' (17 Dec. 1966); 'The Pope's Puppets – Made in Scotland' (8 July 1967); 'Romanising Britain' (14 Oct. 1967).

[42] O'Leary, 'Northern Ireland 1945–72', p. 160.

May an extreme republican list of suggestions for future action focused on subversion in the north, considerably raising Unionist apprehension.[43] In the same month Paisley, as part of his campaign against biblical back-sliding by mainstream Protestant churches, heckled the Queen's representative Lord Erskine and his wife as they left the Presbyterian General Assembly building, occasioning the latter's illness.[44] In the run-up to the Queen's visit Paisley was acquiring a reputation for civil disorder and was rumoured to be planning to make the visit the occasion of a series of protests.

As the visit approached, public debate in Northern Ireland was focusing on the dialectical conflict between Paisley as the figurehead of an indigenous ethnic – and inevitably sectarian – identity, attacking O'Neill and the monarch's representative, Lord Erskine,[45] and that of modern tolerant Britishness represented by O'Neill, who saw those values emblematised in the crown.[46] Conflict between the two versions of Unionism found a focus in a controversy over the naming of a new bridge for Belfast.

As a major landmark in the Belfast cityscape the naming of the bridge was a signifier of identity in a context where indigenous traditions were coming under attack; and for a highly suspicious people who had constructed the meaning of monarchy in terms of those traditions, a belief existed that the Queen's representative was a 'traitor' who had conspired to thwart its naming in honour of Ulster's saviour, Edward Carson. This could be construed as merely the latest in a series of betrayals in which the monarch had been implicated. Paisley had engaged in a series of unsuccessful protests by letter and street demonstration about treacherous concessions to Catholicism – O'Neill had failed to prevent the celebration of the fiftieth anniversary of the 1916 Rising in Northern Ireland, and had invited Lemass, a veteran of the Rising, to Stormont Castle the previous year – and to combat which he began his own newspaper, the *Protestant Telegraph*, in February 1966.

Against this background the issue of the naming of the bridge became a fundamental issue of identity: it was indicative of Paisley's outlook that he was not mollified by the decision to name it in honour of the Queen instead of Carson. This proposal, reluctantly agreed to by Belfast Corporation, had come from Lord Erskine, concerned about a number

[43] *News-Letter* [*NL*; formerly *Belfast News-Letter*], 21 May 1966.

[44] O'Neill, *NIPD*, 15 June 1966, cited in Patrick Marrinan, *Paisley: Man of Wrath* (Tralee, 1973), p. 108; O'Neill, *Autobiography*, p. 80.

[45] Marrinan, *Paisley*, pp. 109–10.

[46] *NL*, 8 June 1966. O'Neill framed condemnation of the Presbyterian Assembly protests in terms of loyalty to the Queen.

of recent Government decisions that had a distinctly anti-Catholic inflection,[47] and anxious to avoid more. Paisley, allegiant more to the memory of 'King' Carson than to the existing monarch, enlisted Carson's son in the campaign to redress the 'insult' to his father's memory, and thereby enhance his own claims as the inheritor of the father's authority.[48] The question was, would he follow the logic of his campaign and make the Queen's visit to Northern Ireland on 4 July[49] the climatic focus of his activities? Initially it seemed that this was his intention, but, forced on to the defensive, Paisley postponed a planned protest at Hillsborough Castle: 'We are not the Queen's enemies. We support the Union Jack.'[50]

Nevertheless, given the clash of political values that characterised the public arena of Northern Ireland, the Queen's visit could not be established on a non-political plane as in 1953. For Unionist modernisers the presence of the monarch would be a validation of O'Neillite reformism, presenting 'a truer picture of the Province for all to see'.[51] But O'Neillite hopes for the visit were already undermined by the bad publicity of previous events. Shortly before the Queen's arrival that usual friend of the regime, *The Times*, which had resoundingly endorsed the regime and all its works in 1953, carried, in its Sunday edition, an indictment of dubious political practices under the title 'John Bull's political slum', exposing religious oppression, ballot-rigging, and job and housing discrimination, and identified Paisleyism as evidence of a deep-seated sectarian problem that ultimately faced Westminster: 'The loyalist cheers for the Queen tomorrow should not be allowed to soften a very hard line on John Bull's political slum.'[52]

In fact, nationalist anger at the discrimination and injustices of Unionist rule impacted dramatically on the royal party when a labourer decided to make a protest by dropping a concrete block from a building under repair on the Queen's limousine as it proceeded along Royal Avenue in Belfast. The perpetrator was quickly apprehended and sentenced to four years in prison,[53] but there could hardly have been a more dramatic illustration of the conflictual nature of the north's political environment.

---

[47] A new city for County Armagh was to be named Craigavon, in honour of an Ulster Unionist leader known for his anti-Catholic opinions; a new university was to be built in Protestant Coleraine instead of mainly Catholic Derry which already had Magee University College on which to build.

[48] For the details see Molony and Pollack, *Paisley*, pp. 128–30.

[49] See 'Royal Visit Still On', *NL*, 13 June 1966.   [50] Ibid.   [51] *NL*, 4 July 1966.

[52] *Sunday Times*, 3 July 1966; also Peter Rose, *How the Troubles Came to Northern Ireland* (Basingstoke, 2000), ch. 2.

[53] *NL*, 5 July 1966; 'Day Queen Got Stoned', *Daily Ireland*, 28 June 2006.

The major features of the visit were the opening of the Queen Elizabeth II bridge and a review of veterans commemorating the fiftieth anniversary of the battle of the Somme at Balmoral showgrounds. Both went off without incident, though Paisley was affronted by the involvement of a Catholic priest in the Balmoral proceedings.[54] However, O'Neillite expectations that the visit could be a mechanism to advance the reform project and discount right-wing fundamentalism were not to be fulfilled. When he personally requested from the Queen a public endorsement of his policies he was politely, but firmly, rebuffed. A reference to improved community relations had been left out of her speech on her arrival and she was impressed by the fact that Paisley had attracted 10,000 people the previous night. Stating that northern Catholics did not like her, she asked: 'What happens if the Protestants also turn against me?' And she remained unmoved by O'Neill's insistence that the constitutional position of Northern Ireland was at stake. Her resistance, O'Neill believed, was an inhibiting effect of the brick-throwing incident.[55] In his memoirs he claimed that one could read support for his position between the lines of the Queen's farewell speech, to the effect that she 'hoped that with the growth of mutual respect and understanding between all people in the Province, Northern Ireland will enjoy a prosperous future'.[56] It is Prince Philip, however, not the Queen, who is described as 'very understanding and anxious that community relations should improve'.[57]

At one level the Queen's position is consistent with an established royal policy of remaining above politics; her grooming for the monarchical office was deeply influenced by courtiers trained in the observation of tradition and ritual, leading to caution and a deep reluctance to do anything 'outside the normal run of things'.[58] And her acknowledgement of the potential strength of Paisleyism suggests she may well have sensed that O'Neill would fail in any event. At any rate, it is unlikely that had she complied with O'Neill's wishes reformism could have surmounted the serious difficulties it faced from traditional Unionism; and by avoiding public support she kept the monarchical office on its proper plane above politics. Nevertheless, and while acknowledging the differences in royal status and personal maturity between the two periods, the Queen's diffidence in 1966 certainly contrasts with her overt and enthusiastic commitment to Ulster Unionism in 1949. As it was, Northern Ireland

[54] Marrinan, *Paisley*, pp. 118–19.
[55] O'Neill's account of conversation with the Queen cited in Marc Mulholland, *Northern Ireland at the Crossroads: Ulster Unionism in the O'Neill Years 1960–9* (Basingstoke, 2000), p. 102.
[56] Queen cited in O'Neill, *Autobiography*, p. 82.   [57] Ibid.
[58] On this aspect of the Queen's character, see Pimlott, *The Queen*, pp. 244–5.

continued its downward path to civil conflict in 1969, a process reflected in the ending of royal visits to the region for nearly ten years, to the accompaniment of Paisleyite protests against royal treachery[59] – the Duke of Edinburgh was accused of having a streak of republicanism.[60] The last royal occasions were entirely private affairs with no public dimension, with the Prince of Wales in November 1969, and Princess Alice of Athlone in June 1970.[61]

III

The chronology of the Northern Ireland troubles in the 1970s is well established: civil conflict in August 1969 which initiated a series of developments that, against a background of state oppression, saw the revival of militant republicanism in the form of the Provisional IRA and the reactive emergence of loyalist paramilitaries, especially the Ulster Defence Association; the splintering into a number of factions of the Ulster Unionist Party; the prorogation of Stormont in 1972 – which also entailed the abolition of the office of Governor – followed by an unsuccessful attempt to establish a power-sharing government for the region, and stern law and order policies thereafter as the Queen's Silver Jubilee approached in August 1977.[62] What is significant for our purposes, however, is the effects of socio-political upheaval on the region's relationship with the monarchy.

The splintering of the monolithic Ulster Unionist Party resulted in a number of political formations. To a considerable extent the O'Neillite faction of the party left to help form the non-sectarian and cross-community Alliance Party; the bulk of the party remained committed to the restoration of one-party Unionist rule after prorogation, while the neo-Fascist Vanguard movement, a political faction with paramilitary links, threatened a sectarian war against the Catholic community and the possibility of Ulster independence if the IRA was not dealt with. Outside the party, the political development of Paisleyism proceeded with the creation of the Protestant – later Democratic – Unionist Party. And despite a continuing campaign against treacherous British concessions to Rome involving the Queen, the party leader, Paisley, responded

---

[59] 'Paisley to Protest "in Front of the Queen"', *PT*, 31 May 1969; 'Popery in the Palace', ibid. 21 Feb. 1969; 'Protest at Prince of Wales Investiture', ibid. 2 Aug. 1969.

[60] *PT*, 3 Aug. 1968 cited in Geoffrey Bell, *The Protestants of Ulster* (London, 1976), p. 41.

[61] Lord Grey of Naunton, Governor of Northern Ireland, to R. W. Porter, Minister of Home Affairs, 8 June 1970; Grey to Prime Minister, James Chichester-Clark, 7 Nov. 1969, PRONI, CAB9R/240.

[62] See, for example, Loughlin, *The Ulster Question since 1945*, chs. 2 and 3.

to the prorogation of Stormont with a demand for the formal integration of Northern Ireland with the rest of the United Kingdom.[63]

For all sections of Unionism, however, the monarchy remained a fundamental cornerstone of their ideas for resolving the Ulster problem; especially so as they disconcertingly observed British neutrality between the contending forces in Northern Ireland, with the clear implication of the denial of authentic membership of the British nation; a perception confirmed in British opinion polls which exhibited that sentiment starkly.[64] Given the absence from Northern Ireland of royal personages, the sense of desertion by even the hegemonic emblem of the British nation was palpable, especially in the months following prorogation. It was caught in a loyalist reaction to the complaint that rioting on the Queen's birthday was a desecration: 'What did she ever do for us?'[65] The only unqualified support in Britain Unionists found was on the extreme right, from the National Front, but even it was not interested in the sectarianism of Ulster Unionism, while rank and file supporters had little conception of 'the Irish thing'.[66]

Clarity of purpose within Unionism emerged in March 1973 when the Government produced a White Paper proposing a power-sharing assembly for the internal administration of the north together with a Council of Ireland to deal with issues common to the whole island.[67] It created a fundamental division between those supporting the initiative, such as the party leader, Brian Faulkner, and his followers who were prepared to accept some form of extra-territorial Irishness as part of their British identity, and those, mainly lower-middle-class and working-class Unionists, who saw Stormont as an expression of fundamentalist Protestant Britishness defined in opposition not only to northern and southern nationalists, but also to modern secular Britain. This sentiment informed popular support for the Ulster Workers' Council strike of 1974 which brought down the power-sharing executive.

The strike, however, brought its own uncertainties. It was followed, not by the restoration of the old Stormont, but by British disillusionment and

---

[63] See *Spectator*, 15 April 1972. Ulster Vanguard, *Betrayal in Ulster: The Technique of Conservative Betrayal* (n.p. [Belfast?], 1972), pp. 4–17. Ulster Vanguard, *Ulster – A Nation* (Belfast, 1972), pp. 10–15. Ulster Vanguard, *Government without Right* (Belfast, 1972), pp. 1–2.

[64] One such poll, in September 1971, showed that only 42 per cent of respondents wanted to keep Northern Ireland within the United Kingdom: Douglas Schoen, *Enoch Powell and the Powellites* (London, 1977), p. 106.

[65] Mary Holland, 'Ulster's Reluctant Rebels', *New Statesman*, 16 June 1972.

[66] *Listener*, 28 Dec. 1972; Martin Walker, *The National Front* (London, 1977), p. 159; Neil Fielding, *The National Front* (London, 1981), pp. 41–2, 69–83, 121–2, 154.

[67] HMSO, *Northern Ireland: Constitutional Proposals* (Belfast, 1973).

unsettling intimations of withdrawal from Northern Ireland, encouraged by the Secretary of State for the region, Merlyn Rees, who claimed to perceive Protestant nationalism expressed in the strike.[68] It was something the absence of royalty from Northern Ireland did nothing to mitigate. The issues of Protestant nationalism and Ulster independence, however, were put to the test when first the Vanguard movement and then the Ulster Defence Association took them up. Ultimately, the fundamental sectarian and national divisions in Northern Ireland[69] – and the failure of the Protestant community to support independence – made progress impossible. Moreover, intimations of a British desire to withdraw from Northern Ireland were not followed up. When Jim Callaghan replaced Harold Wilson as Prime Minister in 1976 a 'no pull-out' pledge was made,[70] while the appointment of the coercionist Roy Mason as Secretary of State in 1975 had signalled an aggressive campaign against the IRA. In the spring of 1977 the imprimatur of the state was given to Callaghan's pledge with the official pronouncement that the Queen's Silver Jubilee celebrations would culminate in a visit to Northern Ireland.[71]

IV

This development was no doubt a recognition of political reality – that however much it may have been desired, an arbitrary withdrawal from Northern Ireland was simply not possible. But from the Government's perspective a new and positive development had occurred in August 1976, the emergence of the Peace People. Arising out of public outrage at the killing of three small children by an IRA get-away car being pursued by the police, it led to the establishment of a non-political peace movement calling for a complete end to violence from all sides. It produced memorable scenes such as Catholic nuns being greeted rapturously on the Protestant Shankill Road and attracted huge rallies.[72] It seemed to offer objective evidence of the existence of a non-sectarian majority opinion that at last was finding its voice. Certainly, its historical significance should be noted. It was exactly the constituency that all British Governments struggling with nationalist movements had sought, without success, to mobilise since the early 1820s. And certainly for at least a year

---

[68] Merlyn Rees, *Northern Ireland: A Personal Perspective* (London, 1985), pp. 91–3.
[69] Sarah Nelson, *Ulster Uncertain Defenders* (Belfast, 1984), pp. 108–12.
[70] *Ulster Commentary*, Aug. 1976.   [71] Ibid. Feb. 1977.
[72] 'The North: Ten Years of Violence', *Magill: Ireland's Current Affairs Monthly Magazine*, Oct. 1978, 31.

or more – for those so beguiled – it offered the prospect of the defeat of paramilitarism. It is in this context that we should see the re-engagement of the monarchy with Northern Ireland.

As Prochaska has argued, the mid-1970s in Britain was a period of profound social and economic upheaval, in which the viability of state-directed enterprise and the post-war welfare-state consensus came under attack from a revival of free-market economics, and with a more valued role for voluntarism envisaged in an increasingly Thatcherite zeitgeist. It was one in which monarchical values of personal service, self-help and local initiative had a more central place.[73] With the emergence of the Peace People in late 1976, it could well have seemed that a particularly Northern Irish, and striking, version of self-help was manifesting itself to great effect, and which appeared to mark a definite turn towards peace. Increasingly it was seen to do so in terms congenial to the Government as the movement, perhaps inevitably, aligned itself with the officially sanctioned forces of law and order. Moreover, keen to support the movement in a period when forceful action against republican paramilitarism was proceeding, Roy Mason, in the run-up to the Queen's Silver Jubilee visit, announced a major investment of £1,000 million in the local economy.[74] Accordingly, as the scene-setting for the visit took shape, a constitutionally seductive scenario emerged, one that – misleadingly – promised a return to 'normality'.

Northern Ireland was a dangerous environment, but, given the symbolic import inherent in the royal presence, the Queen had to come. As *The Times* remarked, not to have done so would have given the unacceptable impression that the north was a 'no-go' area for the monarch.[75] Northern Ireland had demonstrated its loyalty by contributing £60,000 to the Queen's Silver Jubilee Appeal, with the sum expected to rise to £100,000 by the end of the year.[76] Thus the perils of a visit would have to be endured. When the IRA detonated an explosive device at the New University of Ulster, at which the Queen was due to deliver a major speech, it both intimidated the monarch – 'she showed none of the excitement and interest that had been so evident the day before'[77] – while at the same time ruling out the possibility of the visit being cancelled. As Mason recalled: 'To call off the visit now would be a defeat for Britain and the monarchy, celebrated in IRA song and legend for years

---

[73] Frank Prochaska, *Royal Bounty: The Making of a Welfare Monarchy* (New Haven and London, 1995), pp. 261–9.
[74] Roy Mason, *Paying the Price* (London, 1999), p. 205; *Ulster Commentary*, Sept. 1977.
[75] 'A Part of the United Kingdom', *TT*, 10 Aug. 1977.   [76] *TT*, 10 Aug. 1977.
[77] Mason, *Paying the Price*, p. 204.

to come. Unthinkable.'[78] So while the visit went ahead, it did so against a background of paramilitary and state killings and with a level of security that practically created conditions of martial law.

Nationalist areas were saturated with troops and a security cordon was thrown around Belfast; 32,000 soldiers were detailed to guard the Queen while only 7,000 people of a population of 1,500,000 had any hope of seeing her. Those not specifically invited to Jubilee occasions were advised to stay away.[79] As such, the visit could not perform the traditional function of royal ceremonial of *affirming* the authority of the state in its territory; rather it would be a constitutionally less certain *assertion* of that authority. In her speech at the New University of Ulster the Queen perceived 'hopeful signs of reconciliation and understanding. Policemen and soldiers have told me of the real cooperation they are receiving. I have sensed a common bond and shared hope for the future. People everywhere recognize that violence is senseless and wrong and that they do not want it.'[80] The speech could have been written by the Peace People whose sentiments it mirrored, and the movement's two Catholic leaders, Mairead Corrigan and Betty Williams, met the Queen on the royal yacht *Britannia*. The significance she placed on their activities was indicated by a conversation of several minutes.[81] She could only have been impressed by the claim of Betty Williams that the people of Andersonstown, in strongly republican west Belfast, really wanted to greet her.[82]

It was a highly misconceived belief, reflective of a leadership that only imperfectly understood the political environment of Northern Ireland. Politically inexperienced, their alignment with state forces effectively compromised their independence, while the genuine goodwill they generated from both sides of the community, under abstract slogans such as 'Peace for All', tended to disguise some very traditional and divisive understandings of how peace should be achieved. The movement made no significant contribution to a solution to the northern conflict and would effectively disintegrate in the late 1970s with little to show for its efforts other than a Nobel Peace Prize for leaders whose decision to keep the prize money for their own personal use caused controversy among their followers. At the time of the Silver Jubilee, however, they may well

---

[78] Ibid. p. 203.   [79] *TT*, 8, 9, 11 Aug. 1977.
[80] *Northern Constitution*, 13 Aug. 1977; *TT*, 12 Aug. 1977.
[81] Ciaran McKeown, *The Passion of Peace* (Belfast, 1984), pp. 235–6. McKeown was a central organiser of the movement.
[82] James Daly, 'One Man's Jubilee', *Hibernia*, 19 Aug. 1977.

have functioned to deceive the Government about the prospects for peace on its terms.

The presence of the Queen in Northern Ireland, a region permanently on the news agenda since 1969, brought an intense international focus. Six hundred media representatives had official accreditation for the visit and the Government sought to influence their coverage of the occasion through an offical press centre based at the Europa Hotel in central Belfast.[83] But the conditions for shaping, in the state's interest, reporting of the visit were not good. The occasion served to stereotype sharply – and illuminate – the political divisions of the region, with all shades of minority opinion from moderate nationalist to extreme republican opposed. It identified the monarchy closely, as one moderate Catholic put it, 'with hard line Unionism for the past 50-odd years'.[84] It was recalled that the Queen's coronation ceremony itself demonstrated a close identity with Unionism, while the impression of her visit as an exercise to reassure loyalists drew confirmation from a political background in which the extension of Northern Ireland's parliamentary representation at Westminster was being actively processed.[85] But the most significant challenge to the visit came from republicans, who organised an anti-Jubilee celebration – energised by the heavy-handed action of troops detailed to make Belfast safe for the royal visitors.[86] Demonstrations were held across the north during the visit, the centrepiece of which was a 2,000-strong march from Andersonstown to Belfast City Hall. It was a route which would not be allowed, but the prevention of which, as the organisers expected, would occasion conflict that undermined the normalising claims of the authorities and the Queen.

The Queen's Silver Jubilee visit invoked a historical narrative framed in the context of George V's inaugural visit of 1921 – pointing up how little had apparently changed. But while the latter initiated the process that led to the peace settlement of 1921, no such hopes were expressed for this royal occasion.[87] Negotiations for republicans in 1921 were to a large extent driven by anxiety about their ability to sustain their campaign; a concern in Government about the public reaction to excesses by British forces; and the non-partisan *activism* of a monarch concerned to facilitate peace in Ireland. In 1977 none of these conditions applied.

Unlike George V, Elizabeth II's conception of her role was virtually identical to that of the Government, while her identification of 'people of

---

[83] *TT*, 11 Aug. 1977.   [84] Ibid.
[85] Andrew Boyd, 'She Came – And Saw Little', *Hibernia*, 19 Aug. 1977. Ibid. 5 Aug. 1977.
[86] Daly, 'One Man's Jubilee'; McKeown, *Passion for Peace*, pp. 235–6.
[87] *TT*, 6 Aug. 1977.

goodwill'[88] in Northern Ireland with the Unionist community – repeated in her Christmas broadcast of 1977, an occasion when the Queen gives expression to her own views without Government advice[89] – demonstrated a remarkable inability to understand the outlook of the minority community and its experience at the hands of state forces. For its part, the Provisional IRA was under pressure, but would respond by changing its operational structure to function more effectively;[90] while the Secretary of State was strong on security but of limited political imagination, and in thrall to both a misleading version of late nineteenth-century conciliationist Unionism and the misleading prospect of peace that the emergence of the Peace People seemed to herald. In the latter context, T. E. Utley's comment on the importance in the British political mindset of the flawed assumption that all problems were resolvable once the concerns of the 'centre' – supposedly consisting of the great, politically moderate, majority of the population – were identified and addressed[91] should be noted.

Only indirectly and in completely unforeseeable ways can the Silver Jubilee visit of 1977 be said to have made some contribution to peace in Northern Ireland. One could see in the street demonstrations organised by the republican movement useful experience as a precursor to the Hunger Strike demonstrations of the early 1980s, which led to active political engagement and the eventual end of military struggle. As for constitutional nationalism, the royal visit convinced John Hume – the ablest of leading nationalists and who had called for its cancellation[92] – that a solution to the Ulster problem framed by Westminster alone was impossible. International, especially USA, opinion needed to be mobilised, creating discomfort for Westminster Governments and leading ultimately, and very disconcertingly for Unionists, to the Anglo-Irish Agreement of 1985, itself a landmark on the road to the Agreement of Easter 1998.

For the community reassured by the Queen's presence in 1977 the security it offered was misleading, made more so by her claim that 'nowhere more than in the rest of the United Kingdom' was there more heartfelt concern at 'such a conflict taking place *within our country* [my

---

[88] She repeated the sentiment in her Christmas broadcast of 1977: Tom Fleming (ed.), *Voices Out of the Air: The Royal Christmas Broadcasts 1932–1981* (London, 1981), p. 145.

[89] Pimlott, *The Queen*, p. 499.

[90] M. L. R. Smith, *Fighting for Peace? The Military Strategy of the Irish Republican Movement* (London, 1995), p. 145.

[91] T. E. Utley, *Lessons of Ulster* (London, 1975), p. 13.

[92] *TT*, 9 Aug. 1977; Loughlin, *Ulster Question since 1945*, p. 116.

italics]'.[93] It suggested a 'horizontal' community of identity with Northern Ireland across the state that simply did not exist.[94] Moreover, reassured about their constitutional position,[95] Unionists used nationalist protests to maintain their refusal to contribute to a political settlement: under power-sharing, it was argued, no royal visits would be allowed.[96] But, arguably, the visit entailed profound personal consequences for the royal family. It served to politicise the monarchy in a way it had not been before and thereby to 'legitimise' the royal family as a focus of attack. It may well have been the case that the Provisional IRA would have attempted to murder Lord Mountbatten in any event, but the fact was that it occurred two years after a highly politicised royal visit.[97] The Queen's uncle, Mountbatten was a figure of enormous influence on the royal family and a greatly felt loss, especially to Prince Charles, for whom he was a mentor.[98]

V

The Jubilee visit to Northern Ireland marked a departure in royal policy on Northern Ireland. Preceded by the visits of the Duke of Gloucester and Princess Anne in February and March respectively, the tradition of royal visits to the north was resumed. There would be a further twenty by members of the royal family between 1977 and 1985,[99] with the Prince of Wales following the Queen in December 1977 in connection with the Silver Jubilee Fund. And while it was accepted that Britain had secular- ised in a way that created a gulf between themselves and Britain, certain actions of their Protestant Queen enhanced Ulster Unionists' constitu- tional security, such as limiting the Prince of Wales's contact with Pope John Paul II during his British visit of 1982[100] and again during the

---

[93] *TT*, 12 Aug. 1977.

[94] Neither of the two most significant books associated with the Jubilee made any mention of Northern Ireland or the Queen's connection with it: Robert Lacey, *Majesty: Elizabeth II and the House of Windsor* (London, 1977); Philip Zeigler, *Crown and People* (London, 1978).

[95] See, for example, William Ross in *LS*, 17 Aug. 1977.   [96] *LS*, 10 Aug. 1977.

[97] It occurred while Mountbatten was taking his annual holiday on a fishing trip at his County Sligo home at Mullaghmore in August 1979. In addition to Lord Mountbatten, the deaths included his grandson Nicholas, an Irish crew member Paul Maxwell, and, some hours later, Lord Brabourne's mother. Others were severely injured: Pimlott, *The Queen*, p. 470; Jonathan Dimbleby, *The Prince of Wales: A Biography* (London, 1995), p. 323.

[98] See extract from Prince Charles's diary, ibid. pp. 323–4.

[99] Information supplied by the Northern Ireland Office.

[100] Dimbleby, *Prince of Wales*, pp. 423–4.

Prince's visit to the Vatican in 1985.[101] Royal reassurance for Unionists, however, could not prevent the occurrence of unwelcome developments.

The 1981 census, for instance, had indicated a significant demographic shift, with Protestants emigrating from the north in greater numbers than Catholics, while recurrent British opinion polls favoured withdrawal from Northern Ireland. But the greatest shock was the Anglo-Irish Agreement of 1985 (AIA), an agreement largely engineered by John Hume and which provided for a substantial input into the administration of Northern Ireland's affairs by the Government of the Irish Republic. The weakness of the Unionist position was illustrated by the abysmal failure of attempts to mobilise popular opinion in Britain against the Agreement.[102]

And yet despite its limitations as a security for their position, in a context where they seemed surrounded by enemies, it was to the royal relationship that Unionists continued to look for psychological reassurance. This took the form of a petition to the monarch that included 500,000 signatures. For Dr Paisley its significance was twofold: it allowed Ulster Unionists to assert – and have accepted – the authenticity of their British nationality while at the same time successfully releasing tensions that came perilously close to provoking civil war in Northern Ireland.[103] Precisely because the monarchical relationship served to contain Unionist anxieties, the Tory Governments of both Margaret Thatcher and John Major happily facilitated that relationship.

Thus whereas from the Silver Jubilee in 1977 to the signing of the AIA in November 1985 twenty-one royal visits to Northern Ireland took place, in the following eight-year period to September 1993, sixty-one occurred.[104] Indeed, the relationship with the sovereign may well have been emotionally consolidated by the perception that Unionist antagonism to Margaret Thatcher apparently paralleled that of the monarch – a pre-Thatcherite 'one nation' Tory[105] – who had a fraught relationship with the Thatcher Government in the mid to late 1980s over a range of issues from apartheid South Africa and the Commonwealth to domestic social policies.[106] Certainly it would appear that the Queen personally was keen to offer comfort to a disillusioned and anxious Unionist

---

[101] See Moloney and Pollack, *Paisley*, pp. 309, 422.

[102] Loughlin, *Ulster Unionism and British National Identity*, pp. 211–13.

[103] Paisley interviewed on *The Monarchy*, London Weekend Television, 1992; Paisley interview with author, 31 Aug. 1993.

[104] Information supplied by the Northern Ireland Office.

[105] Simon Targett, 'As Blue as Her Blood', *Times Higher Educational Supplement*, 25 Oct. 1996: Interview with Ben Pimlott.

[106] Pimlott, *The Queen*, pp. 499–515; 'The Politics of the Queen', *Sunday Times*, 31 May 1988.

community. Her 'great love' of the north was well known and readily evident: 'She always goes out of her way to talk to anybody she hears comes from Ulster.'[107]

Her sympathy was evident in her visit to Northern Ireland on 29 June 1991 – her first since the Silver Jubilee of 1977 – made for the purpose of presenting colours to four of the nine battalions of the Ulster Defence Regiment (UDR). Her speech on the occasion reflected the mythic Unionist view of the regiment, ignoring its controversial character, links with loyalist paramilitarism and involvement of many of its members in sectarian crimes, including murder: 'The UDR stands for those who are not prepared to stand by and let evil prosper. It provides for everyone in Northern Ireland – regardless of faith or background – the opportunity to make a contribution to the defeat of terrorism.'[108] It is of course true that in the great majority of her speeches a Government hand is clearly evident; nevertheless, the monarch clearly had the choice of delegation of the task and there is often room for visual or verbal nuance to indicate personal disposition. Monarchy's ability to offer constitutional reassurance to Ulster Unionists came into question, however, as throughout the 1990s a recurring campaign to modernise the institution, especially by the removal of the ban on Catholics holding the office, proceeded.[109]

It was something Unionists found unsettling.[110] Revd Martin Smith, a leading member of the Ulster Unionist Party and the Orange Order, thought that a Catholic monarch who did not seek to impose his or her religion in affairs of state might be acceptable to Ulster Unionists,[111] though he strenuously opposed any break of the link between church and state.[112] For Ian Paisley, however, a break of the personal link with Protestanism would render the monarchy redundant as an institution which embodied the British identity of Ulster Unionists; indeed, he was inclined to see recent scandals that were creating difficulties for the monarchy in Britain as the work of the Catholic Church intended to undermine it.[113] During a sermon in the crypt of the Palace of Westminster to mark the fortieth anniversary of the Queen's coronation,

---

[107] Lady Kinahan, wife of the former Lord Lieutenant for Belfast, Sir Robert Kinahan, interviewed on 'House of Windsor or House of Cards?', *Counterpoint*, Ulster Television, 1993.
[108] *TT*, 30 June 1991. For the latest exposure of the regiment's links with loyalist paramilitarism, see 'Collusion', *Irish News*, 2 May 2006.
[109] *ST*, 29 Nov. 1992; See MORI opinion poll results in *ST*, 21 Jan. 1990.
[110] *NL*, 27 June 1994.   [111] Smyth interview with author, 9 Aug. 1993.
[112] 'Allegiance Put to the Test', *Belfast Telegraph* [*BT*], 11 July 1994.
[113] Paisley interview with author, 31 Aug. 1993.

he warned that any monarch who breached the Williamite Settlement would be a usurper.[114] And yet, at the same time, Paisley indulged the thought that the inevitable crisis produced by any attempt at amendment could create a moment of British national epiphany in which the shared Protestant values that underlay the alienation between the British population and Ulster Unionists would rapidly come to the fore as a basis of unity.[115] It was and is an unlikely scenario. Prince Charles gave expression to the verdict of opinion polls on the subject when he declared his wish to be regarded a defender of faith, rather than any one Protestant creed, when he visited Belfast in early July 1994.

VI

The visit was significant. Its political background was one in which negotiations for an IRA ceasefire had been ongoing, and it would culminate on 31 August 1994 with the declaration of an indefinite cessation of hostilities as the republican movement embarked on a political route. In partnership with the constitutional nationalist Social Democratic and Labour Party, and the Government of the Irish Republic, that route would eventually lead to the Agreement of Easter 1998.

In fact, the visit marked the opening of a distinctive and ongoing phase in Anglo-Irish relations. As the troubled history of that relationship entered what can be regarded as its endgame, an opportunity arose for royal personages to help develop a harmonious Anglo-Irish community of interests and identity in a context defined by John Hume as one encompassing the totality of relationships within the British Isles.[116] It was very much in this spirit that Prince Charles's visit was conducted. He made visits to both loyalist and republican areas in Belfast, explicitly denouncing terrorism on both sides, denying that loyalist paramilitaries could claim allegiance to the crown, while condemning the republican killers of his uncle, Lord Mountbatten. Londonderry was also included in his visit, a location that, given the Prince's position as Commander in Chief of the Parachute Regiment, attracted protestors calling attention to the killing of fourteen unarmed civilians by the regiment in 1972.[117]

---

[114] 'MP Marks Royal Rule', *NL*, 15 July 1993.
[115] Paisley interview with author, 31 Aug. 1993.
[116] For sustained argument informed by this theme, see John Hume, *Personal Views* (Dublin, 1996).
[117] 'Charles Crosses Divide', *BT*, 7 Aug. 1994; *TT*, 8 Aug. 1994.

Nevertheless, the Prince's visit was well intentioned and astute, not least in the wider British context. The facilitation of peace would demonstrate the value of monarchy to counter attacks on the institution,[118] especially indictments of its supposed irredeemably reactionary character.[119] And it was followed up by an even more path-breaking and highly successful official visit to Dublin in early June 1995,[120] a visit for which the ground was effectively laid when the Irish President, Mary Robinson, paid a courtesy call on the Queen in 1993, the first such visit since Irish independence.[121] In the same context, but more personally, an Anglo-Irish role could reposition Prince Charles more positively in the eyes of the British public at a time when his estranged wife, Diana, was carving out a distinctive royal persona for herself – populist, glamorous, caring, identified with universal good causes such as the struggle against AIDS and landmine removal – exploited by, and no less exploiting, the tabloid press for her own ends. Princess Diana was a media phenomenon, a liminal figure with the ability to register symbolically with popular opinion in a complex mix of identities – part saint, part celebrity star, and exploiting her own brand of welfare monarchism to position herself successfully as a self-styled 'Queen of Hearts'. As such she developed a popular cult following that can be truly said to have made her a rather unique authority figure.[122] Certainly her appeal transcended national narratives and the problematic history of Anglo-Irish relations to engage with Irish public opinion.

The streets of Dublin were deserted when her funeral was broadcast as around 500,000 viewed the proceedings; floral tributes lined the wall outside the British embassy; tricolours flew at half-mast – even over the sacred site of modern republicanism, the General Post Office – and the Irish soccer team took the field in Iceland wearing black armbands.[123] Perhaps most surprising, in a way unthinkable for any other British royal, an apparently active trade in Diana funeral memorials exists (Fig. 24), itself suggestive of an extended Irish family identity and ownership.

---

[118] For an insight into the debate on monarchy in Britain at this time, see Anthony Barnett (ed.), *Power and the Throne: The Monarchy Debate* (London, 1994), *passim.*

[119] See Tom Nairn, *The Enchanted Glass: Britain and Its Monarchy* (London, 1988).

[120] 'Royal Road to Reconciliation', *ST*, 1 Nov. 1998.

[121] John Burns, 'Royal Return', *ST*, 31 May 1998.

[122] There is a substantial literature on the Diana phenomenon; for a useful survey of the variety of ways in which it has been approached, see Tony Walter, *The Mourning for Diana* (Oxford, 1999).

[123] John Burns, 'Royal Return', *ST*, 31 May 1998.

24 Diana memorial in Irish funeral parlour, 2004.

VII

The accommodation of conflicting traditions that a resolution of the
Northern Ireland problem entails necessarily involves an adjustment of
constitutional symbolism; and by 1996 the place of royal symbols in
Northern Ireland was under debate, with Unionists firmly resisting
change in opposition to a nationalist position which asserted the
co-equality of 'competing symbols'.[124] This debate was a preliminary to
the negotiations that produced the Agreement of Easter 1998 in Belfast.

The Ulster Unionist Party, the SDLP, Provisional Sinn Fein, parties
linked to loyalist paramilitaries – the Ulster Democratic Party and the
Progressive Unionist Party – and the British and Irish Governments
agreed to a solution of the Northern Ireland problem that would include
a power-sharing government at Stormont together with the engagement
of wider national interests embodied in a Council of Ireland and an
east–west Council of the British Isles. But most importantly for our
purposes, alive to the fact that in Northern Ireland constitutional status

[124] 'Does Ulster Need a Monarchy?', *BT*, 19 April 1996.

and national identity were, for many, not complementary, the Agreement eliminated the connection between the two, declaring

the birthright of all the people of Northern Ireland to identify themselves and be accepted as Irish or British, or both, as they may so choose ... their right to hold both British or and Irish citizenship is accepted by both Governments and would not be affected by any future change in the status of Northern Ireland.[125]

 Breaking the connection between constitutionality and nationality – even if it only strictly applied to Northern Ireland – allowed the monarchy's relationship with Ireland in general to be imagined and discussed in a shared conciliatory British–Irish arena, one which indicated that the gulf of alienating traditions dividing Britain and Ireland identified by Burke was at last being overcome.

The re-evaluation of a shared history, for example, provided a site for a deeply symbolic expression of Anglo-Irish amity when the Queen and the Irish President, Mary McAleese, together attended the opening of a battlefield memorial at Messines in Belgium to the Irish dead of the First World War.[126] The sense of liberation from the constraints of the past were perhaps most strikingly evident the same month when the Irish Taoiseach, Bertie Ahern, leader of Fianna Fail, the self-styled republican party, stated that there would be a debate 'within Ireland about rejoining the Commonwealth', pointing out that the situation was different now 'than it was 50 years ago', when the Commonwealth had very distinct imperialist associations.[127] Such suggestions had been made before in the 1990s,[128] but when voiced by the Irish Taoiseach they had much greater import.

It was a personal initiative by Ahern, and quite significant, given that as late as 1994 an attempt to restore to its original pedestal a statue of Queen Victoria which had lain buried in the grounds of University College Cork had created controversy.[129] Moreover, with the hare running, a historical narrative of Ireland's role in Commonwealth evolution could be easily identified as a justificatory context for a re-engagement that might conciliate Unionists and reinvent Ireland's relationship with Great Britain.[130] Press reports that the British and Irish Governments were considering the creation of 'a joint knighthood for heroes admired both north and south of the border' drew credibility from Dáil discussions on

---

[125] *The Agreement* (Belfast, 1998), p. 2.
[126] *ST*, 8 Nov. 1998; 'Side by Side, in Tribute to the Fallen', *TT*, 12 Nov. 1998.
[127] 'Commonwealth Option for Ahern', *TT*, 26 Nov. 1998.
[128] David Norris in Irish Senate, *Dáil (Seanad) Debates*, 133 (1 July 1992), col. 1216.
[129] *TT*, 25 June 1994.
[130] Fintan O'Toole, 'Rejoining Debate Not a Monarchy Fantasy Trip', *IT*, 4 Dec. 1998.

the creation of an honours system in Ireland[131] and added to the belief in a new Anglo-Irish zeitgeist.

In sum, post-Agreement Anglo-Irish relations constituted a liminal arena in which old enmities were breaking down, one in which welfare monarchism could be undertaken to good effect. Accordingly, in the period from the signing of the Agreement at Easter 1998 to 4 May 2006 a sustained engagement by members of a royal family having putative Celtic roots[132] with Northern Ireland took place, involving eighty-six visits;[133] and with care taken to balance gestures to both communities.[134] The British dimension of the new era was reflected in the Queen thanking the Pope for his assistance in Northern Ireland,[135] while Prince Charles – against a background of demands for changes to the Act of Settlement[136] – suggested arrangements being made for a Catholic to assume the throne.[137] Certainly it was the welfarist activities of Prince Charles that were noted especially at this time, described as his taking on 'Diana's caring role'.[138] That he missed the funeral of his aunt, Princess Margaret, to confer British honours on five Irish citizens at the British embassy in Dublin[139] was a measure of the importance he placed on the Irish dimension to royal activities. Certainly the imagery of the Prince in the Irish capital and meeting the President[140] served to identify royal personages as acceptable and normal features of the Irish public arena. From the signing of the Agreement to 26 May 2006 seven official royal visits to the Irish Republic occurred.[141] The extent to which Anglo-Irish relations were being transformed was registered in January 2004 when Michael Kennedy became the first former Irish Government minister to be made an honorary Companion of the Most Distinguished Order of St Michael and St George.[142]

Within the British state itself 2002 was a crucial year. It marked the Golden Jubilee of Elizabeth II's accession to the throne and, against a

---

[131] 'Ireland's Heroes Set To Get Knighthoods', *ST*, 7 March 1999.
[132] Ian Adamsom, 'Millennium Monarchy', *Fortnight*, Feb. 2002, p. 14.
[133] Freedom of Information Team, Northern Ireland Office to author, 19 May 2006.
[134] *BT*, 5–7 May 1999; *TT*, 13 April 2000; *IT*, 18 July 2000; *BT*, 4 Aug. 2000; *NL*, 29 May 2003; *BT*, 19 Sept. 2002. Sir Kenneth Bloomfield and Cardinal Cathal Daly quoted in Deborah and Gerald Strober, *The Monarchy: An Oral History of Elizabeth II* (London, 2002), pp. 391–2;
[135] *TT*, 18 Oct. 2000.   [136] *TT*, 21 Feb., 15 Nov., 6–7 Dec. 2000.
[137] *TT*, 24 Oct. 2000. For dissent by the then Archbishop of Canterbury, Carey, see *ST*, 29 Oct. 2000. Charles would make another significant gesture in 2003 by taking on a Catholic as a senior advisor: *TT*, 28 Feb. 2003.
[138] *TT*, 24 Nov. 2000; for the Royal family in general, *Guardian*, 31 Aug. 2002.
[139] *BT*, 14 Feb. 2002.   [140] *IT*, 15 Feb. 2002.
[141] Robert Wace, Foreign and Commonwealth Office to author, 26 May 2006.
[142] *IT*, 9 July 2004.

background of repeated demands for the repeal of the Act of Settlement,[143] the Queen continued to make important symbolic gestures, becoming the first monarch since 1688 officially to listen to a Catholic sermon when the Roman Catholic Archbishop of Westminster, Cormac Murphy-O'Connor, preached at Sandringham in January.[144] Moreover, the Northern Ireland leg of the Golden Jubilee tour of the United Kingdom was politically the most significant. Its obvious reference point was the Silver Jubilee visit of 1977.[145]

Troubled and unfortunate in its political consequences as that visit was, it served to highlight the great changes that had occurred since then, and how a royal gesture could help the peace process.[146] Thus, whereas popular contact with the monarch was highly restricted then, in 2002 public access was widespread, while the nature of royal ceremonial and public engagement was much less formal and more immediate: violent conflict was effectively over and she was greeted on the steps of Stormont by the Unionist and nationalist leaders of a power-sharing Government. At this highly symbolic site the Queen spoke to Assembly members, not in a formal address to the chamber, but *informally* in the central hall of the building, a decision made in deference to nationalist sensibilities so as not to suggest an assertion of British sovereignty. Moreover, her speech, unlike that of 1977, made acknowledgement of the suffering endured by all sections of the community, and – given that Ian Paisley's DUP was officially opposed to the peace settlement of Easter 1998 – was subtly pro-Agreement in its reference to the Assembly as a means of building a new Northern Ireland in circumstances arranged to meet the aspirations 'of those who are proud to be British and those who feel a strong sense of Irish identity'. The conferring of city status on two towns in the region, Newry and Lisburn respectively, one nationalist and the other Unionist, enhanced the conciliatory theme of a highly successful visit, as it did the approach of royal personages generally now to Ireland.[147]

The occasion was boycotted by Sinn Fein.[148] This was to be expected, but in keeping with the 'parity of esteem' for community cultures at the heart of the Agreement, any kind of hostile dissent would have been unthinkable. And republicans had much to gain. The Agreement was concerned to establish a neutral environment in which both sides of the community could develop faith in the processes of law and order. Accordingly, and much to Unionist dissatisfaction, a process of removing the royal crest, pictures of the Queen and the Union Jack from police and fire stations was under way. By January 2003 forty-one royal coats of arms

[143] *Guardian*, 31 May 2002.   [144] *BT*, 16 Jan. 2002.   [145] *BT*, 13 May 2002.
[146] *ST*, 12 May 2002.   [147] See extensive reporting in *BT*, 15 May 2002.   [148] Ibid.

had been removed from seventeen court buildings across the region, while the badge of the RUC – now renamed the Police Service of Northern Ireland and with recruiting based on a 50:50 Catholic/ Protestant intake – was reshaped to remove the dominance of the crown.[149] For many Unionists an underhand process was underway to remove all vestiges of British culture from Northern Ireland.[150] A controversial resignifying of the ritual and symbolic landscape of Northern Ireland – exacerbated when Sinn Fein councillors on Belfast City Council refused to accept the positioning of a statue of Queen Victoria on its original site in a now nationalist area because of her assumed contribution to the Great Famine[151] – was bound to be discomfiting to Unionists. The frequent presence of royal personages in Northern Ireland helped them to cope with these changes.

VIII

The engagement of members of the royal family with Ireland, north and south, in the period since the Agreement has been unprecedented, both as to the number of visits, and as to the way that formal ceremonial, traditionally believed to add to the mystique of monarchy, has been discounted in favour of immediacy of personal and social contact. It has taken place in a liminal context where the power of traditional narratives of nationality and belonging have begun to break down – Sinn Fein is the dominant political party in the nationalist community, but most nationalists apparently would not vote to end partition[152] – thus providing an arena in which, as Irish acceptance of royal honours and suggestions about the possible re-entry of Ireland to the Commonwealth indicate, the reforging of Anglo-Irish relations can include a reforging of identity. Garret FitzGerald, a former leader of Fine Gael, has opined: 'Queen Victoria never came to live here, and never showed an interest in Ireland. It would have made a difference . . . if she had.'[153] The implication that a permanent royal presence in the nineteenth century would have transformed Anglo-Irish relations is, as we have seen, mistaken, but the real significance of FitzGerald's statement lies less in its credibility about the past than in its implications for the Anglo-Irish relationship in

---

[149] *ST*, 2 Sept. 2001; Loughlin, *Ulster Question since 1945*, pp. 208, 223–4.
[150] See *ST*, 2 Sept. 2001; *DJ*, 14 Jan. 2003. See also 'The Queen's Adviser may be a Republican', *NL*, 14 Aug. 1998.
[151] 'Queen Victoria Statue Sparks Row', *BT*, 2 Nov. 2002. Controversy also surrounded the siting of Boer War memorials in Omagh: *BT*, 27 Feb. 2002. *IT*, 27 Feb. 2003.
[152] Polling evidence, *Sunday Times*, 9 July 2006.
[153] Garret Fitzgerald quoted in Strober and Strober, *The Monarchy*, p. 387.

the future. A leading member of his party has suggested that for Ulster Unionists to accept Irish unity an Irish role for the monarch is necessary.[154]

There are, however, obstacles of varying significance. For instance, the symbolic sense of national inclusion that the abolition of the Act of Settlement would provide for Catholics in the United Kingdom is unlikely to transpire as the Blair Government has refused the necessary legislation, and as a substratum of continuing anti-Catholicism has been identified.[155] This was remarked upon by commentators in the Irish Republic concerned that a public infatuation with monarchy not be taken too far, or be misread.[156] A bomb hoax associated with a visit by Princess Anne to Cork reflected this sentiment.[157]

Nevertheless, such opposition is not yet, and may not be, a significant phenomenon; and the normalising of the royal presence in Ireland is nowhere better conveyed than in the fairly regular personal meetings between the British and Irish heads of state.[158] The ultimate purpose of these visits is to prepare the ground for a state visit by the Queen to Dublin. This has been on the cards since 2000 but the Irish Government has failed to issue an invitation.[159] In large measure this is due to the halting political progress in Northern Ireland since the signing of the Agreement in 1998, resulting from difficulties over IRA decommissioning, Unionist rejectionism and paramilitary criminality. It was fortunate that a Government was in place during the Queen's Golden Jubilee visit of 2002; but it collapsed later in the year.[160] Only in late March 2007 – after Sinn Fein had agreed to endorse fully the Police Service of Northern Ireland and an election which confirmed Ian Paisley's Democratic Unionist Party as the dominant Unionist Party – was agreement arrived at to restore desolved government, which took effect on 8 May.[161] As a state visit by the Queen to Dublin would be profoundly symbolic it is recognised that the most appropriate time

---

[154] *Daily Ireland*, 22 Aug. 2006.

[155] Christine Odone, 'The British Still Fear a Popish Plot', *TT*, 18 Oct. 2004; Adrian Hilton, 'Render unto the Pope', *Spectator*, 30 Aug. 2003; Adrian Hilton, 'The Price of Liberty', *Spectator*, 8 Nov. 2003; Peter Osborne, 'How Blair Betrays the Crown', *Spectator*, 9 April 2005.

[156] See commentary by the Fianna Fail Government advisor Martin Mansergh, 'For Better or Worse Royal Weddings Made History', *IT*, 19 Feb. 2005; also letters page, *IT*, 16 Feb. 2005; 'Marriage and Monarchy', *DJ*, 15 Feb. 2005; Charles Lysaght, 'The Queen and Us? A Step Too Far', *Sunday Independent*, 12 June 2005.

[157] 'Bomb Hoax Fails To Deter Princess from Irish Visit', *IT*, 18 Feb. 2004.

[158] See *North West Telegraph*, 8 Dec. 2005; *IT*, 9 Dec. 2005.

[159] 'Dublin Stalls on Queen's Visit', *TT*, 3 July 2000.

[160] For coverage, see Loughlin, *Ulster Question since 1945*, ch. 5.

[161] *IT*, 31 March 2007.

would be when self-government is securely restored to Northern Ireland. With that in mind, the process of normalising the monarchical presence in the Irish Republic has proceeded. The most significant instance to date was the celebration of the twenty-first anniversary of the Irish President's award scheme for young people, and the fiftieth anniversary of the Duke of Edinburgh's awards, in April 2006, hosted jointly by the Duke and the Irish President.[162] It has been followed by a call from the new Primate of the Anglican Church in Ireland, Bishop Alan Harper, to end the ban on Catholics acceding to the British throne.[163]

[162] See *IT*, 26–7 April 2006.   [163] *IT*, 18 Jan. 2007.

Conclusion

One of the most striking aspects of the Irish question under the Union is the contrast between great demonstrations of 'organic' unity between the Irish people and royal personages as against periodic mass nationalist agitations. At first sight puzzling, it becomes more comprehensible if we abandon the notion of one 'people' and think instead of multiple constituencies called into existence by diverse issues and mobilisations. Certainly in assessing the monarchy's relationship with Ireland we are faced with a variety of complex factors. Under the Union that relationship was mediated by royal/viceregal ritual serving a need to deny the credibility of nationalist claims. Nevertheless, great royal occasions were impressive in their effects. Far from being, as often assumed, merely exceptional incidents of little explanatory value to an understanding of the Irish question, each major occasion deserves close attention. The great outpourings of enthusiasm for the royal presence in 1821, 1849, 1853, 1868, 1903 and 1911 – and to a lesser extent on other royal occasions – appeared to provide striking evidence of visible mass loyalty to the state. The deceptive function of these occasions, however, served to disguise their limitations, limitations in comparison with nationalist ritual and ceremony illustrates.

Drawing on indigenous cultural and national traditions, the great meetings of O'Connell and Parnell were moveable feasts repeatable at any number of locations around the country. The successes of royal occasions, however, were *situationally* determined products of contextual dynamics that were difficult to extend beyond their time and place. Accordingly, the attempt in the 1820s to establish George IV's presence in Ireland as a narrative basis on which Ireland's future development and that of Anglo-Irish relations could be reimagined proved unsustainable, as was also the case with royal occasions of the more favourable 1850s. Even the most enduring product of welfare monarchism in this period – royal and viceregal engagement with popular opinion in the holding of industrial and trades exhibitions – was vulnerable to the effects of economic crises and the stimulus they gave to nationalist mobilisations.

The weakness of the crown in Ireland is illuminated by the work of Lukes and Baker on the disjuncture between appearance and reality in popular responses to royal occasions. Baker's suggestion that, despite appearances, monarchy informed indigenous British working-class culture only to a very limited extent[1] is a recognition of separate national and local spheres of meaning with clear Irish parallels. Steven Luke's argument that the compliance of 'subordinate classes' with hegemonic state interests reflects the absence of consistent values and beliefs that could provide them with realistic oppositional alternatives[2] also applies in the Irish case, though to a much more limited extent. The argument is most plausible for the 1850s when organised nationalism was in abeyance, but not to the O'Connellite or Parnellite periods. Ultimately the alienated historical traditions and popular memory of Catholic Ireland made possible an imagining of the country outside the existing constitutional structure of the United Kingdom in a way not really feasible for anti-state groups in Britain where, as James Vernon points out, popular constitutionalism had a hegemonic influence for all political organisations across the political spectrum, as the collapse of English republicanism in the early 1870s demonstrated. A problematic variable not automatically an agency of mass mobilisation, in the right circumstances national memory was yet capable of engaging a significant enough section of popular opinion to support a challenge to the state, as the aftermath of the 1916 Rising evidenced. While both the crown and nationalist movements had difficulty negotiating the localist sphere of Irish everyday life, nationalists were ultimately better placed to interact with it. The failures of the crown in Ireland during the Union thus had greater import. Yet the break-up of the Union cannot simply be put down to nationalist traditions. The public realm within which royal occasions took place was itself deeply problematic.

Defined by the constitutional entity of Great Britain and Ireland, it was geographically discontinuous – itself a central factor historically in the development of antagonistic national, religious and cultural traditions – while modernisation had variable effects. It appeared, persuasively, to make the Viceroyalty redundant, but functioned no less to enhance the efficiency of nationalist mobilisations, thereby inhibiting viceregal abolition. Also, in functioning to create a greater consciousness in Ireland of how it was perceived within the state, it effected changes in Irish

---

[1] P. S. Baker, 'The Sociological and Ideological Role of the Monarchy in Late Victorian Britain', unpublished MA thesis, University of Lancaster (1978), p. 5.
[2] 'Political Ritual and Social Integration', in Steven Lukes, *Essays on Social Theory* (London, 1977), pp. 56–64.

self-perceptions of appropriate modes of reaction to the royal presence. Relatedly, the media's role in shaping the meaning of royal events could seriously destabilise the environment in which they took place, as in 1885, while the enhanced awareness of the public realm in general that it facilitated illuminated the realm's internal diversity, especially the distinctiveness of the regional sub-spheres of north-east Ulster, southern Ireland and Scotland.

The metropolitan tendency to generalise stereotypically on the nature of 'Celtic' character had posited – through a monarchical prism – the latter as a model for Irish integration into the state, ignoring the considerable religio-cultural differences between the two regions. With Balmoral as its emblematic site it gave proposals for an Irish royal residence undeserved significance. But this issue only served to point up the singularity of Ireland's place in the state, attracting trenchant monarchical opposition during the Victorian era, crystallising situational difficulties and, especially, highlighting the absence of a hegemonic and integrating myth of state identity. Only in north-east Ulster did an enthusiastically loyal Irish sub-realm exist, but there the exclusivity of loyalist myth sectarianised the monarchy, complicating its identity role in Ireland as a whole. Moreover, the tendency of these arenas to produce Geertzian figures of authority, articulating regional agendas, set limits, to varying extents, to monarchical allegiance.

As the example of the Duke of Wellington and – to a more limited extent – Gladstone demonstrates, such figures were not unknown in England, but while sometimes appearing as oppositional poles of authority to the sovereign they did not threaten the constitutional order – Gladstone's Home Rule schemes intended limited reform to secure it. The case was otherwise in Ireland, with O'Connell and Parnell functioning as sources of national identity and allegiance, and promoting radical constitutional revisions constrained only by perceptions of British military might and the limits of what Westminster might be persuaded to accept. Even in loyal north-east Ulster, it could be argued, Edward Carson's activities were no less state-destabilising than those of nationalists, illuminating the contrast between a conception of monarchy framed in the context of loyalist myth and the sovereign's actual role in the state.

The extent to which the monarchy's engagement with Ireland could be deemed successful on any given occasion was dependent on a range of variable factors, such as socio-economic conditions, expectations of reform, the strength or weakness of oppositional forces, and the perceived attitude to Ireland of individual royal personages. But there were also related, enduring problems, affecting the royal relationship with Ireland.

Of fundamental importance was the failure of Ireland to prosper economically to the same degree as other regions of the state. No Government under the Union successfully grappled with Ireland's relative poverty, and while this was largely a function of lack of natural resources, poverty lent powerful credibility to nationalist narratives of British exploitation, with the catastrophe of the Great Famine functioning to provide overwhelming proof (at least for radical nationalists) not only of British genocide but of the complicity of the hegemonic signifier of the state – the Queen – in the 'crime'. And yet the problem of economic development did not necessarily *determine* the failure of the Union. There was also a failure to address serious grievances affecting the Catholic community.

Some of these, relating to land and religion, would have been difficult to address under any circumstances, and, arguably, up to the 1870s, the periodic successes of Irish royal occasions and the zero-sum outlook they facilitated encouraged the view that they might not have to be. Nevertheless, the demands of the rising Irish tenant class that Parnellism would exploit to effect in the 1880s – the 'Three Fs', fixity of tenure, fair rent and free sale – were formulated in the crucially important 1850s when the opportunities for royal influence in Ireland were greatest. But the failure to address the religious grievances of the Catholic community was possibly more serious and the monarchy was closely implicated in this failure.

In 1800 George III's refusal of Catholic emancipation allowed anti-Catholicism to become the basis for anti-state mobilisation, while the conditions of royal accession and the Declaration which gave it voice expressed the mindsets of monarchs throughout the nineteenth century. Thus authentic belonging was denied to a Catholic people growing increasingly pietistic from the 1850s. Had land and religious grievances been addressed in a more timely fashion nationalist traditions would, of course, still have remained, but given their role in energising national memory a resolution of these issues would arguably have done much to neutralise its emotive power. As it was, it remained to be exploited in a crucial period of nationalist mobilisation from the late 1870s. By the time the stance of the monarchy towards the majority of the Irish population changed under Edward VII, and especially George V, a resolution of the Irish question on the basis of the existing Union was no longer feasible. Accordingly, the scenario of love the authorities hoped to establish in Ireland on the British precedent for the greater part of the Union – a state-consolidating myth underpinned by economic progress with welfare monarchism cultivating mass allegiance focused on the sovereign – proved elusive.

The settlement of 1921 registered the failure of the Union project as traditionally conceived and it had a profound effect on the monarchy's relationship with Ireland. The reduction of the Irish dimension of the United Kingdom to the six counties of Northern Ireland from 1921 quickly facilitated the Ulster Unionist tendency to exploit the monarchy for its own ends. While George V, the future Edward VIII and, perhaps to a lesser extent, George VI – whose attitudes to Ireland had been conditioned by its pre-independence constitutional position – could maintain a personal distance from the region, this was less easy for the present Queen. Her outlook on Ireland was necessarily framed through a Northern Ireland lens during the formative period of the Second World War – during which Northern Ireland remained loyal while Eire apparently consorted with the axis powers. In this context, it was only too likely that the young Queen would easily identify with a loyal population whose strong Protestantism would resonate with her own religious beliefs.

In fact, not since the reign of Queen Victoria had a British monarch so strongly identified with Ulster loyalists. It was an unfortunate mindset as the revival of the national question at the end of the 1960s ushered in an IRA paramilitary campaign and nationalist alienation, leaving the monarchy politically compromised. And yet it can be seen as a measure of the adaptability of the institution that the new political era inaugurated by the IRA ceasefire of 1994 has allowed it to make a meaningful contribution to the improvement of Anglo-Irish relations.

This new Anglo-Irish context is certainly significant, and fundamentally different from that of the Union. The onset of peace and the Agreement of 1998 has facilitated the dissolving of alienating national traditions in Britain and Ireland, while the posture of the royal presence in the public arena has changed significantly. Accordingly an arena has been created in which welfare monarchism not only continues to facilitate the adjustment of Ulster Unionist sensibilities to uncomfortable realities, but has a wider Irish role in a context where an opening to a shared Anglo-Irish identity has emerged.

Thus the monarchical strand in Irish nationalism – established by O'Connell and long submerged – has reappeared, allowing many Irish politicians to reimagine Ireland's future in ways which could allow possible re-entry to the Commonwealth and a place for the crown. And, arguably, the monarchy's role in the Anglo-Irish context adds significantly to its authority in the British state. Now, as in the 1820s, Ireland provides a distinctive context for the evaluation of the monarchy uninfluenced by the criticism that attends the institution in Britain. But perhaps the closest parallel is with the early 1870s, when Gladstone sought to neutralise criticism of the crown in Britain through a royal role in Ireland; only now there is a better prospect of success. The monarchy is not expected to establish legitimacy for a constitutional order lacking popular endorsement.

Index